Useful to the Church and Kingdom

Useful to the Church and Kingdom

THE JOURNALS OF JAMES H. MARTINEAU,
PIONEER AND PATRIARCH, 1850–1918
VOLUME 2

EDITED BY
Noel A. Carmack and Charles M. Hatch

SIGNATURE BOOKS | 2023 | SALT LAKE CITY

Dedicated to
Everett L. Cooley
(1917–2006)
and
Andrew J. Simmonds
(1943–1995)

Useful to the Church and Kingdom: The Journals of James H. Martineau, Pioneer and Patriarch, 1850–1918 is comprised of two individual volumes:

Volume 1 hardback ISBN: 978-1-56085-461-6

Volume 2 hardback ISBN: 978-1-56085-462-3

© 2023 Signature Books. All rights reserved. Signature Books is a registered trademark of Signature Books Publishing, LLC. Printed in the USA using paper from sustainably harvested sources.

Join our mail list at www.signaturebooks.com for details on events and related titles we think you'll enjoy.

Design by Jason Francis

FIRST EDITION | 2023

LIBRARY OF CONGRESS CONTROL NUMBER: 2023938532

Contents

Continued from Volume 1

5. Serving the Church in Gila Valley, 1883–1889 601
6. "Everything I Touched Turned to Ashes": Surveying in Southern Arizona, and Northern Mexico, 1889–1897 . . .739
7. "Oh That I May Have Power to Do Good to the Fulness of My Desires": Patriarch and Good Samaritan, 1897–1908 . .945
8. "To the Father Be All Glory": Sunset Years, 1908–1918 . . 1203

Appendix 1: Conversations with John C. Fremont 1265

Appendix 2: Letter to F. E. Eldredge, 1907 1273

James Henry Martineau's Family Pedigree 1281

Photographs and Illustrations 1283

Bibliography 1293

Index 1337

5
SERVING THE CHURCH IN GILA VALLEY
1883–1889

[Page 528L]

1883/ Leave Ogden. Idaho. Sacramento. Lathrop.

Mch. 13/Tues./It is hard to leave so many dear friends as I do in Logan, but I hope not only to keep my old ones but make many <u>new</u> ones. Hardest of all to leave my dear, true and loving wife—Susan, for So long a time; for not having sold out the place She and the rest must stay here awhile. May God bless them all forever!

We reached Ogden at 9 A.M. and in the afternoon I sent Lilly to S.L. City to stay until we should be ready to leave Ogden. I paid M. Thatcher the $12.50 I owed him. at Ogden.

W. 14/ Bought 1000 lbs flour, 1000 lbs Barly, 200 lbs. Lucerne seed, 23 bu. Potatoes + garden seeds, and Also 8 kegs nails and some garden tools. Began to load the car. The boys did not arrive with the wagon until this morning.

15/ Finished loading the car, with Groesbeck and Jones with Groesbeck's team and mine in the Car, for which I paid $350.00 to Benson ^my part, $600 in all for the car^. Also paid for our passage $52.50 for Adults. Our fares came to $236.25 including Seth, [in margin: Leave Logan] who came up with Lilly on this mornings train. At 2.^40^ P.M. we left Ogden, 25 Souls in all.

16+17/ In Idaho. Nothing worthy of note.

Sun. 18/Wake on the Sierra Nevada. Pass through many miles of Snow Sheds. Scenery beautiful and in some places Sublime. Began to see flowers, and trees in bloom. Reached Sacramento 2.30 P.M. and changed

Cars. Seth and Jesse went away and neglected to get their bedding out of the car, and so lost it, which was quite a serious matter to us afterwards. Left Sacramento about 5 P.M. and reached Lathrop about 9.30 P.M.—56 miles, where we changed Cars again, waiting until 3 A.M. next morning.[1]

Mon. 19/ Left Lathrop at 3 A.M. Cold and foggy. Telegraphed to the Supt. about my bedding We pass through a poor country. Bought

[Page 529R]

1883/ Los Angeles. Yuma. Benson. St David, Sury Canal.

Mch./Some shoes for Lilly, and a looking glass
[Blank line]

20/reached Los Angeles 2.30 P.M. having passed through a dreary desert for hundreds of miles. Bought parasol and a mattress, also about 100 oranges @ 1¢ each. Left at 6.^10^ P.M.

21/ Wake at Indio, 260 feet below the level of the Sea. Passed, and visited Volcano Springs, where hot mud boils up constantly.[2] Reached Yuma about 2 P.M. and learned there are 40 cases of Small pox here. Saw indians, men and women, nearly naked. weather quite warm, and the Colorado rising. Left about ^5^ P.M. passing along the Gila.

Thurs./22/ Stopped 2 hours in Tucson. Thermometer 84° Reached Benson at 5 P.M. and found Br. Layton's team waiting for us and his daughter's family. Reached St David at 8 P.M. and stopped with Br. Wild's family.[3] Groesbeck's and Jones families remained at Benson all night.

---

1. Lathrop is approximately sixty miles south of Sacramento. It was founded in 1868 by Leland Stanford and named for his wife, Jane, and her brother, Charles Lathrop. See Ralph Lee and Chrisi Kennedy, "Lathrop Founded by Stanford to Bypass Stockton," *Lodi News-Sentinel,* December 17, 2005, 14.

2. Volcano Springs, now known as Mundo, is an unincorporated community in Imperial County, California. It is located approximately 7.5 miles southeast of Frink. A Volcano Springs post office was in operation from 1901 to 1902. The mud pots can still be visited, 2.9 miles southwest of what is now Niland, near the southeastern shore of the Salton Sea.

3. St. David, located approximately nine miles southeast of Benson on the San Pedro River, was settled by four families of Merrills in 1877. It was named and dedicated by Alexander McDonald in honor of David W. Patten who was killed in Missouri. See J. A. McCrae, "History of St. David," *Deseret Weekly* 38 (March 2, 1889): 317; Barnes, *Arizona Place Names,* 374; and Jenson, *Encyclopedic History of the Church,* 725–726.

23/ Got teams to bring up the others at Benson. They were much discouraged to find so poorly built up a place, after living so long in Logan—the garden.

Sat. 24/ Looked over the city plat, and found a block to build on. Afterwards went to Benson to see of our Car had arrived. Found it had, and gone up the Sonora R.R. to Contention, 8 miles above St David. Got back home, and found Albert had arrived with the horses, and word we must unload tomorrow.

Sun. 25/ Sent the boys to Contention to unload the car. They got back after dark, with everything. I went to Meeting and preached, and felt well.

Mon. 26/ Unpacked our things, and found two bowls and a picture broken, also a glass jar. Other things all right.

27, 28 +29 [see format]/ Surveyed on St David canal, with Jesse and Seth Jones, a distance of about 6 miles. Grade 5 feet pr mile.

[Page 530L]

1883/Set apart H.W. Brizzie on Mission to Sonora.

Mch. 30/Friday/To day Brs. Layton, Kimball and I blessed and Set apart Henry W. Brizzie and his son Arthur, aged 14, as missionaries to Sonora. Br. Brizzie understands the Spanish well.[4]

Board/ourselves/on 26th After coming here we boarded a week with Wilds' family, and began to keep house ourselves on Monday Mch. 26th I let Wilds have 100 lbs of Potatoes, $5.00 and half sack flour $250. also 2 lbs butter 85¢

Sat. 31/ Surveyed land for DP Kimball and myself.

---

4. In a letter to President John Taylor, Christopher Layton reported that he had been to Benson and Tombstone to find out what he could do about potatoes and inquired about railroad freight. "Br. Martineau has arrived all safe. Br. [David] Kimball has been down in Sonora, and found a place on the Vanbuto river that can be rented for a term of five years, and we thought it would be wise to send two or three families, and feel their way in gradually, if it meets your approval." Layton also reported that a Brother Henry W. Brizzie was well versed in the language and customs of the people. It was then suggested that Brizzie travel to Sonora to investigate the possibility of settlements there. "We have got it planned, if it meets your mind, for him to go to Hermosillo and Guaymas, and look around generally, and see what can be done." C. Layton, David P. Kimball, and James H. Martineau to President John Taylor, March 30, 1883, First Presidency, John Taylor Presidential Papers, 1877–1887, CR 1/180, Letters Received, box 13, fd. 5, LDSCHL.

Sun. 1/April/ Brs. Layton + Kimball went to Tucson to enter land, for themselves and for me, (160 A.)

3/ Finished planting about an acre of potatoes. Got a good letter from Charles. Went out north + picked out some good land for our family.

Wed. 4/ Went to Tombstone to make filing for land. Was introduced to Gen. Wardwell Judge Peel + others.[5]

5/Returned at Noon. The whole country is up on account of So many indian massacres round us during the last two weeks. Men are volunteering to go against them, and they Call on us at St David to furnish some horses to help mount the men. We held meeting in the evening, and decided to send 8 or 10 horses to help them. We think best to do this, as the indians richly deserve death, and otherwise we would be looked upon as favoring the indians. Paid $2.00 for entry D.P. Kimballs

Fri. 6/ Today is Jesse's birth day—20 years old. May he have many more to come. Alberts was on the [blank] of [blank] The boys have been clearing land, + Albert plowing.

7/ Wrote to W.D. Johnson, informing him he is called to be a bishop over St David.

Sun. 8/ Lilly was taken very Sick in meeting.– a hot fever. A Man came from Tombstone to get horses to help fit out the Rangers.

9/ Got some poor hay. Lilly still Sick, and I

[Next page is an unpaged newspaper article titled "A Second Alamo. That Will Bring Light and Liberty to the Mexican People. Temochia, Mexico, Annihilated"]

[Page 531R]

1883/Lilly Sick. Plant corn. peas, onions +c

April/cannot get any woman or girl to help. Jesse cooks

---

5. General David K. Wardwell (1823–1908) served in the Mexican War and under Brigadier-General Franklin Pierce. He led the Fifth Volunteer Militia ("The Minute Men of '61") at the Battle of Bull Run. After the war, he moved to Tombstone and served in several local offices. Judge Bryant Lorindo "B. L." Peel (b. ca. 1820) was a prominent judge in Tombstone. His son, Martin R. Peel, was killed in a robbery and shootout at Charleston, Arizona. See Thrapp, *Dictionary of Frontier Biography*, 3:693.

10/ Got another load hay today. Recd some grapes and Bamboo cuttings from Cala to day.

11/ Bought two loads hay + sold one to Grosbeck, $5.00

12/ Lilly still Sick. Every one tells me to give her quinine. Both she and I have more faith in administrations. Br. Reed fixed some drops for her.

To day bought a house of 3 rooms, and lot of C. Bingham, for $250.00 down and $150. more in 2 months. Also, I paid J.McRae $20. of the $60. I owe him for a city lot under the Canal. I buy it so as to have some garden this Summer.

13/ Lilly seems a little better

14/ Seth and the ~~boys~~ ^Jesse^ leveled on ~~upper~~ ^lower^ canal. Albert plowed and I set out the 150 grapes and 11 Bamboos.

15/ Lilly up and dressed to day

16/ Went to Benson and bo't garden seeds. I was to day elected Prest of the St David Irrigation Company. I did not wish the office, but Prest Layton + Kimball wished me to take it.

Recd a letter from home, + one from Henry, who is called to a mission among the Navajoes

Tues. 17/ Wrote home and to the Utah Journal.[6] Planted peas. Lilly worse again. Planted corn

18/ Surveyed for Br. Kimball

---

6. Martineau's letter to the *Utah Journal* included a description of St. David and the agricultural prospects of localities in the Gila River Valley and south. In describing St. David, he wrote:

> It is a healthy climate, and in general there is less sickness than in Utah, rheumatism being unknown except as brought from some other country, and diphtheria also. A few persons have had chills and fevers, generally traceable to bad locations, such as proximity to swamps and stagnant water, and other maladious spots; also to living in poor homes with dirt floors and roofs, and to the many discomforts necessarily endured in a new country.
>
> The settlers here are engaged in making other improvements, and have this spring set out many fruit trees, grape vines, eucalyptus, and pepper trees, and I think two or three years will show a beautiful little town here.

See J. H. M. to Editor, April 17, 1883, "St. David," *Utah Journal* April 27, 1883, 2.

19/ Paid Cash to Mrs. Wild, $3.00. Also flour $2.50 and potatoes $4.50, on room rent.

Sat. 21/ Planted 10 lbs onion setts. Also 3 qts peas. Grosbeck's baby died to day.

Sun. 22/ Spoke at funeral. Lilly about well again.

23/ Got 683 lbs. potatoes, on credit, of C. Layton, to plant.

24/ Let out some work on Canal.

25/ Leveled on upper canal

26/ Planted 1/2 acre of potatoes yesterday. Leveled on lower canal to day.

27/ Lilly + I went to tombstone, + I bought a plow. price $19.00 and 4 chairs $8.00

[Page 532L]

1883/ Horse thieves chased.

April 28/Finished planting garden, 2 acres in all.

Sun. 29/ Some horse thieves passed here at 2 A.M. with 9 horses. I got men on their trail in about an hour, who followed them and in two days recovered the horses.

30/ Resigned my office of U.S. Land + Minl Surveyor.

Tues. May/1/ May day. Seth, King consort. A nice exhibition.
[Blank line]

Sat. 5/ Went to Benson + paid $80.00 to enter 320 acres ^Desert^ Land

Sun. 6/ Went as far as Layton's this evening, on our way to the Settlements on the Gila.[7] Br. J. Hill goes to take me. Brs. Layton and Kimball, in another buggy.

7/ Start at 6 A.M. and drove 67 m. to Hopkin's Ranch.

8/ Drove to Smithville, 43 miles, arriving at 7 P.M.

---

7. Layton, located three miles southeast of Thatcher on the Gila River, was named after Christopher Layton. It was established in the May of 1883. It was formally organized as an LDS ward on November 4, 1884, with John Welker as first bishop. See Jenson, *Encyclopedic History of the Church*, 420, and Barnes, *Arizona Place Names*, 242.

9/ Drove up the Gila on N. Side, visiting settlers. Then to Stafford, and looked at Grist Mill, which we had some thoughts of buying. Dined at J. Moody's. In evening held a council meeting.

Thurs. 10/ Went to Curtis, 8m below, and held meeting. Called a Bishop and two councillors, for Curtis. Held a priesthood meeting at Smithville in the evening.

Fri. 11/ Spent the day in Council. Dined at E.W. Easts.

Sat. 12/ Meeting today, at 10 + 2 P.M. Well attended. We named the following places:—Graham, Curtis, Thatcher and Changed the names of Smithville to Pima, as the Government will recognize no other.[8]

Sun. 13/ Meeting today. I spoke and felt well.

14/ Started home, drove 67m to Hudson's ranch. Br. Layton quite unwell, with cold.

15/ Reached home at evening. Br. Layton's mule nearly died on the way, which delayed us.

16/ Rained hard to day.

17/ Planted Squashes and melons. Plowed in field ^N.^

18/ Wrote letters

19/ Surveyed on town Site.

Sun. 20/ Meetings at St. David.

21/ Seth went to Benson to get work

---

8. A few days later, Christopher Layton wrote a letter to President John Taylor submitting the names of new settlements in the lower Gila Valley and made recommendations for bishops and councilors. The recommended names included Pima (formerly Smithville), Thatcher, Graham, and Curtis. He also requested plans submitted for surveys, writing "The people will be unable to move ahead with their improvements until we get an answer from you." He also indicated, "Elders Kimball + Martineau are with me in our public matters + always on hand to go or help, and I have no occasion to find fault but rather thank God for all his mercies extended to us." The impermanence of the settlements was described when he concluded by writing: "It would be pleasing to get an answer from you as early as possible, the rainey season coming on about the 10th of July and many would like to build, and are living in their tents and wagons." C. Layton to President John Taylor and Councillers, St. David, Cochise Co, Arizona Territory, May 16, 1883, First Presidency, John Taylor Presidential Papers, 1877–1887, CR 1/180, box 13, fd. 5, LDSCHL. See also William R. Teeples to Editor, May 16, 1883, "Correspondence," *Deseret News* 32 (June 6, 1883): 307.

22/ " " Contention to get work. He did.

[Page 533R]

1883/[Blank line]
May 23/ Watered garden, and planted Sorghum.

24/ Moved into our <u>own house</u>. It seems nice to be in our own home again, even of it be a bumble one. Br. Kimball lent me a stove, and a load of hay. I hoed corn and peas.

Fri. 25/ Got a new wagon of Br. Layton, and Sent team to Benson for Some freight for Tombstone. Jesse got back ^at^ dark

26/ Albert went with freight. Quite hot. 92° in house.

Sun. 27/ Very hot. 95° in house. Albert got back at noon. $12.00

Mon. 28/ Went to Benson with Lilly. Bought tub + wash board also a ham, and 2 sack feed, and lumber to make a kitchen table. Hauled some things for Groesbeck. Saw a wreck of freight train on S.P.R.R. near Benson. One man killed. Begun to haul adobes for back and [addition]

Tues. 29/ Heard that Br. Bingham was killed Sunday last. while freighting. Laid foundation, and a few adobes.

Wed. 30/ Br. Bingham's funeral today.

Thurs. 31/ Worked on house. Jesse helped Widow Bingham 1 day.

Fri. June/ Jesse helped repair canal.

Thurs. May 31./ [See bracket] Sold my wagon to T. Jones for 40 acres land. Arranged for wire (10 bales) with D.P.K. and got loads of hay of him. Wrote home and to Charly + Journal.

Sat. June/ Conference today. Well attended from the Gila, 110m.

Sun. 2/3d / do do Spoke and felt well. We organized another new Ward—McDonald, 4 miles above here. with H.J. Horne as Bishop.[9]

4/ Worked on house. Got 2 Sacks feed at Benson. Therr 95° Recd letters from home.

---

9. For minutes of the conference, see "St. Joseph Stake Conference," *Deseret News* 32 (June 27, 1883): 356.

5/ Settled with Layton for 2 wagons $120.00 each (exact cost) one of which I turn to Kimball to pay for wire, and gave Layton note for $277.50

6/ Bought Spring wagon of D.P.K for 100$ 9mo time. Also borrowed 403 feet lumber of T.O. Office. Work on house. Ther 98°

7/ Paid 11.20 for adobes.

8/ Bought 1166 lbs fence wire of DP Kimball for $157.41 + gave note to C. Layton, in all $277.50, interest 10/01

[Page 534R]

1883/[Blank line]

June 8/from date. This am't covered pay due C. Layton on a wagon I bought from him at $120.00

    Surveyed for D.P. Kimball. Finished wall of house.

9/ Gave note to DP Kimball for $100.00 for wagon, 9 mo.

13/ Got lumber for Stable $52.00 Began shingling.

14/ finished this evening.

15/ Attended Lulu Hill's funeral today.

16/ Seth came back to live.

18/ Seth got team to plow his land. He and Albert camp out at Layton's. Thermometer 104°

19/ Finished stable. Cost $50.00 + 15 = $65.00

20+21/ Worked in garden. 104°

22/ Made bedstead

25/ Irrigated. 106°

26/ Planted corn. 107°

27/ Funeral of Br. Newel, kicked by a mule at Chiricahua. Sent my papers for filing on land to Tucson.

28/ Sowed 180 lbs lucern Seed, on 6 ½ acres. Rain. 102°

29/ A little rain. Considerable on Whetstone + Dragoon Mts. Planted Sweet corn + fought potatoe bugs. 80°

30/ Shingled for A. Cluff.

July 2/ Recd certificate of deposit of $80.00 for entry of 320 Acres desert land. Wrote letters. Boys in field.

3/ Went to Benson and got $300.00 Sent by Lyman for land I had Sold. Paid debts

4/ Celebrated, + danced.

5/ Paid Mrs. Bingham $120.00 ^on^ house. Also Pd for lumber and Some smaller debts.

6/ Went to tombstone, and gave County deed for road through my land.

10/ Began to build a Section house of adobes.

    Seth went to Benson to get work.

12/ Recd letter from M. Thatcher. Planted 50 lbs beans.

14/ Hired 3 Mexicans to clean out my well, at $8.00

16/ Got letters from G. Clements + others. Made me a bedstead.

17/ For some time thermometer ranged from 82° to 88° Surveyed on town plat ½ day, with Jesse + Albert.

[Page 535R]

1883/[Blank line]

July 18/ Surveyed ½ day on town plat, with Jesse + Albert.

20/ Built privy.

22/ I came to Utah 33 years ago today. Prest Layton got home from Utah. Lilly + I went to meet him.

27/ Made me a stand. Considerable rain for Some days.

28/ Seth returned home again, having quit work. Rain.

Aug. 2/ Jesse + Albert began work on upper Canal.

4/ Began fencing my 80 near Layton's. Rain.

7/ Traded wagons with F. Campbell

11/ Finished setting 1 mile of posts, (351 in No.)

13/ Letter from Moroni. His son Howard died Aug. 3. Netta still sick with rheumatism, began in July. Also learned that Charles is Sick in Tennessee, very.

15/ Began to stretch wire on fencing

16/ Brs. Layton, Kimball + I visited the Whetstone Mts, 12m The boys finished wiring the fence—1 mile.

17/ Recd check for $75.00 Next day went to Tombstone to get it cased. [cashed] Lyman sent it to me to come home with Netta. being very Sick.

23/ Started back to Utah today, taking Some large Cacti for Lyman and Prest Preston, weighing 140 lbs. Went by Emigrant Cars. In San Francisco took a severe cold, and was sick all the way to Logan, arriving there

Sept. 1/ Sept. 1. 1884.[10] Found all well but Netta, who is very weak and ill, though Somewhat better. From this time till Conference was busy Settling up with people and working around home.

Oct. 2/ Started to Conference.

5/ Conference. Prest Taylor Said "Each stake. is a perfect organization in itself, just as the Church is." HJ Grant Said "Those who do not pay their tithing cannot go to the Temple.

Prest Taylor:– Stake presidents should encourage Quorums and see that people join them. Each Stake is a perfect facsimile of the Church. Stake Presidents must be careful not to assume responsibilities of other peoples sins. They must

[Page 536L]

---

10. Four days later, the *Journal* noted that Martineau had called at the newspaper office and exhibited "two fine specimens of round cactus" weighing nearly sixty pounds each. See "From Arizona," *Utah Journal* (Logan), September 5, 1883, 3. On his way north to Logan, Martineau stopped in Ogden and gave a description of farming and irrigation near St. David to a reporter for the Ogden *Herald*. It was later posted in the *Millennial Star*. See "From Arizona," *Ogden Daily Herald*, September 1, 1883, 3, and "Utah News," *Latter-day Saints' Millennial Star* 45 (October 1, 1883): 640.

1883/ Conference

Oct. 5/ get right after wrong doers. They must wake up to the duties of their callings. When you administer to the sick always say "<u>if not appointed unto death.</u>"

7/ "The Spirit of God is not a part of the Gospel. It is in all people of intelligence."

8+9, 10th/ Attended a special meeting of First Presidency. Apostles, Stake Presidencies, Prests of Seventies + the Presiding Bishopric. Many things taught, and a glorious time.[11]

11/ Visited flowing well, + inspected the Brockett Auger.

12/ Came home. Took Dora, she is about 5 weeks old—^a waif^

17/ Snow storm today. Dora sick and feeble—hardly alive

18/ Went with Theodore to S.L. City to See About Auger. While in S.L. City attended Bishop Hunter's funeral. Also inspected the working of the Brockett Auger.

26/ Wrote to Prest J. Morgan relative to releasing Charles, who is quite sick with chills + fever.

27/ Came home.

Nov. 2/ Br. Moses Thatcher + I administered to Netta. He gave her a very god blessing.

4+5/ Quarterly Conference. Cold + raining.

14/ Went to Provo to see ^and J. Stewart, and^ if I could collect what he owes. He would not pay me—he owes me over $400.00 for work I did for him, Surveying in Cache Co. 1875.

16/ Returned to S.L. City.

18/ Attended Tabernacle. Was called to the stand + prayed. Preached in evening in 15th Ward.

---

11. While attending administrative meetings after the conference, President Layton reported on the promising resources at St. David. See "The Southern Country," *Deseret News* 32 (October 17, 1883): 623.

19/ Snowy.

20/ This morning Charles arrived by Denver R.G.RR feeing pretty well. Had one chill on train. I am very thankful he has returned safe + Sound.

21/ Went to Logan. Heard of DP Kimball's death yester^day^

23/ Charles began work at U.N.R.R. Shop, his old place.[12]

29/ Susan + I had thanksgiving dinner with M. Thatcher's family, + had a pleasant time.

Dec. 8/ Netta much worse today, coughed hard and spit blood, We called in Dr. Ormsby. Joel came home from

[Page 537R]

1883/ Netta's sickness <u>1884</u>.

Nov. 29/the Cañon with his foot cut.

[In margin: Dec. 10]/ Netta much worse, dropy [dropsy] having set in. Her feet and legs begin to Swell. Sat up all night in her chair and coughed very hard. Failing rapidly, and it seems as if nothing but the power of the Lord can save her.

Dec. 11/ I sat up all night with Netta, who passed a very bad night. Dropsy increasing. She slept not more than 5 minutes at a time.

12/ The doctor says the water is accumulating round Netta's heart, and that she cannot possibly live. I pray for and administer to her often. I know God is able to heal her, if it is his will.

21/ Up to this time Netta has been in a very precarious situation. We have had the Elders many times to administer to her, and for a few days she has improved. Last night is the first night for a long time I have not been up with her. For weeks she has not been able to lie in a bed, but has Sat day and night in a chair. Poor girl, she has suffered much.

22/ Netta much worse again, the swelling ascending into her body.

---

12. On November 26, Martineau submitted a letter to the *Utah Journal* showing the elevations of points on the Utah and Northern Railroad, "[a]s a matter of interest to the people of Cache County." This information had been furnished to him by George Wheeler. See James H. Martineau, "Altitudes," *Utah Journal* (Logan), November 28, 1883, 3.

1884 Dora very fretful and weak. Was almost dead when we took her. [It appears that this line had only 1884 then was filled in]

Jan. 1/Tues./ Nett looks better, the swelling is nearly all gone. Susan sick last night and sick abed all day. Very cold.

2/ Susan still quite sick. Alley came down to help.

3/ Gertrude has a very bad Cough. Susan can sit up.

[A margin note between Jan 2 and 5: Jan. 6. 1884/Charles was ordd a Seventy by Sylvester Lowe]

5/ By letter we learn that Jesse is called to learn Spanish, with others, with view to future mission in Mexico. Netta's dropsy nearly all gone.

Tues. 8/ Have been married 32 years. Got a gold ring for S.

10/ Began work in T. Office today.

17/ Lyman got me Suit of clothes—$34.00

21/ Joel began in the Journal Office, asst Book keeper. Did not sit up with Nett last night for first time.

24/ Nett not So well. Dora has been sick for a week with Canker.

[Page 538L]

1884/ Lay out Temple Grounds.

Jan. 24/ Truly I have had my hands full, but the Lord has thus far preserved all our lives, for which all praise to His name.

Feb. 24/ Was Called to sit in the high council, and was chosen to Speak, in case of Brown vs Hopkins. Settled with T.O. for my labor in settling the Stake accounts, + recd $100.00 work.

March 18/ Dora walked today across the room! Paid Kimball's note ($100.00) by Lyman's help. I gave Lyman my note for $185.00 due in 6mo at 1 % per month interest

20/ Snowing still.

Apr. 1./ Went to Conference

4. 5+6/ Conference. At priesthood meeting strong preaching on plurality.

All presiding officers must accept the law or resign. Br. Preston was appointed Presiding Bishop.

7/ Special meeting of Presidency, Apostles + Stake Presidents. Prest Taylor explained Sec. 132 (on Plural Marriage) very fully, Section by Section; and it was voted unanimously that all presiding officers must obey it, or resign.

Tues. 8/ Attended Central Board of Trade, and was added, a member. Also Prest Layton.

9th/ Another Meeting of the Grand Council, Much good teaching.

10/ Came home to Logan.[13]

25/ Sold desk to TB Cardon for $45.00 in goods.

26/ Snowy and cold.

May 1/ Began collecting statistics of the Temple for the Utah Journal today.

Mon. 5/ Last night Nephi had a son born to him at 1-50 A.M. (Standard time—28min fast of true local time) Began to lay out the ornamental walks and drives around the Temple, according to plan furnished by Don C. Young.[14]

10/ Nett rode out in carriage for the first time to day. I was today appointed by the Logan Temple Committee (per. F.D. Richards) to make out a full report of the work from the first, for the Temple Committee, for record in the Church history and for the Temple record.[15]

---

13. Even at this time, Martineau was trying to sell his home and business property in Logan. See "For Sale," *Deseret News* 33 (June 25,1884): 368.

14. Joseph Don Carlos Young (1855–1938) was born in Salt Lake City on May 6, 1855, to Brigham and Emily Dow (Partridge) Young. In 1875, after attending the Deseret University in Salt Lake City, Don Carlos enrolled at the Rensselaer Polytechnic Institute at Troy, New York. He graduated with a degree in engineering but his principal career interest was architecture. He is known for his contributions to Mormon architecture, including the towers of the Salt Lake Temple, the Church Administration Building, the Eagle Gate, and the tabernacle in Paris, Idaho. Young was sustained in general conferences as church architect, a position for which he served from 1889–1893. He died in Salt Lake City on October 19, 1938. See Westwood, "The Early Life and Career of Joseph Don Carlos Young."

15. James H. Martineau, "Report on the Logan Temple." This report was also published without attribution in Utah newspapers. See "The Logan Temple," *Utah Journal* (Logan), May 17, 1884, 2; "The Logan Temple," *Deseret News* 33 (June 4, 1884): 320; and "The Logan Temple," *Ogden Daily Herald*, May 20, 1884, 2.

15/ Henry Lunt + wife arrived from Cedar city to be at the dedication of the temple. Mrs. Lucy B. Young, + her daughter Susy Y. Gates + child also stop with us.

[Page 539R]

1884/ Dedication of Logan Temple.

May 16/ Quarterly Conference began today. Visited temple.

17/18/+/19/Myself, Susan and Netta attended the dedication of the Temple. About 2000 present, all having Cards of invitation. My seat was in the Stand, left side, assigned Presidents of Stakes. The ceremonies were simple but impressive. After the prayer of dedication was read by Prest Taylor, and Singing and addresses by G.Q. Cannon, Jos F. Smith, W. Woodruff, L. Snow, Prest Taylor asked all to rise and shout "Hosanna! hosanna! hosanna to God and the Lamb! Amen! Amen! Amen!

After this Prest Taylor led all the people through the building from Top to bottom. Similar ceremonies were held the two following days so that others might be gratified. I went all three days by invitation.

We have with us, besides Br. + Sister Lunt and L.B. Young and daughter, Br. + Sister Russell, and Seth Johnson, who came unexpectedly, and was very welcome indeed. Besides this, quite a number from places around, stayed with us, making our house pretty full.—over twenty sleeping and eating with us.

20/ To day Path H. Lunt blessed Susan, Netta, + Joel Susan, Nett and I got a recommend to do work in the Temple. Sister Young gave me a name to be sealed to me—Marie St Pierre, who died in 1872 ^born. 1833^ also Clara St Vincent, died 1872, born 1854. afterwards, Susa ^Young^ gave me four more.

Temple Work.

May 21/Began work for the dead, with Susan and Netta. I was endowed for my father, being ordained for him an Elder by Erastus Snow. Susan acted for Marie St Pierre, who was sealed to me by Prest Geo. Q. Cannon, E. Snow and Orson Smith witnesses. Netta acted for herself, though very weak

23/Susan and I in the Temple. I acted for my father Susan for Clara St

Vincent. As all this work is specified in full in my genealogical record, I only give the names we worked for each day.

24/ Worked laying out Temple grounds.

26/ Gave list of names for baptism + worked on grounds.

[Page 540L]

1884/ Temple Work. Dora adopted

May/Sister Young gave me three more names—five in all—of women to be endowed and sealed to me, they are

    Sophia Gilmier, born 1818 died 1872
    Mary Essebrous   "   1820   "   "
      Mary Gertrude   "   1840   "   "

May 27/To day I was baptized to renew my covenant + for 26 dead Netta for her health and for 7 dead. Sister Young was very kind to Netta—took her into a private room + prayed ^with her^

28/ I acted for my mother's father, James Mears, + Susan for Sophia Gilmier, who was sealed to me. Netta acted for my mother, and was proxy for her in sealing my father and mother, I acting for father. What a blessed privilege to reunite my father + mother!

29/ I endowed for my uncle Peter Martineau, Susan for
    Mary Essebrous and Netta for gr. mother Ellenor Haughout.
"   "   was sealed to me. Susan being proxy.

30/ I endowed for Chauncey Mears, my uncle; ^+^ Susan for Mary Gertrude (Sealed to me) Nett went on pic nic to day.

June 3/ Was baptized with Nephi for 55, Nett + Virginia for 55 = 110

4/ I endowed for my step father Wm G. Babcock, Susan for Jane Varley, father's 1st wife, + to whom she was sealed. Nett for gr. mother Lois Sprague, who was sealed to Gr. father Jas Mears.

5/ I ~~ordained~~ ^endowed^ for Stephen Martineau. Nett for his wife + Susan for Mary E. Sherman, her cousin—my wife. Sealed

6/ I endd for Uncle Wm A. Mears, Nephi for my brother Chas Sprague Babcock, Susan for Aunt Mary Dean, Nett for my Sister Julia.

Dora was sealed to me as my daughter + Susan's The ceremony was witnessed by many with interest Some with tears of joy. All thought she was fortunate, and Susan and I feel very thankful—felt as if a child was just born to us. We each had a powerful testimony that the matter was right with the Lord.

This was the first adoption of the kind performd in the Temple. Dora acted very well all through the ceremony.

[Page 541R]

1884/ Temple Work

June 10/I was baptized for 55, Nephi for 28, Joel 27 Theodore 28 Gertrude 10 Emma for 15. Finished 8.45 P.M.

11/ I endowed for Elie Martineau, ancestor, Susan for Aunt Caroline Ferguson Mears, Nephi for Gaston Martineau.[16]

12/ I endd for France's Martineau, Susan for Susan Macon, who was sealed to me. Nett too ill to go to temple.

13/ I endd for Uncle James R. Mears, Susan for his wife Francis Russell.

17/ Emmeline was bapd for 15, Anna for 10, Jene 43.

18/ I endd for Ethan Allen, Susan for Mrs. W.G. Babcock, my step fathers 1st wife.

Eliza came today, with Harry Chamberlin + Mary Lamb, to visit the temple.

19/ I endd for Uncle John Mears, Susan for Margaerite Barbesson (ancestor) Elie + Marguerite Sealed.

20/ I for Stephen Martineau, S. for Charity Christopher (my Aunt)

23/ Wrote the following lines in Mrs. Rhoda Y. McAlister's Album, using some "Maya" indian words:—taught me by Br. O.V. Aoy, of Merida, Yucatan:—

[Blank line, poem follows]

---

16. Gaston Martineau (b. ca. 1654) is the first documented progenitor with the surname Martineau. See note at entry for February 25, 1903. See also Martineau, *Notes on the Pedigree of the Martineau Family*, 10–16, and Smiles, *The Huguenots*, 488–490.

I think I'll write a little "Maya,"
So here I scribble—<u>Kottain gwayah</u>? (come here)
"No sir, I wont," perhaps you'll say.
My footsteps point another way."
If that's the case, then "<u>Bash-ah-kattah</u>" (where go you)
(This, too, is Maya—not Mahratta)
If to answer this you do not wish
   I'll cease, and say "<u>Yos-bottick-tich</u>." (good luck to you)
Query.
You've read good authors by the score
Byron Shakspeare, Scott and Moore
And other poets;
Now dont you think these lines of mine
Than theirs more soulful—more sublime?
 I'm sure they show it.

[Page 542LR]

1884/ Temple Work

June 23/In the Maya language kottain gwayah means "<u>Come here</u>;" "Bash-ah-Kattah" = <u>Where are you going</u>;" <u>Yos bottick tich = Good luck go with you</u>.

Wed. 25/ Endd for Abram Martineau, Susan, Mrs. Abram M. Susan Smith for aunt Laura Mears, Eliza A Benson for Aunt Mary A. Mears (Martineau) Emma for Ellenor Martineau;

   Prest McAllister and Bp. DH Cannon dined with us.

26/ Endd for John Mears, Susan, Mrs. John Mears (E.A. Benson for Aunt Maria Louisa Mears

27/ Endd for Henry Mears; Susan, Huldah Hutchinson (Sealed to me) Elizabeth G. Benson for Maria Martineau, Eliza A. Benson for Elizabeth Martineau Anna Crockett for Ann Martineau

29/ Susan took an overdose of Iodine for rheumatism, and was poisoned, almost fattally. She took mustard Egg, + other things to vomit, which saved her, together with administration, but was very sick.

30/ Better, but still very weak

July 1/ Nephi baptized for 10, Anna for 17

2/ Endd for Uncle Daniel Van Slyke, Nephi for Harvey Abrahms, John Laird for Abraham Merrill; Susan for Susannah Martineau. The following were sealed to me Susannah MArtineau, Mary Martineau, Hannah Martineau Sarah Columbine, Elizabeth Brewer, Beatrice Sumner. My four Uncles + wives were sealed.

3/ Endowed for Abraham Decker, Susan for my Sister Lucretia Martineau (Mears) Lucy B. Young for Judith E. Blake,

E.A. Benson for Eliza Martineau; Presinda Smith (Young)

for Catherine Martineau; Susan J. Smith for Sarah Martineau; Lucy Cardon for Ann Martineau; EG Bensen for Emily Martineau.

The six last named were Sealed to me.

4/ Endd for Jos Christopher, Susan for my Sister Francis E Martineau; Prescinda Smith for Ellen Martineau Lucy Cardon for Lucy Martineau; E.G. Bensen for Lois Hutchinson + Elizabeth Townsend for Marianne

[Page 543R]

1884/ Our Second A.

July 4/ Martineau; all of them were Sealed to me.

Wrote to Prest Jos F. Smith + offered him my two Sisters Lucretia and Francis, which offer he gratefully accepted.

6/ [Note a diamond—like dingbat to the left of the 6] He also said Self and wives might (Prest Taylor said) have our Second Anointings.[17] For this, Father, I thank Thee, and pray we may prove worthy so great blessings.

9/ Endd for Stephen Hutchinson, Nephi for Benj. Martineau, Susan for Miss Rand; Emma for Margaret Haughout; Mrs. Lijenquist for Elizabeth Haughout; E.A. Benson for Catherine Haughout; Anna Crockett for Cathe Keteltas Mrs. McNeil for Cornelia Haughout, Mrs. Morrell for Ann Haughout, + E. Crowther for Elenor Haughout; all these 8 were Sealed to me.

---

17. Martineau indicates here that he and his wives had been authorized by the church president to receive their second anointing together. A second anointing is the highest saving ordinance that can be conferred upon a church member and his or her spouse. See Buerger, "Fullness of the Priesthood."

Thurs. 10/ Endd for Isaac Haughout; Susan for my cousin Mary Poole. Mrs. M.A.S.R. Smith for Rachel Haughout Lucy B. Young for Allatta Cozine, Mrs. Crowther, Alijay Webb; Mrs. McNeil, Elizh Martineau, Anna Crockett, Charity Martineau; E.A.P. Benson, Margaret Martineau, Mrs. Morrell, Miss Rand; Mrs. Liljenquist, Gertrude Martineau. of these last, ~~Eight~~ ^four^ were Sealed to me. (on the 11th)

[In margin: 2d A]
[Note lines in margin]

2nd A.

Myself, Susan E. and Susan J. recd our 2d A. from Prest Mariner W. Merrill; Witnesses Thos. X. Smith + Samuel Roskelly, about 4.30 P.M. Father, I thank Thee. Help us to be true and faithful to the end I ask Thee, in the name of Jesus, our Redeemer. Amen.[18]

11/ Endd for Wm Sprague, Susan for Margarette Haughout; Margaret + Elizth Martineau, Allatta Cozine + Alejay Webb were sealed to me. After this, Mrs. Robbins recd her 2d A. and I acted for her dead husband.[19]

[Left margin has lines and 2d Anointing, with arrow]

14/ Virginia and Anna were baptized for 37 persons. Mrs. S.J. Russell and Nels L. Hagberg and Sarah Westwood arrived from S.L. City,\; The latter to be married, and all stopped with us.

Mrs. Russell gave me the name of Sophia Billatt, her aunt, to be endowed and Sealed to me. Also Br. Hagberg gave me his mother—Anna Maria

[Page 544L]

1884/ Temple Work. Mary E. Johnson. Lyman + Della Sealed

July 14/Hagberg, to be endowed and Sealed to me.

---

18. According to Samuel Roskelley's "Register of Logan Temple Ordinance Work July 1884," a total of eighteen second anointings were performed in the Logan temple during the month of July 1884. See Samuel Roskelley Diary, July 28, 1884, Roskelley Collection, MSS 65, box 2, Book 2, USUSCA.

19. The following day, temple recorder Samuel Roskelley wrote: "We have done the largest weeks work since the Temple was opened, on Thursday we had to turn away a number as the building would not accommodate them for Endowments for the dead." Roskelley Diary, July 12, 1884.

16/ Endd for Egbert Martineau, Susan for Harriet Martineau, the English Authoress.[20]

17/ Endd for Uncle John Hudson Poole; Lyman for Uncle Vornelius Martineau; Susan for Mrs. Wm Sprague, E.A. Benson for Mary Martineau;

Recd a letter from Margaret Johnson, giving me her daughter Mary Elizabeth to me (Susan's ½ Sister)

[In left margin, next to the following stricken sentence: This was an error]

~~Also a letter from Sixtus E. Johnson giving me permission to be adopted to father Joel H. Johnson.~~

This evening Susan looked in a crystal for the first time, and could see clearly in it—Saw many things of much interest.[21]

18/ Endd for Wm Sprague, Lyman for <u>Wm Sherwin</u>, Susan for <u>Mary Elizabeth Johnson</u>; E.A. Benson for <u>Anna Maria Hagberg</u>, ^who with^ Mary E. Johnson were sealed to me.

23/ Endd for <u>Nels Hagberg</u>, Susan for <u>Martha Monson</u>, Nett for <u>Mrs. Wm Sprague</u>, Mrs. Maughan for <u>Margaret Williment</u>, Mrs. Burnham for <u>Mrs. Ethan Allen</u>, E.A. Benson for <u>Rachel Martineau</u>.

---

20. Harriet Martineau (1802–1876) was an English writer, philosopher, social activist and feminist. She visited continental Europe and America and wrote of her travels. She also wrote in support of abolition and the rights of the poor. She was a regular contributor to the *Monthly Repository* and the *Westminster Review*. Her brother, James Martineau (1805–1900), was a noted Unitarian clergyman and philosopher. He wrote a number of philosophical works, including *Endeavors after the Christian Life* (1843; 1847) and *Hours of Thought* (1876; 1879). He was editor of and leading contributor to the *Monthly Repository*, the *Christian Reformer*, the *Prospective Review*, the *Westminster Review*, and the *National Review*. See Riedesel, "Who Was Harriet Martineau?" and Logan, *The Hour and the Woman*. For James Martineau, see Carpenter, *James Martineau, Theologian and Teacher*, Jackson, *James Martineau*, and Schulman, *James Martineau: This Conscience-Intoxicated Unitarian*.

21. This indicates that both James and Susan were still dabbling in magic. Crystal gazing (scrying) and other forms of divination were still being practiced by superstitious Latter-day Saints as late as 1885. By this time, however, astrology and divination were considered "dark arts" and the saints were admonished "to carefully avoid any association with or practice of these doubtful and unreliable pursuits that must of necessity lead the mind into darkness, and if continued will finally lead to apostasy." From A Lover of Knowledge to editor, "Astrology and Kindred Arts," *Deseret News* 34 (March 18, 1885): 143. See also "Divination," *Deseret News* 18 (May 12, 1869): 168, and "A Class of Humbug," *Deseret News* 33 (September 24, 1884): 566.

[In left margin by next paragraph says: Note. This sealing of children was needless, as afterwards decided.]

Lyman Royal and Delcena Diadamie, Susan J's children, born before she had her endowments but after she was sealed to me, were this day sealed to me, Netta acting for her mother, and Virginia For Delcena, and Lyman for himself. Thankful.

24/ Endd for Saml Hawkins, Susan for Mrs. Wm Sprague M.A. Maughan for Margaret Martineau, E.A. Benson for Mrs. Gaston Martineau. Mrs. Poppleton for Margaret Jardine; E. Tounsend for Mary Alice Martineau; (These three last were Sealed to me.)

25/ Endd for Seth Sprague, Susan for Elizabeth Marriott Martineau M.A. Maughan for Amelia Columbine; Mrs. Burgess for Mary Martineau; E.A. Benson for Mary Martineau, Mrs. Poppleton for Jane Martineau. All these were sealed to [name missing]

Susan was then Sealed to her father, Nephi proxy for his grandfather Joel H. Johnson (Susan's father) and Sister Zina D.H. Smith (Young) [note appears to be a line from Susan to margin note which looks like: Measles, or Mission]

[Page 545R]

1884/ Susan Sealed to her father. Lyman's child born

July 25/acting for her mother Anna Pixley Johnson Johnson, Prest M.W. Merrill Sealed them. (needless)
[Blank line]
This morning Lyman and Alley had a little girl born to them, at 4-30 A.M. (Standard time, 4 A.M. local time) She was afterwards named Harriet Ann after Sister H.A. Preston.)

30/ Endd for Cornelius Martineau, G.W. Cummings for John Sprague; Susan for Mrs. Seth Sprague; Mrs. E.F. Sweet for Esther Sprague; Mrs. Hughes for Hannah Maxon; M.A. Maughan for Eunice Sprague;

July 28/Monday/ To day I was blessed by Wm J. Smith, Patriarch, in Substance as follows:—Br. Martineau, I place my hands upon your head and confirm the anointing with which you have just been anointed, and seal and confirm upon you all your former blessings. The Lord loveth thee for thine integrity, + has given his holy angel charge over thee, who shall never leave nor forsake thee, and who shall preserve thee from the power of the wicked, and deliver thee from thy enemies in time of danger. Thou shalt have health and strength, and vigor of body and of mind; thou shalt run like a deer and be strong as a lion. No enemy shall prosper against thee, but thou shalt have power over all thy enemies. Thou shalt be blessed in all you put your hand in righteousness to do, and have power to fill any mission or station appointed ^to^ you. You shall be mighty in the priesthood, and have mighty faith, even like to the Brother of Jared, even to perform any miracle that ever was done on the earth—to cause the Sun + moon to Stand still, and to move mountains if necessary for the prosperity of the work of the Lord; and thou shalt have power to heal the sick and afflicted, the dumb, ~~and~~ the blind, the deaf and the lame, to cause the drooping head to look up and comfort those who mourn, and shall be a great blessing to all you may be associated with. I Seal upon you the Second Comforter. You shall live to be full of years, and shall be full of life and vigor to the end, and shall see and converse with the Savior

[Page 546L]

1884/ Blessings by Wm J Smith. Susan's

July 28/face to face. You shall do a great work in bringing souls to Christ, and shall do a mighty work among the Lamanites, and shall have power to learn tongues and languages, and shall be preserved from every evil. The Lord will open your way before you that you may move your family to Arizona, therefore be of good cheer, for when the time comes for you to go your way shall open, and you shall be greatly prospered in that land. You shall do a mighty work in Mexico, and the Angel of the Lord will be with thee, to deliver thee in time of danger, and from prison walls, that shall not be able to hold thee, and thousands of the Seed of Lehi shall rejoice to hear thee and see thee, and to comfort and bless thee. And thou Shalt be faithful to the end of thy life, and be exalted to a throne in the celestial glory. Therefore rejoice and trust in God thy Friend.

This blessing and Susan's was given in our parlor.

Susan's Blessing.

Sister Martineau, We lay our hands upon your head and seal the anointing which has now been administered to you and confirm it upon you, together with all your former confirmations and blessings, and say they shall be sure unto you. The Lord loveth thee, and will bless thee all you desire in righteousness, for no good thing or blessing shall be witheld from thee. Thou shalt have great faith, and great power to heal the sick. You shall be sent for far and near, and many shall bless thee and rejoice because of thee, for you shall cause the drooping head to rise, and comfort those who mourn, and shall be filled with wisdom, that your counsels shall be full of life and salvation to those to whom you shall speak. You shall have visions and dreams, and be a prophetess and seeress, and shall be taught great and mighty principles by heavenly messengers, and shall see and converse with the Savior face to face. Sickness and disease and death shall flee from before you, and you shall truly be a mother in Israel, and a Comfort and help to your husband, and a blessing to your family.

[Page 547R]

Susan's Blessing (Contd)

1884/July 28/(Susan's contd) Your name shall be honorable in Israel. You shall do a great work in the Temples of the Lord, and be a Savior to many of the dead, in acting for them in the ordinances of the Gospel. You shall have health and strength of body and mind, and shall live to be old and full of days, and your last days shall be your best. Rejoice therefore in the blessings which God has and will bestow upon you, for no good thing shall be witheld from thee. You shall have a numerous posterity, who shall be mighty in the priesthood. Your children and all your father's house shall be Saved. You shall be a wise counsellor ^and a comforter^ to your husband, and shall help him to fulfill his mission in the lands to which you are sent, and shall have wisdom to govern and control all your family affairs in wisdom and in righteousness.

J.H. Martineau Scribe

In giving these blessings Path Smith said he felt impelled by the Spirit to bless us, and said when he was done that he saw great and mighty things which he had not specified, and said he felt the Lord would greatly bless us. For all this I feel very thankful to our Father, and hope I may be faithful to the end.

Thurs. 31/ Endowed for Wm Sprague, Geo. W. Cummings for James Sprague, Susan for Mrs. John Sprague, Sister Hughes for Mrs. James Sprague, Mrs.

Maughan for <u>Mrs. Jesse Sprague</u>, Mrs. Burgess for <u>Rebecca Martineau</u>, Anna Johnson ^Henstrom^ for <u>Rebeca Johnson</u>, Henstrom, Mrs. Cummings for <u>Elizabeth Martineau</u>, Mrs. Maria F. Smith for <u>Mary Martineau</u>

Aug. 1

Endd for <u>Danl Sprague</u>, Susan for <u>Mrs. John Martineau</u>, Mrs. Maughan for <u>Mrs. Stephen Martineau</u>, Mrs. Hughes for <u>Caroline Martineau</u>, Mrs. Hewett for <u>Hannah Martineau</u>, Mrs. Burgess for <u>Elizabeth Martineau</u>.

In the evening assisted Lyman to name and bless his baby—Harriet Ann—named for Sister Preston.

Wed. 6/ Endd for <u>Stephen Keteltas</u>, Susan for <u>Mrs. Stephen Keteltas</u> M.F. Smith for <u>Sarah Neave</u>, M.A. Maughan for <u>Margaret</u>

[Page 548L]

1884/ Lyman Bapd for the dead, also Anna

Aug. 6/<u>Martineau</u>. Sarah Neave + Margaret Martineau sealed to me.

7/ Endd for <u>Abraham Egbert</u>, Susan for <u>Mrs. Ann Egbert</u>, N.F. Smith for <u>Harriet Sprague</u>, Mrs. Cummings for <u>Mary Ann Sprague</u>

8 Endd for <u>Peter Haughout</u>, M.F. Smith for <u>Emeline Martineau</u>, E.A. Benson for <u>Mrs. Addra Perrine</u>.

Susan was too ill to go to the temple today—the only time. We both regretted it very much, for it is like being in heaven to work in the temple for the dead.

Sun. 10/ Joel was today ordained Priest by Bp. B.M. Lewis and on

[In margin: 11]/ began his duty as a Teacher in the ward.

13/ Endd for <u>Ichabod Babcock</u>, Susan for <u>Alley Haughout</u> Miss Mary Ellen Wright for <u>Margaret Haughout</u>, Mrs. ^C^E Hughes for Caroline Martineau (sealed to me) Eliz H Martineau (sealed to me)

14/ Endd for <u>James Cozine</u>, Susan for <u>Mrs. Jane Haughout</u>. Emeline Martineau was sealed to me.

15/ Endd for <u>Nicholas Haughout</u>, Susan for <u>Mrs. Nicholas</u> H E.A. Benson for <u>Mrs. Hannah H</u>.

18/ Settled with Temple Supt. Card for my labor laying out the ornamental grounds around the temple, and for making the temple report—$54.00[22]

19/ Paid the U.O. Co. $41.30 in full

Lyman was baptized for 17 and Anna for 14 persons.

20/ To day Niels Larsen Hagberg came to Logan to be Sealed to me as my son, his mother having already been Sealed as my wife. He was accordingly Sealed.

I was Endowed for Peter Haughout, Niels for Benj. Martineau, Lyman for Peter Haughout, Susan for Mrs. Benj. Martineau, M.A. Maughan for Mrs. John Martineau, Netta for Mrs. Elenor Haughout, Mrs. Smith for Elizabeth Hawkins, Mrs. Maughan for Sophia Billott; The last two were sealed to me.

When N.L. Hagberg was sealed to me, Susan acted for his Mother at the alter. Hagberg gave me $60. to get him some of my land in Arizona.

21/ Went to .L. City to sell part of my lot. Paid Mrs Teeples 24$ in full.

22/ Saw Asmussen about my lot. The body of John H. Gibbs

[Page 549R]

1884/ In S.L. City. Br. JH. Gibbs body brought home. Seth Married

Aug. 22/the Martyr, arrived from Tennessee. A great demonstration in the city in his honor.[23]

23/ Sold part of my city lot to Asmussen for $1645 Cash and a gold watch and chain at cost price ($85.00) for Susan.

---

22. The ornamental walks and grounds were designed by Joseph Don Carlos Young. See notes for entry of May 10, 1884.

23. Missionaries John H. Gibbs (1853–1884) and William S. Berry (1838–1884), and two local members, W. Martin Conder and John Riley Huston, were shot and killed by a mob at the home of W. James Conder on Cane Creek, Lewis County, Tennessee, on August 10, 1884. See "The Tragedy in Tennessee–Interesting Particulars," *Deseret News* 33 (August 27, 1884): 499, "A Detailed Description of the Cane Creek Massacre," *Deseret News* 33 (August 27, 1884): 511. The Denver & Rio Grande train car carrying the body of Gibbs arrived at the Salt Lake Depot on Friday, August 22 and a large procession and ceremony awaited the car as the body was transferred and taken south to Millard and Washington Counties, before being taken to Logan and finally to Paradise on the Utah and Northern Railroad for burial. See "The Martyred Elders," *Deseret News* 33 (August 27, 1884): 508, and "The Martyrs and Home," *Deseret News* 33 (August 27, 1884): 509.

Sun. 24/ Memorial service in the Tabernacle in honor of the Martyrs.[24]

25/ Bought Iron bedstead + mattress $15.00 + 3.75.

26/ Eliza and Seth went to Kaysville. I saw Prest J.F. Smith who said my two dead wives Mary Elvira Sherman and Mary Elizabeth Johnson should receive the 2d A.[25] Said he would have my two Sisters, Lucretia and Francis, sealed to his father Hyrum Smith ^or to himself.^ Went to the Lake and bathed

27/ Went to Logan.

Thurs. 28/ I endd for <u>Stephen Martineau</u>. Lyman for <u>John Martineau</u> John R. Barnes for <u>Jesse Sprague</u>. Susan for <u>Charity Beatty</u>, Mrs. Lufkin for <u>Frances Haughout</u>, M.. Maughan for <u>Mrs. Alley Haughout</u>, Mrs. Layton for <u>Mrs. Wm Sherwin</u>, Mrs. Andrews for <u>Mrs. J.H. Poole</u>, Eliza Jones Martineau for <u>Mrs. Cornelia Haughout</u>.

    Seth Jones and Anna Layton married today. Charity Beatty was sealed to me.

30/ Sold Mirror to Lyman for his, ($15.00) and $60. to be applied to my note for $185. which he holds.

Tues. Sept./[Blank line]
2/Susan was baptized by R. Bain, for her health and to R. cov.t [renew covenants?]

3/Nett came from the City with a bad cough. Made deed to Asmussen for the land.

4/ Went to Ogden + Stopped at Layton's, in Kaysville.

5/ Arrd at S.L. City. Got recommend for my two dead wives M.E.S. + M.E.J. [Note, names appear to have been filled in later thus: M.^ary^ E. S^herman^ + M.^ary^ E. J.^honson^] to have their 2d A. Had talk with Prest Taylor about Arizona and Mexican Mission. He dont want people to leave their posts. Quite cold.

Sat. 6/Got my pay from Asmussen.

---

24. The memorial services started at 2:00 p.m. There was reportedly "a vast congregation present, every seat being taken in the body of the hall, while but little room remained in the galleries." See "Honoring the Martyrs," *Deseret News* 33 (August 27, 1884): 505.

25. The letters "2d A" are code for second anointing. See entry for July 4, 1884.

Sun 7/ Cold + rainy. Saw uncle David LeBaron and Don.

9/ Got home.

10/ Paid debts—$300.25.– Mrs. Palmer $4.95 S. Layton $8.00 J Irvine (note + int) $273.00 Goods $14.30

[Page 550L]

1884/ 2nd A. for two. Leave Logan

Sept.11/Thursday/ Susan and I went to the Temple and recd 2d for Mary E. Sherman Martineau and Mary Elizabeth Johnson Martineau from Prest M.W. Merrill.[26]

12/ Paid Z.C.M.I. $84.60 Gave them note for balance $100.00 1 % pr. Mo. Paid 4th Ward Store $464.00 + gave note for balance due ($170.00) 1 % pr. mo. Lyman gave Susan + me each a nice ring. I gave him my Utah Garnet.

13/ Went to Church farm + Spent the day with Nephi + Em

Sun 14/ Lyman + Alley, Nephi + Emma, spent the day with us, I gave them my parting counsels.

15/ We all sat for a family picture at D. Lewis', at Lyman's expense.[27] He also got rings for Nett + Lilly. I sent a silver teapot ^each^ to my sisters Netta and Lotie by Exp.

Tues 16/ Began packing up, Lyman and Charles helped. Sold them my parlor chairs for $60.00 and the Carpet to Lyman for $60.00 Gave Lyman the Sofa ($40.) + to Charles the Rocker, $20.00 and the Parlor Stove $25.00. To Nephi our Bismark Range for his Small stove + gave him chairs, tables, and many other things. Gave Charles the Bedstead + Mattress.

17/ Finished packing, + Sent things to depot. In the evening went to Lyman's to Sleep. (and to Br. Preston's)

Thurs. 18/ Rose at 3.30 and left Logan at 4.30 A.M. Lyman going with us to Ogden. Our parting with our family and Br. Preston's was sad—the sundering of ties that have been binding us together for many years. But these are stirring times, and no one can Say where we may all be in five or ten years. We have lived here over 24 years, and have formed close

---

26. Martineau's receiving "2nd" refers to the second anointing.

27. David Lewis was a photographer in Logan. This photograph appears in the photo section of this volume.

friendships with many dear friends; but at the call of duty we should be ready always to respond, without regrets or unwillingness, for the Lord loves a willing heart. I was 32 when I came here and am now over 56—getting on the silvery side of life, and I can say truthfully, that in all this time I have not knowingly injured or defrauded a single soul, not at any time oppressed the poor.

[Page 551R]

1884/ San Francisco

Sept. 18/My conscience is clear and void of all offense to <u>all</u> In all things and at all times I have ever sought the public good in preference to my own.—have always placed <u>my</u> affairs second to the public welfare and good. I have never been found opposing the priesthood and ruling authorities, but have always been in unison with them. I do not boast in this, but render thanks to God, that <u>he</u> has caused one to be willing to do this, and has helped one to be faithful thus far; and I pray He may help me to the end.

We arrived at Ogden at 8 A.M. and stopped at the "Central Hotel." Our baggage consisted of 5 trunks + 2100 lbs freight—I got a shot gun at Ogden, with ammunition +c. for $30.00 also some clothing for Susan. Lyman Got some also for the girls and Lilla. Paid $300.00 for our fare (3d class)— 6 full tickets, and left Ogden at 6.15 P.M. (Pacific time) 7.25 Ogden time. Lyman was with us till the train Started.

19/ Awoke at Terrace, Elko about 10 P.M. Cool.

20/ Sunrise at Battle Mountain. Paid 25₵ for a potato at the "Capital Hotel." Winnemucka at noon, and Rye Patch at dark.

Sun. 21/ Reno at 5 A.M. Waited till 9 A.M. on account of a R.R. wreck ahead. by which man or two was killed. Began to ascend the Sierra Nevada's snowy range. At Truckee 2 P.M. Left there with three engines. Passed Donner Lake, and reached the Summit at 4 P.M. reaching Auburn 9. P.M. We passed through over 40 miles of Snow Sheds, most of it continuous, and very disagreeable to us, as it hid from us much of the grand scenery we passed.

22/ Wake near San Francisco Bay. Reach Oakland at 9.40 A.M. and San F. at 11.30 A.M. Went to the "American Exchange"—a pretty good "cheap" place, $1.25 per day—board and room. Good tables, but

[Page 552L]

1884/ Los Angeles. Tucson. <u>Home</u>.

Sept. 22/ poor rooms. Bought hats for Susan, Lilla + Virginia also Theodore; coats for the Girls. Foggy and cold.

23/ Foggy this morning. We all went to the Cliff house by Cable road and Carriage, Saw hundreds of Seals, also the head bones of a whale, played on the shore with the waves and returned by train to the city; then visited "Woodward's Gardens," and returned to the Hotel. Then I went to C.P.R.R. general office, saw Mr. R. Gray, Genl Ft. Agt, and got a reduction on household movables, boxes, from $6.70 to $3.80 per hund, for our people moving to Arizona, from Ogden to Benson. Left San F. at 7 P.M. and at the Oakland Pier met Eli and Harry Dennison—old school mates of Elbridge Left Oakland 10.30 P.M.

Wed. 24/ Woke at Lathrop, 82m at 5 A.M. Met Uncle D.T. LeBaron and Don, on their way to Mesa, Arizona. Tulare, at dark. Plenty of melons and grapes 2 ½ ¢ pr lb.

Thurs. 25/ Tehatchapi Loop about Sun rise. Los Angeles 2 P.M. being attached to the Express trains at Tehatchapi. Left Los Angeles 10. P.M. Here we bought Sugar, C. oil + other provisions, also grapes @ 2 ½ ¢ lb. apples +c.

26/ Wake on San Gorgonio Pass in a cloud + rain Storm: Indio ~~8.30 A.M.~~ ^noon^ 350 feet lower than the Sea; Very hot. Yuma 3 P.M. The new R.R. bridge nearly finished. Left Yuma 4 P.M.

Sat. 27/ Uncle D.T. + Don got off at Maricopa Sta. at 2 A.M. to go to Tempe, reached Tucson at 9 A.M. + were hitched on to Express train, reaching Benson at noon. After we had tried in vain to get a team to St David, Seth and Lilla appeared with Wm Laytons team, and wagon, and we reached St David at 4 P.M. <u>Our new home</u>.

Sun. 28/ Went to meeting, and next day. Jesse at hay field.

29/ Went to Benson + got map $1.15 Expr. Charges. Our baggage not yet arrived. Thermometer 90°

30/ Went for my freight. Paid $5.00 Storage + $88.40 frt.

Wed. Oct/1+2/ Unpacked out things. Our house is too little to hold them all.

[Page 553R]

1884/ Survey Thatcher. Blessed by Path McBride.

Oct. 4/ Started for Pima, to attend our Conference, by S.P.R.R.; reached Bowie 4 P.M. 64 miles + found no way to go on.

Sun. 5/ Hired team to take me to Solomonville—3 miles—$8.00 Staid there all night, and hired teams to go to Safford, 5 miles, for $2.00 Reached there at 9 A.M. and met Prest Layton.[28]

12/ Preached at Layton; also Bp. Roundy, an "<u>Emigre</u>."[29]

13/ Began to Survey a city plat at Thatcher. (Moody's)[30]

14/ Finished Survey for the present. Var. by U.S. Sur. 12° 34'E.

15/ Went to Pima, and met Aunt Harriet Johnson, her two daughters Diadamie and Blanche, also their husbands James H. Carlton + Geo. Aikin, who live 6 miles below here. Saw Co. Sur. J.D. Holladay, who made me his Deputy.[31] Patriarch Wm McBride told me I should <u>be prospered + blessed from this day forth</u>, being constrained to do so by the Holy Spirit. This comforted me very much, for I was very low spirited, having a large family and no means of Support for them—no team, cow, chickens buggy,

---

28. Eleven days later, Layton wrote to President Taylor telling him of the difficulty of conducting stake affairs on his own: "I very much regret that I could not be with you at conference, our conference came off on the same date as the general conference in Salt Lake. We had a good deal to do and I had no counselors here to help me Bro Martineau arrived a few days ago, and if you have another councilor for me he [Martineau] will be very exceptable [sic]." C. Layton to Prest John Taylor & Council, from Safford, Graham Co., Oct. 16, 1884, First Presidency, John Taylor Presidential Papers, 1877–1887, Letters Received, CR 1/180, box 15, fd. 1, LDSCHL.

Solomonville was named after I. E. Solomon opened a post office there on April 10, 1873. The Graham County seat was moved from Safford to this place in 1883, but it was moved back again in 1915. See Barnes, *Arizona Place Names*, 415, and "Solomonville," in *Arizona Bulletin Supplement*, 21–22.

29. This probably refers to Bishop Wallace Wesley Roundy (1848–1918) who was forced to seek exile (on Émigré) in northern Mexico for polygamy. He was the first presiding elder of the Colonia Juárez settlement. See Jenson, *Encyclopedic History of the Church*, 381.

30. This probably means that Martineau corrected or extended John M. Moody's first survey of Thatcher in order to conform to the rectangular survey system. See note at entry for October 19, 1885.

31. J. D. Holladay was elected Graham County surveyor in 1881 at the organization of the county. Martineau was appointed deputy surveyor in 1884 and listed as candidate for County surveyor in the *Clifton Clarion* on August 11, 1886, 2. See also *Arizona Bulletin Supplement*, 11.

plow, nor provisions. He invited me to dinner, after which he gave me the following blessing:–

Patriarchal Blessing by Wm McBride, given in Pima, A.T. Oct. 15. 1884, upon the head of James, son of John Martineau and Eliza Mears Martineau, born March 13. 1828 in Port Jackson, Montgomery Co. N.Y.

Br. James, in the name of the Lord Jesus I lay my hands upon thy head, and by the authority of the Holy Priesthood I Seal upon thee a Patriarchal blessing, and also seal and confirm upon thee all thy former blessings + ordinations, and I say unto thee, be thou comforted, for thou art of the blood of the House of Israel and lineage of Ephraim, and called, chosen, ordained and set apart before the foundations of this world were laid to come forth in the dispensation in which we now live, to bear thy part in the redemption of Zion and the restoration of the House of Israel, and to lay the foundation for the Salvation and exaltation of thy father's house for many generations, back, both for the living and for the dead, and to teach them how to save

[Page 554L]

1884
Surveyed Graham, Pima + Curtis. Meetings at Pima.

Oct. 15/themselves with their dead; and to perform this work thou mayest yet have to travel and hunt up the sons and daughters of Jacob, teach them the plan of Salvation, and to build temples, that they may administer ordinances therein, that will produce their Salvation, both living and dead; and the Lord requires that thou should teach thy children to build upon the foundation that has been laid, that thy work may be complete, for unto this end wast thou born, and by obedience to the new and everlasting covenant thou shalt secure to thyself, thy wives, thy children, relatives and friends an everlasting inheritance; for I seal upon thee the blessings of life and health and Strength, and thou shalt receive a crown of eternal lives, and thy part in the morning of the first ressurrection with all that are near and dear unto thee in the name of Jesus. Amen. [blank space] I was scribe for him

Thurs. 16/ Went to Graham to survey a town plat. Saw peanuts growing, also Sweet potatoes; and the 2d crop potatoes

17/ Surveyed Graham today and the next.

18/ Letter from Sur. Genl of Arizona, saying he would appoint me Deputy U.S. Surveyor.

Sun. 19/ Prest Layton and I went to Pima + held meeting.

20/ Began to Survey Pima, and

[In margin: 20–24]/ Finished. Rainy for several days.

25/ Priesthood meeting at Central.

Sun. 26/ Preached at Central.

27/Wrote to Des. News.[32] Went to Carlton's to Survey his land. Went across the Gila in a skiff.

28/ A light frost (the first) last night. Surveyed.

29/ Went to Curtis, + began Survey of town plat.

30/Finished the Survey

31 Went to Pima. Recd letters from home. Wrote letters.

Sat. Nov. 1/ Apostles Young + Grant arrived at Pima

Sun. 2/ Meetings to day. At evening meeting Several members of the High Council were ordained by Apostles Young + Grant, Prest Layton and myself. I ordained Hiram Weech a High Priest and set him apart as a High Counciller. Attended a party at Bush's in the evening.

[Page 555R]

1884/[Blank line]

Nov. 3/Went to Curtis and held meetings. in forenoon, then went to Central and held another. then returned to Pima. After meeting at Central. I ordained Jacob G. Bigler a High Councillor and High Priest, after which

---

32. Martineau described the climate and agricultural resources in St. David and other Mormon settlements in the Gila Valley. He noted that qualified tradesmen and teachers would be needed in these new settlements. "Town plats have been surveyed at Thatcher, Graham and Pima, and Curtis, Layton and Central will be as soon as possible," he wrote. "With energy and skill of our people we hope this country will soon exchange its wild and primitive appearance for a more attractive one, and become, as it may be, the garden of the south." From Jas. H. Martineau to editor, October 27, 1884, "Correspondence. A Prolific Region," *Deseret News* 33 (November 19, 1884): 702.

Prest Layton and I returned to Safford, while Apostles Young and Grant held meeting at Thatcher.

Nov. 4/ Tues. Went to Graham and held meeting. and met there Brs. Young + Grant. I preached, followed by Brs. Young + Grant. Meeting at Layton at 3 P.M. In the evening a Council was held, after which I went to Central, arriving there at 11 P.M.

" 5/ Walked 5m. to Pima. In afternoon went back to Layton

" 6/ Walked to Alred's, and examined the Canal, 6 miles.

" 7/ Borrowed Bp. Welker's horse, and rode over the Country.

" 8/ Went to Central to a Canal meeting.[33] After meeting Prest Layton and I ordained Alfred Cluff a High Priest and set him apart as a High Councillor; Prest Layton officiating.[34]

Sun. 9/ Meeting at Layton. Blessed a baby. After meeting went with Prest Layton to his land, and rented 40 acres, with water for ¼ the crop (for him)

Mon. 10/ Prest Layton and family moved away this morning before daylight, to avoid arrest for polygamy. I went to Layton to resurvey their Canal, but abandoned it. Earned $6.00 Hear many rumors of impending trouble.

11/ Went to Fonda's Ranch, 10 miles, to Survey for some Stock men. (Bert E. Veatch)

12/ Surveyed, running 4 miles through thick Mesquite.

13/ Surveyed all day. Earned $26.00

14/ Surveyed for Mr. Dowdle " $10.00

15/ Returned to Safford. Found the Mill closed and Joseph Layton gone to Tucson, by subpoena before Grand Jury. Hear that Roundy, Rogers,

---

33. The river supplied a steady source of water for irrigation in the Gila Valley. A complex system of some twenty-three canals were in operation at this time in the valley. See Colvin, "First Came the Water and then the People." Many of the original canal company records are preserved at the Graham County Historical Society and Museum in Thatcher.

34. Alfred Arron Cluff (1844–1930) was born at Nauvoo, Illinois, to David and Elizabeth "Betsy" (Hall) Cluff on November 4, 1844. Cluff was one of several Mormon settlers who helped found Showlow and Forestdale, Arizona. Cluff died on February 2, 1930, in Mesa, Arizona.

Fuller, Loving + others have fled, to avoid arrest for polygamy. By letter from home learn that nearly all the family are sick. Wrote to Henry.

Sun. 16/ Walked to Thatcher and held meeting.

17/ " " Pima, and heard that U.S. officials had been there, acting very suspiciously. Attended a party in the evening, given to the Sonora missionaries.

[Page 556L]

1884/ Return from Safford. Missionaries start to Sonora.

Nov. 19/Started for St David with our two teams and missionaries for Sonora. The Giles Settlement furnished 2 4 mule teams and wagons, four extra riding horses, and 7 men. The Salt River brethren at Mesa are to furnish others. At Noon met J. Layton returning from Tucson.

19/ Last evening Br. Montieth and family, with Br. Layton's 4 sons, arrived from Utah at dark, having left home in Utah Sept 3d 1884.

20/ Drove to Wilcox and nooned there 12m, further = 32m

21/ Reached home 2 P.M. having ridden 5 hours in rain Found my family better—most of them well. Found Apostles Young+ Grant at St David. Went to a party at Bp. Johnson's in the evening. Rainy

22/ Rain all last night. We set apart Wm D Johnson as 1st Councillor in place of D.P. Kimball. Br. Brigham being mouth. Br. B. Young Said I had better move to the Gila valley, to obtain a living, as I had no chance here. And then if I should be called into Mexico would have something to go with.

Sun. 23/ Netta thinks she is threatened with dropsy. Had good meetings today. Br. Brigham speaking with power. In the evening Apostles Young + Grant administered to Netta, and promised her life and health.

24/ The apostles ~~and missionaries~~ started to day, the teams having gone previously. I wrote letters to Utah.

Dec. 1/Monday/ Went to Tombstone with Mother, Netta + Jesse. Netta stood the trip pretty well, but was worse in the night. Paid my Co. Taxes $19.00 Bought rocking chair.

2/ Went for wood, with Susan and Netta. She got tired.

3/ Party. Susan + I went a little while. At bed time Nett found dropsy in her ancles, and she coughs very much.

4/ Went to Benson to get medicine for Nett, + walked home 8 miles. Quite tired.

5 6/ Wrote answer to JR. Rogers from Casas Grandes, Mex. for Prest Layton

6/ Water meeting this evening. St David canal, at which the canal was voted to extend to our land.

[Page 557R]

1884/ Missionaries return from Sonora. I go home.

Dec. 7/Sun. Went to meeting, After which Prest Layton called on me and Br. Johnson to go with him to Safford, to try and settle the difficulty between him and Dr. Groesbeck. Slept at Layton

8/ Started at 7 in a rain storm, and drove to Fisk's 46 miles, through rain most of the time.

9/ Crossed Chiricahua Mts. via Stockton Pass, going for ten miles in a dense cloud, with rain and hail. Reached Safford at dark, 40 miles. Cold + Stormy journey. In the evening Johnson + I went to See Groesbeck.

10/ Attempted to compromise, but poor success. Rainey.

11/ Prest Layton and J. Hill started back before daylight Johnson + I settled with Groesbeck, so far as to get the case out of court.[35]

12/ Settled in full with Groesbeck. Heavy rains + snow.

13/ Still cold and rainy, also a little snow—melts.

14/ Preached at Layton. Storm over, clear and cold.

15/ Br. Montieth and I run trial for canal.

16/ Surveyed for Anderson

---

35. On this date, Martineau wrote to the *Deseret News* describing the plentiful resources in Gila Valley settlements. He described abundant opportunities for enterprising men and women to become prosperous. See J. H. Martineau to editor, December 11, 1884, "A Prosperous Country," *Deseret News* 33 (December 31, 1884): 798. This letter was reprinted under "A Prosperous Country," *Latter-day Saints' Millennial Star* 47 (January 12, 1885): 29–30.

19/ "   " D. Groesbeck. Met my old friend, the daughter of Saml West, formerly Nancy West, now Mrs. JH Rollins.

Sun. 21/ Wrote to Lottie. Preached in Layton, and ordained Geo. Morris a High Priest and set him apart as 2d Counselor to Bp. John Welker. Heard that Netta is worse yesterday.

22/ Started home with Br. A.M. Montieth, and young Roundy.

Drove 30 m. and Camped

23/ " 34 " " "

24/ reached home about noon, having driven 22m total 88m Found Netta's dropsy much worse, her swelling having reached her body. Found Jesse just going for some freight sent us by Lyman, some 350 lbs, for which the charges were $39.50. We got the sewing machine, 14 jars of fruit, and some goods sent by Lyman + Charles as a Christmas gift, for which we were very thankful, as it came in good time.

25/ Br. Montieth went home today. Storm at night.

26/ Stormy all day. Conference commenced. Yesterday the expedition arrived from Sonora all right.

[Page 558L]

1884/ 1885. Joel + Theodore ordained

Dec. 26/H.M. Merrill was voted to be sustained as Presiding Elder here.

28+27/Sat. +/Sun./ Conference two days. We set apart MH Merrill as Presiding Elder over St David today. I let Br. Layton have my revolver, scabbard + about 40 Cartridges on my debt, at $24.00 I also spent 8 days in his service, helping him to compromise with Groesbeck, for which I charge him $26.00 Rains day + night.

Mon. 29/ Storm all night. Cold this morning. Netta not so well. and I sat up with her all night.

30/ Netta seems a little better, but the swelling increases. Settled, partially, with Mrs. Kimball, who claims $12.00

31/ Netta had a bad night. Held council at Laytons with Brs. Layton, Johnson + Macdonald.

[Blank line] with dingbat

1885/Jan. 1./Thurs./ Br. Layton + Macdonald went away today.[36] Netta about the same.

The storm is over for the present, but nights are cold. And the ground freezes a little at night. Telegram from J. Taylor

Fri. 2/ Netta seems little easier this morning, but at times she seems smothering. She has more faith in administration than last winter. Her appetite is almost gone. and she can not turn or raise in bed, nor help herself in the least. Her stomach is so weak as to reject almost everything she swallows. Wrote to Br. Layton

Sat. 3/ Netta about the same, but growing weaker. Has no rest but is in constant distress, wishing all the time to be moved into some easier position, but each move hurting her much. Snowed about an inch in the night—a remarkable thing for this climate. It all melts at sunrise. Wrote to Henry about Netta, and to see if they can help me to a team in any way.

Sun. 4/ At meeting today I presented the name of Joel H for ordination as Elder, and Theodore for Deacon. After meeting they were ordained. I mouth in each case. In the evening Joel assisted in laying on hands for the first time, on Netta, who seems better today.

5/ Netta had a very bad night and is worse to day. The swelling increased, and water oozes from her

[Page 559R]

1885/[Blank line]

Jan./feet and legs, which are swelled almost to bursting. Met with Br. P.C. Merrill and other refugees on the river bank, and appointed P.C. Merrill Prest John S. Merrill Capt, and Geo. W Lake Recorder of their party. Also

---

36. A. F. MacDonald and Christopher Layton left St. David on January 1, 1885, for the state of Chihuahua, Mexico, for the purpose of finding suitable land to purchase. Upon reaching San Jose, a small station on the Mexican Central Railroad about eighty miles south of El Paso, they met John W. Campbell, Joseph Rogers, John Loving, and Peter McBride. From there, they went to Corralitos, Ascension, and Janos. After sending a favorable report on these locations to President Taylor, the party went to Casas Grandes and the Corrales basin where Pacheco is now located. For an account of this trip, see "'Mormons' in Mexico," *Deseret Weekly* (October 10, 1891): 481–482. See also Romney, *Mormon Colonies in Mexico*, 55.

told them not to start till we hear from Prest Taylor, but be ready to start any time and keep out of danger in the mean time.

Tues. 6/ Netta still worse. She coughs and spits blood. We held her for some time in a blanket to give her rest.

Wed. 7/ No improvement, but weaker. Wrote to Lizzie Smith for Netta. Last night She took a change and became easier, sleeping much of the time; and all day she has lain free from pain, and sleeping most of the time, raising now and then for a drink or to vomit or cough. I fear this is a change heralding her departure. I went up into the hills, and dedicated her to the Lord, asking if she is to go that she may do so quickly and without any pain or suffering, for she has suffered so long. She can eat nothing or keep anything on her stomach, and can speak but little above a whisper. She does not realize her low state, till I talked to her about it, and told her to give my love to her mother if She should see her before I do. She said she would, but Said She would not do so yet awhile—she was all right—far better than she had been; "Why," said she, "I dont have any pain now." I played on the organ for her, as she loves to have me do. The last tune was "Sweet home," which she noticed and spoke about.

The day was so warm we kept both doors open. We all feel that our darling is nearly gone. She has always been lovely in character, and now, when she asks for anything does so with such a heavenly Smile on her poor weak face. When I said to her "My poor girl," she said "No Pa, not poor—I'm quite a size," ^with a lovely smile, and^ referring to her dropsical swelling.)

[Page 560L]

1885/ Netta's death.

Jan. 7/Wed./This evening Prest Johnson returned from the Gila, and recd a letter from Prest Taylor saying he and a party of nine will be here in a day or so, on their way to Mexico.

Prest. Johnson, Bp. H. Merrill and I laid our hands upon her and dedicated her to the Lord about 10 P.M. This evening she spoke to Susan, saying what a good mother she has been to her always. She wished her to sit where she could see her. She sleeps or dozes most of the time, rousing occasionally to ask for something, and when she does, her face is lighted up with a lovely and heavenly smile.

Thurs. 8/ She seems stronger, and sat up a long time, sleeping most of the time. She drinks often, but vomits directly She eats nothing but a little broth. Her general condition is like yesterday's. I went to Benson + back.

Fri. 9/ This morning at 6.16 She passed peacefully away without a struggle. She had been sleeping, when all at once she said "Oh Huldah," and raised her hands to be raised up. She was raised up and expired in a few moments.

It all seems a dream. Netta was almost 20, and in all her life never gave me cause for trouble or grief. She was most lovely in character, and was loved by all who knew her. he had made her exaltation sure, and last summer did a good work in the temple for the dead. In her temple robes she looked more like an angel than a mortal, and many noticed it. I can only Say "The Lord gave, the Lord hath taken away. Blessed be the name of the Lord." For many days before her death I prayed that if it be the will of God to heal her, that he would do so soon. If it is His will for her to be taken, that He would do so speedily, that she might not linger in pain and distress.

Our neighbors have been very kind + good. For several nights they have set up with us, and especially Alex. McRae and Huldah Hubbard and

[Page 561R]

1885/ and Burial. Prest Taylor arrives. Sonora trip.

Jan. 9/Fri./Esther Walmsley, also Sister Beebee, whom may the Lord bless.

Sat. 10/ Funeral today at 11 A.M. The choir sung "Sister thou wast mild and lovely," which was sung at her mother's funeral also. Path P.E. Merrill spoke, also Prest Johnson and Bp. M.H. Merrill. The day was warm and very delightful.

Sun. 11/ Good meeting today. I ordained ^Jos^ Alex. McRae an Elder, and we Set him apart as Prest Y.M.M.I.A. of St David. Took Supper at McRae's by invitation.
[Blank line]

Tues. 13/Prest J. Taylor and party arrived this afternoon, as follows:– J.F. Smith. M. Thatcher. E. Snow. John Sharp. Geo. Reynolds. H.J. Grant. Jesse N. Smith. Lot Smith + others. Brs. Thatcher + J.N. Smith came to our house. Lyman sent me a check for $50.00 recd today. Held meeting in the evening, when Prests Taylor + Smith and J.N. Smith spoke.[37]

14/ Meeting at 10 A.M. Remarks by Prest Taylor, E. Snow. M. Thatcher. John Q. Cannon + Geo. Reynolds. Prest J.F. Smith dined with us. By invitation I joined Prest Taylor's party for the trip to Sonora.[38] We Started at 4.20 P.M. We travel in the Utah Central Director's Car, arranged for Cooking, dining, and sleeping—everything nice and comfortable. We reached Los Nogales, a R.R. Station on the boundary line at 10 P.M. The Mexican officials were very courteous, not examining our baggage at all, and offering money +c if we needed. It was decided in Council that M. Thatcher, myself. J.N. Smith + Lot Smith ~~+ I~~ should be a committee to examine lands +c for Sale, with view to buying if satisfactory, with M.G. Trejo as interpreter.[39] We took leave of Prest Taylor + the others at bed time, as we are to leave the train in the night. At 2 A.M. we reached Magdelina + left the train, stopping at the "French Hotel." ^ "Hotel Frances"^[40]

[Page 562L]

1885/ Magdelina. Imuris.

Jan. 15/Thurs./Walked around Magdelina, admiring the orange trees loaded with fruit, saw also lemon trees, palms, pomegranates +c. Cactus (flat-leaved kind) grows 25 feet high, with a regular trunk 6 to 8 inches in diameter. Visited a fine church. About 11.30 we saw some 6 or 7 armed police, running down the street, and immediately heard heavy firing near by, which continued till about 40 shots were fired. heard that the police were trying to arrest a man + did so, after shooting him in the side of his head. Magdelina has about 3000 popn Streets are narrow and all houses,

---

37. On this date, Jessie N. Smith wrote: "Attended meeting at 7 p.m. Joseph F. Smith, F. M. Lyman, myself and Pres. Taylor spoke. Slept at J. H. Martineau's." Smith, ed., *Six Decades in the Early West*, 302.

38. For a brief account of this trip, see "Mexico and the Mormons," 149. It was also recorded by Jessie N. Smith. See Smith, ed., *Six Decades in the Early West*, 302.

39. On this date, Jessie N. Smith wrote: "Our party increased by the addition of J. H. Martineau, M. G. Trejo, and R. Collett. At Nogales the American Consul, Mr. Goodwin, called in and paid his respects to Pres. Layton at Dragoon station on the Southern Pacific." Smith, ed., *Six Decades in the Early West*, 302.

40. Magdalena is located approximately fifty miles south of Nogales on Mexico 15. See note at entry for January 9, 1883.

nearly, built in Mexican style. Got Some oranges and lemons from trees, for 2¢ each. Learned of ranches for sale near Imuris.[41]

16/ Started at 8 A.M. with a hired carriage for Imuris, 12 miles up the Magdelina river. Our team was a poor, little, Scrawny team, and balky as we found to our sorrow. Went 5m. and came to a ford of the Magdelina R. but were detained there two hours or more, by our horses balking + in trying to get another animal. We finally hired a horse which the Mexican Said was "buena" but when we got into the river he, too, balked, and we were there a long time. Br. Thatcher got on a horse and crossed, and I finally took off my pants and waded the river—about up to my waist. Finally myself, Jesse N. + Trejo started to walk the rest of the way to Imuris—7 miles, leaving M. Thatcher + Lot Smith with the team + baggage. We got to Imuris about half an hour before the team—pretty tired. Staid at R.R. Sta. and had to sleep on a dirty floor. Br. Thatcher + I being, as we always are on such trips, mates.[42] After Supper I visited Senor Col. Hilario Gabilando. His daughter speaks good English, and explained about her father's ranches which he has for sale. One, "Rancho de San Nicolas" South of Frontura, has

[Page 563R]

Prest Taylor + party return home. Netta

four sq. leagues = ~~about~~ 17305.6 acres. Price $8000.00 Also a ranch 3 m. from Imuris. price $12.000, ^va. 12° 8'E.^ which has about 700 + 800 acres. It is called the Rancho de la Galera, de Gavilondo, and is mostly under fence. It is a good piece of land. He lives in a pretty good house, with flat dirt roof and brick floor. We Also visited during the day several other ranches.

---

41. Jessie N. Smith's diary entry for this date was quite similar:

At 2 a. m. Moses Thatcher, Lot Smith, J. H. Martineau, M. G. Trejo and myself got off at Magdalena being instructed to look at the country with a view to purchasing a small place for the Church. Stayed at the French Hotel. Looked about town. Talked with different people with the aid of Bro. Trejo as interpreter. Not many Americans in the place. While in a public house asking some questions we heard a sudden fusillade and going out ascertained that a party of policemen were arresting a citizen. Some twenty shots were fired though no one was seriously hurt. Up to this time there had been no frost. Saw ripe oranges still on the trees. Partook of some of them.

From Smith, ed., *Six Decades in the Early West*, 302.

42. Martineau had known Thatcher for nearly twenty-five years. They had grown to be fast friends and this was one of several trips during which they bonded.

17/ At 2 A.M. boarded the return train, and got home about noon. We were immediately summoned to Council meeting, which continued till night. At the meeting were Prest Taylor + party, and Prest Layton, Johnson + myself. Discussed our present situation, and necessary moves for us to make. In the evening held meeting in the School house.

Sun. 18/ Council meeting in the morning, and public meeting at 10 A.M. Prest Taylor preached, after dinner the party went in Carriages to Benson + took train for San Francisco + Ogden. On the way down Bp. J.Q. Cannon proposed I should be appointed Bps. Agent for this Stake, which would require me to move to the Gila. I was appointed, subject to the approval of Bp. Preston.[43] Bp. Cannon gave me considerable instruction in regard to my duties. At the station I offered to give Prest Smith my Netta. He eagerly assented and said he had wished for it, but hesitated to ask me for her, but as he already has two of my Sisters would be very glad to have her also. Hoped he would be worthy of her, and thankful for my Confidence in him.[44] They left at 2.15 P.M. Prest Layton with him. We decided unanimously in the council to locate in Chihuahua, and a Committee was appointed to purchase land there.[45]

I sent by Br. Thatcher, Netta's napkin ring to Nephi + Emma; a ring of hers to Charlie, and a beautiful locket to Lyman + Alley, as mementoes of our dear girl.—now gone to rest. She is

[Page 564L]

---

43. With abolishment of regional presiding bishops in 1877, Brigham Young instituted a system of bishop's agents, an individual who would oversee tithing and financial matters in the stake on behalf of the Presiding Bishop in Salt Lake City. In this case, Martineau—as bishop's agent—would concurrently serve as counselor in the St. Joseph Stake Presidency, under President Christopher Layton. For more on bishop's agents, see Pace, "Changing Patterns of Mormon Financial Administration," 4–7.

44. This means Martineau gave his daughter Julia Henrietta to Smith to be sealed to him as a wife. She died unmarried only a few days before this date, on January 9.

45. Of this, Jessie N. Smith wrote:

Our train came along about 2 a. m. Reached St. David at 1: p. m. Pres. Taylor decided to send Bro. Lot Smith and me home to warn the brethren liable to prosecution for polygamy to go to Chihuahua, Mexico, upon the Casa Grandes River. Some of the brethren were already there with Bro. A. F. MacDonald. Bro. Layton who was just from there made a flattering report of the facilities of that country. ... Attended evening meeting in St. David. Bro. Lot preached; I followed. President Taylor appointed Moses Thatcher, A. F. Macdonald, Christopher Layton, Lot Smith, and myself a committee to purchase lands for the latter-day Saints in Mexico.

Smith, ed., *Six Decades in the Early West*, 303.

1885/ Albert starts for Springville, with J.N. Smith + Lot

Jan./18/well worthy, I think, for the exaltation in Store for her.

19/ I procured horses + Saddles for Lot Smith + Jesse N. to go over the mountains to warn their people. I + Susan went to Tombstone and cashed Lyman's check. Jesse went to haul for Allred. Had a surprise party in the evening.[46]

20/ This morning Lot + Jesse N. Smith, <u>Albert</u>, and some others, started with pack animals for St Johns.[47] I Got some blanks from Goodman, needful for me as Bps. Agent.

Wed. 21/ This morning Prest Johnson and I started for the Gila valley to warn polygamists to escape from their enemies, and to instruct the Bishops.[48] Stopped for the night at Wilcox an Eureka Hotel.

22/ Arrived at Safford, + visited Bp. Welker.

23/ Went to Thatcher and Central + talked to the Bishops, thence to Pima, to Bp. J. Taylor's

Sat. 24/ Went to Curtis—found three in danger there + advised them

---

46. Of this party, Jesse N. Smith wrote: "By invitation I attended a kissing bee at Bro. Martineau's, though I was not told beforehand what kind of an entertainment was in store. I felt very uncomfortable and was sorry I was there." Smith, ed., *Six Decades in the Early West*, 303.

47. This trip is recorded in Smith, ed., *Six Decades in the Early West*, 303–305.

48. Nine days later, Jesse N. Smith wrote a letter marked "Private and Confidential" to Bishop David K. Udall at St. Johns:

> Left the Presidential party at St. David. A place of refuge has been found on the Casas Grande in Chihuahua. Pres. Taylor wants no more of the brethren imprisoned. If they are exposed, let them at once repair to the place of refuge via Williams Valley or Pleasanton, taking seeds, grains and farming tools. It is estimated that each man will require $200.00 for his share of the ranch. Let them take all the money they can but keep up their places at home also, if they can. The entrance will be the Custom House called La Ascencion, near San Jose on the Mexican Central Railway. Brother Moses Thatcher and the four Presidents of Stakes in Arizona are locating Committee for the purchase.
>
> Mules and mares are duty free, also cows, bulls and stallions. There is also duty on provisions and groceries. Talk personally to all exposed persons in your ward or Meadow, but keep the movement strictly secret.
>
> Brother Nobel will see you. Make arrangements promptly and let all be on hand at once.

Jesse N. Smith to Bishop David K. Udall, January 30, 1885, Udall Papers, MS 294, box 2, fd. 3, UASCA.

to go immediately. Returned to Pima. Learned that U.S. marshals are about—hunting.

Sun. 25/ Went to Sunday School + Spoke. Meeting in the afternoon. Sent a messenger to Curtis to notify them about the Marshals. At dark drove to Safford. Think of getting Some land and city lot at Central.

26/ Went to Graham with Prest Johnson. Found the Bishop and his counsellors gone to Mexico, having left P.O. Peterson in charge. We appointed him acting Bishop, until Bp. Yorgensen returns. Returned to Safford + went to Layton and held meeting in the evening.

27/ Br. Johnson returned to St David, and I began Settling tithing at Layton, and finished next day.

29/ Went to Thatcher Ward to settle tithing. Finished

30/ " " Central on same business.

31/ Went to Pima to attend priesthood meeting, and then returned to ~~Central~~ Graham

[Page 565R]

1885/ Bought house. Settled tithing. Jesse + Lot Smith came.

Feb. 1/ Held meeting at Graham, and set apart Br. P.O. Petersen as Acting Bishop. After meeting returned to Central to finish there.

Mon. 2/ Finished settling at Central, and got a city lot of Bp. Jos Cluff for $22.50. Returned to Pima in the evening. Br. P.H. McBride returned from Mexico this evening.

3/ Worked on tithing books.

Wed. 4/ Bought a house and lot and a half share of water for $425.00 of S.F. Wilson. Am to pay him $100.00 down, + gave him my note for $275.00 payable Jan. 10. 1886. Also a note for $50.00 in 3 mo. Went to Curtis in the afternoon, after paying Wilson $50.00 which I borrowed from the T. Office.

5/ Attended fast meeting in Curtis, after which I settled tithing and returned to Pima. At meeting, blessed and named Septemma Layton's baby

6/ Wrote home + to W.C. Basset. Worked on books.

7/ Went to Solomonville to get a desk. Got one for $9.25 On my return to Safford, found Jesse,—just arrived.

Sun. 8/ Attended meeting, after which went to Sister Rogers by her invitation, to board. Before this, I staid at Bp. J. Taylor's, who were very kind to me.

9/ Got clay to plaster my house. Seth Jones moved in.

Tues. 10/ Began work on house. My letter of credentials as Bishops Agent for St Joseph Stake, arrived[49]

11+12/ Began plastering to day, at 15¢ pr yd.

13+14/ Went to graham to settle tithing

15/ Meeting at Graham, and returned to Pima.

17/ Finished plastering house

19/ Went to graham and Layton

20/ Got Bp. Yorgensen's Spring wagon to bring my family from St David. Sent $15.00 to Deseret News. This evening Jesse N. Smith + Lot Smith arrived, to meet Br. Moses Thatcher. Prest McDonald and the Presiding of this Stake in council. They left a large company on the road to Chihuahua. Br. Thatcher not being here, they determined not to wait here, but return to their company.

[Page 566L]

1855/ Arrive at Pima Mch. 1. Gertrude taken Sick.

Feb. 21/ Started for St David for my family, with Webb's, + Norton's teams and Nuttall's horses. Drove 40 miles and stopped at Williamson's ranch in the Graham Mts. Station Pass, one of my horses being sick all the afternoon.

Sun. 22/ Near Croton Spring met Prest Layton + Johnson, who Said I was needed in council at Pima, but excused me. Began to Storm heavily, but Jesse + I determined to go clear through to St David if we drove all night. After a few miles we got lost in the drenching, driving rain, and Camped about 11 P.M. cold, wet and hungry.

---

49. This authorization letter, signed by William B. Preston, R. T. Burton, and John Q. Cannon, dated February 5, 1885, was inserted at the back of Martineau's journal, book two. See Godfrey and Martineau-McCarty, eds., *Uncommon Common Pioneer*, 726.

23/ This morning the storm had ceased, and we found ourselves about half a mile from Dragoon Station. At 10 A.M. Met Brs. M. Thatcher and McDonald. Got home at noon. Sold my corral to Tho. Jones for $12.00 to be paid in tithing.

24/ Rained all night and most of to day.

Wed. 25/ Sold my house and lot for $300.00 tithing—^mostly^ to Peter A Lofgreen, 5$ store pay + 35.00 in a cow. Began packing up. The two teams arrived that are to help me move.

Thurs. 26/ Started at 1 P.M. Sold stable to J. Christiansen for $15.00 Went about 12 m. + camped without water.

27/ Four horses gone this morning but found them by 9 A.M. Stopped for the night at Wilcox

28/ Started at 8 A.M. by the Cienga road, and Camped at Mays well, 20 miles.

Mch. 1 ~~29~~/ Arrived at Pima 7.35 P.M.—50 miles. Found Henry and Albert at the house, having arrived about an hour before, from the Little Colorado, Eastern Arizona. They had been nearly two weeks on the road, + had traveled through much Snow in Crossing the Mogollon Mts.

2/ Began to unload, and fix things. Breakfasted at Sister Rogers, who was very kind to us.

3/ Got Some lumber to make a cupboard. Gertrude was taken with a chill in the afternoon, which soon resulted in a violent fever

6/ Plowed some in Garden.

7/ Went to Layton + Got a desk for the office $35.00

[Page 567R]

1885/ Gertrude's Blessing

March 9/David T. LeBaron—a skipper [?]—arrived. Got some trees of him.

10/Set out my peach trees and grape roots. Peach trees here are now in bloom.

11/ Have paid Wilson to date, $150.00 Cash and order to Frank Thurston for grain $64.00 total $214.00

12/ Went to Layton + Safford. Got 111 lbs potatoes for seed. at $5.55

13/ My birthday—57 years old. Planted potatoes.

14/ Planted peas

15/ Patriarch McBride administered to Gertrude and gave her the following blessing:–

A patriarchal blessing by Wm McBride, given in Pima, Graham Co. Arizona. March 15. 1885, upon the head of Gertrude Martineau, daughter of James Henry + Susan Johnson Martineau, born Sept. 28. 1870 in Logan Cache Co. Utah.

Sister Gertrude, in the name of the Lord Jesus I lay my hands upon thy head, and by the authority of the holy priesthood I seal upon thee a patriarchal blessing; and I seal upon thee all thy former blessings, and I confirm and seal upon thee the blessings life and health and strength, and of wisdom and understanding, that thou mayest know how to take care of thy body that thy life may be prolonged; for thou wast called, chosen, and set apart before the foundations of the Earth were laid to bear thy part in the redemption of Zion, and in the restoration of the daughters of Israel, for thou art of the house of Joseph that was Sold into Egypt, and of the blood of Manassah. Thou shalt become an instrument in the hands of the Lord in doing much for the restoration of the daughters of Manassah, in teaching them the gospel in languages that thou dost not now understand, and administer ordinances unto them in the temples of the Lord that will produce their salvation Thou shalt teach them and learn them how to save themselves with their dead; and thou shalt do a great work for thy father's house, for the living, and the dead for many generations back. And thou shalt have visions and dreams + manifestations of the Holy Spirit, and shall learn to ~~understand~~ read the whisperings of the still small voice that shall make known unto the the mind and will of the Lord.

[Page 568L]

1885/ Quar. Conference. Survey Solomonville. Alex. McRae asks.

Mch. 15/And the Lord will give thee a companion if thou desirest it with all thy heart, that will be true and faithful, and will assist thee in thy mission upon the earth, and will secure unto thee an everlasting inheritance and a crown of Eternal Lives, and a part in the morning of the First

Ressurrection, with all that is near and dear unto thee, for I Seal the words of this blessing upon thee, in the name of the Lord Jesus. Amen.
[Blank line]

Thurs. 19/ Finished my settlement of tithing for the Stake, after a very arduous labor, the accounts being in very bad shape. The total of accounts, notes, and means received was ~~over~~ $10.605.00 Planted melons and other seeds.

20/ Planted garden corn.

23/ Went to Safford, and Surveyed for Mr. Anderson. $10.00 Got a bale of fence wire, 97 lbs = $9.70.

25/ Got 2000 lbs of flour from C. Layton to sell, and another bale of wire, 119 lbs. to fence N. Side of tithing lot.

26/ Fenced north and South sides of my lot with wire. Sunday School Jubilee to day, and Female Relief Conference next day.

28/ Conference (Quarterly) today and tomorrow. Wrote to Baldwin about my debt, and arranged to send him the money due him by Alex. McRae. Set apart Hiram Welch Prest H. Priests Quorum, with JG. Bigler 1st + Tho Jones 2d Counsellors. I set apart Br. Jones. Also Jas Duke Prest and Wm J Ranson 1st + Levi Curtis 2d Counr to Prest of Elders Quo. I set apart Br. Curtis. Also Seth C. Jones was ordained a High Priest, to act as prest Y.M.M.I.A. Prest C. Layton did not attend meeting, not deeming it wise.

20/ Conference. Prest Layton at meeting. Left for St David in the afternoon. I sold a horse to Tho. Jones for $50 tithing, to be paid in one year

30/ Shingled the new kitchen. Sent for letter press to San F.

31/ Alex. McRae asked me for Elizabeth. I gave consent. Went with Jesse to Solomonville to Survey a Mexican town plat. Agreed to do it for $120.00

April 2+3/+ 4th/ Surveyed town plat

[Page 569R]

1885/[Blank line]

Apr. 5/ Came home with Br. Welch. On the way met Br. Lines, and bought his farm—35 acres—for ten cows or $500.00, half to be paid down, the rest in 6 months. Bo't cow of H. Welch for $50.00 and cow + calf of mrs. Gale $55.00; also one from T. Office.

6/ Bo't cow of D. Norton for $45.00 Went back to Solomonville. Jesse surveyed for Jesus Aros, $5.00 I worked on map.

7/ Attended Session of Supervisors, and applied for books, for Surveyor's office. Mapped in Afternoon.

8/ Finished my 2 plats for Judge Hyatt

9/ Settled with Rejino Chararria for survey of town. Donated $3.00 to the Mexicans to help them build a church. Surveyed a Section for I.E. Solomon, $20.00 Our board bill, 8 days. $25.00. My trees arrived from Los Angeles, 2 orange, 2 pepper, 2 Eucalyptus. Freight chgs. (Express) $16.25

10/ Surveyed for Jesus Aros. Settled with Solomon + came home.

13/ Wrote to all the Bishops in regard to Defense fund, and gave them their several apportionments. Went to Solomonville with Br. Welch to see about entering our Town Site and our land. which we accomplished. Br. Welch entered the Quar. Sec. on which is my land and his, under Desert Land Act.

15/ Set out 120 tomato plants

18/ Went to ~~Layton~~ ^Safford^ and settled with C. Layton. Paid him note and interest $180.77. Potatoes + meat 21.69 Horses + harness $275.00 Total $477.46 He owes me on a/c $27.00 Bal. due him $450.00 which I paid him. Took his order on the mill for $128.49

Sun. 19/ Recd the horses and harness

20/ Letter pres came. Total cost, $35.70, with letter books +c

21/ Went to Safford for medicine for Gertrude, who still lies helpless in bed.

22/ Surveyed our (Welch) Quar. Sec. very cold wind from North which killed wheat in fields, melons +c in gardens.

23/ Made plats of Pima, and sent plats to Solomon of his sur.

24/ Boys hauled rock for well. I worked in field. Got mower.

25/ Started mower, cutting alfalfa for East + others. Storm.

27/ Went to Central and held meeting

28/ Delivered three cows to Lines, for his land. Owe 7 still

29/ Plowed, and sowed some lucern—1 acre

[Page 570L]

1885/ Apaches break out. Forts Thomas + Grant

May 1/ May day celebration. I went to Solomonville + bought a grindstone

2/ Heavy rain to day.

3/ Went to Thatcher with Prest Johnson and held meeting.

4/ heavy rain. We all worked in field.

6/ To day the Sisters (East, Ransom, McBride + Moody) washed and anointed Gertrude, and blessed her. She was immediately made much better, and became free from pain, which for many weeks has been agonizing.

    My two orange trees begin to bred. They have cost me $26.00. Figs and grapes are growing.

12/ Potatoes, peas, + some melons in bloom; peanuts growing nicely.

13/ Wrote historical letter to historian F.D. Richards relative to St Joseph Stake. Recd wedding cake from Wm B. Preston + Kate Pyper.

Thurs 14/ To day Henry started home to bring his family accompanied by Albert. We ordained Albert an Elder, he having been accepted by vote last Sunday. at which time my family were admitted into 2 Wards.

Fri. 15/ Surveyed M. Cluff's ranch.

Sat. 16/ Planted Corn

Sun 17/ Went to Safford and held meeting with Prest Layton + Johnson. Apaches broke out again.

Mon. 18/ Paid Gurmain Co. 1.15 in full on trees

Wed. 20/ Bought a Carriage of JD Holladay for $150.00 and paid $100.00 down

Thurs. 21/ Jesse + I started for near Fort Grant to Survey Camped at the Cienega.

Fri. 22/ Reached Fort Grant 2 P.M. having crossed the mountains by Stockton pass. Arrived at Wicks at 3 P.M. tested lines.

Sat. 23/ Surveyed for H. Wicks ¼ Sec. of land. 40.00 and started for Fort Thomas. Camped in the Cedar Spring Pass.

Sun. 4/ Reached Fort Thomas at noon, a Hole.

[Page 571R]

1885/ Surveyed town at Fort Thomas.

May 25/ Surveyed for Thompson. 20$. and returned home.[50]
[Blank line]

---

50. Three days later, Martineau reported that the settlers of Pima had commenced harvesting barley and wheat. The planting of corn, potatoes, beans, and squash would begin in June. Martineau then reported that the Indians, although they had broken away from the reservations, did not do much damage in Arizona but had killed quite a number of people in New Mexico. "I do not advocate a needless and wholesale slaughter of Indians simply because they are Indians, but it seems as if the Indians now gone to the Sierra Madres under Geronimo have forfeited all claim of sympathy by their murders two years ago and the present season." J. H. M., "From Arizona," *Utah Journal* (Logan), May 10, 1885, 1.
On May 29, Martineau signed his name to the following letter:

Dear Brother
Your letter of May 19th came to hand to day, and in reply will say that no one has as yet been imprisoned in this stake for polygamy. Those who were in danger fled to Mexico in time to avoid arrest. Quite a number have thus fled, leaving their families, in general, pretty comfortably provided for; but all the Bishops and Female Relief Societies have been pointedly instructed to look after the families of all such in the absence of their heads, and not to allow any one to suffer.

In addition to those who have fled, there are at times other who come from the north, who are in need of provisions, feed, &c. All such have received the aid they needed. It was in view of this latter class, who come among us unexpectedly from time to time, that the Bishops Agent here, J. H. Martineau, requested tithing aid for the poor to the amount of $140.00 from the General Tithing office. Many of these wanderers are not poor at home, but are in temporary need.

In conclusion we will say, we shall continue to look after the classes you refer to, and will see that none shall suffer, unless through ignorance of their condition.
We remain your brethren
C. Layton
W. D. Johnson
J. H. Martineau
P.S. Prest Wm D Johnson has removed from St David to this locality.

C. Layton, W. D. Johnson, and J. H. Martineau to President John Taylor, May 30, 1885 [in Martineau's hand], First Presidency, John Taylor Presidential Papers, 1877–1887, CR 1/180, Letters Received, box 17, fd. 6, LDSCHL.

June 1.2.3/ Built Stable and Carriage shed. Lumber cost $85.00

Sun. 7/ Went to meeting in Pima. Prest Layton present.

8/ Recd letter from Lyman. "Clarion" arrives.

10/ Went to Safford to consult with Prest Layton in regard to our policy in indian matter.

11/ Held mass meeting in Pima.

13/ Went to the county Mass meeting in Solomonville.

14/ " " Graham with ~~Pres J~~ ^Susan^ + held Meeting

15/ To day we cut our lucern 2nd time

19/ Sent my two mares to the top of Graham Mt. to herd

Sun. 21/ Attended meeting in Pima. Very warm weather

22/ A little rain this morning. Paid Holladay in full for my carriage, $25.00– total $150.00

23/ More rain. Planted beans yesterday + today—1 ½ acres.

25/ Watered my lucern in garden for the first time.

Fri. 26/ Went to Central to attend Ladies Quarterly Conference. Had a very good meeting in a bowery. Susan went.

Sat. 27/ Regular Quarterly conference at Central. Present the Stake Presidency and Patriarchs and Bishops of all the Wards but McDonald. Had a very good meeting.

Sun. 28/ Conference again to day. I spoke several times during the two days, and felt well.
[Blank line]

July 1/Watered land in field. Got word to Survey a town plat at Fort Thomas, 13 miles below here, on the Gila.

2/ Begun Survey of Thomas, + finished next day, 3d Recd $75.00 for the work. Returned home. 3d inst.

Sat. 4/ Gave Crockett my order on him for a cow, bought of W.M. Clifford. Attended celebration, and was Orator of the day. Lizzie and Virginia sang "Far away." After meeting went with Susan to a pic-nic on the banks of the Gila, and there met the Johnson family.

Mon. 6/ Attended priesthood meeting in Pima. It was determined to make a large canal from Layton to Pima, and myself, W.D. Johnson + R.A. Allred were

[Page 572L]

1885/[Blank line]

July 6/appointed a committee to draft articles of incorporation for the company.[51] Still planting corn. 100°

Sat. 11/ Susan's birthday.—49-May she have more until she has enough, and would rather go home, but I dont want her to go before I do. I bought boots.

Sun. 12/ Went with ~~Susan~~ ^Lizie^ to Curtis, and preached. Hot

13/ Wrote to all the bishops relative to tithing +c. 102°

14/ Sent east for some liquid glue. Put in a large head gate in Smithville canal. Thermometer 102° The rainy season is at hand, with showers on the mountains around us. We need rain very much.

15/ Still at work on head gates. Jesse cut lucerne 3d time

16/ Boys hauled hay. Showery all around. Virginia has a Sowing bee in honor of her birth day—her 15th In the evening had Singing and guitar music.

17/ Finished hauling our hay.

21/ The hardest rain I ever saw for an hour.

Thurs 23/ Last night about midnight. Henry and family, + Albert arrived from Apache Co. having been 16 days on the road. They expect to settle here.

    Last Sunday (19th) Went to Layton with Prest W. D. Johnson to hold meeting. Prest Layton quite sick.

---

    51. The next day, Martineau wrote of a decision to build a branch of the Mill Canal, beginning at Layton and ending at Pima. He also wrote of the abundant crops in the Gila River Valley. See J. H. M. to Editor, July 7, 1885, "Arizona Items," *Deseret News* 34 (July 22, 1885): 431.

Sat. 25/ Took Gertrude riding for the first time, lifting her Carefully in + out of the carriage,—the first time Since March 1.st

Sun. 26/ Went to Thatcher, + held meeting. Afterwards went to Safford to See Prest Layton who is still sick. In the evening attended High Priests meeting in Pima.

27/Wrote to Bp. Preston. Planted potatoes in field.

Wed. 29/Jesse started to day to help drive stock from near Camp Thomas to Apache Co. to be absent 4 to 6 weeks in company with several others.

Sat./[Blank line]
Aug. 1/Susan and I, with several of the children went fishing. They caught 70 fish.

Sun 2/ Meeting at Pima. Wrote to Charles + others.

Mon. 3/ Went to Safford to Survey a new canal, with Joel.

[Page 573R]

1885/ B. Young arrives from Mexico.

August/4+5/Surveyed on canal. Returned to Pima on 5th as Br. B Young came at 6 P.M. on the 5th on his way from Sonora to join Some of the Apostles at El Paso.

Thurs. 6/ Two meetings were held at Pima today. Br. Bingham gave an account of his journeys in Mexico, and the good prospects of our work there. He also made a demand for $200.00 Cash tithing from the Stake. which I collected from the various Wards. Br. B. spent considerable time with us, and enjoyed himself.

7/ Went with Susan to Safford to See Br. B. away, and to pay him the money.

8/ Sent to Tucson for wagon bow

11/ Finished my well, 28 ft deep—good water. Bought 5 bales of wire for fencing, $48.00

14/ David Johnson and family, also Alley his brother, arrived from Apache county, to settle.

21/ Heavy rain last night. Went with Susan to the Hot Springs to see about taking Gertrude there for her health.

22/ To day a Mr. John Stiger arrived from Texas. He says he has come to investigate Mormonism in consequence of reading some of my articles in the Deseret News.

23/ Attended meeting in Pima.

27/ Went to Solomonville. Susan is very sick, with a hot fever.

28/ Jesse returned from St Johns, Apache County, well.

29/ Attended priesthood meeting at Pima.

30/ "   meeting at Pima.

Sept./[Blank line]
5/To day Dora is three years old. She had some gifts.

6/Prest Layton, Johnson + Self held meeting in Pima. In council decided to visit St David soon.

7/ Susan's fever has gone, and now she has what seems erysipelas in her finger and arm. I took her to Safford for medical examination.

Tues. 8/ Started to St David. Stopped at Layton's.

[Page 574L]

1885/ Visit St David and return. Susan sick.

Sept. 9/ Left Layton's at 5.30 A.M. Drove to Wilcox, 55 miles

10/ Arrived t St David, 4 P.M. 40 miles. Heavy storm. I took Jesse as far as Wilcox, there to take train for Logan where he is to go to school for a time. Felt very sad to part with him. For many years he has been with me in all my journeys Surveying, and together we have passed through many hardships, as well as good times. At Benson he had to lay over for a day, because of a Washout near Pantana.

11/ Held council meeting at Prest Layton's, and attended a trial in the evening of H. Blair + Huldah Hubbard.

12/ Went to Benson to See Jesse, but he had gone on. Saw in the paper the notice of ^death of^ my daughter-in-law Sarah Westwood Hagberg, who was married last summer. In the evening attended a trial of 4 young men for sacrilege.

Sun. 13/ Held two meetings in St David.

14/ Went to Tombstone to see about well-pipes. Got a new lamp shade for our lamp.

Wed. 16/ Started home. Drove to Wilcox

17/ Reached Safford, and Staid at Prest Layton's

18/ Home, and found Susan Some better, but her arm still quite Swollen and inflamed.

Sat. 19/ Took Susan to Safford and had her arm lanced.

Sun. 20/ Meeting in Pima. Weather very warm yet. Got letter from Lyman, with offer to take his sisters if I feel willing. I ordained Robt Ferrin an Elder.

Mon. 21/ Went to Central to consult with Prest Johnson. We appointed 3 new High Councillors, one of whom is Henry.

Tues. 22/ Wrote to Egan, at Clifton, about surveying for him. David T. LeBaron goes from Pima back, to meet his wife, who is on her way to Mexico.

25/ Attended meeting of the High Council, the first regular one in this Stake. No business was done, no quorum present.

Mon. 28/ High Council organized. Tried O.D. Merrill, also Morgan, Lot and Rialdo Merrill, + cut all from the Church.

30/ Attended a canal meeting at Safford, + engaged to Survey the new Canal

[Page 575R]

1885/[Blank line]

Oct. 3/Sun./ Went to Safford. Found Prest Layton and Johnson had gone last night to Mexico, to avoid arrest.

Mon. 4/ Began Survey of Canal. Surveyed all the week. Soon after Prest Layton left, a U.S. Marshal came for him. Took Mrs. H. Groesbeck to Tucson.

12/ Ordered a Sulkey plow, + paid $35.00 on it.

15/ Finished survey to Pima Canal, about 14 miles. Prest Layton returned.

Fri. 16/ Bought 160 acres of Prest Layton for $1000.00 to be paid in two years, from the crop raised. Interest, 10 %.

18/ Held meeting at Thatcher, Susan went with me.

19/ Went to Thatcher to help locate a new ^town^ Site.[52]

20/ Surveyed for Mr. L. Frye

22/ Heavy rain—first for many weeks. Gathered beans in.

12th/[See left margin dingbat and brackets] Henry and Albert Started to cut hay near Bowie Sta. taking my mower, rake and span of mares.

22/ Recd a long letter from Moses Thatcher, relative to disfellowshipping, cutting off and restoring.

28/ Beebe wrote me saying I can have his machine for boring artesian wells for $175.

Nov/[Blank line]
2/ Surveyed additional lots at Thatcher

3/ Started to Duncan, to Survey that place. Staid all night at Solomonville.

4/ Drove in mail wagon to Sheldon 36 miles. The train having gone I hired a passage 8 miles further to Duncan by private wagon. Stopped with Mr. G.W. Parks

5/ Surveyed in forenoon in rain. Quit at noon and went by Arizona + New Mexico R.R. to Clifton, 32 miles. Very expensive road, passing for miles through rocky gorges, over high bridges 60 to 90 ft high. Clifton lies on San Francisco river, deep in towering cliffs + hills. It is a mining town—mostly Mexican, of some 500 people. Full of low gambling places, brothels, and saloons. It is the center of great copper mining works. Called at Clifton Clarion Office

[Page 576L]

1885/ Men killed by Apaches.

---

52. Francis W. Moody wrote in his diary on October 19, 1885, "I in company with President Layton & Martineau, Bps Claridge and others laid out the town site of Thatcher." Moody Diary, October 19, 1885, 102. The settlement had initially been laid out by John M. Moody, James Pace, and Joseph Cluff on July 30, 1883. See Cole, ed. *100 Years in Thatcher, 1883–1983*, 11–12.

Nov. 7/Returned to Duncan, + Surveyed in afternoon.

" 9/Still Surveying. A great indian scare, caused by recent murders near Deming.[53] Reports of Indians at Ash Springs, which is on my road home. Do not think it safe to travel that way home.

" 12/ Have earned about $100.00 and recd $55. of it Still due me from Parks $45.00. Started home by A.+N.M.R.R. to Lordsburg. Found on arrival there the S.P.R.R. train had gone West, + I had to Stay all night. Lordsburg is 4700 feet above the Sea. Duncan is about 3800 ft. From Duncan to L. is 39 miles.

13/ At ~~noon~~ ^9.30^ took train for Bowie. Got there 11.30 50 miles, and have to remain all night. Bargained with Wickersham for his boring outfit, at $380.00

14/ Started at daylight by mail for home, + reached there 5 P.M.—55 miles. Found all well. Paid 20$ J.D.H.

Susan had gone to get her arm lanced again, and did not get home till after dark.

15/ Meeting at Pima.

17/ Surveyed lots in Thatcher.

Wed. 18/ Sent Joel with team to Bowie to get Sulkey plow Hired W. Owens for a few days while Joel is gone.

20/ Rained to day.

Sat. 21/ Recd $75.00 from Lyman and Charles for Lilla's passage money to Logan. Got my buggy home fixed all right, and paid $3.00 on it. Owe 3$ more

22/ Joel got home in the night with plow. Held meeting at Safford. Prest Layton having got home last night.

23/ Went to visit Carlton's

24/ Met Prest Layton + Johnson at Thatcher, to select lots for public

---

53. The victims included a Mr. and Mrs. Yater whose bodies were discovered beaten, bruised, and stripped of clothing. John T. Shy, his wife, and 11-year-old son survived a shooting attack while sitting at their dinner table. See "Indian Massacre," *Clifton Clarion*, November 18, 1885, 2.

buildings and for ourselves. At night Theodore got home from the hay camp with three of the horses. Wrote to Jesse.

25/ Surveyed more lots at Thatcher. Gertrude went, and drove team, threw out stakes +c.

[Page 577R]

1885/ Meetings of the Apostles. Lilla goes to Utah.

Nov. 26/ Went to Solomonville + paid taxes $17.70 + 2.00 = 19.70 Gertrude went also. Heard of two men being killed by Apaches.

27/ Wrote to Sur. Genl for appointment as Deputy. Also for field notes + plat of Tp. 8S. R. 26E.

28/ Priesthood meeting in Pima. Dismissed at noon as we expect Apostles E. Snow, Young + Lyman.

29/ Meeting at Pima, at 10 A.M. Apostles not present. Large attendance both forenoon and afternoon. Jacob Hamblin spoke very interestingly.

30/ Another man killed 10 miles from here and one about 7 miles. Set corners for meeting house in Pima

Dec. 1/[Blank line]
Tuesday/ Went to meeting at Thatcher + Central, and met Elders E. Snow + wife, F.M. Lyman, and our old friend Emma Smith. Heard at noon of the killing of two of our Layton boys—the Wright brothers, by indians this morning, about 12 miles from Solomonville, while in pursuit of stolen horses. In the evening Elder B. Young arrived. Held Council at Br. Snow's place

2/ Went to Layton to funeral of Wright brothers, with Susan, and took B. Young and Emma Smith. In the evening took B. Young + F.M. Lyman to Curtis, and held meeting there.

3/ Returned with them to Pima, and held meetings. At 4 P.M. Elders Snow + wife, Young, Lyman + Layton dined with us. About 6.30 P.M. I started with Lilla to Safford, to start from there in the morning to Utah. Held Council till near midnight.

4/ Left Safford about 7 A.M. I took F.M. Lyman + Lilla. Reached May's well at noon, 25 miles. Here our Escort of Six mounted men returned. We reached Wilcox about sun set.

5/ Drove to St David by Sunset. Took leave of Lilla this morning, and again at Dragoon pass where the train overtook us. She went with Aunt Harriet Johnson and Leslie Webb.

[Page 578L]

1885/ Charles Married Jan. 20. 1886

Dec. 6/+ 7/Meeting held in St David each day. Held council meetings each day with the Apostles. B. Young started to Hermosillo on the 7th Arranged for a Small party to go by wagon into Sonora, with B.Y. + F.M.L.

8/ Went to Hill's with Br. Lyman. Wrote letter to the "Star" by request of Br. Snow to correct false statements of Dr. Groesbeck.[54] Returned after night to Br. Layton's place. Very cold weather.

9/ Went to Wilcox. Contracted to deliver D.H. Smith + Les 5000 lbs Chop feed at 2¢ Got some goods on credit that we needed very much, $27.58

10/ Reached Pima about 6 P.M.—55 miles.

11/ Attended Women's Conference.

12+13/ Quarterly Conference. Traded Carriages with Br. C Layton Ordained J.A. Burns a High Priest and set him apart as Bp. Taylor's 2d Counr

25/ To day we had a family dinner—about 30 present.

26/ Albert went to Wilcox for the well-borer outfit.
[Blank line]

---

54. Dr. Groesbeck of Safford had written to the *Daily Star* on December 4 in relation to a recent murder near Solomonville, intimating that universal feeling among Gila Valley residents was that if not protected by the government, they should "march upon the Apaches wherever found, reservation or no reservation, and exterminate them." Martineau's letter, written in behalf of the stake presidency, disputed Groesbeck's claim, saying that

> while we deem it the indisputable duty of every citizen of the United States to assist in defending its laws and institutions, the lives and property of our fellow citizens, and our families, we do not think it just to wage war upon those who are so far as we know, innocent of crime. While there may be Indians now on the reservation who have committed murders, and are therefore worthy of death, we think that if such be the case, and their guilt can be proved, they should be tried, condemned and executed by due process of law, and not by an indiscriminate massacre of the innocent and guilty.

From C. Layton, W. O. [sic] Johnson, and J. H. Martineau to editor, "A Temperate View of the Situation," *Arizona Daily Star*, December 11, 1885, 4.

1886/ Rain today turning to snow at night. Cold. Albert came Jan. 1/[Blank line]

Fri. 8th/ Our 34th Wedding anniversary. Had company + dinner.

9th/ Albert + Theodore started to St David for the mares.

    To day I was elected one of the Directors of the S.C.M.I. Store

11/ Qualified as Director. Recd letter from Charles who is going to be married soon to Miss Eva Rice.

12/ Applied to Gov. Zulick to be Notary Public

Tues. 19/ Wrote to Prest Taylor about Tithing paid to M. Curtis Also sent receipt—of B. Young for $200. cash paid him in July last.

Tues. 26/ The boys went to Thatcher to begin plowing.

Jan. 21/ To day Charles was married to Miss Eva Rice

Feb. 4/ In crossing the Gila, was nearly carried down stream. Got my books and papers wet.

Sat. 6/ Got home. Letter from Charles + Eva, also Lilla

Sun. 7/ Wrote to Chas + Eva. also to Lillie

[Page 579R]

1886/ Albert + Joel ordained Seventies at Conference.

Feb. 9/ Set out grape cuttings

Sat. 27/ Finished tithing settlement to day. Have had all the work to do myself

Sun. 28/ At meeting at Central, I ordained J.P. Johnson High Priest and set him apart as 2d Counr to Bp. G.M. Haws.

March/[Blank line]
2/Acted to day as Notary—first time in Arizona. I was appointed By Gov. Zulick Jany 20th

12/ Recd word that land has been bought in Mexico by Br. Teasdale[55]

---

55. George Teasdale (1831–1907) was born on December 8, 1831, at London, England, to William Russell and Hariet Henrietta (Tidey) Teasdale. He was educated in

Sat. 13/ I am 58 years old today! How the years fly! Joel sick yesterday and today.

Fri. 19/ Conference of Female Relief Societies.

Sat. 20/ Our Quarterly Conference begun today. At noon Prest S.B. Young from S.L. City Came to organize the 89th Quo. of Seventies.

21/ The 89th Quo. organized today. Joel + Albert were voted to be members. Joel was ordained a Seventy by Prest James R. Welker; Albert by Prest Joseph East

Henry was voted a Home Missionary.

Y.M.M.I.A + Y.L.M.I.A. Conference in evening.

22/ Took Br. Young and wife and Susan riding; and in the evening to Safford.

23/ Meeting at Safford to day (evening).

24/ Ordered a washing machine pr Br Layton. Came home. Found offer from Grant. Odell + Leo, of farm machinery, wagons +c to start that business here.

26/ Put our cows in herd. Declined Grant + Co's offer. Ordered a "Binder" by J.D. Holladay. I am to pay freight when it comes, $50.00 on tithing, and the balance in 6 + 18 months, equal payments. The first payment to be next Nov., the Second one year after.

27/ Priesthood meeting at Central.

28/ Meeting at Layton. Three Mexicans baptized.

30/ Letter came addressed to <u>Mr. Bowker</u>. Got an arm chair $4.00.

31/ Got 5 gal. oil.

---

public schools and at London University. He joined the church in 1852 and presided over several mission conferences in England. Teasdale immigrated to Utah in 1861 and served missions in the *Millennial Star* office in Liverpool and in the Southern States. He was called as an apostle on October 13, 1882, and presided over church membership areas in Idaho, southern Utah, Arizona, and Mexico. He served in the European mission presidency from 1886 to 1890, when he returned to Utah. He died on June 9, 1907 in Salt Lake City. See Jenson, *LDS Biographical Encyclopedia*, 1:144–147.

For these Mexican land purchases, see Teasdale Diary, entries for November 19, 20, and 21, 1885, Teasdale Papers, box 15, fd. 4, UUSCM.

[Page 580L]

1886/ Temple Memoranda.

April 3/ Answered letter from John Q. Cannon.

4/ Meeting at Safford. Grape vines opened their leaves.

Mon. 5/ Began to lower my dry well. Got 2 feet water

8/ Recd notice I am appointed to examine for Site for a Bridge across Gila river, and report probable expense for building (By the County) Got a petition started to get a Money Order Office in Pima.[56]

Sat. 10/ In looking through my records of Temple work I find the following items:—

Temple items.

"May 21/1884/Began work in the temple, as one of the first company—Self, wife, and Netta.

Sept. 11/ Finished temple work.

July 10/84/ Self and Susan recd our 2nd A. Also for Susan J. [Note margin writing]

Thurs./[Blank line]
Sept. 11/Recd 2d A. by Susan, for Mary Elvira Sherman Martineau and Mary Elizabeth Johnson Martineau. Finished Work

July 11/ I recd 2d A. for John Robbins

Sept. 2/ Susan was baptized for her health, + to renew Covenant.

<u>Netta</u>/ Netta began work in the Temple May 21st—, but was very weak. She worked a few days from time to time, [in margin: Aug. 20] until Aug. 20th which was her last work in the temple.

The temple workers were very kind to her, especially Sisters Prescinda Kimball, Lucy B. Young, Minerva Snow Zina D.H. Young, young Zina Williams, E.G. Benson and others, whom may our Father ever Bless.

---

56. The Pima Bridge crossing is located where Main Street (Bryce-Eden Road) crosses the Gila River. The bridge was replaced in September 1915 and again in the 1980s. It is still a local landmark in Pima. See Burgess, ed., *Mt. Graham Profiles: Ryder Ridgway Collection, Volume 2*, 127–128.

Baptisms/for dead/ Myself, Netta, Gean (Virginia), Gertrude, Anna, Joel Charles, Theodore, Lyman, Nephi, + Emmeline performed baptisms for 470 dead.

Endowments/ Of this number about 200 were endowed, and nearly all of them Sealed; most of them to former companions, and quite a number to me, who had no husbands, to be united to. The names of those Sealed to me are on the next page.

Dora/June 6/84/ To day Dora was sealed to Self and Susan by J.T.D. McAlister, the first of the kind in the temple. [See date bracket]

[Page 581R]

    Temple Memoranda, cond
Sealed to me [illegible older writing]
[Left margin says 2d A for first name, and " for next two names]

#	Name			
1/	Susan Ellen Johnson Martineau	May 13. 1852	Sept. 12. 1860	
2/	Susan Julia Sherman	Jan. 18. 1857	" " "	
3/	Mary Elvira Sherman	— 2 A	" " "	
4/	Marie St Pierre	May	21	1884
5/	Clara St Vincent	"	23	"
6/	Sophia Gilmier	"	28	"
7/	Mary Essebrous	"	29	"
8/	Mary Gertrude	"	30	"
9/	Susan Macon	June	12	"
10/	Huldah Hutchinson	"	27	"
11/	Susannah Martineau	July	2	"
12/	Mary "	"	"	"
13/	Hannah "	"	"	"
14/	Sarah Colombine	"	"	"
15/	Elizabeth Brewer	"	"	"
16/	Beatrice Sumner	"	"	"
17/	Judith Elizabeth Blake	July	3	1884
18/	Catherine Martineau	"	"	"
19/	Sarah "	"	"	"
20/	Ann "	"	"	"
21/	Emily "	"	"	"
22/	Ellen "	"	4	"
23/	Lucy "	"	"	"

24/ Marianne "	"	"	"
25/ Miss Rand	July	9	"
26/ Margaret Haughout	"	"	"
27/ Elizabeth "	"	"	"
28/ Catherine "	"	"	"
29/ Cornelia "	"	"	"
30/ Ann "	"	"	"
31/ Elenor "	"	"	"
32/ Catherine Keleltas	"	"	"
33/ Gertrude Haughout	July	10	"
34/ Miss Rand	"	"	"
35/ Margaret Martineau	"	"	"
36/ Charity Martineau	"	"	"

[Page 582L]

1886/Temple Memoranda. Contd

37/ Alujay Webb	July	11	1884
38/ Allalta Cozine	"	"	"
39/ Elizabeth Martineau	"	"	"
40/ Rachel Haughout	"	"	"
41/ Margarette Haughout	"	"	"
42/ Mary Elizabeth Johnson [in margin: 2d A]	"	18	"
43/ Anna Maria Hagberg	"	"	"
44/ Rachel Martineau	"	20	"
45/ Mary Alice Martineau	"	24	"
46/ Margaret Jardine	"	"	"
47/ Margaret Martineau	"	"	"
48/ Elizabeth Marriott Martineau	"	25	"
49/ Amelia Columbine	"	"	"
50/ Mary Martineau	"	"	"
51/ Jane "	"	"	"
52/ Mary "	"	"	"
53/ Sarah Neave	Aug	6	"
54/ Margaret Martineau	"	"	"
55/ Caroline "	"	13th	"
56/ Elizabeth "	"	"	"
57/ Emeline "	"	14	"
58/ Elizabeth Hawkins	"	20	"

59/ Sophia Billott (Billow)	"	"	"
60/ Charity Beatty	"	28th	"
61/ Harriet Martineau	July	16	"
62/ Mary Martineau	"	17	"
63/ Margaret Williment	"	23	"

   Nelly Benson   2a
[Last line is in older, shaky hand]

[Page 583R]

1886/[Blank line]

Apr. 15/ Sent recommends to Jesse N. and Elizabeth, so they may join the Logan Ward, and be able to labor in the temple.

16/ Several of my grape vines are in blossom.

Sat 17/ Recd letter from W.B. Preston, who wished to meet me at St David. ~~In half an hour myself and Br. Layton were on our way to Safford~~.

Mon. 19/ Br.s Thurber and Bean, of Br. Preston's company ^came.^ Got a new washing machine, cost about $13.50. Sent back the blank bonds to Sur. Genl Office, as I cannot find any one to sign such high bonds $10.000. Sent a conveyance for Br. W.B.P. at Bowie. but he was not there.

23/ Letter from W.B.P. to meet him and R.T. Burton at St David to-morrow. Started in 10 minutes, to Safford.

Sat. 24/ Started from Safford at 5 A.M. Arrived at Wilcox. 50 miles at 3 P.M. Stopped two hours and camped out at Croton Sps. 60 miles.

Sun. 25/ Started 5 A.M. Reached St David 10 A.M. 40 miles. Found the brethren had not yet arrived, but they did in two hours, and had meeting at 2 P.M.

26/ We all went to John Hill's and staid all night.

27/ Went to Tombstone. Got my watch cleaned. Bought a suit of clothes $20.00 the first for almost 3 years.

Wed. 28/ Back to St D. found Br. Thurber had arrived from the Gila. Advised Bp. Merrill to let Jos G. Allred have the church stock to herd, at $2.00 pr year, he to be responsible. Hear reports of hostile indians near by in the Whetstone mts.

29/ We started for home at 7 A.M. with Mrs. Allred + son. Sleep at Wilcox. At Dragoon Station found the Agent barricaded and much alarmed, on account of Apaches near by. Some troops had passed a little before in chase.

30/ Started at 5.30—May's well, 20m 9.15 Safford 2.15 P.M. 50 miles. I got home in the evening. Theatre.
[Blank line]

Sat. May 1st/ Forward letter to Bp. Preston. La Ascincion Mexico.

6/ Read that U.S. Atty. Genl Maury said "it would have been infinitely better if the Mormons had all

[Page 584L]

1886/ St David Henry's son Jesse died.

May 6/ been put to the sword long ago." Susan prophesied that his hair should fall from his head, his teeth fall out, + his flesh rot upon his bones." I believe it. She also said "Edmunds Shall die a beggar in the Streets." and be esteemed most infamous forever." They are worthy.

7/ Albert arrived from Wilcox with 3887 lbs Chopd grain I had there. To day I was assessed for taxes, personal 690.00 Real 900.00 = $1590.

13/ Finished planting my garden in Pima,—peanuts corn, squashes, melons + big sunflowers. Tomatoes

15/ High Council met to try W. Hawkins for profanity + drunkeness. Recd my new carriage spring. $7.00 ^6.72^

19/ Got my carriage fixed.

20/ Started for St David with Susan. Staid at Layton's Heard reports of late indian murders, but I must go on

21/ Susan felt impressed to return, but did not tell me then. Arrived at Wilcox. Heard of men being killed yesterday close to our intended route.

22/ At Dragoon pass were told that indians crossed the road just ahead of us, and Soldiers had gone in chase. Arrived at St D. at 5 P.M. the horses much jaded + lame. Staid at Bebee's. Folks much astonished to See us come alone amid so many murders.

Sun. 23/ Meeting. We learn by letter Jesse died yesterday of croup.

Mon. 24/ Transacted business with Bp. Merrill. Heard of eight more murders committed yesterday, all around us.

25/ Start home much against the wish of the people who all think it very dangerous. I offered to Send Susan by train and mail to Pima, so she might go safe but she would not leave me. Went to Wilcox.

26/ We are told by Genl Miles and citizens not to go without company, but I know of no Company, and I <u>must</u> go to meet Bp. Preston. When we turned off into the "Cilenega road," which lies many miles among hills, ravines, rocks and brush, and therefore very dangerous. I felt the danger fully but said

[Page 585R]

1886/[Has a title but in old hand and illegible]

May/nothing to alarm Susan. At May's well we both felt a sense of great danger. The place was deserted, the Cattle gone and many horse tracks at the troughs. We only watered, and drove quickly away for six miles to a place out the hills, and there fed the team and ate lunch, then drove on reaching Laytons at 5. Br. Layton was greatly pleased to see us. He had greatly feared for us, and had tried to have an escort go to meet us, along with Albert. We heard while at St David, Monday, that our dear little grandson Jesse B. died Sat. morning. He was taken with croup the night we left, and soon died. This was why Susan felt impressed to stay.

We found at Br. Layton's Bps. Preston + Burton, E. Snow, wife, girl and boy. And spent 2 hours resting, then went on and got home at 8 P.M. after a very dangerous journey. Susan explained why she sat so much of the time with her head close to mine. She wished the same ball that should strike me to kill her too.

We also learn that our neighbor on the same block, Frank Thurston, was killed by Apaches on Sunday evening about 6 miles from Pima, and ^they^ also took horses from Curtis the same night. Troops had gone in pursuit.

We (Susan + I) gave thanks to God for our preservation, for it was only by His power we were preserved.

27/ Worked on my accounts with Bp. Preston. We heard some indians were seen near Pima, and a party of men went out to see. They found them to be indian scouts, and nearly had a fight.

28/ Bps. Preston and Burton start home to day. Also Brs. Thurber and Bean. Wrote to Bp. J.Q. Cannon.

29/ Priesthood meeting at Layton.

31/ Started my new Binder today. Henry manager. It cost 200$ + 60$ + 9.60 = $269.60

[Page 586L]

1886/[Blank line]

June 2/This evening B. Young and Brs. Preston + Rogers Came and stop with us.

3/ Br. Young left this afternoon, after a pleasant visit.

5/ Examined the Gila for location of Bridge, having been appointed Chairman of that committee by Suprvr meeting at Pima.[57]

Sun. 6/ Meeting at Pima.

7/ Leveled and Surveyed for bridge.

10/ Have been estimating cost of bridge till now.

Fri. 11/ Relief Society Conference. I attended.

Sat. 12/ Quarterly Conference, also Sun. 13. A good time.

14.15.16.17/ Estimates for bridge.

18/ Made plan for Sun dial

19/ High Council at Central. Bp. Welker vs Campbel

Sun. 20/ Meeting at Mathews Branch. Br Layton Sick. We located spot for new town.

Tues. 22/ I married ^Benj Willard Johnson and Sarah May Weller to day at 2 P.M. at Carlton's

Sat. 26/ Worked on my accounts all the week. Found some lines composed long ago, and not recorded:– (Also, priesthood meeting.)

---

57. There are now five bridges that cross the Gila River at various locations in Graham County. These include: Eden Bridge (Eden Road), Pima Bridge (Bryce-Eden Road), Thatcher Bridge (Rea Lane), Safford Bridge (8th Avenue), and Solomon Bridge (Sanchez Road). See note at entry for April 8, 1886.

My Loved ones are gone.

<u>The missing ones</u>
Some of my loved ones—my children—are gone!–
Where, where are they?
I miss their sweet prattle—their jubilant Song
That day after day So joyously rung—
Where, where are they?
[Blank line]
With hearts light and happy they played round my door
Day after day;
Or tumbling and frisking about on the floor—
How with play things and toys they littered it oer—
Gone, now, are they.
[Blank line]
How often in sport have they climbed on my knee!
Not there, are they;
With arms soft and loving circling me—
With kisses so sweet and so tender—ah me!

[Page 587R]

   1886/[Blank line]
Where, now, are they?
Shall I seek for the little ones missing, to night,
Gone for my fold!
Will they ever—or never more gladden my sight
With their bright winsome ways, and their eyes tender light,
Precious as Gold?
[Blank line]
Not <u>here</u> shall I search—twere futile and vain—
Not here are they;
But fled from this region of ~~sorrow~~ ^trouble^ and pain
Where they shall see sorrow—oh never again—
Safe—safe are they.
[Blank line]
To the heavens above—to the mansions of light
 There have they gone;
No grief will enshroud like a shadow of night,

Nor sorrow nor parting their happiness blight
Safe, now, at home.

S.L. City. Jan. 29, 1882.

June/[Blank line]
27/<u>Sunday</u>. Went to Curtis, with Susan. Good meeting. Coming home, was overtaken by a Cavalry Soldier with orders to warn settlers of another band of indians.

Mon. 28/ Wrote certificate of Willard Johnson's marriage This evening, at 9.40 P.M. Henry had another daughter born to him. She weighed 9 lbs.

<u>Tues. 29</u> Wrote in Tithing books

July 2/[Blank line]
Friday/Settled with Henry about our land. He has paid hay 57.33 Cow 40.00 = $97.33 I sell him 10 acres land for $225.00 with $35.00 in canal stock included) he to have two years to pay it in.

Mon. 5/ Celebration in Pima. I worked at my books all day.

6/ Went to Solomonville, and presented Report on Bridge Also presented bill for services, $58.00

7/ wrote to Fabes. C.R.R.R. agent, Ogden, about special rate.

[Page 588L]

1886/[Blank line]

July 7
Wrote to Bp. Merrill about Church Cattle. Heavy rain—the first since last January.

Thurs. 8
Henry started the binder again.– has been broken.

Sat. 10
The boys bring word that the heading machines cannot Cut our grain. It will be a great loss—one year's labor. and many debts to be paid. for which I had depended upon the crop. But I think all will be right in the end, though now it seems dark—very.
[Blank line]

Sunday/[Blank line]
11/To day Susan's 50 years old. It seem but a little while since I married her, a young, slim girl of 15. It seems so strange, that only fifty years ago she lived in Heaven, associating with God, the Savior, and the spirits of light, as brother and Sister. I wrote the following lines in honor of her birthday:–
[Blank line]
    To my dear Wife
    on her fiftieth birthday.

1
Fifty years! as future, the time seems immense
But fifty years past—how speedy ~~its~~ ^their^ flight!
And doubtless, when we shall be called to go hence
Our life here will seem as a dream of the night.
2
How strangely it seems that so lately you dwelt
In the Heaven of Heavens—with the Father and Son.
And ~~the~~ ^with^ Spirits of Light, who kept their estate
 When Lucifer fell, with the Spirits he had won!
3
You kept your Estate, and a promise received
In the Second Estate that you should Come forth;–
Should there be anointed a Priestess and Queen—
Be mother of Spirits—be Eve to an Earth.
4
How wondrous the love of Our Father in Heaven!
How wondrous His mercy—how wondrous His grace!

[Page 589R]

[Poem continues]

    Virginia returns to Logan

    July/That we, after all the offense we have given
May again be permitted to look on His face!
5
How trivial and worthless this World's honors seem;–
    How transient ^trivial^ our Sorrows when ^once^ they should/
be ^are^ past;!

Twill seem like the ills of a night's troubled dream
When through this Estate we safely have passed.

Pima July 11, 1886

[Blank line]

July/[Blank line]
12/Began cutting our grain with the mower. Finished 15th

Mon. 19/B. Young arrived from Mexico today, and staid with us, till 4 P.M. and then went on to Apache Co.

Tues 20/ Henry finished work with the binder. Has cut 79 ½ acres @ $2.00 = $159.00

23/ Threshed grain. Had 52 Sacks, expected 600.

Wed. 28/ Recd my tithing schedules and went to work on my amended report. Cut Lucern again yesterday.

29/ Began boring for water with my Auger. Next day broke Shaft, + left Auger in well 26 ft deep. Dug it out. Have been quite lame for a week, caused by cutting brush on my farm.

Aug/Wed. Aug 4/ Went to Thatcher + chose site for Tithing office.

7/ Laid out the foundation for it.

Sat. 8/ Went with Stake Presidency + held meetings in Curtis and Mathews

Tues. 18th/ Started with Jean to Wilcox, to put her on train for Utah. Camped at the Cienega. Heavy storm at evening.

19/ Arrived at Wilcox. Heard that the R.R. is blockaded by washouts for the last four days.

Thurs 19/ Jean started on train at 9 P.M. in company with the two widows Wright, whose husbands were killed by indians last fall. I felt sad to part with her, but think it is for her best good to go to her brothers in Utah—Logan. Anna went with us. Started for home next morning, and got there about 8 P.M.

[Page 590L]

1886/ Lyman and Moroni's children born.

Aug. 23/ Sent to JB Alden for book. From this time on worked Continually on my report to G.T. Office, to date of [in margin: Sept. 4th] and then waited for a few days.

" 7/ To day Henry, Albert + Joel went haying.

" 9/ A good rain.

16/ I cut my Lucern

17/ Today Lyman + Alley had a son born, 12.20 M. weighed 11 lbs. Named him

To day the Presidency located place for a new town in Mathews Ward. Attended F. Relief Conf. in afternoon.

18+19/ Quarterly Conference.

Mon. 20th/ Began Auditing my tithing report, with Prest Layton and W.D. Johnson, which he approved + Signed.[58]
[Blank line]
A girl was born to Moroni and Laura [Sarah?] today.

Sept. 30/ Finished auditing my tithing reports, with Br Layton.
[Blank line]

Oct. 4/ Sent my T.O. returns to S.L. City.[59] Plowed weeds.

5/ Plowed weeds, + did not quit till after sunset + quit work wet through with sweat. Got chilled in coming home.

6/ Taken with rheumatism, + took to bed.

---

58. Bishop's agents neither received nor disbursed tithing. They imparted instructions given by the Presiding Bishop to local ward bishops relative to tithing matters and bookkeeping. They also audited ward accounts with bishops and submitted a report to the Presiding Bishop. Stake president Layton and his counselor, William Derby Johnson Sr., would be responsible for reviewing and signing the report. See Pace, "Changing Patterns," 6–7.

59. In a letter dated October 2, Martineau submitted his tithing report for 1885: "Dear Brother, I send herewith the amended Tithing report for 1885, which has long been delayed by lack of word from St David in consequence of Bp. Merrill's absence from home. Also, Prest Layton has taken over two weeks investigating tithing matters of 1883-4-5. The complicated condition of matters up to the date of my appointment made it difficult to get at exactly. But this report, as amended, is, I think, as near right as it can be." J. H. Martineau to Bp. W. B. Preston, October 2, 1886, St. Joseph Stake Letterpress Copybook, 1885–1888, p. 46, LR 7781/21, LDSCHL.

23d/ Up to this time I have been confined to bed, with a severe season of sciatica, unable to sit up and suffering greatly.

    To day R.A. Allred visited me on behalf of others to see if would run for Legislature. I said no. He said I would have the full vote of the gentile towns. Judge Hyatt also sent to me for the same purpose.
[Blank line]

Oct. 21/To day Susan was set part as Prest of the R.S. of Pima, by Bp. Taylor

26/ Henry + Albert came home from haying to day. Yesterday recd letter from Bp. Preston acknowleging receipt of my returns. O.K.

[Page 591R]

1886/ Elvira's boy born, at Mesa. Also Charlie's

Oct. 29/Cut my lucern for the last time this year.

Nov. 4/Was carried to the Hot Springs today. Susan went with me, and Henry.

6/ Began to feel better from the hot baths

9/ Gertrude came today to try the baths for her lameness.

12/ Joel got home from haying ~~Nov.~~ today.
[Blank line]

Nov. 1/ To day Elvira presented another grand child. Born at Mesa, Maricopa Co. A.T. at 1.30

17/ I walked about 6 rods to day.

22/ Cold. Snowed a few minutes.

27/ Much worse last night and to day.

29/ Last night slept from 9 P.M. to 4 A.M. the first sleep since Oct. 6th of more than one or two hours in the twenty-four. Have had no sleep, for months, only from one to two hours each 24 hours. I have taken laudanum and morphine, but it only lulls the pain—does not make me sleep.
[Blank line]

Dec. 1/Wed./Went home by Prest Layton's advise, to be nearer the help of the priesthood.

4/ Gertrude came home from the springs.

10/ Femal Relief Conference. I did not attend.

11th + 12th/ Quarterly Conference. I went in Carriage. Spoke once

Wed 22/ Having been appointed by Probate Court one of appraisers in Collins estate. Went to Thomas to Survey the place to set off the widow's portion.[60]

Thu. 23/ Surveyed

Fri. 24/ Ditto. Came home in afternoon for Christmas.

27/ High Council at Central.

----- ----- ----- ----- -----

Dec. 20/To day Charles + Eva had a son born to them at Logan at 1.30 P.M.

----- ----- ----- ----- -----

28/ Returned to Collins to finish up

29th/ finished + returned home. My bill $35.00.

Henry got his hand hurt blasting. He came home.

[Page 592L]

1886/ 1887.

Dec. 31/Recd box of C. gifts from Lyman + Allie. Wrote them.

1887/--

Jan. 1/To day F. Gunnell, W. Maughan, Baxter + Poppleton came. Exiles.[61] Moroni admitted Jan. 2d a member of Pima Ward, with his family.

---

60. The Collins estate refers to the estate of Jerome B. Collins (1840–1886), a frontiersman and post trader at Camp Thomas (later Fort Thomas), who settled in Gila Valley ca. 1875 and founded the town of Maxey near the camp. He was shot and killed by William Williams, a cattleman of Aravaipa, on August 1, 1886, in a dispute over some unresolved business. See Thrapp, *Encyclopedia of Frontier Biography*, 1:300, and Barns, *Arizona Place Names*, 269.

61. In May 1886, Francis Wilson Gunnell, Robert Wright Baxter, William H. Maughan, and William S. Poppleton, were indicted for cohabitation. To avoid arrest, they fled Utah for Mexico. After nearly three months of travel, they reached Gila Valley. On January 1, Baxter wrote: "At 9 a.m. we pulled up and traveled along the banks of the river for 12 miles, and nooned, thence we traveled three miles and crossed the Gila at Fort Thomas.

5/ Resurveyed part of Union Canal.

7/ Attended justice's Court as witness in A.M.M. Case

8/ Our 35th Wedding day. Had a house full of family + friends.

10/ To day attended City Council as Mayor of Pima.[62]

11/ Self + F. Gunnell start for St David, in tithing business. Drove to Layton + stopped with Packer's.

12/ " " Wilcox, next day to St David. F. 13th

14/To Tucson. Saw Sur. Genl Hise, in relation to making copies of U.S. Surveys in Graham Co.

15/ Made plats all day. Next day, very lonesome.

17/ Copied plats, ^18th^ also next day. Went to a fire.

19/ Finished. Got my watch fixed

20/ Returned to St David. Found M. Thatcher there, just from Mexico. Goad to meet each other, also to see Br. Gunnell. Held meeting in the evening.

21/ Start home. John Hill came to bring Br. M.T. to the Gila. While riding with Br. Thatcher, talking with [in margin: Dead.] him, and without any premonition or ill feeling of any kind, I was suddenly struck dead, to all appearance. Br. T. hastily called the others up, and they all thought I was dead for a time. After a lapse of 30 minutes I came too, but was weak. They hurriedly drove on to Wilcox, 16 miles. Br. T. having first administered to me. He asked if I would call a doctor. I said no, I wanted nothing but the administrations of the priesthood.—had no faith in any thing else. The brethren were all as kind as could be to me, especially Br. T. He said I must quit work for a time and go to Utah to recuperate. In this, they all joined. Next day drove home, Br. T. Staying at Thatcher Ward.

This is a large military post. We continued our journey 12 miles and arrived at Pima. Here we put up in the Tithing yard, and had supper with James H. Martineau. ... Jan 2nd, Sunday morning, all is well, had breakfast at Brother Martineau's and agreed to board at his house while we stayed at Pima." The party remained in Pima until February 3 and departed on horseback, following along the Southern Pacific Railroad line to Deming and then on to Casas Grandes and Juárez. See Robert Wright Baxter, "Life History of Robert Wright Baxter," 13–22 (quote on p. 18).

62. Martineau was elected mayor of Pima on January 4, 1887, but resigned the office after a few months because of a prolonged stay in Utah. See James H. Martineau, "Col. James H. Martineau," 79. See also "Life History of Robert Wright Baxter," 18.

[Page 593R]

1887/[Blank line]

Jan./Br. Thatcher thinks my attack was apoplectic, or else exhaustion caused by my work.

22/ Br. T. Came in to day + stopped with me. He Says I must give up the Bishops Agency, and take a rest of 2 or 3 months in Utah. I said I had no means for the trip, but he said he would give me $50.00 for that purpose.[63]

Sun. 23/ Meeting in Pima. Br. Thatcher preached, and was filled with the Holy Spirit. Prest Layton also spoke.

Tues. 25/ Br. T. held meeting again this evening.

Wed. 26/"   "   Started for St Louis this morning, with John Campbell, to buy saw and grist mills +c for Juarez in Chihuahua.[64] He left me a check for $50.00 and told me to go to Utah and rest. May God ever bless him, and repay him a hundred fold. He approves my moving to Mexico, if Bp. releases me from the Bps. Agency. Br. T. wrote him to recommend it.

I feel drawn to Mexico, although I understand well the great amount of heavy labor required in a new country, and my own lack of physical strength. But I think a great work awaits me there, in helping to save the

---

63. This should not be perceived—at least not entirely—as a disciplinary action. Between 1887 and 1889, bishop's agents were replaced by stake tithing clerks. On March 1, 1888, the Quorum of Twelve Apostles chose to discontinue the office of bishop's agent in all stakes of the church, so Martineau's release was as much a welcome conclusion to a stressful situation as it was an act of discipline. See Pace, "Changing Patterns," 6.

64. Colonia Juárez was founded in 1886, after a group of Mormon polygamous families from Arizona camped on the southwest bank of the Piedras Verdes River southwest of Casas Grandes, Chihuahua, Mexico. LDS Apostle George Teasdale appointed George W. Sevey as the presiding elder. In the fall of 1886, the townsite had to be moved to a location two miles north because it was not on the land to which they held title. On June 5, 1887, the Colonia Juárez Ward was organized with George W. Sevey as bishop and Miles P. Romney and Ernest L. Taylor as counselors. The town is located in a narrow valley on Rio Piedras Verdes in the state of Chihuahua, Mexico, approximately ten miles southwest of the town of Casas Grandes, sixteen miles southwest of Colonia Dublán, and 150 miles west of El Paso, Texas. The valley is about three-fourths of a mile wide (on average) and bordered by high bluffs varying in height from 100 to 200 feet. The town is laid out in regular square blocks, the streets crossing each other at right angles, but instead of following the cardinal points of the compass the streets run parallel with the bluffs and the river from the northwest to the southeast. See Hatch, *Colonia Juarez*, 1–38, Romney, *Mormon Colonies in Mexico*, 85–94, Jenson, *Encyclopedic History of the Church*, 380–382, Sudweeks, "Miracle of the Piedras Verdes."

seed of Abraham in that land, who must have the gospel brought to them; and I am willing, if it be the Lord's will, to labor in that cause. My past blessings by various patriarchs, all point to this work in that land.

29/ Priesthood meeting and High Council meeting to day I read Prest Taylor's instructions to me in letter just received, relative to ordination of High Priests. I was appointed to make a plan of our proposed Tabernacle and Send it to Prest Taylor for approval. I bought to day of Prest Layton a large ditch plow for use in Mexico. I paid $100.00 for it. Also arranged for Albert to go with Br. Gunnell, drive team, and take up a place for me there.

   Sunday 30. Meeting in Pima.

[Page 594L]

1887/ Go to Utah. Snow Blockade in Sierra Nevada.

Feb. 8/To day went to Solomonville to file affidavit for my pension for service in the Mexican War.

10/ This evening attended City Council, as Mayor. As I intend to start for Utah tomorrow, and Susan feels apprehensive about my traveling alone in my poor health, I went to Patriarch Wm McBride for a blessing He gave me a good one, saying I should go and come in peace and safety. After he sat down again, he suddenly said "He that is unjustly accusing you to injure you, shall Serve you." I said—"Why no one would do that against me." He repeated his former words, and I said again "I am sure no one would try to injure me—I injure no one." He said, "Some one is doing this. I am not deceived by the Spirit." I said, "Even if any one is trying to injure me, I dont wish him to serve me." He said, "Why, what would you do." I said, "Why, I would forgive him, and let him go."

Fri. 11/ Started this morning, Moroni going with me to Wilcox. Staid all night with a stock man, Wm Fonda.

12/ Took train this evening about 7.30 P.M. in a Sleeper, as I did not feel able to go such a way in a 3d Class.

13/ Breakfast at Yuma. Dine at Indio, sup at Los Angeles

Mon. 14/ " at Tulare. Dine at Lathrop, San F. at 4.40 P.M.

Tues 15/Left San Francisco 3. P.M. and reached Colfax 11 P.M. Here we found several trains blockaded by Snow.

Thu. 17/ Many trains and hundreds of passengers here. Start at 2.15 P.M. with 3 engines and 12 Cars. At Blue Cañon met 2 trains going West. Snow 8 to 10 feet deep. Sup at Truckee.

18/ Breakfast at Elko, Nevada. Reach Ogden 10.45 P.M.

Sat. 19/ Got to Logan 2 P.M. and found all well. The girls did not expect me.

Mon 21/ Visited Nephi's family, and next day visited Eva.

Wed. 23/ Went to S.L. City, and found Eliza well.

Fri. 25/ Found charges against me, sent by Br. Layton, who had been fair to my face.

[Page 595R]

1887/ Charges made by Layton.

25/Bp. Preston said he did not believe them, and told me to write a full refutation of them which I did, on

26th]I copied Layton's letter, and sent reply to Prest Taylor.[65]

March/[Blank line]
Tues. 1/ Saw Sister Grieve to day—a pleasant visit.

Thur. 3/To day we got positive assurance of the passage of the new Edmunds-Tucker Bill. I then determined to fulfill the law of God so soon as He will open my way to do so. This evening I saw for the first time Jessie Grieve—a pleasant companion.[66] Great rejoicing Among the Gentiles. They ^say^ Mormonism is doomed, <u>now</u>. A momentous question propounded Jessie.

Fri. 4/ Wrote to our Bishops on tithing matters, especially, stock.

5/ At priesthood meeting, it was said that points relating to doctrine must be submitted to the High Council.

Fri. 11/ Hunted names of ancestor's in Historian's Office, about 105.

Sat. 12/ Lyman came last evening. To a question of mine—Si Senor

---

65. See note at entry for March 19, 1887.
66. The Edmunds-Tucker Act was, in fact, signed into law on the day of this entry. Martineau was obviously more concerned with complying with the "Law of God" (D&C 132: 4–6, 12) and felt the urgency to find another wife. See entry for April 18, 1887.

Sun. 13/ Lyman took Eliza and I riding to day, before meeting.

14/ Attended practice of the Choral Union this evening.

Tues. 15/ Went to top of Ensign Peak today—a hard jaunt for me. In the evening got word that deputies were watching me, so I left Eliza's and went to Bp. Preston's to stay.

Sat. 19/ Got my recommend from Prest Taylor, O.K. for temple work.[67] Jesse came this evening with Church team. Arranged to do Some baptizing for Bp. Whitney on Monday next. viz:– Miss Jessie Grieve, who desires to do some work in the Logan temple. [above line from viz appears in slightly different hand]

Sun. 20/ Jesse is Engaged for the Church for the summer, by Bp. P.

Mon. 21/ Got tickets for self and May Preston, to Logan. Baptized Jessie Grieve by request of O.F.W. in the Bath House.

Tues. 22/ Went to Logan, found all well. Visited Zina Young, and "Young Zina", and had a pleasant visit.

23/ Charly came from Pocatello to see us.

24/ Wrote letters to Susan and Anna. Visited with Charles.

26/ Attended Choir practice, but was disappointed—so many faces gone—so many new ones. Not like my old choir, of which I was a member 24 years.

Sun. 27/ I preached, to day. Weather Cold and Snowy.

---

67. Martineau's letter of February 26 was received by President Taylor. Taylor responded by writing:

> Your lengthy communication upon the subject of the charges made against you by President C. Layton, of St. Joseph Stake, have been received and carefully perused. It seems necessary in order that a proper settlement be reached of this difficulty, that there should be an investigation of the affairs mentioned, at which you both can be present. This, therefore, is to enquire of you at what time you are likely to return to St. Joseph Stake. When we learn this we shall try and arrange to have one or more of the Twelve visit there, and give a full hearing to both sides. We enclose your recommend to the Temple properly endorsed. We see no objection to you moving from Arizona into Mexico, if you desire to do so and can make it convenient.

John Taylor to James H. Martineau "c/o Bishop Wm. B. Preston," March 16, 1887, First Presidency, Letterpress Copybooks, Vol. 15, p. 319, CR 1/20, LDSCHL.

29/ Arrival ~~of~~ at Sister Zina's of Jessie H.R.A. Grieves.

[Page 596L]

Jessie H. endowed

1887/Jessie Helen R.A. Grieves endowed to day for herself, not sealed.

Mch. 30/Began in Temple. I was endowed for <u>Abraham Martineau</u>, <u>Margaret Martineau</u>, endowed by S.M. Benson; <u>Marie Martineau</u>, by E. Nankevin; <u>Sarah Martineau</u> by E. Lundberg. <u>Elizabeth Finch</u>, by M.R. Henderson; <u>Catherine Martineau</u> by J.C. Christianson. <u>Margt Martineau</u> was sealed to me, Mary T. Richards, proxy, saw Jesse G

[In margin to left of next paragraph is: Mrs. M PW Young Sealing proxy]

" 31/ I endowed for <u>Daniel Carson</u>, <u>Susan Colembine</u> was endowed by M.R. Henderson; <u>Marriott Margt Bunny</u> by S.M. Benson, <u>Fanny Martineau</u>, by S.B. More; <u>Elizth Rankin</u> by J.C. Christiansen; <u>Caroline B. Parry</u>, by Lavina Parry. To day <u>Marie Martineau</u> and <u>Susan Columbine</u> were sealed to me. Jessie H. returned home. Sealing could not be done in the Temple, so Jessie returned home.

April 1/I endowed for <u>David Martineau</u>, <u>Ann Columbine</u>, by Mrs. Benson, <u>Mary Columbine</u> by J.C. Christiansen, <u>Susan Martineau</u>, by E. Lundberg, <u>Elizabeth Brewer</u> by E. Nankevin <u>Mrs. Gaston Hogle</u>, by M.R. Henderson.

To day I wrote to Prest Taylor, relative to doing a work for Jeanne d'Arc and Charlotte Corday.[68] Zina showed one of the arrow found in the skeleton by Jos Smith when on the road to redeem Zion. He gave it to Brigham, and he to his daughter Zina.[69] The one slain was Zelph a Lamanite general.[70]

---

68. Martineau had requested to be sealed to these two French political martyrs. In response to Martineau's letter dated March 30, President Taylor gave him permission to endow and seal these women to him. He was, however, instructed to check with the Logan and St. George temples to be sure that the work had not already been completed. John Taylor to James H. Martineau, April 13, 1887, First Presidency, Letterpress Copybooks, Vol. 15, p. 499, CR 1/20, LDSCHL.

69. This was Zina Presendia (Young) Card (1850–1931) who, according to James Talmage, was in possession of the arrow before giving it to Wilford Woodruff. See Godfrey, "Zelph Story," 41.

70. The Lamanite general "Zelph" is the identity given by Joseph Smith as the person whose remains were found on a mound in Illinois by members of Zion's Camp on June 3,

2/ Wrote to Susan, Prof. J.W. Mears, and Joel

4/ Went to S.L. City, on way to Conference, in [unspecified]

5/ In the evening went with Jessie H.G. to Path Hyde for a blessing. He then blessed me ^(See p. 601)^ and then wanted me to bless him, which I did, giving him great pleasure. He said I told him just what Jos. Smith had said to him before + gave him the same blessings. It was a very good time.

6/ Went to Provo, to Conference. Met Jesse N. Smith there + we both went to Bp. Jas R Johnson's who was very good to us.

+8th+7th/ Meeting again. Lyman at afternoon meeting, and went back same day. At evening Jessie Grieves came with several others, supposing Conference would last till Sunday.

9/ Returned to S.L. City.

10/ Visited Della's grave. Very cold and Stormy.

11/ Still cold and Stormy.

[Page 597R]
While going to S.L. City April 4th I wrote the following lines, to the tune and Song "I'll remember you, love in my prayers,"—a beautiful tune.
[Blank line]
    I'll remember you, love, in my prayers.
                            [illegible text, may have been added later]
    In the heaven of heavens, together we dwelt
With our Father and Mother in love,
    And often together in unison Knelt
As we worshipped with spirits above.
    Then first were we parted, when came we to earth
To dwell on this planet below
    To forget all we knew—e'en our heavenly birth
To suffer affliction and woe

                                                    Chorus

1834. Included among the bones, unearthed from a large mound about one mile south of present-day Valley City, Illinois, was an arrow that was believed to have caused the death of this Lamanite warrior. According to the varying diary accounts, Smith further revealed that Zelph was a white Lamanite warrior who fought under a man of God, Onandagus "known from the East sea to the Rocky Mountains." This revelation has been a significant point of speculation in formulating theories about Book of Mormon geography. See Godfrey, "Zelph Story," and Cannon, "Zelph Revisited."

Be where we may—at home or away—
We'll share all our joys and our cares.
And at morn or at eve, when to Father I pray
I'll remember you, love, in my prayers.
2
But all is not sorrow, nor is it all pain
That we are here Called to endure;
What we fancy a loss is an infinite gain—
A glory, eternal and sure.
Then let us be happy, whate'er may betide,
If sunshine, or clouds round us spread,
Up the [illegible] [in margin: pathway] of Life we together will glide—
[in margin: Brier]/Together life's pathway we'll tread.

               Chorus

3
Should Sorrows assail us—should false ones forsake—
Our footsteps grow feeble and sore,—
We'll trust in our Father, and fresh Courage take—
To each other be true evermore.
In joy or in Sorrow together be one,
Cheered by an unchangable love;
And when Exaltations and ^heaven is^ ~~thrones we have won~~
We'll reign with our Father, above.

               Chorus.

[Page 598L]

[[written in top margin and indented is:

April 18. 1887
* Jessie H. Sealed to me in Endowment House by Apostle F.D. Richards, very secretly. John Lyon Witness holding a lighted candle. Richards hidden from my view.[71]]

1887/[Blank line]

---

71. This marriage—Martineau's third plural marriage—would have been in violation of the Edmunds-Tucker Act which had been passed only six weeks earlier, on March 3, 1887, disincorporating the LDS Church and the practice of polygamy. Richards undoubtedly performed the marriage behind a curtain in order to avoid the liability of being an eyewitness to this unlawful union. For more on the Endowment House's sealing room, see Brown, "'Temple Pro Tempore,'" 45–46, 65–66.

Apr. 12/Wrote to Alby Sherman, about doing work for his father and mother. Also to Susan.

Wed. 13/ Bought a gold watch Case for my watch—$32.00 Went to Church farm with Lyman.

14/ Visited M. Sloan. Lyman went home.

15/ Went to theatre with Alley. Saw ^E.^ Booth, in Shylock + [in margin: 16] Saw him in Othello.

Sun. 17/ Rainy and cold. Went to 17th Ward also to tabernacle.

[In margin to following para says: Jessie/Sealed to/me]

Mon. 18/ To day C. Fullmer and Ella went home. *Dos sunt ein quite Cold. At about 8.30 P.M. ^I and JHRA Grieves^ went to endowment house, each one alone, + entering by a different gate. Sealed at 9 P.M. one witness [under the word Sealed says: to Jessie Helen Russell Anderson Grieves]

Tues. 19/ Wrote letters home, Walked. Also visited at house of Jessie's mother. Jessie born Nov. 23. 1864. near Edinbury Scotland[72]

Wed. 20/ Had a narrow chance for escape this morning—team

21/ Snow, cold and muddy.

[In margin of following says: Jessie/2d A.]

22/ WB Preston went away to day. May follow tomorrow. This evening, at about 8.30, The 2d A. was administered in the Historian Office ^to Jessie H.R.A.G. Martineau^ by F.D. Richards, and myself laying on hands with ^him^[73]

Fri. 29/Returned to Logan, with Allie and Harriet. At Ogden we met the Queen of the Sandwich islands on her way east.

30/ Quarterly Conference in Logan. In the evening we went to hear the opera "Chunks," in which Jesse, Lilla + Virginia have part. It went off very well.

---

72. Jessie Helen Russell Anderson Grieve (1864–1896) was born to Simon (1835–1915) and Helen Russell (Anderson) Grieve (1836–1916) on November 23, 1864, in Edinburgh, Scotland. She died in Salt Lake City on October 28, 1896, and was buried in the Salt Lake City Cemetery.

73. The second anointing was administered to Jessie Grieve. This entry indicates that the ordinance does not have to be performed in the temple.

Sun. 1/May/ Snow on ground this morning, and quit cold. Wrote to Prest Taylor relative to Joan d' Arc and Charlotte Corday.[74]

[In margin of following says: MPW Young S. Proxy]

May 4/[note bracket] I was endowed for Paul Columbine to day.[75]

I was endowed for Gaston Martineau, Mrs. E.B. Smith for Catherine Skottowe, M.R. Henderson for Margaret Martineau. MH Anderson, for]Elizabeth Martineau, EB McNiel for Sarah Martineau, JM Thomassen for Marion Martineau. M.P.W. Young for Ann O.Brien.
[Blank line]
Read in Times + Seasons, p. 746 vol. 5 that Shem was Melchisedec.[76]

6/ I endowed for Mr. Haughout, EB McNeif for Nelly ^Haughout.^

[Page 599R]

1887/[Blank line]

May/MR Henderson for Elizth Francis Beatty, MH. Anderson for Jane Taylor.

6/ Also Chas Blackwell for Francis Columbine[77]

7/ Writing my biography for publication by E.W. Tullidge in his "History of Northern Utah," finished it next day.[78] Have some thoughts of going

---

74. Martineau may have been acknowledging the receipt of a letter from George Reynolds in which it stated: "some years ago Sister Josephene Ursenbach was baptized for quite a long list of deceased French ladies of note, amongst them, according to my best recollection, Empress Josephene, Marie Antoinette, Ninou [?] D'Euclos, Madame de Maukusu [?], Jeanne D'Arc, and Charlotte Corday. I also have the impression that she had them sealed to different bretheren, but of this I am not so certain, as I am of their baptism." Reynolds then suggested that the temple records needed to be examined closely. George Reynolds to James H. Martineau, April 15, 1887, First Presidency, Letterpress Copybooks, Vol. 15, p. 500, CR 1/20, LDSCHL.

75. Paul Columbine (1698–1784) was listed as one of the congregants of the Walloon Church at Norwich, England. According to the inscription on his tombstone, he was descended from a family in the Province of Dauphiny, France, from whence his father, Fraçois la Colombine, a man of piety, probity, and learning, withdrew at the revocation of the edict of Nantes in 1685. See Smiles, *The Huguenots*, 389–390, and Smith, "Walloon Church at Norwitch in 1589," 100, 147.

76. This statement was presumably made by the editor, John Taylor, under "Ancient Ruins," *Times and Seasons* 5 (December 15, 1844): 745–748, quote on p. 746.

77. This refers to François la Colombine, the father of Paul Columbine of Norwich, England. See note at entry for May 4, 1887.

78. Martineau's autobiography appeared in Tullidge, *Tullidge's Histories, (Vol. II)*, Biographical Appendix, pp. 68–79.

on a trip to England, Lyman wishes it. But there will not be enough time for me before I must return to meet some of the 12 in Pima on important business relative to myself and Prest Layton.

Wed. 11/ I was endowed for Peter Martineau, Sarah Moffat for Marriott Martineau, MR Henderson for Margaret Martineau, MH. Anderson for Catherine Martineau Foss. BB Hoth for Eliza Barnard. EB McNeil for Margaret Ronalds.

[In margin between here and 13 says: Mrs. J. T. Richards Sealing proxy]

To day were sealed Peter Martineau + Margaret Ronalds; Mr. Haughout + M. Martineau. Francis Haughout + Mrs. Francis Houghout, and Paul Columbine + Elizabeth Brewer and Catherine Skittowl

Nephi was endowed for Joseph Martineau and M.M. Burris for Sarah Meadows, and C.A. Henderson for Melia Hardingham.

12/ I was endowed for John Martineau, MH Anderson for Theodora Martha Dyball, EB McNeil for Catherine Harris, M.M. Burris for Margaret Williment, BB. Hoth for Susan Macon.

13/ To day were sealed Joseph Martineau + Caroline B. Parry. Peter Columbine + Marie Martineau. John Martineau + Marriot Margt Burnny, Richd Williment + Mary Martineau

I endowed for Peter Columbine. Nephi for Richd Williment. EB NcNeil for Elizabeth Humphrey. MM Burris for Ann Dorothy Clark. MR Henderson for Catherine Marsh, M.H. Anderson for Susanna Scott. BB Hoth for Elizabeth Bromton.
[Blank line]

Tues. 17/To day Lyman was baptized of 65 and Lilla for 37.

[Page 600L]

1887/[Blank line]

May 18/I endowed for Philip Meadows Martineau. MR Henderson for Mrs. Ann Haughout, MH Anderson for Mrs. Peter Haughout, MM. Burris for Elizth Haughout. M.B Kent for Mary Haughout

[In margin from 18 to 20 says: Mrs. Jane T. Richards Sealing proxy.]

There were Sealed Philip M. Martineau + Elizth Humphreys and Ann Dorothy Clark.

19/ I endowed for Hewett Raved, Nephi for Peter F. Martineau, MR Henderson for Mary Davis Guild, MH Anderson for Elizabeth Mears, MM. Burris for Hannah Mears. MB Kent for Mary Mears. M.A. Kent for Ann Bogart. Sealed to me M.D. Guild, E. Mears, + Mary Mears.

20/ I endowed for David Columbine, Nephi for Peter Columbine, MH. Anderson for Allette Haughout, M.M. Burris for Elizabeth Martineau, MB Kent for Mrs. Elizth Blackburn. M.A. Kent for Theodore Martha Blake, MR Henderson for Elizabeth Mears.

There were Sealed Peter Columbine + Melia Hardingham. David Columbine + Theodora Martha Dyball (pr J.T. Richards) and Myself and Elizabeth Mears, also myself + Millie Benson, (pr A.B. Benson)

21/ Wrote to Prest J. Taylor for 2d A for Nellie Benson.

24/ Finished reading proofs of my biography.

24/ I endowed for David Martineau, Nephi for Francis Columbine, M.M. Burris for Mary Mears, MH Anderson for Winnifred Sprague.

[In margin from 25 to end says: M.P.W. Young—S. proxy this week]

There were Sealed David Martineau + Sarah Meadows, and Francis Columbine + Susan Macon.

26/ I endowed for Jacques d' Arc (father of Jeanne) Nephi for Mr. Egbert, MR Henderson for Mrs. Sarah Dexter, MH. Anderson for Catherine Mears, MM. Burris for Sarah Mears. MB Kent for Isabeau de Vorethon (mother of Joan of Arc) EB McNiel for Elizth Mears.

There were Sealed Hewett Rand + Mary Columbine, Jacques d' Arc and Isabeau de Votethon, Mr. Egbert + Elizth Martineau.

I acted as proxy for Peter Stubbs, dead, Sealed to two wives. (dead

[Page 601R]

1887/[Blank line]

May 27/I endowed for John Dexter, Nephi for Thomas Vernon MR Henderson for Elizabeth Johnson MH Anderson for Mary Mudge. MM

Burris for <u>Catherine Mears</u>. EB McNiel for <u>Mary Catherine Mears</u>, MB Kent for <u>Margt Ketelas</u>.

[In margin, under May 27, says: M.P.W. Young./Sealing proxy this week]

~~Re~~ There were sealed <u>John Dexter</u> + Winnifred Sprague <u>Thomas Vernon</u> + <u>Mary Mears</u>.

Received permission for 2 A. for Nellie Benson, Also a letter from F.M. Lyman. Settled with those who have assisted in the temple, by Nephi's liberality, to amount of $33.00 besides some other I paid myself.

28/ Charles went to Pocatello to day, after two days visit, which I much enjoyed. He feels well in the gospel.

<u>Memoranda</u>. He was born 24 July 1861, married Eva Rosetta Rice 21 Jan. 1886. Their son Chas Freeman Jr. born 20 Dec. 1886. Was ordained Elder by C.W. Hyde. Aug. 6. 1865.

Apr. 5/1887/The following blessing was given me in S.L. City by Patriarch Charles W. Hyde, April 5. 1887.

Beloved Brother, I place my hands upon thy head and Seal upon you a patriarchal blessing. And thou shalt yet be called to proclaim this gospel from land to land and from Sea to Sea, and no power shall stay thy hand; and you shall proclaim the gospel from city to city, even to the house of Israel, and they will call thee blessed of the Father. And you shall see Zion redeemed, and stand with your Redeemer and with the prophet Joseph when the Saints will be free. And be comforted, for Zion <u>shall</u> be redeemed; for they shall bind up the law and seal up the testimony. For you know not the blessings which the Lord thy God has for you. For thou art of Ephraim and a lawful heir to the fulness of the priesthood. And if thou desirest it thou shalt converse with the three Nephites, and they shall unlock to you things that shall not enter the heart of man. And I seal upon your head eternal life, with all thy father's household. Even so. Amen and amen.

(Recorded in Book J. folio 178.) See p. 596

[Page 602L]

1887/Jessie H.^R.A. Grieve^ received her blessing at same time, I being scribe.

May 30/To day our family and the Thatchers decorated the graves of our dead. Sister Preston had a large box of flowers brought from her garden in S.L. City, for the purpose. Very warm.

June 1/Br.[Blank; note bracket]
Wed./To day I was endowed for <u>Peter Columbine</u>, and Nephi for <u>David Martineau</u>. There were sealed to day <u>Gaston Martineau</u> + <u>Mrs. Gaston Hoyle Martineau</u>; <u>Peter Columbine</u> + <u>Elizth Brunton</u>; <u>David Martineau</u> and <u>Catherine Harris</u>. I acted for the males, and Sister May T. Richards for the females, in sealing.

I also acted as proxy for Wm Lea, dead, in sealing two wives to him, by Mrs. Stubbs.

I wrote to Bp. C. Pulsipher, Huntington, Emery Co. Utah relative to Albey's standing in the Church, as what he will do about working for the dead (his father +c) so that if he will not do anything for them my children may. Lyman Sherman has waited long for his blessings, having died in full faith and fellowship, in 1838, in Far West, Mo. a <u>martyr</u>, as I have been told by H.C. Kimball and Geo. A. Smith. He was one of the first Seven Presidents of Seventies, and shortly before his death was called to be an Apostle, but died before he was ordained. He was father to my wife Susan Julia Sherman.[79]

---

79. On June 20, Martineau wrote to President John Taylor, asking permission to perform the work for his deceased father-in-law, Lyman Sherman, and Emmeline Wallace Cranney Drake (1815–1887), the deceased plural wife of his other father-in-law, Joel H. Johnson. In the letter, he wrote:

> I feel anxious that a work may be done for Lyman P. Sherman, my wife's father, who died in Far West in 1838. I would like to have him and his wife receive the 1st and 2d anointings, to have them sealed together, and have their children sealed to them. My wife's brother, Albey, the eldest of the family living, has no desire, apparently, to do anything for his parents, though I have urged him to do so. He has for years been on the back ground and seems to think nothing of these things. I do not wish to curtail any of his rights, but do wish that a work may be done for my wife's parents while the present opportunity exists. My son, Lyman, of Logan, could act for his grandfather, and I could, if approved, receive the 2d A for him. My daughter acting for her G. mother. I will be satisfied, whatever your decision.

J. H. Martineau to John Taylor, June 20, 1887, cited in Woodford, "The Historical Development of the Doctrine and Covenants," 2: 1433–1434. Taylor responded by writing that he needed to check with B. F. Johnson before proceeding with any temple work so there won't be any confusion. John Taylor to James H. Martineau, June 22, 1887, First Presidency, Letterpress Copybooks, Vol. 16, p. 429, CR 1/20, LDSCHL.

2/ I endowed <u>Arthur Martineau</u> and Nephi, <u>Philip Martineau</u>; Sister Adaline B. Benson endowed for <u>Mary Mears</u>. There were sealed <u>Arthur Martineau</u> and <u>Ann O'Brien</u>. Also <u>Philip Martineau</u> + <u>Elizth Frances Beatty</u>. After which I was proxy, in sealing two wives to <u>John Stubbs</u>. At 2.30 P.M. Nellie Benson Martineau received her 2d A. Sister Adaline B.A. Benson being proxy. This is the first case of the kind in this dispensation, I am told, of a Lamanite woman receiving this ordinance. I rejoice to be one of those counted worthy to save and exalt one of the daughters of Lehi, and I believe that Lehi and Moroni and other holy ones will also rejoice, and will bless and aid me in my labors for the Salvation of

[Page 603R]

1887/[Blank line]
June/2/the living children of Lehi, whose redemption is very near at hand, and to whom I am to be a messenger + a hunter, if I forfeit not my blessings. I feel as if my great life labor is just about to commence; although, in one sense, I have labored faithfully for 36 years, striving to build up Zion in my humble capacity.

Fri. 3/ I endowed <u>Mr. Neave</u> ^by^ Nephi, and I endowed <u>John Martineau Lyon</u>, my nephew, Emmeline was endowed for <u>Ruth Mears</u> and Mary A.B. Freeze for <u>Mrs. Thomas Vernon</u>. Sister Freeze is my dear friend, and helped me to day for friendship's sake. There were sealed, <u>Mrs. Neave</u> + <u>Catherine Martineau</u>, M.A.B. Freeze being proxy.

I have been quite feeble all this week, having at times strange sensations. I know I stand very near the vail,—so near I can almost see <u>beyond</u> it, and I can see so many principles of truth—oh, so plainly. Oh Father, I thank Thee for the work I have been permitted to do for my dead—even to be a savior to so many. Help me, my Father, to continue, and to be true to the end;—help me, Father, to become pure in heart, that I may not forfeit my kingdom and exaltation in Thy presence. In my last letter to my dear wife Susan I made a covenant with her and me, to be a ~~such~~ ^covenant^ forever between us;— that no woman shall ever come between her and me—no one shall ever take her place in my love;—for she is the wife of my youth, and has <u>always</u> been true and faithful—has always been a help. Help me, my Father, to keep my covenant, and to be a blessing to her. And not only to <u>her</u>, but to <u>all</u> whom Thou doest give unto me, for thou hast said, my Father, that I shall be blessed in every gift that is given unto me. Oh, help me to be worthy.

Sister Preston returned to S.L. City to day, and her son Will started for Chicago to meet his father and May.

Mon. 6/ I went to S.L. City, stopping at Bp. Preston's not feeling Safe to go Elsewhere.

7/ Took Sister P. to hear "Belshazzar" in the big Tabernacle.

[Page 604L]

1887/[Blank line]
June 13/I obtained some names for baptism from the "Encyclopedia Brittanica," of Martini's (from Italy) back to the year 1256

14/ Went bathing at Garfield, on Salt Lake.

Thu. 16/ Went to closing exercises of the University with Sister Preston

Sat. 18/ Went driving with Sister P. and Nett + Lutie Thatcher. Also to Garfield, + bathed, which does me good.

20/ Recd letters from Susan and Albert, and answered. Commenced writing my collection of "Pearls."[80]

21/ Ordered 1000 tithing receipts for Pima T. Office. Wrote

23/ Went to Garfield + bathed. Wrote in "Pearls."

---

80. Martineau's collection of "pearls" refers to a compilation of quotes and dictations taken from published works and speeches by LDS authorities. These quotes and dictations were kept in what might be called a commonplace book—a small ruled book of quotations. When it was completed, he made handwritten copies and gave them to his children. In the prefacing note to his children, Martineau wrote:

> In making this collection of keys of wisdom and knowledge, my object has been to bring together in compact form many precious truths that are widely scattered among many publications of the Church, and therefore beyond the reach of any save a few, whose time and means will permit them to read and search for wisdom.
>
> As we will be exalted in proportion, not to our goodness but our intelligence, it is of vast importance to gain all we can: by study, faith & prayer, by the aid of the Holy Spirit; and to help and assist my children to obtain this intelligence and so to help them become wise unto their eternal salvation in their celestial kingdoms and never ending dominions is the object of this work.
>
> May my beloved ones profit by my labors, and become great and mighty in doing good, great and mighty in the Priesthood, and great in their celestial exhaltations in the celestial glory through obedience to every law of God, is the earnest prayer of their loving father, Patriarch, Prophet, Priest and King. Logan August 18, 1887.

James H. Martineau, "Pearls Collected from Church Works by James H. Martineau, 1887," p. 2.

24+25/ Wrote in my "Pearls."

27/ Letters from Susan and Henry. C. Layton still devilish.[81] Attended Teacher's Institute at University.

28/ With Mrs. P. drove Mr. + Mrs. Rouse around town, and then Went to Garfield with them, at opening of that Resort. A large number present. Wrote to Susan.
[Blank line]

July/[Blank line]
1/Friday/Went to Garfield with Teacher's Institute Excursions. Had a good dinner for 10¢ Bathed twice, + had a good time. On return visited Br. Norman with my friend. He gave me a good blessing and Comforted me much. Also the same for my friend. In the evening Bp. P. got home, with May +^N^

Sat. 1/ I returned to Logan. At Ogden ordered Shoe for Trudie. Found Charlie + wife living in my house for which I am glad. He has quit the R.R. Service

4/ Spent to day at home (Lyman's) Nephi + Emma there— In the evening a big fire near to Stores, in Logan.

Wed. 6/ Temple work. I endowed ~~John Mears~~. Oliver Burt. I find some temple work done while I was away, as follows:–

June 8	Nephi	endowed	John Mears
	Emma	"	Tirza Colly
June 9	Nephi	"	Oliver King
	Emma	"	Lucinda Cooley
June 10	Nephi	"	Wm Hancock
	Emma	"	Jerusha Cooley

<u>June 8</u>. Nephi endowed   John Mears.
Emma   "   Tiza Colly

June 9 Nephi   "   Oliver King
Emma   "   Lucinda Cooley

---

81. This comment reflects the kind of suspiciousness and intimidation Layton must have been exerting with regard to Martineau's handling of the tithing books.

June 10 Nephi   "   Wm Hancock
Emma   "   Jerusha Cooley
[Note brackets]

Also the following work done by Sister Elizabeth Pyper Angell:–

[Page 605R]

1887/[Blank line]
July 6// June 22d <u>Catherine Stevens</u>; 23d <u>Mary Haughout</u>, 24th <u>Mary Langston</u>.

7/ I endowed <u>Oliver Collins</u>. Sealings to day:—<u>Oliver Burt</u> + ~~Lucinda~~ ^Jerusha Cooly; <u>Oliver Collins</u> + <u>Lucinda Cooley</u>, Zina D.H. Smith was proxy both times in sealing.

8/ I endowed <u>Peter Terry</u>, + had him sealed to Tirzo Cooley. Margt W. Young, her proxy in Sealing.

Sat. 9/ Sent Pension Papers to Gelston + Co. Washington D.C. To day Lyman + Alley + kids went to S.L. City.

Sun. 10/ Rain last night. A man in the girls room at 3 A.M. I could find no one. Believe it was Jesse.

Rain all day. Letter from Susan.

11/ Sent her + girls some things from Allie. Also wrote to her.

12/ Wrote in "Pearls." Letter from Susan.

13/ I endowed <u>James Mears</u> and had his wife <u>Elizabeth</u> Sealed to him. Letters from Tullidge and others. Rainy.

14/ I endowed <u>Samuel Mears</u>. Sent pay for T.O. book.^$6.50^ Recd a letter from Annie W. Mears, my cousin, Albion, Neb.

15/ I endowed <u>Levi Woodsum</u> for Sister Lufkin.

16/ Wrote to Albert + to Susan—particular—and to J.W. Young. To day is Virginia's 17th birth day. May she have very many happy ones, and much happiness in this life, and life eternal. Copied two of my poems for Sister H.A. Preston, by her request, "Bells" + "memories."

Mon. 18/ Lyman returned from S.L. City.

Tue. 19/ Wrote in "Pearls." Sent a cork shoe to Trudie.

Wed. 20/ I endowed for Thomas Vernon, b. 1740

Thu. 21/ Jessie came. I sent T.O. Blank book to Pima $6.85

Fri 22/ I endowed John Dexter, b. 1639, Jessie G. endowed Mary Mears, B. 1699. I had Sealed to day, Saml Mears + Mary Mears, also John Dexter + Mrs. Sarah Dexter.

Wrote for my new recommend to temple, the old one having expired July 31st proximo.

25/ Wrote to A.M. Cannon for renewed recd for Jessie

26/ I was baptized to day for Seven persons, some of them as Simone di Martino, Lippo Memmo, and Guglielmo Memmo, being born as early as 1256 to 1283. Jessie was

[Page 606R]

1887/
   Elizabeth first endowed
July/26/
baptized for four of my dead, and also for 84 or her own dead.

Wed. 27/ I endowed Samuel May, Lilla was endowed for herself. To day I sealed Samuel May + Catherine Mears, also Thos Vernon + Mary Mears. Jessie for J. Thompson.

28/ I endowed (another) Thos Vernon, Lilla, Ruth Cooley Eva, for Margaret Cooley; Jessie for Margt Thompson.

   I had sealed to day, Thos Vernon + Mrs. Thos Vernon, Oliver King + Ruth Cooley, Wm Hancock + Margt Cooley I acted Proxy at the Alter for Edwd Taylor, in sealing.

Fri. 29/ Memorial Service in the temple in honor of Prest Taylor, who died July 25, I was one of the speakers appointed.

   I endowed John Mears, b. 1790, Jessie, Susanna Story Lilla, Antie Boden, Eva, Sarah Pierce; and had Sealed John Mears + Susanna Story.

[In margin from here to end of page says: Note I fasted from Tuesday, 2, to Sat. 6th hoping for a blessing from the Lord.]

Yesterday, Jessie had her eyes anointed by Prest Merrill, and was blessed by him, Br. Edlifson + myself, and her eyes (nearly blind) immediately healed, so that she removed her glasses, and could see to read well Several others were healed of deafness in the temple. The Lord has not forgotten His promises and his people.

August/[Blank line]
Mon. 1/ Election today. I had the honor of being a witness in the marriage of Bell Harris, who was in prison so long for her former husband's sake. In throwing off such a woman, he threw away a pearl, + showed himself unworthy.

Tues. 2/ Jessie was baptized for 308, all at one time, the greatest number ever done at any one time by one person.

Wed. 3/ I endowed <u>Abraham Keteltas</u>, Jessie <u>Helen Anderson</u>

Wed. 4/ I " <u>Pierce Pool</u>. There were sealed, <u>Abraham Keteltas</u> + <u>Antie Boelen</u>, <u>Pierce Pool</u> + <u>Sarah Pierce</u>

5/ Eva endowed for <u>Cornelia Haughout</u>, Jessie went home.

Sat. 6 Conference to day and tomorrow, H.J. Grant present, + on Sunday forenoon M. Thatcher spoke powerfully. Recd directions from Bp. Preston, relative to cattle, and I wrote to our Bishops in Arizona accordingly. Nettie Thatcher gave me her Photo.

[Page 607R]

1887/[Blank line]
Aug. 8/ Sent orders to the Bishops of St Joseph Stake, relative to the Church cattle. Also to Joel. Nettie Thatcher gave me her photo.

9/ To day Alley + Sister Preston came home. The baby, Royal, has been very sick, but is better. Recd Trudie's shoe, to be first.

Wed. 10/ I endowed <u>Stephen Martineau</u> (over again) and had him again sealed to his wife Elenor.—an error in first sealing.

10/ Letter from Tullidge,—says he has given order on me to G.Q. Cannon + Co. for $100.00

Thu. 11/ I endowed <u>Robt Mears</u>

Fri. 12/ I " <u>Lucas Covert</u>. Had sealings—<u>Robt Mears</u> and <u>Elizabeth Johnson</u>, also <u>Lucas Covert</u> + <u>Cornelia Haughout</u>. I was proxy at the alter in sealing, for <u>Wm Little</u> <u>dead</u> and Eliza Little <u>alive</u>, Also <u>Wm Philtpot</u>, <u>John Allen Jr</u>. and <u>John Pingriff</u>, <u>dead</u> and <u>Martha Ann Chandler</u>.

I began to fast this evening, hoping God will bless me.

Sat. 13+14/ Still fasting.

Mon. 15/ Still fasting all day. Gave in names for baptism,

Tues. 16/ Ended my fast this morning, having eaten nothing since last Friday—3 days + 5 nights. I was baptized for 56 persons; and Miss Josephine Johanna Riser baptized 13 for me—may God reward her.

Wed. 17/ I endowed <u>Cajeme</u>, a great Yaqui chief, of Sonora. I was proxy at the Alter in sealing, for <u>James Lindsay</u> <u>dead</u> + Agnes L. Scroggie; Also for <u>Isaac Williams</u>, <u>Thos Bowen</u>, + <u>Benj Evans</u>, with Mary Evans Jeremy;– Also <u>William Worvill</u>, <u>Thos Worrvill</u>, and <u>Robt Plumb</u>, with Mrs. Harriet Worvill.

18/ I endowed Benito Juarez, Prest of Mex. (full blood indian) Mrs. Henderson, for <u>Hilena Haughout</u>, M.H. Anderson, for <u>Mehetabel Davenport</u>, <u>Hilena Haughout</u> was sealed to me, Mrs Jane T. Richards, Proxy.
[Blank line]

19/ I endowed <u>Montezuma</u>, Mex. Emperor, Mrs. Henderson for <u>Mehetabel Dawes</u>, MH Anderson for <u>Catherine Bloomfield</u>.

20/ Went to Nephi's. <u>Sun</u>. 21 Returned to Logan.

21/ Lilla, Charles + Eva returned from a week in Logan Cañon. Coming home, Eva + baby were thrown from the

[Page 608L]

1887/[Blank line]
Aug. 21/wagon and somewhat hurt—not seriously.

Tues. 23/ Charles was baptized for [blank] dead. Mrs. Preston went home. Susan writes that C. Layton still tries to injure me, + has called in all the tithing books to find something against me. The Lord judge.

Wed. 24/ I endowed Simone di Martino, Born 1283, Italy, Mrs Henderson for Jane Smith.

25/ I endowed Comonicus, indian chief, Mrs. Henderson for Giovanna Memmo, wife of Simone di Martino. Had them Sealed to day.

Fri. 26/ I endowed Wm Maycock, Mrs Henderson for Mrs. Roswell Mears, Mrs Morrill Benson for Mrs Joseph Mears, Josephine J. Riser for Helen Bourne, + M.B. Kent for Louisa Day.

Sat. 27/ Wrote all day, in my Temple Books. Charles sick to day

Sun. 28/ Charles sick—Cholera Morbus—administered. Last evening Saw Moses Thatcher and J.W. Taylor. Recd letter from St George Saying I can have 2d A for Emmeline Drake, wife of my father-in-law Joel H. Johnson, for which I rejoice much. I had applied some time previously, to Prest Taylor for the privilege, which he gave conditionally, (if the other wives had recd their 2d A.[82]

Tues. 30/ To day Josephine J. Riser was baptized for 51 names for me, Among them, Lady Hester Stanhope, who lived and died in Syria, at June 23, 1839, eldest child of Charles 3d Earl of Stanhope, and grand daughter of Earl of Chatham + of Lord Chesterfield. Jessie came today.

31/ I endowed Aaron Cooley, Jessie Virginia Johnson, Mrs. Staines, Cora Rice, J. Farraday Henry Stanley, MR Henderson Ahenatic, C. Henderson, Magus, S.M. Benson, Cacica. All five latter were sealed to me, by M.P.W.Y.

Sep. 1/ I endowed Thayendanega (Brant) G.A. Godfrey for Benj. Withwell, F. Lunberg for Isaac Haughout; Jessie for Lady Hester Stanhope, M.R. Henderson for Mary Blackburn C. Henderson for Fanny Ann Clark, S.M. Benson for Mary Martineau, Mrs. P. Staines for Jane Martineau

---

82. Emmeline Wallace Cranney (1815–1887) married James Drake on April 8, 1847. It is not clear when she married Joel Hills Johnson. See note at entry for June 1, 1887. A few days later, Martineau was denied a request to perform the second anointing ordinance for Viroqua Johnson, an Indian girl whom Joel H. Johnson had adopted in 1851 while at Fort Johnson: "Dear Brother: The Indian girl Viroqua Johnson concerning whose second anointings you write to me, I think is a case that should be deferred for the present. You are at liberty to have her baptized for and have someone have Endowments for her: but at present I think it is improper for the ordinance of Second Anointing to be administered in her behalf. With kind regards Your Brother. Wilford Woodruff." Wilford Woodruff to Elder James H. Martineau, September 2, 1887, First Presidency, Letterpress Copybooks, Vol. 17, pp. 124, CR 1/20, LDSCHL. Transcription taken from the *New Mormon Studies* CD. For more on Viroqua, see James H. Martineau, "Indian Reminiscences," *Deseret Weekly* 52 (May 23, 1896): 718.

I had sealed, Henry Stanley + Harriet Sprague; Benj. Withwell + Mary Ann Sprague.

Sep. 2/ I endowed Pontiac; G.A. Godfrey Peter Haughout

[Page 609R]

1887/[Blank line]
Sept./2/John M. Lewis for Roswell Mears, John Farraday for Jacob Johnson, Jessie for Wectamoo, M.H. Henderson for Mary Fisher, C. Henderson for Mary Wright, S.M. Benson for Patience Scott, P.M. Staines for Mrs. Hester Stanhope, M.A. Bingham for Ann Burrows, Ida Lewis for Caroline Martineau S.E.D. Hanks Isabella Wilds, Josephine J Riser for Marie Jourdain. [blank] Sealed Roswell Mears + Mrs. Roswell Mears.

4/ DH Wells staid at Lyman's today.

5/ Wrote to Bp. Preston, relative to T. Office cattle. Also home. Gave in names for Baptism.

Tues. 6/ Was baptized for 308 of Jessie's relatives. She was baptized for four of mine and 106 of her relatives. ^7th^ Jessie retd

Wed. 7/ I endowed Wamsutta, J. Faraday for Chas Stanhope (3d Earl) W.C. Lewis for Anthony Housman, G.A. Godfrey for Wm Bodine. Eva for Louise La Vallier, M.H. Henderson for Dorothy Waugh. [blank] Sealed Peter Haughout + Mrs. Peter Haughout, Isaac Haughout + Mrs. Ann Haughout, Jacob Johnson + Elizabeth Haughout, Anthony Housman + Mary Haughout. [blank] Sealed to me Ann Burrows. Also G.M. Thompson for Mr. Holland,

[In margin for next para says: Jessie retd S.L. City]

8/ Nephi endowed Joseph Mears, Eva for Elizabeth Mary Jillard, W.J. McColleck for Mr. Cunningham, Jessie returned to S.L. City. Wrote home to Susan + childn Recd letter from Prest Woodruff, giving consent to my adoption to Joel H. Johnson which I desired, as it was agreed upon between JHJ. and myself many years ago. Also in relation to 2 A. for Emmeline W.C. Johnson.[83] Wrote to him in reply, asking that Sister Adaline

---

83. In addition to granting permission to be "adopted into the family of Brother Joel H. Johnson," the letter also responds to a request to perform temple ordinances for deceased Indian Chiefs. Woodruff counseled Martineau: "you have gone too fast" in trying to perform ordinances for the Indian Chiefs mentioned. "There must be order observed in

B.A. Benson receive the ordinance for E.W.C. Johnson in place of my wife, who is in Arizona.⁸⁴

Fri.9/ Recd letter from W.B. Preston, relative to Cattle. I endowed <u>Guilliaume Pierre</u>, Nephi, <u>Charles Martineau</u>, Alley P. Martineau for <u>Mary Martineau</u>. [blank] <u>Sealed</u>. <u>W. Bodine</u> + <u>Alletta Haughout</u>, C. Stanhope + <u>Mrs. Hester Stanhope, Mr. Holland</u> + <u>Fanny Martineau, Mr. Cuningham</u> + <u>Susan Martineau, Joseph Mears</u> + <u>Mrs. Jos Mears, G. Pierre</u> + <u>Marie Jourdain, Charles</u>

[Page 610L]

1887/ Albert married to Emma Allred.

Sept. 9/<u>Martineau</u> + E.^M.^ Jillard. Wrote to JN Smith about Cattle.

Mon. 12/Very cold. Snow in mountains. Saw Bp. W.B. Preston + got permission to build a tithing office in Pima.

Tues. 13/ I was baptized for 240 for Jessie and 4 for myself. Wrote to Joel + appointed Welch and Webb to assist in trading Church cattle with Layton.

Wed. 14/ I endowed <u>John Blackburn</u>. Sealed <u>him</u> + his wife <u>Elizth Blackburn</u>. Wrote to Prest Woodruff about 2d A for E.W.C. Johnson.

15/ I endowed <u>Samuel Dexter</u>, + had him sealed to <u>Catherine Martineau</u>.

Fri. 16/ I endowed <u>John Martineau</u>, + Sealed to <u>M. Mudge</u>. Sealed to me, <u>Mary Fisher</u>.

Mon. 19/Continued copying my "Pearls" for Alley.

Wd 21/ I endowed <u>Edwd Haughout</u> + sealed him to <u>A Bryant</u> Recd permission for E.W.C.J.s 2d A.⁸⁵

---

the House of God in regard to these ordinances for the dead or confusion of the gravest character may arise. A little reflection will show this to you." Wilford Woodruff to James H. Martineau, September 5, 1887, First Presidency, Letterpress Copybooks, Vol. 17, pp. 154–156, CR 1/20, LDSCHL.

84. See entry for September 21.

85. This is in reference to permission received for performing the second anointing for Emmeline Wallace Cranney Johnson, a plural wife of Joel Hills Johnson. Wilford Woodruff to Elder J. H. Martineau, September 19, 1887, First Presidency, Letterpress Copybooks, Vol. 17, p. 235, CR 1/20, LDSCHL. Transcription available on *New Mormon Studies* CD-ROM. Also see entry for September 29.

22/ I endd J. Hilyard + had him sealed to A. Columbine Had sealed to me Patience Scott and Mary Wright.

Fri.23/ I endd Saml Mears, + sealed to his wife Mary C. Mears. Had sealed to me Dorothy Waugh + Mary Martineau.

Sat. 24/ Saw W. Webb to day, from Pima. He tells me Geo. Albert was married on Tuesday Sept. 13. 1887, to Emma Alred.

Lyman got me a suit of clothing, shirts +c. for which our Father will bless him, as I do.

This morning before light I had a vision:—I was sleeping soundly, and was suddenly waked by several distinct taps like a pencil striking a table, + was instantly wide awake. I saw with my eyes a procession of people or spirits, walking two and two, towards a cloud on my left, wherein were some personages in authority, but veiled by the cloud so that I could not see their faces. Each person carried in his hand, elevated, something like a leafy ^branch or^ bough, seemingly as a symbol of joy or triumph, and the procession extending far away into the distance. Over our heads was a scroll on which was written

[Page 611R]

Sept/1887/"Come to me all ye weary and heavy laden, and I will give you rest." There seemed to be a thin ^silvery^ veil between them and me, making them a little dim or not quite plain. I saw on my right, faces peering from a cloud, oh, how full of malice and hatred and wickedness, saying at those who were walking towards the place of rest; but they were powerless to do harm, and this made them look so hideous and evil. The scene was lighted with an indiscribable silvery or pale light, although it was a dark, moonless night. I saw this for quite a while. This was given for my comfort, and to teach me to whom to go for help and rest in time of trial or anxiety and care. If we go to God in the right way, in humility, repentance + faith, He will give us rest, and the spirits of evil cannot prevent. Oh, what a comfort to know we have a true Friend. And oh, may I be worthy, like Abraham, to be called the Friend of God.
[Blank line]

Mon. 26/Letter from Susan. Albert had started for St George temple with Emma to be sealed. He went on 14th

Tues. 27/ Eva was baptized for 8 persons for me.

28/ I endowed James Mears. Sarah Burns for Mary Mears. I had sealed J. Mears + M. Davenport. I was also proxy for Sister Berry in sealing two wives to her husband. Saw W. Webb and S. Burns married. Isabella Wilde was sealed to me.

Tue. 29/ I Endowed John Mears. W. Webb, Wm Dawes, S.B. Webb, Mary Mears. Adaline B.A. Benson, Mary Mears. Had the following Sealed:– John Mears + Mary Mears, Tho Blake + Theodora M. Blake. Wm Dawes + Mehet Dawes, Francis Fletcher + Marriett Martineau, Tho Martineau + Elizth Rankin, Wm Henry Blake + Louisa Day, Thos Martineau + Helen Bourne. Robt R. Martineau + Jane Smith.

[See margin note, like: 2d A <arrow> Sep. 28 1887]

2d A.
To day my father's wife, Emeline Wire Cranney Johnson, Born June 1. 1815. Ohio. wife of Joel Hills ^Johnson^

[Page 612L]

1887/[Blank line]
Sep. 29/was anointed to him by M.W. Merrill, Adaline Brooks Andrus Benson sitting for her, I for him, Samuel Roskelly witness and recorder. How I thank Thee, Oh Father, for this privilege to me, blessing to Emmeline, and added glory to my Father-in-law Johnson. They have both passed behind the vail, they are both Safe, and both have now entered into their glory as King and Priestess—Priest and Queen. Help me, my Father, also to be true to the end, that I may gain _my_ exaltation. [blank] She died Aug. 11. 1887 Logan.
[Blank line]

Fri. 30/ I endowed John Mears. Lyman, Thos Mears. Nephi Cornelius Martineau. Alley, Mrs. Mary Mears, Emma Mrs. Margt Martineau. [blank] Sealed. To J.H.M. Louise La Valliere; other sealings. Cornelius Martineau and Mrs. Margt Martineau, Thos Martineau + Mary Martineau John Mears + Mary Mears, Wm Mason + Elizth Brewer Columbine, David Jardine + Sarah Martineau, James Lee + Margaret Martineau, Edwd Foss + Catherine Martineau.

In this Sealing Lyman + Alley officiated for Thos Mears + wife, Nephi and Emma for Cornelius + wife, myself and Emma for the other dead.

Oct. 1/ After temple hours, we all went through the temple. In the morning I went to Nephi's, returning on the [in margin: Sun. 2] next day. All the children and grandchildren assembled at Lyman's today. At dinner there were 16 besides me. A very pleasant day.

5/Went to S.L. City with Gene. Lyman and the 2 Chiln stopped at Bp. Preston's. Conference lasted 4 days. and Prest Woodruff came on the stand and spoke having been a long time hidden. Very cold weather

12/ Had a very pleasant visit at Br. Norman's. He is 87. but is full of the Holy Spirit and the gift of prophecy. Sister Grieve and Jessie Helen were there also. Br. Norman gave me a good blessing, after which we blessed all the others, and were happy.

[Page 613R]

1887/[Blank line]
Oct. 13/Visited J.H. Smith and had a pleasant visit, in relation to affairs in Pima, in connection with Prest Layton. Russells

14/ Staid this evening at Bp. P.'s house with Jean.

15/ Came home, found all well.

16/ Began fasting this evening, for 3 ½ days.

17+18/ Writing names in my temple record—1048.

19/ I endowed Benjamin Martineau ^(68)^ Full temple.

20/ " " Gerritt Keteltas. Wrote to Joel. Gertrude, Henry and mother (Susan) Recd letter from Sherman relative to business in Engineering on S.P.R.R. While in S.L. City, the hand of the Lord was upon me for good in a remarkable manner, in two cases. the first, on the 12th when a teacher was engaged for a school; and on the same day when I received authority to do temple work for certain dead. For all these blessings, I thank our Father in heaven. On Wed. evening I finished my three ^and 1/2^ days fast. I fasted, that God would open the way for me to go speedily to my home, + with means to pay all my debts. The testimony of the spirit came to me like this, "Be patient, for in the Lord's own time you will go in peace, and all will be well." I believe this, but it is hard to wait; may I be patient, and trust in my Father who is in heaven, who doeth all things well. Jesse N. came home.

Fri. 21/ I endowed Samuel Mears + wrote to Jessie. I was proxy at the altar, for John Bucherfield and Joseph Wallett. I had sealed Gerritt Keteltas + Catherine Stevens.

Sat. 22/ Got additional names for baptism, among which are the Earls Chatham, Chesterfield, Bedford and Stanhope, all related to my father by marriage. Also five Popes of Rome, my ancestors, viz:—Martinus 1st, 2d 3d 4th + 5, the first being born in the year 600. Also St Martin, who was born about 316 Died 400. Also an ancestor, Martina, a young girl, a martyr, killed in 235 for her Christianity.

[Page 614L]

1887/[Blank line]
Oct. 23/ Lyman's baby, Royal, begins walking to day, for himself.

Mon. 24/ Still very cold weather Recd letter (farewell) from Jes Charles and Nephi start for Star valley, Wyoming Ter.

25/ Snowing this morning. I was baptized for 36 and Mary T. Richards for 9 of my relatives, including Martina. I felt happy in having this privilege to help the dead.

Wed. 26/ I endowed Samuel Guild, Lilla, Martina. ^my friend departed to day.^

27/I   " : James Pool. Had sealed to me, Mercy Mears and Martina; also sealed the dead:– Samuel Guild + and Sarah Mears; also James Pool + Mary Langdon. Wrote to D.P. Anderson;– told him I had been baptized for his dead—543. Wrote to Sixtus Johnson;– told him of my work for his father's wife Emeline W. Cranney Johnson Yesterday wrote to my friend, who started for Ogden on Tues. the 25th having heard from the day before.

Fri. 28/ Wrote to Susan. Last eve saw M.T. on eve of departure. and told him he should not be molested. This I felt to say by the spirit of prophecy, and may our Father grant it. Bought a fountain pen. I endowed Leffert Haughout, and sealed to his wife Mary Haughout. Recd letter from Prest Woodruff, with permission to do temple Work for some of the early martyrs.[86]

---

86. Woodruff advised Martineau that he should wait before giving Nellie Benson her second anointing but allowed him to perform saving ordinances for the women martyrs:

> Dear Brother, Your letter of the 18th inst. in which you express your wishes concerning an Indian girl who has been sealed to you receiving her second anointing, and also

Sat. 29/ A dull day for me—nothing much to do.

Sun. 30/ Dined at G.W. Thatcher's with Lyman's and Preston's families

Nov. 1st Tues./ Was baptized today for 17 persons, for some sisters who needed male help, and was glad to help so many more of the dead. Sister Elizth Russell Hamblin was baptized for five persons for me, martyrs of the 3d century in Rome. Yesterday I wrote of Jessie. Also to W. Woodruff, in regard to the five martyrs, I desire them as wives.

Wed. 2/ I endowed Judge Crittenden.

3/ I " Peter Haughout, and had him sealed to his wife Cornelia. Also had sealed two indians, a chief and his wife, who lived some 200 years ago in Masss—Wamsutta + Watamoo, I believe they are the first dead Lamanites endowed + Sealed in this dispensation.

[Page 615R]

1887/[Blank line]
Nov. 3/I feel honored in doing this work for the dead, of the house of Lehi, and I greatly desire to do much more.

Also Sealed Judge Crittenden + Eunice Sprague. Recd a letter from Vallejo, Cal. Nephi and Charles returned from their trip to Star valley, Wyoming. Recd letter from Susan, Joel + one from my son Neils, from Sweden. Spent the afternoon and evening at Moses Thatcher's, with Lyman's folks, and Sister W.B. Preston, also Langton's and Jeppeson's families. A pleasant time.

Fri. 4/ I endowed Thos Michael Greenhow. We all went to H.E. Hatch's, and spent the afternoon and evening.

---

respecting her doing work for 7 or 8 of the early martyrs, unmarried women, and having them sealed to you, has been received. I think it is better for you to defer the ordinance of second anointing for this indian girl who has been sealed to you since her death. It will be no lost to her for the present. As to the martyrs of whom you speak, we see no impropriety in having the ordinance of baptism attended to for them, especially if you know who they are: but before having them sealed to you, you should certainly have some knowledge of them and of your right to have them, as others may claim that they have a better right than you hereafter. With kind regards, Your Brother, Wilford Woodruff

Wilford Woodruff to Elder James H. Martineau, October 26, 1887, First Presidency, Letterpress Copybooks, Vol. 17, p. 421, CR 1/20, LDSCHL. Transcription taken from *New Mormon Studies* CD-ROM.

Sat. 5/ Sister Preston and Grandma Thatcher went home to day.

Sun 6/Wrote to Susan and Vallejo. Recd letter from A.M. Monteith.

7/Also wrote to Annie S. Mears, of Albion, Neb. + to Nettie and Lois. After noon, went to Nephi's.

Tues. 8/ Lyman. Bassett and others on U.G.

Wed. 9/ I endowed John Martineau. Margt A. Kent, Rufina ^M.^ and Sariah Moffett, Secunda ^E.^

Thu. 10/ I endowed James Lee, Nephi, J. Alison. S. Moffett, Denisa ^R^ Mrs. Thomassen, Apollonia ^R^ Emma, Julia ^S^ These five were Christian, virgin martyrs, slain ~~from~~ in 238, ~~to~~ 250, 257, + 457. They were sealed to me by Authority of Prest Woodruff.[87] I also had sealed:—

John Martineau Lyon   and Caroline Martineau
Thos Michael Greenhow " Elizabeth "
James Lee   " Sarah   "
John Martineau   " Jane Taylor—

[Blank line]
Mon. 14/Borrowed $500.00 of Logan Bank at 1 % pr Mo. Lyman Secy

Tu. 15/Went to S.L. City, Charles went also. to work in D+R.G. shops

16/Returned, having visited Eliza, Prestons and others in S.L. City

17/Got things for Susan and children

18/A family meeting to day—sad to me. In the evening I gave Alley a patriarchal blessing, by her request, which is on record in my "Temple record."

Sat. 19/ Left Logan, with Lyman at 4 A.M. parting from him at Ogden. I took C.P. fast train at 8.30 A.M. I secured a ½

[Page 616L]

1887/ Leave Logan for Pima.

---

87. See note at entry for October 28, 1887. Martineau was given further council by President Woodruff regarding temple work for martyrs mentioned in letter of October 26. See Wilford Woodruff to James H. Martineau, November 3, 1887, First Presidency, Letterpress Copybooks, Vol. 17, p. 504, CR 1/20, LDSCHL.

Nov. 19/1st class rate to Deming for $37.50, as a clergyman, by virtue of my certificate as such, and an appointment as missionary in Arizona, New Mexico and old Mexico. While I have been in Logan, my children have done all they could for my comfort, and on coming away, they sent many things for Susan and the children, for which may God forever bless and prosper them.

The last nine or ten months have been important to me in many ways. In the temple, I have had baptisms for about 600 men, and for about as many women; have procured Endowment and sealing for nearly 200 Souls; have had 36 wives (dead) sealed to me + endowed; and obtained the 2d A. for two of them—one living and one dead—an indian girl—the first Lamanite who recd that holy ordinance in this dispensation—Nellie Benson.[88] I also procured the 2d A. for a wife we sealed to father Joel H. Johnson—Emmeline Wire Cranny Johnson—. The Lord also blessed me in the gift of a companion, who received the 2d A. mentioned above. I spent much time searching after truth, gleaning from many church publications precious truths—keys of intelligence—which I compiled into a book which I named "Pearls." This I copied for Nephi, also for Alley.[89] In attending to all these, and my temple duties, I worked almost without intermission, day and night, and so accomplished a great work, for which all praise be to our Father. for his goodness and blessing. I spent no time in traveling around, never going to any other town, although often invited to do so. In the Temple, Prest M.W. Merrill told me I had done a mighty work—none excelling me.[90]

I dined at Terrace, supped at Elko, and there telegraphed to Jessie, to meet me at Sacramento tomorrow afternoon.

Sun. 20/ Breakfast at Reno. Arrived Sacramento 3.20 P.M. No Jessie. Took room at Western Hotel, and waited there all next day.

---

88. This is a significant milestone for Native American membership, since the "2d A" refers to the second anointing ordinance, the highest ordinance that can be performed for a member of the church.

89. See note at entry for June 20 above. The holographic volume of "Pearls" housed at MerrillCazier Library contains handwritten notes (post1921) by Nephi Martineau, suggesting that it is his copy.

90. Logan Temple recorder Samuel Roskelley inserted his "Register of Logan Temple Ordinance Work for November 1887" in his diary entry for November 27, 1887. He listed endowment totals for living/dead males and females (1404), sealing totals for living/dead males and females (452), totals for sealings of children to parents (219), adoptions (2), and second anointings, living/dead (11). See Samuel Roskelley Diary, November 27, 1887, Roskelley Collection, MSS 65, box 2, Book 2, USUSCA.

Tues. 22/ Telegraphed J. Started for Vallejo + arrd 6.30 P.M. Found Mrs. Lizzie Russell, Jessie's aunt, but Jessie was absent in San F. since the last ten days. Next day Telegraphed for Culmer's address in San F. Visited the Mare Island Navy Yard, and

[Page 617R]

1887/[Blank line]
Nov. 23/ Saw the French ship-of-war "Duchesne," armored with huge steel breech-loading guns, and Gattlings, and 600 crew.

24/ Wrote to Mrs. Grieve, and telegraphed by Mrs. Russell in answer to mine. Spent the evening at Mrs. Russell's, who was once a L.D.S.

25/ Went to San F. this morning at 8.10 reaching there at 9.45. Put up at American Exchange. Immediately started out to find Culmer's friend, at Elgin Park, and did so, but no Jessie to be heard of, as she has not been there. Where, in this great and wicked city, is she? No one can tell my agony of mind when I went to bed—and only when I cried unto the Lord—"thy will, not mine, be done"—only then did peace come to me, and my agony assuage.

26/ Hunted the streets and cars all day—unsuccessfully—and at 3.30 P.M. started on my homeward way, feeling that I was leaving hope behind—some one who might become a prey to wolves,—worse than dead. Oh Father preserve and shield her from evil.

27/ At 6 A.M. this morning, I was awakened by a violent shock, and found we had collided with another train, ascending the mountains near Caliente. Our engine,—the front one—was used up, the tender smashing entirely through the next car, and several of them being splintered into small kindling wood. It was a miracle our sleeper was not thrown off the high trestle on which we stopped; had we fallen, many must have been killed, and burned alive. For this deliverance I thank thee, my Father. We were detained half a day, arriving at Los Angeles at 2 A.M. (the 28th)

28/ at 9.15 A.M. Started again for Pima. Arrived at Colton 11.45 and stopped off to try for employment on the S.P.R.R. having had some encouragement. Found there is no opening for me. All right.

Tues 29/ Took train at noon; dined at Indio. Supped at Yuma 7 P.M.

Wed.30/Tucson at 5.0 A.M. Benson 7.00 Wilcox 8.30 + Bowie 9.15 A.M. Took room in R.R. hotel, waiting for conveyance home.

Fri./Dec. 2/Started home in Stage, as my team did not come. Met Joel about 18 miles coming for me. Reached home at 6. P.M. in a cold rain storm, and found all well as usual. No place like home.

Sun. 4/ Meeting in Pima, and spoke. People glad to see me.

5/ Visited some to day.

Tues. 6/ Saw B. Young to day. He went to St Johns. Albert went with him.

[Page 618L]

1887/[Blank line]
Dec. 11/Wrote to Alley and Lyman. Cold and windy.

12/Went to Solomonville, surveying. Surveyed, also next day.[91]

14/Rain all day—did not work

Fri. 16/Paid $30.15 taxes. Returned home next day—Saturday 17th

18/Meeting in Pima. B. Scavy, of Juarez, Mex. spoke. Wrote to J and to Nephi[92]

---

91. Isadore Solomon's original forty-acre homestead grant, which was preempted from Bill Munson in 1880, became the townsite of Solomonville. Martineau surveyed and subdivided the land; a map, on file in the Graham County Recorder's Office, was drawn by Samuel Logan. See Ramenofsky, *From Charcoal to Banking*, 109.

92. In addition to writing to Jessie Grieve and to his son Nephi, Martineau expressed some of his frustration with President Layton in a letter to Bishop Preston:

> Last January Prest Layton urged me to procure a studebaker 2-seat side spring wagon with cover, for use in this stake, and I ordered one, to cost about $180.00 Before I started for Utah, he told me that if I thought best, he would keep it and probably sell it to M. Thatcher; and I told [him] to do so. I find on returning here, that because he did not see Bro. M. T., he claims that it is a tithing Office vehicle, and has kept and used it as such till the present time; that is, he says it is a tithing wagon, but keeps and uses it constantly. I expect to go into Mexico soon after the stake T. O. settlement, and would like very much to take it for sister M. and myself to ride in, being responsible for all injury to it,—to be gone 4 or 5 weeks. I wish to find a location there to settle in, (either willingly or not.) If you do not wish to keep the vehicle for use in the emergencies that sometimes arise here, through the arrival of U.S. persons, I am willing to take it, charging it to my salary a/c for the year. I think we ought to have such a vehicle, and also a church team, as it is sometimes different to get one on short notice.

J. H. Martineau to Bp. William B. Preston, December 18, 1887, St. Joseph Stake Letterpress Copybook 1885–1888, pp. 61–62, LR 7781/21, LDSCHL.

19/ Went again to Solomonville, surveying.

Wed. 21./Finished the Canal, and farm land surveys. Came home Weather very cold, with snow enough to whiten the ground.

Thu. 22/ Attended Y.M.M.I. Conference in Pima.

23/ " F. Relief Conference in Central

Sat. 24/ Quarterly Conference to day and next. Good meetings. Albert and Joel were voted to be home missionaries for Stake.

26/ Worked on my county survey maps.

27 to 29/ Surveyed for A. Baker 500 acres. Letter from Alley.

Fri. 30/Worked on my plats. Elvira and her four children came from Mesa. Have not seen her for 13 years before.

31/Priesthood meeting in Thatcher. Had settlement of some difficulty with Prest Layton.

1888/[Note double lines above and below year]

Jan. 1/Sunday meeting. Also had a family gathering, 24 present.

2/Surveyed. Letter from Jessie Helen, from Oakland, Cal.[93]

---

93. Jessie Grieve had gone to Alameda, California, to hide from U.S. Marshals. She was using her mother's maiden name, "Russell," as an alias. In her letter, dated November 30, 1887, Jessie wrote, in part:

> My Dear Friend,
> You surely have not received two letters which I sent to you. One addressed Great Western Hotel, Sacramento, and the other to Vallejo. In my last I wanted to see you and tell you fully why I thought it safer not to go South with you. D. P. A. sent to Vallejo a long letter telling everything. how they found it out I know not, and they sent to know if I were there and my aunt telegraphed back to him that I was not there, that I had been + gone again, and that she knew nothing about me. They say if they find you, they will make you suffer, you know in what way I presume. That was the motive for me acting as I have done since I knew of that D. P. A.'s letter. My aunt thought also it was better for me to go away, so that she would feel free, should anything serious take place. ... I do feel so lonely at times with no one to talk to about things that are nearest and dearest to me. You know what it is having been in the same position yourself, yet I can always find a refuge in prayer, oh, never forget me at any time, even though we are separated by distance. I think the old adage is true "Absence makes the heart grow fonder."

Jessie Russell to James H. Martineau, November 30, 1887. This letter was inserted at the back of Martineau's journal, book two. See Godfrey and Martineau-McCarty, eds., *Uncommon Common Pioneer*, 737–742.

3/Went to Solomonville to sell my plats to the county.

4/Sold them—31—for $155.00 Co. warrants. + returned home.

Sun. 8/ To day Susan and I have been married 36 years. From 2 my family, with grand children, and sons wives = 60; viz:—21, children; 27 Gr. children, with 100 wives, living or dead. Truly has God blessed me most bountifully.

Mo. 9/ Had our annual wedding dinner, and a full house.

10/Surveyed for O. Elmer. Cold and windy.

11/ " Canal for Jerry Taylor + others.

Thu. 12/ made out deeds for Baker

13/Wrote to Nephi to come and visit us soon.

16/Letter from W.B.P. Next day Sent resignation as Bps. Agt.[94]

17/Began the mason work for T. Office in Pima.

21/Sent to Gurley for Mex. Vara chain, also for paper at Boston Worked on my plans for the tithing office.

[Page 619R]

1888/[Blank line]
Jan. 24/ Went to Fort Thomas, surveying; returned 26th

Sun. 29/This evening Ada Johnson, Susan's Niece, was married to Tom East, by Prest W.D. Johnson. I fear, a very poor match.

---

94. The letter, addressed to the Presiding Bishopric and dated January 17, read:

Dear Brethren
I hereby respectfully tender my resignation as Bishop's Agent for St. Joseph Stake, A. T. to take effect as soon as I make my Stake report for 1887.
    I intend to remove to Mexico shortly after making the stake settlement, with the intention of making my home there. I retire from the position I have occupied, with the knowledge that I leave tithing affairs in much better shape than I found them, and the consciousness that I have labored faithfully for the interests of the Church, to the best of my ability.
Respectfully your Brother
James H. Martineau

James H. Martineau to Presiding Bishopric, January 17, 1888, St. Joseph Stake Letterpress Copybook, 1885–1888, p. 67, LR 7781/21, LDSCHL.

30/Went to Safford, surveying.

31/ Sent $150.00 Cash to G.T.O. and next day $100.00 more

Feb. 1+2/ /Went to Thatcher, to settle tithing. Returned 3d Gave to Prest C. Layton my Defense fund Book, together with 145.10 in full payment. Check for 108.50, cash $36.60. Susan very sick, with sinking spells.

4/ Surveyed Pima Canal. Was subpoenad to go to Tucson as witness in trial, Vodkel vs Mrs. Collins.

5/Wrote to Jessie. Meeting in Pima.

6/Surveyed new Canal, at Pima.

7/ Started to Tucson, as witness in Mrs. Collins' land trial. By stage to Benson reached Tucson 2 A.M. 110m from Bowie.

15/Finished my business as witness and started home 5 P.M. Stopped at Benson, and next day went to St David, to settle tithing.

17/Finished at St David, went to Benson, took train + reached Bowie 11 P.M.

18/Home again, and glad. Have still a very bad cold.

20/Went and settled tithing at Curtis and Graham.

21/At Layton, same business. Home next day.

23/Went to Solomonville, to survey a canal. Home next day.

Mch. 3/Recd letter from John W. Young, Washington. Wishes me to go to Gila Bend and examine as to location +c for a big dam and Canal.[95] In order to telegraph him, had to go to Fort Thomas.

4/finished my Tithing Report today

5/Surveyed for L. Vodkel and returned next day.

10/Went to Safford to settle with Bp. Merrill

11/Attended funeral of little Coz. Damie Carlton. Charli + family and Virginia moved to S.L. City to day.

---

95. This refers to a canal and dam project that was initially financed by Morris R. Locke of Jerseyville, Illinois. See note at entry for December 15, 1888.

Tues. 13/I am 60 years old today. Had a family dinner.

16/Susan taken very sick, from night exposure at Mathews.

17/Letters from Lyman and Lilla. Ansd next day

Sun. 25/To day I drop my calling as Prests Counsellor, having resigned on the 15th inst. to remove into Mexico. I recd permission from Prest Taylor to do so in March 1887.[96] I have always felt out of place, and as if not wanted by Br. Layton.

[Page 620L]

1888/[Blank line]
April 1/Relinquished my entry of land at St David. Also wrote to Br. Seth Johnson, to Jesse, and others. About this time finished my Tithing reports.

5th to 7th/ Surveyed at Solomonville. Got home and found Dora sick. Gertrude was also taken quite sick with fever. In evening she was administered to, and healed; Dora also. Letters from Lilla + Gean.

Sun. 8/Not feeling well, myself. 10th unable to sit up, with lame back.

16/Up to this date, I have been confined to house, but better now. Recd choice roses and other plants from the east + set them out. Recd letter from S.E. Johnson, Juarez Mex.; gives good report of things.

19/Sent part of my Tithing report to Bp. Preston, also letter to him.

24/Took my tithing Reports to Prest Layton for his examination + signature, but he did not take time to attend to it. This is now the fourth time I have gone to Thatcher to see him for that business. It seems to me he delays on purpose to bring me into disrepute with the general authorities.

May 2/Bought a new Wood Mower, $90.00.

3/Began cutting our Lucerne hay. Quite lame in my back.

---

96. Martineau received a letter in early February from Wilford Woodruff acknowledging his resignation as Bishop's Agent: "A letter addressed by you to Bishop Preston, in which you tender your resignation as Bishops Agent in the St Joseph Stake was read to the council of the Apostles, and after some deliberation it was decided that your resignation should be accepted. I deem it proper to advise you of this action, that you may be made familiar with the decision in the case." Wilford Woodruff to James H. Martineau, February 4, 1888, First Presidency, Letterpress Copybooks, Vol. 18, p. 191, CR 1/20, LDSCHL.

9/Delivered tithing keys and books to Bp. J. Taylor. Good riddance.

Sun. 13/My Brother in law, C. Lyon died in St Paul, Min.

15/Recd 2 Nos of Western Galaxy, from E.W. Tullidge, with request to write for the Magazine.⁹⁷

16/Wrote article for Galaxy "Visit to Sonora, Mexico."⁹⁸

21/Recd blank deed to fill out, for sale of my house + lot in Logan ^$3000.00^

22/Got the deed acknowledged and returned in on 24th

25/Narrowly escaped a bite from a "Gila Monster" while surveying today. It is more fatal than a rattlesnake. It is a kind of lizard.

June 1/Bought a carriage of C. Layton to day, $175.00 Sold one to him about a month ago, for $180.00 Again tried to get him to examine the Tithing + Church papers.

5/Sold my plow (Sulky) and binder, $150.00

Since my return from Utah I have had much surveying to do, for gentiles, mostly, which has brought me several hundred dollars, so I have not needed to draw any of that resulting from Sale of the old home.

Again took my church papers to turn them to Layton, but he had no time to attend to them.

[Page 621R]

1888/[Blank line]
June 8/I turned over 27 head of Stock to C. Layton, for Albert

25/ Bp. W.B. Preston came from Pima. Appointed to meet tomorrow.

26/ He examined my Tithing reports for 1887 and found them all right.

Wed. 27/Examined my personal account, and accepted it. I turned G.T. Office orders +c to him, also delivered some Stock by his verbal order.

---

97. The *Western Galaxy* was published by Edward Tullidge from March to June 1888. Martineau had published a poem in the previous month's issue. See James H. Martineau, "Twilight Memories," *Western Galaxy* 1 (April 1888): 193–194.

98. This article never appeared in the *Western Galaxy*, as it was discontinued after the first volume (ending June 1888).

Dined with us. ^He^ left next day. He said we could change Susan's cows from Kanab to Pima

July 8/ Settled tithing business (Stock a/c) with Crockett and ^Albert.^ and finished up all my tithing business. Thankful. Bp. John Taylor, of Pima, having unjustly witheld from me water in the Canal Co. to am't of $42.00 which I had bought and paid for last year. I thought best not to contend about it, but my garden and trees are dying for want of the water.

11/ Susan's Birth day. Had a family dinner, + house full May she have many more such anniversaries.

I let Henry have H Blair's note (due me) for $33.70, he to pay me when he can.

At our family party to day Patriarch Wm McBride + wife were present, and in the afternoon gave the following blessings, which I took down as clerk:—

Susan's Blessing:

Sister Susan, in the name of the Lord Jesus I place my hands upon thy head and by the authority of the holy priesthood I seal upon you a patriarchal blessing, and I say unto thee, dear Susan, lift up thy head and rejoice, for thy name is recorded in the Lamb's Book of Life never to be blotted out, for the Lord is well pleased with thee, and thy Sins are forgiven. For thou hast had many troubles, trials, and afflictions; but they have been brought upon thee for thy exaltation and glory; and for thine own faith thou shalt be exalted very high, + thou shalt preside over queens; for thou art of the leading blood of Israel, of the lineage of Ephraim; but thy lineage is so closely connected with that of Manassah, that it cannot be separated, for they cannot be made perfect without thee, neither canst thou be made perfect without them.

[Page 622L]

1888/[Blank line]
July 11/the Lord will grant thee life, health and Strength, wisdom and understanding. For thou shalt begin to have joy and pleasure in thy last days, for thy last days shall be thy best days; for thou shalt live to see knowledge cover the earth, and see thy household redeemed; and all things shall appear before thee for thy honor and thy glory and thou shalt extend

blessings to thy household, and to thy friends and to thy Relatives, and to thy Father's house in general. Thou shalt be blessed with wisdom and understanding that none shall excell; and in connexion with thy companion, thou shalt fulfill thy mission upon the earth, both for the living and for the dead, and receive an exaltation, inheritance and crown of eternal lives, and thy part in the morning of the first ressurrection, with all that are near and dear unto thee; and I seal and confirm upon thee all thy former blessings, in the name of Jesus. Amen.
[Blank line]

George Albert's Blessing:

Brother George Albert, in the name of the Lord Jesus and by Authority of the holy priesthood I lay my hands upon thy head and I seal upon thee a patriarchal blessing; and I say unto thee, be thou faithful unto the End of thy days; for thou wast called, chosen and set apart to bear thy part in the redemption of Zion, and the bringing about the restoration of the House of Israel, and to lay the foundation for the Salvation and exaltation of thy father's house for many generations back; for thou art of the holy priesthood after the order of Enoch; for thy lineage is in Ephraim, who is the first born of Israel, holding the keys of the blessings of the gospel in every land; and thou shalt be a mighty instrument in the hands of the Almighty in restoring peace to the earth and turning the government into the hands of the just; for unto this end wast thou born, and in performing this great work thou shalt travel much for the gospel's sake, and bringing the Sons and daughters of Jacob from their long dispersion, which the Lord made known to them by their forefathers, and the land shall be blessed for their sake. Thou shalt assist them in building temples, and shall administer ordinances unto them therein,

[Page 623R]

that will produce their salvation; and thou shalt teach them how to be saved, and how to save themselves for many generations back, both for the living and the dead. And by obedience to the new and everlasting covenant thou shalt secure unto thyself and unto thy wives and children, friends and relatives, an everlasting inheritance and crown of eternal lives, with all that are near and dear unto thee; for I seal these words upon thee, in the name of Jesus. Amen.
[Blank line]
Anna Sariah's Blessing:—

Sister Anna Sariah, in the name of the Lord Jesus I lay my hands upon thy head, and by virtue and authority of the Holy Priesthood I seal upon thee a patriarchal blessing; and I say unto thee, honor thy father and thy mother, and thy days shall be many upon the earth, and if thou wilt give heed unto this blessing it shall be a comfort unto thee in time and a guide unto thee through thy future life. For thou art of the house of Jacob through the loins of Ephraim; and thou shalt be a blessing and a comfort to thy father's house, and shall be an instrument in the hands of the Lord in doing much for their salvation and exaltation; And thou shalt be a blessing to the daughters of Jacob, for thou shalt become a teacher and a counsellor unto them, and shall administer ordinances in the temple of the Lord that shall be the means of their salvation and exaltation; and thou shalt administer ordinances in languages that thou dost not now understand and teach them to save themselves with their dead for many generations back; and when thou shalt commence this work the Lord will give thee dreams and visions and manifestations of his holy spirit; and thou shalt learn to read the whisperings of the still small voice that shall make known unto thee the mind and will of the Father; and will teach thee how to choose a true and faithful companion that will assist thee in thy mission upon the earth and make thy journey through life easy and comfortable; and thou shalt labor upon the foundation that has already been laid for the Salvation and exaltation of thy father's house for many generations back; for thy children shall be as numerous as the sands upon the sea

[Page 624L]

1888/[Blank line]
July 11/shore and thou shalt be blessed in thy labors from this time forth with health and strength; and the blessings of the heavens shall be thine and the blessings of the earth shall not be witheld from thee; for I seal this upon thee with all that is near and dear unto thee, in the name of Jesus. Amen. [Blank line]

11th/Joel H. Blessing:—

Br. Joel, in the name of the Lord Jesus Christ I lay my hands upon thy head and by virtue and authority of the holy priesthood I seal upon thee a patriarchal blessing; for thou wast called, chosen, ordained and set apart before the foundations of this earth were laid, and did there covenant and agree that thou wouldst come forth in the dispensation in which we now live, and bear thy part in the redemption of Zion, and the restoration of the House of Israel; for thou art of the lineage of the house of Israel through the loins of Ephraim; and this was all recorded in the heavens and in the law before thou left the eternal worlds. I say unto thee that thou shalt fill thy mission with honor to thy Father in heaven and to thy father on earth, and to thy exaltation. And is so doing the Lord will bless thee with every blessing that is necessary to thy Exaltation, and will give thee wives and children to suit thy circumstances. And thou shalt become an instrument in the hands of the Lord in doing much for the redemption of thy father's house; and shall build upon the foundations already laid for their salvation and exaltation. For thou shalt have wisdom and understanding in all thy movements; and thy brethren shall seek unto thee for counsel; and through obedience to thy counsel they shall be exalted; for the Lord will give thee mighty wisdom in the counsels thou shalt bear to the house of Israel. For thou shalt become a savior on Mt. Zion, and thou shalt judge the house of Esau; and they will acknowledge thy kingdom to be the Lord's. And thou shalt hunt up Israel from the ends of the Earth, and bring them to the Zion of the last days; And among the house of Israel thou shalt be called the Wonderful Counsellor; And thy heart shall be filled with wisdom and thy tongue shall be loosed; and thou shalt speak with understanding and to the comfort of all the subjects of

[Page 625R]

1888/
July 11/Israel. And thy faith shall increase, and thou shalt have power over all evil spirits; and by obedience to the Everlasting covenant thou shalt receive an everlasting inheritance for thyself, thy children and friends, and be crowned with eternal lives, and come forth in the morning of the first ressurrection and receive thy exaltation; for I seal these words upon thee with all thy former blessings and ordinations, in the name of Jesus. Amen.
[Blank line]
Theodore's Blessing:—

Brother Theodore, in the name of the Lord Jesus I put my hands upon thy head and by the authority of the hold priesthood I seal upon thee a patriarchal blessing. I say unto thee, be thou faithful and true, and the spirit of the gospel shall follow thee in all thy ups and downs in life. I say unto thee, prepare thyself for thou hast a mighty mission given unto thee on Earth, for thy calling is to labor for Zion; and for the restoration of the house of Israel, and to carry the gospel to those that sit in darkness. For thy lineage is of the house of Israel, through the loins of Ephraim. And to perform this work thou wilt have to travel much for the gospel's sake, from land to land and from Sea to sea, and bring them in from their long dispersion to their own land that has been bequeathed to them by their fathers, of old; And I say unto thee, prepare thyself, for thou shalt have many difficulties to pass through. Thou shalt see thy fellow man fall upon thy right and upon thy left. Pestilence and famine shall stalk through the land, and thou shalt see great distress among the nations; but through faith thy life shall be preserved. Thou shalt gather in the house of Israel, and the Angel of the Lord shall go before thee; and when it is necessary he will give thee power over the elements. Evil spirits shall flee from before thee, and thou shalt cause springs to break forth from the desert of it be necessary to quench the thirst of this house of Israel; and rivers shall be turned out of their courses as will lead them over dry shod. For the Lord will give thee a faithful companion that ~~will~~ shall labor with thee for the Salvation of the living and the dead, and bring about the salvation and redemption of thy father's house; and their exaltation for many generations back.

[Page 626L]

1888/[Blank line]
July 11/For thou shalt administer ordinances for them in the temple in the order of the holy priesthood, through blood of Ephraim who is appointed to preside, and a king upon the earth in the latter days. And thy posterity shall be numerous, and thou shalt be blessed above thy fellow men. For thou wilt be true, because thou art faithful, and angels shall meet with thee and converse with thee, and tell thee what to do; for I seal these words upon thee in the name of Jesus. Amen.
[Blank line]
11th/ Dora's Blessing:—

Sister Dora in the name of the Lord Jesus I lay my hands upon thy head and by authority of the holy priesthood I seal upon thee a father's blessing which is after the patriarchal order. And I say unto thee, thou art of the loins and blood of Ephraim. And be faithful and true to thy father and mother and learn to honor them. For the Lord will hold them accountable for all that they may teach thee in relation to the gospel in preparing thy mind to receive the same, until thy mind shall become matured, and then the Lord will begin to hold thee accountable for thyself.

I seal upon thee the blessing of life, of health and of strength, that thou mayest be able to enjoy life while thou hast the privilege of sojourning here upon the earth. I seal upon thee knowledge, that thou mayest know how to take care of thy body, that thy life may be prolonged and preserved. For there is much for thee to do in bringing about the restoration of the daughters of Jacob, in teaching them the gospel of life and salvation, in administering the ordinances that will produce it. And in this labor thou shalt be blessed and strengthened in body and mind; for thou art of the blood of the house of Ephraim, who is the first born, according to the priesthood which belongeth to thee according to thy sex. Thou shalt do much in blessing and comforting thy father's house, in bringing about the salvation and exaltation of the same. For God will give thee the wisdom and understanding in all things pertaining to thy mission; for I seal these words upon thee, and leave room for a greater blessing to follow, in the name of Jesus. Amen.

[Page 627R]

1888/ Start to visit Mexico with Joel.

July 12/Thurs./To day Joel and I started to Mexico, to look for a place in which to settle my family. We drove 10 miles and camped. Next day we drove 30 miles, having a heavy thunder storm in the afternoon. We reached the S.P.R.R. next evening, and were in a tremendous storm which beat into the wagon, and wet our bed and things. Going east along the railroad track, we passed Stein's Pass at noon, + camped within 8 m. of Lordsburg. We passed through Lordsburg on the 16th where we got some spoons, bread, +c On the 17th we passed Sopar, where we bought water from a well 750 ft deep. We passed Gage next day, and reached Deming, 170m from Pima, on the 18th Here I spent about 20$ for provisions, ammunition, skillet, + other things.

18th/I here met Br. Eaton, and traded my horse Bob to him for a mule, as horses have to pay 40$ duty entering Mexico. Camped 12m from Deming. Up to this time we have had storms almost every day. At Deming I got a pass from the Custom House officer, to enable me to return free of duty.

19th/ To night we camped on Mexican Soil, and next day 20th got to Boca Grande at 10 A.M. and arrived opposite Diaz at noon of

21/Saturday 21st Called to see Coz. W.D. Johnson, then went on to La

Ascencion, where is the Mex. Custom House, but did not get all papers fixed, so had to return to Diaz.

22/ At meeting spoke, and felt well, and as if in presence of a Select company of Saints.

23/ Finished at the Custom house. I had to pay 34.00^7^ for my wagon and harness, as duty, and for my papers. To day Br. M. Thatcher passed Ascencion, returning to Utah.

24/ Attended celebration dance this evening. Br. Thatcher + others spoke eloquently. O.F. Whitney and ladies were also there. Felt a slight earthquake this morning. To day my animals strayed away, not being hobbled. Rains heavily, every day.

25/ This afternoon the Administrator, Plutarcho Enriquez, with other Mexican gentlemen, came and remained till late, then staid all night, on account of the storm. We had a very pleasant time, and a good feeling prevailed. All the Mexicans wrote in Spanish, sentiments in Br. Thatcher's Album.

26/ To day Brs. Thatcher and Whitney, with their ladies, returned to Utah. Have hunted my team, unsuccessfully.

[Page 628L]

1888/ In Mexico

July 30th/Up to this time we have had heavy daily rains, and have sought for my team, but without avail. To day Coz. David Wilson + family came. [Blank line]

Aug. 1st/Sent letter to Susan. Can not find my horses. Must buy a team.

Sun. 5th/ This evening we started South at 5.30 P.M. having bought a team of A. Peterson for $300.00 on credit (to be paid in 10 cows + calves.)

6/Obtained pass to south, at La Ascencion. Passed the inner, or State guards at noon, at "Ojo del Paraje." reached Casas Grande river at evening + camped.

7th/ Passed Coralitios in forenoon, Casas Grande 5 P.M. and reached Juarez 9 P.M. = 46m Distance from Diaz 70 m. and from home 340m. Stopped with my brother Sixtus E. Johnson. Glad.

8/ Wrote home to day, + looked round next day, seeing what is best to do, +c also the 10th

11/ Started for Corallis. Saw some antelope on the San Diego Ranch. Camped high up in the Sierra Madre, in the "Park," + among pines.

Sun. 12/ Reached Lower Corallis, or Cave Bally, and Saw mill, at noon.

12/ Visited the ancient caves. An Alla 11 ft high 15 ft diameter.

13/ Went 7m to Corallis, and stopped with J.N. Smith Jun. A lovely place miles of green grass, flowers and pines. Cool atmosphere, cold night. An altitude of about 6800 feet—almost on the summit of Sierra Madre I felt a spirit of freedom and liberty here—more than in the vallies below. I felt this to be a refuge for Liberty, whence she should never be driven, and embody my feelings, in a limited degree, in the following lines, addressed to Sierra Madre—the "Mother Mountain."

   Lines to the Sierra Madre Mountains.
I am here, in thy heart, oh "Mother of Mountains,"
I am tired and weary—oh here let me rest!
Let me lave my hot brow in thy cool sparkling fountains,
And rest my worn head on thy motherly breast!
2
I have fled from a land full ^of^ sorrow and sadness;–
From a land filled with turmoil, disunion and strife;
Where the leaders of men seem stricken with madness
And where Anarchy threatens fair Liberty's life.

[Page 629R]

[Poem continues]

1888/[Blank line]
Aug./
3
Oh Madre! be thou unto Freedom a haven!–
A strong place of refuge no foe dare assail!
Whence Liberty fair shall never be driven.
Nor longer her children's misfortunes bewail!
4
May thy crags give defiance-each gorge be a fortress—

Each valley a stronghold that none may invade;
Thy foes boasted power be turned into weakness!—
Be scattered their legions, and broken, each blade!
5
Oh Madre! as children we seek thy protection!
Oh be thou our refuge!—we cling to thy breast!
And while the world rages and seeks our destruction
'Mid thy vallies and peaks—'mid thy clouds will we rest.
[End of poem]

Bought a house + 2 lots in Juarez of F. Spencer for $210.00 (Mexican).

15/ Start home this morning, having spent yesterday in looking around. Reach Juarez at 9 P.M. in a heavy rain. Distance 33 miles, and the road over the mountains very rocky, and steep in places.

16/ Recd a letter from Susan. Start home next day, the [in margin: 17] after buying a house and lot of Br. F. Spencer for $210.00[99]

    Arrive at Ascencion about noon. Applied for papers to re-enter Mexico 3 mo. from date

21/ Passed through Diaz, and reached Deming on 24th

24/ Traded my team with J. Eaton for a pair of mules. Had 2 heavy storms, lately, and once I nearly had my left hand shot off, while taking my gun from the Wagon. A spirit whispered me to change the position of my hand, and the gun discharged the next instant burning my wrist and shirt cuffs. Reached home

29th/Wed. Aug 29th having been absent just 7 ~~months~~ ^weeks^, + traveled 750m Heavy rain at home.

    I made application, directed to Henry Eyring 1a Calle De Soto no. 2 City of Mexico, for papers as Colonists, for myself, Joel, and Moroni, and asked for ~~exp~~ exemption from Custom house duties for the following articles:–

---

    99. Martineau purchased his home from Franklin Spencer (1836–1915), who was born at Augusta, Bracken County, Kentucky, on June 26, 1836. He died at Colonia Dublán on December 10, 1915. The home was located north of the townsite, at the middle of the valley, and on the east side of the Piedras Verdes River. See Hatch, *Colonia Juarez*, list of early property owners on unnumbered pages 294–295, and Dale-Lloyd, *El Proceso de Modernización*, 28–29.

[Page 630L]

1888/[Blank line]
Aug. 29/For myself: 2 wagons, with covers, harness for 4 Animals 1 stove, furniture + pipe, 1 table, 1 stand, 4 chairs. 1 Cabinet Organ, 1 Iron bedstead, bedding for family 1 spring mattress, ~~fen~~ fc 1 Saddle, 2 mirrors, Books + instruments, map paper and d. instruments, Scales food, (100 kilos flour 25 k. bacon) arms + ammunition.

For Joel

2 wagons + 2 setts harness + 2 wagon Covers, 100 k. flour 25 k. bacon, 2 plows, shovels + tools, 1 mower, + Ag. implements, 2 chairs, Box of books + photos in frames, Arms + Ammunition, China + glassware, 4 Silver ware, knives forks + Spoons.

For Moroni.

1 Wagon, cover, 2 S. harness, 1 stove + furniture + pipe. household furniture. Ag. implements + tools, bedding 100 k. flour 25 k. bacon, Books, Saddle, Lamp + oil. Arms + Ammunition.

Sept. 2/ Have been busy at my correspondence. I wrote to Lilla, Jesse (who is called to a mission in Germany) Mrs. S.J. Russell, H. Eyring, Mexico, and others.
[Blank line]

5th/To day Dora is 6 yrs. old. She had a little party. I went to Solomonville and prepared my pension papers, which I Sent off to Washington. I hope my pension may be granted.

6th/ I find in Websters Unabd Dictionary, the following in reference to my family name:—Martineau—:

In Latin, Martinus, male, Martinea, female
" Italian, Martino, also Martini (plural)
" Spanish, Martino, ~~also disevative, Martinez~~
" French, Martineau, sometimes Martin
" Portuguese, Martinho
" German, Martin
" English, Martin

This is important, as an aid in trading our genealogy.

11/ Recd letter from F. Gunnell offering to sell me 500$ stock in the Juarez (Mex.) Saw Mill Co. which I directed on

12/that Lyman should pay him for from my funds.

[Unstamped page]
[A genealogical note, over a page titled Application for Pension Sept 6th, 1888]
[Page end]

[Page 631R]

1888/[Blank line]

Sept. 15th/Had an interview with Apostle J.H. Smith and Bp. R.T. Burton, relative to false accusations made against me by Prest C. Layton. After meeting (Quar. Conf.) in the afternoon met with the High Council.[100]

Sun. 16/ Was rebaptized this evening + Confirmed next

Mon. 17/morning, by Apostle Smith and R. Burton, having confirmed upon me all former blessings, gifts, ordinances, sealings and keys.[101] Prest Layton said in afternoon meeting yesterday, that Bp. Preston had fully exhonerated me from anything wrong in my tithing business as Bps. Agent, my accounts being found all right.

Tues. 18/ This morning, at 7.45, Albert had a son born to him. To his increase may there be no end. Brs. Smith and Burton leave the valley to day. Wrote to Mexico by Henry's request, for apapers [papers] to admit him as a Colonist to Mexico. Asked for the following to be exempted:—

4 chairs, 1 old Bureau, 2 pr horses, 2 S. harness ^double^
2 Wagons 4 log chains 1 Sewing machine
1 Chest Carpenter tools, 1 Small mirror + dishes

---

100. On this date, John Henry Smith wrote in his diary: "Bp. R. T. Burton and I had an interview with Bp. John Taylor and J. H. Martineau about his, Bro. Martineau's immoral conduct.
"We held three meetings today, one being that of the High Council. It was unanimously agreed that Bro. J. H. Martineau should make a public confession of his wrong doing and if forgiven by the people to renew his covenants by Baptism. He said he would do so." White, ed., *Church, State, and Politics*, 208.
101. According to Smith, "Bro. J. H. Martineau was forgiven by the people and was baptised." The following day (17th), Smith wrote: "Bro. J. H. Martineau took Bro. Burton and me to Thatcher and we blessed Bro. M. [and] admonished him to guard himself for the future." White, ed., *Church, State, and Politics*, 208.

1 Stove, furniture + pipe, Beds + Bedding
1 Small Stand [blank]A few photos, framed
Arms + Ammunition, Plow + Ag. tools.
100 kilos flour 20 kilos Bacon, 1 Wash. machine
200 lbs nails + a few groceries for present use.

19/ Sent $6.80 to Dr. G.A. Scott for magnetic articles: 1 flesh Brush, 1 no. 3 hair Brush, 1 Sciatie appliance, + 30¢ for postage.

21/ Wrote to Patriarch H. Norman + Virginia. Delivered Peterson 3 cows on team acc't. Recd letter from Gelston

25/ Wrote Gelston + Sent him $1.00 more, also to M.E.J.

27/ Laid out new Co. Road, also next day.

30/ Recd letter from City of Mexico, as to what I may bring into Mexico free of duty, also the same for Joel and Moroni, and letter explaining same from Henry Eyring.

[Page 632L]

1888/[Blank line]

Sept. 30/We may enter, free of duty, as follows:—

<u>for Myself</u>:— 2 wagons + covers, 2 pr harness, 2 tables 4 chairs, iron bedstead + mattress, 1 sett scales, 100 kilos flour 25 kilos meat, Bedding, agricultural tools, Books.

<u>Joel</u>: 2 wagons + Covers, 2 Setts harness, 2 chairs 100 kilos flour 25 kilos bacon, 1 sett crockery and glass ware 1 Sett nickel plate wares, books +c

<u>Moroni</u>: 1 Wagon + Cover, 2 Setts harness, furniture for the use of family, 100 kilos flour 25 k. bacon, 1 Lamp + Oil, Books +c

Upon all other articles duty must be paid.

Mon. 1st/[Blank line]
Oct Recd long letter from Lyman, also 2 from Nephi.

3d/Wrote to Lyman, telling him again, to buy Gunnell's $500.00 interest in the Juarez Saw Mill Co. Paid Peterson 3 Cows + 1 Calf on horse team a/c. Sick

4/Surveyed for J. Blake, at Safford; home next day.

5/ Sent Scott $7.58 for 1 M. Belt 1 W. Belt, 1 k. Cap. 2 no. 1 Brushes 2 pr insoles + .58¢ postage.

7/Joel has hot fever. I am still unwell.

8/Recd first goods ordered from Scott.

Note 2/ By letter from Nephi, I learn he had a narrow escape from a fearful death, on Tues. Oct. 2. His horse jumped, the saddle turned, his foot hung in the stirrup and he was furiously dragged a 100 yds. He had given himself up to death, when his foot came loose. He was badly bruised, but broke no bones. Thank God for his mercy.

11/ Sent to JB Alden, no. 393 Pearl St N.Y. $7.89 for books; also for Life of Jos Smith and History of Mexico = total $17.39 Also wrote to Lyman for $300.00

13/ Wrote to Bps. Preston + Burton, and Apl. John H. Smith.

Sun. 21/ Susan and I dined with Patriarch Wm McBride. As I entered, he said he felt as if he must give me a blessing, and asked if I wanted one. I said yes, and he then gave me the following; which is very much like others I have had before:—

[Page 633R]

Moroni's boy Born

    Br. Martineau, I feel a desire to bless you, although I am in pain all through my body with rheumatism. But my heart is free, and it is full of blessings for you. I say unto you that you shall be greatly blessed, with Susan and all your wives and children, and shall be blessed and prospered in all you undertake in humility. You shall be great and mighty in the priesthood. You and your sons shall reign and rule over Kings and Princes and Nobles, and Susan shall preside over Queens, and you, over kingdoms and over a great posterity. Your word shall be strong and powerful, even to cause the hypocrite to tremble, and the wicked to flee away from before you. Your daughters shall be filled with the spirit of the Lord, and your Sons become mighty in the priesthood, and shall be mighty rulers in the land. Your wives and children shall increase like a fruitful vine, and your children shall become a great people. And I say unto you in the name of the Lord, that if any shall interfere or meddle with your family, to cause disunion, without your consent, they shall burn their fingers. I seal upon you every blessing you desire in humility that is for your good, and I seal you up to eternal life in the name of Jesus. Amen.

Br. McBride Seemed full of the Holy Spirit, and spoke with much power. His blessing was a great comfort to me and to Susan.

By letter from Lyman I learn that Jesse N. Started on Oct. 10th for his mission in Germany. May God preserve and bless him always. He arrived at N.Y. City Oct. 16th and Sailed in the Alaska
[Blank line]

Oct. 26/Moroni had a son born to him this morning at 3-10 A.M. He weighed 10 lbs. [blank]I ordered $70.00 worth of fruit trees, vines and plants of Cluff, and paid him $31.00 down. Bought a plow, $14.00 and recd my books from Alden N.Y.

28/ Recd my magnetic goods from Dr. G.A. Scott, 843 Pearl st. N.Y.

[Page 634L]

1888/ Pension papers

Nov. 6/Election to day. I voted for the first time in Arizona. There is too much trickery and ring work in politics to suit me, and it is very nauseous to me. I recd ~~my~~ transfer from F. Gunnell for $500.00 stock in Juarez Saw Mill Co. by letter from Lyman. Also recd my certificate no. 17226 for Mexican War Pension, which is $8.00 pr month, from Jany 29. 1887, which, to Sept. 4. 1888 is $153.33 From this is to be deducted $25.00 to Gelston + Co. Attys

7/ Joel started to Mexico this afternoon, with load. I wrote to Lyman. Weather quite cold.

8/ I sold my transit, level, 2 chains, and protractor to C. Brown, the new Co. Surveyor, for $400.00 taking his mules, harness and wagon in payment. Yesterday morning the plants were killed in the garden, for the first. Wrote to E.H. Gelston + Co. to Lyman, and to T.H. Allen.

9/ Finished survey of Pima Canal.

[Left margin note about first pension payment in shaky hand]

10/ Paid Welch $100.00 for my land. Executed vouchers for my first payment of pension, at Solomonville. Cold.

13/ Sent For Froisseth Chronicle $1.34 Des. News $3.00 Herald $8.50[blank]Yesterday Sent for my pension Check of 153.33 also for Mexican Laws $5.00, to Gurley .70¢ Wrote again to Bp. Preston about cows, T.O. orders +c

14/ Sent $30.00 to Montgomery Ward + Co for goods

15/ Wrote article for Tucson Star, defending Prest Layton from certain unjust charges[102]

16/ Sent a lot of old notes to Lyman, Sum $743.50 some of it paid

17/ Sent for Cloak for Anna and suit for Theodore, to California

18/ Moroni and Albert got home. Rainy.

19/ Wrote to Lilla. Killed a beef steer

22/ Sent $31.45 to W. + L. Cal. for goods

23/ Sent 3.93 for lasts. Shoe nails +c Also 12.00 for Electric goods from Dr. Scott, and on

26/ Bought wagon of Bp. Taylor + Sold my old one.

27/ Gave my level to Brown (sold him) Recd my Trois-sart.

---

102. A correspondent at Bonita made the charge that President Layton had ordered the Mormons in Pima to vote him into county office. Martineau responded by writing:

> Every man has not only the right to vote as he pleases, but to induce everybody else to favor his favorite candidate—if he can. Bishop Layton is and has been for years a straightforward democrat, but he is not the fool your Bonita correspondent would cause one to infer. There is no more 'union of church and state' among Mormons than among Baptists, Presbyterians or other Christian sects. This is clearly shown in the election just held, in which his son was defeated as candidate for supervisor by an overwhelming majority; and this too, in the Mormon precincts. If he had carried the Mormon vote in his pocket, his chosen candidates would have had a majority in the Mormon settlements. The contrary being the case, proves the falsity of the charge made against him in this regard—a charge at once disgraceful to him and to the Mormon community of this county.

From J. H. Martineau, "All Right," *Arizona Daily Star*, November 18, 1888, 4. For the charges against Layton by the Bonita correspondent and others, see "Notes from Western Graham," *Arizona Weekly Star*, November 1, 1888, 2; "Bishop Layton's Opportunity," *Arizona Weekly Star*, November 1, 1888, 3; and E. D. Tuttle, "What They Say," *Arizona Daily Star*, November 11, 1888, 4. For Layton's defenders, see "From Graham County. A Short Talk on the Political Outlook There," *Arizona Weekly Star*, October 25, 1888, 4; Elder R. A. Allred, "Falshood [sic] and Truth," *Arizona Weekly Star*, November 22, 1888, 3.

28/ Recd suit of clothes for Theodore:— too small. Sent for ^another^

[Page 635R]

1888/ Lyman's baby born, my 30th grand child

Nov. 29/Sold my house and lot to H. Lines, for $600.00 in horses, cattle, goods +c. It is less than it has cost me. But I want to sell every thing I have in this place.

30/ Sent 6.17 to Vickery and 6.50 to W.L. + Co for mdse. Also sent Old level to Gurley to be repaired, with 15.00 Cash. Finished my index to "Pearls."[103]

Dec. 2/ Special conference, held by John Morgan

3d/ Alley + Lyman's baby born at 5 P.M.

4/Recd $39.00 mdse from W.L. + Co. and $30.00 from Chicago with a beautiful ring for Susan, emerald and diamond.

5/Wrote to Jesse, who is now in Berne, Switzerland. He arrived at Liverpool Oct. 29. by the "Alaska". Spent a little time in London, also in Paris. Paid $27.03 tax

8/We measured height, with shoes +c on, as follows:—myself 6'11 ½" Susan 5'5" Gertrude 5'6" Dora 3'9" Anna 5'3" Theodore 5'9 1/2"[blank]Yesterday drew my first cash in pension, to Sept. 4. 1888, = $128.33. I resigned for Joel, his post as Secretary + Treasurer of 89th Quo. of 70s and as ditto for Stake Y.M.M.I.A. He and David Johnson arrived from Juarez, Mex: 370m in 12 days. and brought the mule we lost near Diaz last summer.

10/ Got my iron lasts, and Shoe nails from the east. Traded wagons with Moroni.

12/ Bought of N.P. Worden, a mare of his in Mexico, for $55.00 Sent $10.00 to W.L. + Co. Cal. for goods; also for shoe findings. Sold my stove to Moroni for $10.00 and traded cow with him.

Got the following Ague Cure from R. Silva, a Mexican. Into 2 oz vinegar put white of 1 Egg, beaten up, add tablespoonful Sugar, and add half teacup of water. Drink once a day. It will cure the Chills + Fever in 2 to 4 days.

---

103. The copy of "Pearls" at Utah State University does not include this index.

The boys started to Globe today, with 3 span each.

13/ Recd letter from Lyman, telling of the birth of his little girl, Dec 3d at 5 P.M. Also sent checks for $400.00 I recd letter from J.F. Wells, editor of "Contributor" asking me to write for that magazine[104]

14/ Heavy rain. Wrote Lyman

Mem./ While in Utah, last year, I recd the following blessing from Pat. C.W. Hyde, April 5. 1887:—

[Page 636L]

1887/ Memorandum—of April 5. 1887

Beloved Brother, I place my hands upon thy head, and seal upon you a patriarchal blessing. And thou shalt yet be called to proclaim this gospel from land to land and from Sea to sea, and no power shall stay thy hand. And you shall proclaim the gospel from city to city, even to the house of Israel, and they will call thee <u>Blessed of the Father</u>. And you shall see Zion redeemed, and Stand with your Redeemer and with the prophet Joseph when the Saints will be free. And be comforted, for Zion <u>shall</u> be redeemed; for they shall bind up the law and seal up the testimony. For you know not the blessings which the Lord thy God has for you. For thou art of Ephraim, and a lawful heir to the fulness of the priesthood, and if thou desirest it thou shalt converse with the Three Nephites, and they shall unlock to you things that shall not enter the heart of man. And I seal upon your head eternal life, with all thy father's household. Even so. Amen and Amen.

At the same time he gave the following blessing to Miss Jessie Helen Anderson Grieve, I being scribe:-
[Blank to end of page]

[Page 637R]

1888/[Blank line]

Dec. 15/Recd letter from JW Young, requesting me to go and see Gila

---

104. The *Contributor* was published by Junius F. Wells from 1882 through 1896 as the organ of the Young Men's and Young Ladies' Mutual Improvement Association. Martineau had published an article, "The Magnetic Needle," in 1884, but began to be published more frequently between 1888 and 1891.

Canal[105] Subscribed for the books published for a course of reading for the Y.M.M.I.A. as prescribed by the Genl Supt

16+17/ Quar. Conference On 17th I went to H Thomas and telegraphed MR Locke, El Paso, Texas, relative to going to visit the Gila Bend Canal, below Phoenix A.T.[106]

18/ Recd goods from Vickery

20/ Wrote to JW Young. Joel arrived from Mexico on Sunday night. Dec. 19th David Johnson, his cousin, also. (Note. Error. They arrived Dec. 9th) Sent to S. Ward + Co Boston. for writing case + rubbers. Wrote to M. Thatcher

21/ Sent essay—Arizona—to "Contributor." Recd letters from Mr. Locke, El Paso, relative to taking charge of his canal (the construction) near Gila Bend. An Rainy, still.

---

105. Young's letter read, in part:

Mr. Morris R. Locke, of El Paso, Texas, is the principal owner and has direct charge of the St. Louis Canal Company's scheme which I wrote you about some time last Spring, that is being constructed and to be constructed at Gila Bend, Maricopa County. You write him at El Paso in care of M. R. Locke & Co., telling him when you can meet him at that place. If you can agree on suitable terms, I would like you to go with him to examine the Canal and possibly, if he chooses to make arrangements with you, for you to take charge of the work. I have recommended you to him as a thorough engineer in the construction of Canals, and I can fully recommend Mr. Locke to your most favorable consideration and confidence, as he is a gentleman in whom I have great confidence, and feel that all the arrangements that are made with you will be satisfactory and honorable. Take this matter into immediate consideration and write Mr. Locke immediately, so that no time may be lost in the arrangement of this Canal.

John W. Young to James H. Martineau, December 6, 1888, Letterbook, May 1888–December 1889, pp. 67–68, box 3, fd. 3, John W. Young Papers, MS 1237, LDSCHL.

106. Morris Roberts Locke (1842–1920) was born at Lexington, Lafayette County, Missouri, on October 31, 1842, to David and Caroline Matilda (Burford) Locke. He received his primary education in the private schools at Lexington and later attended the public schools until he was fourteen years old. Locke joined the Confederate forces in the Civil War and after its close in 1865, he moved to Jerseyville, Illinois, where he practiced law, engaged in real estate, and insurance and newspaper publishing. In Jerseyville, he built (with his brother James A. Locke) the St. Louis, Jerseyville & Springfield Railroad, now known as the Chicago, Peoria & St. Louis Railroad. He was editor of the *Jerseyville Republican* and for fifty-two years was a correspondent of the *St. Louis Republic*. In 1886, he left Jerseyville for Texas to engage in the railroad business. In 1888, the Morris R. Locke Co., of Jerseyville, Illlinois, was awarded a contract to build the Monterey and Tampico Railroad in Sonora, Mexico. From Texas, Locke promoted several railroad and canal building projects. He died in Abilene, Texas, on September 9, 1820. From unmarked obituaries and biographical information kindly provided by Lois Lock of the Jersey County Historical Society, Jerseyville, Illinois. See also Locke, "Reminiscences of Morris R. Locke."

26/ Started this morning for El Paso, Texas, to see Mr. Locke.

27/ At El Paso, Mr. Locke engaged me as engineer in charge of St. Louis canal, near Gila Bend. Ariz. with Salary of $200.00 pr month and all necessary expenses. Started home at noon for Mesa.

29/Arrd at Mesa, + Saw C.I. Robson on canal business

30/Went to Nephi, and saw Sam + Elvira the first time for years.

1889

Jan. 1/Took dinner at Don LeBaron's

2/Went to Phoenix to see C.S. Masten, canal business[107]

8/Went to Gila Bend with Masten + Robson. Started up river 40m.

9/Reached head of Canal. Quite cold nights. Did some leveling. Started home, + Stopped at Benson, to visit St David.

10/At St. David, Agreed with Calvin Reed for him to build + fence around Netta's grave, for $8.00 returned to Bowie

11/Reached home. All well.

16/Got recommends for Quarez Ward for self and family.

18/Prest Layton came to me for information as to making out Tithing settlement for 1888. Showed him how to do it.

19/Our house filled with a surprise party—a pleasant time.

---

107. Having received a letter from Martineau on December 20, John W. Young responded by writing:

> If circumstances are propitious, I would like to have you join Mr. Locke in helping to get through the Canal at Gila Bend. I presume you have written to him ere this, as a letter would be sure to find him, and perhaps a telegram might not be so readily delivered. Possibly you did not put your telegram in care of Morris R. Locke & Co.; that may have caused the delay. If you do not join Mr. Locke in assisting through that work, I believe I can furnish you with something to do in making some explorations for me. You will probably know by the time you receive this letter whether you are going to Gila Bend or not, and if not, write me immediately both to this address and Salt Lake City, as I may go there, but possibly be here so that I will get one or the other of your letters, and can answer you immediately what I want done.

John W. Young to James H. Martineau, December 31, 1888, Letterbook, May 1888–December 1889, pp. 91–92, box 3, fd. 3, John W. Young Papers, MS 1237, LDSCHL.

Gave accounts due me of $136.00 to Albert + Moroni to collect Sold my carriage for $150.00 Prest Layton owes me for the survey of Thatcher about $200.00 which he will not pay

[Page 638L]

1889/[Blank line]

Jan. 22/Gertrude and I start in stage for Bowie. She is going to Utah I to Gila Bend, to take charge of Canal work. The stage was robbed the day before, but we got to Bowie all right, after dark. Took train 8 P.M. and reached Maricopa next Morning 5 A.M. Thence to Tempe + Mesa, reaching last place on 24th

24/ Went to Phoenix to See Masten, returning next day to Mesa. Visited David Johnson, and found the following verses in Julia's Album (once her mother's)

    To Aunt Julia
Dark night has now her mantle cast
On mountain peak and Vale serene,
While softly sighs the passing blast
And glimmering stars are faintly seen.
[Blank line]
But soon the sun's enlivening ray
Will tinge with gold the mountain height,–
Will chase the gloom of night away
And storm clouds banish from our sight.
[Blank line]
Thus oft our souls are plunged in grief,
Afflictions too, our steps attend,
Our hours of joy so few and brief
that Death appears our truest friend.
[Blank line]
But soon will dawn a brighter day
Than this, which now upon us lowers,
For brightest are the sun's warm rays
That follow soon a chilling shower
[Blank line]
Then let us still in hope look up
And make the most of each bright hour

And strive to fill life's crystal cup
With honey gathered from each flower
S.L. City, April 11. 1855.

[Blank line]

27/Went to Sam's + Elvira's camp, 7 miles distant. They are clearing land for Some one.

[Page 639R]

1889/[Blank line]

Recd word from Joel, Mother and family left Pima on the 25th with five wagons. Henry + family and J. Carlton and family also went with them, driving cows + horses.

I had sold my house and lot in Pima for about $550.00 much less than it cost me, and failed to get five head of Cows + steers I had bought of the Church. My move makes me lose several hundred dollars, but I am glad to get away from Pima, and move into Mexico.[108]

---

108. Martineau had sold his home and property to H. Lines. See entry at November 29, 1888.

On January 18, Martineau wrote to John W. Young asking him about the desirable qualities of rock for tunneling. In answer to a personal query about the possibility of employment in Mexico, Young responded by writing:

> if you wish some of the work South of the <line>, I think I can give it to you, but I do not wish to disturb your relations with Mr. Locke, if you feel perfectly satisfied yourself with them, and are not obligated so that you cannot honorably withdraw.; but if you find it necessary or desirable to go into Mexico, you go to Diaz and see Bishop Johnson and write me from there. I can probably give you work that would be very satisfactory to you, though not at a high price per month; but I am willing to do what is fair, and can undoubtedly assist you so that it will be satisfactory.

John W. Young to James H. Martineau, January 23, 1889, Letterbook, May 1888–December 1889, pp. 116–117, John W. Young Papers, MS 1237, box 3, fd. 3, LDSCHL.

6
"Everything I Touched Turned to Ashes"

Surveying in Southern Arizona, and Northern Mexico, 1889–1897

Feb. 1/ Arrived at Gila Bend, leaving Gertrude at Elvira's, 6 A.M.

4/ W.C. Masten came + went again. I began to take inventory of Company tools, carts, scrapers +c. at Gila Bend.

6/ Finished inventory. Started to El Paso. Fare $21.80

7/ Arrived in Deming 6 A.M. and at El Paso 9.30 A.M. 80m farther Saw Locke but got no money. Returned to Deming next day.

9/ Hired carriage and went 5 miles to meet Susan + family.

11/ Left Deming 3 P.M. with teams, for Mexico.

12/ Lost 3 horses last night. Joel went to look for them

13/Joel returned with horses this afternoon, having had nothing to eat since he left yesterday. Traveled a few miles.

14/ Rained this morning, + cold wind. Camped near Las Palomas.

15/ Theodore + David joined us with the cattle this morning. Met Br. Taylor, merchant, and paid him $50.00 Mexican money for Spencer, due on the house + lot in Juarez. Arrd in Palomas, and got our wagons all inspected by 5 P.M. very cold and windy. Duties were about $95.00

16/ I here left my family, they to go on into Mexico. I to return to Gila Bend. But I hated the parting. I leave the family in the care of our Father. Went by Stage from Palomas to Deming—44 miles—in one day. Ticket to Gila Bend $22.15

17/ Arrived in Gila Bend 6 A.M.

21/ Began journey to head of canal, with party of Surveyors. Spent a few days leveling and examining river fall and returned to Gila Bend on 24th

Mch. 5/ Started again on Survey, and began at junction of Salt and Gila Rivers. Exposed to heavy rain, and slept in wet bedding. No fire.

10/ Examined tip of Robbins Butte. An ancient wall still

[Page 640L]

1889/[Blank line]

March 10/fortifies its summit. Indian hyeroglyphics mark the rocks on the summit.

11/ Leveled in the pass. Very hot + suffered for water

12/ Returned to Gila Bend, to prepare notes and report[1]

13/ My 61st Birth day.

14/ Lon Hall proposed to me to leave employment of Locke + Co. Saying I could make $200.000 by the change I told him I was bound in honor to Locke + Co. and did not agree to abandon them for another company.

15/ Locke, Masten, Barnes + I held consultation on Canal matters, after which they returned east.

18/ Went up the river 40 miles to locate another head of ^Canal.^

20/ Returned to Gila Bend, thence to Phoenix. Examined records.

30/ Started out with full survey party to locate a line for Canal, the previous line being abandoned on my recommendation, as being a very poor one.

April 28th/ Finished 60 miles of location, and quit for the present.

30/ Went to Elvira's at Nephi, + to Mesa.

May 3/ " to Phoenix. Hall made his proposition to me again.[2]

---

1. An advertisement announcing James H. Martineau as Deputy County Surveyor and Civil and Hydraulic Engineer was printed in the *Valley Bulletin* beginning on April 12, 1889 and continued through August of the same year.

2. Hall's proposition must have been difficult to resist, as Martineau was beginning to question Locke's ability to pay debts incurred in surveys and his room and board, etc.

4/ At Nephi, Sam + Elvira had an ice cream party. Nice.

While camping on the Gila in March (2d) I wrote the following lines

To my darling Netta.
Oh darling Netta! mournful was the hour
When from thy loving Father thou didst part!
He dearly loved thee, but he had not power
To keep thee longer near his aching heart.
[Blank line]
He loved thee, darling, more than tongue can tell!
And more! much more than thou coulds't ever guess.
In life he loved thee, and he loves thee still
Though now beyond all reach of fond caress.
[Blank line]
But dearly as he loved, he would not call
Thee back to dwell in mortal form again!
Exposed to grief and sorrow, and to all
That tends to disappointment fear and pain.

[Page 641R]

[Poem continues]

No! thou hast safely passed those trials dread
That all <u>must</u> pass who dwell in this estate,
Thy griefs are o'er—thy pains forever fled.
And safe from Snares and pitfalls are thy feet.
[Blank line]
Oh that mine eye the silvery veil might pierce
That hides from mortal eye thy radiant light!
That I again might see thee face to face—
Might see thee now, So beautiful and bright!
[Blank line]
But tis not so ordained, and all must wait
Their own appointed time, with patience meek;
And in this life so live, that at the gate
Of Paradise, our loved ones we may meet.

Two months later, Martineau asked John W. Young if the company had been successful in obtaining money to build the Excelsior Canal. James H. Martineau to John W. Young, July 2, 1889, John W. Young Papers, MS 1237, box 7, fd. 8, LDSCHL.

[Blank line]

May 8/ Returned to Gila Bend. Begun work on Survey notes of Canal and profile.[3]

10/ Today Elvira's baby girl was born. Weighed 11 ½ lbs. They named her Anna Gertrude.

19/ Sent $20.00 to Susan by mail. She never got it.

21/ Recd letter from L.H. Poole, U.S. Agent at Tucson He says 3 Poole brothers came from England years ago. One settled in Delaware, one in Maryland. The other, I believe, is ancestor of my Cousin D.C. Poole, U.S.A.

22/ Went to Nephi, for Gertrude.

25/ We left Sam's + Elvira's. Patriarch B.F. Johnson gave her and Samuel the following blessings:–

Note/ These two blessings are recorded in my temple and blessing record, which is now in Mexico. (See page 660.)

Gertrude and I went to Maricopa. Staid over night, gave her much fatherly counsel.

26/ Arrived at Gila Bend. Gertrude staid at Rawley's.

27/ Gertrude started for Logan, Utah, today. I had felt worried about her going 2000 miles alone, but after I blessed her I felt that all would be well with her. Mrs. Rowley went with her as far as Lathrop, Cal.

[Page 642L]

1889/ Gertrude goes to Logan. I nearly died in [blank]

May 27/ She went to Logan Safely, except that on the 28th she was very

---

3. A few days later, the newspaper reported on canal projects under way in the Gila Bend Valley:

> J. H. Martineau, whom the reporter had the pleasure of meeting is in charge of the construction of the Excelsior canal now building. He has had more experience ten to one than any other man in the United States in this particular business. He is also a civil engineer of some eminence and reputation.
>
> The valley has been surveyed on the south side of the river. The north side will be surveyed soon as an appropriation for the purpose has already been made.

From "The Lower Gila Bend Valley," *Arizona Daily Star*, May 12, 1889, 4.

sick—pain in her side. Gov. Waterman + wife and daughter were very good to her, and did all they could to help her. May God reward them.

29/ Sent claim for loss of tithing stock to Washington and informed Bp. Preston.

June 6/ Sent essay to "Contributor" for publication.

23/   "   2 articles to Contributor.[4]

29/ Was judge at School election

July 8/ Went to Phoenix, and next day to Sam's.

12/ Returned to Gila Bend.

14/ To day Jose Manuel, a Yaqui indian, was killed a few yards from me, while resisting arrest. I was foreman of the Coroner's jury. He was about 28 years old. I must do temple work for him, or have it done.

15/ People much alarmed. It is reported indians from Mexico are coming to revenge Manuel's death.

17/ Sent final claim for indian depredations in 1886 to amount of $235.00 (Cow $50 Loss on horse $185.00)

21/ Another scare about indians coming.

25/ To day narrowly escaped death from thirst. I went about 35 miles away on horseback, with no water, and had a hard time crossing a high rocky ridge, which much exhausted me. I dug in bottom of dry gulch for water but found none. Then rode a few miles until I could hardly keep the Saddle, then dismounted and lay on the sand about two hours to gain strength. I then crawled to my saddle and rode a few more miles, then had to lie down again for a long time. But I grew weaker all the time instead of stronger, and lay in a hazy, dreamy state, with no inclination to move. I thought I would let the horse go, but I knew when he arrived at home without me, all the people would be alarmed and might hunt all night for me. Then I thought of the work I still had to do, according to my blessings, and prayed God to strengthen me so I could get home.

---

4. This probably refers to a series of articles published under Santiago, "Frontier Life in Utah," *Contributor* 10 (July 1889): 349–352, *idem*, 10 (August 1889): 364–367, and *idem*, 10 (September 1889): 404–406.

[Page 643R]

the desert of thirst. Up the river again

July/Before this I felt too weak to rise; but after prayer I felt stronger, so that I got upon my feet and stood awhile by my horse, holding by the saddle. Then I prayed again, and was strengthened so I could climb to his back. Then, holding by both hands to the saddle, my horse took his own way to Gila Bend. Who can imagine my joy when I first saw the trees at the Station. Arrived there, the people were very kind to me, helping restore me, but they said I was crazy all night. It was only by the blessing of God I was saved + to Him be all the glory and praise. I had eaten three cactus fruits, which helped me somewhat, and was careful to keep my mouth shut and breathe through my nose. This prevented me from suffering such an agony of thirst as otherwise I should have done—learned in my former experiences in the deserts. A hot wind was blowing all day, which seemed to dry out all the moisture of my body, even to my very blood, and to dry up the kidneys. I had not thought the desert winds so deadly, though I had known of men before now, perishing on the deserts. Those who use spirits cannot stand it as well as those who do not. This I know.

26+27/ Still quite weak and feeble, otherwise, all right. I had received a letter from Susan, in Mexico, just a day or two before I went into the desert, warning me to take care of myself. The Spirit had warned her, but I was not careful enough, thinking myself too tough and hardy to fear anything.

28/ Wrote to Lyman to Send Jesse $75.00 So he Could go to the Paris Exposition.

31/ To day Locke, Masten, myself, Hodnett + L. W. Locke, with tent + camp outfit went up to the head of canal, to inspect line. In the Afternoon Masten was overcome by the heat, and we camped early.

[Page 644L]

1889/[Blank line]

Aug. 1//Reached Gila river about noon. Masten again overcome with heat. We laid him down and poured water, all over his body all the afternoon to keep him alive. I walked up the river a mile or more, to examine river at the head of the line, and concluded to change its location. I was nearly overcome, at one time, by the heat. [blank] At evening, moved camp two miles ^down.^

2/ The directors accepted my last location, as best Start home in the morning. At noon stopped under a Cottonwood for dinner, and Masten was again overcome by heat. We doused him continually with water until night to keep him alive. One of our horses while standing under the tree, also fell. We poured water over him, and I secretly laid hands upon and blessed him. This restored him. At night we started for our long march, while the darkness should make it cool, traveling until midnight, and camped at a deserted house + well.

3/ Reached Gila Bend 10 A.M. Heard that two other men had been prostrated on the 2d and a horse died from heat. So this shows the intense heat we endured.

6/ Read that in Guatemala is a lake ~~Amitlan~~ Amatillan, in the bottom of which lies a City sunk. No doubt this is one of those which sunk when the Savior was crucified. See Book of Mormon.

7/ Received word from Masten to go to Tucson to stay. ^Went.^

8/ By Judge W.H. Barne's request I wrote a description of our canal line, the land + general particulars for presentation to capitalists in New York. Judge Barnes complimented the article very highly. From this time, I was very busy making estimates of Canal, working on profile, copying U.S. Survey plats, and making map of the Gila Bend Country.

27/ To day the Great Feast of St. Augustine begins celebrated by the Catholics for a month. They have Bull fights by day by Mexican Matadors Mexican Circus, horse racing +c. And at night

[Page 645R]

1889/[Blank line]

Aug./thousands gather at the fair grounds. Here are many Booths for sale of liquors, fruits, suppers, fancy work, shooting galleries, and about 18 gambling tables. These are surrounded constantly by crowds of men and women, betting on roulette, renge et noir, faro, keno and other games whose names I did not know. There was also an excellent Mexican band and a band composed of Papago indians, who presided at a dancing floor, which was occupied by Mexican indians dancing. Sunday is the greatest day of all for these things. While looking upon these people, Sundays, thus desecrating the Lord's day without thought of wrong, I thought of Jonah and the people of Nineveh, of whom the Lord said there were 120.000 besides many cattle, who knew not their right hand from their left. So with these—in dense darkness—and God will, I believe, be merciful to them because of it.

Sep. 2/ Sent a map to M.R. Locke in N.Y. for his use.

5/ The Senatorial Committee on Irrigation visited Tucson one day and took testimony. I was invited by the Committee to speak for Graham Co. but declined. Afterwards, by invitation, I rode with them all around Tucson.

10/ Was requested to help temporarily in the Sur. Gen Office, Tucson, the Chief clerk being about to go away for awhile on account of sickness. I Continued at this work until Oct. 12th at $5.00 pr. day. Gen. R.A. Johnson seemed satisfied with me.[5]

13/ Received a letter from Lyman with $75.00 He wrote that Allie had had a dream that Susan was away from home in a strange town and destitute of money. She gave Lyman no peace till he sent me the $75.00 for her use. I suppose she is safe at home in Juarez Mex. as I told her lately not to start from home for Utah until I could send her money needful,

[Page 646L]

1889/[Blank line]

Sept./13th/and she had answered me she was not so green as to start on a 2000 mile journey without money. In a few minutes a telegram came from

---

5. Royal A. Johnson (1854–1906) was born to Hiram A. and Emaline Amelia (Jacobs) Johnson in Whiteside County, Illinois. The family moved to New York City and made their home there until 1871, when Royal went to Europe and spent two years in England and France. In 1873 he returned to the United States and in the latter part of that year he went to Venezuela to help with the construction of the Caracas and La Guaria Railroad. He spent several years in New York working in his father's law office and serving in public office. He married Francis Morrison of Brooklyn, New York, on February 14, 1877. After moving to Tucson, Arizona, he was appointed chief clerkship of the Surveyor-General's office, under General J. W. Robbins. Johnson succeeded Robbins as surveyor general of Arizona in 1883 and served until December 1885, when President Cleveland replaced Johnson with John Hise of Globe. Johnson was reappointed when Hise was released in July 1889. Johnson served in the office until 1892 when Eli H. Manning was placed in the position. See McClintock, *Arizona*, 3:539.

her, from Deming N.M. asking for money to come on with. I was utterly astonished, but sent her the money just received from Lyman, which the Lord had caused him to send. (by Allie's dream) just in time for her use. Our Father is very good and watchful over those whom He loves as He does Susan, whom He has styled "Beloved of the Lord." I telegraphed her to come at once.

14/ Got telegram from Susan. She has started.

15/ Susan Came with Dora this morning at 2 A.M. I had been up all night, waiting for her, and walked miles upon the track in my impatience. We talked until morning. I had not seen her since in January 1889.

16/ We attended the Mexican Celebration of Independence. A fine affair. Thousands of Mexicans present, not one drunk, noisy, or ungentlemanly in any way. Not so an equal number of Americans. The Mexican ladies were dressed with exquisite taste, as to Colors in dress. Fireworks at night. I felt one with them.

17/ Susan must go on, so as to have her visit in Logan before cold weather. I dread the parting. I blessed her, got her a ticket to Ogden $71.15 also sleeping birth $13.00 and got for her $25.00 pocket money. Truly has God opened my way and hers. She suddenly determined, in Juarez, to Start north. Borrowed $20.00 of Cardon Saw a covered wagon in the street, asked for a ride to Carlton's, 15 miles, Seized Satchel + Dora and went to Carlton's. Found him just going on the next day to Deming, N.M. and he gave her passage to that place. There my money met her, and so the Lord prospered her at every moment + turn. She safely reached Logan on the 21st all well, and met Lyman at Ogden, where he went to meet ^her.^

[Page 647R]

1889/[Blank line]

Sept. 18/Susan and Dora start to Logan at 2.50 A.M. ^Sad.^ Continued work in the Sur. Genl Office. He offers me a contract of Surveying 120 miles of the west boundary of the San Carlos Reservation, at $22 pr ^mile.^

25/ To night I felt impelled to make the same covenant relative to tithing that Joseph Smith and Oliver Cowdery did, as recorded in the life of Joseph. This covenant of theirs seems a more particular covenant than it is usually thought, and I desire to be in the same bonds as Br. Joseph. This

Covenant I have written in the back part of my Temple Record in full. God help me to keep it.

Oct. 3/ To day I felt impelled to bless the Gila Bend canal enterprise, that it may be completed, and be for the final benefit of the Saints when they shall possess the land, that the land may be made fruitful and productive. This I did, + asked the Father to ratify it.

By Judge Barnes request, I wrote a description of the Gila Bend Canal line, the land, productions +c +c to Mr. Murphey, of Phoenix, who desired to answer New York letters.

7/ Sent an article for publication in Young Womans Journal, in answer to Susa Young Gates request.[6] Sent $10.00 tithing to S.L.T. Office.

12/ Finished my work in Sur. Genl Office.

15/ Paid $15.00 more tithing, which is all I owe. Wrote to my adopted Son Niels L. Hagberg, S.L. City.

18/ By letter I learn Moroni and family start to Mexico to day, having sent the cattle two days before.

19/ Judge Barnes told me he would see that I should have a share in the Canal, as a "promoter."

20/ Wrote a frontier Ball in 1851 for Y.W. Journal.

25/ Received a letter from Prest Woodruff, asking me to do some Surveying for the Papago indian mission.[7] I answered that I would, with pleasure.

30/ heard of the death of my old friend Francis Gunnell.

[Page 648L]

1889/[Blank line]

---

6. The article appeared in the first volume of Gates's new periodical, under Santiago, "Pioneer Sketches. A Ball in Early Days," *Young Woman's Journal* 1 (December 1889): 78–81. This article told of a dancing party in the early days of Parowan and the customs of social etiquette at these parties. See also J. H. Martineau, "An Old Time Dancing Party," *Deseret Weekly* 55 (August 7, 1897): 240.

7. This letter requested that Martineau accept a surveying job for Indians in the Maricopa Stake under the direction of President C. I. Robson and counselors. Wilford Woodruff to James H. Martineau, October 19, 1889, First Presidency Copypress Letterbooks, Vol. 21, p. 259, CR 1/20, LDSCHL.

Oct. 30/ who died Oct. 20, of heart trouble. A good man.

Nov. 2/ Sent to Gurley for a new Survey chain.

24/ Recd a letter from Virginia with the following lines:–

[Blank line]
To Netta's Memory.
by Virginia
[Blank line]
In a lonely spot some miles away
We laid our darling Sister.
Oh yes! She was as fair as day
And oh! how much we miss her!
[Blank line]
She was but young—a budding flower
when she was called away.
We waited for the fearful hour—
She could no longer Stay.
[Blank line]
We left the home we loved so well
And to the southward went.
We thought 'twould thus her health improve
And give her life and strength.
[Blank line]
But 'twas not long before Death came
And took her soul away.
But in the other world again
We hope to meet some day.
S.L. City Nov. 18. 1889
[Blank line]

27/ Recd Tullidges History of Northern Utah, containing my biography, in garbled form.
[Blank line]
    Hearing Lt. Donaldson and wife Sing a hymn Called "Flee as a Bird," and liking very much the Soft plaintive air, this evening I hastily wrote some other lines of my own to the same tune, entitled "Hark to the voice of the Shepherd."

[Page 649R]

(poem title): Hark to the voice of the Shepherd.
Air. "Flee as a Bird."
[Blank line]
Hark! tis the voice of the Shepherd
Calling His flock as of old;
List to His voice and be gathered
Safely and sure in His fold!
Haste! for the wolves are about thee:–
Raging and fierce to destroy thee,–
Fly, for the arms that await thee
Would thee so gladly unfold.
Oh! would thee so gladly enfold!
[Blank line]
[In margin of following: Forever in glory shall reign.]
Why will ye wander in danger
Sorrow and darkness and pain.
Come! be no longer a ranger!
Come to thy Father again!
He in His love will enfold thee!
He with His might will defend thee!
He to a throne will exalt thee!
Ever with Him thou shalt reign.
In glory with Him we shalt reign!
[In shaky hand:] forever to reign
[Blank line]

Dec. 1/Letter from Susan and Gertrude. They wish to return home. I wrote in answer—Come!

　Elvira wrote me, and sent this little verse expressive of her love to me:–

[Poem follows:]
When you are sitting all alone
Reflecting on the past
Remember that you have my love,
Which will forever last.
[Blank line]

During this month the celebrated trial of men suspected of complicity in the Wham robbery was being conducted in Tucson.[8] About 200 witnesses were present from Graham County, on the two sides among them Cousin Melissa Johnson and daughter

[Page 650L]

1889/[Blank line]

Dec./8/–in-Law Emma. Alberts wife, who were witnesses for the prosecution.[9] I walked with Melissa to see the old Catholic convent ruin, about 300 years old.

9/ Emma testified in Court to day.[10] Complimented highly.

10/ Paid Welch $10.00 for share of taxes on land, Pima. Gave Emma a nice dress and Albert a book.

15/ Today the Pima witnesses all returned, the Wham trial being over, and accused acquitted.[11]

This trial was called the "Mormon robbery trial," the accused being ostensible members of the Church but only one of them in fellowship. It was part of a crusade against the Mormons.

---

8. On May 11, 1889, a group of masked men ambushed Major Joseph Washington Wham, U.S. Army Paymaster, and his guards on a road between Fort Grant and Fort Thomas, near Pima, Arizona. The escorting soldiers engaged the robbers in a lengthy gun battle, which resulted in eight of the soldiers being wounded. The perpetrators made off with $28,345.10 in gold and silver coins. Seven local Mormons were tried for the crime. See "A Bold Robbery," *Arizona Daily Star*, May 12, 1889, 4; "The Robbery," *Arizona Daily Star*, May 14, 1889, 4; "The Robbers," *Arizona Daily Star*, May 17, 1889, 4; "The Particulars," *Arizona Daily Citizen*, May 13, 1889, 1; and "The Robbery," *Arizona Daily Citizen*, May 13, 1889, 4. For more on the Wham Robbery, see Upton and Ball, "Who Robbed Major Wham?, 99–134, and Ball, *Ambush at Bloody Run*.

9. See "The Wham Robbery," *Arizona Daily Star*, December 7, 1889, 4; "The Wham Robbery," *Arizona Daily Citizen*, December 9, 1889, 4. The testimonies of Emma Martineau and Melissa Johnson are briefly discussed in Ball, *Ambush at Bloody Run*, 128, 142–143.

10. Emma Martineau lived on the same lot as defendant David Rogers and testified that she did not see him at his home on May 11, the day of the robbery. She also testified that when she passed through Rogers's orchard to visit his home, she noticed that it had not been irrigated on that day. See "The Wham Robbery," *Arizona Daily Star*, December 10, 1889, 4, and "The Wham Robbery," *Arizona Daily Citizen*, December 10, 1889, 4. Emma's testimony is discussed in Ball, *Ambush at Bloody Run*, 160–161.

11. See untitled, *Arizona Daily Star*, November 16, 1889, 2; "The Verdict," *Arizona Daily Citizen*, December 14, 1889, 4; and untitled, *Arizona Daily Citizen*, December 16, 1889, 2.

18/ Susan writes she will be at Gila Bend Newyears. Glad.

22/ Began to fast for 24 hours, pursuant to request of Prest Taylor sent to all the Saints.

23/ Fasted until night.

26/ Copied names in Temple Record still unworked for, into a Smaller book, so I can send the Temple Record home.

30/ Left Tucson for Gila Bend. Have been in Tucson 5 months, nearly, and have been very busy, mapping + other work. I have written many letters to my family in Mexico, Logan, Pima, and to Jesse N. who is in Switzerland on Mission. I have constantly taught them principles of life in my letters, and stimulated them to be Saints indeed. I have prayed much, and fasted; and have sought to gain a victory over all my sins, and to be filled with the Holy Spirit. Many times I have had precious answers to my prayers, + many principles of truth have been unfolded to my mind in answer to prayer. I have tried all I could to exert a good influence for Mormonism, and think I have done some good. I have become acquainted with many prominent men, and in short, I have labored for Zion the best I could. By request, I have been a constant writer for the "Contributor," as a general thing writing of early days in Utah, so that the youth of Zion may have some idea as to the

[Page 651R]

1889/[Blank line]

Dec./labors and trials of the early settlers of Utah. May the father bless all these, my labors; for my heart's greatest desire in this life is to help build up and establish Zion, to do good to all, and to bring Souls to God. That I may do this, I ask Him constantly to give me health and strength, and every other blessing needful, spiritually, and to bless my labors temporarily, that my hands and time and labors may be free and untrammeled, so I can the more effectually help to establish Zion and labor for the Salvation of Souls, especially the Lamanites, so long driven, oppressed, robbed and Slain. Oh! Father! hasten the time for their redemption, and the time when Zion shall be free! Grant that I may stand among my children as a patriarch and father indeed, to teach and help in the way of life, that not one may be lost, but all saved in the Celestial Glory; and that all my family may be one with me in this great work. Amen.

[Blank line]

31/Was today arrested by Noonan for a debt due him by the Canal Company. Found Security. Wrote to Lock, also Judge Barnes Concerning it.

1890/   1890.

Jan.1/Telegram from Susan. She started Dec. 31st glad!

2/Letter from Locke + Co. My hotel bill at the San Havier, Tucson, is $270.40 Copied my blessings and Susan's, in small book which I can have with me.

3/Recd Letter from Susan. She, Trudie + Dora came at 7 P.M. All well. How thankful I am to see them.

 She came on the only through train from Sacramento that has come for a month, all railroad travel through California having been interrupted by wash outs. At Sacramento the officials recommended her to go by sea from San Francisco to Los Angeles, as she could

[Stamp page 652L]

1890/[Blank line]

Jan. 3/not go through by rail. Susan and Gertrude consulted, and finally decided to stick to the train, and try it by land. The succeeded, though sometimes in much danger. On one occasion the train was all night going ten miles, over washed out and hastily fixed road, creeping slowly and carefully along. But they came right through to Gila Bend, the only through train for a month previous and for two weeks after; for the very day they reached Gila Bend the track was all washed out behind them near Cloton, Cal. Truly the blessing and hand of God has been over them for good. Had they left Logan a day sooner or a day later, they could not have come through, except with vexations delays and expense. I thank the Father for His goodness. My joy at meeting my family was great.

4/ To day Noonan was glad to withdraw his suit.

5/ This morning we left Gila Bend at 2 P.M. the train being many hours late. Reached Maricopa at 4 A.M. and Tempe at 6 A.M. ^Sam met us there.^ Uncle Benja quite sick. I blessed him, and cheered him up, and he felt better. Rained on us as we went to Nephi. Found Elvira + children well, and very glad to see us after so long separation.

6/ Went to Mesa, dined at Prest Robison's. Saw ~~Gr~~ Mother Susan Johnson, Susan's Step mother, lately came from Apache Co. Saw many of our relatives.

8/ Our Wedding anniversary. Elvira had a nice dinner. Gertrude taken quite sick. Wrote article for "Contributor" "A journey in 1854 in Utah."[12]

9/ Gertrude better. Visited C.I. Robson, 10th on Canal matters.

14/ Gertrude well of La Grippe, but Elvira takes it.[13]

17/ Bought a Sewing machine for Elvira. Gave note. 90 days for $50.00 to Stewart. Interest 1 ½ % from maturity.

[Next paragraph has floor plan drawing on left, text on right]

19/ Letter from Joel, with size of our house, as follows:–

I wish to build a good house in front + joining to the old one, and for this reason I have sent for dimensions of the old house I bought in Juarez.

[Page 653R]

1890/[Blank line]

Jan. 21/Susan down with La Grippe, quite bad. In the evening she asked me to administer to her, which I did, The Lord gave each of us strong faith, and she was healed almost immediately. Thanks be to the Father for His mercy.

23/ Wrote to Charlie + advised him to come to Gila Bend and set up blacksmith Shop. This I did, to get him into a warmer and better climate than where he is now, in S.L. City, threatened with consumption.

28/ Took Susan to Phoenix, and bought some dress patterns.[14]

31/ I went to Phoenix to meet Murphey. To no purpose.

---

12. This article appeared under Santiago, "Pioneer Sketches. II. A Journey in 1854," *Contributor* 11 (March 1890): 180–184.

13. Two days later, B. F. Johnson wrote that "President Robson & J. H. Martineau, with their wives, came and stayed over night. A pleasant occasion." Diary entry for January 16, 1890 in Johnson, *My Life's Review*, 320.

14. Two days later, on January 30, B. F. Johnson wrote that "Bro. James Henry Martineau and wife came for their Patriarchal Blessings. She is my niece and the mother to B. Samuel's wife. A noble woman." From Johnson, *My Life's Review*, 320.

Feb./3/ Wrote to Murphey I would not be a party to any plan that would injure Locke + Co. If he can sell his franchise as he thinks and make $5000 each, for us, without hurting Locke + Co. all right. If not, I will not join in with him. as, to me, honor is worth more than gold. just as when the Hall's offered me $200.000 to kill Locke + Co. scheme Locke + Co. have employed me, and they <u>trust</u> me; so I must not forfeit the confidence they place in me.

9/ Wrote for "Contributor" "<u>A Mystery of the desert</u>." and of Walker's (Indian Chief) Nephite money.[15]

16/ Wrote for "Contributor" Elvira's story of the indian outbreak of 1882, and killing of Robinson near Showlow.[16]

21/Sent to Lyman for $200.00 so Mother can get home.

27/ Renewed my subscription to N.Y. World[17]
[Blank line]

March/4/ Bought goods for Susan at Mesa, credit, $27.60 of which $7.00 was for Sam.

6/ Bought additional goods " " 11.35

        $38.95

11/ Susan and I sat for photos at Mesa. Ordered 3 doz. cards @ $9.00 and 1 doz of Gertrude + Vira @$ = $15.00 Went to Tempe to negotiate load by Mortgage of Sams 160 acres. Did so, for $1000.00 Previous to this we went to Uncle Benjamin's—Patriarch—and got patriarchal blessings for her and me; and again, we (Uncle B. and I) ordained and set her apart as a nurse and comforter to the sick and the troubled, and as a midwife, as follows:–

[Page 654L]

1890/[Blank line]

---

 15. See Santiago, "Pioneer Sketches. IV. Seeking a Refuge in the Desert," *Contributor* 11 (May 1890): 249–251, and Santiago, "Pioneer Sketches. VI. A Mystery of the Desert," *Contributor* 11 (July 1890): 342–344.

 16. These experiences were published under Santiago, "Pioneer Sketches. III. A Time of Fear and Death," *Contributor* 11 (April 1890): 224–227.

 17. The *New York World* was a newspaper published in New York from 1860 to 1931. Among its publishers was Hungarian-American publisher, Joseph Pulitzer (1847–1911), for whom the Pulitzer Prize was named.

March/11/ Blessing by Benj. F. Johnson, Patriarch, upon Jas H. Martineau given in Tempe, Arizona Jan. 30. 1890

[Blank line]

 Brother James, in the name of the Lord Jesus and by virtue of the priesthood of the fathers I place my hands upon thy head to say such things unto thee relating to the past and the future as the Lord shall give ^to^ me by the inspiration of His Spirit. I say unto thee, lift up thy head and let thy heart rejoice before the Lord, for He hath thee in His remembrance, even to fulfill unto thee every desire of thy heart, and bestow upon thee every blessing that His servants have pronounced upon thy head. For he hath a great purpose in thee, even from before the foundation of the Earth, and for the accomplishment of His purpose He hath gathered thee out, and in blessing raised thee above thy fellows. And from the days of thy birth His angel had charge concerning thee, the arm of His power hath been around thee, and the hand of the Lord hath led thee, even in ways that thou knewest not, and for a purpose plainly known unto Himself which thou didst not understand. In all the circumstances of thy life He hath been near unto thee to strengthen thee; and the arm of His power and the Spirit of His might shall never be withdrawn from thee. For thou shalt raise up and go forward, and no power shall turn thee backward from fulfilling the purposes of the Almighty. The spirit of wisdom and council hath been sealed upon thy head, and it shall be more fully developed within thee; and thou shalt lead forth in the redemption of the covenant people of the Lord, to assist mightily in the re-establishment of Jacob upon the land given them by the Father. Unto them thou shalt become a Prince and a Patriarch, a Prophet and a Seer; and thou and thy Sons shall be an arm of power, even to be as the horns of Ephraim in assisting to push together the people, and to establish them upon the land of their inheritance. And when the cities of the Gentiles are waste, behold thou shalt go forth with thy children and thy children's children to redeem the waste places, and to inhabit the cities that are made desolate. Thy years shall be many upon the earth, even according to the fulness of the desire of thy heart. The Lord hath given thee wisdom to lead thy family in the ways of the just, to honor Him, and thy shall rise up and call thee blessed all the days of thy life, and carry thy name and thy fame

[Page 655R]

1890/ Susan's Blessing

in honor throughout all generations of Time. The treasures of the earth shall be unto thee in great fulness, whereby thou shalt be able to assist in bringing to pass the redemption of Zion, the rearing of His holy temple, the gathering and sustaining of the meek of the earth, whereby the blessing of the poor shall ever be upon thy head. All the blessings that have been conferred upon thee in priesthood thou shalt hold forever, and shall lack in no good thing, to prepare thee to fulfull every degree of usefulness and to attain to every greatness that is according to the desires of thy heart. Thou shalt stand as a Savior in thy father's house, and be numbered among those who are Saviors upon Mt. Zion, even to the accomplishment of a mighty work among the living and the dead. For it is even thy privilege to live to see the holy temple reared in Zion, and the glory of the Lord resting upon its towers, and to minister therein, when His glory shall fill its courts. Now all these blessings I seal upon thy head, and I seal thee up unto eternal lives, to come forth in the morning of the First Ressurrection, clothed in glory, immortality and eternal lives, in the name of Jesus. Amen. [Blank line]

<u>Patriarchal Blessing by B.F. Johnson, upon Susan E.J. Martineau, given in Tempe, Arizona, Jan. 30. 1890.</u>

Sister Susan, in the name of the Lord Jesus and by virtue of the patriarchal priesthood, I place my hands upon thy head in blessing, that the Lord may speak through me to the joy and comfort of thy heart, or to admonish and strengthen thee in the path that leadeth back into His presence. Thou art one of the Beloved of the Lord; thou wast valiant for the truth, and before the earth was thou didst shout hosanna that it would be thy privilege to come forth in this dispensation to assist in bringing forth and establishing Zion preparatory to a reign of peace upon the earth. To this end the Father blessed thee and sent thee as with a crown of glory upon thy head, that through thee mighty men and women should live upon the earth to be prophets, seers and mighty men, to lead forth in establishing righteousness and truth, to the rebuke of iniquity and sin, whose arm shall be strong against opposition, and in avenging innocent blood.

[Page 656L]

1890/ Blessing upon Susan

Thou hast earnestly sought to fulfill the Law of Sarah and to lead thy children to honor the Lord thy God. Because of this He shall honor thee, and all thy children shall remain steadfast before Him. Thy shall rise up and bless thee all thy days, and carry thy name in honor through all generations of time. The Lord shall bestow upon thee more fully the Spirit of wisdom and Council, and of the mothers and matrons of Zion thou shalt stand among those who are the most honored, because of the words of wisdom and comfort that as rubies shall fall from thy lips. The spirit and power of blessing and consolation shall rest upon thee in mighty power, even that all whom shalt bless shall be blessed indeed. The blessings of the earth shall be unto thee, and when the meek shall flee unto Zion in the great day of tribulation, thou shalt feed the hungry, clothe the naked and give shelter to the homeless; and thy words of consolation will bind up the sorrowful and the broken-hearted. And when because of wickedness the cities of the land shall become desolate, thou, together with thy husband and all thy family shall go forth to inhabit the cities that are desolate, and to inhabit the waste places. The Lord knoweth the integrity of thy heart and all thy sacrifices, and He will never leave thee alone that thy Spirit shall droop before Him, for His angels shall camp around thee, to be as thy companions. His arms shall sustain thee, his hand shall lead thee, His spirit shall fill thy heart with consolation and joy continually, while the vision of heaven shall be opened unto thee, to rebuke affliction, to command the Destroyer that no power shall invade thy inhibation to destroy thy peace or take away thy loved ones. Years shall be multiplied upon thy head, and thou shalt live even to the fulness of thy desires; and it is thy privilege to assist in the work both for the living and the dead, in the holy temple that shall be reared in Zion; to strike hands with the Son of Man when He shall descend to his holy temple, and to associate with those loved ones whom He will bring with Him. And in blessings thou shalt lack in no good thing. Thy inheritance shall be forever in Zion, which thou shalt receive with thy companion and family when the Ancient of Days shall sit. I rebuke from thy heart and mind every principle of doubt that might trouble thee, or any principle of

[Page 657R]

1890/ Susan's Ordination Blessing

fear that might spring up in thy heart, and say unto thee that thy way shall ever be open before thee. Now all these blessings I seal upon thy head, and seal thee up unto eternal lives, to come forth in the morning of the first ressurrection clothed upon with glory, immortality and eternal lives in the name of Jesus. Amen. (See page 660 for Elvira's

[Blank line]

<u>Blessing and Ordination by Patriarch B.F. Johnson
and James H. Martineau upon Susan E.J. Martineau,
given in Tempe Arizona, Feb. 25. 1890. (B.F.J. mouth)</u>

    Susan, we lay our hands upon thee and ask God to give unto us His Spirit, that our words may be dictated by it. Thou art of the Seed of the Blessed; thou art a Princess and a Priestess and a Queen; and thou hast by inheritance a right to all the blessings of the daughters of Abraham. In these thy rights are unlimited, even to all the rights and blessings of Sarah. Thou shalt be filled with great wisdom as a Nurse, and be a great comfort, a help and a blessing to the sick, the afflict^ed^ and to those who are bowed down and distressed, of the poor of the earth. Many shall seek unto thee of the poor and also the rich; and health and peace shall drop from the ends of thy fingers, and consolation and Comfort from thy lips. We ordain thee and set thee apart as a Nurse and as a Midwife, and thou shalt administer peace and comfort to the afflicted. The sick shall rise up at thy touch, and sickness and death shall flee away from thy presence. No blessing thou shalt desire, that pertains to the daughters of Abraham, shall be denied thee. Thou shalt be filled with words of peace and comfort to those whose hearts are bowed down in grief or trouble, and they shall rejoice greatly at thy presence. And all that is good and womanly and pure shall be with thee and in thee continually, even to the fulness of thy desires. All these blessings, and all that you desire we seal and confirm upon thee in the name of the Lord Jesus Christ. Amen.
[Blank line]
    Father, I thank thee, for these blessings

[Page 658L]

1890/ Elvira's Blessing.

The following blessing was given to Elvira by Path Joel H. Johnson, at Johnson, Kane Co. Utah. Jan. 19th 1879. Born in Parowan, Utah Aug. 14. 1856. She was then wife of B.S. Johnson.

    Susan Martineau Johnson, in the name of the Lord Jesus Christ of Nazareth I lay my hands upon thy head to give thee a fathers or patriarchal blessing, and to confirm all the blessings thou hast received from the Elders of Israel. Thou art of the seed of Ephraim, and entitled to all the blessings of the holy men and women of old, therefore I bless ~~thee~~ you with the Spirit of the loving God to abide in your bosom forever like a well of water springing up unto everlasting life. Thou shalt be an assistant with thy companion in teaching the daughters of Ephraim the principles of eternal life, civilization and economy. Thou shalt have many children, and thy seed shall be great in the earth. Inasmuch as thou wilt bring them up in righteousness, thou shalt have power to drive the Destroyer from their midst when thy companion is absent. Messengers from behind the vail shall visit thee in times of sorrow and trial, and give thee counsel and comfort. No enemy shall cross thy path and prosper while thou art faithful to do the will of God. Thou shalt be beloved by all faithful Saints, and thy name shall be had in honorable remembrance by all the pure in heart. Thou shalt live long upon the earth, and when the ressurrection are given thou shalt be quickened I seal ~~all~~ upon thy head all the blessings that thy heart can conceive or desire, and seal thee up unto eternal lives with thy companion, to inherit thrones, powers and dominions, and come forth in the morning of the first ressurrection shouldst thou fall asleep, with glory, immortality and eternal lives. All these blessings are thine, if thou art faithful to hearken the words of wisdom and eternal life, in the name of Jesus Christ. Amen.

<u>Note</u>. The foregoing was not recorded in Joel H. Johnson's Record through inadvertence. I therefore send it to B.F. Johnson Patriarch, to be recorded in his Record of Blessings.

Copied from the original, Nephi, A.T.
March 6. 1890

[Page 659R]

1890/ Family leave Deming for home.

March 12/left Samuel's for Tempe, on our way to Mexico. Got $1000 at Tempe Natl Bank, less bank charges $48.90 which includes 3 mo. interest @ 1 ½ % = $15.00 pr month. Gave Sam $7.00 Elvira $15.00 paid D.T. LeBaron's family, by Sam $35.00 pd Armstrong for goods $16.80. 3 Tickets to Maricopa

13/7.50. Left Tempe 5 A.M. Arr. Maricopa 6.15 A.M. Took S.P.R.R. at 11.00 A.M. 3 Tickets to Deming $45.90 + .65 extra for excess of 40 lbs baggage.

14/ Arrived at Deming N.M. at 2 A.M. Staid at R.R. hotel. met Joel and

Anna. All were overjoyed to meet again. After breakfast, moved to St. James hotel. Our bill at R.R. hotel for 2 rooms + breakfast, was $6.75.

15/ Deposited $700.00 in First National Bank, Deming.

17/ Met Peterson, of Diaz, whom I owed $15.00 horse trade, in full.
I find I still owe in Juarez, for house + Lot ^Mex^ $135.00
I owe Clough for trees (U.S. Money) bal. old a/c $39.00
   "   "   " Joel's trees $31.30

                            $70.30

Susan also owes P. Cardon, cash $20.00 + 1.40 = $21.40

I gave her the money to pay it him. Also gave her $400.00 Mexican money and to Joel $13.00 Mex. cash.

In Deming we traded over $410.00 including a wagon $120.00 Also bought harness $48.00 on time, of H. Nordhaus. In settling up, I gave Checks for $304.00 (for the $400.00 Mex. money @76¢) and $300.00 for use. Also deposited $200.00 Thatcher Bank and drew $50.00, Paid St James Hotel bill for 6 ⅓ days $35.75 Our expenses have been heavy, but the family needed much clothing and household goods. We waited 6 days for Company, and I enjoyed myself very much with my family together, and it was a dread to part from them. Joel hired span of mules of Hainey to haul the new wagon and load as far as Diaz. The folks made up considerable clothing in Deming, and were busy [in margin:20/Thurs.] as bees. The family at last left Deming in the afternoon—4 P.M.—a dreadful windy day with clouds of sand filling the air. My Consul papers Cost $6.25.

[Page 660L]

1890/[Blank line]

March 20/I went a little distance with Susan, she driving the mules with Gertrude, and Joel and Anna driving the other team. At last I alighted with tearful kisses, and stood and watched the teams as long as I could see them, then sorrowfully returned to my desolate room. It will be very good, in the next estate, that there will no more be sorrowful partings from loved ones. I took train for Gila Bend at [in margin: 20] 9 P.M. and arrived there at 9 A.M. Next morning, the [in margin: 21st] on Friday. I found plenty of letters + papers, and spent next day in answering letters +c. I also sent to [in margin: 22] "Contributor" some poems, "Title of Liberty," "Boyhood's Days" and "Missing ones." Also to Y.W. Journal, "Lines to my wife" + "Truth."[18] Also sent for pension.

24/ Got photos of Susan, Gertrude + Dora from Logan, and sent Some to Elvira and Albert. Wrote to Genl Raum, U.S. Pension Commissioner, about my pension.

25/ Sent two articles to Contributor; Seeking a refuge in the desert, including the lost company, Snake dinner +c +c[19] I have spent all spare time in writing up my journal from my pocket notes, copying blessings into it, +c to date of 26th[20]
[Blank line]
Patriarchal Blessing upon S. Elvira M. Johnson by B.F. Johnson, Tempe A.T. Jan 30. 1890. Born 14 Aug, 1856

Elvira my daughter, in the name of Jesus, by virtue of the patriarchal priesthood I place my hands upon thy head in blessing, praying that the Lord may give me through the inspiration of His Spirit, words of counsel, admonition and blessing, to be keys of knowledge and principles of faith to govern thee all thy life. Thou art one of those born in Zion in the new Covenant, entitled to all the blessings, dominion, increase and exaltation pertaining to the daughters of Abraham. Because of thy love for the truth and the integrity of thy heart, Thou art one of the most loved of the ~~Lord~~ Father. He sent thee to the earth with a crown of joy upon thy head that thou mightest become a medium of Salvation and restoration upon the earth. To this end He gave His angels charge concerning thee, to hedge thee round about from evil, and to open the

[Page 661R]

pathway of thy feet, to protect thy life to the fulfillment of the missions

---

18. See Santiago, "The Title of Liberty," *Contributor* 11 (June 1890): 312–313; Santiago, "Boyhood's Days," *Contributor* 12 (January 1891): 113; Santiago, "To My Wife on Her Fiftieth Birthday," *Young Woman's Journal* 1 (May 1890): 246; Santiago, "To My Wife," *Young Woman's Journal* 1 (August 1890): 405; and Santiago, "Truth," *Young Woman's Journal* 2 (October 1890): 10.

19. These experiences, including a famished Indian's feast of four snakes, a mouse, and two field rats, were published under Santiago, "Pioneer Sketches. IV. Seeking a Refuge in the Desert—I," *Contributor* 11 (May 1890): 249–251, and Santiago, "Pioneer Sketches. V. Seeking a Refuge in the Desert—II," *Contributor* 11 (June 1890): 296–300.

20. This is another entry that describes Martineau's process of transferring diary entries from pocket notes to the larger journal. See entry for April 1, 1874.

for which thou hast come to the earth; for which purpose He hath given thee a companion, and shall multiply unto thee children until they shall be around thee as thick clusters of grapes upon a fruitful vine, whom thou shalt lead in the way of the Lord to honor Him, and they shall honor and bless thee all thy days, and carry thy name in honor throughout all generations of time. Thou dost delight in the way of the Lord, and because of thy love for the truth, the Lord shall make thee great. For thou shalt stand as a counsellor among the honored of thy sex, and by the example thou shalt teach them to honor, the laws of Sarah. Thy husband shall love and honor thee, and thy house shall be a house of joy and peace, and all who dwell therein shall rise up to bless thee. The blessings of the earth shall be multiplied unto thee, even in the fruits of flocks and herds, orchards and gardens, and thou shalt dwell in costly habitations; and when the meek shall flee to Zion, through the abundance that shall be around thee, thou shalt feed, clothe and comfort the poor and the needy, and give habitations to the homeless; and the blessings of the poor shall ever rest upon thee; and with thy husband thou shalt do thy full part in all the works of righteousness pertaining to the building up of Zion, gathering her children, rearing her holy temples, and laboring therein both for the living and the dead; for thou shalt see the holy temple reared in Zion, shall strike hands with the Son of Man when He shall descend to the earth, and shall minister therein when His glory shall fill its courts. Thy days shall be many upon the earth, and thy power for usefulness shall be great. for the spirit of blessing and consolation Shall rest upon thee and faith shall spring up in thy heart, to rebuke affliction, to command the Destroyer that no power shall invade thy habitations to destroy thy peace or take away thy loved ones. The angels shall camp around thee, if thou wilt be admonished to call upon the name of the Lord thy God, and ~~to~~ forget not to call upon His name.

[Page 662L]

1890/[Blank line]

For thou art among the most favored of the daughters of Abraham, and entitled to every privilege that belongs to the wives, the mothers and the matrons ~~of~~ ^in^ Zion, to stand in thy place as a counsellor to admonish to teach, and to cultivate the younger of thy sex; and all who hear thy voice shall cleave unto thee and love thee; and all thy kindred shall rejoice in thee because of the wisdom and spirit of consolation and blessing which shall drop as pearls from thy lips. Associated with thy husband thou shalt stand in thy place and officiate for thy sex in the great day of Israel's crowning under the hands of the children of Ephraim. And thy inheritance shall be forever in Zion, which, with thy companion thou shalt receive when the Ancient of Days does sit. All these blessings I seal upon thy head, together with all thy former blessings, and I seal thee up unto eternal lives, to come forth in the morning of the first ressurrection, to inherit thrones and dominions, in the name of the Lord Jesus Christ. Amen. [Blank line]

Patriarchal Blessing by B.F. Johnson, given in Tempe A.T. May 25. 1889, upon Benjamin Samuel Johnson, Son of Benj. F. and Mary Ann Johnson, born in Santaquin, Utah Co. Utah April 20th 1853.

Benjamin Samuel, in the name of the Lord Jesus + through the priesthood of the Fathers, I lay my hands upon thy head to give thee a father's blessing. Thou art one of those who were valiant for the truth and didst shout hosanna to the Most High before the foundations of the earth were laid, that it would be thy privilege to come forth to assist in bringing forth Zion and in gathering her children from the four corners of the earth. Thy blessing is in Ephraim, and the Lord has a mighty work for thee to do assisting to bring to pass His purposes. He has given thee a Companion, ^+^ He will continue to multiply blessings unto thee, according to the fulness of thy desires to serve and obey Him; and inasmuch as thou wilt accept it, thou shalt become a minister of Salvation, and one of the mightiest of ^among^ the sons of Zion, +

[Page 663R]

1890/[Blank line]

thy voice make the wicked to tremble in nations afar off. And the meek of the earth shall rejoice in thee, + gather around thee as flocks unto their shepherds. The winds and the waves shall obey thee, Devils shall flee before thee, while the sick and the lame, the blind and the halt, shall be healed by thy command. The Spirit of the Lord Shall be within thee, and His wisdom shall be as a well of water springing up unto eternal life. Thy arm shall be strong to resist oppression and to avenge the blood of the innocent. The poor shall ever rejoice in thee, for the Lord will open unto thee the treasures of the earth, + thou shalt feed the hungry, clothe the naked, and be mighty in assisting to rear the temple, cities and bulwarks in Zion and in gathering her children. Wives and children shall be multiplied unto thee, and thou shalt lead them in the way of the Lord, and they shall honor thee, + they shall carry thy name and fame in honor to all generations of time. Thy days and thy years shall be multiplied unto thee. Thou shalt assist in rearing the holy temple in Zion, and thou shalt minister therein with thy companion, when the glory of the Lord shall rest upon its towers and fill its courts; and when Israel returns from the north Country to receive their crowning in Zion, thou and thy companion shalt minister unto them. Thy habitations shall ever be in peace, and abundance of the earth shall ever be unto thee. Faith shall increase with thee; wisdom and the treasures of knowledge shall shall fill thee. The Lord shall loose thy tongue, + thou shalt become a mighty councillor in Zion; and every blessing that thy heart shall desire the Lord will bestow upon thee. All these blessings I seal upon thee with power to accomplish every good purpose of thy heart; and I seal thee up unto eternal life, to come forth in the morning of the first ressurrection, to be around with glory, immortality and eternal lives, in the name of Jesus. Amen.

J.H. Martineau Scribe

[Page 664L]

1890/[Blank line]

March 27/Went to Nephi. Found Elvira and family well, but Susan was not there and it seemed very lonesome to me, although Elvira was as good to me as she could be, and so were they all. I spent several days in copying keys of principle from the "Times and Seasons," of 1884, into my book of "pearls." Among other things a description of the City of Zion, as it will be laid out, and its twelve temples.[21]

April 3/ Started back to Gila Bend, Prest Robson having declined to do anything with the canal work. At Gila Bend I found letters from Susan, Joel, and others. My duties in the Mexican Custom House at La Ascencion amounted to $145.00 of which $32.67 was on new wagon, $39.49 on new harness, $11.80 on side saddle (worth about $8.00) on 100 lbs Sugar $6.81, Advance papers $20.45. So you can see it costs something to go into Mexico.

---

21. A number of items were copied from the *Times and Seasons* into "Pearls." The explanation of the plot of the City of Zion, provided by Joseph Smith in a letter, dated June 25, 1833, was published in the *Times and Seasons* 6 (January 15, 1845): 786–787. This description, however, is not found in the copy of "Pearls" Martineau gave to his son, Nephi. See, Martineau, "Pearls," esp. pp. 55–71.

6/ Letter from Locke to go to Tucson. He sent $10.00 for expenses. Arrived in Tucson 2.15 P.M. Began to make estimates (canal)

8/Changed from Palace Hotel to the Russ House.

9/Made Canal report to Col. Snead, our N.Y. broker and agent. Also began to board (day) at Cosmopolitan hotel, + sleeping on a cot in Barnes' office.

10/Sent report and map of Canal lands, to Locke. Letter from Jesse N.

11/ who s traveling in Germany.

12/ Good news about canal from Locke. On strength of it I bought 2 Collars and 20¢ worth (6) of oranges.

15/ Letter from Virginia, who is in S.L. City alone, in debt, trying to earn her own living. Sent her $15.00

16/ Engaged by Barnes and Capt. A.E. Miltimore U.S.A. as Engineer to bring water from the Rillito creek 10 miles from here, near Fort Lowell. Went with Miltimore to look at it. Began making estimates and Surveys on the work (Rillito)[22]

19/Locke expects to begin Work right away on our canal. Wants me ready

20/Woke suddenly and thought I heard Susan cry out "Oh James," as if Sick. I prayed for her—which is all I <u>can</u> do for her now.

22/ Caught bad cold on the Rillito, by sitting in Shade with coat off. From this time continued canal work and making plan and estimates for reservoir +c.

[Page 665R]

1890/[Blank line]

May 5/To day the Mexicans celebrate their victory over Maximilian—the Cinco de Mayo—(5th of May). Receive and write many letters.

12/Wrote a kind, good letter to Jessie, enclosed under cover to Jas Sharp, where she is teaching his children. The letter and money I Sent Virginia returned to me. Sent it her again, care of Charlie. Sent my article to Contributor "A leap for life or death." I sent monthly, articles to it for publication.

---

22. See entry at July 3, 1890, and March 21, 1890.

21/Sent $48.00 to Nordhaus, Deming, to pay for the harness.

23/Sent articles to Young Woman's Journal "Woman's Power," also poetry, "I'll remember you love in my prayers."[23]

25/Wrote article for Phoenix "Gazette," in defense of Mormonism.[24]

26/ "   "   " Tucson Star,"   "   "   "   "[25]

31/ "   "   "   "   " on our religious belief, by request.[26]

June 6/Sent $50. to pay for Elvira's Sewing machine + $20.00 to Store.

10/Went to Gila Bend and returned Tucson 12th

13/Sent $60.00 to Susan. Attended Capt. Miltimore's Court martial.

19/Got a letter from Jessie's mother. Forbids me to write again. All my enemies shall finally fall away, and God will give me the victory. Genl R.A. Johnson offered me a small Survey, of part of township near Yuma. Accepted it.[27]

21/ Executed Bond, as U.S. Dep. Surveyor, $1200.00

22/ Sent plan of house to Susan.

---

23. See Santiago, "Woman's Power," *Young Woman's Journal* 1 (August 1890): 405–407.
24. See J. H. M., "Justice Upheld," *Arizona Daily Gazette*, May 30, 1890, 1.
25. This article was written in defense of the constitutional rights of a fair and impartial trial and a right to vote for all citizens of the United States, including Mormons. See J. B. [sic] M. to editor, "Constitutional Rights," *Arizona Daily Star*, May 27, 1890, 3.
26. This article could not be found in any subsequent issues of the *Daily Star*.
27. A few days later, Martineau received written confirmation that his contract (no. 15) in Tp. 8 S., R 21 W. was approved by the Commissioner of the General Land Office. Royal A. Johnson to James H. Martineau, June 21, 1890, Letters Sent, box 6: Vol. 23, April 22, 1890–June 11, 1891, pp. 86–88, CSGAZ. On June 21, a brief entry appeared in the *Weekly Citizen*, saying:

> Mr. Martineau, of Gila Bend, is in the city. Mr. Martineau reports that Gila Bend is a country with a great future in the agricultural line. The Gila Bend canal is being built, which will be 60 or 70 miles long and 40 feet wide, opening up to settlement about 150,000 acres of land, which there will be a great rush to occupy. This region is a fine fruit region, and a specialty will be made of oranges, which, with lemons and olives, will be raised in considerable quantities, to compete with California fruits, as this region like the Salt River Valley, can get fruit in the market a month earlier than California can. Mr. Martineau also reports that a canal is to be built by eastern parties about 30 miles west of Gila Bend which will open a large tract of valuable land to cultivation.

See untitled, *Arizona Weekly Citizen*, June 21, 1890, 4.

24/ ~~Recd a check from "Contributor" for $20.00 my first pay as an Author. Also A~~ letter from Adaline Benson, of Logan.

29/ My friend J.A. Heatley was very sad. No work, no money. I felt impressed + told him he should have his way opened from this time. He said he believed my words.
[Blank line]

July 1/Recd a letter from F.R. Nebaker. He wants to marry Lilla.

5/Sent articles to Contributor, "Scout," and "Wonderful ride."[28]

7/Sent Theodore $3.00 at Deming, a little bit, but nearly all I had.

5/Wrote a blessing letter to Susan. Received a letter from her next day. She dreamed she wanted to come to me but a Swift river intervened. She went into a room, went to the door, saw she was near the Shore, jumped about 5 feet, and found me not expecting her

9th/ I had a singular dream, which I believe will at some future time be fulfilled. (See next page.)

[Page 666L]

1890/Scene 1.

July 9/I seemed to be in a large room with 3 or 4 men whom I knew but do not now recollect. One of them told me I was to move a large flock of sheep—700.000—from where we were to the South. It seemed to me an immense undertaking, so great a number, and I spoke of it, when one said quickly, "Why, there are 500.000 of them already there." (in the South) I felt relieved as the labor seemed so much less, now.

<u>Scene 2nd</u> Got ready to travel, with teams +c. Found the well dipped almost dry—so many getting water. Then started out with a team of 7 or 8 spans of mules + big wagon.

<u>Scene 3</u>. I was in the South, and saw a tall palm tree, with a large fruit hanging just under its leaves. Looking closer, I saw a braided basket hanging there—the fruit inside, and the object of the basket was to protect the fruit until it should come to maturity. The basket was much in shape of a thimble 18 or 20 inches long, mouth upward.

---

28. See Santiago, "Pioneer Sketches. VII. A Scouting Party," *Contributor* 11 (August 1890): 395–397, and Santiago, "A Wonderful Ride," *Contributor* 11 (August 1890): 397–398.

My interpretation. I believe the 700.000 sheep was to show that a <u>great many</u> sheep—endless, or seed of Joseph—are to be gathered into the fold of Christ in the land South, and that I may be called at some time, to help gather them. And it is not generally known there are so many sheep now there.

The draining of the well, seems to show the fulness of our preparations for the work, and using all our resources as for it.

The fruit growing on the palm, hidden and protected by the basket, shows God has good fruit ripening there, hidden from the world for the present, but quietly growing and ripening, and will be preserved from evil. The palm, shows a warm southern climate, perhaps, Mexico, Central or South America.

When I went to bed, I was anxious about my debts and prayed for a comforting dream. This dream was given, not in answer to my temporal anxieties, but in relation to our spiritual labors, as more important.—the salvation of Souls.

16/ Received $450.00 from Logan, being the remainder that I had in the Bank there—the last of my $3000.00 All right. My Father will provide.

[Page 667R]

1890/A wonder. Contributor sent me $20.00 for my writing. This is the first I ever received so.

17/ Deposited $450.00 in Consolidated National Bank of Tucson. Paid Des. News $6.00 for 2 copies of paper.

21/ Recd my written instructions as U.S. Dep. Surveyor, from Johnson.[29]

22/ Thermometer 109°, hottest day thus far.

31/ Began to Copy my Book of "Pearls," so Henry can have a copy.

~~July 3~~/ Began surveying Rillito Canal.[30] Very hot, 107° Caught in a [in

---

29. He received information for his surveying contract, a manual of instructions, and a drawing of the western boundary of the township. Royal A. Johnson to James H. Martineau, July 18, 1890, Letters Sent, box 6: Vol. 23, April 22, 1890–June 11, 1891, pp. 123–125, CSGAZ.

30. The Rillito Canal, northeast of Tucson, was known for its unique engineering design in obtaining seepage water by the aid of a concrete flume submerged in the bed of

margin: August 3] cloud burst and flood. Worked on canal from day to day to [in margin: 9th] Sent Bank of Tempe $400.00 to apply on Sam's note. ($1000.)

Also send interest for the month—$9.00 which continues every month until April 1891. I constantly receive and write letters, 10 to 15 a week, which, with other work, keeps me very busy.

11/Spent today in regulating the Solar transit I will survey with.

13/Recd a letter from the Bank of Tempe, giving me more time in which to pay Sam's note of $1000. This was in answer to my prayer for help from the Lord. The note was given due in 6 mo. and secured by mortgage on Sam's entry of 160 acres, containing the homes of himself and six brothers. I feared lest the bank foreclose, and take their homes, + such a disgrace to me, robbing them of their homes seemed to me worse than death. After I prayed, the voice of the Spirit whispered that I should <u>not</u> come to any disgrace or evil but should pay all my debts in due time to the full satisfaction of all concerned; that no one should suffer any loss by me, and that God would bless me and give me my desires, also other precious promises, which greatly cheered me.

17/ Sunday. Fasted all day till night, and prayed much.

18/ A letter from my sister Netta (Mrs. D.C. Lyon) She says our father's first wife was a Mrs. Hawkins, widow of Captain Hawkins of the British Navy, who had two children, Samuel + Elizabeth, both dead many years ago. Mrs. Hawkins was daughter to Earl Stanhope, who at his death willed her £8.000 and £1000 ^each^ to ~~Samuel + Elizabeth, her children.~~ Julia and Lucretia, her children by my father,—my half sisters.

[Page 668L]

1890/[Blank line]

Rillito Creek. Several other smaller ditches along the Rillito removed seepage water by means of open cuts to the extent of a few hundred miners' inches. See note at entry for March 25, 1891.

According to the newspaper, "Col. Martineau left this morning on a surveying trip to a few miles beyond Ft. Lowell, to survey the course of a projected canal there which if found practicable will when finished, be of immense benefit to Tucson. It is intended to make a water storage, taking the water from the Rillito. To do so the reservoir will be dug down about 10 or 12 feet, taking out the gravel on the surface, to the water tight stratum below." See untitled, *Arizona Weekly Citizen*, August 2, 1890, 3.

August/18/I believe Mrs. Hawkins was originally [blank] [blank] daughter to Earl Stanhope, who is related closely to the Earls of Bedford. [Blank line]

Recd a letter from Nephi. He had endowed No. 8 George Hows, on May 15. 1890. Ordd by Robt Henderson + S. Roskelly.

Emma endowed Mrs. Maria Margaret Hows, his wife + was proxy in sealing by Prest M.W. Merrill, May 15/90

On May 16. 1890 Nephi Endowed David Elwin, ordd by M.W. Merrill. Emma endowed Mary Clementine Stuart. Sealed by N.C. Edlefsen, witness R. Henderson, J.A. McAlister.

23/ To day Lyman had a boy born to him, who weighed 10 lbs. He was named Preston Martineau, after Bp. Preston.

25/ Copied into "Pearls" from Prest Woodruff's sermon.[31]

29/ Letter from Susan. She says Gertrude, Anna + Dora were poisoned and nearly died, by eating toadstools in a mistake for mushrooms. They were only saved by prompt emetics, and especially by the power of the priesthood. Gertrude was very sick a week or ten days. The others got well sooner. Susan had been warned in a dream the previous night, but forgot all about it until they were poisoned. I thank thee, my Father, for thy goodness. [Blank line]

Sept./[Blank line]
2/ A good letter from M. Thatcher. He says Lyman has a new boy. Have not heard from Lyman yet about it.

5/ Letter from Lyman, who says his boy was born Sat. 23d Aug. + weighed 10 lbs.

11/ Finished my surveys, estimates and plans of the Rillito dam and Canal

13/ Borrowed $175.00 from Bank for my survey, in addition to my $50.00 in bank. Wrote an article for the "Star" by request, condemning the Fiesta de San Augustin.[32] Also finished copying my "Pearls." By letter from

---

31. This sermon is not found in the copy of Martineau's "Pearls" given to his son, Nephi. See Martineau, "Pearls Collected from Church Works," USU Special Collections & Archives.

32. Martineau called the feast a "hideous conglomeration of whiskey saloons gambling tables" and advised that "such things should be abolished in Tucson." See A Tender Foot, "The Feast—The Views of a Visitor," *Arizona Daily Star*, September 14, 1890, 4.

Charles I learn <u>his</u> new baby boy was born Aug. 11th at 12 P.M. His is Bryant Sherman Martineau.

14/ My bill for Engineering +c on Rillito creek, amounts to $217.05, against Pima Land and Water Company.

[Page 669R]

1890/[Blank line]

Sept. 15/Started today for Yuma, to Survey U.S. public land.

16/Arrived at Yuma, 240 miles, and arranged for Mexicans. Was detained at Yuma by rain and washout until the [in margin: 18th] I went to Blaisdell, 10 miles with my party of four men to begin work on Survey.[33] Found beginning point, + Survd ½ miles.

19/ Very hot. Ran 4m and then had to walk 5 miles to Camp Arrived late, tired out. Almost stepped a big coiled rattle Snake, but saw him in time to miss stepping on him. He was coiled up in thick grass and weeds.

20/ Not so hot today—only 120° in shade.

28/ Have been surveying all last week, + suffered much from intense heat, thirst and fatigue, climbing steep rocky hills + mountains, or going through dense thickets of thorns. One day I was toiling up a high mountain, almost exhausted with heat + thirst, and in my distress prayed for a little cool wind to revive me. Immediately a gentle, cooling breeze came, unspeakably refreshing to me. I was so glad tears of joy flowed as I thanked the Holy Father for his mercies. He also heard and answered my prayers for aid at other times. The Lord is very merciful.[34]

---

33. Blaisdell is located eleven miles east of Yuma on US-95. It was a SPRR station named after Yuma pioneer Hiram W. Blaisdell, chief engineer of the Mohawk Canal Company, who built the Araby Canal in 1888. See Barnes, *Arizona Place Names*, 53.

34. On this date, Martineau wrote to Surveyor General Johnson:

Dr Sir
I drop a line to say I am nearly done with my survey, but may be a few days beyond Oct. 1st having been detained two days by clouds to get observation on Polaris, and also several days by high water in the Gila, but I am working hard to finish as soon as possible Hoping for your indulgence a few more days I am
Yours respy
J. H. Martineau
U.S. Dep. Sur.

29/ Went from Blaisdell to Gila City, 6 miles, to finish the rest of the Township on North side of the Gila river which is high, broad and deep. Crossed in a Mexican's boat.

Oct./[Blank line]

2/Finished my survey, and returned to Blaisdell. I also had meandered both banks of the Gila—over 17 miles—all of which was in dense thickets of thorns or river mud, + suffered greatly from heat + thirst. Often had to creep on hands and knees under the brush to get through, my clothing wet through with sweat. It was the hardest job I ever had to do in my life.[35]

7/ Detained by another washout since last 4th inst. My expenses of Survey are $250.00 Went to Gila Bend.

8/To Tucson.

11/To day Judge Barnes said he would no longer pay for my board on behalf of the Gila Bend Canal Co. I have only $5 or $6.00 money. What I shall do I do not know, but

[Page 670L]

1890/[Blank line]

October/11/I believe God will open my way for me, though it seems very dark, naturally speaking. I can get no employment of any kind, to pay for food, much less to pay for any thing on the debts I owe or the monthly interest of $12.00 which must be paid or I be disgraced, the note + mortgage foreclosed, my kindred lose their homes—all by my act. A gloomy picture—a failure would be worse than death to me, because of the Shame, grief and dishonor. I can get nothing from the Canal Company, which owes me nearly $5000. But God has made precious promises to me—and says I will be able to pay all honorably;—I shall not be disgraced; and my time of payment on the note will be extended for me.

Recd a note from the Bank saying the note had been extended (for

---

J. H. Martineau to Royal A. Johnson, September 28, 1890, Letters Received, box 38: Vol. 20, August 10, 1890–May 21, 1891, letter #33, CSGAZ.

35. The highest temperature reported by a regular station of the Signal Service for September 1890 was 110° F at Yuma, Arizona, on the 4th. United States Army Post surgeons and voluntary observers reported a high of 116° at Gila Bend during the month of September 1890. See "Maximum and Minimum Temperatures," *Monthly Weather Review* 18 (September 1890): 231 and Table of Miscellaneous Data, p. 250.

payment) a year longer. Oh what a joy to me! How thankful I am to the Father that He has granted this to me, and that He had promised it + <u>fulfilled</u> His promise; thus greatly increasing my faith, + knowledge of the influence and voice of the Holy Spirit I have fasted and prayed much, and sought to put away all evil and to draw near to God, who has said "Draw near unto me and I will draw near unto You."[36] I have claimed his promises, in humility and as much faith as I could exercise, and in answer to prayers have received precious promises. But I have doubted, and thought perhaps I was deceived by my own <u>anxiety</u>, mistaking it for the voice of the Holy Spirit. This caused me to pray more, and to ask for light. The answer came in plainness, just as I would reason with my son. The Spirit said "These are but two powers, that of God and of Satan. Satan does not incite to do any good, but only evil, but the heavenly influence incites to do good, put away all sin, keep all the commandments of the Lord, + to live a holy, pure life. Hath not the voice unto you taught you to do all this? Yes, verily. Was it not good? yes, verily. As no good comes from Satan, but only from God, this was the voice of God unto thee. Dost thou not see it!" Oh, the mercy and goodness of the

[Page 671R]

11/Father to condescend to reason thus with me, so full of doubts and unbelief, and yet striving by all means in my power to gain faith and holiness and put away all my evils and my unbelief. So I knew it was the voice of the Lord unto me by the Holy Spirit. And the Lord says in a revelation "I will tell thee in thy heart and in thy mind" (See Doc + Cov Sec. 8 v.2) "Now behold this is the Spirit of revelation, behold this is the spirit by which Moses brought the children of Israel through the Red Sea on dry ground."[37]

Thus I learned the voice of the Holy Spirit—the spirit of revelation, but only in weakness and trembling. But I prayed and fasted much, asking for the Spirit of revelation, that I might <u>know</u> the voice of the Holy Spirit, even as plainly as did Moses, and that I might not be deceived by any other spirit. And the Father, in His mercy, and for His own purposes, has greatly blessed me in this, and hath many times answered my questions and instructed me in regard to principles I did not understand, as plainly as one talking with another. All honor, and glory be to the Father for His mercy forever.

---

36. See James 4:8 and D&C 88:63.
37. See D&C 8:2–3.

19/ Went with Mr. Thomas, Engineer of the Royal Albert docks, London, to look at my proposed work on the Rillito. He greatly approved what I had done, and my plans. Prayed, and was told the Lord was going to prosper me soon. So I went and bought me a hat, out of my little money. I was told to wear good clothes, and not to doubt, So I also bought a shirt and some collars and neck tie, believing the intimation of the Spirit.

20/Wrote to Susan, and blessed her. She deserves it all. She prays for me and comforts me, prophecying good for me.

22/ Presented my field notes of Survey to Sur. Genl Johnson. Sent article for "Contributor," and article for "Star" on the "Manifesto" of Last Conference.[38]

30/Recd a letter from F.K. Nebeker, who asks me for Lilla.

31/Told Nebeker "yes"—if he would be good always to Lilla and be a true L.D. Saint. Recd a letter from Don LeBaron who is distressed about the mortgage, as he wants to sell.

[Page 672L]

1890/[Blank line]

Oct. 31/I felt very badly about it, and asked for help. I was greatly comforted. Told I should be able to pay every debt and no one should lose by me, but be benefited for they should sell for a better price than they could obtain now. So I was comforted; for I believe it, though I cannot See any way for it to come true, naturally speaking. Samuel + Elvira are also much distressed, for their kindred are very angry with them, and treat them Shamefully, which adds much to my grief. Wrote to comfort them, and prophesied good for them.

November/[Blank line]
2/Wrote article for "Star" and "Gazette."[39] Fasted + prayed, and had precious principles explained to me by the Spirit. I fast now each Sunday and

---

38. The article for the *Star* appeared unsigned and under the title "Fair Play," *Arizona Daily Star*, October 26, 1890, 4.

39. This was an editorial letter, criticizing a speech by James G. Blaine and the so-called "great steps" or "movements of advancement" made by the Republican Party. See Santiago, "Blaine's 'Republican Advancement,'" *Arizona Daily Star*, November 4, 1890, 4, and Santiago, "Blaine's 'Republican Advancement,'" *Arizona Daily Gazette*, November 5, 1890, 3.

Thursday—all day, striving to gain power ^favor^[favor is placed directly above power] with the Lord, faith, and spirit of revelation. I also pray regularly morning, noon and night, besides other times. We are so counseled to do by Apostle Lyman, and I find the more I pray, the more I gain in faith and the Holy Spirit, which testifies to me when I pray that my prayer is heard and will be answered. But I am told that although what I ask for is <u>right</u>, it is not expedient to have every thing at once, but a little at a time, lest the top of the tree outgrow the root; and thus grow more steadily, slowly and safely. I can see this is best. So if I do not get what I desire <u>now</u>, it is because it is not for my best good; therefore I am content, knowing that the Lord doeth all things well.

5/ Letter from "Contributor." Praise for my articles + wish me to continue writing. Wrote "<u>A Stolen child</u>."[40]

6/fasted, ^7th^ revised my article for publication.

8/A good comforting letter from Br. M. Thatcher. Hear good news about our Canal. Am desired to make profile and report, for parties in New York. This took me several days, but only in the end for disappointment, and double discouragement.

13/Had a letter from Mr. Blaisdell. I had given him a check for $22.00, and it was found I had no

[Page 673R]

1890/[Blank line]

funds in the bank. His letter was a scorcher. I was very much distressed. Disgrace was before me, and I had no money to pay it nor any way to earn any. I had eaten nothing from Tuesday to ~~Thursday~~ ^Saturday^ evening for want of money for meals, keeping 50¢—all I had—for an emergency. I fasted and prayed "Oh Father help me in my distress, and help me that I may not be disgraced." He comforted me, and said my way should be opened. To ask Judge Barnes (who had told me he would not advance another cent upon any consideration) for money; that he would let me have it, and be a friend to me. So I felt comforted, though it was hard to believe I could get any money from Barnes, knowing his cold, greedy Spirit for wealth, and his inordinate selfishness. I prayed earnestly for faith.

---

40. See Santiago, "A Stolen Child," *Contributor* 12 (December 1890): 75–78.

[In margin next to following paragraph: Henry's baby girl was born Nov. 14. 1890/ of Melissa.]

14/ I asked Barnes for $30.00 to pay Blaisdell and for a week's board at the restaurant. He would not, but when I said I had not eaten for so many days, he let me have it without a word. I will remember him for it. It was the answer to prayer, and fulfilled the promise of the Father to me, in every particular. Oh my Father, I thank Thee, and praise and adore thy holy name for all thy goodness to me a sinner. Oh that I may be able to spend the rest of my life in doing the will of my Father, who is so good to me in thus teaching me faith in Him, and how to know the voice of the Spirit by so many testimonies—promises + fulfillments.

I feel that surely God is preparing me for some thing great—that I may yet do a great work for Zion, and thus preparing me for it. I paid Blaisdell, and got a week's meal ticket = $5.00 with $3.00 left.

16/Sunday. Fasted as usual, and climbed Sentinel Hill It was shown me that Moroni stood on this hill and viewed the camp beneath of his retreating host of Nephites, who marched past this point on their way from south, coming by where Nogales now stands, the only natural pass west of the Sierra Madres. As I call it

[Page 674L]

1890/[Blank line]

November/Moroni's Hill. Prayed and had a blessed time.

20/Wrote "Utah in 1850" for "Contributor."[41]

23/Sunday. Fasted and prayed. Was told I should begin to prosper from this very hour; my way will open; friends will be raised up to me, and I shall be blessed.

26/ Was engaged to work as special draughtsman in office of Surveyor General, to make a map of the west boundary of the White Mountain Indian reservation, 92 ½ miles long, at $125.00 per month. Thus hath the Father begun to fulfill His promise in blessing me. Father, I thank thee.

December/[Blank line]

---

41. This article gave a description of early life in Parowan. See Santiago, "Pioneer Sketches. Utah in 1850," *Contributor* 12 (January 1891): 93–96.

4/ Recd letter from Col. R.J. Hinton, Interior Dept, Washington, requesting me to send statistics about canals +c.+c[42]

10/ Henry says in his letter Melissa's baby was born Nov. 14/90

Susan says we now have 38 grand children, as follows:—Henry 7, Moroni 7 Elvira 7 Nephi 4 Albert 1 Lyman 5 Charly 3, Hagberg 4 = 38 The promise to me is that my Children shall become a great nation, and it will be fulfilled.

11/ A letter from Susan. She has had a hard time and has done nobly. Her brother Almon went to Deming, took smallpox came home and died. Then his wife and two children died in a week or two, and his three remaining children were quarantined 1 ½ miles in a house all alone, no one daring to go to them, only to bring them provisions. Susan and her niece Anna Hilton, went one day to see them and determined to stay with the poor little stricken flock of 15, 11 and 8 years of age, although neither of them had had the disease, and were therefore almost certain to take it. and there was no physician or medicine in the country. So they staid several days, until some one was sent as nurse who had had the disease, and they returned home. But God wonderfully blessed them, so that neither of them took the disease nor infected any of their families by their clothing. It was a true miracle, or exhibition of the power and blessing of the Lord, and of faith and heroism in Susan + Anna. May the Father bless them forever. I blessed her in letter.

[Page 675R]

1890/ 1890–1891

December/13/ Was in great need of money to pay tax on my land in Pima, to prevent its being sold by the Sheriff, and today got $60.00 Sent me by Susan, who sold our new wagon to Henry for $150.00 So I sent money for taxes to Pima.

14/ Sat. Fasted 24 hours. A letter from Susan, telling of her danger. Does not know yet if She will have Small pox or not. Prayed much for her. Elvira + Sam write that Uncle Benjamin, Don LeBaron and others had to flee to Mexico on a few hours notice to escape arrest for polygamy.[43] I had just

---

42. Martineau provided Hinton with statistics showing mileages of ditches, acreages of irrigated land, and sources of water supply. See Hinton, *Progress Report on Irrigation*, 290–91.

43. At this time, rumors were circulating in the east of a Mormon exodus to Mexico. See "The 'Mormons' and Mexico," *Deseret Weekly* 42 (January 3, 1891): 40.

written Uncle Ben that his place was in Mexico, and he skipped while my letter was on the way to him, + reached him in Mexico. So I was led aright.[44]

17/ Nephi writes he has bought a lot of church cattle on credit, of Bp. Preston.

21/Sunday. Fasted as usual, all day

25/Thursday. do   do do   do

27/Wrote for Contributor "Athirst in the desert."—my own experience near Gila Bend some months ago.[45]

28/Fasted.

29/Sent $4.00 for Juvenile Instructor for Susan + Henry.

31/Recd $131 $126.40 for this Month's work, also $20.84 for November.

January 1891 Thursday.

1/Fasted, to begin the year humbly and faithfully, in hopes I may do better this year than ever before.

Wrote article for Contributor "Legends of the Deluge."[46]

2/Believing that the Lord is going to bless me and open my way more fully, I bought an overcoat—$10.50—which I much needed in this cold weather

4/Fasted, as this is Sunday. Took a 5 mile walk. Wrote as usual to Susan

7/Snt $2.48 to Montgomery Ward + Co. for chess men + bible.

12/Very cold. Was obliged to buy a mattress for my Cot. $3.00 To day Joel started with three others across the Sierra Madre mts. into Sonora, to see a tract of land offered for Sale. This I learned from letters from Susan.[47]

---

44. The following day, Martineau wrote a letter to the *Deseret Weekly* regarding the climate and adaptability of the Salt River Valley for agriculture. See J. H. Martineau, "A Mild Climate," *Deseret Weekly* 42 (December 27, 1890): 18.

45. This article appeared under J. H. Martineau, "Athirst in the Desert," *Contributor* 12 (February 1891): 155–158.

46. J. H. Martineau, "Traditions of the Deluge. I. The Chaldean Story," *Contributor* 12 (March 1891): 167–171.

47. John W. Young had requested Bishop George W. Sevey to go with a small party as far as Onavas on the Yaqui River in Sonora, with a Mr. Morris who wished to sell a large tract of land for colonizing purposes. Joel H. Martineau left Colonia Juárez in company with Bishop Sevey, W. R. Stowell, and Peter N. Skousen on January 21 and went to Caretas

18/Fasted, being Thursday. I fast Sundays and Thursdays.

[Page 676L]

1891/[Blank line]

Jany 19/Subscribed for Sunday Republican for Susan. By Request of Agricultural Dept. Washington, I made them a report of Canals +c of Arizona.[48]

20/ By letter from Jesse N. I find he has been traveling through Germany, Switzerland, and Italy, Lyman having sent him money for that purpose. Lyman is a good son and a good brother, and has done much for his mothers children.

21/ Had fun with a phonograph this morning at Genl R. A. Johnson's house for the first time in my life.[49]

22/ To day I was greatly frightened. The Sur. Genl (Johnson) told me he expected my Survey would be rejected. The Gov. Inspector had reported to him that a certain corner was not as represented in my notes, +c +c If my survey be rejected I will have no means to repay my loan at the Tucson Bank ($200.00) nor redeem Sam's mortgage, and disgrace and shame will cover me. I walked in the public Square until late in the night, + besought the Father to avert such great disaster. I prayed that He would take me, rather than have it happen me. The Holy Spirit comforted me, and said I should _not_ be disgraced; all will be well; to see Bussey (Govt Inspector of Surveys) and he will be my friend.

23/and will help me. I saw Bussey, and explained about the Corner to Bussey's satisfaction. He said he will do all he Can for me.

I have continually extraordinary trials and contradictions (Spiritual) but I believe they are to test my faith, and to prepare me for something better and greater, that I may do a greater work. Also to teach me to know and trust the voice and teachings of the Holy Spirit, that it may be a guide

---

Ranch where Mr. Morris met them. See Joel H. Martineau, "Colonia Oaxaca Settled," *Improvement Era* 53 (November 1950): 889–890, 892, and 894.

48. See note at entry for December 3, 1890, above. James Hinton's progress report for 1890, prepared under the direction of the secretary of agriculture, named Martineau as the compiler of the tables providing the number of ditches and irrigated areas in Graham, Maricopa, Pinal, and Yuma counties. See Hinton, *Progress Report on Irrigation*, 290–291.

49. General Royal Johnson was Surveyor General of Arizona from 1883–1885 and again from 1889–1892. See note at entry for August 10, 1889.

to me. The promise "Come unto me all ye weary and heavy laden and I will give you rest." is a great comfort to me, and I do strive with all my might to come unto Him.

Sent another article to Contributor "Traditions of the Deluge."[50]

27/ Bad word again about my Survey. It seems sure to be rejected. No hope, naturally speaking. Prayed, and the Lord comforted me, just as He did before, repeating the same promises. It gave me faith, though I can

[Page 677R]

1891/[Blank line]

Jany/not see how it can come about.[51]

31/ Recd my pay for this month, $129.60.

February 1891 Sunday

1/ ^Sunday^ Walked upon the mountain west of Tucson + prayed. I found beautiful flowers growing there among the rocks. I Sent Albert $10.00 to help pay his taxes. Fasted

8/ Fasted all day as usual, being Thursday. Paid my note in Bank for $175.00 + $13.00 interest = $188.00 I thank thee, my Father, that one big debt is thus paid.

11/ To day Albert's baby was born (learned subsequently)

14/ Letter from Virginia Says she is going to marry Edd Sudberg in a few months, and desires my approbation.

15/ Sunday. Fasted as usual and wrote to Virginia.

16/ Sent 38¢ for book on chess, also for a book for Dora. Letter from Elvira. Says her baby had been very sick, saved only by faith and the priesthood. She feels very thankful, continually, She was taught by her parents to pray to God while a child. Her prayers have often been answered.

---

50. This was probably the second installment of two articles. See Santiago, "Traditions of the Deluge. II. Greek and Other Traditions," *Contributor* 12 (April 1891): 213–217.

51. Two days later, Martineau wrote to Susan Ellen with counsel about teaching the children moral principles. See James H. Martineau to Susan Ellen Martineau, January 29, 1891, Martineau Collection, MS 4786, box 1, fd. 6, LDSCHL.

17/ Albert writes me of the birth of their baby girl, born Feb. 11th She is named Emma. He had sold his place and will move into Mexico next fall.

18/ Last Monday Morning about 2 A.M. I awoke + prayed, + asked how I might know positively the voice and teaching of the Holy Spirit, and how did Moses know it, being taught, as the revelations tells us—"I will tell you in your heart + in your mind" +c (See Chap. 8 Doc + Cov.) which is called the Spirit of revelation. I was shown how Moses was taught, and ^he^ proved it by his obedience, which brings not only faith but <u>knowledge</u>. Also, it is right to anoint my own body or members when diseased to bless it, and rebuke disease from it as from the body of any one else. I asked this because of my rheumatism, catarrh and injured voice, + lungs. So I arose, lit a candle, and anointed and blessed various parts, + rebuked disease. The

[Page 678L]

1891/[Blank line]

Feb. 18/pain all left every part. I was told I should be healed by so doing, and not to buy drugs + medicines. I had been thinking to buy some catarrh medicine + liniment. I felt a strong faith in this ordinance and in the promises, and will not buy drugs any more. I felt overflowing with joy to think the Lord would so teach me so sinful as I am. But He is full of mercy.

19/ Recd a letter from Edward Sudbury, asking for Genie. I told him in reply—yes, if he would love + cherish her, and so live as a Saint as to gain his celestial glory. Not knowing him myself, I wrote to Lyman, + sent him Sudbury's letter, if he could say nothing against him.

20/ Wrote to F.F. Hintze, late a missionary in Armenia, asking for date +c on monument of an ancestor—a Roman Officer, whose ancient tomb he saw in Armenia.[52] Erected in memory of one Martinus.[53] The Encyclopedia Brittanica Says my name—Martineau—was Martinus in Latin,

---

52. This was Ferdinand Friis Hintze (1854–1928), of Copenhagen, Denmark, who was appointed president of the Turkish Mission in the fall of 1886. See Frederick Stauffer, "Turkish Mission," *Latter-day Saints' Millennial Star* 53 (December 14, 1891): 797–799.

53. This probably refers to an inscription found at Cyrrhus (Nabi Huri) in the province of Aleppo, Syria, and is believed to be related to the Parthian wars of the third century. The person named on the tomb, Martinus Aurelius, appears to have been a *miles* (soldier) of *legio IIII Flavia*. See *Corpus Inscriptionum Latinarum* (CIL), III, pt. 1, no. 195. See also Pollard, *Soldiers, Cities, and Civilians in Roman Syria*, 262, and Dean, "A Study of the Cognomina of Soldiers in the Roman Legions," 226. Also see notes at entries for March 15, 1891 and January 1912.

Martino n Italian, Martiniho in Portuguese, Martino in Spanish, + Martin in German and English. I have ascertained my ancestors were of ancient Roman stock. Besides this ancient Roman Soldier—Martinus, in the year 235 A.D. another relative—a young girl 15 years old, was burned as a christian martyr. Her name was Martina—feminine form of Martinus. I have had her baptized, endowed, and sealed to me as a wife. Poor girl! She waited a long time for her redemption—over 1600 years. She was burned because she would not abjure her religion, only 15 years old. How many L.D. Saints would do that to day? Would I be able to do it. I would not like to be tested.

22/ As I was going to my room to night about 12.30 (midnight) a fellow wanted to rob me as I was returning from playing chess, but he did not make it out.

[Page 679R]

1891/[Blank line]

Feb. 26/ Word came from Washington that my Survey is approved! Words are feeble to express my joy and thankfulness. The amount—$518.14 was almost like a gift, for the Surr General had said the survey would be rejected; though I tried, as much as possible, to have faith in the promise made me by the Holy Spirit that I my survey would be approved and I would get my pay.—a promise made me when in anguish of Soul I cried unto God for help, almost wishing for death. The Father gave me peace and comfort, but when I began to think about it naturally, it seemed so unlikely that I feared lest I had been deceived, and that some other—some evil had deceived me. But when I prayed to know about this, the answer was always the same—I should <u>not</u> be disgraced but should get my pay, and this would be another testimony to me that the voice which had spoken to me was the voice of the Holy Spirit—the same that spoke to and led Moses in the wilderness. This, then, was my greatest joy—to know that the Lord hears and answers my prayers, weak + Sinful as I am, in His wonderful mercy + goodness. How merciful should <u>we</u> be to those who injure us, when the Lord is so merciful to <u>us</u>! I pray thee, oh Father, to forgive my weakness and doubts! Help me to put away all doubt, and have full trust in Thee, and help me that I may <u>know</u> the voice of the Spirit as plainly as did Moses thy Servant!

28/ Recd my month's pay, $92.40

March 1891

1/ Fasted, Sunday. Wrote to Susan as usual. All this winter I have written many letters each week, to Susan and the children, teaching them principles of truth and holiness to the best of my ability, that I may be clear, and that they may be one with me in the building up of the work of the Lord, and that the promises made me may all be fulfilled, as I believe they will be, for I have faith that the Lord will help me.

[Page 680L]

1891/[Blank line]

March 4/ Took a very bad cold—like La grippe.

4 7/[4 crossed out] This morning after prayer I received instructions about my

7/ house I shall build in Mexico, and a room in it dedicated to prayer +c And of blessings I shall receive in it. Also that I shall receive all my canal pay in due time; also great and glorious promises of blessings and prosperity + usefulness in Mexico, which I believe but will not write now, lest I seem like boasting. It is not boasting in me, but a wish to show the goodness of the Lord to me, and how He fulfills His promises—that I write these things for an example to my family.

8/ Sunday. Fasted as usual.

10/ Finished my Maps to day, and cease work in the office. I have received in all, these, $402.63 and $5.00 besides, making $407.63. This has enabled me to pay much of my debts, but I still owe Tempe $600.00 and $110.00 at Deming, both at 1 ½ % pr. month interest, which I do not know how to pay, having now no more work. But I have a promise from the Lord that I will soon be able to pay all honorably, and I believe it. My pay is $34.65 making as before stated $402.65[54]

---

54. On February 20, the Commissioner of the GLO notified Gen. Johnson that the notes and plats of Martineau's survey of Tp. 8 S., R. 1 E. (under Contract No. 15) were approved. Even though there were a few discrepancies in the measurement of lines, he wrote, "this may result from the exceedingly rough character of the country." According to the Commissioner, Martineau's field notes were "examined and compared with the accompanying plat, from which it appears that the work has been fairly well executed in conformity with the Manual of Instructions." Two weeks later, on March 4, the Commissioner's office indicated that an adjustment and correction had been made to Martineau's account

13/ My Birthday—63 years old!. I, who always used to think I would not pass 40. At first I thought I would have a treat to day—a good 50¢ dinner (as I usually eat but twice a day, often only once a day for several days together) Then I thought best to begin my 64th year in humility—fasting and prayer, that I may do better this year than the last. So I fasted all day, and had many precious keys given me to understand why I was led to leave my beautiful home in Logan for the South with a miserable house and poverty; why I had been afflicted and tried as I have been—all of which have been for my experiences and good. Also received precious promises, which will all be so many additional testimonies when fulfilled. Recd loving letters from Susan and Henry. Also a call from J.W. Young, to go to Deming and be Engineer on his new Railroad which he is to build through Mexico to the Pacific.[55] Answered him. Said I would come.[56]

[Page 681R]

from $574.04 to $518.14. See Lewis A. Groff to Royal A. Johnson, February 20, 1891 and March 4, 1891, Letters Received, box 110: Vol. 13, November 25, 1890–October 23, 1891, letters #27 and 36, CSGAZ.

55. The officers for the new railroad consisted of: John W. Young, president; Thomas "Tomás" MacManus, vice president; Judge J. F. Crosby, Messrs. Storrs and Prevost, counsel; William Derby Johnson Jr., general manager; Ladislao Weber, chief engineer; Will Crosby, right of way agent. As Directors: John W. Young, Salt Lake City; J. F. Crosby, El Paso; Tomás MacManus, Chihuahua; Luis Hüller, Mexico City; W. Derby Johnson, Jr., Colonia Diaz; C. H. Dane, President of First National Bank, Deming; Gustav Wormser and Judge Murat Masterson also of Deming. Information from "A New Turn in the Railroad Matter," *Deming Headlight*, December 13, 1890, p. 3; "New Railway Organization," *Deming Headlight*, February 21, 1891, 3; and "Chihuahua, Sonora and Sinaloa," *The Mexican Financier* 17 (March 7, 1891): 564–565. See Hardy, "The Sonora, Sinaloa and Chihuahua Railroad," 269–279.

The Salt Lake newspaper reported on the railroad project with optimism: "We hope it will succeed. It will be a good thing for that country. And as it may open the way for colonists from crowded parts of the United States it will be a benefit to this country." From "The 'Mormons' and Mexico," *Deseret Weekly* 42 (January 3, 1891): 40.

56. This was the Mexican Pacific Railway enterprise initiated in the fall of 1890 by John W. Young to facilitate overland travel for Latter-day Saints to and from Utah. It was initially reported that Young was seeking to gain control of the Arizona and New Mexico Railroad route and extend it northward to connect with a road coming south from Salt Lake to make "a continuous north and south road from Utah to Sonora." Company headquarters was established in Deming, New Mexico, and Martineau would work under the direction of Chief Engineer J. Fewson Smith who was expected to arrive from Denver on March 14. See untitled, *Deming Headlight*, January 17, 1891, 3; "The Mexican Pacific," *Deming Headlight*, February 21, 1891, 2; "Mexican Pacific," *Deming Headlight*, February 28, 1891, 3; "Another Road to Mexico," *Deming Headlight*, March 7, 1891, 3; "The New Railroad," *Deming Headlight*, March 7, 1891, 3; and "The Mexican Pacific," *Deming Headlight*, March 14, 1891, 3. See also William Derby Johnson Diary, March 10 and 14, 1891, pp. 115–116, MS 1506, box 1, fd. 16, BYUSC.

1891/[Blank line]

March 15/Sunday, fasted. Recd telegram from Ex. Gov. Wolfley to Meet him and moneyed men from Illinois at Gila Bend and with them visit the site of his proposed dam across the Gila River and see, as an Expert, what damage, if any, the late tremendous flood had caused to the site.[57] Previous to this, by Wolfley's request, I had given him a plan for a timber dam at that point which he much approved.[58] I prayed about it, and was told to go—I should be blessed.

Recd letter from F.F. Hintze, the returned Missionary. He says the tomb of Martinus, the Roman soldier, is in the province of Aleppo, Syria. The inscription was much defaced by time, and the dates illegible. Says Br. Lecander was the one who saw it.[59]

---

57. Lewis Wolfley (1839–1910) was born in Philadelphia, Pennsylvania, on October 8, 1839, to Louis and Eleanor (Irwin) Wolfley. When both parents died, he and his brother were raised by an uncle in Pomeroy, Pennsylvania. During the years he lived with his uncle, Wolfley learned surveying and mining skills. While he looked for work in Kentucky, he joined the Third Kentucky Cavalry as a captain and helped stop Confederate incursions into the state. After participating in several mining ventures, Wolfley worked for Arizona Surveyor General Royal A. Johnson in 1884 and 1885. On April 9, 1889, Wolfley was appointed the eighth governor of Arizona. At the time of his appointment, he was a resident of Yavapai County and was a mining man and surveyor. During his term of office, he founded the *Arizona Republican* and initiated the Gila Bend Reservoir and Irrigation Company. His partisan politics divided the party, making it so unpleasant for his associates that he was forced from office before finishing his term. His mismanagement of the GBRIC caused him to lose ownership and led to subsequent civil suits with the Arizona Construction Company. He died in Los Angeles after being struck by a streetcar on February 12, 1910. See Keen, "Arizona's Governors," 11–12, Wrighton and Zarbin, "Lewis Wolfley, Territorial Politics, and the Founding of *The Arizona Republican*," and Peden, "Land Laws, Water Monopoly, and Lewis Wolfley in Gila Bend," 47–83.
The flood damage to Wolfley's canal and dam was reported under the headline, "High Water Again," *Arizona Republican*, February 24, 1891, 1.

58. See "The Progress of Irrigation: A Great Arizona Reservoir," *Irrigation Age* 3 (June 1, 1892): 67, and "Not Discouraged," *Arizona Republican*, March 12, 1891, 4.

59. This was probably Charles Urban Locander (1863–1927), who was called to serve in the Turkish Mission in the fall of 1888. See "Farewell Sociable," *Deseret News* 37 (November 14, 1888): 659, and "Arrivals and Appointments," *Latter-day Saints' Millennial Star* 50 (December 3, 1888): 779.
Martineau's son Joel later wrote: "On the 15th [of March 1891] he received a letter from Brother Hintze, who said that the tomb Martinus, a Roman General (possibly an ancestor) was in the province of Aleppo, Turkey [Syria], and that a Brother Locander had seen the tomb. Later Locander moved to Colonia Juarez and described the tomb to Father as built of white stone." Joel H. Martineau, Untitled Biographical Information on James Henry Martineau, p. 28. For more on this inscription, see notes at entries for February 20, 1891 and August 4, 1908.

16/ Letter from Edd Sudbury, thanking me for my consent.

17/ Went to Gila Bend, arrived at 8.30, breakfasted, then went with Wolfley, and William and Samuel Jack of Peoria Ill, up the river 24 miles to the Site for dam.[60]

18/ Made Some measurements of river bed. Dam will be 1800 ft long, and about 20 or 24 ft high. Returned to Gila Bend.

19/ Made Calculations for my report. Recd $45.00 fee.

20/ Returned to Tucson.

23/ Sent $100.00 to Bank of Tempe to apply on Benja's note. Wolfley wants me to Copy my map for him—4 copies.

24/ Recd draft from Washington for $518.14 ^of^ which I sent to Tempe $500.00 to finish payment of Benja's note. Oh how thankful I am it is all paid, just as I was promised, when all seemed so dark, and no earthly way to pay it. But the Lord fulfilled his promise to me, thanks and honor be unto Him forever. Wrote to Benja + Elvira to tell them the good news, that they and I are free!

26/ Sent my report to Wm Jack, Peoria Ill. Today Judge Barnes proposed to give to me and Geo. J. Roskruge a 1/12 share in the Tucson Land and Water Company in return for Preliminary Surveys we should make to bring water from the Santa Catalina Mts, to Tucson, 12 or 15 miles, in pipes. I believe I will be blessed in it, and so accepted the offer.[61] My share

---

60. This site was described three months later in the *Irrigation Age* and it was believed that the reservoir would irrigate from 200,000 to 300,000 acres of land. See "Arizona," *Irrigation Age and Western Empire* 1 (July 1, 1891): 93, and Arizona Construction Company, *Irrigated Lands*, 21.

61. George J. Roskruge (1845–1928) was born at Helston, Cornwall, England, on April 10, 1845, to John and Anne (Kendall) Roskruge. In October 1870, he immigrated to the United States and settled in Denver, Colorado. On May 26, he moved to Arizona where he was engaged in the surveying of public lands until July 1874, when he accepted a position as draftsman in the Surveyor General's Office in Tucson. After leaving that office in 1880, he entered into business as a surveyor and was appointed U.S. Land and mineral surveyor for the district of Arizona, and city surveyor of Tucson. In 1881, he was appointed superintendent of irrigation ditches for the Papago Indian Reservation. That same year, he was also appointed a member of the Board of Trustees School District No. 1. He was elected Pima County surveyor November 1882. Roskruge was appointed chief clerk in the Tucson Surveyor General's Office on July 1, 1893. In 1896, he was appointed U.S. Surveyor General of Arizona by President Cleveland, an office he held until 1897. He served as president and member of the Board of Education in Tucson at intervals from 1881 to 1914

[Page 682L]

1891/[Blank line]

March 25/would be 2000 Shares. The Company own a 1000 acres of good land near Ft Lowell—10 miles from town, and a Canal franchise.

28/ Got my receipt from Bank of Tempe for payment in full of Samuel's note and Mortgage. Finished my 4 maps for Wolfley + received for them $20.00 Wolfley wants me to make full plans and estimates for his dam and canal, and says I can be Engineer of the work.[62] Also Sur. Genl R.A. Johnson offered to give me another U.S. contract for a land survey of several townships. "When it rains, it pours."

29/ Fasted. (Sunday.) Went on the hills to pray + be alone.

30/ Began estimates +c for the Dam. Sent my monthly Gila Bend Canal Co. Account. The Company owe me at this date $6000.00 which I hope to get some time.

31/This morning had a joyful time and precious promises. Recd 2 volumes (bound) of Contributor, and one sent to Netta

---

and was an important figure in education in Tucson. He was instrumental in founding the University of Arizona and served as a member of the Board of Regents of the UA under governors Zulick, Brodie, Kibbie, and Sloan. Roskruge was active in the Masonic fraternity in Tucson and died in that city on July 27, 1928. From biographical information in Roskruge Papers and Surveying Documents, MS 0697, box 1, fd. 1, AHSL.

 The water project refers to the Rillito Canal Company's conveyance of the Rillito River water and its tributaries from the Santa Catalina Mountains to Tucson by canal and partly through redwood pipe, four hundred sixty-eight feet long and 4'6" in diameter. By means of a design engineered by Alexander Johnson Davidson (1843–1938), seepage water was obtained by a 1,300 foot concrete flume submerged in the bed of Rillito Creek and extended with this redwood pipe. See William E. Smythe, "The New Era in Arizona: The Rillito Canal Company," *Irrigation Age* 4 (February 1893): 287–288, and illustrations on p. 291.

 62. The water appropriation for the canal project was filed collaboratively in 1887 by members of the Gila River Irrigation Company; the land for the dam site was located and claimed by Lewis Wolfley and Royal Johnson of the Gila Bend Canal Company on October 27, 1887. A chain of subsequent sale and trust agreements gave Wolfley and Johnson the oversight of construction. Wolfley's part in construction was disrupted in 1888 when he was appointed eighth Governor of Arizona. Although Wolfley had conducted the initial location surveys, Martineau must have been contracted to carry out engineering assessments and surveys for the dam site. The Arizona Construction Company hired N. R. Gibson as engineer, but Wolfley, who trusted Gibson as an engineer, didn't trust him as a contractor. In response, he hired Alvin A. Dougherty of Los Angeles as engineer. See Peden, "Land Laws, Water Monopoly, and Lewis Wolfley in Gila Bend, Arizona," 51–68, and "The Progress of Irrigation: A Great Arizona Reservoir," *Irrigation Age* 3 (June 1, 1892): 67.

April—1891.

1/ Had a precious season of prayer this morning. Went to Santa Catalina Mts. this morning to see if we can bring water thence in pipes to Tucson. Returned on

3/ The plan is feasible and good.

4/ Recd my trunk from Gila Bend.

5/ Sunday, fasted as usual. Albert says they named their last baby girl—Elzadie, after Emma's mother.

6/ Wrote again to J.W. Young to know if he wants me still on his Mex. Pacific R.R. Survey.[63] I would rather be there, on less salary, than work here among Gentiles And Mexico is to be my home for a time, and I would rather build up that land. Sent Spencer's Mex. map to him. Started out again to survey water route to Tucson from the mountains. We spent some days in this work, returning to Tucson on Friday 10th Found

10/many letters, as usual. Also letter from J.W. Young to Come to Deming as Engineer on R.R. @ $150.00 pr mo.[64] I prayed for guidance whether to go, or stay here and take the U.S. Surveying offered me, by which I can make much better wages, but be away from my family

[Page 683R]

1891/[Blank line]

Apr. 10/ My desire is to be near my family, and I decide to go to the new R. Road, and this the spirit teaches me.

11/ Wrote to Albert about my farm—to sell it. Wrote J.W.Y. I will come

---

63. The name of the railroad was officially changed from the Mexican Pacific Railroad to the North Mexican Pacific Railway. See untitled announcement, *Deming Headlight*, March 28, 1891, 3; untitled announcement, *Deming Headlight*, April 11, 1891, 3; and "Hon. John W. Young's Latest Enterprise," *Deseret Weekly* 42 (April 25, 1891): 564.

64. By this time, the railroad had progressed approximately fifty miles from Deming to the Palomas tract. See "The North Pacific Railway Route," *Deming Headlight*, April 4, 1891, 2. John Fewson Smith was employed as superintendent of construction and Ammon M. Tenney was contracted for the grading of the road from a point nine miles south of Palomas to Corralitos, a distance of ninety miles. The grading on this section of the road was to be completed by September 15, with "about one hundred teams and a proportionate number of hands at work." From "Hon. John W. Young's Latest Enterprise," *Deseret Weekly* 42 (April 25, 1891): 564.

and assist on his work.⁶⁵ Made plans and estimates for Wolfley, for his dam and Canal.⁶⁶

12/ Sunday. Fast + pray. Wrote some in my journal. Recd letter from Home as usual. Also from W.D. Johnson Manager North Mex. Pacific Ry, saying he would Send a pass for me.⁶⁷

13/ Made plan of dam for Wolfley, + recd $10.00 for it.⁶⁸

14/ Estimated on Sabina Cañon water works.

15/ do do do do Sent $4.50 to Deseret News for 1 yr. Some to Susan + 6 mos. Weekly to me.

16/ Sent $5.00 for books on Hyd. Engineering to Greely, Tony N.Y.

Worked in Sabina Cañon water works as usual. Up to date I have spent this season all my time since Mch 1st 1891 and previous to that time 3 months in 1890.

18/ The Baron von Wendt started to N.Y. City to day to sell [in margin: Sat.] his placer gold mine or get money to work it. He made me promise to go and survey for a Storage dam and pipe line, to work his placer, and

---

65. At a special meeting held March 19, 1891, J. Fewson Smith told the people of the work to be had in building Young's railroad from Deming to Corralitos. Many settlers from Colonia Diaz took contracts for grading, responding "willingly and with enthusiasm." At this time, a number of colonists were suffering from an outbreak of smallpox and diphtheria and the railroad project was seen as an economic boon. See Martineau, "Mormon Colonies in Mexico," Colonia Diaz, p. 41. See also Hardy, "Sonora, Sinaloa and Chihuahua Railroad," 272–273.
66. Martineau was probably asked to do engineering assessments and initial surveys for the dam site. Alvin A. Dougherty was ultimately hired as the project engineer. See note at entry for March 28, 1891.
67. William Derby Johnson, Jr. (1850–1923) was born at Council Bluffs, Iowa, to William Derby and Jane C. (Brown) Johnson on May 2, 1850. In 1871, Johnson settled in Johnson, near Kanab, Utah. In 1872, he accompanied Major John Wesley Powell on his second expedition down the Colorado River. He later moved to northern Mexico where he helped settle Colonia Diaz. He was bishop of the Colonia Diaz Ward, Juárez Stake, from 1886 to 1911. Johnson was general manager of the North Mexican Pacific Railway. He died on October 17, 1923 in Tucson, Arizona. See note at entry for March 13, 1891. For biographical information on Johnson, see Jenson, *LDS Biographical Encyclopedia*, 4:500, and Haver, "Exploring Southern Utah, 1872."
68. In March, under the newly passed Right of Way Act, the Gila Bend Reservoir and Irrigation Company (GBRIC) filed a right-of-way application and map with the General Land Office for the Gila Bend dam and canal. This gave ownership of diversions off of the canal to the GBRIC in addition to all other holdings. Martineau had probably prepared a map for this application. See Peden, "Land Laws, Water Monopoly, and Lewis Wolfley," 66.

promises to help my interests.⁶⁹ I felt impelled to tell him he should be prospered + blessed in his trip and business, which pleased him much.

Recd Letter from the Genl Manager of the N. Mex. P. Ry. Saying I am engaged as Engineer on that road.⁷⁰

19/ Sunday, fasted as usual

21/ Prest Harrison visited Tucson. I saw him. Great doings

23/ Sent article to Contributor "Trials and tribulations of a Surveyor."⁷¹ Directed Contributor and Journal to be sent to me here. I had a heavenly time this morning in prayer, and received great promises from the Father.

26/ Sunday, and fasted. Next day sent pay roll for Apr.

27/ Started with J.C. Scrivener for the placer gold mine at foot of Santa Rita mts.⁷² Camped 33 miles away.

---

69. Alexander von Wenden, or Alexander von Wendt (1849–1897) was born at Riga, Latvia, Russia, on August 12, 1849. He was evidently betrothed to a Margaret Leavitt (ca. 1851–1869) of Leith, Scotland. He and Martineau would later become close friends and roommates. He died on May 25, 1897.

Von Wendt's placers were located on the "Doxology" and "True Blue" mining claims in the Silver Bell Mining district, forty miles west-northwest of Tucson. He evidently needed Martineau's engineering expertise to determine the availability of water and devise a plan for storing and conveying the water to run the placers. In 1882, when the Director of the U.S. Mint made his annual report, he wrote of their prospects for silver:

> The Doxology, True Blue, and Spring are new discoveries, but promise to become important mines.
>
> The Doxology is opened along the ledge by eight different cuts, from each of which good ore has been extracted. These different openings were made in prospect for the location of the main shaft. Eight hundred tons of ore are now on the dump, as a result of these workings.
>
> The True Blue is on the same ledge, to the west of the Doxology, and has 200 tons of gray and yellow carbonate and chloride ores upon its dump, which give assays of from $15 to $122 to the ton.
>
> The Spring is still better developed than the Doxology or True Blue, and is said to show very flattering prospects. Twelve men are now employed, working in day and night shifts.

From U.S. Bureau of the Mint, *Report of the Director of the Mint*, 308.

70. Martineau was assigned to a surveying party charged with locating a section of line between Chihuahua and Guerrero.

71. See J. H. Martineau, "An Engineer's Tribulations," *Contributor* 12 (June 1891): 317–320.

72. Apparently Scrivener was an invested partner in von Wendt's mining venture. The journal never discloses the circumstances, but by mid-February 1892, von Wendt had severed his relationship with Scrivener. See untitled, *Arizona Weekly Citizen*, February 20, 1892, 2.

28/ At destination 58 m. from Tucson.

29/+ 30th Worked on Survey of dam and pipe line.

May 1. 1891

1/ Finished survey and started back to Tucson at 1 P.M.

[Page 684L]

1891/[Blank line]

May 2/ Reached Tucson 1 P.M. tired, hot and dusty.

5/ Editor L.C. Hughes of "Star" Said Miss I.C. DeVelling, a lady organizer of W.C.T. Union, who had read my poem "Twilight Memories," in the paper, wished me to call on her.[73] I did so, and spent a pleasant evening. She is a talented + good lady.

6/ Wrote an article for "Star" in reply to attack in "Republican" entitled "No polygamy in the Mormon Church now."[74]

8/ Finished estimates, map and report on the Santa Rita gold placer, and Sent to Baron von Wendt.[75] Also worked on Sabina Cañon water supply.

10/ Sunday, fasted as usual. Have been very busy on maps estimates and family correspondence all the time. I am still trying to gain the victory over all my sins, and trying to draw nearer to God. I am very happy, except that I so greatly desire to be with my dear family, but I feel that the Lord is leading me, and I desire to be fully subject to his will.

11/ This morning after prayer, the Lord gave me precious promises relative to priesthood and its calling, and in regard to temporal and spiritual prosperity—that from this time I shall prosper. Help me, my Father, to draw near to Thee.

---

73. He probably meant the poem, "Boyhood's Days," which was published in *Arizona Daily Star*, April 23, 1891, 4. The poem, "Twilight Memories," does not appear in the *Star*, but was closely related to "Boyhood's Days" as they were originally conceived together. See poems entered on October 1, 1867.

74. Martineau's article indicates that the authorities of the church and all members throughout the world had submitted to the laws of the land and were no longer teaching or practicing polygamy. See Santiago, "No Polygamy in the Mormon Church," *Arizona Daily Star*, May 8, 1891, 4.

75. This report is probably one of two or three surveys done to assess the availability of water for sluices. See note at entry for May 30, 1894.

12/ Election day for members to Constitutional Convention.

13/ Still working on my plans and estimates for Sabina water.

14/ Letter from Jesse N. in Berlin, Germany. He has been honorably released, and expects to leave England May 9th He had been to Munich, Nuremberg, Leipsie, Dresden and other places. He had gained a testimony for himself of this Gospel, and had baptized 12 persons into the Church. Father I thank thee for all thy goodness.

15/ Felt sad to day. Prayed and was much comforted + blessed.

17/ Sunday. Fasted as usual, and was blessed.

18/ The Baron Alex. von Wendt wrote me from New York, saying he wants me to do his Engineering for his placer mines.[76] I asked the Father, who gave me a testimony in regard to it. So I wrote him favorably.

20/ W.D. Johnson wrote me to come to Deming as Engineer on the New North Mex. Pacific Ry.[77]

[Unstamped page]
[Two-page letter of missionary release of Jesse N. from his mission, dated Mar. 19th 1891.]
[Page end]

[Page 685R]

1891/[blank line

May 21/Went to Nephi to visit B.S. + Elvira.

23/I went to Phoenix to See about Sam's mortgage. On our return Elvira and I crossed the Salt River on the ties, the river being dangerous to ford.

27/ To day D.T. LeBaron and family, Vilate Johnson and Aunt Susan Johnson and daughter went to Mexico. Surveyed Samuel's 160 land entry, Sub dividing it. Recd pass R.R.

29/ Started for Deming, and arrived there June 2 at 2 A.M. Stopped one day in Tucson to get my things. Read that Gen. B.B. Eggleston, gr. nephew of Ethan Allen, died 27 May 1891 at Wichita, Kansas. My relative.

---

76. See entry for May 30, 1894.
77. See notes at entries for April 6 and 10, 1891.

June 1891

2/ Find I must go to Chihuahua City to locate line to Gurrero, instead of being near my family. Disappointed.[78]

3/ Met Henry, first time in more than two years.

7/ Sunday Meeting at W.D. Johnson's. I spoke, first time in a year.

10/ Lilla was married to day to Frank K. Nebeker.

12/ Went to El Paso 6 a.m. At 6.15 P.M. left Juarez on Mex. Central R.R. and arrived at Chihuahua on

13/ at 6.30 A.M. on Saturday.

14/ Wrote letters to my family and others. Visited places.

15/ In Company with Chf. Eng. Smith examined Surveyed route for 16 miles on horseback.[79]

16/ Examined other possible routes.

17/ Made alteration in completed line ¾ mile. Broke inst.

19/ Began locating line from Completed portion (8m) and Continued at this work until Aug. 14th

20/ Moved into Camp at Las Escobas ravine, 8m away.[80]

---

78. While John W. Young sailed to London to close the business with the English syndicate supporting him in the construction of the road, the news reported:

> Work on the Mexican Northern Pacific south from Deming has been partially suspended the last few days, owing to the rulings of the officer in charge of the customs house, who will not permit supplies to cross the line without paying fully duty. The result is that everything has to go to Ascension 100 more miles from the border, for inspection and payment of duty, and then back to the locality. Efforts are being made to straighten out this complication. In the meantime the affairs of the road are otherwise very bright. Division Engineer Martineau shortly goes to Chihuahua to relocate the line of the branch of the M. N. P. between Chihuahua and Guerrero, preparatory to beginning the work of construction on that branch.

From "The Mormon Road," *Rocky Mountain News*, June 16, 1891, 5. See also *Arizona Weekly Citizen*, June 6, 1891, 4.

79. Of this, Martineau's son Joel wrote: "On the 15th he [his father] examined two routes on horseback from the Mexican Central Depot to a line that had been traded from the southeast part of the city and running southwest about 6 miles." Joel H. Martineau, Untitled Biographical Material, 28.

80. On this date, Martineau wrote: "I have been here about ten days, having been

25/ A.J. Stewart came as my transitman. It was unfortunate for me, causing my Subsequent departure from the work.[81]

July 1891

4/ Went to Chihuahua in the evening to the celebration.[82]

19/ Discharged Stewart for incompetency.

25/ Turned over the party to Mr. Mathewson, and began duty as topographer.[83]

---

detailed to this city [Chihuahua] to locate a line of the Railway from Chihuahua to Guerrero, a distance of about 160 miles, there to connect with the main line of the Mexican Northern Pacific Railway. This road will run from Deming, N. M., through the states of Chihuahua, Sinaloa and part of Sonora, traversing a country full of natural advantages, most of which today lie dormant for want of American energy and vim to utilize them." From J. H. Martineau, "The Prospects in Chihuahua," *Deseret Evening News*, June 26, 1891, 8.

Despite John W. Young's difficulties in securing capital, the *Deseret Evening News* was still reporting on the construction with optimism: "… earnest progress is being made, and the contract is let for 125 miles of grade, to be completed by September 15, 1891. About seventy miles of grade is now ready for the ties, while a hundred men and teems, besides a large force of Mexicans with the shovel, are pushing the work with vigor. As a promoter of the enterprise, Bishop Wm. Derby Johnson, Jr., of Diaz, stands next to Hon. John W. Young, and his object from the first has been to give employment and bring prosperity generally to the Latter-day Saints in Mexico." See L. A. Wilson, "Regions of Chihuahua," *Deseret Evening News*, June 6, 1891, 9. See also "Mormon Progress in Mexico," *Deming Headlight*, June 13, 1891, 1, and "United States of Mexico," *Deseret Evening News*, June 17, 1891, 5.

81. After losing his two-and-half-year-old daughter, Kathe, from diptheria on June 2, Bishop William Derby Johnson Jr. fell ill with a kidney infection (probably the E. coli virus) from drinking unclean water at Boca Grande. On June 28, he wrote in his diary:

> Today up for first time in 3 weeks. been very low with kidney heart trouble. one thing made me very much worse was John [Young] not honoring my draft on him for 5,000.00 which makes it very hard for me as everyone feels there is something wrong. Lindauer + Wamser would not let me have any more supplies for the RR. others the same, feel terrible bad down hearted + sick of John W's promises being unfulfilled + many think I am lying to them.
>
> The Engineers desire to quit work but I promised them to make them secure by holding the land I have of John W. in my name + Judge Crosbys until they get their pay.

William Derby Johnson, Jr. Diary, June 28, 1891, pp. 124–125, Johnson Collection, MSS 1506, box 1, fd. 16, BYUSC.

82. The next day, Martineau wrote: "Our railroad survey party worked all day some miles from town, but went in the evening to the city to witness the fireworks and hear the music of the two fine military bands of the Eleventh Infantry and Fifth Cavalry, both of which regiments are stationed here, as also a force of state troops, making several thousand in all." For more of his report on the festivities, see J. H. Martineau, "The Fourth in Chihuahua," *Deseret Evening News*, July 14, 1891, 8.

83. Six days later, William Derby Johnson Jr. wrote in his diary: "During this month I have passed a terrible period in my life worry + bother I never before felt + could stand

[Page 686L]

1891/ Home again in Juarez

Aug. 12/ Was transferred to the office in Deming, and will quit work. Was promised by J. Fewson Smith, Chf. Eng. that my pay should be continued to end of the month at full rate of $150.00 which promise he broke in settling, in Deming. I am glad to leave the Company, and to go home.[84]

14/ Joel and I left Camp, and in the evening left for Deming. Joel joined me in camp on June 19. having left home on the 15th Recd a letter from Smith to pay our way home, $40.00 Mex. Equal to $32.20 U.S. cash.[85]

15/ Arrived at El Paso 7.30 a.m. Joel left train at Galligo. At Las Escobas we left some good Mexican friends—Luis Anchendo + Wife, and daughter Tomasa. Catarina, Maria and Jesus, Also a little boy José. Arrd Deming at 8.30 P.M. Sunday, and fasted all day. Blessed.

17/ Wrote Susan to Come for me. Wrote Genie, and sent her names for temple work. Said names are noted in pencil in my temple record. Taken very sick.

18+19/ Sick. Fasted all day. Better to night (19th)

John W. [Young] went to England in June still there + does not send any money." William Derby Johnson, Jr. Diary, July 31, 1891, p. 126, Johnson Collection, MSS 1506, box 1, fd. 16, BYUSC.

84. By this time, it was probably becoming evident that wages would not be forthcoming. It was intended that the road would pass through Díaz, La Ascension, Corralitos, Dublán, then through the Chocolate Pass to Galeana and El Valle, but since Young was unable to secure financial support from investors, the work came to a halt. According to Martineau's son Joel, the grading was stopped ten miles beyond the Espia, a high hill that rose out of the plain south of the Boca Grande. See Joel H. Martineau, "Mormon Colonies in Mexico," Colonia Diaz, pp. 46, 58–61, and Hardy, "The Sonora, Sinaloa and Chihuahua Railroad," 275–276. Joel later wrote of his father: "He was a conpetant [sic] civil engineer with many years of experience, but on account of his trouble with A. J. Stewart, who was an incompetant [sic], and made trouble in camp, and was slow—Stewart made a big story out of it, and Father lost his job. On August 14th, Father and I left camp and took the evening train. I got off at Gallegos, and he went on to Deming." Joel H. Martineau, Untitled Biographical Material on James Henry Martineau, p. 29.

85. Of this, Joel wrote: "Before we left, Father received forty pesos' worth, $32.35 in American money, of which $12.10 was mine. At Deming he received a check for $183.47. They still owe him $147.36, and me more than $100.00 which I had hoped to have for my wedding stake, but which I never received." Joel H. Martineau, Untitled Biographical Material on James Henry Martineau, p. 29. The North Mexican Pacific Railway became known as the "Mañana Railway" because of the repeated delays of promised payrolls. See Bishop, "Building Railroads for the Kingdom," 79.

21/ Saw Albert and his little George, first time in 3 yrs.

22/ Settled with R.R. Co. They only pay me $362.14 instead of $450 as agreed before in Chihuahua. John Fewson Smith, the engineer, has deliberately lied to me about my dues.[86]

24/ Am tired of waiting for Susan to come for me and so took advantage of my R.R. pass to go to Los Angeles and Santa Monica, Cal. Was absent 5 days in all, bathed in the sea, and bought some clothing +c. Also passed near the new lake in Southern Colorado desert.—Found no one in coming for me and got a chance to ride as far as Diaz, paying $6.00 to Mrs. Black. Left Deming at ~~noon 5~~. 1.00 P.M. 29th Reached Diaz

Sept. 1/Sept.1. having had heavy rains all the way. Mrs. Black was very good to me on the journey for which may the Lord reward her. As I passed Boca Grande I saw Br. Gilt [Gilbert] Webb, who has been a friend to me, and blessed him.[87]

3/ Started for home, hiring Mrs. Black's son to take me for $5.^00^

4/ Reached home at Sunset, and met Theodore the first time in three

---

86. Smith was probably trying to put a positive face on a desperate situation. John W. Young was virtually incommunicado during this time, as William Derby Johnson pleaded with him to send money to pay creditors in Deming. Smith was undoubtedly told that money was forthcoming, when in fact it wasn't. Of this, Joel wrote: "The company that was backing John W. Young failed for some reason, and he could not get the necessary money to pay for the work already done, about one hundred miles from Deming, and from Chihuahua, so they had to shut down. The people of Colonia Diaz who had spent so much time on the road, and neglecting their farms and home work were nearly ruined." Martineau, Untitled Biographical Material on James Henry Martineau, 29. See also Hardy, "Sonora, Sinaloa and Chihuahua Railroad," 276.

In the spring, Johnson wrote to George Teasdale and Presiding Bishop William B. Preston, seeking aid for the people of the Díaz ward, indicating that they were in "destitute circumstances" and did not have sufficient flour. To Preston he wrote: "This state of affairs has been brought about by the extreme drought of last year which destroyed the crops and the failure of the brethren to receive all their pay for work done on the R R." William Derby Johnson to George Teasdale, April 23, 1892, Letterpress copybook, vol. 3, "Private letters," Deming, 1892, pp. 6–7, box 2, fd. 3, and William Derby Johnson to William B. Preston, May 17, 1892, Letterpress copybook, vol. 2, 1884–1893, pp. 557–561, box 2, fd. 2, W. D. Johnson Collection, MSS 1506, BYUSC.

87. Probably Chauncey Gilbert Webb (1836–1923), who was born in Kirtland, Ohio, to Chauncey Webb and Eliza Jane Churchill. He married Georgiana Kate Cropper on December 20, 1867, in Deseret, Millard County, Utah. He served as mayor of Pima, Arizona, and was charged as the ringleader of the Wham Paymaster Robbery. See Ball, *Ambush at Bloody Run*, 22, 24, 28, 34, passim. (See also journal entries beginning on page 649 above.) He died on December 11, 1923, in Casas Grandes and was buried in Colonia Juarez.

years, it being a year and a half since I had seen any others of the family. I thank the Lord.

[Page 687R]

1891/ October

Sept. 5+6./ Conference (the first) in the Mexican Mission at Juarez. Apostle Teasdale presiding. A very good time.[88] Manager A.F. Macdonald engaged me to Survey the boundaries of the Caralles [Corrales] Purchase, 5 ¾ miles wide 23m long, all in the Summits of the Sierra Madre mts.

16/ Today we held a celebration of Mexican Independence.

20/ Sunday. A boy was born this morning to Henry by Mary A. Thurston, at 12.10 A.M.

30/ To day Moroni's wife came to us much alarmed because her husband did not come home, and she feared he was dead. Susan told her all was well with him, and I afterwards said the same to her, having asked God about it, and having received an answer that all is well with him.

Last Sunday I felt impressed to say by the same spirit of prophecy to Bp. J.N. Smith Jr. when he was in very low spirits because of charges brought against him, that he would be fully vindicated and come out all right. He was greatly comforted, and I was glad to comfort him. Three days after, he came and said my words had proved true to the letter, and he rejoiced. I thank Thee, Father, for thy blessing to me, in giving me a portion of the Spirit of prophecy, for which I have fasted and prayed much.[89]

---

88. On September 7, Benjamin F. Johnson wrote that, while visiting Colonia Juárez, he spoke to the women at the Relief Society conference: "With kindred and friends took dinner at Bro. J. H. Martineau's. Blessed Winnifred's [Winifred Fredrica Johnson Guthrie] baby, ministered to and blessed 'Aunt Susan' my eldest brother's widow now aged and infirm and all present appeared to feel it a pleasant occasion." Johnson, *My Life's Review*, 338.

89. On this date, Martineau wrote to the *Deseret News* with a description of Colonia Juárez and the abundant resources to be had by its settlers. The letter read, in part:

> There is a much larger area of farm land than I had expected to see, fields of corn, cane and lucern extending up the river four miles. The cane is now being pressed for molasses. Many miles of ditches are in use, and another ditch is in process of construction. Everyone appears busy, for in new settlements a hundred things must seemingly be done at once. ... Juarez is principally adapted to mills and manufactures, the river affording abundant power which may be used over and over again; while the lands at Casas Grandes (twelve miles below) are rich and unexcelled for field crops.

> Despite its abundance, the colony was too far from a temple:

October

1/Thursday. Fasted as usual. Today Hermandes, wife + child were baptized into the Church, Mexicans.

3/ Sat. Started this evening with Theodore and J.M. Macfarlan Surveying Corrales Boundary line. Drove to Pratt's, 12 miles, and camped, remaining all next day, Sunday. Before I left I bought a stove of H. Shumway for $56.50. Henry took us with his team and wagon. Theo killed a wild turkey.

5/ Started up the cañon, and had heavy rains all day. Camped at O. Allen's dairy, and waited there all next day for men from Pacheco to help on our Survey.

8/ four men came from Pacheco, and we went to the place of beginning in Strawberry vally and camped, in a cañon of grand precipeces and cliffs.

[Page 688L]

1891/[Blank line]

October 9/Started on Survey of east boundary, running south. Had to climb a high mountain with our pack animals. Henry going round into Hop valley another way. Theo. killed a fine deer to day. Heard the cry of a mountain lion or Jaguar last night.

10/ Hard work crossing deep Cañons and precipices. Reached Hop Creek at sunset, and found Henry camped there. Henry had killed 5 wild turkeys.

10/ Spent the day in triangulating across Hop valley, wide and deep. Henry shot a bear, but did not kill him.

12/ Sunday. Henry and Theo. looked for the wounded bear, found him and killed him, and four men brought it to Camp. I did not eat any of

---

All countries have their disadvantages and Mexico is no exception; but the Lord has greatly, even wonderfully blessed His people here notwithstanding, and the people are full of hope.

And especially do we hope a temple may be built in this land before long, that we may work for the dead without being obliged to expend a year's revenue in a long and tedious journey to Utah. Scarcely any here can afford to go by rail, but have to go by wagon nearly a thousand miles across a desert or mountainous country, spending weeks in the journey each way. But we are willing in this to await the Lord's time, as in all things else.

J. H. Martineau, "Letter from Mexico," *Deseret Weekly* 43 (October 24, 1891): 589. Also see note at entry for November 28, 1897.

him. It was a large brown one. Henry went home for supplies. I went up to a cave once dwelt in by Cliff dwellers, high up the side of a cliff,[90] on the wall was traced a picture like this, some 20 feet long:–

[Drawing of cave art on left of page, text on right]

I was very tired, and under its influence wrote the following lines:–

[Poem follows:]
The Saint's Rest.
Rest for the weary hands
Folded across the breast!
Now that are sundered Life's silver strands—
Rest ~~for the weary~~ ^from thy labors^—rest!
2
Rest for the weary feet
Treading on stones and thorns!
Bruised and torn at every step—
Rest in the coming morn!
3
Rest for the weary eye
Tired with piercing the night!
Shineth now brightly the light on high—
Darkness hath taken its flight.
4
Rest for the ~~silent~~ ^weary^ tongue!
Long hath it plead for ~~right~~ ^light^!
[Last line older shaking hand and illegible]

[Page 689R]

[Poem continued]

1891/[Blank line]

~~Soon will its~~ ^Now shall its^ song of triumph be sung—
Truth hath put Error to flight!
5
Rest for the weary heart [shaky writing to right]

---

90. A number of ancient cave dwellings were discovered by Mormon settlers in Strawberry Valley and Cave Valley, through which the Piedras River flows. For more on the cave dwellings in these valleys, see Lumholtz, *Unknown Mexico*, 1:60–79.

Throbbing so oft in pain!
Never again shall the tear drops start—
Never, oh never again!
6
Thou who wast weary and faint
Rest, ^for Earth's^ ~~thy~~ labor is done!
Open to thee ^is^ the heavenly gate!
Now is thy glory won![91]
[Blank line]

12 ~~13/~~ Some more came from Pacheco, making 11 in all. I took the latitude by Solar Compass 30° 3' N. We moved camp, climbing difficult steeps with our 5 pack horses, + not knowing where we would find water. Camped at dark in a deep cañon, at ruins of ancients, but Theo. and W. Porter were not in camp. We fired guns, shouted, and I went up on hill side and kept a large fire burning for hours, shouting every few minutes. Other men went up on a high peak and built a fire. At last in answer to my shout we heard a faint answer a mile away, and heard a distant gun fired, and knew they were coming down the cañon. I had prayed much, and was answered that the young men were safe, but the sound of the answering voice was sweet indeed to my ears, and the dew dimmed my eyes. The boys got in all right. The shot we heard was one from Theo. which killed a fine deer. Oh, how good the Father is to hear my prayers! The Spirit also told me that Gertrude and Anna shall both have mates who will love and cherish them always, and gain a celestial exaltation. I received also many other precious promises.

13/ I started two deer today but did not shoot, as we had meat enough, and we must not shed blood unnecessarily One of the men killed a deer today, and one next day. Established a Stone monument for S.E. Corner of the Survey. 8700 meters from place of beginning

[Page 890L]

1891/ At the Rio de Gabilanas.

---

91. A version of this poem was published under the title, "Rest," in *Improvement Era* 5 (September 1902): 880. In explanation, Martineau wrote: "I was utterly exhausted, climbing precipices and descending almost impassable gorges, and was resting in a prehistoric cave which showed evidences of its ancient inhabitants. Upon the wall was engraved the form of a serpent about fifty feet long, with a human head and face. I thought, as I reclined, that perhaps I was then surrounded by the spirits who dwelt there—wondering who I was, and why in their ancient abode. I felt, but did not see them."

Oct. 20/We have steadily cut our way through heavy pines and across steep and high mountains and tremendous Cañons, until to day, when we descended the precipitous sides of a deep gorge of the Rio de Gabilanas, [below Rio de Gabilanas is written: (River of Hawkes)] 1000 ft deep, and only wide enough at the bottom for the rushing torrent. Strangely enough, we found our camp by an old stone ruin—Toltec—and enjoyed much the clear, cool water. I lay down early while the boys sing songs round our fire, and thought of the littleness of man compared with the works of nature, which suggests the following lines:–

[Blank line], poem follows
Song of the Torrent.
My couch is spread
In the rocky bed
Of a Cañon dark and wild
Whose craggy steeps
Full a thousand feet
Are cliffs and boulders piled
2
The Oak and pine
And clinging vine
And rocks that arch o'er head
Safe covert make
For Bear and Snake
And Jaguar, fierce and dread
3
There's a stealthy tread
About my bed,
And the panther's wailing cry
Is borne on the breeze
As it stirs the trees,
With ~~as~~ ^its^ Solemn, Eerie sigh.
4
The Torrent's Song
As it leaps along
Its rocky, devious way

[Page 691R]

[Poem continues]

Corrales Boundary Survey

Hath now a tongue
As it rushes on
And this I hear it Say:–
-------- 5 --------
"Vain man! who art so proud and strong
In self conceit so wise,
What is thy life? An infant's span!
what see'st thou with thine eyes?
[In different hand: Behold there open thine eyes!]
That grand old oak was strong and firm
Five hundred years ago!
What is thy life! A passing gleam—
A flake of melting snow!
6
That huge gray rock ~~that~~ ^which^ thee o'er towers
Counts ~~centuries~~ ^1000 years^ by scores;
Its years pass quick as summer showers—
Compare its age with yours!
And I, the Book that speaks to thee,
Through centuries ^thousands of years^ untold
Have sung my song unceasingly—
Cans't <u>thou</u> be called old?
7
~~And~~ ^Here^ mighty nations have been born—
Grown haughty in their pride;
Have waged great wars—been overthrown—
Decreased—decayed—and died!
And generations, too, have passed,
A countless, misty throng,
Have lived and died, until at last
Their names are e'en unknown.
8
Here, by thy couch old ruins lie
Of a race now lost and dead;
Unseen, their spirits hover nigh
And cluster round thy head.

For centuries they dwelt—increased—
And roamed these mountains grand,

[Page 692L]

[Poem continues]

1891/ Corrales Boundary Survey

October/Now, even Memory hath ceased
Of those who held this land.
9
Then what is man!—A passing sigh—
A note that floats in air,
Like clouds, a moment seen on high
That quickly disappear.
Then art <u>thou</u> old, thou passing Breath?
Dost <u>thou</u> lay claim to age?
A moment here—and then comes Death
To close thy earthly page."
-------- 10 --------
For a moment dumb
Is the Torrent's tongue
And ceased is its Sermon grand;
Our camp fire bright
Bathe with ruddy light
~~The cliffs on either hand~~
[added in shaky hand: Brightens the cliffs around]
11
Then again begins
The Brook to Sing
Its interrupted Song
And Stars shine bright
With Silvery light
As I lie and ponder long.
[Blank line]

23/Friday. Macfarlane, my aid, was unwilling to stay any longer on the Survey, and decided, against my protest, to go home, when we were within five miles of the end of South boundary. Our position was indeed difficult. We were on the brink of an immense gorge 2000 feet deep, down which it was almost impossible for our pack animals to go; but I had triangulated across it—1 ¼ miles—and got a point located on the farther ridge. So we turned back

24/ Sat. Descended to Gabilanas river 8 miles, thence up and over the main Summit of the Sierra Madres to Pacheco, reaching there at Sun Set, tired and hungry.

[Page 693R]

1891/[Blank line]

Oct. 25/Sunday. Attended meeting in Pacheco, then went to Br. Henry Lunt's to stay until we could get to Juarez

31/ Arrived at home, having staid last night at Br. H. Pratt's ranch, 12 miles from Juarez. Apostle Teasdale was there.[92] Took Lat. of Juarez with my Solar Compass and John M. Macfarlane's transit. It is 30°20' N. Long. 108°W Found my family well, for which I thank thee, my Father. During this trip He has strengthened me most wonderfully to endure the hardships entailed by high, steep mountains and almost impassible gorges; and He has blessed me in answer to prayer, with many precious promises. He also heard and Answered the prayers of Theodore on several occasions.

November

Nov. 5/Attended fast meeting and blessed Henry's last baby Frank Thurston, by Mary A. Thurston, his wife for time

12/Sowed lucerne seed on city lot + in field.

16/Began my map of the Corrales Survey.

22/Quarterly Conference of the Mex. Mission. G. Teasdale, presiding[93]

23/Today Joel H. Martineau and Mary Ann Thurston were Sealed for time by Apostle Teasdale in my house.[94]

---

92. See George Teasdale Diary, October 25, 1891, 47–49, Teasdale Papers, box 17, fd. 5, UUSCM.
93. For a summary of this meeting, see Teasdale Diary, November 22, 87–90, Teasdale Papers, box 17, fd. 6, UUSCM.
94. Of this event, Teasdale wrote:

We had a glorious conference in all our meetings and our Social Party was indeed a pleasant gathering. At the close of the afternoons meeting, upon invitation I went to

25/ While laying up adobes I was taken with lame back so as to be almost helpless. Continued Several days

December

Dec. 5/ Settled my herd bill with Moroni + paid him $67.00 I find we have 28 Cattle, and 8 belonging to Susan, and 29 horses including four of Gertrudes and 3 of Anna's

17/Killed a steer for beef.

25/Christmas. Worked all day laying adobes.

26/ My ranch account, for am't due the Colonization Co. for 1891 mounts to $30.00 being due ^wood $2.00^ on 29 ^$11.00^ horses + 32 ^$11.50^ Cattle also for rent of 5 acres ^$2.50^ land and two city ^$3.00^ lots.

On Christmas, I was able to buy only a pair of cotton Stockings for Susan's Christmas gift. Quite cold, 15°

29/fell from Scaffold while laying adobes, Somewhat jarred

30/finished the adobe house. Blizzard + Snow on 31st

31/just enough to whiten the ground.

[Page 694L]

1892/January/5/ Wrote these lines for a Song to the tune "Sounds from the ^Shore"^

[Poem follows:]
It breathes of Scenes forever fled—
Of happy hours to come;–
Of loved ones resting with the dead
Gone to their glorious home
It breathes of childhoods happy hours

Bro. James Martineau's and expected to have met Bp. Geo. W. Sevey to attend the marriage of Br. Joel H. Martineau and Mary Ann Thurston. But the Bishop did not come. So after waiting nearly, or over an hour, by request I performed the ceremony of marriage between Joel H. Martineau, son of James Martineau and Mary Ann Thurston, whose father was shot by the indians in Arizona some time ago. After the ceremony there were the usual congratulations and some refreshments.

Teasdale Diary, November 22, 92–93, Teasdale Papers, box 17, fd. 6, UUSCM.

And scenes of youthful glee
Of meadows green and wildwood flowers—
That sweet sound from the sea.
[End of poem]

24/Was put into office as one of the field and fence committee.

25/Helped lay off fence for the field.

Feb.-/ February

4/Started up the mountains to meet Col. Kosterlitzky Mexican manager of public lands of Sonora.[95] Camped.

5/ Reached G.C. Williams' house. The Colonel came in afternoon with his escort. Drew article of agreement

6/for sale of his land to G.C. Williams and others for $35.000 The estate is called "Los Horcones," (the forks) and has about 118000 acres, lying on the Bavispe river, in Sonora.[96] We have three years in which to pay for the land.[97] I believe God has brought this about, that we may get a foothold in Sonora. Br. Williams promises me the Surveying of the land, and Col. Emilio Kosterlitzky will make me State or Govt Surveyor for public lands in Sonora. I like the appearance of the Colonel much.[98]

---

95. Col. Emilio Kosterlitzky (1853–1928) also known as Emil Kosterlitzky was born in Moscow, Russia, on November 16, 1853, to Earnst Kosterlitzky (a Russian Cossack) and Emily Lenbert (a German). As a teen, he joined the Russian Navy and worked as a midshipmen until he deserted his ship in Venezuela, at the age of 18. He traveled to Sonora, Mexico, where he changed his name to Emilio and joined the Mexican Army. During the 1880s, he fought in the Apache Wars on the side of Mexico. He also assisted American troops pursuing Apaches across the border under the 1882 United States-Mexico reciprocal border crossing treaty. Kosterlitzky became known to the American troops as the "Mexican Cossack." Beginning in 1885, Kosterlitzky worked for the Mexican customs guard or *Gendarmería Fiscal*. He was captured in 1913 by revolutionaries during the Mexican revolution and after his release in 1914, he moved to Los Angeles, California, and worked as a translator for the US Postal Service. He died on March 7, 1928, and is buried in Calvary in East Los Angeles. See Smith Jr., *Emilio Kosterlitzky*, esp. 29–47, 95–126, and Truett, "Transnational Warrior, 243–246.

96. The Río Bavispe begins in Chihuahua and crosses the region from the north, cutting through Bavispe Valley and flows into Río Yaqui. See West, *Sonora*, 1–2.

97. See Naylor, "Mormons Colonize Sonora," 337–341.

98. As Borderlands historian Samuel Truett has observed: "Americans seemed irresistibly drawn to this immigrant officer. Perhaps it was the juxtaposition of a Russian horseman with the equally romanticized Mexican countryside. The idea of the Cossack as a free and 'wild' hero had currency among nineteenth-century audiences who equated this Old-World horseman with the American cowboy." Truett, "Transnational Warrior," 244.

7/ Started home, weather very cold. Heavy snow storm from Noon until 9 P.M. with cold piercing wind. Got home at 8.30 P.M. Glad. Found letters from North. Lyman's little girl Reita has died in Logan, age 3 yrs. Also got a letter from Gov. Wolfley, offering me charge of construction of a Canal 30 miles long, near Gila Bend, with good salary of $200 pr month.[99] I prayed for light and was told not to go there to labor for the wicked gentiles but labor in Mexico, and God will bless me.

9/ Wrote Wolfley, declining, with thanks. Also to Br. M. Thatcher, telling him what we have done. I decline Wolfley's offer because I wish to be with the Saints and help build up Zion; and not to help build up that

[Page 695R]

Go to Sonora.

1892/Feb./Gentile nation, for this was shown by the spirit to be my duty in answer to my prayer.

16/ Started to day with Theodore and Anna, also ^Moroni, Eddie, Br. Sixtus +^ others, to go over the Sierra Madre mts, to the new purchase on the Bavispe or Yaqui river, Sonora. Camped near some old Aztec ruins, the walls being yet about 30 ft high and 4 ft thick, built of adobes. It was once a large and important place, surrounded by outworks and walls.

17/Camped near Ramus, 25m Moroni joined us this evening, with our band of 22 horses.

18/ Drove to Casa de Janos, 20m thence 4 m. and camped.

19/ Nooned near Punta de Auga, and camped near Caritas.

20/ Laid by all day for rest of Company to arrive.

21/ Sunday. Br. G.C. Williams, our leader, came. Sixtus + David Johnson and Gruwell also came. Moved 3 miles.

22/ Mon. Began work on road over mountains, cutting oak and making dug ways. I was appointed president of camp. Col. Kosterlzky and his party camped with us on lost Cr.

---

99. The Gila Bend Canal and Dam was a water reclamation project initiated by Lewis Wolfley's Gila Bend Reservoir Company and later developed by the Arizona Construction Company of Peoria, Illinois. See Arizona Construction Company, *Irrigated Lands*, ii.

25/ Working every day on road. Rained heavily

26/ Still raining, till noon. Some of the company moved on.

29/ We moved over the Summit, about 2 ½ miles, + camped in deep ravine. Cold weather.

March 1892.

1/ Anna climbed a high mountain peak, alone.

2/ Heavy winds and rain, turned to snow in the night.

4/ Still snowing and blowing, + very cold, until 5th

6/ Moved 2 ½ miles to top of high peak. Moved again 1 m. on 8th

9/ Reached Bavispe River (Yaque) and camped. Met here a Company of Mexicans from Bavispe to welcome us. They brought a beef Steer and keg of mescal. Had songs +c.

10/ Began to cross a rough hilly Country, towards purchase. Very rough and bad roads 10 miles. It took us till the

15/Arrived at Los Horcones, and settled for work.[100]

16/Began to Survey the canal

20/Sunday. To day held meeting. How many centuries have elapsed since any saints have had a meeting in this land! Probably 1500 years. I presided. My thoughts were difficult to analyze.

[Page 696L]

At Camp Ferrochio Dora baptized

---

100. In a letter dated March 14 to the *Deseret Weekly*, Martineau wrote: "We arrived today—a new colony planted in Mexico, and the first in the State of Sonora. We are located on the estate called Los Horcones (the Forks), lately bought from Col. Emilio Kosterlitzky, commanding in northern Sonora, who has charge of public lands in connection with Gen. Juan Ferrochio of Hermocillo." After describing the land, acreage, and plan for financing the purchase, Martineau continued, writing, "Our beautiful townsite we have named Ferrochio (with the accent on second syllable) in honor of Gen. Ferrochio, a firm friend to our people. The leading men of Sonora have been desirous of having our people in their State to help build it up, knowing our reputation for industry and thrift, and in this the common people share fully. 'Now,' say the latter, 'we will have mills and machinery and good roads, and someone to show us how to get along.'" See "A New Mexican Colony," *Deseret Weekly* 44 (April 16, 1892): 554.

April   1892   May

1892/Constantly working on canal. Cool nights. Ice in wash dish.

March 25/Took latitude of Camp. Ferrochio—30° 27' N.

April/ April 1

1/Friday. Ice this morning on still water.

5/Snow on Mountain peaks around, + cold nights. Dora baptized.

6/Water in Canal at last, but dam is not yet finished.

7/Fast day. I fasted. Sixtus + David went to Juarez.

17/Got letters. Elvira had a new baby girl, born March 5th Her name is Emma Vilate. Nephi is called to go on a Mission to Europe next fall. Got letter from Ex. Gov. Powers relative to Canal near Gila Bend.[101]

20/Col. Kosterlitzky, wife, and escort come to visit us. Had a pleasant party in the evening, Songs +c +c[102]

---

101. Ridgley C. Powers (1836–1912) was born to Milo and Lucy Ann (Dickenson) Powers in Trumbull county, Ohio, on December 24, 1836, where he lived until adulthood. He attended the Western Reserve Seminary, and later took a scientific course at the University of Michigan. He completed his education at Union College, Schenectady, New York, where he earned a Bachelor of Arts degree in 1862. After leaving college, he enlisted in the 125th Ohio Infantry and was promoted to first lieutenant and then became captain of his company; he fought in several campaigns during the Civil War and participated with the army of the Cumberland. He was elected lieutenant governor of Mississippi in 1869. In 1871, when J. L. Alcorn was elected to the US Senate, Powers became governor, serving as such through 1872 and 1873. At the expiration of his term, Powers returned to his plantation which he sold in 1879, in order to remove to Arizona. During his years in Arizona, he was engaged in civil engineering and was a deputy mineral surveyor. See *Portrait and Biographical Record of Arizona*, 123–124.

102. In his news correspondence, Martineau was quick to acknowledge Kosterlitzky's generosity:

> Co. Kosterlitzky said to me, 'we have 3800 men in the Bavispe district, and all of them together would not have done so much work in three months as you have done in this short time.' The presidente (mayor) of Bavispe and other officials came to visit us while we were blasting our roadway, and were astonished. They have furnished us three beeves, gratis, and will aid us more if needful. Col. Kosterlitzky has been especially kind, and should be held in grateful remembrance by our people. The governor, also, has directed the presidente of Bavispe to give us any assistance we may need. ... The Colonel refused two offers for the estate, cash in hand, in order to have the 'Mormons' colonize it. One of these offers was from a Catholic party in Illinois and the other from some stockmen.

From "A New Mexican Colony," *Deseret Weekly* 44 (April 16, 1892): 554. See also Naylor, "Mormons Colonize Sonora," 331–332.

28/ The water in the canal got to the field, for the first time. I planted Squashes, corn +c Set out our fruit trees.

May 1

May 1/Sunday. Up to this date I have presided over the camp, by vote of the colony, but Br Williams, lately returned from Chihuahua says Bp. J.N. Smith had appointed P.A. Dillman to act as Presiding Priest over the Colony. So today at meeting I stated this, and resigned to him.

2/ Surveyed our field, and find we have only 25 acres in it,—about an acre to each family. Our Canal and dam has cost us nearly $2000.00 making cost of our water $80.00 and more, for acre. This is owing to the bad management of Br. G.C. Williams, who will have everything his own way, as he is the purchaser of the Ranch of Los Horcomes, which consists of 26 ½ Sitios of 4428 acres each, making about 118000 acres in all. Theodore and I have constantly worked on the road and Canal, most of the time living on dry graham bread and water, having no groceries, meat, butter nor milk. I dip a piece of dry coarse bread in water, and am very thankful for it. The Lord has caused the Mexicans to be very good to us, bringing us meal, beans and sometimes beef, which we got on credit, and have told us not to go hungry. They think we have done a great work. Col. Kosterlitzky said to me in March

[Page 697L]

1892/May/"We have 3800 men in this District, and the whole of them would not have done as much work in 3 months as you people have done in two weeks." There never was a road from Sonora to Chihuahua, until we made it,—a small party of 22 men. There was a <u>burro</u> trail, but that was a very steep and difficult one

4/ Today Anna is 17. She is bright, cheerful, strong and healthy, a favorite with all in camp, and a great blessing to me on this trip.—never complaining at any hardship or discomfort. And the same with Theodore

11/ Planted potatoes, and cane, also squashes and melons.

16/ We started home today, but not being able to get up the steep hills, had to return. Yesterday, 11 P.M. Col. Kosterlitzky and his troops passed our camp in pursuit of hostile Apaches who had stolen some horses. He returned on the 24th having killed the indians and got the horses.

24/ I went to Bavispe, 21 miles, to rent land for corn. On the way I asked the Father to open my way to do so if it was best, and to close it up if it is not for the best. The Col. Said he had got a good farm for me, and I went to see it. The land belongs to <u>Donaciano Parra</u>, the

25/Guide. Accepted the offer. I take his field of about 15 acres, for three years, to pay no rent, but bring it into cultivation by ditches, plowing +c. Got all the papers made out and returned to Ferrochio. This old place—Bavispe—was destroyed by earthquake 5 years ago, and many people killed. Altitude of the place, by U.S. barometer = 3600 feet.

30/ Finished up our field fence and Moroni's. To day Patriarch Lunt gave Gertrude a blessing:–
[Blank line]

A blessing by Henry Lunt, Patriarch, upon the head of Gertrude, daughter of James Henry + Susan Ellen Johnson Martineau, born Sept 28th 1870 Logan Cache Co. Utah.

Beloved Sister Gertrude inasmuch s thou hast desired a blessing at my hands I feel to comply with thy wishes as thou art worthy through obedience

[Page 698L]

Gertrude's blessing

1892/May/30th/to the gospel, also by lineage, being of the blood of Ephraim, and a daughter of Zion born under the new and everlasting covenant, and being pure in heart and meek in Spirit. The Lord loveth thee for thine integrity, and for seeking after the imperishable riches of heaven. Thou shalt realize every desire of thy heart in righteousness, and shall be blessed in the own due time of the Lord with husband, by whom thou shalt raise up a numerous posterity, that shall become great in goodness and virtue and righteousness; and in connection with thy husband thou shalt reign as a Queen in heaven in celestial glory. Thy name is written in the Lamb's Book of Life, and thy guardian Angel watcheth over thee. Thou shalt be healed up of all thine infirmities and injuries that thou hast received to thy body. I seal upon thee a renewal of health and strength, and reconfirm upon thee all thy former blessings, ministering angels shall visit thee + converse with thee in a familiar manner as one friend with another, and shall reveal unto thee many important things that shall fill thy soul with joy and gladness unspeakable. Give thy heart unto the Lord in thy young and tender years and great wisdom shall be given unto thee, and thou shalt become a bright and shining light amongst the daughters of Zion. Keep the Word of Wisdom and thou shalt have a healthy body, and live until thou art satisfied with life, shall sleep but for a little season, and come forth in the morning of the ressurrection, crowned with glory, immortality and eternal lives in connection with thy husband, all of which blessings I seal upon thy head in the name of the Lord Jesus Christ. Even So. Amen.

31st/[Blank line]
Monday/Theo and I went to our farm near Bavispe, to begin planting

June/ June 1

Tues. 1/Leveled a ditch for our land to bring water upon it, over half a mile long. Watered land, plowed, and planted corn and cane.

4/Returned to Fenochio (our Camp, named in honor of Genl Juan Fenochio)

Monday 6/ Paid G.C. Williams on provision a/c, or land, $10.00 Cash, and a Stove, $15.00 – $25.00 Sold my farm in Pima to John Kartchener for $600.00 Amer. money, to be paid for in Cash $30.00 and good American Cows and heifers at $25.00 and $12.50 respectively.

[Page 699R]

June. Return to Juarez

1892/Then started home to Juarez, with Theo. Anna, Self, and Dick Bloomfield. Went 8m and camped. Reached home on Friday June [in margin: June] 10th tired and hungry, and our team given out. Theo. walked 5 miles into town and got Joel's horses to help us in. Found all well but Gertrude, but she is much better, and can walk around now, having been blessed by Apostle Teasdale.

Mon. 13/Wrote to Lyman and Geo. Roskruge. Also to M. Thatcher to get him to buy my mill shares, as we are so destitute. Susan had eaten her last corn meal, and knew not where to get any more in this time of famine, when lo! a letter from Lyman with $40.00 Sent by him ($25.00) Nephi $10.00 and Jesse ($5.00) She said tears of joy ran down her cheeks. With this she got flour, $10.00 Sent me $10.00 and sot some things in the Store She needed very badly. Truly God is good to us, and hears our prayers, and fulfils his promises, for He has sealed upon me that I shall not want for food nor clothing, neither my family. Once before Lyman sent Susan money when she needed it, being impelled by a dream his wife Alley had.

16/ Sent my pension papers to B.Y. McKeyes, Deming, a notary, by Benja Johnson. Visited Prest Teasdale, and told him of my habit of Asking God to direct me, and of his goodness in answering me, but as I had heard he was opposed to out Los Horcones Colony I feared I might have been deceived by a lying spirit that had told me God had opened up that land to us and that I should be blessed by Him. It is a thing I cannot afford to be deceived in, and so came to him. He said I had <u>not</u> been deceived, "No! no! no!" said he. Said it was a good thing for one of experience, like me, to be there, and gave me much comfort. I had asked the Father the night previous, and He told me by His Spirit, to See Br. Teasdale, and he would be a friend to me and bless me, as he <u>did</u>.

A glorious and blessed privilige it is, to ask the Father and receive an answer, just as one answereth another. For over two years has God thus blessed, led, and taught me, praised be His holy name, for such goodness to me So poor and weak as I am. Help me, oh Father, to grow and increase in the gifts + knowledge of the Spirit.

[Page 700L]

1892/ June. Went to Galeana.

June 17/Planted beans and Squashes. Next day [blank to end of line]

21/Theodore and Moroni started back to Sonora. Lost horse same night.

Wed. 22/Boys started again. Rain next day. Cucumbers on 28th

Wed. 29/Started to Galeana with letter from Macdonald, to try and get the surveying of Galeana. Joel + his wife and Gertrude also went. Camped 17 miles in Chocolate Pass, famous for indian atrocities.

Thu. 30/Galeana at noon. Saw the Presidente Salomí C. Garcia, who Said I could do the work if I would obtain proper license from the Governor. I sent my application for license by him, and started home at 2 P.M. Camping again in Chocolate Pass, where a large Company of Mexicans were killed by Apaches. At sunset a big thunder storm came on. Joel + I who had tried to lie on the ground, got into the wagon with the Girls at 1.30 a.m. wet to the skin, and sat up all the rest of the night, wrapped in wet quilts. Prayed that none of us be taken ill in any way.

July/ July 1892

1/ Got home at 2 P.M. no one being hurt by the storm. Thankful

2/ Planted corn. Got letter from W.D. Johnson Jr. asking me to ^go^ South into Mexico to examine an estate a Syndicate think of buying, and report as to farm land, water for irrigation +c.[103]

6/ Letter from Sam and Elvira. Also letter from Genie, who has a new baby, born 25 June 1892, weighs 8 1/2 ^named Sherman Edward^ lbs. Sam's letter gave me much comfort, and I insert part of it:–

"Am sorry times are so hard there with you, and I feel as if the hand of the Lord is in it, for if there was plenty to eat and drink there and a land of plenty, it would be just as bad there as here; it would soon be run over with devils and wicked men, and you would soon have to move on or be persecuted. The Lord is trying you to see if you can stand that kind of trouble, and my faith is, after He has proven you in that, then He will open the door to plenty again to you; for as sure as the Sun Shines the Lord has got His eye ^up^ on you, and He loves you, and He is not going to see you go hungry nor destitute of anything that you and Mother needs. So the Spirit said to me, when it spoke to me that you was in destitute circumstances, and for me to write to the boys in Logan; and So we did. And it also said you was doing a good work, and out of your work would spring a great work for us as a family to go on with."

Much more, in the same spirit. It comforted me much.

---

103. The letter, preserved in the William Derby Johnson collection, read:

Dear Bro:
In a letter from John W. Young he desires that three brethren should go on to some land (to be designated hereafter) owned in Mexico by English Capitalists and make a report in relation to its resources + capabilities of agriculture, grazing + irrigation. the trip will take about a month or six weeks. you will be paid $150.00 month + all expenses paid. Can you go if so let me know at once so I can inform him + get further instructions.
I expect to get my father and Bro A. M. Tenney to go with you.
RR matters still hanging fire.
Let me hear from you <u>at once</u> Love to you + all Your cousin
W. Derby Johnson Jr.

William Derby Johnson to J. H. Martineau, June 25, 1892, Letterpress copybook, vol. 3, "Private letters," Deming, 1892, p. 52, W. D. Johnson Collection, MSS 1506, box 2, fd. 3, BYUSC.

11/ Susan's birthday, 56 years old. Had a family dinner.

[Page 701R]

Joel's baby born + died

1892/July 11/By letter from Moroni I learn he traded my Pima farm to Br. Kartchener for 14 Amer. Cows, 9 Calves 1 heifer 1 horse + tent +c to amount of $79.30

23/ Up to this time I have been busy in the garden, hoeing, planting corn and lucern seed. To day Joel's wife Annie, was confined with a 7 mo. baby girl, at 10 a.m. which lived only 5 hours. I blessed and named her Mary Ann, after her mother.

Annie is quite low, having suffered much the last 6 days. The midwife finally had to take the placenta by force.

24/ Buried the baby today, Sunday.

25/ Celebrated the 24th, I was Chaplain, games + dance in after part of the day. Wrote to Lyman, Nephi, Morris Murphey and others.

27/ Sent blank deed to John Kartchener for the farm I sold him in Pima for $600.00 (37 3/10 acres) taking cows +c for pay. Also Sent order to Weech to make the deed to him.

Aug. 2/ August
Letter from Theodore, who is alone on farm near Bavispe. He is lonesome, poor fellow, all alone. He sent us the following verses:—(his first attempt at poetry)

[Poem follows:]
To the Loved ones at home.
While sitting here thinking of home, mother
My thoughts turn insensibly to thee
I seemed to see you a sitting
'Neath the spreading cottonwood tree.
[Blank line]
You appeared to be reading, dear mother
For you held a book in your hand,
But I believe you were thinking of me, mother
Alone in this far distant land.

[Blank line]
Whenever I let my thoughts stray, mother,
I begin thinking of father and you,
Which makes me feel so lonesome + friendless
That I dont know what on earth to do.
[Blank line]
I've oft wondered since leaving home, mother
If I've one friend on the earth that is true;

[Page 702L]

[Poem continues]

Gertrude goes to Arizona.

1892/But though all the world hate me, dear mother
Aug.2/ I still have dear father and you.
[Blank line]
Do any brothers and sisters at home, mother
Ever think of the one far away;
Who is living alone among strangers
In Solitude, day after day.
[Blank line]
But things will change sometime, dear mother
When we will be parted no more;
Our family will be gathered together
In union and peace ever more.
[Blank line]
I pray for you day after day mother,
That you may ~~be~~ become well and strong,
For I know that our Father can heal you
From the pains you have suffered so long.
[Blank line]
I hope that you'll not think me foolish, mother,
For sending these verses to you;
They express my thoughts, feebly, dear mother
But every word written is true.
[Blank line]

Thu. 4/Fast day

Fri. 5/ To day Gertrude starts for Arizona, to visit awhile at Samuel + Elvira. Gathered 10 qts grapes from our vine, our first vintage.

21/ Theodore got home from Sonora. He says cattle had eaten all his corn and cane. Anna went to San Diego ranch to work for a few weeks.

22/ Joel got home with goods from Gallego for store, 135m I am still planting corn in garden.

29th/ Moroni got back from Sonora. Has come for his family.

30/ To day Theodore went to work in Saw Mill. We had a family reunion in honor of Mother Susan Johnson's ^80th^ birthday[104]

September

5th/ Dora is 10 yrs old to day. Had a little party.

10/ Henry's baby was born this morning at 3.35 weighed 10 lbs.

[Page 703R]

1892/Sept. 12/ I began work in grist mill as a helper, and to help reweigh 32000lb wheat for the Corralitos Co. about which there is some dispute as to weight.

16/ We celebrated Mexican Independence day.

17/ To day Apaches took a horse from C. Whipple, a few miles from here but he escaped unhurt. They have also stolen others from San Pedro ranch. Pursued by mounted men.

For some time I have been in much doubt as to what is best for me

---

104. Three days later, on September 2, Martineau wrote a letter to the *Deseret Weekly*, giving an account of the events of the past season, noting that "The long-continued drouth has ended at last, to the joy of people and range stock." Though the area had experienced little rainfall, farmers near Casas Grandes had produced some grain and those in Colonia Juárez had yielded a substantial amount of peaches, apples, plums and other fruit. In addition to reporting on the quarterly conference, Martineau told of the establishment of a new settlement in Sonora: "We learn by brethren from our new settlement in Sonora that Colonel Kosterlitzky, military commandant in northern Sonora, had lately returned from the City of Mexico with very generous concessions of government for the settlers in Sonora. He stated that President Diaz is much interested in the welfare of the Sonora colony, and that he gave it the name of Oaxaca, in honor of his birthplace." This was followed by the stipulation of the colonization law issued by Diaz, including duty-free importation of staple goods and livestock. J. H. Martineau, "Letter from Mexico," *Deseret Weekly* 45 (September 24, 1892): 441.

to do or where live, having no means of support here, as an Engineer or otherwise. I asked the Father in prayer and received this answer:–

That I should not go back to live in Utah or Arizona. That He had led me to Mexico for a purpose of His own, and here I shall make my home; build a good house of brick and make it nice + beautiful, for in it shall be entertained some of the leading men of this State and Nation.[105] After I have lived here a few years, and am called to go farther South I shall sell out at no loss, and go to a place or land where there will be room for me and my family and friends to gather about me; and begin to grow into a nation as has been promised me. Also that I Shall prosper spiritually and temporally from this day forth. Also many other precious promises. For all this I am thankful to the Father, who heareth our prayers.

Mon. 19/ This morning Apaches killed Sister Thompson and her son and shot another boy through the body. He and a little girl about 6 years old started through the woods 2 miles for help, but the boy fainted on the way. A party went from here after the indians but did not find them in a weeks

20/hunt.[106] Another party went out, found their trail, and followed it for days. We hear no word from them.

October/ October

Sat 1/I quit the mill today, 12 days time. Another alarm today Some Mexicans from Corrallitos at the mill said indians had stolen 16 mules. We Sent a party out at dusk and [in margin: 2] another at 3 a.m. Sunday, who found the mules and think they may only have strayed away. We have made a military organization here, of a Company of five tens each. Miles P. Romney Capt. J. Harper Lieutenant.

[Page 704L]

---

105. Based on the family photograph taken in 1908 (see photograph section), Martineau's home was a modest-sized brick Victorian home with a modified hip roof. It would have provided a remarkable level of American comfort, compared to native adobe and framed structures in Chihuahua at that time.

106. Karren Tomson (1833–1892), wife of Hans A. Tomson, was shot and killed by Apaches at their home in Colonia Pacheco, Chihuahua. Their oldest son Hyrum was also shot and killed in this ambush. Two young children, Engmark, a son, and Annie, a granddaughter, escaped. The Indians ransacked the house, taking bedding, clothing, ammunition, and about fifteen head of horses. See "Murdered by Apaches," *Deseret Evening News*, September 29, 1892, 4; "More of the Mexican Tragedy," *Deseret Evening News*, September 30, 1892, 4; and Willard Carroll, "Murderous Apaches," *Deseret Weekly* 45 (October 29, 1892): 593.

Anna married

1892/October 2/Theodore quit the mill + came home to go to school. Also Anna quit work at San Diego—6 weeks. Yesterday I sent an article "The Cross" to Contributor.[107]

5/Wrote to John Wedderburn, Washington D.C. relative to my claim for Indian depredations (for the church) filed 1890 amounting to $225.00

6/ Went to San Diego Rancho to Survey a canal. Gone 2 days and earned $10.00 was very thankful to earn something.

10/ Began taking lessons in Spanish. Henry Eyring, teacher.[108]

26/ Learn by letter from Lyman, that Jesse has gone to Chicago, to attend a business College.

November/ November

1/Moroni came from Sonora, to hunt his cattle + horses. Susan and I are going to start to Deming tomorrow.

2/ Rained and Snowed all day and last night

3 + 3/ The same. We gave up our journey.

11/ Wrote to John W. Young, 85 London Well E.C. London.

14/ Wrote to President Porforio Diaz, Mex. relative to what I can do in engineering, and what I would like to do. Blessed the letter, that a good influence may go with it. If not, it will all be right, for God knows best what is good for us.

---

107. See Santiago, "The Cross," *Contributor* 13 (September 1892): 487–488.

108. Henry Carlos Ferdinand Eyring (1835–1902) was born at Coburg, SaxeCoburg-gotha, Germany, on March 9, 1835, to Edward Christian and Ferdinandine Charlotte Caroline (von Blomberg) Eyring. He immigrated to New York in 1853 and traveled to St. Louis, Missouri, in March 1854. After converting to the LDS Church in 1855, Eyring served a mission to the Indian Territory, Tennessee and Kentucky, from 1855 to 1860. From 1862 to 1874, he and his wife, Mary Bonneli, lived in St. George, Utah, where he served as bishop of the Second Ward from 1863 to 1874. From 1874 to 1876, he served a mission to Germany and assisted in the publication of *Der Stern*, a church periodical, and the translation of the Doctrine and Covenants into German. After returning from Germany, he served as a counselor in the St. George Stake presidency from 1877–1887. In 1887, he moved to Colonia Juárez, Mexico. He served as first counselor to Anthony W. Ivins, president of the Colonia Juárez Stake from 1895 until his death in 1902. He died in Colonia Juárez on February 10, 1902. See Jenson, *LDS Biographical Encyclopedia*, 3:311–312.

Fri. 18/ To day at 3 P.M. Anna S. married Henry Samuel Walser at my house. The ceremony was by Apostle George Teasdal, who Sealed them for time and eternity, and gave them a good blessing. We had a house full, and a good dinner. I had been suffering two days with an attack of pleurisy, in my left side, suffering severely. Prest Teasdal, Sixtus E. Johnson + J.J. Walser administered to me, Br. Teasdal being mouth. He also blessed me in other particulars, Saying I had been led here by the Lord and should be able to do what I had been appointed to do, and that wealth and prosperity should flow unto me to enable me to do my work.

19/By letter from Gertrude she says she had had a bad fall from a horse that ran with her under a low shed and scraped her off. She falling on top of his head, and narrowly escaping a broken neck. But she had now recovered from the fall.

[Page 705R]

1892/Quarterly Conference begins to day, lasting 3 days

Nov. 26/27th was at priesthood meeting chosen an alternate in the High Council.

December

1/Finished article for "Contributor," a table of dates of births and deaths of ancient patriarchs.[109]

Learn by letter Lyman's baby was born on Nov. 24, 1892, at 9 a.m. Her name, Martha ^Claytor^

7th/ Started to Mesa, Arizona, with Br. Spillsbury, at noon. We hear that Gertrude is very sick and needs me. Cold weather. Drove to Dublan and stayed with Br. F.G. Williams.[110] Br. Williams at first said he could not

---

109. The table was compiled from the Bible, Doctrine and Covenants, Pearl of Great Price, and *Times and Seasons*. See J. H. Martineau, "Important Chronology," *Contributor* 14 (November 1892): 44–45.

110. Colonia Dublán was first settled in 1888, after George M. Brown negotiated the purchase of a 73,000-acre tract of land for colonization with a German-Mexican, Lewis Huller. Dublán became a branch of the LDS Church on April 14, 1889, with Frederick W. Jones as presiding elder. It is located sixteen miles northeast of Colonia Juárez in the Casas Grandes Valley and 150 miles west of El Paso, Texas, in the state of Chihuahua, Mexico. See Stout, *History of Colonia Dublán*; Romney, *Mormon Colonies in Mexico*, 95–101; and Jenson, *Encyclopedic History of the Church*, 199.

Frederick G. Williams II (1853–1918) was born at Salt Lake City on March 29, 1853,

take me, his team was so poor. But the answer of the Spirit was that I <u>should</u> go, and with Br. Williams. So next day Br. W. Said I <u>could</u> go with him, and I did.

8/Drove 25m and camped. Very cold weather

9/Arrived at Diaz, and went on next day, reaching Las Palomas, the custom house in the evening.

12/In the Territory of New Mexico. Snow on mountains and bitterly cold.

13/Reached Deming at noon. Paid Williams $5.00 passage money, got a hat and a few little things, and R.R. ticket to Tempe $16.90 and left Deming 8 P.M.

14/reaching Tucson 5 a.m. next day, Maricopa Stan 8 a.m. Tempe 10.45, and Son-in-law B.S. Johnson's 12.30 P.M. Found Gertrude very ill with agonizing pain behind her eyes. For weeks she has been unable to see, or have her eyes unbound. All the rest of Sam's family were well.

15/ I wrote to Susan to come, and to bring Dora.

18/ Quarterly Conference at Mesa. I spoke + felt well. I spent some days in copying items from an old copy of "Times and Seasons" of 1844.

25th/ Christmas, but not as if at home. Preached in Nephi.

27/ Gertrude improves daily, but is very feeble still.[111]

28th/ Went to Franklin Johnson's wedding at Mesa. He is eldest son of Joseph, Sam's brother.

[Page 706L]

<u>1893</u>

---

to Ezra Granger and Henrietta Elizabeth (Crombie) Williams. He was the grandson of Frederick Granger Williams, lived in Ogden and Fairview, Utah, and was an early settler of St. Joseph, Arizona. He married Amanda Burns in 1876, Hansena Kathena Hegsted in 1884, and Nancy Burns in 1889. Under threat of arrest for cohabitation, he was advised in 1889 to take his wives to Mexico, where they lived in Colonia Diaz for a short time, then settled in Dublán. The family ultimately lived out their lives in Binghampton, Arizona, a small Mormon community near Tucson. Williams died at Binghamton on January 20, 1918. See Rogers, "From Colonia Dublán to Binghampton," 19–46.

111. The previous evening, B. F. Johnson wrote: "At B. Samuel's met Bro. J. H. Martineau and gave Blessing to his daughter Gertrude." Johnson, *My Life's Review*, 347.

1892/ Br. John Reidhead, an old friend of Sam's came to stay.

Dec. 28]I received a letter from Sur. Genl Royal Johnson to go to Tucson and work in his office as draughtsman[112]

30/ Sent my account for indian depredations to Washington, and made plats for Br. Cosby, of Mesa. Made out a bill for Sam of indian depredations he suffered in Apache Co. some years ago, in being driven from their home, farm, and all they had, narrowly escaping with life.

31/ Went 6 miles to Tempe. Gertrude went with me, the first time she has been out in 6 weeks.

<u>1893</u> [note lines in margin]

Jan. 1893/ Took dinner at James Turman's in Mesa, and had a pleasant time with him, who are my true friends.

Lyman's baby is named Martha Claytor, after Bp. W.B. Preston's mother.

3/ I blessed Gertrude, and started to Tucson, reaching

4/there 3.15 a.m. Began work in Surr Genl office at $4.00 per day. Took a room with board at $7.50 per week[113]

---

112. A copy of the letter is preserved in the Arizona Surveyor General's Correspondence:

J. H. Martineau Esq
My dear sir:–
I understand that you are in Mesa, and desirous of going to work. If you desire I can give you some work at four dollars for the working day, excluding Sundays. I know you are worth more money, but unfortunately this is all I am able to pay.
Please let me know at once by telegraph if you will come as I shall want you at once.
Respectfully Yours
Royal A. Johnson [signed]
U.S. Surveyor General.

Royal A. Johnson to James H. Martineau, December 27, 1892, Letters Sent, box 7: Vol. 25, May 6, 1892–February 15, 1893, p. 364, CSGAZ.

113. On this date, General Johnson reported Martineau's appointment and salary:

Sir:–
I have the honor to inform you of the following changes to the clerical force of this office: James H. Martineau, is appointed ^a^ Mineral Draughtsman, at $4.00 per day, to date from the morning of January 4th, 1893, vice- Charles R. Allen, who ceased work on the evening of December 31st 1892.

Royal A. Johnson to Commissioner of General Land Office, January 4, 1893, Letters Sent,

6/ Recd a letter from Susan at Nephi, where she arrived on the fifth, being 9 days on the road from Juarez to Deming, in cold weather and poor food + bedding. At Deming her cousins David T. and Harriet LeBaron did not even invite her into their house, which was adjoining the corral in which Susan camped all night, in cold winter weather and nothing but a crust of dry bread and some water for supper and breakfast. I was very angry when I heard of it.

8/ Our 41st anniversary of our marriage. I sat for photo.

11/ Moved to the "Cosmopolitan Hotel," at $25.00 pr month.

15/ The Baron Alex. von Wendt called to see me, with Mr. Lavagnino, a Rothschild mining expert. Gave him my opinion of the Santa Rita gold placers belonging to von Wendt.[114]

19/ I am tempted to take a contract for U.S. land Survey, but the answer I received is not to do so. The Lord hath other work for me,—I shall have a place in Mexico where I may gather my family, kindred

[Page 707R]

1893/and friends about me and grow into a great people—a nation—which shall <u>not</u> go into captivity as ancient Israel because this is the last dispensation. Also, my brethren shall receive a testimony in my favor, and shall lift me up among them and make me mighty in Israel. Help me, Father, to receive all promised me.

I have now been a member of the Church 42 years, and in that time how many changes,—ups and downs—lights and shadows—joy and sadness,—health and sickness and death—plenty and poverty!

21/ Spent my last dime, but today my pension came of $24.00 so I did not go hungry.

25/ Moved to Gibbons' room, $10.00 per month.

28/ Bought 3 opals of a traveler, because of their beauty.

Feb/ February

---

box 7: Vol. 25, May 6, 1892–February 15, 1893, p. 372, CSGAZ. See also untitled entry, *Arizona Weekly Citizen*, January 14, 1893, 4.

114. Martineau visited the placers at Santa Rita the following year. See entry for May 30, 1894.

4/ I asked the Father if I should take a survey contract offered me by Genl Johnson. The answer was "Yes," and shall be blessed in it from beginning to end thereof.

6/ Sent $40.00 to Sam and Susan, Sam having sent Susan $20.00 to help her on her way from Mexico.

11/ Br. Spillsbury came along on his way home to Colonia Juarez. I sent some things to Anna, and arranged with him to take a can of honey to Juarez for me, giving him $3.00 to pay duties on things Sent Anna.

12/ Sent for "Lives and times of the Roman Pontiffs," in the hope to learn something of my Roman or Italian ancestry.

I know my ancestry was Col notable in Italy, mostly in the church, as Popes (Martin 1, 2, 3, 4+5th also as eminent painters and scholars, and hope to learn enough about them to do temple work for them.

14/ Wrote again to my wife Jessie Helen, who utterly and without any reason known to me, refuses to correspond with me. I am satisfied it is because of her mothers influence, though I have never, to my knowledge, done anything to incur her dislike nor can I guess at the cause of her enmity.

[Page 708L]

1893/

1893/Feb./ As she is a member of the Salt Lake Choir I sent her letter to Evan Stephens, the leader, to deliver to her.

March.

Mch. 8/ Sent $20.00 to Susan

13/ To day I am 65 years old, but I cannot realize it, only as I see how old some of my children are.

On Thursday morning, the 9th as I prayed, a voice Said to me "I ordain thee a patriarch in my Church." This is <u>spiritual</u>, and I may now exercise the gift of prophecy when moved upon by the Holy Spirit. And the time will come when I shall be ordained by my brethren. I celebrated by birthday by an oyster stew, 50¢ doing without one regular meal, to make up for it. I eat but two meals a day, 25¢ each, to save money and get ahead a little. Two meals a day is all I ever have eaten in Tucson for some years, and for weeks at a time only <u>one</u> meal a day, when I had but little means to live on. Upon ^one^ occasion I went from Monday afternoon until Saturday without eating anything at all, having but 50¢ in the world and no way to get any more. So I kept the 50¢ in reserve in case of emergency, but it was not pleasant.

14/ Received my "Lives of Roman Pontiffs" +c but was much disappointed, as it does not supply the items I want.

15/ I received $150.00 by letter from Lyman. He sent me $9.00 and Nephi and Charles $30.00 each, so I could come to the dedication of the Salt Lake temple. Sent Susan $15.00 to help her to get ready for the journey.

28/ Susan and Gertrude started for S.L. City

29/ I joined them on train at 3 a.m. going via Deming N.M. Left Deming 11.30 a.m. and went north by Atchison, T + Santa Fe R.R. Our fare from Deming to S.L. City was $36.40 each, and from Tucson to Deming $11.00

30/ At Colorado Springs 3.30 and Summit of Mountains 4.35 P.M.

31/ At Aspen Junction 5.30 a.m. and Grand Junction at 10.00 a.m. Lay by until 2.00 p.m. We passed through Leadville about midnight, altitude 11.000 feet. Cold,

[Page 709R]

1893/Mch./with Snow all about us, and Pike's Peak rising high to the South east many miles distant. Grand Junction is on the West Side of the Rocky mountains. We have passed through grand mountain scenery, pine clad, cold and sno^w^y. In the afternoon we cross Green river (the upper Colorado) and soon enter Utah, and begin the ascent of the Wahsatch Mts, descending through Spanish Fork Cañon and arriving at Ogden

Apr. 1/about 9 P.M. arriving at S.L. City 12.40 A.M. and stopped with Eliza

4+5/ Conference was held 4th and 5th So the temple can be dedicated April 6th just 40 years from its commencement.

6/ Lyman took us to the Theatre.

7/ The 7th was the time Set for people from Mexico to attend the dedication services, which were very impressive. But there was not such manifestations of holy influences as when the Manti Temple was dedicated, owing, I believe, to the fact that <u>now</u> all are permitted to enter who have any standing at all in the church, good or poor standing; so that many attended who were utterly unworthy to do any temple work. About 1000 gentiles and apostates were permitted to go through the building before it was dedicated, who were filled with amazement at its beauty, grandeur and magnificence. The "Tribune" our deadliest foe, described it as a "dream of Supernatural beauty."

When my son Nephi, a member of the famed Logan Choir went through a few days after, he heard heavenly music that entirely overcame him. He is one of the pure in heart, if there be any such living.

In the evening we attended a grand concert of over 600 children, dressed in the costumes of many countries, and who sang songs in various languages.

8th + 9th/ Cold, and snow 4 inches deep.

10/We went to Logan and found all well, and all glad to see us, as also Gean and Eliza in S.L. City when we arrived there. Gean's husband

[Page 710L]

1893/Edward Sudbury, is absent on a Mission on the Society islands. Gean lives near his parents, and has a fine boy. A snow storm the evening we got to Lyman's place in Logan. It seems so strange and Logan seems strange also, after an absence of 5 ½ years. The Streets seem narrow and the trees appear stunted, compared with those in Arizona.

12/ Yesterday was cold and Snowy. Saw Nephi and his family, and had a joyful time

15/ Spent the day at Nephi's, who gave a family dinner.

16/ Administered again to Apostle M. Thatcher, who is very low—not able to sit up, with dyspepsia, and is in much danger. Bp. + Mrs. W.B. Preston came from S.L. City to be with him.

17/ Returned to Lyman's, as Nephi is going off to his farm to sow wheat.

18/ Snow this morning, and quite cold.

20/ Began work in the temple, myself, Susan + Gertrude I endowed David Martineau, born in Eng. 25 Jan. 1788, Died June 1836. Bap. 10 June 1884 [blank] His wife Caroline Elizabeth Hyde, born 1796, Eng.—Bap. Sept. 1887. Gertrude was endowed for her, and my wife Susan proxy in Sealing April 21st.

20th/ Mrs. Benj. Martineau born in N. York 1770 died — Bap 19 Aug. 1887. Her husband was previously endowed, Susan proxy in Endowment and Sealing, April 20, 1893.

J. Alison, Born 1770 Eng. Bap. 10 June 1884, Endowed Nov. 10 1887, and his wife Margaret Martineau, born Eng. 1778. Bap. 15 July 1884, Endowed 5 May 1887, were Sealed. I and Susan officiating for them.

21/ I endowed George Martineau b. 5 Apr. 1792, Eng. bap. 10th June 1884, and his wife Sarah Greenhaw, Endowed by Susan, born 1797, Eng. Bap. 19 Aug. 1884 Sealed to day, by Susan + me.

Gertrude was ~~ordained~~ ^Endowed^ for Caroline E. Hyde. All above Sealings were by Br. N.C. Edlefsen, who also blessed Gertrude to heal her eyes, which pain her very much, assisted by me and Cousin W.D. Johnson Jr. In the evening we went to

[Page 711R]

1893/the Theatre. I presented to the Logan Temple Library 4 April 21/ volumes of "Life and Times of the Roman Pontiffs," cost $8.70

22/ Snow again to day.

23/ We all went to Nephi's, and had a good time,—we, Lyman's + Allie, Genie, Frank Nebeker and Lilla. Had Songs and a very pleasant time.

25/ All met at Lyman's, and had a good time with a family supper in the evening.

26/ I went to the Temple. Lyman gave us considerable dry goods, for which may God bless him with plenty.

30/ Attended Conference and had a good meeting, also May 1st

May

May 2/ Went to S.L. City, Virginia went also. Susan and Gertrude remained at Logan.

3/ Talked with Mrs. Jane C. Young, about getting an interview with my wife Jessie, whose mother prevents her from coming to me. She said she would do all to help me she can.

4/ Lyman came to see about having an examination of Gertrude.

5/ Saw Sister Young. She had visited Jessie, but can not say if Jessie will see me or not. Susan and Gertrude came to day. We all stay with Virginia.

7/ We went in Street cars to Camp Douglass, very cold.

8/ I determined to see Jessie, and went to the house, but her mother shut the door in my face and forbade me entrance. I went away out of sight and waited until I saw her mother go away, and then went again to the door and had a talk with Jessie, but she said I must not enter, as her mother had forbidden it. She looked sick and bad, and seemed to feel very badly, but did not dare to let me come in, and told me I must not even write to her, only I might send her a fig leaf, but no writing in the letter. Poor girl, I know she longed to come to me. And she will Sometime.

9/ Went to Bp. Prestons and spent the day, and staid all night. They were very kind indeed.

10/ Started 11 P.M. to Station and had to wait there until

11/3 a.m. before we could start, via Denver + Rio

[Page 712L]

1893/May/ Gertrude remained in S.L. City, hoping it would be better for her. Crossed the Wahsatch Mts. amid snow + ice, also, the Rocky mts, arriving at Colorado Springs at 7 a.m.

12/and waited there until 4.40 P.M. reached Pueblo 5.50 P.M. and La Junta 8.30 P.M. and lay over until next day

13/at 9.50 a.m. Reached Trinidad 1.15 P.M. Socorro

14/7.15 a.m. and arrived at Deming 12.40, noon. From Logan to Deming is 1149 miles. Stopped at a hotel

15/found Some L.D. Saints here,—Br. + Sis. Farnsworth, who made Susan welcome at their house. I am anxious to return to Tucson to work in the Sur. Genl office, + so I left Susan here, she to return to Colonia Juarez with Br. Macdonald's Company. I hated to leave her here, for her to make such a long journey—5 or 6 days—with wagon, camping out at night, but I knew there was no work there for me to do, and I could best show my love by earning means for her comfort. So at 2.20 P.M. I took train for Tucson, reaching there at 10.45 P.M. Susan was obliged to wait in Deming ten days for a chance to get home, finally returning in company with Apostle Teasdale and others, and found all well in Juarez.[115]

16/ Saw Sur. Genl Johnson, who said there was no work for me in the office, as his time of office was nearly expired. This is a great disappointment to me; here a long distance from home, and with money enough to keep me 3 or 4 days, and no means to leave Tucson. What shall I do? It is all so dark.[116]

17/ This morning I prayed for help, and received answer that all will be well with me, and my way shall be opened for me. I will trust in the promise of the Spirit. My room (the cheapest I can get) is 20¢ pr day, and I eat but one meal a day, 25¢, trying to make my few dollars hold out as long as possible.

20/ Still looks very dark, and as if I must beg or starve. Prayed and received a comforting answer.

21/ Wrote to Jessie Helen and sent the fig leaf as she

[Page 713R]

1893/wished me, but nothing in words, as she told me.

May 21/ Fasted 24 hours and prayed and was comforted.

22/A letter from Susan, full of comfort and prophecy of good to me, saying my way will be opened and all will be well with me.

In the afternoon Genl Johnson promised me work in the office, to continue until he should resign. Oh how thankful I am—rescued from apparent starvation, and still more thankful because I see the voice which promised me blessing was truly the voice of the Holy Spirit. I am striving hard, to learn to know his voice, and thus my faith strengthens.

---

115. Susan had been waiting at David Wilson's home in Deming. See Teasdale Diary, May 25, 1893, 58, Teasdale Papers, box 18, fd. 1, UUSCM.

116. Fortunately, Martineau was able to obtain work under Johnson's successor, Levi H. Manning. See entry for June 19.

23/ Began work in the office as draughtsman, at $4. per day. I thank thee, my Father, for thy goodness.

24/ I prayed, and asked concerning Anna M. Hagberg,—dead many years ago—and sealed to me as wife. She was the mother of my Sealed son Niels M. Hagberg. I received answer that she had joyfully received all my temple work for her—endowments and sealing to me. So Niels is ^as^ truly my own son as any from my loins, and I must cultivate him as such.

May 2/ May

Made a map for Howe and got $4.00 for it

Sun. 4/At about 2 a.m. I dreamed about Jessie Helen. I was at a Sunday meeting and was called to lead the singing. As I went to take my place, Jessie also came to take her seat near by on my left hand, but just as she was about to sit down two women slipped into the two chairs before she could sit, and she had to sit partly on their laps, and seemed annoyed at them. We sang some hymns, and as she turned away she spoke of taking to her notes again.

I awoke, and the meaning of the dream and if it had any meaning, I was told it had, to have comfort in it, have faith in it and write it down so that I may remember it more perfectly when I see the fulfillment of it. The full importance will not be made known to me now, but will be in the future. And

[Page 714L]

June 1893 [blank] July

1893/the dream is for my comfort. Even now she desires [in margin: June 4] in her heart to correspond with me, and will in due time when opposing influences are removed, as they will be, and she will come to me as a true and loving wife.

And the Spirit said to me "I seal upon thee at this time the gift of dreams and interpretation that thou mayest be comforted, instructed or warned, and if thou wilt receive this in faith and do according as thou art shone thy gifts shall grow and increase, + prepare thee for the blessing of heavenly messengers, even of angels + the Three Nephites; and this because thou hast long sought these gifts because my servant the Prophet counseled my Saints to Seek for them. Thou shalt write thy dream, and in due time thou shalt know concerning the two women who sat where Jessie expected to sit ^more^ fully."

I was instructed more fully, and referred to Joseph when he was warned to flee into Egypt, with the infant Savior; how he at once awoke, told Mary, arose and prepared his beasts for the journey, while Mary prepared the child for the journey, and took food and water. And so, if I am instructed in a dream, and do as I am told, I shall be blessed. Oh my Father, I thank thee for thy goodness to me in this, and in giving me money for my needful food and lodging.

19/ Sur. Genl Manning offers me a contract to Survey 5 townships.[117] I asked the Father, and was told I shall be blessed in doing the work and in receiving my pay.

24/ Files my bonds of $4500.00. Contract No. 30

27/ Have 2 more townships to Survey, Contract No. 32; bonds $2000. I thank thee of Father, for giving me work.

28/ Got my Second bond (contract No. 32) fixed today.[118] This evening Ex-Gov. Wolfley engaged me to survey for the Gila Bend Canal + Irrn Company along the line of their Canal, and to pay me $10.00 pr day and board. I felt as if this was a great blessing to me, and that my way is opening wonderfully. Sent money to Susan.

July

3/ Received my Commission as Deputy U.S. Surveyor, also

[Page 715R]

---

117. Levi Howard Manning (1864–1935) was born to Van H. and Mary (Wallace) Manning in Halifax, North Carolina, on May 18, 1864. He attended the University of Mississippi. Manning arrived in Tucson in 1884, where he served as general manager of the Tucson Ice & Electric Light Company. He married Gussie Lovell in 1897. He was appointed Arizona Surveyor General in 1893 by President Grover Cleveland and served in that office until 1896, when he resigned. See *Portrait and Biographical Record of Arizona*, 110–113.

118. Manning obtained approval of Martineau's contract (No. 32), providing for the survey of Tp. 15 S. Rs. 16 & 17 E., for a liability of $1,000, fiscal year 1892–93. Levi H. Manning to Commissioner of the General Land Office, June 28, 1893, and Levi H. Manning to James H. Martineau, [hand dated September 5, but placed in sequence after June 28, 1893], Letters Sent, box 7: Vol. 26, February 15, 1893–October 3, 1893, pp. 336–340, CSGAZ.

July

1893/July 3/was appointed Chief Engineer of the Gila Bend Canal and Irrigation Company.[119] I got trunk, bedding, +c, and Started to Gila Bend at 9.45 P.M. arriving next morning at

4/2.25 a.m. Before accepting the work Jas McMillan Superintendent of the Canal, agreed in writing to pay me the sum agreed upon at the completion of my work, and paid me $20.00 in advance. At 8 a.m. the Same day I and McMillan started in a carriage up the river to the dam 20 miles. The canal and dam has cost up to this time over $700.000.00 and they are still unfinished.[120] My work is to connect the line of canal with the U.S. public land Survey Section corners, and make a map of the same for the whole length of the canal, 38 miles. The weather is very hot, but I am glad to have employment, to earn means for my family.

5th/ Got my help and began work, continuing from day to day until Sunday the [blank to end of line]

9th/when I went to Gila Bend for letters. Last night I had a dream, and awoke and thought about it. I thought I was in some public meeting, standing just at the entrance and some one at the other End of the room said "Let three men come forward." Without knowing why, I at once stepped forward and then stopped, ashamed at my own forwardness, but was in a moment at the far end of the room. I then heard read the ~~notes~~ ^minutes^ of the meeting, which said I was ordained 1st Counsellor to the President of the Stake and also President or to act as President

---

119. In a letter to Martineau dated July 5, Manning wrote: "Your commission as Deputy U.S. Land Surveyor for the District of Arizona, has this day been mailed you, the receipt of which you will please acknowledge." Martineau was instructed to take the oath of office before a certified notary public or a commissioned officer authorized to receive oaths and return it to the office. Levi H. Manning to James H. Martineau, July 5, 1893, Letters Sent, box 7: Vol. 26, February 15, 1893–October 3, 1893, p. 352, CSGAZ.

120. The dam of the Gila Bend Reservoir and Irrigation Company was located approximately 23 miles north of the town of Gila Bend. See "Gila Bend Canal," in Davis, *Irrigation Near Phoenix*, 47–49, also plates IX, X, and XI. A brief entry in the *Irrigation Age* gave a description of the work to this point: "The Wolfley Dam at Tucsan [sic] is filled with water and eight inches flowing over the top. This means that there is the largest lake in the territory impounded. It is 2,100 feet wide at the dam and wider farther upstream for a distance of four miles. This large volume of water is to supply the farms in the Gila valley. All the water rights have been sold, and as the water supply is sufficient, some extra fine fruits and vegetables are expected from this valley." See "Arizona. The Wolfley Dam," *Irrigation Age* 5 (August 1893): 72.

because the President would be absent so much of the time that I might act as Such more properly, and hence was ordained President as well. Also that I would have $1200 a year, also $200. which would be enough to sustain my family in Comfort.

The dream was so vivid and strange. I asked that if it had no real meaning for me it might all pass from my mind. If it <u>has</u> a meaning, that it may remain in my memory.

11/ Worked all day in intense heat—124° in Shade, without a breath of air. At one time was nearly over come by the heat and all became dark and I felt like death was

[Page 716L]

1893/upon me, but I had sufficient thought and life to rebuke

July 11/the Evil One that my life might be spared. As soon as I prayed and rebuked the evil powers, it passed away + I continued my work. Day after day my instrument became so hot I could not touch it without burning my hands severely, and we drank enormous quantities of Water, which immediately came out through the skin like as through a sieve, and our clothes from head to foot wet as though I had been in the river. Had I not thus perspired I would have died.

19/ Reached Gila Bend—20 miles—with my survey

25/ Finished the field work of my Survey, and will now have easier time, as I will be at work in the office, making my maps, in Gila Bend. Have received and written many letters from my family and Sent Gertrude and Eliza a little money.

26/ Received my "instructions" for the Survey I am to make.[121]

August/ August

---

121. The Commissioner of the GLO having approved Martineau's contract (No. 30), dated June 21, 1893, providing for the survey of fractional Tp. 3 N. R. 3 E. and Tp. 4 N., Rs. 2 & 3 E., and Tp. 5 N. Rs. 2 & 3 East, authorized him to proceed with the work according to the Manual of Instructions. Manning provided him with specific instructions to the survey. The boundaries of the survey were established by Andrew Barry, R. C. Powers, and G. P. Ingalls. Levi H. Manning to James H. Martineau, July 19, 1893, Letters Sent, box 7: Vol. 26, February 15, 1893–October 3, 1893, 322–328; appended to this, 329–330, was "Desert Land Declarations on File Embraced within Survey to be made Under Contract No 29, James H. Martineau, Deputy Surveyor, Tp 4 North R. 2 East," CSGAZ.

1/ Got $40.00 from McMillan, which, with $20.00 before makes $60 in all. Went to Tucson to finish my work.

Sun. 6th/ Took a long walk, and wished I could see the family.

13/ Reci'd my pay for the Month of June, $104.00 and wrote to Theodore to come and help on my Survey.

22/ Finished my maps of the Gila Bend Canal Survey My time has been 44 days in all, hard work, and the balance due me is $304.75 which is promised me in a few days.

26/ I lent von Wendt $10.00 He was in great need and was about discouraged. Settled my accounts in Tucson and Started to Mesa about midnight

27/ Reached my Son-in-law Samuel Johnson about 10 a.m. and went to Conference in the afternoon, and preached.

Sept./ Sept. 2nd

2/ I went to High Priests meeting to day at Mesa. At the place of meeting I found Br. Charles Allen in horrible agony He was bitten on the toe this morning by a small black Spider, with ~~bac~~ round, black and shiny, about

[Page 717R]

1893/Sept./the Size of a buck shot. He could not have suffered more had he been in the fire. I learned afterwards he suffered two or three days and nights before his pain left him.

6/ Have tried to borrow money to commence my Survey, but the panic in business is still so great that I have not been able to raise a cent. I went to Tempe to see if I could borrow there. The Cashier said they were not making loans to any body—times were to dangerous.

8/ I went to Phoenix to see if I could get money there. I must have money to buy a transit, get supplies, teams +c for my party. I went to several banks, but got the Same answer from all—"We are not making loans now." What to do I did not know. Phoenix was my last hope and without I get money my Contract must forfeit. I had had a promise that I would be blessed in it. But it seemed now impossible, and I began to wonder "have I been deceived—was it an evil spirit, and not the Holy Spirit which promised me a blessing upon my contract? If I have been deceived, what have I to cling to! In this Sad state of mind I stood on a Street corner and saw a bank sign I had never seen before, and thinking "they can only refuse, like the others" I went there and made known my business. Mr. W.K. James said his bank was not making any loans, but he had some money to loan on good security. In the end I borrowed of him $600.00 giving him power of attorney to Collect my Survey pay when it should be due me. For this I must pay him $250.00, or $850.00 in all in return—pretty big interest. But it was my only chance, and I felt that God had opened my way, getting the money from a Stranger as I did, and best of all—I know I had <u>not</u> been deceived and that the voice which had promised me a blessing was <u>not</u> a lying Spirit, but the Holy Spirit. For this I am very thankful, more than words can tell. I am diligently trying to learn the voice of the Holy Spirit, and could not bear the thought that I may be deceived in it. I am thankful I am not deceived,

[Page 718L]

1893/Sept. 8/am gaining faith in God's promises, and gaining knowledge of the principle of revelation and prophecy, as Prest Woodruff has said it is our duty to do.

I returned to Sam's and found letters Saying the Genl Land Dept. Washn, had approved my contract, and Sent me all necessary blank books, field notes and instructions.

14/ Went to Phoenix again and concluded my deal with Mr. James, for the $600.00 I sent $100.00 to W.+L.E. Gurley, Troy, N.Y. in part payment for a transit to Cost about $300.00 also for Survey chain and Steel rule. This to me is a day to be remembered, for God's blessing to me. I Sent more names to Gertrude, in Logan, to be endowed for in the temple.

During all these months I have spent much time in writing to Susan and my children, as well as ^to^ many others. I receive my pension every 3 months, of $24.00 which is quite a help to us, although but a small amount. I send von Wendt money from time to time, dividing with him, as he sorely needs it, and some way I feel very much drawn to him, as well as he to me. He is a Russian Baron of ancient lineage (of the Knights of Malta) who conquered East Prussia many hundred years ago, the Country of the <u>Wends</u>, whence his family name of von Wendt. He is a mine operator and expert, who has lost his means and is about discouraged. I have cheered him up all I can, and he Seems to think me his only trusted friend in Tucson, having no confidence in any other person here. It is, I believe, from the Lord.

23/ Albert writes me their last baby is named <u>Ernest</u>.

27/ Nephi has another baby, dont know the name yet. Sent 25$ for Susan to come to Mesa. Got a letter from Joel saying my Solar Compass and other things had been Sent from Juarz and were now at Bisbee A.T. My boys are not coming from Mexico, as they think they are too late, all but Theodore, who I think will come.

Oct. 4/ My new transit is come to Tucson, and my Solar has been Sent me from Bisbee.

[Page 719R]

This finishes the first volume—a book so large that I never expected to fill it, and yet the story of my life is not all told. In this volume are noted many things not worth record, while I find, on looking back, that I have omitted many that should have been noted. In part, this has been because some things appeared at the time of some importance, which time subsequently disproved; and some things, of apparently little moment afterwards proved to be important as time unfolded the future.

I now leave this volume and begin again in volume two, a book of 500 pages. How many of them my remaining years may require I know not, neither is it important. I wish to remain here only so long as I can do good and help to advance the work of the Lord. When the time comes that I can no longer do so, then it will be much better to go on to the next and higher life. I have received promises, which entitle me to get many years in this, my second estate, and if I do not fail too grievously in my duty and so forfeit them, or forfeit them by want of faith—doubt and unbelief,—fruitful source of loss of blessings—I may continue, until I may assist in building the City of Zion and her twelve temples, and do a work therein for many of the dead, which I greatly desire to do, if it be the will of the Father, in company with my dear Susan—the wife of my youth, the companion and sharer of my toils, my trials, my sorrows and my joys—always my help and comfort—always filled with hope, comfort and consolation, whom may our Father forever bless with his choice blessings.

[Unstamped page]
[Between page 719 and beginning of second book follows 31 pages of notes, letters, certificates, and newspaper clippings]
[JHM's second book of My Life follows]
[Page end]

[Page B01R]
[Second book begins, all centered]

My Life
[Blank line]
James H. Martineau
[Blank line]
Vol. 2
[Page end]

[Page B03R]

1893/[Blank line]

Oct. 5/ I went to Phoenix and got Some goods, and on the 6th

6/got my Solar Compass, Chain and a few other things I had sent for to Mexico.

8/ Sent money to Theodore at Wilcox so he could come to Tucson.

14/ Started to Tucson, arriving 2.15 a.m. Got my transit and new chain, and had them tested by Chief Clk. Geo. J Roskruge. They were found in good condition.

17/ By letter from Nephi I learn his last baby was born in September, and named Elva. Theodore came.

19/ My party of Surveyors came from Mesa to day having been 5 days on the journey

20/ Bought supplies for our Survey party.

21/ Started for my field of work about 20 miles away, my party consists of Saml Johnson and Arthur Openshaw, chainmen, Theodore, flagman, J.W. Johnson, Cook, Alanson Reidhead, teamster, John J. Tucker, axeman + self, 7 in all, with tent, 1 wagon, and two deans. ^teams^ Camped at Crane's place.

22nd/ Sunday, rested

23/ Began the Survey of the ^4th^ Standard Parallel South Ranges 16 + 17 East

25/ Last night I dreamed of the Savior and of being with him. It gave me much Comfort.

Nov. 4/[blank to center]Nov. 4[blank]To day I finished the Survey of Tp. 17 E. and tomorrow begin on Tp. 16 East.

17/Finished my Survey of Contract No. 32 and Started to Tucson. The work has been very hard, being in a very rough, mountainous and rocky country, full of Cactus and prickly shrubs. Some days it was all we could do to run a survey of 1 ½ miles, starting at Sunrise and not getting into camp until late at night, tired out completely. Our Shoes soon were off our feet, and I bought two raw hides with which to tie up our feet, but which were soon cut through by the sharp rocks. We had to haul all our water for miles, and, all in all, it was a hard trip, quite cold at the end. Spent the night in Tucson of 18th

[Page B04L]

1893/[Blank line]

Nov. 18th/We arrived in Tucson at 2 P.M. and all went on towards home but ^me.^ ~~Theo and I.~~ Cold, with prospect of rain.

20/ I began work on my plats and field notes.

23/Still working on my field notes. Received telegram from Susan, who is at Bowie Station with Dora, + will be at Tucson to night at midnight. I borrowed $5.00 to help me to Mesa, and met Susan on the train. I had not seen her since May, nor Dora since 18 months, when I left Colonia Juarez. We arrived at Tempe at 3 a.m. and lodged at a hotel, going then to Sams by Stage, reaching him at 10 a.m.

    Susan had Stopped off at Bowie Sta, on her way to Arizona to visit Albert and Emma at Thatcher. She had an uneventful journey from home to Deming, and was blessed in all her journeys.

    Anna's baby girl, Phyllis, was born Nov. 13/93 10.45 P.M. and weighed 9 lbs.

Was very glad to ^see^ my family after so long separation, and was warmly welcomed by Samuel and Elvira. From this time I continued work on my field notes and plats

December/ December

9th/ I went to Phoenix today to See R.C. Powers, in order to have him give me the knowledge of where to begin my Survey, Contract No. 32, he having surveyed near. Theodore was rebaptized today by Bp. Openshaw.

Sun. 10/ At meeting to day I was mouth in confirming Theodore. He is trying to live a pure and holy life.

12/ To day I finished my field notes, plats + sent to Tucson

13/ Got supplies for my Survey north of Phoenix, and on

14/ Started out with my party, the same as before, except I had one more in party than before. Camped in Nevada Corral at Phoenix

15/ Bought additional Supplies

16/ Left Phoenix, and drove 10 miles to my work near ~~Hardin's place~~ Mail Station 18m from town

[Page B05R]

1893/[Blank line]

Dec. 18/ Began Survey, but was quite unwell all day, with a burning fever.

22/ Again began work, and ran line 6 miles + returned.

23/ Heavy rain all last night and today. Could not work.

24/ Still very sick, with much cough. All thought best to quit and take me home. We reached home at 10 P.M. I having lain on a bed all the way. Samuel also was quite unwell. From this time on I got worse, having with my fever an incessant cough, and my friends thought my condition dangerous.

28th/ When I prayed early this morning I received a promise by the voice of the Spirit, that my faith shall increase from this hour, until it shall become like that of Abraham, Noah and the brother of Jared, also that I shall Soon be restored to health and finish my Survey in the time appointed, and shall be blessed in it from beginning to end. Lilla + Gertie wrote me from Logan, and Sent my Prest Woodruff's remedy for kidney complaints, as follows:–

1 oz hops, 1 oz Senna, 1 oz celery Seed, 1 oz Buchu leaves all steeped in a quart of water. When done, strain into a a pint of holland gin. Dose, a table spoonful 3 times a day. But the teaching of the spirit to me was, not to trust to medicines, but rather to consecrated oil and administration.

[In margin of following paragraph is: Twins born Dec. 8, named Joel and Joseph Franklin]

31st/ Still very sick with fever, incessant cough. Some throat and headache, But I believe in the promise that I shall be healed soon. We received a letter from Mexico, stating that Joel and Anna had a pair of twins born, boys, who lived only a few hours—long enough to be named + blessed.

1894/ January 1894.

Jan. 1/ Still sick, threatened with pneumonia. Slept last night.

8/ Our 42 year of marriage. I feel much better today, and so are Elvira and Wilmirth, both having la grippe.

The Father has been very good to me and mine all these 42 years, and I thank and praise him.

Still sick, distressing cough, headache and fever. I use consecrated oil as my medicine. I prayed to the

[Page B06L]

1894/[Blank line]

Jan. 8/Father to know if I ought to have a doctor as my friends recommended me. The answer, by the voice of the Spirit was, not to depend upon doctors, but use holy oil with prayer, faith and administration by the Elders, and I should be healed. And so I follow it out the best I can, knowing God is abundantly able to heal me if he will.

13/ To day Theodore split his foot with an axe, and bled so much he became very faint. I am now able to walk out but am very weak. I was hoping soon to be able to go back to my Surveys, but Theodore's accident will hinder.

16/ To day we counted up our family, as follows:

Self and 4 wives, = 5 [blank] Children, 21; Grand-children 55, Sons wives (mine) 10, total, 91. Forty two years ago I stood alone. But god has given a promise that I Shall become a great people,—a nation, and I hope I may not forfeit it.

20/ To Day I Surveyed a piece of Sam's land for him, and hope soon to go to work again. The Father has verified his promise, and healed me without a doctor.

21/ To day I again attended meeting, and spoke.

22/ At 2 P.M. I again set out with my party to finish my U.S. land Survey, and went to Phoenix, 18 miles.

23/ I borrowed $150.00 at the bank to obtain supplies, and Sent $80.00 to Gertrude, so she may come to us. We went on to where we had left our tent and supplies when we came home in December, and found about $10-worth of provisions had been Stolen.

24/ Began to Survey again, and lost a screw from my transit which disabled it, until I thought, and made one out of a leaden bullet, which enables me to go on until I can send to the factory in Troy, N.Y. for another.

29th/ This morning Alanson went home, very ill with pain in his ear, which was almost unbearable, and Sam volunteered to cook in his place, besides his duty as Chainman. Theodore drives team, being able only to hobble about a little. His foot has healed remarkably, and from the time he was administered

[Page B07R]

1894/[Blank line]

to at first, has had no pain to speak of although the bone was cut. It is by the blessing of the Lord.

Feb. 1/ To day Sam's boy—Joseph—came from home to help in Alanson's place. I went to Phoenix on business.

6/ Moved camp, having finished T.3N. R.3. East

8th/ Have sold my old Solar Compass, which Cost me $460.00 to the factory, for a Barometer, worth $50.00. My Solar compass had a history. In 1877 I did the field work for A.J. Stewart, who had a U.S. land Survey, and earned between $800.00 and $900.00 Stewart paid me the Compass, worth about $150.00 Charging me $400.00 for it, and afterwards cheated me out of the balance due me—$440.00 But with this instrument I afterwards considerable government Surveying, which I could not have done without it.

9/ To night at about 11 P.M. I prayed, and received an answer, in which, among other great promises, I was promised the Apostleship "whether in the Quorum of the Twelve or not, it mattereth not to thee." This seemed too great, almost for one like me, but it was repeated twice. Once before, a month or so, this was said to me, "Behold I have chosen thee to be mine apostle to the Lamanites." This was in connexion with other great blessings; but I felt as if it might probably be that I would be one "Sent" to them, as the word Apostle means "Sent," but not ordained as an Apostle. And I was told this should be an incentive to live a holy life; also, that He will not suffer me to be tempted more than I can bear, that I may do the work to which I have been appointed from before the foundation of the world. I was again promised a land of promise, where I and my people may rest in Safety, while judgement shall go forth upon the earth; and it shall be among the Lamanites, who shall be a bulwark of defense to us. And they shall have mighty faith, even as when Jesus appeared to them, so that their dead shall be raised Some of the elder ones become white through faith, and their children be born white, for so shall the curse be removed. And also many other glorious promises. Help me, oh God,

[Page B08L]

1894/[Blank line]

Feb. 9th/to so live that I may not forfeit these blessings.

10/ We got caught some miles from camp in a heavy rain storm, wetting and chilling us as it turned to icy sleet. Got to camp nearly chilled and frozen.

13/Alanson returned, nearly well, and Jodie went home.

19/I went to Phoenix and thence to Mesa and found all well. Got my new Aneroid Surveying Barometer, the best of its kind.

25/I find the elevation of our Camp, 15m North of Phoenix is 2358 ft.

March 1894.

March 6/Finished T.5N. R.2E.

" 13/Finished all my survey contract to day, five townships in this contract. Started home at noon. Truly God has blessed us very much, according to his promise.

14/ Got home to Nephi, and found all well, and Gertrude come from Logan, Utah. Immediately commenced to make my plats and write my field notes, which I finished on the [in margin: 30th] and sent them to Tucson,—the Sur. Genl Office.

[In margin left of next says: Reciepe for/Blk. ink.]

I found the following receipe to make black ink:—

½ oz Extract of Logwood, 10 grams Bichromate of potash, dissolve in 1 qt. hot rain water, When cold, pour into glass bottle and leave uncorked a week or two.

Baking Powder. 5 oz tartaric acid, 8 oz Bi-carb. of Soda, 16 oz potato starch, all dried in Cool oven, mix by a Sieve. Dase ½ teaspoonful for a pint of flour. Mix with cold water and bake at once in hot oven.

April/ April 1894

11th/Br. and Sister Truman Sent for Susan to help with their sick baby. We both went, and remained with them.

13/ Borrowed $50.00 of W.K. James, paid some debts in Phoenix.

20th/and Saw J.M. Rice, attorney for the Peoria Canal Co. He wants me to do Some more work on the canal. Left Phoenix 9 P.M. on my was to Tucson, where I went to expedite my Survey business. Arrived there at 3 a.m. on the 21st

May 4th/ May 4

Went to the University to compare and test my barometer with that at the university, a mercurial one. Mine agrees nearly in reading, being 0.07 of an inch higher.

[Page B09R]

1894/[Blank line]

May 4/Mr. D.T. Horton of New York City Sent von Wendt $100.00 which is a great blessing to us, he and I living together and doing our own cooking on a Small coal oil lamp-stove.[122] He is a first class cook.

23/ Sent a dress each to Susan, Gertie and Dora. Von Wendt my friend and chum, gave me $5.00 for the purpose.

30th/ To day von Wendt and I, with teamster, started for the Santa Rita Mt. about 45 or 50 miles distant, to look at a Silver and lead mine we have thoughts of bonding, to Work it or sell it.[123] Watered at Davis' Ranch, which is 1300 ft. higher than Tucson. We camped a few miles below Greaterville, among beautiful oaks and grassy hills.[124] Night Cold.

31/ Rose at 4 a.m. and at 9 a.m. reached Greaterville, a small village at the foot of Santa Rita peak, which is 10,000 ft high.

June 1894

June 1/We examined three mining claims owned by Mr. John Anderson, and filed location notice on an old abandoned gold mine. The elevations are as follows:– Greaterville 5114 ft. the mines, on a high ridge 5390 ft. on pass of the ridge 5500 ft.

2/ I obtained a bond on Anderson's 3 mines, good for 3 mo. If they turn out well and we desire to keep them, I must pay him $1500.00 for them. Started home at 4 P.M. and Camped near a well. Night quite cool.

---

122. It is not clear from the historical record who "D. T. Horton" was. Several pharmaceutical magazines list a "D. T. Horton" of Buffalo, New York, working as a representative of the laboratory of Strong & Cobb drug manufacturing company. Evidently Horton was an early shareholder of the Doxology and True Blue mining claim. Von Wendt later indicated, however, that Horton backed out of his dealings with the mines. See Alex von Wendt to Selim M. Franklin, May 21, 1895, and Alex von Wendt to Selim M. Franklin, May 27, 1895, Franklin Papers, AZ 336, box 44, fd. 8, UASCA.

123. It may have been during this visit to the placers that Martineau surveyed the geological prospects for mining and the availability of water for sluices. Von Wendt relied on Martineau's report as a selling point to generate interest in the placers. Alex von Wendt to Selim M. Franklin, June 6, 1895, Franklin Papers, AZ 336, box 44, fd. 8, Special Collections, University of Arizona Library. See also entry for May 8, 1891.

124. Called Santa Rita in 1873, Greaterville was settled as a placer gold mining community and established a post office in 1879. It was located in Tp. 19 S., R. 16 E., approximately thirty-eight miles south of Tucson and six miles west of AZ-83 (at exit 281). Although it is considered a ghost town today, it is still home to a few residents. See Barnes, *Arizona Place Names*, 190.

3/ Arrived at Tucson at 7 P.M.

12/ Made out my account against the U.S. for my contracts as follows:— Contract No. 32 $838.93. Cont No. 32 $2441.72 total, $3280.65. I gave Alex. von Wendt a power of Attorney, so he may sell the mines I have bonded. I recd a telegram from Gila Bend saying I need not come to work on the canal, which somewhat disappointed me, but I know all will be for the best.

21/ Recd word from Horton, who reports against our mines and Cannot use them. Having finished my business here I start [in margin: 22] for Mesa, arriving there next day, 10 a.m. Found Susan still at Br. Truman's, ~~helping with the sick baby~~.

24/ Went to meeting, and spoke. After, I went with Susan to Sam's, and in the evening Theodore and Celia Johnson

[Page B10L]

1894/[Blank line]

June 24/ Came to me and announced their engagement, asking my blessing, which I cordially gave, with my consent, in which Susan coincided. Susan made a good liniment for rheumatism, as follows:– 1 oz each of oil cinnamon and chloroform, 2 oz Alcohol.

July 3

July 3/ To day Gertrude was severely ill all day. We administered often. The next day she was better and free from pain.

7/ This evening Susan, Theodore, Gertrude and Dora Started with Celia and Joseph Johnson and family, for the hills. I remain at Mesa to write up Uncle Benjamin's journal in his book. The family went on and I spent a week in writing up his journal.[125]

Sat. 14/ At noon all returned from the hills, having had quite a pleasant outing. But Gertrude had not improved any and in the night was taken

---

125. Martineau must have been recording entries for Benjamin Franklin Johnson, whose autobiography and journal were published as *My Life's Review*. Details relating to Johnson's marriage to Susan Holman and Martineau's courtship and marriage to Susan Julia Sherman suggest that Martineau added them at this writing. See note at entry for 15 January 1857 and Johnson, *My Life's Review*, 191.

with severe pain in her side. We administered often, but she obtained but temporary help.

Sun. 15/ Gertrude is in extreme pain in her side—it seems like some internal inflammation. Administration helps her for the moment only, giving her a five minute sleep.

16/ Gertrude still worse, and wants a physician, as she

17/thinks something is wrong internally. I walked to Mesa 4 miles and return, and Dr. Sabin, who thinks her in great danger, through inflammation caused by a stoppage in her small intestines—peronitis—and gave her opiates to relieve her agony, and took means to remove the obstruction by means of a fountain syringe.

18/ She is still the same, but indications are better.

19+20/ Improving a little, and fever decreasing. The obstruction is removed, mostly, and her pain less.

21/ Sat up a few minutes while her bed was made. Fever gone, but She is very weak

23+24/ We remained by her bedside, to fan her and help her all we can.

26/ Dr. Sabin will not call any more unless we send for him, as he thinks she will not need him, if she will continue with the medicine he left her.

[Page B11R]

1894/[Blank line]

July 27/ Gertie not so well today, but I hope nothing serious.

28/Uncle Benj. F. Johnson's birthday, celebrated by many of his family gathering at Don M LeBaron's place, where a fine dinner was prepared in a grove of fig trees. Songs sung, and kind speeches by myself and his sons and friends. There ^were^ several hundred present at this, his 76th birth day.[126]

31st/ Gertrude slowly improving, but not able to stand on her feet, nor to eat anything, more than 2 or 3 oysters at a time. She has very severe pain behind the eyeballs.

---

126. For a detailed account of this party and a short biographical overview of Johnson's life, see James H. Martineau, "Birthday Reunion," *Deseret Weekly* 59 (August 11, 1894): 250.

August.

Aug. 2/ Gertrude wishes to be moved to Mesa, where Br. and Sister James Turman invite her to come to their house. We carried her to a carriage and took her there, receiving a kindly welcome from the family who gave up a room for her, and a place at the table for us all, Susan, Dora + me. May God bless them, they may never want friends in time of need. I board at Uncle Ben's, and am writing up his journal.

7/ Gertie walked a few steps today. Theodore received a patriarchal blessing from uncle Benjamin to day:–

[Blank to end of page, and stamp page B12 is blank]

[Page B13R]

1894/[Blank line]

Aug. 21/ Received instructions from the Sur. Genl L.H. Manning in regard to resurveying the line between my line and Powers', to see which is correct, as they vary somewhat. I quit writing for Uncle Benjamin for the present.

Susan has fears that she has dropsy, but I hope it is not so.

22/ Borrowed $60.00 from the Mesa Bank at 2 % pr month. Administered to Susan, and she is better in health.

23/ I went to Phoenix to meet Powers, who will assist me in making the resurvey. We Started to work on the next day.

25/ Very tired to day, also raw and so lame I could hardly get back to our camp. Glad tomorrow is Sunday.

29/ Have finished all I have to do, and leave Powers to make a resurvey of part of his contract.

30/ Started home by Stage, arriving at 9 P.M. and found Gertie pretty well, also Susan and Dora. We have my tent pitched under the trees at Turman's place, and Gertie and Dora sleep in the house, Susan and I in the tent. We have a small folding table, a few dishes and an oil stove to cook on, and Sister Truman and Jim are as good and kind as can be. I pray that they may never want for anything needful while they live. No blood-relation could be kinder than they have always been.

September 1895

Sep. 1/ Must go to Tucson on my Survey business, and von Wendt writes he has something good in view—gold mines.

3/ Started to Tucson. Found von Wendt well and glad to See me. Thinks he has a good mine in view through Mr. Horton of N.Y. City. Am working up our last notes of joint Survey and making plat of the same.

24/ Sam and Elvira have a new baby, born Sept. 24 They named her Rita. (Margaerite)

October 1894

Oct. 1/ As I am doing Powers work in the making of all our Survey notes +c, also in re-writing his old field notes, he Sent me 25$ on my application, which will keep us on a while longer. I sent Susan $5.00.[127]

24/ By letter from Jesse N. I learn he is in Streator, Ill

[Page B14L]

1894/[Blank line]

Oct. 24/working as a hotel clerk there.

November 1894

Nov. 4/ Saw James F. Johnson on his way to Mexico, he wants me to go to Mesa, keep the Store books until his return home, and write for his father, Uncle Ben, and says he will pay me a little wages for it. So I return home, having filed the notes in the Sur. Genl office of our new Survey (Powers + mine) Left at 12 midnight.

5/ Got home. All is excitement about the election.

6/ Election day, but I did not vote. I began writing again, for Uncle Benjamin

19/ Surveyed a small piece of land for Sam.

23/ I moved my family into two rooms, instead of the one Susan had hired while I was in Tucson. I pay $6.00 pr month for the new place. Susan has

---

127. At this time, Martineau was corresponding with the *Utah Church and Farm*, a semi-official weekly church periodical inserted in the *Salt Lake Daily Herald*. See J. H. Martineau, "Maricopa Stake of Zion," *Utah Church and Farm* 1 (October 6, 1894): 101.

a swelling and sore in her breast, which all think a cancer. Dr. Bailey also declared it a cancer. We prayed, and both received the same testimony—that it is **not** a cancer, but an ulcer, and she shall be healed of it.

December 1894

Dec. 1/ The Swelling in her breast is increasing and more painful. We anoint and rebuke it. Theodore is

7/anxious to got to Utah to school, and has saved money enough for his passage there. I got some clothing in the Store for him, gave him my new overcoat and Some shirts +c, to help fit him out and gave his a blessing. He starts tomorrow

8/ Theo Started at 9 P.M. accompanied to Tempe by quite a number of relatives besides my own family. Many tears were shed, and many hearty good byes. He goes to enter the U.S. Agricultural College, Logan, Utah, and fit himself for a higher usefulness in Zion. He had worked hard all the fall and summer, helping at farm work, in order to get the money necessary for the journey. As I have not received my pay for my U.S. land Survey I am unable to help him much, but wish I could, as he is a good son and one every way worthy.

[Page B15R]

1894/[Blank line]

Dec. 8/I am still busy every day writing for Uncle Benjamin.[128] Frank credited me the munificent sum of $25.00 on my Store account for over a months service. Gertie is able to go to parties now and then, but suffers very much nearly all the time. She says that when she goes to a dance, it only puts her usual pain in another part of her body, for she is never without pain.

20/ I am invited to go to Tucson by Sur. Genl Manning to do mapping, to begin Jan. 1st—one months employment. I answered I would come Jan. 2nd 1895.

---

128. Martineau was probably compiling and emending Benjamin F. Johnson's autobiography and diaries, later published as *My Life's Review*. In addition to writing for Johnson, Martineau submitted an article to the *Utah Church and Farm*. See J. H. Martineau, "Mexican Indians," *Utah Church and Farm* 1 (December 15, 1894): 181–182.

I am very thankful to have even a month's work, to earn something for my loved ones, and for this, O Father I thank thee.

25/ By invitation we had our Christmas dinner at Turman's and had a pleasant time together.
[Blank line]

January 1895.
Jan. 1/ To day we had dinner at Uncle Benjamin's, but I had to hurry away from the table to take the coach to Tempe. I blessed my family before departure, and reached Tempe in time to see a balloon ascension by a woman, who came down in a parachute safely. reached Tucson next day,

2/at 3 a.m. Began mapping in the office.[129]

7/ Bought a nice brooch for Susan, for our wedding day.

8/ Our 43d wedding Anniversary. Greatly has God blessed us in our married life. We have had sorrow, sickness and death, plenty and poverty, pleasure and pain; but only enough for our good, to perfect us in faith, patience and knowledge,—knowledge gained only by experience. And in no other way can we become perfected. If we have sorrows we know how to sympathise with others who are sad, for we can understand their troubles.

But I have been blessed as have been but few men, in my beloved Companion—one among ten thousand; and in my children, who thus far all proved honorable and true to the truth. One other there is, who holds aloof, but why I know not, unless it be by the unity of her

[Page B16L]

1895/[Blank line]

Jan. 8/mother, whom I never injured in the smallest particulars. But I have a testimony that she will yet return to me as a true and loving companion.[130]

To day poor Gertie is sick in bed with lagrippe, as I learn by letter.

9/ I am lodging again with Baron Alex. von Wendt. We do our own cooking,

---

129. No documentation of this temporary appointment as draftsman is found in the Tucson Surveyor General's office correspondence. The appointment was undoubtedly made under authority of approval contained in a departmental letter, dated March 6, 1894.

130. This is in reference to Jessie Helen Russell Anderson Grieve. See entries for February 14, May 3–8, 21, and June 4, 1893.

and although forced to be economical and eat but twice a day, we get along very well. I bought a quilt, as nights are cold.

14/ I bought a silk dress pattern for Susan, the first she has ever had. The cost was $8.35. She deserves one, if any one does.

28/ I felt quite anxious, as my month draws to a close, hoping I may have one or two more months employment. I prayed for this, and received testimony that I <u>shall</u> have two or three month's work. At noon, the Chief Clerk told me I could continue on, next month and perhaps two months; thus verifying the whisperings of the Holy Spirit to me. In the evening one of the draughtsmen resigned his position and told me I could have his place, as he had something else he could do.[131] Truly God is very good to me, in giving me words of comfort by the voice of his Holy Spirit when I ask him, unworthy as I am.

29/ To day my Survey papers were sent to Washington.

February 1895

Feb. 1/ To day Manning told me I could have 3 or 4 months work.[132] Truly the promise of the Father is being fulfilled. And I am learning more and more to know the voice of the Spirit when he whispers to me.

---

131. At this time, Martineau and von Erxleben were listed as "draughtsmen" working in the Tucson Surveyor General's office. See *A Historical and Biographical Record of the Territory of Arizona*, 271.

132. On this date, Manning wrote to obtain permission for Martineau to take Contzen's place in the office:

Sir:–
Philip Contzen, appointed on September 15, 1894, as draughtsman in this office, appointment authorized by Department letter of date August 25, 1894, initial "A", resigned on January 31, 1895. Mr. James H. Martineau, an expert draughtsman, formerly employed in this office, has this day been appointed to fill the place made vacant by Mr. Contzen. Complying with instructions contained in Department letter "A" dated January 9, 1894, I have the honor to request approval of this action. Mr. Martineau's appointment to date from and include February 1st, 1895, salary $100.00 per month.
Very respectfully,
Levi H. Manning [Signed]
U.S. Surveyor General.

Levi H. Manning to Commissioner of the General Land Office, Washington, February 1, 1895, Letters Sent, box 7: Vol. 28, October 28, 1894–April 1, 1896, p. 77, CSGAZ. This appointment was approved a few days later. S. W. Lamoreaux to L. H. Manning, February 7, 1895, Letters Received, box 112: Vol. 17, September 9, 1894–August 13, 1895 (180–311), letter #238, CSGAZ.

2/ Br. and Sister Pierce called to see me, on their home to Mexico. I Sent a few little things to Anna by them.

4/ By letter from Susan I learn Wilmirth was married to Alanson Reidhead on January 31, 1895. This is the first marriage of any of my grand children. Wilmirth was about 14 or 15 yrs old I think.

[Page B17R]

1895/[Blank line]

Feb. 4/ To day the U.S. inspector examined my Survey of the two townships near Tucson.[133] I naturally felt a trifle anxious, as upon his report would depend the acceptance of my Survey. So I asked the Father to cause his to accept it,—to see nothing that might be imperfect, or that would keep him from accepting the work; and I receive a clear testimony he would receive the Survey.

6/ The inspector returned to Tucson, and reports my Survey excellent,—the most perfect he has ever seen; and said the Authorities in Washington might suspect him of putting up a job, +c. As I know all land Surveys are very imperfect, through errors in chaining and courses. I was very much astonished, and could plainly see that God had led him to go over only such portions as were exact; or if not, the inspector had made just the same errors I had (if any there were) so it all appeared right to him. I do not mean that God caused him to accept work that should not be, for my work was really much better than average surveys, and therefore should be accepted. The Father fulfilled the promise of the spirit to me; and for this I praise his holy name, and am thankful I am learning more and more the voice of the Spirit, which said to me not long since in Mesa, to "do nothing except thou shalt ask the Father, and if the Spirit saith unto thee "do it," thou shalt do it; and if he saith "do it not," then thou shalt not do it, and so thou shalt be blessed in all thou shalt do."

But for a year or more it has been my custom to ask for guidance and many times—always—has an answer come in words spoken to me by the Holy Spirit, and it is the same with my dear wife Susan. Notably, on one occasion in Juarez when my old friend John Macfarlane was sick she prayed for him, and an answer came in words

---

133. About this time, Martineau sent an article to the *Church and Farm*, giving a description of the population size and prominent historic landmarks of Tucson. See J. H. Martineau, "An Old American City," *Church and Farm*, February 9, 1895, 49.

[Page B18L]

1895/[Blank line]

Feb. 6/"He shall depart, it is the will of the Father." At this time he was apparently nearly well, and went to Utah, but suddenly died. This blessing is to me about all price—to know God actually hears and answers me, weak and sinful as I am. How wondrous is his mercy and goodness, and how little I can do in return! But it is the great desire of my soul to do all I possibly can to help redeem Zion, and redeem the Souls of men and bring them to God. This I desire more than all earth can give could I have it all.

7/ I have thought much of moving my family here from Mesa, so I can provide better for their comfort, but have feared evil influences here. This morning I asked if it is best to bring them here,—shall it be well for them! The answer of the Spirit to me, in answer to my prayer was,—"Bring thy family here unto thee; they shall be blessed, and no evil shall come to any of them nor to thee, and all shall be well with thee."

I had some fear that Gertrude might be led to love my friend Alex. von Wendt, who is social and attractive, but not a member of the Church. He and I have "bached" together many months and like each other very well; but I do not want any daughters to marry one not a member of the Church.[134] I understood from the answer given, that no evil should come to Gertrude through him. And so I at once announced to him I would bring my family to Tucson, as he had often urged, and I wrote my family to get ready at once and I would come for them. Engaged a house of 6 rooms conditionally.

14/ Bought wood and family supplies, and stored them.

15/ von Wendt Started to day to visit some mines, and in the evening I started to Mesa.

16/ Settled some bills in Mesa, and we all went to Sam's, and remained all night.

---

134. This was a heart-wrenching dilemma for Martineau. He had grown to respect von Went as a trusted friend. Yet, granting him permission to marry his daughter Gertrude would go against his belief in marriage "under the covenant"—or the invocation of Abrahamic blessings which are entitled to members of the church who are married in the temple. See Lane "Protecting the Family in the West," 1–17, esp. 10–15.

17/ Started from Tempe at 9 P.M. Sam and quite a number of the relatives going there with us.

[Page B19R]

1895/[Blank line]

Feb. 18/ Got to Tucson at 3 a.m. and resumed work in office.

20/ Wrote to Joel to buy a ⅙ interest in a threshing machine.

23/ To day Von Wendt got back and called to see us. He reported well of the mines he has Secured, as being rich in Silver, with some copper and gold.[135]

My sons in Mexico wish we may buy land in the new Chuichupe country, situated in the mountains about 50 miles South of Pacheco. A lot is 5000 meters square, equal to 6175 acres. Price $1.00 pr hectare, equals 40¢ per acre. The payment to be made in 3, 6 and 9 yrs after 1st payment, colonists to have many concessions for a term of ten years. Br. Macdonald gave me all these particulars, and I will buy land there if I can. Being in the tips of the mountains the climate is delightful and salubrious, with plenty of timber, grass and wild game. Each colonist over 12 years old will receive $50.00 which will apply in part payment for the land.

March 1895

13/ My 67th Birthday. We had a nice Supper which von Wendt shared with us. Got word that Aunt Sally Tuttle, the only Sister of my dear wife's mother, died Feb. 11th quite suddenly. She had been for years a temple worker, and was an excellent woman. Her exaltation is gained, for she has been true to the end.

16/ Got word from Washington my Rincon Survey is approved. The value is $839.93 I believe. I am very thankful, not only for the money but because I see that God <u>has</u> heard and blessed me, and that the voice which promised it was the voice of the Holy Spirit,—not that of any lying Spirit. And this increases my faith.

22/ My Sister Henrietta says my niece Bertha is the matron of the Children's Hospital, Columbus, Ohio, and her sister Jenny is teacher in the U.S. indian School at Fort Felton. Joel has sold my saw mill for lumber $500.00

---

135. For a written description of the Doxology and True Blue mining claims, see footnote at entry for April 18, 1891.

26/ Received word that my other Survey is approved, value $2349.93. This is as the Spirit had said to me would be, and I am thankful.

[Page B20L]

1895/[Blank line]

April/ April 1895
2nd/ Mr. von Wendt came to us, having badly burned his foot, scalding it badly. We fixed him a cot in the front room and made him as comfortable as possible. Messrs Horton, Barney and another, who came from New York to examine a so-called placer gold claim have returned from visiting it, much disgusted. They found nothing of value, and this is as I told von Wendt it would be.[136]

14/ This evening Mr. von Wendt surprised me very much by asking me for Gertrude as a wife. I had not thought of such a thing. I had given him a home in his illness from his burn, and I knew he liked our family, but I did not think of any wish on his part to marry my daughter. I felt much disturbed at the thought of my daughter marrying one not of the faith, and told him it was contrary to our principles to so permit. He plead his love, and Said that although he did not believe in any of the churches or religions of the day, he did believe the Mormons were nearer right than any of them, and his religion consisted in doing good—doing all the good he could, and no harm or evil to any. I told him I would consider, and tell him in the morning. I wanted an opportunity to ask the Lord for guidance. I asked the Father concerning the matter, and the answer of the Spirit was "Be of good cheer, and fear not, for no evil shall come to thy daughter Gertrude through him or any other man. He is one who is honest in heart, and will receive the gospel, and do a mighty work in Zion." Therefore I felt to trust in God, and that it would be right to give my consent to Gertrude's marriage to him, relying upon the promises given to me. But it was

---

136. Martineau was an experienced mining surveyor and had probably given von Wendt his opinion regarding the mineral prospects in the area where the placers were located. Von Wendt respected his friend's opinion and defended his expertise when it was later questioned by his lawyer, Selim Franklin: "I am just in receit [sic] of your letters May the 26 also in receit of the Bonds, ect [sic] and note what you say, but may dear friend your are mistaken when you say that Mr Martineau don't know nothing about the Placers, in the contrary he knows all about it! As he made the Water Survey ect ect!" Alex von Wendt to Selim M. Franklin, June 1, 1895, Franklin Papers, AZ 336, box 44, fd. 8, Special Collections, University of Arizona Library.

quite a trial to my faith, seeming to me such a serious matter,—a thing I had always firmly set myself

[Page B21R]

1895/[Blank line]

April/against, especially in case of covenants made in holy places. So it was with fear and anxiety I determined to give my consent, which nothing would have induced me to do, except the promise of the Spirit.[137]

15/ This morning I told von Wendt he had my consent provided he and Gertrude continue of the same mind when he returns from New York City a few months hence, as he intends soon to go east to sell mining property.

This morning before daylight the voice of the Spirit came to me, repeating what I have previously written, and saying also God had brought von W. and me together, for a purpose of his own; that von W. would bless me in temporal things and I should be a blessing to him in Spiritual things; that noble spirits should be sent to them who will never turn away from God, but be exalted with Gertrude and von Wendt in the celestial glory. And this was said to me three times, giving me great comfort.

And Susan, praying also, received the same testimony; for she too, had the same anxiety about the matter, and the same fears, that I had, especially as Gertrude said she would leave it all to us, although she loves him with her whole heart. This responsibility in our heads makes Susan and me more anxious to be guided by the Holy Spirit in this important matter.

All we can do is to receive and believe the word of the Spirit, and trust our father in Heaven. Gertrude says he is the first and only one who ever attracted her and she loves him, but does not wish to violate any covenant she has made, nor do anything wrong.

16/ I wrote to Lochrin, Pension Commissioner, withdrawing my application for increase of pension as a Mexican War veteran from 8$ per month to 12$, agreeable to the late law, because I would have to Swear in an "indigent circumstances—a beggar—which I decline to do, although I am poor, with nothing but my daily labor to sustain us.

---

137. Despite his misgivings about giving consent for him to marry Gertrude, Martineau knew that von Wendt was an honorable man. After receiving a promise that "no evil" would come to his daughter, Martineau felt assured enough to give his consent. See Lane, "Protecting the Family in the West," 12–13.

[Page B22L]

1895/[Blank line]

April 17/ This morning when I prayed, I received precious promises by the whisperings of the Holy Spirit. I was told von Wendt was appointed before the world was, to be Gertie's husband, and he shall become a man after God's own heart and do a mighty work in Zion. Gertie will not be obliged to violate her covenants in marrying him. When he is ready to go to New York he shall have money to go with for his way to obtain it will open to him; and he shall be prospered then in his business to the fulness of his expectations, and even more so. He shall love and be true to Gertie all his life, and wealth shall in abundance flow to him and to me. Also that I shall be mighty in Israel, a leader, a mighty prophet, with power to do mighty miracles and a mighty work in bringing Souls to God; besides other great promises. I thank thee, oh my Father, and ask thee to help me to live so as to attain these great blessings, which have been already sealed upon me by patriarchs.

May.

May 1/Up to this date von Wendt has been slowly improving, but has been mostly confined to his cot. My wife and I, notwithstanding the testimonies we have received, feel anxious about Gertie's union with one out of the Church, and have frequently prayed about it, but we both have always the same comforting answer, that "no evil shall come to thy daughter through von Wendt," and so we comfort ourselves, and feel to trust in God that all will be well, although we cannot see how it will come about. But we know God is fully able to do his own will in all things.

I borrowed $300.00 in the bank to day, and Sent $40.00 to Susan, who is in great need, and gave $200.00 to von Wendt, he having obtained $150.00 or more from a Mr. S. Franklin, his lawyer.[138] It was with difficulty I could borrow the money,

---

138. This was Selim Maurice Franklin (1859–1927) born at San Bernardino, California, on October 19, 1859, to Maurice and Victoria (Jacobs) Franklin, early pioneers of San Diego. Franklin graduated from the UC Berkeley Law School in 1883 and was elected to the Arizona Territorial Legislature in 1884. He is often referred to as the "father" of the University of Arizona for his work in obtaining passage to the bill leading to its founding. Franklin worked in private practice in Tucson for many years. He died on November 22, 1927, in Tucson. See *Portrait and Biographical Record of Arizona*, 235–236.

Von Wendt went to New York for the purpose of selling his mining claims, "Doxologie"

[Page B23R]

1895/[Blank line]

May/1/having no property in this country. But in this way the promise was fulfilled that von W. would have money necessary for his journey when the time for it arrives.

2/ To day von Wendt started for New York City to sell his mining property, which we hope he may do.

5/ I received a letter from Sam in which he says I shall be greatly blessed. He says "I do know you will have the privilige to pay all you owe; and that yours and mother's last days will be the best days of your lives, and the happiest days; for you are going to have plenty, and you will live to see your children and your grand children all around you, and they will rise up and bless you; and you will both be a blessing to others." He testified that ^he^ knew this by the testimony of the holy Spirit. I feel thankful and happy, for I believe his words.

6/ Got word that my Second Survey contract has been ordered paid me, amount, $2349.93 being $143.31 less that what I applied for.

I thank thee, my Father, for this fulfillment of thy promise to me!

14/ Recd a treasury draft for the amount, and at once Commenced paying my debts. I had borrowed of WK James, of Phoenix $650.00 for which I paid $930.00 I borrowed 150. of Hickey and paid him $210.00 I paid my note to the bank here and $3.60 interest, also many other debts which reduces my money almost to 0, but I am glad to be able to pay all honorably. At this time I had not told Susan I had received my money, wishing to be able to Say I had recd it and had paid my debts, which we had worried over, and was free. I had sent the draft to Phoenix to pay Mr. James, and it did not come back till

18th/the 18th. This morning before I received my draft from the post Office, Susan was awaked in the early hour about daylight by the sound of clinking money, as if I was counting it, like silver dollars.

---

and "True Blue," but soon ran out of money for food and lodging when he arrived. See Alex von Wendt to Selim M. Franklin, May 12 and May 13, 1895, Franklin Papers, AZ 336, box 44, fd. 8, UASCA.

[Page B24L]

1895/[Blank line]

May 18/ She heard is so loud and plain she feared a burglar was in the room, robbing me of money, and because I made no sound feared I had been made insensible until she heard me breathe, as usual. As soon as I awoke, she told me of it. When I went to the post I found my draft for $1416.93 waiting me. So she was enlightened by the Holy Spirit.

19/ This morning I had a vivid dream, relative to the power and might of the United States. I saw a tall liberty pole, about 250 or 300 ft high, and much admired it height and straightness. As I looked again I saw it was bent over at the lower one of its three splices, the upper ⅔ part being almost horizontal. But I saw the pole was not <u>broken</u> at the bottom splice, although it seemed at first to be I knew this pole represented the United States. I awoke, and the interpretation came, that thus would be humbled the glory of this nation, and seem to be broken and destroyed, but not entirely, the bottom part being firm, sustaining still the upper part. So the great hurt may be healed.

24/ By letter from my nephew Fritz Vaswinkel I learn he is visiting Logan, likes the country, and will bring his wife and two children from Omaha. He was married Dec. 15, 1889 to Emma Phillips, had Emma and Lois. His sister Bertha was born

June 9, 1864. Fritz was born Jan. 27, 1862

29/ Got word my Rincon Survey is ordered paid.

30/ Recd a telegram from Anna S. at Deming. Sent

31/her $20.00 to Come to Tucson

31/ Anna came, with her baby girl Phyllis. We were very glad indeed.

    This finishes my engagement at the office, as there is no money to pay me for June. The Sur. General informed me if I would work next month and wait for my pay, he would insure it to me, which I agreed to do.

[Page B25R]

1895/[Blank line]

June 1/ I continue work in the office. I had been told by the Chief Clerk I could work no more, but the voice of the Spirit had said I <u>should</u> work as long as I desire. I feared some lying Spirit had promised me this, but now I found it was true, and that it was the voice of the holy Spirit which had told me. It makes me very happy to know God hears and answers me, when I know I am so weak, doubting and unworthy. He is very good to me.

2/ Subscribed for Cosmopolitan for 6 months.

7/   "   " "Chronicle" for 6 months.

15/Sent von Wendt $100.00 I still continue to receive the same good testimonies concerning him by the Spirit.[139]

16/ Received my pay for the Ricon Survey,—$838.93 a total for both Surveys of $3188.86. Thus has the father verified his promise that I should "be blessed and prospered in my survey from beginning to end," although for a time it seemed as if my work would be disallowed by the inspector.

20/ At this date I have paid all borrowed money; Store debts and all my survey hands, besides sending $10.00 to $20.00 per month to Theodore, and buying many dresses for Anna and my family besides other goods. I still owe about $350.00 which I hope to be able to pay when von Wendt repays me. I am very thankful indeed to be so nearly free of debt once more, and pray that I may no more be brought so deeply in debt. For 6 years I have earned nothing to speak of—say $500.00—and by sickness of my family my expenses have been constant and increasing. But I am now free from nearly all debt and I am very glad indeed. At many times it has seemed dark as Egypt, and had it not been for the promises I received from the Spirit I should have despaired. For many months at a time I had only 2 meals a day, and for Some months only one meal a day,

[Page B26L]

1895/[Blank line]

June 20/but still I was able to keep up very well. If I got very hungry I

---

139. Von Wendt acknowledged receiving $100 from Martineau a few weeks later when he wrote to his lawyer to update him on the placers. Alex von Wendt to Selim M. Franklin, July 10, 1895, Franklin Papers, AZ 336, box 44, fd. 8, Special Collections, University of Arizona Library.

asked the Father to remove it, and then I forgot all about being hungry for hours at a time. And sometimes I got to my last 50 cents and had no idea where the next would come from. So God has given me a chance to trust Him and to grow in faith, and in the knowledge of the voice and influence of the Holy Spirit,—blessings of far greater worth than millions of money.

Surveyor General Manning offered me a small Contract of a few hundred dollars, to survey the west boundary of the Pima indian reservation, but as I found I would be able to clear very little I declined it especially as both Susan and Gertrude opposed it.

July 1985

July 11/ To day Susan is 59 Years old, more than 43 years of which she has been my wife, a comfort + a blessing.

16/ I telegraphed $180.00 to J.F. Johnson, in part payment for 2500 acres of land in the Chuhuachupe purchase, in the Sierra Madre mts, Mexico, as my sons in Mexico are desirous to settle there in the new settlement. The land is rich, timber and grass abundant, and enough rain to produce good crops. Also sent $20.00 to Theodore as usual, in College, Logan, Utah.

25/ The money I telegraphed J.F. Johnson returned to me uncalled for. I then sent $100.00 to Alex. von Wendt in New York city.

August 1895

Aug. 1/Sent $15.00 to Theodore. Telegraphed to my grand-dau. Bertha Martineau, daughter of Henry A, and who is arrived at Deming on her way to visit us, money for her fare to Tucson.

2/ Bertha came this evening on the train. She is 15, full grown and comely, and we were glad to meet her.

7/Sent a pale Sea green crystal to New York, to find out if it is of value. Henry found it in Mexico. Recd first Weekly Leslie[140]

[Unstamped page]
[Between page B26 and B27, a thank you note to JHM from Susan dated Tucson, July 11, 1895—a lovely note]

---

140. This refers to *Frank Leslie's Illustrated Weekly*, a pictorial newspaper which was published in New York from 1855 to 1922.

[Page end]

[Page B27R]

1895/[Blank line]

August 13/Mr. Laragino, an Italian mine expert, called to see me. Sent for medicine for Susan, to reduce flesh, as she is quite fleshy, weighing nearly 250 lbs, which makes it hard for her to go about much.

17/ Sent $1.30 to Chicago for a blank book in which to continue my journal. (it is <u>this</u> book.)

20/ Sent $8.50 to Juv. Instructor, Salt Lake City, for Moroni.

September

Sept. 9/ To day Elvira, my eldest daughter, came by wagon from Nephi, 5 days journey, with Joseph, Emma + Gertrude to visit us, we not expecting them. It was a very pleasant surprise to us.

Gertrude has now been in bed for about two weeks, while her mother was rubbing her hip as usual, she felt the head of the hip bone move from its place, which rendered her unable to walk without great pain, which she bears, as she always has, with the greatest patience.

12th/ We went to the circus, but Elvira did not go.

13th/ She started home this morning—a long journey—and to Camp out every night in the wilderness. But she is a true pioneer, brave and self-reliant.

15/ Susan was very sick all day, but was healed by faith, in a speedy and remarkable manner, by the blessing of the Father, to whom be all honor and praise.

17/ Dora began going to school. She is 12 years old, but has had no schooling, as she seemed almost unable to learn or remember anything heretofore. I blessed her, that her memory might become good, and she be able to learn and become wise and useful, + I believe she will.

18/ Letter from Alex. von Wendt, who is very sick in New York. He says he has willed all he has to Gertie if he dies. Susan and I each prayed for him, and we both received the same answer—that he should recover, and yet do a great work in Zion. We wrote words of

19/comfort and promise to him. Gertie was very sick during the night, but is better in the morning, She has great faith in administration.

[Page B28L]

1895/[Blank line]

Oct. 2/Von Wendt writes he has been very sick, and did not expect to live, but is better now, and not in danger. It was pulmonary illness.

3/ Sent Joel's level to Troy to be repaired.

5/ Gertrude is slowly improving, but still keeps her bed. Theo writes that he has been part in charge of a squad of 12 men at the U.S. Agricultural College, Utah, and is making good progress in study. Also, that he will soon be put in charge of the class in wood turning.

14/ Received my Deseret Semi News, as correspondent.

15/ Got telegram from Deming that a team is waiting there to take her home to Colonia Juarez, Mexico. She began to pack up at once; also Bertha.

16/ Anna and Bertha started at 9 a.m. for home. We were very sorry to have them go, but they had made us a long and pleasant visit and so we must feel resigned. We will greatly miss little Phyllis with her cute, winsome ways which made her so dear to us.

18/ Joel's level came, repaired. The expenses in all are nearly $20.00

20/ To day I took Gertie and the rest for an hour's ride in a carriage, but it tired her considerably.

27/ Took a walk early this morning and found the body of a man murdered but a short time before, lying in a ravine, soaked from head to feet in blood. He proved to be a miner, killed by two Mexicans.

November 1895

Nov. 13/ Sent $10.00 to von W. Sent article to Deseret News.

14/ Sent $10.00 to Theodore

16/ I am offered another Survey contract of $2000.00 adjoining the Apache indian reservation; but as it will not pay much, if properly done, I do not accept.

18/ Ceased work in the Sur. General's office. When I came from Mesa I had assurance of only one month's work. I prayed, asking that I might have 3 or 4 months additional (In January last when I first came here) and received answer that I should have,

[Page B29R]

1895/[Blank line]

November/and even more, and so this has been abundantly fulfilled. This causes my faith to greatly increase.

19/ By letter from Nephi, to day, we learn he has another Son born, on Nov. 12th weight 11 lbs.

23/ I am still lame with rheumatism in my back + legs. This morning before day light I prayed and received a glorious testimony, which I hardly dare to write;—I am to do a mighty work in Zion—be like Seth a perfect man,—walk with God like Enoch;—be mighty in priesthood and calling among the Saints, and a mighty pillar in the Church;—see my savior in the flesh and remain until He comes, to bring Souls to him,—Susan to remain with me—to assist me and to do a mighty work in the temple in Zion—in the Center Stake—for the redemption of our dead, and to receive great blessings therein.

Great blessings also were promised Gertie;—health and a perfect healing of her lameness,—a husband who shall be one after God's own heart and attain an exaltation in the celestial glory with her and their children + grand children who shall do a mighty work in Zion.

Also many other great and comforting promises. To the natural mind Such things may seem impossible, but we know if we do the works of Enoch we will receive the same reward as he, and attain the same glory. I believe I shall receive these blessings; if I do not, it will be because I do not do my part, for our Father fails not.

26/ Sent an article for publication to the Salt Lake Herald.[141]

---

141. The article to which Martineau refers was published a week later. In it, he describes the changing climate in southern Arizona, the election campaign in Utah, mining matters, and education in Tucson and Phoenix. "Business in general is improving," he wrote, "and the Southern Pacific railroad is rushed to its full capacity, many freight trains passing daily each way, which shows that people east and west have something to sell and something to

28/ Thanksgiving day, and a chicken. We have had much to be thankful for up to the present time. We have been blessed greatly here in Tucson, with much better health, and I with employment, by which to sustain my family.

29/ A letter from Virginia. She writes that her last child named for her, Virginia, was born Oct. 7th 1895, and was blessed by her father Edward Sudbury, Oct. 15, 1895.

December 1895

2/ Received last months Salary, $97.80 and paid

[Page B30L]

1895/[Blank line]

Dec. 2/it nearly all away for our monthly accounts and to Theodore, to whom I send monthly $10. to $20.00

    To day Dora Started to the public school

4/ Mr. Alex. von Wendt returned to us from New York. He had made a partial sale, to a small amount, and gave me $100, on account the money I had sent him.[142]

11/ I sent a nice dress to Emma, Albert's wife. While von Wendt was in New York I sent him $410.00, money which I needed badly for my family, but which I thought he needed worse.

14/ Sent for the N.Y. World for Joel and Anna, having also Sent the San Francisco Chronicle to Henry A.

15/ I received my quarterly pension of $24.00

16/ By letter from Joel we learn he had a fine Son born on Dec. 7th 1895, weighing 10 lbs. His name is Leland.

17/ I sent Theodore $15.00 I ceased work at the office.

18/ Letter from Nephi informs me he will start on his mission on Feb. 15th He seems full of the Spirit of his calling, as the following extracts from his letter indicates:–

---

buy with—a very satisfactory condition of things." J. H. Martineau, "News from Near-by Towns; Interesting Facts about Tucson, Arizona," *Salt Lake Herald*, December 2, 1895, 7.

    142. Von Wendt's return from New York was reported in the local newspaper. See untitled, *Arizona Weekly Citizen*, December 14, 1895, 4.

"Logan Dec. 8, 1895
Dear father, Mother and all

x x x I received my letter from "Box B" which informed me that my mission would be to the Southern States, and I am well satisfied to go there, on account of being a cheaper place to go. Now I will sell a piece of my land and get entirely out of debt, and will still have 120 acres left, which will be enough for the present. I had to mortgage my land for $450.00 to pay for the land, and lawyers fees, and now by selling 40 acres I will be out of debt and have no interest to pay every month. The way is being opened up for me to dispose of every thing so that I can go at the appointed time. The words are true which say the Lord will ask nothing only as he will open the way to accomplish it, and it has been so in my case. I have

[Page B31R]

1895/[Blank line]

December/partly learned one thing—I say partly, because I can not always discern the right Spirit—but can See that as I follow ^its^ the influences that I am nearly always right. I try to give place to that Spirit continually in all my temporal affairs, and find it ever ready to lead me aright, and the more I watch and study it the better satisfied I am. It is good to pray always, or have a humble Spirit, and then that spirit will abide in us continually, to lead us in the ways of truth. How beautiful!

A person who would be happy should be possessed of pure thoughts, humble spirit,—a clean tabernacle, and then the spirit of God could abide therein. How beautiful will be those who fought the good fight and are worthy of the blessings of the faithful. I can see no peace, only as is found in the gospel. My ambition is to be a good man in the Church, in preference to being a governor or Senator, which was plainly shown when the Savior chose the fisherman to follow him. We should honor the priesthood we have, and do our duty in that, and then there would be harmony in all the Church. How nice it would be to see you and talk about these things that are of So much value to us. I am thankful for my parents, who have taught me truth. We as children, owe a debt we can never repay. May God bless you both, and prosper you, and ever give you his spirit to comfort you, and may your last days be your best days, that you may live long and counsel your children in righteousness is my prayer continually." x x x

Your loving Son Nephi.
[Blank line]

I have inserted this letter to show the pure, humble and holy spirit which—as always—possesses him.

[Page B32L]

1895/[Blank line]

Dec. 18/In answering Nephi's letter, I wrote the following as a promised blessing to him:–

Nephi, you shall go and return in peace and safety, be blessed and prospered in your absence and do a good work, and no power Shall hurt you. Your family, also, shall be blessed and prospered while you are away and none shall be taken while you are away but all of them shall greet you on your return with great joy and pleasure. Your mission shall be a great blessing to you, causing you to grow and increase in Spiritual gifts and blessings, in prophecy and revelations, in visions and dreams and interpretation of the same; in the gift of healing, and in faith, and in the knowledge of the influence and power of the Holy Spirit, who will be your constant companion, and fill you with great wisdom and power to do good. You shall be blessed more than your greatest anticipations, and the power of God will be manifested in your behalf. The heavens are full of blessings for you and for your family, therefore do not have any fears nor doubts, but believe, and trust in God, and you shall see the fulfillment of every word of this prophecy and blessing, for I pronounce and seal it upon you by my authority as patriarch to my family in the name of Jesus the Redeemer. Amen.

In writing this, I felt it was by the influence of the holy spirit. It was not so much a <u>blessing</u> as a prophecy, for I do not understand that we have authority to <u>seal</u> a blessing without at the Same time laying on hands. I also wrote that he should "Strive to be like Enoch that God may love you, and that you may walk with him, till the coming of the Savior in his power and

[Page B33R]

1895/glory."

Dec. 18/ I asked the Father if what I have written to him is right, and the answer came—"It is right, write it down." and so I Sent him (Nephi) the letter, and record it here. [blank] our first cold weather to day.

20/ Von Wendt started to examine the Cababi mines he has, and to start work on them.

24/ Sent a box of things to our children in Mexico, Henry being at Deming, N.M. with his team.

25/ Christmas, and a turkey, our first <u>own</u> turkey for years.

28/ Von Wendt returned, having had a very cold time. He brought a dozen chickens, and a Spaniel pup—<u>Molly</u>.

January/ January 1896.

1896/ Had another turkey dinner to day.

3/ Sent to Hall Chemical Co. St Louis, for 80 days treatment obesity pills for Susan, as they seem to reduce her weight.[143]

4/ Letter from Joel. Says they have named baby Leland Knowlton. They say it is a very nice baby. Of course it is.

Mr. von Wendt and I, with a teamster started for Graterville, 48 miles, at foot of Mount Santa Rita, to look at a new gold placer. Arrived at Ensenbergs at 5 P.M.

5/ Looked over the ground some.

6/ Went up the mountain, and took levels for a dam. In the afternoon witnessed the operation of a <u>dry washer</u> (or Winnower) which blows away the dirt and leaves the gold. The ground seems quite rich, say $1.00 to the cub. yard.

7/ Very cold and windy. Prospected in the mountains for a water supply, for hydraulic purposes in mining.

8/ Started home at 9 a.m. arrived at 4 P.M. and found all well.

This is our 44th Anniversary of our marriage, and is always our most enjoyable occasion or holiday.

---

143. This is the first indication of Susan's longtime effort to reduce her weight. See entry for January 31, 1910.

9/ The Surveyor General again gave me work in the office for a short time. And thus is fulfilled the word I received in answer to my prayer that my way may be opened. The answer to me was, my way shall be open before me from this time forth, and that I shall not any more be brought into such poverty and

[Page B34L]

1896/[Blank line]
January/want as in Colonia Juarez and Mesa, and that I shall be prospered in all I do, and abundant wealth will flow to me, that I may do good. I have had this promise several times in answer to my prayers. Truly the Father is very merciful and good to us.

25/ Ceased work again, there being no funds on hand for me, an extra employee. I believe still, it is all right.

Feb. 1/ February 1896.
To day von W. and I went with a Mr. Charlve to survey a copper mine, which we did, returning at night, pretty tired.

5/ Sent Theodore $20.00 This morning Erxleben, a draughtsman in the office, came to ask me to go to work in the office in his place for a week or ten days, as he wished to be absent for a while. I was very glad for the chance to earn something for my family, as our expenses are nearly $3.00 a day. And so my way opens again, if only for a short time.[144]

---

144. Martineau worked for von Erxleben while he was recovering from illness. Ten days later, Levi Manning wrote to the Commissioner of the General Land Office to report on Martineau's appointment:

Sir:–
I have the honor to advise you that Mr. James H. Martineau has been employed temporarily as draughtsman in the Mineral Department of this office, salary $4.00 per diem, to date from and include January 9, 1896. Authority for the appointment of these temporary clerks is contained in Department letter of date March 6, 1894.
Very respectfully,
Levi H. Manning [signed]
U.S. Surveyor General.

Levi H. Manning to Commissioner of the General Land Office, Washington, January 15, 1896, Letters Sent, box 7: Vol. 28, October 28, 1894–April 1, 1896, p. 429, CSGAZ.

Erxleben, a rather pretentious individual, appears to have been using his professed illness and knowledge of the inner workings of the Surveyor General's Office to exert pressure and intimation on Roskruge to increase his salary. On April 12, 1896, Erxleben wrote: "I am sorry I ever resigned. If you raise my salary to $1500 a year I shall return." See Charles von Erxleben to George J. Roskruge, April 2, 12, 15, and May 20, 1896; Letter of

9/ Von W. went to see the Silver bell mine. Susan and I wrote a comforting letter to Nephi.

10/ Von W. returned, bringing a very good report of the mine, which he says is very valuable.

13/ Sent for a galvanic or Electric Battery, also some electric belts +c, and applied for an agency.

von W. Started to his Cababi mines.

16/ I feel impressed to take Mary Harris, a girl of 16, who lately in a fit of despondency killed herself in California, caused be ill treatment and cruelty. I know Suicide is a grivous sin, but I think she will be forgiven, because she was driven wild. But this will be as the priesthood Shall rule.

18/ Von W. returned. He found that the men he was employing at his mines had "jumped" them to deprive him of them, they all the time eating his bread. But he made them undo what they had done. He went in good time, surely.

[Page B35R]

1896/[Blank line]
Feb. 21/ Susan and I sat for our photos to day.

24/ Received a letter from Apostle F.D. Richards, to whom I had written, asking instruction in regard to the letter I had written to Nephi, promising him blessings, Dec. 18th

25/ He said it was right to <u>promise</u> blessings by the Spirit of prophecy to persons absent, but to seal a blessing upon one it was necessary for that one to be present, so that he who would seal the blessing might lay his hands upon the one to be blessed. And this is just as I understand it. In looking over the blessing I sent to Nephi I see that I wrote it in that way,—by promise. Apostle Richards said:—"I see no objection to a man writing a blessing if it be revealed to him by the Holy Spirit, and sending it to the one for whom it is intended; but, the sealing it upon that person is quite another thing, while such a blessing dictated by revelation will just as surely come to a fulfillment as if it had been sealed upon a person.

Recommendation, March 11, 1897; and Hugh H. Price to George J. Roskruge, November 24, 1902 and May 15, 1903, in Roskruge Papers and Surveying Documents, MS 0697, box 2, fd. 23, AHSL.

His letter is very kind, and I will try to profit by it.

28/ Received our Photos, which friends say look natural.

March/ March 1896

7/ This evening Benj. Samuel + his boy James, Cousin James F. and his little boy, and Vaughan Guthrie came, on their way to Mexico. They remained next day, Sunday.

9/ The boys went on their way. We Sent a box of things to the Children in Mexico, also our photos.

13/ This is my 68th birthday. I cannot realize it. Is it possible I am almost 70 years old? It must be so.
[Blank line]
Susan.

I think it right to insert in this record something concerning my dear wife Susan Ellen. She was born in Kirtland, our first temple city, Geagua Co. Ohio, July 11, 1836, being a daughter of Patriarch Joel H. Johnson and Anna Pixley Johnson.[145] Her mother dying when Susan E. was only 4 years old. She was reared by her step-mother, Susan Bryant, whom her father married some

[Page B36R]

1896./[Blank line]
Feb. 13/(Continued)/years after his first wife's death. She spent some years also with her grandmother. By reason of the persecutions of the Saints she was reared in poverty among mobs, who repeatedly drove the family from place to place, keeping them in poverty and distress, and at times threatening their lives. At one period, when living on Crooked Creek, two miles from Ramus in Illinois, a mob one day came to the house, about 30 in number, mounted and armed, their faces blackened, and halted in front of the door. Susan and her brother Seth came to the door in obedience to their call, and stood there hand in hand, trembling with fear.—two little tots, only 8 and 6 years old respectively. Well might they fear and tremble, for mobs had already pillaged and burned scores of

---

145. For more biographical material on Susan Ellen Johnson, see Susan Ellen Martineau, "Record of Susan Ellen Johnson Martineau" and James H. Martineau, "Additional Material Written About Susan Johnson Martineau."

houses, shot or whipped men to death, ravished women and committed other horrible atrocities, until, in the minds of the children, the name "Mob" meant all that was fearful and horrid. The mob asked for father Johnson. The children Said he was not at home. The mob told them to tell their father to take his family in two weeks, or they would come and burn their house and kill them all. Then they rode away to harass other families in like manner.

What could the family do? They had no means for travel—no means to make a new home if robbed of this one. They could only resign themselves to any fate that might overtake them.

In a few weeks the mob came again, about midnight, and with fearful oaths demanded why the family were not gone. Father Johnson told them that all the family were sick and could not go, some of the mobs swore they would burn them out now; others said that would be too bad, as the family was sick; and the discussion terminated in a quarrel between the two factions. In the end they said the family could have just ten days longer in which to leave; if not gone by that time, sick or well, they might look for death.

[Page B37R]

There seemed no hope for escape. All the family were Sick, they had neither team, wagon nor money with which to move and make a new home. But just a day or two before the ten days were out, a forlorn party of four families came along, seeking refuge in Nauvoo. They had but one old, rickety wagon and two poor little scrubs of horses. Susan's father obtained permission to go with this party to Nauvoo, and did so, leaving home, farm, cows, pigs, poultry and household goods to the Spoilers. Think of it! Five families, with but one poor little team and wagon which could carry only a few quilts for each family, with perhaps a bag of corn meal,—the men, women and children trudging painfully along through rain and mud on foot. But, as "a man will give all that he hath for his life"—they were glad to go, even in so Sad a plight.

After most of the Saints had been driven from Nauvoo, Susan remained there with her grand-mother, and witnessed the burning of the Temple, Set on fire and destroyed by the mob. Her father, with most of his family having gone to Utah in 1848, she followed in 1850, traveling in the care of her uncle Geo. Johnson and his family. The Cholera, which killed so many thousands of emigrants upon the plains in that year, attacked the little company in which She journeyed. Day after day Death claimed his victims, for every one attacked in the party died except Susan. She, too, lay desperately ill with the scourge alone in her wagon. Stephen Markham, Captain of the Company, in his rounds found her near unto death. He spoke cheerfully, said she must not die, and asked if she believed she could be healed by the laying on of hands. She answered "Yes." "Well then," said he, "we'll have you out if this right away." He brought some elders, she was administered to and healed immediately, by the power of God, and soon was well as ever. Of this little company of 28 families, 15 persons were stricken, of whom 14 died, she, of them all, being the only one who

[Page B38L]

1896/
recovered; and this, that she might fulfill the work appointed her.

Slowly journeying with their ox teams for some weeks they at length came to the country of the Cheyennes, and met a party of these indians on a hunting tour. The company remained encamped two nights and one day in one place on account of stormy weather, during which time an indian became enamored with Susan, then 14 years of age, and comely to look upon, with a lovely complexion and well formed figure. He wanted her for a wife. A young man, Andy Kelly, an irishman who had deserted from the army at Fort Kearney, and had joined the Company hoping to get to the gold fields of California told the indian he could have her for 5 ponies, some buffalo robes and some other things, just for a joke. But the indian was in earnest, not understanding such jokes, and next day came to camp bringing the five horses and the other things specified in the bargain. Of course he was told it was all in fun—that the whites never sold their girls for wives to any one. But the indian could not be made to understand this; he had made a fair bargain, had fulfilled his part of it and now wanted the whites to fulfill theirs. When he finally found he could not have Susan he was furious, and departed, muttering revenge.

No indian came around afterwards and the company were glad, supposing their visitors had gone entirely away, and had much fun over the poor fellow's disappointment. At night a terrible tempest came on, such as the Platte valley is famous for—tempest, deluging rain, vivid lightening and tremendous thunder. It seemed as though the tent would be blown away, so Susan and Some others went out into the storm to help hold the tent ropes and keep it in place. While thus engaged in holding the tent, which stood close to the bank of the river, which was fringed beneath by a dense growth of willows, she felt herself suddenly seized and placed upon a horse, the pitchy blackness of the night preventing her from seeing who it was, but not

[Page B39R]

for a moment thinking of an indian. Just then a bright glare of the lightening revealed an indian in the act of springing upon the horse behind her, ready to dash away with her. Her screams instantly brought her help, as she leaped from the horse, while her dusky lover—disappointed and baffled in his daring scheme—dashed away down the bank into the thicket and was instantly lost to Sight. She was thus providentially saved from a fate worse than death, and did not soon venture again outside the camp.[146] The morning light showed how the indian had approached the Camp along the river bank and waited till the night became dark as Egypt, then brought his horse up near the tent, and waited for a favorable moment to seize and carry her off. Poor fellow! With him, as with so many others, "the course of true love never does run smooth." That night the indians revenged themselves by creeping into camp and stealing every kettle, frying pan, dish, axe or tool of any kind not put into the wagons but left around the camp fire as they usually were. But the hunting party never came in Sight of the company again.

Kelly, the young man who had caused all the trouble, went with the company as far as Great Salt Lake, then stole all the clothing and blankets from the man who had given him food and passage, and soon got into the city chain gang. What finally became of him Susan knows not.

One day while journeying up the Platte river she and a girl named Ann Howard Strayed away from the road gathering choke cherries. After a pleasant time they mounted a ridge and looked for the wagon train, but in vain. Far as the eye could reach not a wagon was to be seen. Somewhat alarmed at being thus left alone in the vast prairies of the roaming Cheyenne indians, who might at any moment appear, swoop down upon them

---

146. The foregoing story was retold under Susan E. J. Martineau, "Almost an Indian Bride," *Young Woman's Journal* 18 (June 1907): 264–265. A comparison of the language of this and the published version suggests that it was James Martineau who wrote both.

and carry them away into an eternal captivity, they regained the wagon trail as soon as possible, and pressed forward to overtake the company. Thus they went on, mile after mile, still hoping but never coming in sight of the wagons. Night came on, while now and then the distant cry of the prairie wolves

[Page B40L]

1896/[Blank line]
could be heard, but fortunately always in the distance. And so hour after hour in the darkness of the vast and lonely plains, tired out and wearied, these two girls went on until at length the figure of a man suddenly appeared before them in the darkness. They supposed him to be an indian, but the welcome voice of Andy Kelly disippated all their not baseless fears. Knowing they had not arrived in camp, he had come out to meet them at a place where the trail forked, and placed them both upon his horse he conducted them to the camp, where they arrived after ten o'clock at night. Truly a lonesome and a hazardous walk for two lone girls in an indian country.—one which they never repeated.

Susan remained in Salt Lake City until the fall of 1851, when she, in company with Susan West who afterwards became a wife of Prest Geo. A. Smith, and a few families, went to Parowan, Iron Co. Utah. When Patriarch Joel H Johnson, her father, founded Fort Johnson, she went there and remained until I married her there, on Jan. 8, 1852. John L. Smith, now patriarch, united us in wedlock—his first experience in that line, and John D. Lee, who met so tragic an end, was one of the wedding guests. Our nuptial couch consisted of a few quilts spread upon the floor,—afterwards in a wagon box; and when I took her to Parowan, our future home, our bedstead was only a few boards laid across some trestles. At length I became rich enough to buy a regular bedstead, but this, being unpainted, was not stylish—far from it. To remedy this we bought some red face paint from an indian (a Pah Eed) Susan mixed it with some Sour milk, and with it we painted out bedstead and a table. We had no varnish, but took the fat of a prairie dog I had killed, and rubbed it over the parts with a rag until it resembled a French polish. Many were the glances of pride we bestowed upon these articles of furniture I do not believe that Queen Victoria feels as proud to day of any article of furniture She has in her house, as we did when we looked at our brilliant

[Page B41R]

scarlet tinted bedstead and table.

Since then Susan has passed with me through many trying scenes of poverty, sickness, trouble and danger—things that would try one to the center—but never has she murmured nor complained, and "because she has not, She shall be exalted very high," for so saith the Lord. She spent a night moulding bullets by the fireside, while I, with the other men, guarded the approaches to our fort, while the long night was made hideous by the yells of the Utes, as they danced their war and scalp dances not far away. They had told us the previous day that they would kill every soul in the fort. They were 400 warriors, well armed; we, a hundred men, poorly armed, encumbered with women and children and 200 miles from help. And so, at other times, was out little settlement threatened, but never, in any such scenes did she show cowardice. She was always at such times calm and cool, trusting always in God. Of such mothers are born heroes.

And when in 1886 the Apaches filled Arizona with blood and torture—slaying hundreds of settlers—Susan and I had to travel with a team from St David to Pima—a 110 miles—to reach our home in Pima, right through a section where they were murdering people every day—a route which Genl Miles had forbidden any settlers to traverse because he could furnish them no aid—even then she would not leave me. I wished her to go by rail to Bowie Station, thence by Stage home, a route comparatively safe, while I would come on alone with my horses and Carriage. If she came with me she could be of no help if attacked; and if Death was waiting for a victim on our trail it was far better for but one to die instead of both. It is bad enough for a man to be in danger of torture and death, but ten times worse to have a loved and helpless one with him at such a time. But all such arguments fell upon deaf ears. She would stay and go with me, and my fate should be hers. When we started, our friends as they bid us good bye (and said afterwards) believed they

[Page B42L]

1896/[Blank line]
March 13/would never again behold us alive. We traveled for miles through canons and hills, the roadside lined with rocks and bushes, any one of which might hide a lurking Apache; but we prayed our Father to

protect us, and not let the Apaches see us, and he heard our prayer. Once we came so near the indians, who were lurking just over a low ridge near by, that we saw one of their dogs prowling about. We crossed their trails freshly made, and at a watering place, where I intended to rest and lunch, the ground was covered with fresh pony tracks recently made. Pausing only to water our tired but splendid animals, we drove swiftly on, and by sunset were safe. But while passing near the foe Susan forced from me a dreadful promise—the most fearful a man can make, who loves his wife. She said "James, make me one promise:—If the indians come upon us, and you are not yet killed, promise me that you will kill me yourself." Said I, "How can I promise such a thing—I would rather die myself." Said She, "Would you rather have me fall into their hands alive, to be tortured?" "No, but how could I kill you my dear wife!" But she was firm in her request, and nothing could move her. And I knew, too, that a quick death at my hand would be a thousand times more merciful than such tortures as the Apaches had already inflicted upon many women and children. But oh! what a dreadful thing it is to be obliged to make so fearful a promise! No one can begin to realize it until he faces the dread alternative. At last I gave the promise she desired, inwardly resolving that if one bullet ^of mine^ should make her free another should do for me.

But the Father heard our prayers, and though we passed near the Savages they saw us not. In all this days journey, threatened with a fearful death, Susan never once lost her calmness and peace of mind, nor showed any fear. She was a true heroine, and I

[Page B43R]

1896/
March 13/rejoice to be able to chronicle these facts, that her children to the latest generation may honor her forever. But I pray we may never again be in such a straight, if it be according to the will of the Father. What may yet befall us I know not, but my constant prayer is that we may never be parted—neither in life nor in death.

Susan Julia Sherman. (deceased)

I think I have mentioned in the course of this journall all items of interest relating to my wife Susan Julia Sherman and therefore will add nothing more, until I shall find out items of interest of which I am now ignorant, except to say I believe no mother taught her children true and

holy principles more carefully than she. And she died firm in the faith and in full fellowship with the Saints. She now rests from her labors, having attained, through ordinances in her behalf in the Logan Temple, all the exaltation pertaining to a fulness of the priesthood, even to be a priestess and queen in the highest degree of the Celestial glory by obedience to the law of Celestial marriage as revealed by Joseph the Prophet and Seer.[147] Peace to her memory until we shall meet again.
[Blank line]

20/Last night I dreamed of having a handsome service of Gold upon my table. I may yet see this fulfilled; if not, it will be all right. Have dreamed several times of having gold in plenty. I believe the Father will give me all I need.

29/B. Samuel and party returned from Deming, having been unable to enter Mexico, owing to increased stringency of regulations.

April 4/ April. 4.

This evening I felt impressed to visit Gov. L.C. Hughes, who has been removed from Office as Governor.[148] He has been a true friend to the Saints and to me, giving me space in his paper for replies to attacks upon the Saints, when in our darkest hour. For this I pray God to bless him, and I was told to visit and give him words of Comfort, for they shall be fulfilled. I went and did so. He much appreciated this, and said he believed what I told him, for he knew I believed in prayer, and he also did. I told him he should gain the victory

[Page B44L]

1896/April 4/over his enemies, and some of them should yet come to him bending, and asking him for favors. He was affected to Firmness in the eyes, and said he could not tell me how much good I had done him.

---

147. The "fulness of the priesthood" refers to second anointing ordinance, which is only given to a select few who have received their calling and election sure. See Bueger, "Fulness of the Priesthood," 10–44.

148. Louis Cameron "L. C." Hughes (1842–1915) was born at Philadelphia, Pennsylvania, to Samuel and Elizabeth Edwards Hughes. He served as Tucson City Councilman in June 1872 and later as a county attorney in April 1873. He was appointed Attorney General of the Territory of Arizona in 1873, but resigned after only a year. He served as governor of Arizona Territory from 1893 to 1896, when he was removed from office for his liberal views. Hughes started the *Daily Bulletin* in March 1877, which later became the *Triweekly Arizona Star*, and finally the *Arizona Daily Star*, beginning on June 26, 1879. He died in Tucson on November 24, 1915. See Keen, "Arizona's Governors," 13–14.

I am thankful I was able to comfort him.

11/ Ceased work in the Sur. Genl Office—no more work. I know not how we will get along here, without money or employment, but I believe the Father will open up my way.[149]

21/ Filed a bill against the U.S. Land office for $71.72 which is righteously due me on last Survey.[150]

22/ This morning, after secret prayer, I had very comforting answer, and received many great and glorious promises. Truly the Father is very merciful and good to me.

24/ I sent an article to the Dest News in support of the last "Manifesto" in relation to political and other matters.[151]

28/ This afternoon about 2 P.M., after secret prayer I had a greatly comforting answer thereto, by the voice of the Holy Spirit, and things were

---

149. About this time, Martineau sent an article to the *Deseret Weekly* giving an account of the wars between the Apaches and Pimas, and telling the story of the ancient ruins of Casa Grande. See James H. Martineau, "Tradition of the Pimas," *Deseret Weekly* 52 (April 25, 1896): 578–579.

150. Arizona Surveyor General Manning had verbally notified Martineau that his account for surveys under Contract No. 30, dated June 21, 1893, had been approved and allowed to the amount of $2,349.93, being $143.31 less than the account rendered by him (JHM). This disallowance was caused by the rejection of the exterior line of Tp. 4 N., R. 1 E. and by the disallowance of certain exterior lines "which are not described in the deputy's field notes." Since Manning didn't rectify this disallowance during his time in office, Martineau asked that Roskruge refer it to the Commissioner of the GLO. He then objected to the reduction of his account, since he only retraced and resurveyed lines as ordered by special instructions given by Gen. Manning dated December 11, 1893. Since these lines were found to be correct by Inspector Holladay, "I should receive pay for the same, amounting to $42.19," he wrote. Having followed the directions given by Manning, Martineau felt that he was due his pay: "I respectfully submit that my retracement and survey of the S. bdy of T. 3 N., R. 3 E. having been approved, as also the subdivision lines of the north based upon it, I should not suffer loss because of an error made in the office of the Surveyor General of Arizona, and that I am justly entitled to pay for work on this exterior amounting to $29.53 for 2 m. 78.52 chs. at $7.00 per mile, and 63 chs. at $11.00 per mile." Martineau claimed compensation in the amount of: $42.19 + 29.53, totaling $71.72. James H. Martineau to George J. Roskruge, April 24, 1896, letter #159, CSGAZ.

Three days later, Roskruge forwarded Martineau's request to the Commissioner's Office, writing that Martineau's claim was a proper one and that "he is justly entitled to compensation for those lines requested in his said letter, and would so recommend." George J. Roskruge to Commissioner of the General Land Office, Washington, April 27, 1896, Letters Sent, box 8: Vol. 29, April 1, 1896–December 31, 1896, p. 41, CSGAZ.

151. See J. H. Martineau, "More of that Manifesto," *Deseret Evening News*, April 29, 1896, 2, and *idem*, *Deseret Weekly* 52 (May 9, 1896): 665–666.

made plain about which I had been in doubt. For instance, whether it was right for me to be in Tucson with my family—away from the Saints. Also, if I had been deceived by any lying Spirit, or that what I had received as from the Holy Spirit had been from an evil source. I was told to reflect and consider whether I had been taught by that Spirit to good or evil; that the Evil One <u>never</u> incites any one to Good, because there is no good whatever in him; if there were, he would not be the Son of Perdition that he is, but after having atoned for his Sins the good in him would receive its reward.

But the Holy Spirit <u>does</u> always incite to do good, and thus I may know to judge between them. And I was told that the Spirit which had promised me blessings, and that spirit which now Speaks to me is the voice of the Holy Spirit, and therefore to fear not, nor doubt nor be troubled, for the Father loveth me because of my desires to do right. And He saith, "Behold I know the secret desires of they heart, to overcome sin, to work righteousness, to honor and glorify thy Father in heaven, and when thou desirest a blessing shall

[Page B45R]

1896/[Blank line]
April 28/I turn thee away with a curse? Wouldst <u>thou</u> do so to a son who desired to do thy will? And shall I be less just than thou? Verily, no. Therefore rejoice and be glad, for the spirit that speaketh unto thee is the voice of the Holy Spirit, and if thou shalt believe and obey it thou shalt be blessed indeed, and no power shall hinder. And be not troubled because thou art here with thy family, for I have brought thee here for a purpose of mine own, which thou shalt more fully know in due time; but in part it is that thou shalt grow to be mighty in faith; for when troubles make it seem dark unto thee, and my Spirit speaketh words of comfort unto thee, and they are afterwards fulfilled, then thy faith shall grow and become mighty,—thy wisdom also. And the time is near, even very near, when thy friend shall sell a part of his mines and give thee money in plenty, and thou shalt be able to go to my saints and the family, and be free from thy present life. And although thou art out of work and thy money nearly gone, fear not, for I will open thy way, and thou shalt have means for thy food and raiment, and for shelter and other purposes, and be not again destitute as in Mexico and Mesa, for thou shalt have wealth in abundance, even mighty wealth, that thou mayest do a great and a mightier work in

the temporal building up and redemption of Zion, in buying lands, building mills and machinery for the good of my saints, and for doing good in general. For thy friend shall sell his mining property and receive great wealth, and impart freely unto thee, that thou mayest do these things. And fear not for thy daughter Gertrude, for she shall not be led to do evil by him, but shall be true and faithful, and shall suffer no loss by him nor any other man. And he shall have his eyes opened, for he is honest in heart, and when he knoweth the truth he will receive it and do a mighty work in Zion,

[Page B46L]

1896/[Blank line]
April 28/for he shall open the doors of salvation to his kindred, for some of them are honest in heart and will receive the truth. And thou shalt assist him in this, for he shall desire it; and some of the great and mighty shall receive thy testimony, and thus it shall be fulfilled that was sealed upon thee, that "the great and the wise shall submit themselves unto thee, thy shall consecrate their gain to the Lord and their substance to the God of the whole earth; thou shalt lead them to Zion with their riches." And he shall do a mighty work in Zion, and thou, my son, shall do a mighty work in Zion. For this cause I have gathered thee out from among thy kindred, and given thee power to receive the truth and to be firm and unshaken unto the present time. And thou shalt declare my word, and thy voice shall be as the voice of an angel and as the voice of a lion; for the righteous shall rejoice to hear thee, but the wicked shall flee away and tremble. And I will show forth my power through thee, and give thee power to do mighty miracles among the House of Joseph, even to raise the dead to life if needful, to cause the earth to shake and the rivers to turn their course."

And other great and mighty blessings were given me, and I pray I may live so as to obtain them, and I have a sure testimony these sayings are true, and if they be not fulfilled, the fault will be mine, not of the Father. Praise and glory be unto him forever. Amen.

After writing this down on a memorandum, I asked if what I have written is all as it should be, and if any thing is not right that it may be made known to me. Also, shall I record it in my record? The answer to me is—"it is all true and right and pleasing to the Father and to write it, that my children after me may read it and be blessed and strengthened in their faith. I have therefore recorded it in this book.

[Page B47R]

1896/[Blank line]
April 29/Spent considerable time in writing up my journal.

In ~~Feb~~. ^March 4^ last Susan's Aunt, her father's sister Almera died in Parowan, Iron Co. Utah, of old age, at the age of [blank] She was a wife of the Prophet Joseph Smith, being Sealed to him in Nauvoo. After his death she married a Mr. Barton, who afterwards apostatized, by whom she had five children, who all died before she did, two of them in Parowan. She was a true Saint to the end of her life.

In April, 1896 Susan's step mother, Susan Bryant Johnson second wife of her father, died in Diaz, state of Chihuahua, Mex. in her 84th year of asthma.[152] She married Joel H. Johnson in October 1840, he being a widower with five children, Sixtus, Sariah, Nephi, Susan and Seth, Susan being then 4 yrs of age. She received her 2nd A. in the St George temple, and lived many years in Utah—from 1847 and in Mexico [the 7 in 1847 seems to be overwritten with 8] as a pioneer, sharing all its hardships bravely. She was the mother of 8 children, only tow of whom, David and Joel, survive her.

Two or three days after her death occurred that of her Uncle, William D. Johnson, also in Diaz, Mexico, after a short illness. He was one of the younger brother of Susan's father.[153]

Thus do the old veterans of early Mormonism pass away, and soon, if <u>we</u> do not also pass, will we, too be left almost alone. But if we can be true to the end it will all be right.

May/ May 1896

1/Yesterday I received $39.53 for my office work in April, which is not enough to pay last month's living expenses, which are over $2.00 per day.

---

152. Susan Bryant Johnson died on April 7, 1896, in Colonia Diaz, Mexico. See "Obituary Notes," *Deseret Weekly* 52 (May 9, 1896): 671.
153. William Derby Johnson died on April 13, 1896. See "The Mormons in Mexico," *Deseret Weekly* 52 (May 2, 1896): 635, and "Obituary Notes," *Deseret Weekly* 53 (July 4, 1896): 96.

Our rent is $20.00; Ice $2.30 milk $3.00, with wood and grocery bills, not counting what we need for clothing +c. Naturally speaking, with nothing in sight before me, by which to get any means, it looks very dark indeed. The only thing I have upon which to depend is the promise of the Lord through the voice of the Spirit that we shall not want. But sometimes the thought comes to me "<u>Was</u> it the voice of the holy Spirit, or was it a lying spirit, to deceive me?"

[Page B48L]

1896/ Moroni's death.

May 1/Then when I ask the Father concerning this, I always receive the same comforting answer, that the voice which speaks to me is the voice of the Holy Spirit, and reminds me that the Evil Spirit <u>never</u> incited any one to good, but <u>always</u> to evil, because there is no good in him. If there were, he could not be the son of Perdition, for the good that would be in him must be saved. And I do know that the voice which guides me <u>does</u> always incite me to good, and comforts me,—gives me strength and courage and faith in God, and hence I know it <u>is</u> the voice of the Holy Spirit. And I believe the Father thus causes me to be in close places is that I may grow in <u>faith</u>,—seeing the promises of God fulfilled when it seems almost impossible that they can be.

And I know that by this experience, which in some cases has been marvelous, and by the blessing of the Father, I <u>have</u> increased in the gift of faith. And so all these things which seem to me <u>trials</u> are right and for my good. Blessed be the name of the Father. And so I try all I can to exercise faith that we shall not come to want, but that we shall have means for our support, and I believe we will.

4/ Received a letter from my gr-daughter Alley Martineau daughter of Lyman and Alley. Her first to me. I had previously received one from her little sister Harriet; both are precious mementos to me.

7th/Lilla's girl/ By letter from Lilla I learn she has a new baby girl, born April 10, 1896. ~~not yet~~ named. Margorie [note lines in margin]

8th/ We also received a letter from Melissa, dated April 27 [in margin says: Moroni's/death] which conveys the terribly sudden tidings of the death of our dear Son <u>Moroni</u>, which occurred April 22, 1896 in Mariana (or Chuichupe) the new settlement in the tops of the Sierra Madre Mts.

Sonora, Mexico.[154] He was taken ill Thursday Night April 16th with a chill and a stiff neck, but did not complain of being sick or of any pain until he died. On Monday, 20th he began to labor in his breathing, but no one thought him

[Page B49R]

seriously ill, nor did he himself, refusing to take any strong medicine, and desiring only the nursing of his beloved wife Sarah Sophia. They had three elders to administer to him, Henry being absent,—leaving home on a prospecting trip with some brethren on the 21st He had no thought that Moroni was seriously ill, or he would not have gone away.

During the night Moroni's breast and ears turned dark—visible in the morning. He told his son Eddie how to plow a piece of land near by, and Eddie went to do it, but had only plowed two furrows before his father was dead. These are all the particulars I could glean from the letter, but Henry will soon give us a full detail I hope.

Moroni was born Sept. 12, 1854 in Parowan, Utah. In 1860 removed to Salt Lake City, and thence to Logan, where he lived many years and was a great help to me in Surveying and other work. He was called, with Henry and Elvira and her husband B. Samuel Johnson to a mission in the South,—Arizona—and in September 1876 went there, never again returning to Logan, Henry and Samuel had gone the previous Spring, on Feb. 7th 1876. In Dec. 17, 1879 he married his cousin Sarah Sophia Johnson, daughter of Sixtus E. and Editha Johnson, being Sealed in the St George temple. He immediately proceeded to Apache Co. Arizona with Henry and Samuel and their families, and for several years endured much hardship and privation, in settling the country, infested with Mexicans, Indians and renegades who stole many horses and other stock, year after year.

After we removed to Pima, Graham Co. Ariz. he and Henry removed there to join us, and when we moved into Mexico they determined to go

---

154. Chuichupa (first named Mariano) was located near the western border of Chihuahua, eighty-five miles southwest of Casas Grandes, thirty-five miles south of Colonia Garcia, and forty-five miles southwest of Colonia Pacheco. Chuichupa was founded in April 1894, when Benjamin Johnson, Edwin H. Austin, James H. Carlton and son, Ben L. Johnson, and Wallace Edwin Staley of Colonia Dublan pitched camp there in search of a new home. A few days later they were joined by Sixtus Johnson, David E. Johnson, and John McNeil. Martineau's sons, Theodore and Henry Augustus were early settlers of this colony in the Sierra Madre mountains. See Romney, *Mormon Colonies in Mexico*, 112–114.

with us. Moroni removed to Colonia Juarez in the fall of 1889, and afterwards to Pacheco in 1890, thence

[Page B50L]

1896/ Moroni's death

returning to Juarez. Being a raiser of cattle, and there being poor range about Juarez, he and I went to over the Sierra into Sonora and helped found Oaxaca, on the head of the Yaqui river (then called the Bavispe). We left Juarez on the 6th of Feb. 1892 and arrived at the place of destination on the 15th of March 1892. We had to build a road across the mountains, and had to make many miles of heavy dug way, and do much blasting of rock. Theodore and Anna also went with me, Moroni leaving his family behind. We also moved most of our cattle and horses with us.

As we could not get along with our leader "Parson" Williams (who soon apostatised) I returned to Juarez in the Summer, and Moroni came back in 1894. While he resided in Oaxaca, he was appointed constable in the municipal organization there, and was teacher in the Sunday School, and a most efficient worker. In March 1895 he with Sixtus and others settled at Chuichupe on the western slope of the Sierra Madre Mts, (since named Mariano) where he died. He had laid the foundation there for a good home, but died while all was yet in embryo.

He was a character of the truest integrity and unselfish devotion to the work of the Lord, in which he was always a most energetic laborer. He was always full of fun and good humor, and full of bright natural wit and good sound sense. He was a Seventy, and he honored his priesthood to the best of his ability, keeping strictly the laws of tithing and Word of Wisdom, and receiving in his heart sincerely every law, regulation and doctrine of the Church, never in opposition thereto, nor to his presiding leaders in the priesthood.

[Page B51R]

1896/[Blank line]

Few have left a better or more unsullied record, and his exaltation is sure, dying in full faith and fellowship in the church. He had nine children—7 living—and another soon to be born, and died nearly 42 years of age, in his prime. He lived in great happiness with his beloved wife and

family, and taught them principles of righteousness all his days. He has "fought the good fight" and has gone to his sure reward.
[Blank line]

May 9th/ This morning about daylight, I asked why it was that Moroni had been taken, seeing that his patriarchal blessing had not yet been fulfilled. I inquired if it was because of sin in me, or in him, or why it was. I received a very comforting answer, of which this is the spirit:—It was not because of sin in me nor in him, but because he had stayed here his full appointed time. Spirits come to earth according to law and order, in their appointed times and seasons and return to the spirit world and enter into their Third Estate at the time appointed to do so. And so it was with him; he had finished all his labors here, and gone to do other and greater labors in the spirit world. His work is to preach the gospel to our ancient fathers who died without it.—the ancient ones of our own family or lineage, that they may be prepared to receive temple ordinances when they shall be performed for them. He has passed all danger from the power of the Evil One, and has made his calling and election Sure, to attain a throne as one of the Kings of Eternity—one of the Gods. For although he had not received <u>all</u> the Temple Ordinances (the 2nd A. and other) yet, as he has never rejected or opposed any one of the laws of heaven, he is entitled to a full and a complete exaltation, and his anointings

[Page B52L]

1896//[Blank line]
May 9/and other ordinances can be administered to him by proxy in a day to come. And his early death shall cause him no loss, For his work shall follow him.

All this was comforting to me, and especially that referring to the work he is now to do for the ancients of my lineage; and I wondered much, when it was all shown to me so plainly I had never thought of it before. As we do temple work for our dead relatives—each for his own family—so we should, in the spirit world naturally preach to our own family and prepare them to receive the temple work some time to be performed for them. It is as plain as the Sun to me—why did I never think of it before.

But after all, our hearts are sore. Moroni was always good and obedient at home, kind and loving to his mother and sisters and to me. He was always punctual in attendance to Sunday Schools, Y.M.M.I.A. meetings, his Elders and Seventies Quorum meetings, his Sunday meetings; and active in discharge of all his duties. Blessed are the dead who die in the Lord; and their works shall follow him.

Yesterday I telegraphed the sad news to Lyman, and Sent an obituary notice to the Deseret News.[155] Also sent many letters, and words of comfort for poor Sadie and her fatherless children.

To day (9th) I have spent in recording all these things. Also prayed and received a comforting answer. Sent an article to Des. News on the first discovery of lead and Silver in Utah, also about Virginia's escape from Squash head.[156]

16/ Sent an article in defense of the last "Manifesto" of the Authorities relative to acting in accordance with the priesthood.[157]

18/ Received word my claim against the U.S. is just, and to make out an account in due form, which I at once did.

20/ Filed my account to amount of $127.72, the same being approved by Sur. Genl Geo. J. Roskruge.[158] He also offers me

[Page B53R]

1896/[Blank line]
May 20/a contract to survey a township, at rates $20 to $23 pr mile.

23/ Sent article on early settlement of Utah, and its difficulties.[159]

---

155. See "Obituary Notes," *Deseret Weekly* 52 (May 23, 1896): 736.
156. See James H. Martineau, "Indian Reminiscences," *Deseret Weekly* 52 (May 23, 1896): 718, and note at entry for August 28, 1887.
157. This article refuted the notion that the Manifesto on polygamy was not a revelation. See J. H. Martineau, "What is Revelation?" *Deseret Weekly* 52 (May 30, 1896): 739.
158. Roskruge's approval was in reply to Martineau's letter dated April 24, 1896. Martineau's letter was forwarded to the Commissioner of the GLO, with the recommendation that the claim therein for compensation for certain lines be allowed. Roskruge was in receipt of the Commissioner's reply in which the recommendation of the office was approved. Martineau was asked to prepare and file in the office a supplemental account under Contract No. 30, so that the matter could be properly adjusted. George J. Roskruge to James H. Martineau, Tucson, May 19, 1896, and George J. Roskruge to Commissioner of the General Land Office, May 21, 1896, Letters Sent, box 8: Vol. 29, April 1, 1896–December 31, 1896, pp. 89 and 96; and James H. Martineau to George J. Roskruge, May 19, 1896, Letters Received, box 44: Vol. 28, November 14, 1895–July 31, 1896, letter #202, CSGAZ.
159. See James H. Martineau, "Some Plain Truths," *Deseret Weekly* 53 (June 20, 1896): 20.

31/Sarah sent me the following particulars of Moroni's death dated Mariano May 21, 1896:–

My dear Father and Mother and sisters. I will try and write a few lines. It is a month tomorrow since my dear Moroni died. Oh dear! it is terrible to think about; I never get it off from my mind when I am around home. He commenced Thursday (16th April) night with a head ache that lasted Friday, Saturday he had a pain in his shoulder; the pain left his shoulder and went under his left arm. I got that stopped and he seemed to be getting better. He sat up ~~in bed~~ part of the time and walked around. He went down to Henry's on Monday night. (20th) I did not want him to go—he said he felt well enough. I put my big coat around him. In the night he woke me up breathing so hard and such a rattling in his throat. Anything we done for him did him no good. He never wanted anybody to do anything but me. I tried my best to get him to let me go and get somebody to come. He said "You are doing all you can, I dont want anybody else." At last he gave his consent for me to send for Dama (Didame Carlton) She came and asked him how he felt. He said "I am better." Inside of a half an hour he was dead. He was sitting up in bed, his head fell over one side and he died without a struggle. He said he was in no pain after I got it stopped under his arm. He has tried to do better since he came here than he ever did before. He paid a full tithing and took such interest in the Sunday School and anything to teach the young, and he felt so anxious about the children; he wanted them to be better than other children. He has worked so hard since we have been here; when he was sick he would talk about his work so much. But the Lord's will be done, and not ours, but it is a great trial for me. x x x I hope you are all well. From your loving daughter Sarah Martineau"

[Page B54L]

1896/[Blank line]
June 4/Sent article to Deseret News concerning the indian raid at Ogden in 1850.[160]

10/ Von Wendt to day received an offer of $30000.00 per year besides all expenses to go to South Africa to manage mines for an English mining

---

160. See J. H. Martineau, "Plundered by Indians," *Deseret Weekly* 53 (July 25, 1896): 177, and J. H. Martineau, "Plundered by Indians," *Deseret Evening News*, July 3, 1896, 11.

company;—about 41x0000 in all. He to contract for 3 years service. I hope he will not accept.

5th/ On the 5th inst. Sur. Genl Roskruge offered me a Contract to Survey a township, mountainous, at four times the usual price, the work amounting to over $1500.00 I asked concerning it; the answer was—not to take it. So I informed him I would not. It was a temptation for I could probably clear over $1000.00 on it, in a month time.

13/ This morning I was greatly blessed in prayer, and in the answers I received—great promises. It was also Said to me "I ordain thee by promise a patriarch in the Church, to bless the Saints, and those whom thou shalt bless shall be blessed, and whom thou shalt curse shall be cursed. Thou shalt have all the rights and powers and privileges pertaining to this office." But I understood, that no one must curse to avenge a personal wrong, but only when needful to advance the work of the Lord, as in the case of Zeezrom. I will not here record the great promises made me, but it was shown me that the dreams or visions I had over 40 years ago should be fulfilled as I saw them, and I should do the work therein manifested to me. One I will mention: that in which I stood with a multitude on the bank of a mighty river. They were being baptized and as each man stepped forward, I, as a recorder, took down a list of all his property, and then he was baptized. The interpretation to this is,— the time will come when people will be required to consecrate all property when they join the Church, each receiving a portion back as his stewardship. And I believe it will be so.

How merciful is our Father, to hear and answer our feeble prayers—and we so weak, doubting and evil!

[Page B55R]

1896/[Blank line]
June 15/The weather is very hot—108° in the shade. No sunstrokes

16/ I have been greatly troubled in mind because of the deep darkness of my friend A. von W. He desires to marry Gertrude, but he believes not in God nor His Son Jesus, the Redeemer. Why do I have him about my family, if this be so, and I know the result of Such a thing? It is because in some things he has a noble spirit—a desire to do all the good he possibly can; and especially, because, when I asked concerning him and the attachment between him and Gertrude the answer came—"Fear not, no evil shall come to thy daughter because of him; he shall receive the gospel and do a mighty work in Israel. I have brought him and thee together, that thou mayest be a blessing to him in spiritual things, and he be a blessing unto thee in temporal things."

Believing this, I have suffered this intimacy to go on, though to my natural sense very obnoxious.

To day, feeling very sad about this, I prayed again, and received the same answers, and much more to comfort me and my dear wife.

June 14/ To day Albert and Emma had another son born to them. [Blank line]

18/received my pension of $24.00 and paid my rent $20.00 retaining $4.00 for expenses. Naturally speaking, it looks very dark to me, being without money in a land like this, but I hope and trust in our Father's word.

23/ Was today appointed U.S. Deputy Mineral Surveyor for Arizona, by Sur. Genl Geo. J. Roskruge.[161] As I know no one here to whom I would care to go to be bondsman for me in this to the amount of $10,000.00 I sent blanks to Lyman, hoping he may be able to get them subscribed in Utah. If I can get this office I may earn something for my family.

24/ Wrote an article for Deseret News—early history of Parowan, guarding, and the daily life of Settlers, with their toils and dangers.[162]

[Page B56L]

[Note tape at upper third of page]

1896/[Blank line]

---

161. Written documentation of this appointment is not found in the Arizona Surveyor General's Correspondence. It would have been done, however, after Martineau's resignation on June 19 as Public Land Draughtsman. Martineau was then replaced by Charles von Erxleben as draughtsman. See E. F. Best, Acting Commissioner, to U.S. Surveyor General, Tucson, Arizona, June 19, 1896, Letters Received, box 113: Vol. 18, August 14, 1895–July 20, 1896 (312–446), letter #430, CSGAZ.

162. Martineau's article gave a description of the fort and the measures taken to prevent Indian attacks and raids on personal property. He also mentions the organization of one of the earliest Mutual Improvement societies in the territory and the dramatic association which followed. See J. H. Martineau, "Went Armed to Church," *Deseret Evening News*, August 8, 1896, part 2, p. 9, and J. H. Martineau, "Went Armed to Church," *Deseret Weekly* 53 (August 22, 1896): 291.

June 28/ Sunday. This morning, in answer to prayer, I received many great promises, most of which I do not think best to write now, but refer to some.

    I was told not to purchase a home in the north, (Utah) though I might dwell there at times and labor in the Temples. I must make my home in Mexico, for in that land I am to labor, and there I shall be greatly blessed and honored, even to be as was Joseph in Egypt. Then I may do a mighty work among the Lamanites, among whom the power of God shall be shown mightily, even to the raising of the dead, and the causing of the earth to shake. And it was shown to me how the earth shall be desolated by great and bloody wars, causing the death of millions of men, women and children; also tempests earthquakes, tidal waves, pestilence, famine, evil beasts, reptiles and insects, that shall breed worms in people until they shall die. And many also among the Saints shall fall, because of lack of faith and because they keep not the laws of God. I also received a renewal of promises concerning Von W. and of prosperity for my family,—even that from this time forth I shall be prospered, and shall very soon receive the money still due me from Government on my Survey.
[Blank line]

July/ July 1896

7/By letter from Lilla we learn she has named her baby girl Marjorie.

11/ Susan's 60thBirthday! And yet it seems but a little time since I saw her first, a slim, rosy pretty young girl not yet fifteen! The Father has been very [looks like arrow from fifteen to margin saying Sixteen] good to me in giving me such a wife—a help mate in very deed. I pray that she may have many more birthdays, each happier than the other, and that she may have the desires of her heart. Wrote the following lines:—

[Next two pages are unpaged, a poem which begins: "To my wife on her Eighty Second year"]

[Page B57R]

[Poem, first stanza of which appears to be crossed out, and later material added]

1
Dear wife this Sixty years since first thine eyes
In thy last birth,

Opened, to view with wonder and surprise
[Blank line]
So dim, so dark, so dreary—[illegible]
'Twas like an entrance, almost, to a tomb!
2
Was thy first home So glorious? so bright?
Did Earth Seem drear
Because of change from that celestial light
Whey thy obedient Spirit took its flight
And nestled here?
3
Ah yes! No darkness there! No strife! no fear!—
No grief!—no pain!
But all of these assail thee quickly here,
And cause the sigh, the moan, the frequent tear—
That falls as rain!
4
But through the clouds the light of heaven appears—
A glorious light!
Dispelling gloom and doubt,—all griefs and fears;
With promise, too, of joy in future years;—
An end to night!
5
Let us be faithful, while on Earth we dwell
And patient be;
Trusting in Him who doeth all things well-
In hope of joys no mortal tongue can tell-
From Satan free!
6
As we with Father and with Mother dwelt
Through ages vast,—
As Brother and as Sister walked, and knelt
Together in praise,—sweet union felt.-
Again at last

[Page B58L]

[Poem continues]

July 11/[Blank line]

1896/7
We will to Father and to Mother come,
Our trials o'er;
And hear with joyful hearts the words "Well done
~~Reign upon your glorious throne~~
Forever more"!
[Blank line]
This was all the gift I could offer, having no means to buy her a better one.
[Blank line]

14/Sent my new blank bonds as U.S. Deputy Mineral Surveyor to Lyman, for him to find me Sureties in the amount of $10.000.00 He is now absent in Chicago as an Alternate delegate to the Convention which the Democrats have called.
[Blank line]

24th/To day Samuel and Elvira had a son ^(Seth Guernsey)^ born to them at 12 o'clock, healthy and plump,—weighed 12 ½ lbs.

Susan and I had written them previously, to anoint and bless Elvira and all should be well with her and her baby, whom we felt impressed would be a boy.

On the 26th Sam's sister Mary Park died in Childbirth.

"/ Sent article on early Settlement of Parowan, the fort, drouth, +c[163]

"/ Sent a letter to inquire why I do not receive the $127.72 due from the Government.[164]

24/ Sur. Genl Roskruge offers me a contract to run 45 miles of line to cut off the Coal lands in Indian reservation, at $30.00 a mile.[165] It would

---

163. This article did not appear in the *Deseret News* until August 8. See note at entry for June 24, 1896.

164. Martineau's request was to be advised as to what action had been taken on his supplemental account rendered May 21, 1896, amounting to $127.72, for surveys executed under Contract No. 30. General Roskruge then referred to this letter to the Commissioner for reply. George J. Roskruge to Commissioner of the General Land Office, Washington, July 27, 1896, Letters Sent, box 8: Vol. 29, April 1, 1896–December 31, 1896, p. 226, CSGAZ.

165. Martineau was listed among twenty-six engineers who were sent an invitation to bid on the government survey, east of the White Mountain Indian Reservation. This was to close the boundary of the San Carlos Coal Fields. Memorandum, Office of the U.S. Surveyor General, Tucson, July 27, 1896, Letters Sent, box 8: Vol. 29, April 1, 1896–December 31, 1896, p. 222, CSGAZ.

probably take 3 or 4 weeks time. I am now sadly in need of money,—in debt for our living expenses since April, and $40.00 rent, with no visible means to continue here, nor to go away, and it looks very dark, naturally speaking. But I have the promise, by the voice of the Spirit, that all Shall be well with me and my family, and I try to have faith in the promises and goodness of God.

29/ I asked concerning the Contract which is offered me, and which I had desired much to obtain, but was told "touch it not—take it not."

[Page B59R]

1896/[Blank line]

July ~~29~~/31/Being in doubt, fearing I might have been deceived, and that what I have taken as the voice of the Spirit might have been something else, I inquired again of the Lord concerning the Contract offered me, by which I could clear over a thousand dollars, and which in my present poverty seems so desirable, and received an answer, a part of which I insert, as a testimony to help my children in a future time. I was again told "touch it not—take it not, for it is not needful for thee, for I will bless thee abundantly in other ways, and thou shalt know it is from the hand of the Father in Heaven. Thou shalt not be brought into poverty and want, neither shalt thou be brought into Shame because of thy debts, for thou shalt be able to pay them to the full satisfaction of all. Thou hast been brought into trouble and difficulty in order that thy faith may become mighty, and thou hast been brought to this place for a purpose of mine own, which thou shalt know hereafter, but in mine own time thou shalt return to the Saints and to thy family. Thou shalt not labor to build up this nation, for vengeance must overtake it. My Saints have been slain and many hundreds have laid down their lives because of persecution, they have been robbed + plundered and driven, and not one has been punished for these things, but the nation has winked at it all, and as a people have rejected to gospel. Therefore they must Suffer what my servant Joseph has declared concerning them. But they shall not be utterly destroyed, for my Saints Shall be as the Salt to preserve them.

Thou art called to labor in Mexico and in the lands South, and there thou shalt be mightily blessed, for thou shalt be in that land as was Joseph in the house of Pharaoh. They shall Seek unto thee, for thou shalt be filled with

[Page B60L]

1896/[Blank line]

July 31/wisdom from on high. Thou shalt do a great work in that land, for there are millions there who are of the blood of Joseph, heirs to all the promises made to Abraham, Isaac, and Jacob."

Other great and glorious promises were made to me, and the Spirit Saith that this is the voice of the Holy Ghost, and not that of a lying Spirit, nor of my own desires and anxiety. I praise thee, my Father, for thy wonderful goodness, and pray thee to so live as to attain to all that is promised. I will not take the Contract offered me, but trust in the Lord for my blessing. Help me, my Father.

August/ August 1896

I feel impelled to insert here a letter recently received from Nephi, now on a mission in Kentucky, which shows a lovely spirit, and a soul devoted to the work of the Father; and I am thankful indeed that I have a representative who is laboring so energetically.

Campellvill, Taylor Co. Ky.
July 23, 1896

My dear parents

Your ever welcome letter came and found me after I returned from Conference, having been about 4 weeks without any mail of any kind, and then I received a letter that Leigh had been very sick. I fasted and prayed for him and got the assurance that he would be all right again.

Of course you are interested in your son, and he reads your good letters over and over. Dont be afraid to ask questions. I went to Conference and we were there told that the Lord required us to travel without purse or scrip in the future, (read Doc. + Cov. 84 Sec.) I Sent my money to the office at Chattanooga to pay for books and tracts, and went forth on our journey of 125 miles to Taylor Co. being on the road about 10 days, we leaving without money, trusting in the Lord. I did

[Page B61R]

1896/[Blank line]

August/not feel justified in laying in a supply of writing material, but we go out to prove the word of the Lord when he says he will raise up friends to administer to our wants. Just as soon as I quit traveling with money I was more humble and put all my trust in the Lord. The first thing I received was a nice handkerchief, which I was needing, also some soap, which was handed me by a lady in a store, after hearing a gospel conversation. If I had told her what I needed it was those things. We were out of blacking and stayed at a house where we used theirs. I prayed for the blacking and on going to the post office got a letter with sufficient stamps to get everything we needed. These things came just as they were needed, and if they were small things it shows that the Lord is able to help us. People ask to do our washing, so you see we are better off than if we were worrying about money to pay our way with. I have been very busy of late. I wrote home and told Emma that if She got any money for me to sent it to Chattanooga to pay for books and tracts which we distribute. Now if any money comes to me I will use what I need and send the rest to the office, and consider any that might come sent me of the Lord. As President Kimball says, "The bridge is cut, brethren, go forth in this way and you will become mighty in the sight of the Lord." I was humbled Several times in tears, and it seemed that it was necessary, to bring me in the right position. I have had the Spirit of the Lord resting upon me until my frame just shook, and the Lord has shown me just what is required to fill an honorable mission. We can not work in this work without being humble and prayerful, and at times I was not in that way. I repented of my nonsense and fasted and prayed, any my prayers were answered and I have felt

[Page B62L]

1896/[Blank line]

August/good ever since and am very thankful that I was able to see the error of my ways. I prayed to the Lord mightily and asked him to bring me into subjection. I dont tell you these things to scare you and to make you think I hav'nt Enjoyed my labors some of the time, but just as soon as I laid my money away, got rid of it by Sending it away and fasting and praying, having a partner who is strict in prayer, I have the assurance that my labors have been accepted of the Lord, and it is an experience I would not like to do without I have been able to meet men and look them in the face. You know I used to be very bashful, but the fear is fast leaving me.

It is a tough ordeal to pass through for about 3 or 4 months until we get acquainted with the people and the way of preaching the gospel. Now all of that has vanished away.

I guess I better tell you what was the matter with me. My companion was younger than me ~~and~~ and it was his right to preside over me, he being out 16 months. I did not want to be dictated to all the time and was somewhat rebellious, I suppose, like Laman and Lemuel. We went along several days trying to hold meetings under such conditions. He is a young man from Tooele Co. and a good young man, but I could not Stand to be under some one else. One night we retired to the woods to have prayer. We kneeled together asking the Lord to soften our hearts so that we could work in peace and love. We then separated to have secret prayer. I asked the Lord to bring me under subjection and to unite us together in love and union. I finished first and set down on a log. He came near + set down by me. I said we were talking about being out here preaching, and our hearts were softened.

[Page B63R]

1896/[Blank line]

August/That feeling of love came upon us both at the Same time; we embraced each other—tears ~~came~~ flowed from our eyes—we were both melted and asked each other's forgiveness. Such is the feeling the gospel brings to the penitent, and there is a love existing between us which only the gospel brings. That is the same spirit which great men have possessed, and it was necessary, thanks for it. We hav'nt felt the same since, but have a love for each other which unites us together in all our labors. We Could not go along in any other way.

The time has passed by quickly and we are doing a good work which is as follows; Since 3d of July: meetings held 20, miles walked 110, visits 3, revisits 38, tracts distributed 65, gospel conversations 45, which last from 10 minutes to an hour. So you can see that is twice the amount of work we were able to do before. People everywhere kill spring Chickens—have them nearly every meal, but we generally go without our meal when we hold meeting so s to be able to speak better. They are after us on all sides, saying "Come and stay with me," "Aint you coming to my house before you leave?" "Will you be coming to preach in our district?" And it is becoming unpopular to speak against us in any way—men ready to defend us on every hand. The work is progressing rapidly and the people are following us from one place to another, some coming for miles through ^the^ timber to hear the gospel. We are magnified in their eyes, and they think we have been to College for years. Zion is coming to the front and thousands will be found who are seeking the truth and waiting for a chance. We have a branch organized in the next county, a membership of 34 and more getting ready. We are the first elders that have ever preached in this county, and it seems as

[Page B64L]

1896/[Blank line]

August/though the Lord has his spirit striving with them. Think of the people that are visited every day in the South. We have 365 Elders; just think about what a grand work we are engaged in, gathering out the honest in heart from the nations of the earth. I have many dear friends here, and would hate to see them destroyed with the judgements which will come. Prest Kimball said in Conference "Some of you Elders will be called to come out here to preside." Just think of it! being called ^to come out^ here to preside and live and teach the people day after day in the meetings; think of the thousands of children growing up here, and all of them can't be wicked, but they need the Gospel to be preached to them that they may have a chance to grow up in it as our children do. My heart is reaching out after the people, and there are a great many of them waiting for the gospel who will receive it with open arms. Our elders are getting among the bankers and lawyers + doctors; They are all studying it. I dont want to go home. I prefer to stay and enjoy the mission and try to do my part, that I may stand on Mt. Zion worthy of the blessings. I am 5 years younger, only my hair is coming out on top of my head. I could write you as much again if I only had time, but I must get myself ready to speak, not having time to study much. God bless you all

From your loving son

P.S. I will write you as often as I can. Dear parents I know how to appreciate you more every day, and my heart is full of blessings for you. And dont be afraid to ask me any questions. I am your son just the same, and just let Gertie kiss you both for me, and may our hearts be ever bound together in love. Dont think I have forgotten you. We live too far apart,

[Page B65R]

1896/[Blank line]

August/but our hearts can be bound together with the Spirit of the Lord, and I hope to meet you when I come home, and I will be a better man in every way. May you have the peace of heaven to be with you.   Nephi.
[Blank line]
   I sent extracts from this letter to the Deseret News for publication. (forgot to insert)[166]
[Blank line]

Aug. 4/ To day Von Wendt told us he had played his last card and has failed. All his efforts to get means has come to nought, and he did not know what would become of us all. He has no money, and I have been living on credit Since April. To the natural eye it looks black as night.

   Susan and I prayed in Secret, and each had a very comforting answer,—that all shall be well with us, + we shall have means from source unexpected to us, also much more that was very comforting to us and Strengthening to our faith and trust in God. We are surely passing through an experience calculated for our good and to give us a great increase in faith. For now we have to live by faith, having nothing to look to but the help of our Father in Heaven.

14/ I have been quite unwell for some days, but am now much better. It was kidney trouble, to which I am subject.

18/ Susan is very sick. A cold settled on her lungs, and she has a heavy rattling in her throat at every breath. I anoint her and rebuke the disease and bless her frequently, and I have promise she shall be healed. Much better next day.

20/ Susan sat up a little while

21/ Von Wendt feels very blue,—says he dont see how we are to exist. I prayed and received a comforting answer, as I always do, and was told that all shall be well with us. To the natural eye it is black as night. Heavily in debt for rent, grocery account, ice, milk and washing, with no means to

---

   166. This article was published under the title "The Lord Working with the People," *Deseret Weekly* 53 (August 29, 1896): 323.

pay my debts, and nothing in sight for us—not even means to move away. But we trust in God.

[Page B66L]

1896/[Blank line]

August 31/ My account for pay still due me for Surveys came to day, reduced about $50.00 It is very discouraging.[167]

September.

Sept. 3/ My bonds, executed in Utah, for commission as U.S. Mineral Surveyor, came, but were found incorrect. So I Sent new papers to Lyman to be filled anew. My bond is to the amount of $20.000, my sureties, Lyman, Bishop W.B. Preston and Judge C.H. Hart.

6/ Susan's rheumatism is still very painful. For 2 Weeks she has not been able to dress or undress herself, nor to turn in bed without help. She took a hot air bath which seemed to help her.

9/ Susan had another Turkish bath, but was worse [in margin: 10] afterwards. There is much rain, which is probably the cause.

13/ Von Wendt received a letter from Barney, in New York which has

---

167. In reply to a letter by General Roskruge dated July 29, 1896, relative to Martineau's surveys executed under Contract No. 30, the Commissioner's Office enclosed a copy of Martineau's adjusted account which sent to the treasury April 29, 1895, of which Roskruge was notified by office letter "M" dated April 29, 1895. Martineau's supplemental account was returned for amendment. The exterior lines of Tp. 3 N., R. 3 E., "amounting to 19 miles, 62 chains, 81 links were allowed in the account as adjusted, the 9 miles, 21 chains 59 links, ^in addition^ as stated in the supplemental account would be in excess of the exteriors of a township and could not be allowed." E. F. Best, Acting Commissioner, to U.S. Surveyor General, Tucson, Arizona, August 24, 1896, Letters Received from the Commissioner of the General Land Office, box 113: Vol. 18, August 14, 1895–July 20, 1896 (312–446), letter #459 ½, CSGAZ.

Roskruge was sympathetic to Martineau's plight and responded to the Commissioner, indicating that Martineau was advised of the contents of Commissioner's letter and that he (Martineau) had filed a new supplemental account, corrected as required by the Department, the same being transmitted in the amount of $71.72. Roskruge wrote: "I respectfully ask that prompt and early action be taken on this account as the Deputy is old and in straightened circumstances, and much needs this amount." George J. Roskruge to Commissioner of the GLO, Washington, September 1, 1896, Letters Sent, box 8: Vol. 29, April 1, 1896–December 31, 1896, p. 321, CSGAZ.

On this date (August 31), Martineau wrote an article recounting the efforts of several early settlers of Parowan to diffuse an armed confrontation with Chief Walker. See J. H. Martineau, "At the Indians' Mercy," *Deseret Weekly* 53 (September 19, 1896): 419.

entirely discouraged him. He says he has done all he can—can do nothing more; he has no more hope. Says he will go to Colorado if he can get means to go with, and see if he can do anything there. I asked concerning the matter, and was told all shall be well with us; <u>he shall receive</u> the money he needs to hold the mine and work it, and it shall be to his astonishment.[168] He shall be blessed and prospered, his eyes shall be opened, he shall know that God lives and that Jesus is the Christ, and shall do a great work in Zion. He shall have great wealth and shall be a blessing to us, to help us. I was told to trust in the Lord and fear not, for all shall be well. This was repeated three times.

So I went to his rooms to comfort him, but he could not believe what I said—that he should come out all right. But I had a testimony that what I had told him was true.

How wonderfully good is the Father, to hear and answer the prayers of one so weak and sinful as I am, and to give Susan the same comforting testimonies as he has so many times given me! Praise and honor be to him forever and ever.

[Page B67R]

1896/[Blank line]

Sept. 13/ Received a letter from Lyman, who is discouraged [In margin: " 14] about the bonds. I wrote him in answer, to do nothing more about them, but let it go. I believe God will bless me in some other way, for I receive great promises from him. I know if I do not obtain them the fault will be with me and not with the Father.

For a considerable time I have been subject to great and contradictory influences—Evil and Good, from the darkness of night to the glory of the noon-day Sun. I know the Evil One is determined to prevent me from gaining my exaltation, but the voice of the Holy Spirit tells me I <u>shall</u>, for I

---

168. Von Wendt had experienced considerable difficulty in securing enough money to help pay taxes and expenses for the Doxology and True Blue mines. He and his attorney, Selim M. Franklin, tried desperately to sell the mines on several extensions before foreclosure on the title. In late fall of 1895, von Wendt optimistically wrote to his attorney: "I head [had] a hard time and have it still but I and you and Martineau I think will come out <u>alright</u>." Alex von Wendt to Selim M. Franklin, October 18, 1895, Franklin Papers, AZ 336, box 44, fd. 8. See also von Wendt to Franklin, October 24, 1895, von Wendt to Franklin, November 15, 1895, H. H. North to Franklin, May 16, 1896, and F. W. Davis to Franklin, February 5, 1897, Franklin Papers, AZ 336, box 44, fd. 8, UASCA.

shall never be tempted more than I can bear. And this gives me great comfort, realizing how weak I am, and how great the power of the Evil One. But the Father is infinitely more powerful, and I know if I take a course to make and keep Him my friend and helper, no power can hinder me from gaining my exaltation. This is a great comfort. I am passing through an experience fearful to the natural man, but I believe it is to perfect me, and for an increase in faith, patience, humility and in all good gifts.

In all these troubles Susan and Gertrude are great helps; they do not lose their faith no matter how dark things appear; and strengthen my faith greatly.

Dora again began to attend the public school to day. She is hard to learn and remember, or understand, but since I have blessed her in her intellect she has greatly improved, and can now work in the simple rules of Arithmetic, and reads in easy lessons. She has gifts in music and drawing, which I hope I may be able to cultivate.

17/ Received word that my account against the Government for balance due me for Surveys, of $71.61 is allowed.[169] Thankful.

18/ To day in answer to prayer I received many comforting promises, and among others, this, spoken in reference to my desires to do a great work in bringing the Lamanites, or House of Joseph—to the fold of Christ, according to that which has been sealed upon me by authority of the priesthood:—"I ordain thee

[Page B68L]

1896/[Blank line]

Sept. 18/a Prince and a Patriarch, a Prophet and a Seer,"—to the house of Joseph. I desired to know if this is a complete ordination or one by <u>promise</u>, and the answer was very clear and plain, and I write it for instruction of my family:—Although the Lord hath all power both on earth and in heaven, he hath given authority to men on Earth to regulate and rule in the authority of the priesthood all things pertaining to the Church on earth; and He honors each man holding authority in the priesthood in his particular calling. Hence, when Saul was stricken down by the power of

---

169. The letter or memorandum approving Martineau's supplemental account is not found in the CSGAZ.

God while persecuting the saints, and asked what he should do, the Lord, instead of telling him (Saul) himself, told him to go to a certain town, find a certain man, who would tell him what to do.[170] Thus God honored the man who held the authority on earth to govern the Church. And so, though I am ordained to certain callings by the Lord, I may not officiate in them until properly authorized also by the church authorities. And thus that there may order in the Church. A man may hold a fulness of the priesthood, and by it have power to officiate in any office in the church, but he cannot act in any office in a Ward or Stake until he is properly called and appointed to do so by proper authority. A High Priest's office is to officiate as a President, but not until he is appointed specially to do so. A Seventy is to preach as a traveling missionary, but not until he is sent. A man may hold all the priesthood there is, and yet may not act as a Ward Teacher or a Deacon, Even, until properly appointed so to act. If it were not so, all the men in a Ward might be Deacons—or none at all—and all would be confusion.[171]

18/ Received my pension for last quarter,—$24.00 Welcome.

October 1 [See line in margin]

Oct. 1/ To day Von Wendt received $400.00 from Mr. Barney to apply on the mine he has bonded, and the time of which would expire tomorrow. This would be ruin to him,

[Page B69R]

1896/[Blank line]

Oct. 1/and what he had greatly feared, as Barney had said there was no chance to raise any money in New York on account of the Silver-money panic in the east.[172] I had been anxious too, because Von Wendt had given

---

170. See Acts 9:1–20; 22:6–16.
171. See, for example, Heb 5:4 and D&C 42:11. For an official statement supporting this doctrine, see Joseph F. Smith, John R. Winder, and Anthon H. Lund, "Editor's Table. The Priesthood and Its Offices," *Improvement Era* 5 (May 1902): 549–551.
172. The silver-money panic was part of a serious economic downturn in the United States in 1893, which was caused by railroad overbuilding and shaky railroad financing which set off a series of bank failures. Compounding market overbuilding and a railroad bubble was a run on the gold supply and a policy of using both gold and silver metals as a peg for the US Dollar value. People attempted to redeem silver notes for gold; ultimately the statutory limit for the minimum amount of gold in federal reserves was reached and US notes could no longer be successfully redeemed for gold. A series of bank failures followed,

up all hope. Susan and I both prayed concerning the matter, and each received a plain, comforting answer. The voice of the Spirit said he surely should get the money he needed, and should be greatly prospered.

So the greatest joy to me in this (and to Susan) was the knowledge that we had not been deceived by any Evil Spirit, but had been taught by the Holy Spirit, which is a great encouragement in our faith, for its increase.

3/ This morning in answer to my prayer I received a Testimony it was accepted, also myself and family were accepted. And I received a great promise—the same that is recorded in the "Compendium," in the "Gems from Joseph's teachings, where he speaks of "The Other Comforter," saying that when the Father sees fit he will say to me "Son, thou shalt be exalted +c." Even so came the promise to me, "My son, thou shalt be exalted. Thou art not all free from Sin and weaknesses, but because thou dost hunger to become pure and holy, and to do a mighty work in Zion for her redemption, and to do a mighty work in bringing Souls unto me, thou shalt become mighty in priesthood and calling, and be a mighty leader among thy brethren."[173] And other words very comforting, and great promises, which I pray I may be able to attain unto. And if I fail, I know it will be my fault, not that of the Fathers.

14/ For some time my prospects have been very dark, being in debt in Tucson for rent, provisions +c to the amount of $200.00 and the debt of $2.00 a day, with no apparent means to pay it or to leave the town (as I

---

and the price of silver fell. The Northern Pacific Railway, the Union Pacific Railroad and the Atchison, Topeka & Santa Fe Railroad failed as a result.

173. In 1857, Franklin D. Richards compiled a pocketsized compilation of the doctrines of the LDS church. The compilation, or compendium, went through at least nine subsequent editions, revisions, and enlargements, Richards being assisted by James A. Little. The third (1892) edition contained a section entitled, "Gems from the History of Joseph Smith." Martineau was paraphrasing Smith's statement regarding the promise of the Second Comforter:

> After a person hath faith in Christ, repents of his sins, and is baptized for the remission of his sins and receives the Holy Ghost (by the laying on of hands,) which is the first Comforter, then let him continue to humble himself before God, hungering and thirsting after righteousness, and living by every word of God, and the Lord will soon say unto him, Son, thou shalt be exalted, etc. When the Lord has thoroughly proved him, and finds that the man is determined to serve him at all hazards, then the man will find his calling and his election made sure, then it will be his privilege to receive the *other Comforter*, which the Lord hath promised the Saints.

From Richards and Little, comps., *A Compendium of the Doctrines of the Gospel*, 269

could not endure to do in debt) In answer to my prayer that I might have employment in the Sur. General's Office the answer came that I surely shall have employment there while I need it. Also, that I shall be prospered from this time forth in all I undertake. And that no

[Page B70L]

1896/[Blank line]

Oct. 14/hand or voice raised against me shall prosper. And my life, age and strength shall be renewed, that I may yet do a great work for the redemption of the dead, as well as the living, especially among the House of Joseph. Also many other great promises.

It makes me very thankful and full of wonder at the mercy and goodness of the Almighty to thus hear and answer one so unworthy as me, the great desire of my heart is to become pure in heart and holy—to be like Enoch and other holy men of old.
[Blank line]

15/ Sent another article to the Deseret News, on early scenes in Parowan and the death of Walker, the Utah Chief.[174]
[Blank line]

20/ This morning before day light I was reflecting upon the explanation given by Joseph the Prophet upon this quotation from John the revelator:—"Four destroying Angels having power over the quarters of the earth until the Servants of God are sealed in their foreheads. "—" which signifies," Joseph says, "sealing the blessing upon their heads, meaning the everlasting covenant, thereby making their calling and election sure. When a Seal is put upon the father and mother it secures their posterity, so they cannot be lost, but will be saved by virtue of the covenant of their father and mother."[175]

The part I have written at the last in sloping hand was what I could not clearly understand, as to me it seemed to deprive some children of their agency, and saving them whether they seek for or desire it or not. But by

---

174. See James H. Martineau, "Buried Alive by Indians," *Deseret Weekly* 53 (October 31, 1896): 626–627.

175. This is from a statement made by Joseph Smith on August 13, 1843. Martineau had evidently taken it from Richards and Little, comps., *A Compendium of the Doctrines of the Gospel*, 279.

the blessing of the Father it was made plain to me in answer to prayer and I write it for the benefit of my children; not as instruction or teaching to the church, which is not my right, but as words of wisdom and instruction to my own family. It is this:—

When a spirit leaves his first estate where he dwelt

[Page B71R]

1896/[Blank line]

Oct. 20/for ages with the Father and the Holy ones, and filled with the wisdoms of the heavens, and comes in earth, entering his second estate, he forgets all he formerly knew; but Satan has authority to tempt him, to cause him to do evil if he can, Satan learned in the wisdom of the heavens and having forgotten nothing. Therefore, the man could not of his own power stand against the knowledge and power of the Evil One; he can only stand by the aid given him from the heavens. What is this aid? First, it is a portion of the inspiration of the Holy Spirit which is given to all to help them distinguish between right and wrong, evil and good; and secondly, the aid given by our guardian angels, as is written in "Paradites," published in the "Times and Seasons," vol. 6 page 891, as follows"- That none of the work of the hands of the "Son" might be lost, or any of the souls which his Father had given Him might be left in prison, angels were commissioned to watch over Idumia, and act as spiritual guides to every soul, "lest they should fall and dash their feet against a stone." They were denominated "The Angels of Our Presence."[176]

As all <u>must</u> be aided thus from the Heavens to enable them to withstand the Powers of Darkness, their free agency is not destroyed or infringed by the help they receive from above; and when the "<u>blessing</u>" first referred to in the words of Joseph is sealed upon the parents, it is a covenant that this aid shall be given their posterity in time of need.

---

176. The passage, as submitted to the *Times and Seasons*, read: "That none of the work of the hands of the 'Son' might be lost or any souls which his father had given him, might be left in prison, angels were commissioned to watch over Idumia, and act as *spiritual guides* to every soul, 'lest they should fall and dash their feet against a stone.' They were denominated 'the angels of our presence." Joseph's Speckled Bird, "Paracletes," *Times and Seasons* 6 (May 1, 1845): 891–892, quote from p. 892. This passage was also copied into Martineau's "Pearl's Collected from Church Works," pp. 65–70, quote on p. 70, MSS 238, no. 108, USU Special Collections & Archives.

The blessing sealed upon my head by Patriarch John Young that—"You shall never be tempted above what you are able to bear."—is in full agreement with the foregoing, because my sincere <u>desire</u> and my <u>will</u> is to serve God and live a holy life; therefore if I am aided in this, it does not infringe my agency in the least but is in full accord with it. If I should knowingly and with full purpose choose evil and reject good I could not claim this help and blessing, because all blessing can only be obtained through perfect obedience to the Head."

I have not made this so clear and plain as it was

[Page B72L]

1896/[Blank line]

Oct. 20/shown to me; but if my posterity will seek to know more fully than I have shown, let them ask God in humility, faith and prayer and it shall be shown unto them and made plain.

But one may say,—suppose parents who have been thus sealed and blessed have a son—and there are many such—who has no religious feeling or desire; who cares for nothing but worldly things and have no desire to gain any knowledge of heavenly things:—one who barely has a standing in the church but is dead and lifeless;—shall Such a one be saved without any effort on his part? Is not that saving him without his agency?

I answer—No. There is a vast difference between <u>salvation</u> and <u>exaltation</u>; a man may be <u>saved</u> and not <u>exalted</u>. Every soul will be saved in some degree of glory except such as commit the sin against the Holy Ghost—the unpardonable sin—and become "sons of Perdition". And as every one must reap that which he sows, he will receive all that his works entitle him to. So, such a son will be saved in <u>some</u> glory, ever if it be not the celestial, though I do not say he may not attain to a glory, even, in that. For "<u>in the celestial glory there are three heavens of degrees</u>," and only those who attain to the highest may become Kings of Kings and Lords of Lords—the Gods of Eternity.[177] And a man who, as described above, lives as a drone in the Church can <u>not</u> become a Son of Perdition—become <u>lost</u>—because he does not know enough. For to entitle a man to become a Son of Perdition he must be far enough advanced to become a God; and the prophet has said that the number of those who will attain to the

---

177. See Richards and Little, comps., *Compendium of the Doctrines of the Gospel*, 276.

highest exaltation will be very few, because they are not willing, in this life, to make the sacrifice necessary to attain to it. What must a man sacrifice? He must sacrifice <u>all things</u>, or be willing to,—the dearest things to his heart—even life itself, just as Jesus had to do to gain his exaltation. For it is said— "+ it had been agreed by the Gods and the Grand Council of Heaven, that all the family of the "Head"

[Page B73R]

1896/[Blank line]

Oct. 20/that would do as He or his eldest Son did, should be exalted to the same glory."

And as Jesus follows in the path of his Father, so we must follow Jesus if we would attain an exaltation with Him.

25/ This morning I received word from the Treasury Department, Washington, that my <u>account</u> for balance due me on my Survey was disallowed. This account was for $71.62, and had been declared just by the General Land Office Dept and ordered paid.[178] This news was a great disappointment to me, as I had depended upon it to help pay my debts here.

For some time I felt much discouraged; but after I had prayed, I felt comforted. I received answer that no shame or contempt shall come upon me because of my debts here, for I shall have power to pay them all, and shall be blessed and prospered all I need. I believe in the promise I have received, although everything looks to the natural eye as black as ink.

26/ Wrote to the Commissioner of Interior about my claim jut rejected after its approval at the General Land Office, and sent him original papers and instructions received, to show my claim is just.

---

178. Martineau's supplemental "account," dated June 21, 1893, for balance due him was rejected by the Commissioner because it made claim for lines already paid in the amount allowed him ($2,349.93). Martineau argued that the reason he included the lines in his supplemental account was that the Commissioner of the GLO had requested that he make claim with a supplemental account for those lines, since his returns had been accepted for those lines. He stated that it was not included in the original amount and that he is entitled to be paid for these accepted lines. See S. W. Lamoreaux to U.S. Surveyor General, Tucson, Arizona, August 11, 1896, Letters Received from the Commissioner of the General Land Office, box 113: Vol. 19, July 21, 1896–September 9, 1897 (447–625), letter #452; James H. Martineau to George J. Roskruge, August 31, 1896, Letters Received, box 44: Vol. 29, July 31, 1896–March 27, 1897, letter #18, CSGAZ.

30/ Hired an organ at $2.50 pr. month, for the comfort of our family in our lonely condition. We visit no one, and no one visits us, not do we wish it, for there is nothing which is congenial with the wicked people of Tucson.

November

3/Election day. McKinley elected President. Wrote to Locke.[179]

4/By letter from Netta, learn the names of two of family of Martineau in France, which my Niece Fanny found in the Historical Library in Paris:–

Pierre Martineau, Seigneur du Perron, Elector du Beaurais, Picardy, who was declared noble in the Council of Deuce in June 1667; also __ Matrineau, Barroness de Thuré, (Dates not given by Fanny.)

The family arms of Pierre Martineau, are azure field with 3 towers, silver, with cross of Jerusa-

[Page B74L]

1896/[Blank line]

Nov. 4 lem, (Like this)

[Drawing of coat of arms]
[Blank line]

7/Letter from Sarah, Moroni's widow. A son was born to her on Oct. 4th, weighed 10 lbs. She was blessed in her confinement, her sister Anna being with her. She thinks of calling her boy Helaman, after his father. I am very thankful all was well with her. Both Susan and I had testimony that all would be, and that is would be a boy.

9/ A feeling of great darkness and dread came over me this evening, because all looks so dark before me in regard to our means to pay debts, and in regard to going away from Tucson, to be with the Saints and with my family. My way seemed hedged up on all sides, with no way of escape, for all things seem to fail me, and nothing but disappointment remaining. I cannot bear to think of leaving here in debt—so disgraceful—and yet my debts, now about $230.00 here increase day by day, with no way in sight in which to pay them. At no time in my life have I felt in so bad a straight.

---

179. This was Morris R. Locke (1842–1920), contractor for the Arizona Construction Company. See biographical note at entry for December 15, 1888.

We have been in depth of poverty before, deeper than now, but we were among our brethren, and knew they would not suffer us to starve. But here, there are no brothers nor sisters, and we are alone.

But I prayed, and received a comforting answer—a promise that all shall be well with us. Susan read some of my patriarchal blessings to me, and had faith all would be well. I felt ashamed and repented of my doubts and fears, asked God to forgive me, and received testimony that he did forgive me. He is wonderfully merciful to me.

10/ This morning before day light I had a good season of prayer, and received many glorious promises and instruction, some of which I was told to write for the benefit of my children, and I now do so.

I was told to fear not, all shall be well with us; to be filled with joy and peace, for my Father has set

[Page B75R]

1896/[Blank line]

Nov. 10/his hand to bless me. He will lift me up and make me mighty among my brethren in priesthood and calling. The Father had led me to Tucson for his own purpose and I have not sinned in coming here, nor in bringing my family here; and when the time comes for us to leave, our way shall open abundantly before us. I shall have Employment, and means to pay my debts, and not be turned out of our house, nor be brought into any shame or trouble because of debts. The trials, (as we think them) we now pass through, are for the purpose of giving us experience and an increase in faith, to fit and prepare us for far greater work to come, which has been appointed me before I come to earth, and for which I was gathered out from among my kindred. Jesus had to suffer more than any other man could, and live, to gain the experience necessary for him, even as His Father had done before him, and as all Gods have done and must forever do, for there is one path leading to a celestial exaltation, and all must walk in it who would gain that exaltation. My faith shall increase from this hour, and I shall increase in all heavenly gifts, all of which I have a right to, except those which pertain especially to the Presidency of the Church ^[illegible insertion]^ by virtue of holding the fulness of the holy priesthood which has been conferred upon me. I may bless my family with full faith and power, for my words shall be sealed and ratified in the heavens and shall be fulfilled. I must seek continually to the Lord in humility and faith, and be filled continually with the Holy Ghost, and know his voice, that it may be a constant help and guide. It was by understanding this "still small voice" of the Spirit that Moses led the hebrews through the Red Sea, and not by the audible voice of God as a usual thing. And von Wendt shall be greatly prospered in his business, and his eyes shall be opened, and he shall receive the gospel and do a mighty work in Zion, especially in the redemption of his father's family and kindred, in which I may assist him.

[Page B76L]

1896/[Blank line]

Nov. 10/ Many other comforting promises were made me, and instruction given, for which I thank the Father.

How great is His mercy, to notice one so small and so full of evil as I am, He, who has created all the worlds in the Starry heavens, and how I ought to strive to gain the victory over all my sins, and become pure in heart—and this is my great desire to do.

24/ Moved to day to a house of three rooms, being cheaper, and $16.00 a month instead of $25.00 as formerly.

27/ Sworn as a juror to day for the first time in my life.

28/ Sat as juror to day in a burglary case—Luis Naranja.

29/ Today Susan found Moroni's certificate as a Seventy. He was ordained a Seventy by Joseph W. Smith on November 30th 1885, in Arizona, county of [blank] The certificate is numbered 145, and countersigned by Jacob Gates of the Pres. of Seventies and John M. Whittaker, clk, on May 23d 1890. (Book 1, No. 145.)

December/ December 1

1st/Received pas as Juror 3 days, my first experience: $5.35 I also lettered a map for the County Surveyor, price $5.00 I feel very thankful for this chance to earn something, the first, except $5.00 during the Summer, since April of this year. I have been all this time steadily running into debt for rent, Groceries and provisions, milk and ice, and if it were not for the promises I receive, in answer to prayer, I should feel almost to despair. I cannot honorably go away so heavily in debt, and to remain only increases the trouble. But when I pray concerning it, the answer is always the same:—that I shall be blessed, my way opened before me so I shall be able to pay all my debts honorably, and when the time comes for me to go from here I shall have means to go in comfort. I confess it is hard to keep my faith from faltering. And yet I know God is all powerful to do what he wills to perform.

3/ To day is the first general fast day of the Church, it it having been changed from the first Thursday in each month to the first Sunday in the month. Mother and I fasted until night,—twenty four hours.

[Page B77R]

1896/[Blank line]

D 9/December/Finished lettering another map, price $5.00. Very thankful. Sent article to the Des. News, on "Walker, the Utah Chief."[180]

" 10/ To day I weigh 182lbs, Susan 226lbs and Gertie 130lbs

To day on looking for a stamp in my pocket book I found to my astonishment a silver half dollar. I had been without a nickel, having spent my last nickel for postage stamps. I asked Susan and Gertie if they had placed the money there, + they declared they had not, having none they could give me. I felt as this must have been placed there by an angel, as it could have come there in no other way. I asked and was told it was brought by a heavenly messenger; and it made me rejoice greatly, not because of the value, which is small, but because it fulfills the promise sealed upon me, of the ministering of angels. And this shows me I am still in the favor of the Lord to a certain degree, and that I have not forfeited the blessing sealed upon me by several patriarchs as well as by the voice of the Holy Spirit to me. Truly, the mercy and loving kindness of the Lord to me are great!

And in the summer of 1888 my life was saved from instant death when my guardian angel spoke, as with as audible voice—"turn your hand." I did so, and at the instant, my gun was discharged, just missing my body but burning my wrist and sleeve.

Dec. 11/ to be more certain, and not to record something which might be a mistake, I inquired again, and was told the same as before, and that

---

[180]. See James H. Martineau, "Chief Walker's Methods," *Deseret Weekly* 54 (December 26, 1896): 60–61.

the money was given me, not as something of value, but to show me that the eye of the Father is upon me, that he knows my needs, and will not desert me, even in my present deep financial troubles. And for this I thank my Father in heaven

12/ Samuel and Elvira write Wilmirth has been quite sick for a week or more, vomiting continually, day and night.

24/ This morning we received a fine turkey from Samuel and Elvira, which was very acceptable indeed. Wilmirth no better. I received a testimony concerning her, for thus said the voice of the Spirit to me,—"Thy granddaughter hath lived her appointed time, and shall depart in peace, and shall

[Page B78L]

1896/[Blank line]

Dec. 24/suffer no loss, for so hath her time been appointed from before the foundation of the earth. And she shall receive an exaltation in the celestial glory with the Father, and all is well with her." And I wrote this, that my children may realize more fully that the Father hears and answers us when we seek unto him in humility and faith, teaching us by the voice of the Spirit when it is expedient, but sometimes I have been told I should understand at some future time, but not now, the thing I wished to know.

" 25/ Christmas, and a happier one than I expected, for I had only $2.00 to spend, and the shops were filled with beautiful Christmas presents. Baron von Wendt dined with us and brought a bottle of Champagne, the first we ever had at any meal. We did not care for it very much, however.

26/ This morning about 3 o'clock, after a season of prayer, I had a joyful season, receiving many great and glorious promises, and having principles of truth made plain to me. I was told, among other things, that my sins are forgiven, and that I am accepted by the Father, with all my family, although I I and they are not all pure and clean, but the Father knows that in my heart I truly desire to put away all sin, to become pure in heart and to live a holy life; to do good and bring many souls to Him; and for this cause He is merciful to us. Also that I nor any of my family shall be never more than we can bear, and shall all be saved together in the Celestial Glory. I was told that I shall do a mighty work for the redemption of the house of Joseph upon this land and be a restorer to the house of Jacob,—I should be a Prince and a Patriarch, a Prophet and a Seer unto them, as has already been Sealed upon me by the Patriarch. Great and glorious were also other promises made me. And now, I know how weak and sinful I am, and how easily led astray; and if I fail to receive any of these blessings it will not be because God has failed, but because of failure in me. But I pray that I may not forfeit these blessings.

27/ This morning these things were all shown me again, also I was told that my son Moroni shall suffer no loss in

[Page B79R]

1896/[Blank line]

Dec. 27/^being^ called away in his prime, for he was needed there to do a work in connexion with that performed for our dead which could not be done here. Also, that although he had not obeyed the law of plural marriage yet he had never opposed it, but had received it in his heart, and should receive his exaltation accordingly; and that I should have wives sealed to him, and receive the 2nd A for him. Also that he will visit me, yet in this life, for which I am very thankful, having asked that he may be permitted to do so.

" 31/ To day we had a roast goose, the first in our married life. It was furnished by von Wendt, who, with us, watched the old year out and the new one in.

Jan. 1897./ January 1897.

1/To day was rainy and cold.

7/Received a letter from Jesse N.—Chicago. He sent me $12.00 for which I was very thankful indeed, as I found that unless I could pay something on my debt due our grocer, he would not let us have anything more on credit, and as I had no money, we would be brought to beggary or almost starvation. I was glad to be able to pay $10.00 on the account.

I know God put it into Jesse's heart to send it me. Early in December last, Charly sent me $10.00 which I paid on my rent, and thus was able to keep my word given, that I <u>would</u> pay it. And for this I was very thankful, for I would rather be dead than dishonored.

I thank our Father for his care and goodness.

Jan. 8th/ To day is the 45th anniversary of our marriage. I can scarcely realize it can be so. Forty five years, as a future, seems a very long time; but as past, it is all as a dream. Susan and I recalled the names of those who lived in Parowan at that time, and of all the men and women who then lived there, and of many young people—all have passed away except a few, probably eight or ten in all. It seems so strange that Susan and I have been thus left behind, lingering almost alone, while so many strong, robust people have passed away.

And while life, for itself, has no great attraction for me, I am thankful we have been thus preserved, and

[Page B80L]

1897./[Blank line]

January 8/have been enabled to do the work for the dead we have done, to the number of about 2000, and that we have received all the temple ordinances given this side of the veil.

And I have a hope and desire to still, in this life, ^do^ a much greater work, and for this I have the promise of the Lord. If I fail to realize its fulfillment, it will be my fault, not that of the Father.

I have had a strange and hard experience for a long time past; everything I touched turned to ashes, and every hope and every plan, apparently sure, has failed. I had strong hopes of appointment as City Engineer, but on Jan. 4th that hope also failed, and I am left here, in debt here $250.00,—debt increasing daily, with no or probable way to pay it, and unable to leave here. Even if I could go to Elvira's, as they urge me to do, I could not feel satisfied to go leaving my debts unpaid. And yet, every time I ask the Father concerning these things, I always get the same comforting answer:—that I shall be able to pay all my debts honorably and have means to go to the Saints and to my family in due time, and that all shall be well with us. And Susan always has the same answer to her prayers. Sometimes a fear arises in my mind that perhaps I have been deceived, and that my comforting answer has not come from the Holy Spirit but from an evil source. And then I have been plainly shown how to judge the Spirits:—that a spirit which incites to good, tells us to cleave to

God and to righteousness, to do good and to bless is from above and not from beneath; for <u>no good whatever</u> cometh from the Evil One because there is <u>no good in him</u>. I there were, he could not be Perdition, for the good in him must be saved in some glory, even if it be as of the faintest and smallest star. Therefore, nothing good can come from Lucifer but only darkness, fear, doubt and trouble of mind.

[Page B81R]

1897/[Blank line]

Jan. 8/ And by this I know the answers received have been from the Lord by the voice of the Holy Ghost, and so I am better able to bear up against what would otherwise crush my life out.

And I know all this is for my good: to teach me to trust fully in God no matter how impossible his word seems of fulfillment:—to seek more unto him; for He will have all the glory of our salvation. "Without faith we cannot please God," and difficulties,—met and overcome—are necessary to give an increase in faith. If there be no opposition or difficulty we have no need of faith. If the sea has been as solid ground Peter would not have had need of faith to walk upon it; and it is he whose flour bin is Empty who must ask in faith "give us this day our daily bread," not he whose bin is full. And I believe this schooling is to prepare me for a work still greater than any in my past; and I only pray "Father, not my will, but thine be done," and that I may not at any time murmur or sin in thought word or deed because of disappointments.

Von Wendt came in despondent, saying he had lost his gold placers, which had cost him many thousand dollars, and he feels as if all is gone. I prayed, and the answer is—he shall yet be blessed and prospered abundantly; his eyes shall be opened, and he shall receive and obey the truth, and do a great work for Zion, and for his progenitors. And so I endeavored to comfort him, and he felt better. The Father is wonderfully good to hear and answer one so unworthy as I am.

I had no means to get any present for my dear Susan on this wedding anniversary, as I have always done, and so, for a present, and token of my love I composed the following, as I walked out in the evening in the outskirts of town among the brushy chaparal. They seem a little sad, but it is because of our sad surroundings, and of the memory of times and friends long since passed away.

[Page B82L]

[Top margin, in shaky hand: See p 57]

1897./[Blank line]

Jany 8th/ To my dear Susan, on our 45th wedding day.
1
Five and forty years have sped
Since the hour that saw us wed
Years of pleasure mixed with pain,—
Songs of gladness,—tears like rain,—
Happy moments—hours of woe—
So they come and so they go!
2
Friends have vanished from our sight
Entering heaven's refulgent light;
Souls to us from heaven came—
Some have gone—some still remain.
Not to us is given to know
Who shall stay and who shall go.
3
Tears in torrents we have shed
While with grief our hearts have bled.
Hopes ~~we~~ ^once^ chirish'd baseless seem
As bubbles floating on the stream;
And we are tossed—tossed to and fro
As whirl in storm the flakes of snow.
4
But not all somber—not all drear,—
Not all sigh or blinding tear!
Many hours ^years^, like glimpse of heav'n
To us have been in mercy giv'n;—
A fortaste of that peace and love
That reigns forever in heav'n above.
5
Many of our friends are gone—
Those of our youth; Almost alone
We linger now—among new friends
Until our Earthly work shall end

When again with joy we'll greet
Those whom here no more shall meet.

[Page B83R]

[Poem continues]

[Top margin says, in shaky hand: See page 57]

1897/[Blank line]

Jan. 8th/ 6
Soon the clouds shall break away!
Soon shall shine the glorious day!
Heaven's blessings on thee rest—
My Queen!—my princess!—be thou blessed!
Thou, with me, shalt vic'try gain!—
Enthroned, Thou—a Mother Queen.
[Blank line]

8th/Today a letter from David Booth of Brigham City, gives me information relative to Cora Colorado, the indian girl I bought of the Utes in Parowan about the year 1856 to save her life, and whom, when we lived in Salt Lake City in 1860, we allowed Br. Cherry, of what is now called Centerville, Davis Co, Utah, to take as his own child.[181] He said his children were all married and gone, and he and his wife were lonely in their big house. And so we let him have her, he being well off and able to do better by her than we could, who had so large a family and were so poor.

He says Cora went and lived in Mound Fort with Wells Chase and wife for some years, until she died of quick Consumption, and is buried in Ogden cemetery. She had a child—a boy, Joseph Hyrum—having been betrayed under promise of marriage by one Joseph Johnson. Before she died she requested Mrs. Booth to care for her boy, which she did until he died, aged 3 years 3 months 18 days, and was buried in Plain City. I was very thankful for this information, for I did not know what became of her. I want a work done for her in the temple, and I want her sealed to me with her son. I consider her as much married in reality as are all who are married by the gentile law, which has no real authority to join man and

---

181. See note for entry at September 15, 1860, and Cannon, "Adopted or Indentured," esp. pp. 342–345.

wife. And her sin was one of ignorance and of her surroundings, which a merciful Father above has forgiven. And let him who is without sin cast the first Stone. The spirit approves this, and saith unto me—take her to wife and it shall be approved of God.[182]

[Page B84L]

1897/[Blank line]

Jan. 8th (Con)/ To day von Wendt says he has lost his placers, through not having done his assessment work upon them. We hoped to sell them or gain much from them, but that hope is gone and it seems darker than ever.[183] All that enables me to keep up at all is the faith I have in the answers which I receive in prayer, and even then my fears are great, although I pray continually for an increase in faith. I feel that nothing except the overruling blessing of the Lord will lift me out of my troubles. I prayed for help and had a good, comforting answer.

10/ Received a letter from Jesse N, Chicago, Ill. He wrote a kind letter and sent me $12.00 for which I am very thankful indeed, as it will enable me to pay my month's rent, and keep me from being turned out.

Note/(This entry is an error, as Jesse's gift is noted Jan. 7th)

16/ Received an invitation to become a member of the Arizona Association of Civil Engineers, at Phoenix, which I accepted.

19/ Sent an article to the Deseret News relative to Walker, the Utah Chief—"King of the Mountains."[184] Received a letter from Gean, Eureka, Juab Co. Utah, enclosing $15.00, ten from her and Edward, and $5.00 from Charley. Father I thank thee, for it enables me to keep my credit in the provision store by making a payment.

---

182. This seems unusual, but Martineau appears to have done this so that Cora could be entitled to the blessings of those married (or sealed) under the covenant of an LDS temple marriage.

183. The following month, F. W. Davis, the largest shareholder in the Doxology mine, suggested that Mr. Franklin purchase the Doxology property at the sheriff's sale, at which time he would sell the property to Davis, R. R. Richardson, H. H. North, and other owners, "an amount equal to what they owned in the company." The remainder of the sale would be kept by Franklin. Davis then concluded, "I would not advise this course if all paid their share, but I have got very tired of putting up for all and only getting a portion of it back." F. W. Davis to Selim M. Franklin, February 5, 1897, Franklin Papers, box 44, fd. 8.

184. See J. H. Martineau, "Chief Walker's Doings," *Deseret Weekly* 54 (February 6, 1897): 242.

23/ Received a letter from Albert and Emma, inviting us to come and stay awhile with them,—a very kind letter. I answered that we would do so, if we could get R.R. fare as I did not feel it safe for Susan and Gertrude to make so long a journey by wagon in their weak condition. Susan has been unable to dress or undress herself now for over four months, on account of rheumatism in her arms and shoulders, and Gertie's hip is very weak and painful. Paid rent $16.00

Lyman's boy/ To day at 12, noon, a fine boy was born to Lyman and Alley, weighing ten pounds. I learned this a few days later. He sent me ten, and wrote very kindly.

25/ Applied to Comr of Genl Land Office, Washington, for employment in the Sur. Genl Office here.

[Page B85R]

1897/[Blank line]

Jan 28th/By Sam's request I made out a deed from him and Elvira for 6 acres land to Saml Openshaw. Wilmirth, their eldest daughter, is still very sick, dangerously so, and has been for almost two months. But they think she is improving.

-------------- February. --------------

Feb. 4/Recd word from Washington there is no vacancy for me in the Sur. Genl Office here.

6/ Today Jesse N. Smith and C.R. Hakes spent the evening with us, very pleasantly. Jesse was my wedding guest over 45 years ago at Fort Johnson, and Br. Hakes lived with us in Parowan in 1858—both old friends. We had a happy time indeed.[185]

7/ Attended the Consecration of the new Catholic Cathedral here, at which there was an Archbishop, three or four Bishops in their gorgeous gold embroidered robes, with many lesser dignitaries—all of them in official robes and insignia. They were all in woman's dress and all wore a short white night gown, (apparently) made either of lawn or of lace. It was one

---

185. After spending the day in Tucson, Jesse N. Smith, Collins R. Hakes, and an unnamed man toured the San Xavier church. "Upon returning," Smith wrote, "Bro. James H. Martineau and wife, Susan, came to the hotel and wanted Bro. Hakes and me to spend the evening with them, which we did." Smith, ed., *Six Decades in the Early West*, 421.

continued scene of Senseless mummery and show—bowing, kneeling, signing of the cross, scattering holy water +c Gertrude also went, although she had a headache.

16/ Sent another article to the Dest News, relative to early times in Parowan—a plot to take the fort by the Pah.eeds[186]

17/ This morning after awakening I went again to sleep and dreamed the two following dreams. As they seem significant I now record them.

I thought I happened to look at my right foot and was surprised to see a hole worn through the top of my big toe. As I was wondering that I had never seen it before, I saw it growing larger, and was as large as a silver dollar, exposing all my toes, which I did not like. While still looking and wondering, the whole shoe suddenly split apart from the toe upwards, and the two sides fell down flat on each side. After a momentary dismay I said to myself, laughing, "Well, now I wont have to spend any money for mending it." And the dream ceased. Then I thought I was traveling along a road, and saw one or two hawks sailing over my head; one sailed lower and

[Page B86L]

1897/[Blank line]

Feb. 17/finally settled upon my head, its long straight tail projecting in front of me. I seized the tail with my right hand while with the other I tried to secure his legs or head, as he struggled to get away. Having secured him, he spoke as a man, saying, "Come in the house and have something to eat." I said "Why, how can you give me anything to eat?" He answered "Oh, thats all right, come in: my wife will fix up something for you." I looked, and there beside the road stood his house, his wife and his boys and girls standing by, and the hawk now appeared as a man. I saw that my boys were getting out of my wagon, having part of my survey instruments in their hands, ready to accept the man's invitation, so I was getting out also when I found it all a dream.

It struck me so forcibly that I felt it meant something, and I inquired concerning it, asking if it was a dream given for a purpose, or only a vision of the night without meaning. I was told it was (both of them) a significant dream, which I should understand after a while, when they will

---

186. See J. H. Martineau, "In Early Utah," *Deseret Weekly* 54 (March 13, 1897): 403.

both of them be fulfilled; but I did not get the full interpretation, except this,—that there is to be some kind of a change for me, of which these dreams are significant. I was instructed to write them, as I have now done.

19/ I letter from Joel, saying if we will come home he will send money to carry us to Deming and meet us there with team to bring us to Colonia Juarez. I believe he is led to do this by a good spirit, and wrote accepting his offer. As it will require about $50.00 to pay sundry small debts here, I wrote to Lyman, Lilla, Charley and Virginia, asking them to send me ^each a part of^ that sum, so I can go honorably, and not as one running away from his creditors. Even then I will have to make some arrangement with regard to the remaining $200.00 I owe, which I hope I can do. I have several hundred dollars ($650.00) due me, but cannot collect it at present.

[Page B87R]

1897/[Blank line]

Feb. 19/My rent ($16.00) falls due on the 23d, with not a dollar to pay it. But I have a testimony that all will be well with us. If it were not for the help and comfort I receive through prayer, it seems to me I could not endure such anxiety.
[Blank line]

" 24/ In looking through my journal, I find I have failed to note many incidents which would be of interest, now that so many years have passed, but which at the time seemed of little interest; and I think best to record some of them.

About the year 1852 the people of Parowan, where we then lived, thought best to give the Pah-eed indians a feast, to make them feel more friendly. A long table was improvised of boards and trestles, which by the contributions of the people was covered with a bountiful supply of food, nearly all of which was of vegetables, beef being an article of which we had only a very little—say a small piece once in 6 or 8 months. Cows were more valued than gold, and nearly all the team work of the colony was done by oxen; so no one could afford to kill his team. The indians ate all they could—which is saying a good deal—and were told to take away all that was not eaten. Most of what was left was stewed summer squash, and they had no vessels or dishes in which to carry it away. But "where there's a will there's a way," and they soon found a way. Each buck took off his leggings, (made of deer skin. I tied a string around the bottom of the leg, and lo!—a sack big enough to contain nearly a half bushel. All the remnants were scraped into these sacks, cemented into a solid mass by the stewed squash; and away all marched—the men, especially, in a costume very light and airy.

Before they went, however, Prest John C.L. Smith, thought it a good time to advise them how to live, so as to increase and not die out. He made them a long speech, the burden of which was—cease laziness, learn to work like the Mormons. If they would do this they would increase and multiply; if not they would all

[Page B88L]

1897/[Blank line]

Feb. 24/die off until none would be left. We thought they were all convinced, until Kanarra, the wise old chief asked a question which entirely upset Prest Smith's whole argument. Pointing to our cemetery not far away he quietly asked "who lie up there?" That was all he said but that was enough. All who were buried there were Mormons—not one indian among them. All the tribe appreciated the force of Kanarra's question, and expressed their satisfaction as such a knock-down reply, by sighs and grunts of pleasure. It was some time before any of us could think of any answer, or explain why so many of our people lay dead and no indians when they had been told they must imitate the Mormons or all die off. [Blank line]

At another time the tribe congregated near our house and gambled until some had lost all they owned, among them one indian, who, having lost everything else, gambled off his wife. But the squaw did not wish to go with her new husband, and unseen by them slipped hurriedly into our house, without speaking; hid first behind the door, then went and got under some clothing, then under the bed, But not feeling safe yet, she passed out of the back door and down into a small out-door cellar, where she stood behind the open door. Not more than ten minutes had passed when suddenly an indian entered around with a big butcher knife in hand. Without saying a word he began looking for the squaw all through the room and examined every place where the squaw had hid, knife in hand ready to kill her on sight. We looked on in dismay, knowing we could do nothing to save the poor woman, with the whole tribe ready to condemn her. The indian then went out the back door, went down into the cellar and looked in. As it had nothing in ^it^ he went away without entering, while the squaw stood within a foot of him behind the door. He then went to our corral and looked all through it and then to other corrals. When he had gone the squaw followed

[Page B89R]

1897/[Blank line]

Feb. 24/on his track, knowing that he would not look again in any place he had once inspected. And so she escaped, and finally rejoined her original husband, as we understood.
[Blank line]
 One morning old Kanarra came to Prest Wm H. Dame and asked him if there was any Mormon in Parowan whom he did not love much. A peculiar feeling struck Prest Dame and he answered that he loved <u>all</u> in the fort, "But", said Kanarra, "is'nt there some you love only a very little, "<u>me-a-pooch</u>,"—showing about a half inch of his finger, "no", said Prest Dame. "I love them all, heap,—<u>shaunt</u>," opening his arms wide as he said so. After a time he found the reason of all the inquiries. The night previous, around their camp fire, an indian told how his brother had been killed five years before for stealing cattle, and he said his blood had never been revenged, his spirit was lamenting because no white person had been slain to atone for it. So the tribe said they would go immediately to the fort, kill some one, and after the excitement had blown over they could go and explain all about it. But Kanarra said, "No, if we kill some one tonight in the dark, it may be some one that the Mormons love very much, and they will make a big fuss about it. I will go tomorrow and find out if there is any one they dont like much; we will kill that one. It will pay the debt and the Mormons will not be so mad." The tribe thought this was wise, and this was why Kanarra came to ask Prest Dame if there was any one he did'nt love much. It took all day before the Chief could be induced to give up his scheme.
[Blank line]
 In the summer of 1851, I was boarding with Gilbert Moss. One Sunday morning I had discharged my long-loaded rifle in order to clean it; had washed it out and had placed a cap on the tube to dry that part when I was called in to eat breakfast. I set the gun down and went in. While

eating, word came that the indians had taken our herd of loose cattle running on the range about 14 miles

[Page B90L]

1897/[Blank line]

Feb. 24/distant, near Buckhorn Springs, and calling for volunteers to go and recover them. I jumped up, hurried out to get a horse, and as soon as mounted I seized my rifle as it stood outside the house and hurried to overtake the rest of the company. Arriving on the cattle range we found where the cattle had been rounded up in a bunch, but could not find any tracks of indians or horses driving any of them away. The ground was soft, sandy and without any grass, so that I could track a rabbit anywhere, and we wondered greatly that we could find no indian signs. At length we adopted a course which was successful. We formed a line of men about two steps apart, one end of which was at the place of the round up, and circled slowly round and round, scanning every foot of the ground between each man, and gradually widening our circle farther and farther from the center. When we had thus examined every foot of ground for a distance of about half a mile from the center, we suddenly found tracks of indians driving cattle away towards the mountains, and found trails leading to the west, north and east, where the stolen cattle had been driven away. We afterwards learned how the indians had accomplished this. Each indian carried the hoof of an ox, and as he drove away the stolen cattle placed the ox foot over the tracks, pointing it <u>towards</u> the round up, thus making it appear that every track led that way and none from it, thus entirely obliterating all their own tracks for a long distance from the round-up. They knew this would delay us a long time in finding their tracks and give ample time to get away with the body. And they succeeded, for we never recovered any of our cattle.

I found where too indians mounted on ponies had driven away an ox, making for the mouth of Little Creek Cañon, some nine or ten miles away,

[Page B91R]

and I thought I would do something very smart, by without saying anything to the others, I rode off, tracking my two indians, hoping to get back the ox, much to my individual renown. I trailed them until I entered the cañon, and then went forward, scanning every bush or rock to prevent being fired on from ambush, my gun cocked and ready to fire on the instant. I thought if I fired and missed I would wheel and run until out of range, so I could reload, then return to the attack. I followed the trail thus about too miles up the cañon, and then, as it was near sunset, and I was many miles from home and alone. I started home, Arriving there after dark. All this time I had forgotten my gun was empty, for I could see the cap in place, and because we always kept our gun loaded night or day. After eating something, I thought I would shoot off my gun and load it afresh, so stepped out and fired, aiming for fun at the nearly—full moon. To my surprise only the cap exploded—but no gun fire. "Mighty lucky I did'nt see any indians, or I would have been killed," thought I. I put on another cap; still my gun did not fire. I then pricked powder into the tube, put on another cap and pulled the trigger. Still my gun would not fire, and I wondered greatly that my gun, always so sure, failed to explode. I then spent quite a time in pricking powder into the tube, until I knew there was enough to a least force the ball out of the gun, and then with another cap, fired again. Same result. I was nonplussed; then I cocked the gun and blew down the muzzle with my mouth, and to my astonishment heard my breath whistle out the tube! The gun was entirely empty! Then I remembered, all at once, how I had washed out the rifle and how I had left it standing empty beside the door, and had finally siezed it and carried it all day, supposing it was loaded as usual. I was more thankful than ever that I had found no indians, or I would not be writing this now. I did

[Page B92L]

1897/[Blank line]

Feb. 24/not tell anybody of this for many years, knowing I would be made a laughing stock.
[Blank line]

1851/ In the summer of 1851 Walker, the famous Chief of the Utah came to Parowan one Sunday, with his tribe. Walker and Ammon were invited to the stand, and they both spoke a little while. Walker said he had been told the Mormons were good dancers, and he wanted to see us dance, and as he was going away soon he wanted us to dance <u>now</u>. It was thought best to humor him; so meeting was dismissed, and we all went outside to a level place, got a fiddler, and danced several cotillions The day was hot, clouds of dust nearly hid the dancers and begrimed their faces with mingled sweat and dirt. But Walker said "Stop! You dont know how to dance! I will show you how!" Crestfallen, we stood aside, while about 60 warriors took our places, forming an exact circle, facing inward. Then two others began to clap their hands singing "A-ya, a-ya! a-ya! a-ya! And all circled to the left, keeping most perfect time. At a signal all circled the other way; and so on alternately for half an hour. Walker then said "I have showed you how men dance. Dont dance like little children any more!" Their perfect unity of time and motion was wonderful; I have never seen anything equal to it in all my life. It was like the motions of a machine—not that of 60 individuals.

[Blank line]

1851/ I will now narrate an incident which occured in the spring of 1851 while on my way to Iron County with Wm K. Rice. We laid over a few days at American Fork, Utah Co. and hearing there were mountain sheep upon a high mountain east of the settlement I started alone to capture some of them. A few miles brought me to the foot of the mountain which rose above me very steep and apparently quite inaccessible. I clambered up a steep slope of small loose stones which slid down hill as I tried to ascend, so that

[Page B93R]

it was only with the greatest labor and effort that I could advance at all. But at last I reached the foot of the steep precipitous mountain, the top of which seemed about 500 feet above me, almost perpendicular. I saw a large crack which I thought might aid my ascent, and began to work my was up, clinging with hands and toes to rough projections of the rock, my gun slung to my back. In this was I reached to about 20 feet of the top, when a fierce gust of wind almost blew me away from the face of the rock, so that for several minutes I only saved myself by clinging desperately to the rock I hugged. Every few minutes the gusts came again; and looking up, I could see nothing above my head to enable me to get any higher,—absolutely nothing to cling to,—and so, almost at the top, I was obliged to give it up, and descend.

But how was I to descend? As I looked down during a slight lull in the tempest the giddy height—about 475 ft—made me so weak that I almost lost my hold to the cliff; so I could only descend by carefully feeling with my foot for a place to rest on a little lower, then find something to

take hold of a little lower, and carefully change my position to one a little lower down. And so, slowly and with the most imminent danger of a fall to certain death, I worked my way down the cliff side to its foot, thankful indeed to be on safe footing once more. It was truly a marvelous escape from death. Had I fallen and not been instantly killed I would have died there, for no one would have known where to have looked for me. Only the ravens and wolves would have known. I got back to my wagon late that night completely exhausted.
[Blank line]

1851/ But I was in a far worse scrape in the summer of 1851, at Parowan. One Sunday I ascended a high peak South of Parowan to view the country, ascending by a long easy ridge, a distance of about five miles. I had no water, and on arrival at the top was almost famished for water.

[Page B94L]

1897/[Blank line]

Feb. 24/I looked for something green and juicy to chew, for moisture to my mouth, but could see nothing except a species of cactus. I peeled a piece of one, and chewed and ate. At length it made me gag, and I attempted to spit it out, but could not, for it joined some that I had already swallowed, and all clung together in a glutinous mass. So I seized it with my fingers to pull it out. But I was like a necromancer, who pulls out a hundred yards of ribbon from his mouth; for as I pulled the stuff out, that in my stomach clung to it and it all came out in one long slimy string which made me gag fearfully as it came out. When it was all out I sat and laughed until tears ran down my cheeks, thinking how I must have appeared in the operation.

I took a view—a sketch—of the fort and all the surrounding mountains to the north west, including the Little Salt Lake about 8 miles distant, then, as the afternoon was waning, started down the mountain. To reach the bottom sooner, I did not return the way I came, but went directly down the steep side; and to avoid brush and cactus, got into the bed of a small hollow, descending rapidly as I jumped down from one rock to another, and thought I would soon be at the bottom. I finally jumped down some eight or ten feet to a rocky platform, and found to my dismay that my next jump would be at least 150 feet. Of course I immediately attempted to retrace my last jump, ~~but~~ but I could not climb up again. The rock, though not high, was smooth and had no projections on which to place my feet or cling to with my hands. I struggles desperately to ascend the rock, knowing starvation would be my fate if I remained there. But all in vain. I took off my shoes, and tried to cling with my bare toes and hands to the rock. But I could not ascend two or three feet, and then slip to the bottom again. After an hours struggle

[Page B95R]

I sat down to consider what to do. I lay on my stomach and crawled to the edge of the precipice and looked over. Below me, 150 feet, were jagged rocks, and a tall pine tree stood below and rose some little distance from the foot of the cliff.

To more perfectly calm my mind, I made a sketch of the opposite side of the cañon, which was formed of tall pillars of stone over a hundred feet in height, each having a broad cap stone of another kind of rock. These pillars seemed to have been formed by a process of erosion and reminded me of giants guarding the domain of the mountain elves and spirits. By the time my sketch was finished, my mind was perfectly calm, and clear. I knew if I could not get back the way I came, I must either remain there and perish of thirst and starvation, or I must jump down a sheer descent of 150 feet, with a chance to alight safely in the top of the pine beneath, or, failing this, be torn to pieces by its limbs or be dashed to death on the rocks below. These were my only alternatives. I crawled again to the edge and looked. The tree top was full 30 or 40 feet below me, and stood so far out that it was doubtful if I could jump out far enough to land on its top. The view below made me shudder, and my limbs grew weak.

I made another desperate attempt to scale the rock, but could not, and I knew I must die there slowly or risk a violent death by a leap into that awful abyss. It is a fearful thing to be compelled to make choice between two such deaths, with no one to advise with, and the knowledge that no one would ever know what had become of me;—for I was in a place to which no person would ever come. At last I made up my mind to leap for life or death. I had room to take three steps from the wall to the edge, and I ran, to leap. But as I neared the edge and saw into the abyss below all strength left my knees and I could hardly stand. I tottered back to the rock and

[Page B96L]

1897/[Blank line]

Feb. 24/panted until I became calm again. And then I again essayed to leap, but as before all strength left my knees, so I could hardly stand on my feet. Third attempt was the same. I knew if I tried to jump in that state I could not leap out far enough to alight in the tree, and even if I should, what would prevent me from being torn by the branches, falling from so great a height?

I reflected on the promises made by Patriarch John Smith (uncle to the Prophet Joseph) in his blessing upon my head. I could not see that I had done anything bad enough to forfeit them, consequently I must live to fulfill them. And so I gained faith enough to pray for strength and for safety in the leap I must now make. I arose, determined to do, or die and end it all. I rushed again at the brink. And now, instead of weakness my sinews and limbs were as steel; I shot far out into the air, and in a moment found myself clinging to two limbs—one in each hand—with a grip like that of death, but safe and unharmed; not a shred of my clothing torn or disarranged, not a scratch or a mark upon me. How this came about I had no knowledge, for I knew nothing as I fell swiftly through the air, and had no knowledge of grasping at or clutching a branch of the tree. But there I was, safe and unharmed. I know now that I was saved by the power of God. He it was who guided my hands to the limbs by which I hung and enabled me to retain my hold when falling with so great speed, and that, too, without tearing my hands as such a strain would <u>naturally</u> do; he it was He who gave me strength to leap out so far,—who steeled my muscles and strengthened my limbs, for no other power could have preserved me.

I climbed down from one limb to another until the last one, and then hung and dropped from that

[Page B97R]

about 20 feet to the ground—safe and unharmed!

1851/I examined the tree carefully. It was about four feet in diameter, and, judging by other trees of similar size I cut down afterwards, was fully 125 or 130 feet high.

I know that nothing but the power of God preserved my life, and to him be all the praise and honor. I reached the foot in due time, but did not tell any one of my scrape, knowing I would be laughed at for getting into such a predicament.[187]

[Blank line]

1851/ In February 1851, while living at Farmington with William K Rice I went one day upon the high mountain east of the village climbing a sharp ridge from which the snow had been blown off. Arriving at the summit I started down the north slope of the mountain, walking on a hard frozen crust which was covered with four inches of light, new fallen snow. I slipped down and began sliding down the steep declivity, striving vainly to stop my progress by clenching at the hard frozen crust, while quite a big heap of loose snow piles up in front of me—making me a sort of avalanche. I slid swiftly down the slope a quarter of a mile before I could catch hold of any bush or tree top, but at length did so, and holding on with all my strength I stopped while my snow pile went on. What was my surprise and horror to see it slide only a few yards and disappear as it went over a precipice 100 feet in depth, while I remained alive almost upon its very brink! I quickly got upon all fours and by hard work and the blessing of the Father reached a place of safety.

[Blank line]

1850/ On a previous date I went up on the mountain side to get a view of the lake and scenery, and noticing a big object in a Cedar tree, went to see what it was. I found it was the body of a dead indian, wrapped up in buffalo robes and placed there for sepulture to be secure from the wolves as was the custom of the indians of the plains in general. Upon his body lay his gun, which he needed to enter the spirit world in respectable style as a hunter and warrior. I found it

[Page B98L]

1897/[Blank line]

Feb. 24/had no lock, and the barrel was tied to the stock with a string, and so I thought it would be rather a disgrace to him in the spirit world rather than an honor, and took it away, as it might be of some little use to me in this. I afterwards sold it in S.L. City to Peck + McBride, blacksmiths for a small value in gun percussion tubes. It was while in their shop to sell

---

187. A retelling of this story was published under "Pioneer Sketches. VIII. A Leap for Life or Death," *Contributor* 11 (September 1890): 419–23.

it, I inquired of Hezekiah Peck if he had any book to prove the Book of Mormon true. He said he had, and brought out Winchester's Evidence of the Book of Mormon. I sat down and read it through, was convinced by it, and asked him (Peck) to baptize me.

[In margin, sideways is: Bapt Jany 19, 1851]

He being very busy just then called his partner, William McBride, to go and baptize me. We went to the temple block, then not enclosed, through which the west branch of City Creek flowed toward the Jordan river, and hunted up and down it until we found a place, near the center of the block, where he baptized and confirmed me at the water's edge. The day was bitterly raw, windy and cold, but I did not care. I was filled with a joy beyond words and could only say to myself with exultation "Now I am a Mormon! Now I'm a Mormon!" When I asked for baptism I did not believe Joseph Smith was a prophet. I thought all such things, and miracles, were long past. But when I was confirmed I received the Holy Ghost, and by his testimony knew for myself that <u>all</u> Mormonism was true, as I had been told I <u>should</u> know if I would be baptized with an honest heart to know the truth. I knew I <u>was</u> honest in the matter and hence went forward in the holy ordinance of baptism.

And now, (March 1. 1897) my testimony to all who may ever know of me is still firm and unshaken, but on the contrary strengthened by a thousand proofs, that the principles of truth as revealed by God through Joseph Smith the Prophet are the gospel of Salvation to us and are verily true and holy; and I charge and command my children after me, to the latest generation to sustain honor, obey and practice them all their lives.

[Page B99R]

1897/[Blank line]

Feb. 24/So obeying they shall attain not only salvation but an exaltation in the Celestial glory; and without obedience unto this gospel they will lose all, which I pray may never be.
[Blank line]
I acknowledge the hand of the Lord in bringing me to a knowledge of the truth, for he gave me the desire to investigate the doctrines of the Church, when as a gentile emigrant among the Saints no one cared enough for me to teach me anything except two widow women, one of

whom lived in a small house near the temple block on South Temple street whose name I never knew, (but hope to, by-and-bye) and the other, Sister Picket, once the wife of Don Carlos Smith. These two women converted me to the truth of the gospel. I never heard a sermon from an elder until after I was baptized a member of the Church. At this time Widow Pickett and her two grown daughters lived with William Walker, at Farmington, Utah. She lent me the "Voice of Warning."[188]

[Blank line]

July 22/1850/[Date in shaky hand, hard to read] I well remember the day I entered S.L. City. The east "bench" or sloping foothills was covered with a dense growth of sunflowers about four feet high and indian women went through, beating the ripe seeds into their baskets for food.

As we passed along Emigration street, I saw a city lot a little way ahead which was enclosed with a fence made of raw hide strips stretched from post to post. The cow herd was just ahead of us, and an old bull who saw the fence seemed to take offense at it. He walked deliberately to it and with his horns tore it all down and then walked on. In all the city I saw not a sign upon any building to indicate a trade or business. There was not a store or shop of any kind on what is now the main business street—East Temple St.—The street was fenced on each side with a pole fence of two or three poles high, and on each block stood a little house of one story, built generally of adobe, with a dirt roof; not a tree planted, and all new and crude. The "Council House" was but a few feet high, and against its walls I sat leaning when William Walker came along and hired me to work for ^him.^

[Page B100L]

1897/[Blank line]

Feb. 24/him at Farmington. At this time (just before harvest) wheat was worth $10.00 a bushel in gold, but after harvest the price fell to $3.00 at which price it remained several years. Being a printer by trade, my first thought was to enter the Deseret News office which had just started to publish that paper, but as a harvest hand could earn a bushel of wheat a day—$10.00—I thought best not to go into the office at the wages

---

188. Martineau recounted this conversion story many years earlier. See narrative entry for 1850 on stamped page 27.

offered. And so I did not. How small are the things which turn the whole current of our lives! Had I went to printing I would have had an entirely different life from that I have led, and would probably have been dead long ere this, as printers are short lived, owing to the composition of the type metal.

After I went to live with Walker I worked 6 weeks cutting wheat with a sickle,—my first experience—Also made ditch fence and dug and stoned up a well thirty feet deep. Mary Walker, his second wife, taught me to tell fortunes with cards, and I became noted far and near. All the girls round about came to me with their love troubles, seeming to have implicit confidence in me, though I never had tried to pry into their affairs, and never betrayed any of their secrets. I know pretty well who they kept company with, and as I told their fortunes watched their eyes. I could tell if I was anywhere near the truth by looking at them. I had much enjoyment for a while until I tired of it and told them I could not really know or tell anything by cards. They said they knew better; I had told so and so, and it had all come true, +c +c. And so I had, but not by the Cards.[189]
[Blank line]

1851/ While Rice and I were waiting at Peteetneet (now Payson) I determined to remain there, and went and selected a farm. There were about seven families just starting settlement there, who had commenced two or three log houses. I told them I was going to settle there.

[Page B101R]

They said all right, I could have all the land I wanted, but no water for irrigation—the seven families claimed it all. And it was small in quantity. The whole stream when taken out ran in a single plow furrow. Now the who [whole] country round about is a meadow, farm, garden or orchard, with water enough for all. And this brings to mind a prophecy I heard Prest H.C. Kimball make on May 12th 1851 at Parowan. He said as the needs of the people for water increased so should the water increase; and said "write it down." I wrote it at the time, and have seen it fulfilled from

---

189. Many years later, when Martineau was surveying the route for the Utah Central Railroad, Martineau wrote to Susan Ellen from Farmington and expressed his wish to be home with his family: "Do you ever look at the Cards now-a-days? If you do, just see how long it will be before I come home on a visit." James H. Martineau to Dear Wife [Susan Ellen?], July 17, 1869, Martineau Correspondence, MS 4786, box 1, fd. 6, LDSCHL. See also entry for October 28, 1858.

that day to this. I have seen a little spring so small that I could only get a drink by taking a spoonful at a time until I got a cup full; and Some years later I found at that same place five families living; with farms, gardens and orchards—so had the waters of that spring increased. At my first visit I was in company with Geo. A. Smith and Amasa Lyman, Apostles, and other brethren and sisters, on our way to Washington, in Southern Utah. [Blank line]
I here relate an incident that occurred in the first settlement of Iron County. Sep. 1851 [Date in shaky hand]

In the summer of 1852 word came to Parowan that indians had stolen cattle from Fort Johnson the previous night and help was asked to recover them, as that settlement was too weak to retake them and at the same time leave men enough to protect the families. Accordingly about a dozen men went to their assistance from Parowan, the writer among the number. The party left Fort Johnson some 15 or 16 in number, found the trail of the indians and the stolen ox and followed as fast as possible, our progress retarded at times where the indians, taking advantage of hard ground, concealed their trail as is their custom, causing much loss of time in recovering it. It would be a waste of time to try to follow a thieving band or a war party except as guided by their trail, as they use every stratagem to elude their pursuers.

To recover the trail when lost we scattered a little distance apart so as to scan every inch between,

[Page B102L]

1851/watching for signs which would be without significance to an unpracticed eye—a twig freshly broken—a spear of grass broken or bent aside, or a pebble lately displaced. Sometimes the ground was so hard for a considerable distance that even an ox track was only very faintly discernible; and the course of the thieves was surmised by supporting the course <u>we</u> would take it we were ourselves the guilty party.

After many miles we found that the ox, driven most of the time on the run had tired, and his captors to hasten his movements had shot him repeatedly with their small arrows but not so as to seriously wound him; and occasionally we found then on the way as they had dropped out of his skin.

At length we saw some ravens circling high above a small rocky hill and were satisfied the beast had been killed there or that his flesh had been there hidden. Hastening to the spot we found we were right, and after a search discovered the meat cut up and hidden in a cavity and so neatly covered by rocks that had we not been told by the ravens we would never have suspected such a thing, or thought of looking there for any thing.

As the indians had here scattered we divided into two parties, one to scout the country north of the Iron Mountain and the other south of it. Each man took a big piece of meat and tied it to his saddle for supper as we had no other food with us, and then away to find the indians. Our party scouted on the South of Iron Mountain and at night camped at the Iron Springs—the scene of many a bloody deed of the natives—and next day returned to Fort Johnson. Here we found the remainder of our party, who had had a more exciting experience.

They had suddenly come upon two indians and a boy of bout 7 or 8 years hidden in a bunch of willows, had captured them and had taken away

[Page B103R]

their bows and arrows and butcher knives, and then started for Fort Johnson driving the two men before them and one of the horsemen carrying the boy behind him.

Coming to a small stream with banks four or five feet perpendicular, with soft miry bottom, consequently impossible for horses, the indians saw their chance, cleared the stream and fled like frightened deer. By the time our boys had found a crossing the indians were far away. A hard chase brought their pursuers within gun shot and a brisk fire was opened upon them, but apparently without effect, although all were excellent marksmen. As soon as a gun was pointed the indians sprung sideways right and left, so no one could take sure aim with their rifles—their only arms—and many times as soon as a man had fired at an indian, the latter would rush up to him and try to pull him from his horse, and a man had all he could do to get away and load again, and by the time the indian would be far in advance.

At length Samuel Hamilton determined to overtake and seize by main force the one he was after, but the latter seizing Sam by the leg nearly pulled him from his horse before Hamilton fired a shot that stretched the indian on the ground. During the melee the other indian escaped wounded, and the party brought the boy to the Fort where he was adopted in the family of Joel H. Johnson, after whom the place was named—a veteran of Kirtland days. The boy was renamed Sam, was kindly treated, and grew up to manhood.

Kanarra the Chief said it was all right; he had often told the man not to steal of he would get killed, and it was all right. But there was a sequel to all this.

Five years later, as the tribe sat about their camp fire one night the brother of the slain indian said the spirit of his brother was crying for revenge,—some

[Page B104L]

white person must be killed to pay the debt.

1851/[In shaky hand] According to indian ideas this was perfectly correct, and they were about to go to Parowan that night to kill some one; but Kanarra said "No, if we go tonight we may kill some one the Mormons love very much, and they will be very mad. I will go in the morning and find out if there is any one they dont like much. We will kill him, and then the people wont be mad or make war." This was approved. Next morning Kanarra came to President Wm H. Dame and asked if there was any one in Parowan whom he did not love much. The question seemed suspicious to Prest Dame and he said, "No, I love them all." "But," said Kanarra, "is'nt there some one you love ^only^ me-a-posts"—a very little, measuring about half an inch on his finger. "No," said Prest Dame, "I love them all—shaunt!—shaunt!"—very much. At last he found the cause of Kanarra's visit as explained above, and had to labor for hours before he prevailed on the Chief to forego his purposed revenge; and the chief in his turn had a hard task to correct his men to sustain his agreement with Prest Dame. He was only able to do this by showing that the settlers were aware of their purpose, and there would be war; and then they could no longer beg bread nor procure guns and ammunition. And so this danger was averted through the blessing of the Lord.
[Blank line]
I now resume my diary.

Feb. 19/Wrote to my children in Utah for help to return home.

1897/ March.

March 2/Lyman sent me $10.00 Paid $8.00 to Store on a/c. having previously got means to pay my rent.

5/ Theo. sent me $5.00 from his scanty means. I had not asked his for help, knowing he needed it very much himself.

[Page B105R]

1897/[Blank line]

March 8/Bot pants, $2.50—the first for a year.

12/ Albert writes he is unable to send us any money. I know he would if he could. I have written three times to Prest Christopher Layton who owes me nearly $300 dollars, to send me something, if only 40 or 50$, but he does not respond nor answer me. He is rescalltry [rascality?] God judge between us.

11/ Wrote again to Joel, asking him to send me help at once, and we would come home.

13/ My 69th birth day. Getting old. As a great treat I got a Chicken for dinner, cost 75¢

15/ Susan had a dangerous attack of heart failure. I believe she would have died but for the blessing of God and administration. She seemed to see strange things. Said she saw Turkey all devoured save the head and legs—typical of that country.

16/ Susan has recovered. Recd a letter from Geannie, who writes lovingly and promises help soon.

18/ Sent article to Des. News.—Indian feast in Parowan.[190]

19/ Letter from Charles and Virginia with $25.00, ten of which was from Virginia, $15 from Charley.

20/ Letter from Jesse N. Says he can get no money now, will send some later.

21/ Last night Mr. von Wendt had a dream, of climbing up a very high, steep and difficult hill, we following with him. I felt this was a dream from the Lord for his and our comfort, as we all finally reached the top. We are

---

190. See J. H. Martineau, "An Indian Dinner," *Deseret Weekly* 54 (April 3, 1897): 494.

truly in a very difficult way now, and have no hope except in the help of the Lord, which I believe he will give us. This is the testimony to me.

22/ To day our married grand daughter Wilmirth died after an illness of about five months. She died at 11 a.m.

24th/visited several of my creditors, to whom I owe sums for the paper, ice, milk, rent +c, and told them I was unable to pay them now, but would as soon as I could. They were very good, and

[Page B106L]

1897/[Blank line]

March 24/told me not to worry, for they knew I would pay when I could. I know that God softened their hearts, and to him be all the praise.

29/ Wrote to a famous surgeon in New York City, Dr. W.T. Bull, No. 35 West 36th St. (residence) or No. 33 East 33d St. (hospital) detailing particulars of Gertrude's lameness, and asking if he thinks he can help her.

31 I owe store at this date $123.55. I wish I could pay.

---------------- April ----------------

April 3/Recd a letter from Elvira, giving particulars of Wilmirth's last illness and death, which I here record:—(Extracts)
   Nephi April 1, 1897

"Sam left for California on March 30th Baby was quite sick, but is all right now. He is cutting teeth, so I expect a hard time all alone, but we are all in the hands of the Lord. x x On March 14th Wilmirth was feeling better and wanted to go for a ride. x x We made a bed in our carriage for her and she was so happy she cried for joy.

Father B.F. Johnson came at one o'clock and gave her a patriarchal blessing. She slept then for hours but seemed very weak. Monday she did not eat any thing, but drank a little rice water and an egg beat up in milk, and that was all nourishment he ever took afterwards. Tuesday (16) she asked me to put her in her chair. She wanted to fix things in her chest so she could find then when she would want them. She took every thing out, folded them and put them all back. She said "I will give this to Gertie when she gets big," and so on, presents to all the children. The 19th wad

Jodie's birth day. She was much weaker than the day before. Her stomach hurt her so bad she cried "Oh Ma! cant you do something for me! my stomach is on fire! I am almost wild! I anointed her and asked the Lord to take away that awful pain, that she

[Page B107R]

1897/ Wilmirth's last moments

might not suffer any more with it. It left her at once and she was quite easy for an hour. At one o'clock she asked for water. I raised her up and she sank away as if dead. Celia and Mabel were with me. They began rubbing her, but her heart did not move. I said "I think she will never breathe again." Just then she came to, and said "Oh Ma! I want Martin Allred." I knew she wanted him to administer to her. He came and administered to her, and in the mean time Ben had gone for Pa and Alanson. When they came she was much better, but from that time had a deathly expression and could not talk only by the greatest effort, but gradually declined. She knew the end was near, but had faith to the last. She called the children to her and kissed them. She called Jodie. He came with little Gurnie in his arms. She said "Oh I love you so!" and kissed them both, and said "Ma has such good boys." he hugged Alanson and told him she loved him and he must be good. Then he went out and did not see her alive again. I had her head on my arm, pa was kneeling beside her. She said "Oh you blessed good pa!" She then seemed in much pain, but could not tell us anything. She opened her eyes and saw me and said "Oh ma!" and breathed a few times, and her spirit passed away (Mch. 22) I said "Oh I thank Thee, heavenly Father, for this release."

Not long before she and Alanson were sealed by one of the Apostles (Young or Grant) which made her very happy. She had been married a little over two years. She was always a good girl, and a great comfort to her parents and brothers and sisters. All is well with her, and her exaltation is sure.

When I first heard of her sickness I asked concerning her, and the answer came "She will pass away. She has remained her appointed time and shall suffer no loss, but shall receive an exaltation in the celestial glory." And I had the same testimony several times afterward.

[Page B108L]

1897/[Blank line]

April 3/ Sent article to Des. News, on the taking of Sam in 1851 +c[191]

7/ John Angus Johnson came, canvassing for a cabinet.

8/ Received a letter from Henry, saying he will soon come to Deming for us. We were very thankful, and began packing.

12/ Received R.R. tickets from Henry, who is in Deming.

13/ Started this morning at 1 o'clock P.M. Von W. and Angus saw us off on train. We were very ill provided with clothes +c, as we had only $5.00 for all expenses, but were very glad to be able to go at all. I left in debt about $335.00 but arranged with my creditors to pay when I could. I made a not for Ivancovich, our grocer, for $125.55 and one to Drachman, for rent, about $25.00

Reached Deming at 9.30 a.m. and was glad to meet Henry after so long an absence. We left Deming at 3.30 P.M., our goods in a lumber wagon and Susan, Dora Gertrude and I in a covered carriage. Drove 10 miles and camped.

14/ Camped just across the line in Mexico. I felt happy to be in Mexico again.

15/ Reached Palomas at 8 a.m. and were detained 3 hours while our trunks and boxes were inspected. We paid $3.48 duty on our sewing machine and clothes wringer, and camped in the hills. A heavy wind came up, and a great storm threatened, which was bad, as we had no tent, and would have to lie on the ground, wet or dry. But the Lord overruled, and the storm passed one side. The elevation at Palomas is about 4000 feet.

16/ About noon came to the Boca Grande of the Casas Grande river, and about 5 P.M. came to the guard station at the Espia, where we were again inspected.

---

191. The article gave an account of several men from Parowan who pursued Indians who had stolen stock from Fort Johnson during the summer of 1852. During the pursuit, they found that the Indians killed the stock and stored the meat in the cavity of a small rocky hill. When they apprehended the Indians, the men confiscated their weapons and took a young boy eight or nine years of age. The boy, whom they named Sam, was adopted into the family of Joel H. Johnson and later grew to manhood. See J. H. Martineau, "Trailing Indian Thieves," *Deseret Weekly* 54 (April 24, 1897): 578–579. See entry for September 4, 1852.

17/ Arrived at Diaz about 10 a.m. and stopped with our niece Anna [blank]. Elevation of Diaz 4380 ft.

18/ Being unable to get feed for our horses we had to go on. Drove 12 miles and camped near Ascension Lake.

19/ Passed through Corallitos, a mining town, and camped near Barrancos, a deserted mining town.

[Page end]

7

"Oh That I May Have Power to Do Good to the Fulness of My Desires"

Patriarch and Good Samaritan, 1897–1908

[Page: B109R]

[Page has a graphic of a monument]

1897/[Blank line]

April 20/ At noon came to Dublan, and took dinner with Sister Dora Pratt, wife of Heleman Pratt, and at sunset came to our home in Colonia Juarez. Very glad and thankful to be at home after so long an absence,— over four years. The village, of 700 inhabitants, seemed beautiful with its forest of fruit trees and tasteful brick buildings.[1] Our home is small, and, in fact, a hovel, but it is <u>home</u>, and I thank our Father who has finally brought us home again, when it seemed so difficult to attain, and could not, had it not been for our dear children—especially Henry A—in Juarez. Elevation of Dublan, by observation, is 5230 feet.

<u>Tuesday</u> Colonia Juarez again.

We found Joel and family living in our house, and all our family in Mexico well and prospering.

21/ I began pruning fruit trees and fixing up things.

23/ Joel and family moved into another house, ours being too small for so

---

1. The uniquely "Mormon" appearance of homes, landscaping, and village layout is discussed in Francaviglia's *The Mormon Landscape*. For a geographer's characterization of Mormon settlements in Chihuahua, Mexico, see Wright, "Mormon 'Colonias' of Chihuahua," 586–596.

many of us. I took an observation with Solar transit, and find the Latitude 30°15' 30", var. of needle 11°8' E.

25/ Sunday. Was called upon to speak to day. From this time I continued at work in my orchard and garden until

May 1/ May 1st 1897

Plowed part of my lot (Joel did) having watered it. Up to this time we could not procure any meat or butter, but got some milk at times from Joel or Anna (Annita.)

3/ Bought a ham of fresh pork, for $2.50 on credit. Planted seeds.

4/ Watered city lots to day, and got some beef.[2]

5/ Attended the celebration of Cinco de Mayo (5th of May)—a national anniversary of the defeat of the French by Mexican during Maximillian's attempt to rule Mexico. The girls joined in as a may day celebration. I met Elder Lucander, who told me of seeing, between Antioch and Laodicea, on the site of an ancient intrenched Roman Camp, an ancient monument of marble erected by a Roman Officer to the memory of his beloved daughter—Lucilla Martinus—our ancestor.

[Graphic of monument on page left, text to right]

The monument was like this, Br Lucander says, and of a date about the year A.D. ninety. I shall be glad to do a work for her in the temple of the Lord.

[Page B110L]

1897/[Blank line]

May 5/To day attended the celebration of the Fifth of May, a great Mexican holiday in honor of a victory of Mexico over Marshal Bazaines French army, in Maximillian's time.

" 18/ Dr. W.T. Bull, of N.Y. City, 35 West 35th Street, gives little encouragement in regard to Gertrude's lameness, but refers me to good surgeons nearer than N.Y. City, viz: Prof. T.D. Griffiths, Kansas City, Mo

---

2. On this date, Martineau wrote a letter to the *Deseret News* regarding the value of the Mexican dollar. See J. H. Martineau, "No Loafers There," *Deseret Evening News*, May 14, 1897, 12.

Charles a. Powers Denver, Col. and Prof. N. Senn, Chicago, Ill. as being reliable.

20/ By invitation I started to Colonia Diaz, 70 miles dist. to attend Conference, with Path. W.R.R. Stowell, Sister Eyring and Miss Burrows^ull^. Went 40m. and camped.

21/ Arrived at Diaz at evening. Attended a conjoint of the Young men and young women.

22/ Regular Quart Conference met, continuing next day (Sunday) 23d and finished Mon. 24th

[In the margin, sideways is: Anna's boy born.]

23/ This morning at 5.45 Anna Walser gave birth to a fine boy, weighing 9 lbs. She was much blessed in her time of trial, having previously been anointed and blessed for this event by Sister Fife and my dear wife. I had prayed regarding her, and received testimony she would be greatly blessed in her confinement, and that her child would be a boy, one of the noble spirits held in reserve to do a great work for Zion.

26/ Returned home and found all well. I was much benefited in my health by the trip, as I was almost too unwell to be about my work before I went.

27/ Patriarch Henry Lunt and his wife Ellen, friends of 46 years, came to see us. He blessed us after dinner saying we should not from this time forth want for food or comforts of life, for our way shall be wonderfully opened and I shall build my house and have plenty within it.

I gave him a cane, and in return he gave me his whittled stick, saying that as long as I keep it I shall be prospered in all things with the desire of my heart. I will keep it, trusting his words may prove true, as I believe they will.

[Page B111R]

1897/
June 31/May/Wrote Des. News an account of finding the dead body of Francis Schlatter, "the Healer," in the cañon about 12 miles above here.[3] I [in margin: 31] saw his things, which were taken to Casa Grandes.

---

3. See J. H. Martineau, "Schlatter's Death," *Deseret Evening News*, June 11, 1897, 9. See note at entry for October 19, 1900.

Among others was his famous copper healing rod, 3 feet long, 2 to 2 ½ in thick, weighing 28 ½ lbs. Also sent my pension papers.

June 2/ June.

[In margin sideways: Death of von Wendt.]

Wed./By newspaper learn of the death of my dear friend, Baron Alexander Wenden, or, as he styled himself, Alex. von Wendt, which occurred in St. Joseph's Hospital, Tucson, Arizona, on the afternoon of May 26th 1897. He had been sick almost six weeks, being taken down soon after we left Tucson on April 13th For two weeks our cousin John Angus Johnson lived with him in his rooms and tenderly waited upon him, for which von W. was very thankful. von W. rallied from his first attack and wrote me he would soon go to his bonded silver-lead mine and commence shipping ore from it. Soon after this we received word from Dr. W.F. Amith that he was worse and had gone to the hospital, where he could be made perfectly comfortable. But he steadily grew worse, and soon we learned of his death, which came as a great shock to us all, as he seemed to possess a wonderfully strong constitution, and, excepting some lung trouble, seemed in perfect physical condition. He was just on the eve of great financial success. An eastern syndicate was about to commence working his placer mines, from which he expected an increase of $500 or $600 a day; and also expected a revenue from his silver mine of about $250 to 300$ per day, in all which I would have had a fair share. But this was not to so be.[4]

He was a descendant of one of the noblest families of Russia, his ancestral home being in the Baltic Provinces, a few miles from Stetting on the Duma or Divina river. He was a descendant of the Knights of Malta a branch of whom about a thousand years ago, had conquered the <u>Wends</u>, a nation of north eastern Germany Hence his family name—Wenden—or von Wendt.

[Page B112L]

1897/[Blank line]

June 2/He had been an officer in the Russian household "Guards," but

---

4. The indenture, disclosing the sheriff's sale of the Doxology and True Blue mines, indicated that the mines, held under the Doxology Group Mining Company, were sold to the highest bidder for $99.88. A. Marcus to Selim M. Franklin, August 30, 1897, and accompanying indenture, Franklin Papers, box 44, folder 8, UASCA.

came to America about 20 years ago and engaged in mining in Colorado, where he gained and lost several fortunes. He came to Arizona for the benefit of his lungs, which were somewhat afflicted.

He was not a member of any church, but his religion consisted in doing all the good he could, and in making others happy. He thought that the Mormon religion was the nearest right of any, so far as he understood it. He was very jovial, social and genial, a polished, well educated gentleman and the soul of honor in his business dealings,—emphatically an honest hearted man,—one who will receive the gospel and its blessings in a time to come, when I can do a work for him in the Temple of the Lord. [Blank line]

I think proper to record his last letter to me:—as it shows his indomitable will and energy:—

Tucson Arizona May 2, 1897
flush right: P.O. Box 373

My Dear Brother

Your letter of April the 21st at hand, but it was not in my power to answer as I have been for the last two weeks and more on my back with gastric fever and general debility. Oh my! I now know for the first time what sickness is! Oh my! I never want any more of it—<u>never</u>! <u>never</u>! I am just out of bed and am very weak. For nine long days nothing passed my lips but water and a little buttermilk. I have lost 14lbs and I look just like a yellow wax figure, but it seems Providence dont want me yet. I am gaining strength every hour, and expect in a few days to start for the P.W. mine <u>to work</u>.

I must tell you a curious thing. When I fell sick

[Page B113R]

1897/I had not a cent, but enough provisions, so that your cousin had plenty to eat. Well, I was sick, got sicker and sicker. Your cousin attended to me kindly; then he failed entirely with his enterprise. Poor fellow! He took it terrible to heart that he could not make a success of it and besides, he was very short in cash, and I had none. I was laying and thinking—thinking, my head as big as a <u>barrel</u>! burning, throbbing, aching, but I was thinking delirious impossibilities and wishing I had some lemons, some fruit,—something to quench my fearful thirst, when there comes a knock at a door and a telegram telling me he will send me shortly tomorrow the necessary money to see if we cannot make some money by shipping the ore from the P.W. mine. Imagine my relief! I borrowed from Dr. Smith a few Dolls and got medicine and fruit at once. Is not <u>there a Providence</u>? I will start out in a few days to see what I can do in the mountains. I need a little more strength. Your cousin stayed with me two weeks and left Tucson in disgust; he could do nothing here. Poor fellow! Well, he is a kind and good fellow and I think a great deal of him.

I finally have found out Underwood. He is doing everything for Underwood, and is an absolute selfish and disgusting man! I never was more mistaken in my life than in him. Some time I will <u>tell you all</u>.

I have seen all Your creditors, and they all had a kind <u>word for you</u>, and behaved like gentlemen. They all said they were perfectly sure that you would pay them whenever you can. You know very well that as soon as I can scrape the money together that I will pay every cent you owe.

Write me as often as you can and tell me how Gertie is getting on.

[Page B114L]

1897/[Blank line]

June 2/I got a letter very short from your friend Dr. Bull I enclose the same; it seems he has written to you before this letter. You never told me about it. You must have <u>forgotten it</u>. He gives but little encouragement for poor Gertie,—it almost breaks my heart to think that there should be no help; but I dont believe it! She will yet get well and no mistake. Dont, please, show her this letter, or she may lose <u>courage</u>! <u>Be careful</u>! Give my love to the Duchess and ask her if she takes the exercise still? I cannot write more; I am played out. My <u>love to all</u>!

And I remain always yours.
Alex.

The man Underwood referred to was his man of business. The "Duchess" is my dear wife, whom he always so addressed, calling Gertie "Princess."

I afterwards received a letter from his friend Dr. T.M. Smith, saying (date of May 14) that von Wendt had been very sick for 3 weeks, but was in the St Joseph's hospital in good care, and was in hopes he would recover.

Sat. 5/ Wrote a biographical sketch of Solomon Chamberlain, one of the earliest members of the Church, at the request of his daughter, Mrs. Sariah L. Redd and sent it to the Deseret News.[5]
[Blank line]

5th/Gertrude received the following letter from Dr. T.M. Smith, relative to the last illness if her dear friend Alex. von Wendt, which I insert:—
[Blank line]
Tucson Arizona May 29th 1897
Miss Gertrude Martineau

Dear Miss:

It is with feelings of great sorrow that I inform you of the death of a good friend, namely, the Baron. He passed away on the

[Page B115R]

1897/[Blank line]

June 5/evening of the 25th at 5.35. Poor fellow had a hard struggle, and the trip over the mountain was more than he could stand. I insisted on waiting until he was stronger, but he had made up his mind to go, and it was foolish to be complaining all the time, and that he would go if he died on the way. You know when he made up his mind to do any thing he generally carried it out. The next day after getting to camp he wanted to go to Reitz camp, distance of 4 miles, and I told him he was not able to stand the trip, and asked if he would put it off, as it might prove a very expensive trip, as he was not accustomed to riding horseback or to the rays of the sun. But he would go, and before we got through looking at the property, he became prostrated and would have fallen had I not been with him. After resting for a time he managed to get back to camp, and that evening was a very sick man. His fingers to the knuckle were very cold, and he became frightened and thought he was going to die, and wished he were in Tucson. Fortunately I went prepared to administer to his wants, and in a little while he was free from pain and spent rather a good night; and early next morning we left for Tucson. When he came home I wanted him to go where he could have good nursing and plenty of fresh air, which would be very necessary for him to have to ever recover. But he seemed

---

5. See James H. Martineau to editor, June 4, 1897, "Solomon Chamberlain," *Deseret Evening News*, June 15, 1897, 2.

^to^ think differently, so I waited on him day and night, and I had the doctors go see him, and they diagnosed his disease as I had and said that they knew of nothing better to give him than what I had prescribed, but as I am not practicing I ~~am~~ ^was^ only consulting physician. But I will state that I do not believe any Dr. could have saved his life, for in the early stages of his disease he would not take any medicines, and his temperature used to go to 105°,

[Page B116L]

1897/[Blank line]

June 5/and while it got down to normal, and he might have gotten through all right, had not his case become complicated. He had typhoid-pneumonical fever in its worst form. Mr. Johnson was so kind to him, and he insisted on the Baron doing something, but he would not take what he needed. He wanted for nothing, and I seen that he was well cared for while sick, and when he died I seen that he was given a respectable burial. And it is my earnest prayer that he has gone to a happier world than this. He was conscious up to a short time before he died, and he was brave to the last and did not fear death. One of the sisters asked him if he would like to see any of his spiritual friends. He said no, his religion was the "Golden Rule." I have not been well for some time nor do I feel like writing now so please excuse all imperfections. I herewith enclose your letter addressed to the Baron which was received this morning. With best wishes I remain most respectfully Dr. T.M. Smith.
(Hurriedly)
[Blank line]

 This letter gave Gertie much comfort, as she had feared he might have wanted for proper care, needs and burial

6th/ Today Patriarch Wm R.R. Stowell gave Gertie the following blessing, I being scribe:— (omitted by accident)

16/ We were weighed on the mill scales to day: I weigh 163lbs Susan 215lbs and Gertie 121lbs I have lost 10lbs Susan 11lbs and Gertie 5lbs. I guess it is on account of our poor-fare—mostly bread and milk with occasional meat. We got our cow home two days ago. Her milk is a great help to us. On the 15th we bought a tub and other things. Also flour 50#

17/ Attended the funeral of Geo. Hawes' child + spoke.

19/ Henry, Sadie and Bertha went home. Brother Sixtus E. Johnson also went home to Chuichupe.

[Page B117R]

1897/[Blank line]

June 19/Gertie to day received a very kind, sympathetic letter from Dr. T.M. Smith, giving full particulars of the last illness and death of von Wendt. I pray God to bless him forever.

Cement.

I insert 2 recipes which I think valuable:—

To make a good cement:—8 parts furnace ashes, slag or coke, 4 of slacked lime and 1 of clay; Mix dry, then moisten with water, varied proportions for aerial or hydraulic cement.

Mushroom bed.

A box 3 ft sq and 20in deep. In the bottom place a compost four in. deep composed of 3 parts cow-dung + 1 pt. soil. Then a layer 2in deep of compost + broken spawn brick; upon this 8 ins. of compost, pat gently and water well. Mushrooms will appear in 2 weeks and furnish regular supply for 2 years, with one brick of spawn. Must be kept in the shade.
[Blank line]

July
July 2nd/Up to this time I have been very busy, working in my garden, trimming the fruit and other trees; and putting things in good order.

To day the Stake Presidency, (A.W. Ivins, H. Eyring and H. Pratt)[6] engaged me to finish the surveys of the Juarez Colony purchase; I am to have a dollar a day, half in Cash and store pay and half in other good pay. This is only half the rate I ought to have, to be in proportion to the labor and pay given others, but I am thankful indeed for this, having earned nothing to speak of in the last year or two.

3d/ To day, a Mr. Mundy, of El Paso and Mexico City came for me to go

---

6. The Juarez Stake was organized on December 9, 1895. The stake presidency was comprised of Anthony W. Ivins (1852–1934), Henry Eyring (1835–1902), and Helaman Pratt (1846–1909). See Romney, *Mormon Colonies in Mexico*, 130–131, and 139.

over the mountains and survey some land for him in Sonora. Prest Ivins kindly permitted me to do so, and I left home at 5 P.M. going 16 miles to Dublan where I found Mr. Mundy ready to start out. As soon as

[Page B118L]

1897/[Blank line]

July 3/we had supper, about 10 P.M. we left Dublan with a team and wagon of Emanuel Cardon's. After crossing the Casas Grandes river we lost our way and wandered about until near midnight, and then camped.

4/ Arose and started at 4.30; found the road, reached Ramus at 10 a.m. and breakfasted; then proceeded to Casa de Janos, arriving there about 11 P.M. The night was dark and rainy, and we had quite a time crossing the San Pedro.[7] Finally camped in the mud about midnight, wet + hungry.

5/ Started at 4 a.m. passing Ojetos at 3 P.M. Rain. Camped on the bare wet and muddy ground at 7 p.m.

6/ Arrived at Carretas at 10 a.m. and remained the rest of the day. Mr. Boyd, the owner of the estate was very kind.

7/ As this is the end of the wagon road we (Mr. Mundy, his son and myself) proceed over the crest of the Sierra Madres on horseback, my transit + bedding on a pack mule.[8] Our trail was a very bad one; up and down steeps, winding along Steep, rocky mountain sides where a misstep of a horse might send him and his rider tumbling down the jagged rocks. Two or three times I thought best to dismount and go afoot. We reached Bavispe about 2 P.M. This place is still much in ruins caused by an earthquake some years ago, in which 46 persons were killed and many wounded by falling walls and buildings. We finally reached Galerita, our stopping place about night[9]

8/ Surveyed the farm partially

---

7. To reach Carretas from the San Pedro River, the party would have traveled through some of the most rugged country in the Sierra Madre Occidental, including the Sierra Los Ajos.

8. The mule had long been a favored pack animal and mount for surveyors and explorers in the Southwest. See Ewing Jr., "Mule as a Factor in the Development of the Southwest," 315–326, esp. pp. 323–325, and Essin, *Shavetails and Bell Sharps*, 89–121.

9. La Galerita is just south of Bavispe, Sonora, Mexico, and located approximately sixty miles due west of Nuevo Casas Grandes.

9/ Finished the survey of about 170 acres, and at 1 P.M. Started back to Carritas. Going up the cañon Mr. Mundy + I took the wrong trail, but found a Mexican who said he would show us a trail to Carritos. He took us to a disused trail and left us. The trail soon became very bad, and was very difficult to follow, leading us among rocks which were almost impassible for our horses, and finally over a high rocky, steep crest of the mountains. Here a thunder storm overtook us, and night came on, dark as Egypt. We lost our way, wandering about until 9 P.M. when we finally got to Caritos.

[Page B119R]

1897/[Blank line]

July 9/I think Mundy was much frightened, because Indians had not long before killed a mule near the ranch, and many mountain lions abounded. I was not afraid, because of the promises made me from above.

10/ Worked up my field notes for Mr. Mundy. Heavy rain. Received my pay $100.00 Rained hard next day.

13/ Started home on horseback, with a Mexican packer, my things on a pack mule. Road to Ojetos, 24 miles.

14/ Went to Ramus, 35 m.

15/ To Dublan. Got conveyance home, arriving 7 P.M. very much worn with my tedious journey, but happy with $100.00

16/ Paid $11.00 Cash tithing. Heavy rain.

24/ The 24th July—celebrated in good style. Houses broken into.

27/ Began my Survey of Colonia Juarez.[10] Also next ^3^ days = 4

August/ August.

1/Received word from Stockslager + Heard, Washington D.C. that they had collected my claim of $72.52 against U.S. for land Surveys, their fees being $20.00 of it.[11]

---

10. Of this survey, Anthony W. Ivins wrote in his journal: "On the 27th Bro. J. H. Martineau commenced to survey the Juarez lands which work we concluded on the 17th of August." Ivins, Journals, Vol. 2, January 16, 1897–January 29, 1900, p. 19, MSS B 2, box 6, folder 1, USHS.

11. About this time, Martineau wrote an article for the *Deseret Weekly* on a dancing party held in Parowan during the fall of 1851. See J. H. Martineau, "An Old Time Dancing Party," *Deseret Weekly* 55 (August 7, 1897): 240.

Another proof of the goodness of our Father. This account had been allowed in full by the General Land Office, + <u>disallowed</u> by the Auditor of the Treasury Dept. as being just, but that it could not be paid me because the books for 1896 had been closed. I felt sad, for the amount, tho' small, was much to me in my straightend circumstances. I asked concerning it, and was told I should receive it. And yet it seemed to be impossible, because the Treasury Dept utterly refused to pay. After putting it in the hands of Attorneys in Washington and waiting almost a year, I find the word of the Spirit true + faithful. And so my faith is strengthened.[12]

2+3/ Surveyed in very rough mountains. Exhausted and wet through with rain on the 3d. Too tired for supper.[13]

5/ Leveled 1300 feet of Canal for Prest Ivins.[14]

6/ Surveyed West from Mescal Cor. through rough mountains for about 3 miles. I shouted to the chainman in front a distance of two miles, and they heard plainly and obeyed my directions as to locating a monument of stones on the line. Very tired at night.

[Page B120L]

1897/[Blank line]

August 7/Surveyed part of the boundaries of Macdonald's, Davis and Eyring's pastures, in very high, rough mountains, and was very tired at night.

---

12. The original claim, totaling $71.72, was made in April 1896, but had to be corrected and resubmitted as required by the Commissioner of the GLO. General Roskruge wasn't able to do this until September 1, 1896. See note at entry for August 31, 1896.

13. On August 2, Anthony W. Ivins wrote: "Bro. Martineau, John Davis, Antoine and I went to the monument on the Tenaga (Sugar loaf) and chained from there South on a true line 4900 meters where we built a monument on the S. W. Corner of the Juarez corner From there we chained due East 3000 meters and built a monument. It was now dark and we returned home. Antoine stuck [a] pin in his knee." The following day, Ivins wrote: "A. P. Brown, John Davis Bro. Martineau + I went out this morning we went to the monument established last night and from there ran due South building monuments on our West line which we found to be about 2 miles further West than heretofore supposed. It rained hard on us in the afternoon." On August 4, Ivins described the day's work: "With the same help as yesterday I went out on the survey again today. We went to the Mescal Monument and ran a line due west to the line established yesterday." Ivins Diary, August 2, 3, and 4, 1897, Ivins Collection, MSS B2, box 1, folder 14, USHS.

14. On this date, Ivins wrote: "Bro. Martineau, John Davis, his brother Erastus + I went out today. We commenced at a point on our West line due W. from Mescal + ran around the tract of land sold to John Davis as far as his pasture gate." Ivins Diary, August 5, 1897, Ivins Collection, MSS B2, box 1, folder 14, USHS.

Much of the time it was almost impossible for me to get along the steep, rocky slopes with my instrument without falling.

12th/ Surveyed ½ day in the field and spent the rest of the day platting. Heavy rain.[15]

13/ One day draughting and calculating acres. Much rain.

31/ Up to this time have spent some time on my map and in Surveying. In the latter part of the month Albert telegraphed me from the Mexican Custom house at Las Palomas, that he was there and could not cross the line into Mexico. Joel started to help him in, but found on arrival at Palomas that Albert and family had returned home, much to our and his disappointment.

I omitted to say that on Aug. 16th I started to El Paso, and on arriving at Dublan met Theodore, just returning home from his three years in the Agricultural College, Utah.

[In margin: I go to El Paso, and got von. W. trunk/Theo. came home.]

At El Paso I got Baron von Wendt's trunk, which had been sent me by Dr. T.M. Smith of Tucson. It contained his two canes, jewelry and many little trinkets he used to have on his table. I ask God to bless Dr. Smith for his kindness in the matter. I returned home of the 21st in time for our Quar. Conference. It was on the 22nd we got the telegram from Albert, who wished to visit us with his family, and on the 23d that Joel started to go and bring him in.

Henry and Melissa and family also made us a visit in the latter part of August, returning home Sept 2nd

September/------------- September 1897. --------------

1st/ Theodore went away with Guy Taylor to help him buy cattle, to be gone ten or fifteen days. They went South.

11/ Up to this time I have surveyed some and worked on my map Some, but at noon I had to give up, being taken violently ill with diarrhea.

---

15. On this date, Ivins wrote: "Bro. Martineau, A. P. Brown Antoine + I went out today and ran a line from the Mescal Mt. due north to the fence on our N. line and from that point we chained W. to the sugar loaf Mt. a distance of 7880 meters. This will give us the distance but [?] the Mescal Mt. and our West line which proves to be 4880 meters or three miles + 56 yds. or meters." Ivins Diary, August 12, 1897, Ivins Collection, MSS B2, box 1, folder 14, USHS.

17/ Have got worse all the time, having very copious watery stools 12 to 15 times a day, which nothing seems to check, and my flesh seems all turning to water and is

[Page B121R]

1897/[Blank line]

Sept. 17/all running away. I am aware I am in a precarious position, for at my age such a condition is very dangerous. I am not afraid of death, for as I look back upon my life since I received the gospel 50 years ago I find causes of comfort, in this. That I have <u>always</u> held my private interests secondary to duty to the Church; I have never at any time been in opposition to the Holy priesthood, either in word, deed or influence; I have always labored with my might to help build up Zion; and have done all I could for our dead, having done a work, more or less complete for about 2000 souls, and what is still better, have received a testimony that our temple work for them has all been received joyfully. So I knew I shall meet many friends in the next estate.

But I do not like to leave my family, especially in such poor circumstances, living as we do, in a mere hovel, and with no permanent means of support. And I hate the thought of being buried in such a horrible place as our burial ground is—nothing but a mass of Stones and gravel. I would rather choose a soft loaming soil, near some murmuring mountain stream, and where at times the sweet whispering breath of the pines might float above me. But after all, it does not matter. The will of the Father is always best, and I truly say in my heart—"Not my will, Father, but thine be done."

27/ Still very sick and weak—my case still doubtful.

28th/ It seems impossible to keep warm, especially my feet and legs up to my knees, even with hot irons in bed. This afternoon, after I prayed, asking the Father to make known to me if I had committed a sin sufficient to cause me to forfeit my promised blessings, or if I am still entitled to them, I received a very comforting answer:—that although not clear from sin I had not forfeited my blessings, I prayed again that I might be healed. Immediately I felt a warm sensation flow down from my body through my legs to my feet, which at once became warm again, and filled with the spirit of life. It was something which I cannot describe. I felt it was an answer to my prayer—a testimony my work is not completed, and that I shall live. From this time began gradually to improve, but very slowly, as I have had no appetite from the beginning.

To day 6 young men started on missions, among then our dear friend L. Guy Taylor, who has been very kind to us.

[Page B122L]

1897/[Blank line]

September 28/ Able to sit up a little, and wrote letters of introduction for Guy to Lyman and Jesse N.

29/ Better this morning, and with an appetite—the first for weeks. Henry Walsor and Anita went to Guy's house, to stay until his wife, Minnie, comes home from S.L. City.

30/ Received a telegram from Lyman, who wants to know if I am better, or shall he come to me. Guy T. Said he would answer from El Paso.

October/ ----------------- October 1897 -----------------

1/ Measured one of our apples: = 12 ⅛ in one way and 12 ¾ in the other way. Have had some larger than this; all excellent in flavor.

2/ Knowing I have narrowly escaped death, I feel it important to here record certain things pertaining to our genealogy, which would be liable to be lost should I suddenly pass away. I feel best to write to Lyman in relation to it, and here record the letter I sent:—

Colonia Juarez, Mex. Oct. 3, 1897

My dear Lyman

My recent sickness, from which I had slight expectation of recovery for some days, caused me to remember some things which I wish my children to know, and which, had I passed away, would have been lost to them. Among these are certain things pertaining to our family genealogy, and which are of much importance in our work for our dead; and which if I myself cannot attend to it, owing to my distance from a temple, may eventually be of use to my descendants. But I hope I may yet be able to do much in the temple myself.

I have spent a great deal of research to trace back our lineage as far as possible, and have ascertained many facts which will greatly aid in our work for the dead.

The British Encyclopedia shows that first we came of ancient Roman stock, in the days of the Roman Empire, saying that the Latin name of Martineau was <u>Martinus</u>. Also, that <u>Martinus</u>, translated into English, French and German is <u>Martin</u>; in Italian and Spanish, <u>Martino</u>; in Portuguese <u>Martinho</u>, (Pronounced Martinyo) You wonder then why in French it is now [<u>Martineau</u> instead of <u>Martin</u> or <u>Martino</u>. I will explain. During the middle ages, and since, there was much communi-
[Page end]

[Page B123R]

1897/[Blank line]

October/3/-cation and Emigration between France and Italy; and Italions, removing to France had to change the spelling of their name, changing the final o in the name to <u>eau</u> in order to get the proper sound in French; just as I have to do here in Mexico, for here, <u>Martineau</u> does not give our name at all. In Spanish each vowel makes a syllable, so that our name—<u>Martineau</u>—they would pronounce <u>Mar</u>-<u>tin</u>- <u>á</u>-<u>ah</u>-<u>oo</u>; but <u>Martino</u> gives them the correct name at once.

The Encyclopedia also says that Martino and Marino are identically the same, the t being sometimes omitted. So Martineau, Martinus, Martin, Martino, Marino, Martinho, are all of the same ancient stock. In Latin, where a masculine name ends in <u>us</u> or <u>o</u>, the corresponding feminine will end in <u>a</u>;—thus Augustus, Agusta; Julius, Juia, Octavius and Octavia; Claudio, Virgilio +c become Claudia, Virgilia in feminine. So in our family in Latin, <u>Martinus</u>, male, becomes <u>Martina</u>, female, of which there is an illustrious example in Saint Martina, who was burned alive in the year 235 A.D. aged 15 years, during one of the early persecutions against the Christians. She sympathised with an old man about to be burned, and had to so suffer herself or deny her religion. So She died. Br. Locander of this place, while on mission in Syria, found near the ruins of an old Roman entrenched camp near Antioch, an old marble tomb erected by Martinus, the commander of the Roman Army to the memory of his "<u>dearly beloved daughter Lucilla</u>"The date was about the time of the destruction of Jerusalem by Titus,—about A.D. 70.

For generations the family lived in Rome, Sienna and Bologna, and as a rule were eminent as Churchmen, artists and physicians. Seven of the Roman Pontiffs were of the family, as follows:—

A.D.
Pope Eutychianus, son of Pope Martinus, died Dec. 8   283
St Martin, Pope, son of Fabricus, Italy, died Sept 16.   655
Marinus 1st, Pope, of Montefiascone "   " February   884
Marinus 2nd, "   " June   946

[Page B124L]

1897/[Blank line]

Oct. 3d (cont)/ Martin 4th, Pope, died in Perugia, Italy, in A.D. 1285
"   5th   "   " ____   "   " 1417

Besides these were many others very Eminent in the Roman Church, as Marinus, Duke of Rome, in A.D. 720; and Marinus, Papal Legate to Paris in A.D. 948. I have been baptized for all these Popes except Martin V. To obtain these records I searched the "Lives of the Popes Roman Pontiffs," and Rankes "History of the Popes" and other works.

The Duke of Vorgua, who represented Columbus at the World's Fair in 1894, had Martineau blood, his master, the grandson of Columbus having married a Martino of Spain whence he descended.

The Martino's of Italy who went to France adopted the French spelling, and thence to England and America. My father spelled his name Martino at first, when I was a boy. He was connected by his first marriage with some of the noblest blood of England, as the Earl of Chesterfield, Earl of Bedford, Earl of Minto, Lord Russell and Earl Stanhope. He married as his first wife th gr. daughter of Earl Stanhope, who willed to my father's wife £18000 and £1000 to each of her two children by my father, Julia and Lucretia; but these bequests have long since reverted to the Crown of England.

On mother's side, her mother was a descendant of Lord Hutchison, whose son, an officer in the English Army, was killed in the massacre at the Capture of Fort William Henry in 1757 by French and indians under Montcalm. My gr. mother was gr. niece of Ethan Allen of Ticonderoga fame, and was mixed with the blood of the Spragues. My mother's father, James Mears, was of English blood. He fought in the war of 1812; <u>his</u> father was a Commissary under Washington; in the revolution; and <u>his</u> father was captured in the French war of 1754–9 at the taking of Oswego by French troops under Gen Montcalm. All our ancestors have been defenders of liberty of Conscience from the days of the Huguenots. My only brother laid down his life for the Union in 1863, and I, myself, volunteered for the whole war with Mexico, and since then have many times put my life in

[Page B125R]

1897/[Blank line]

Oct. 3/peril in the cause of the L.D.S.

Your grandfather Lyman R. Sherman was appointed an apostle, but died of exposure before he could be ordained. Prest H.C. Kimball and Geo. A. Smith each told me he died as a martyr, and would receive the glory of a martyr. And of the Johnsons—Joseph Smith had four of the Johnson women—your gr. aunts sealed to him, your gr-mother being one; she was sealed to him for time only. She and Eliza Snow lived together as his wives, and your mother often sat on Joseph's lap. He made himself at home often in the house of my father-in-law, Joel H. Johnson, in Macedonia.

So far as what the world call "good blood," we stand with the best, but of course that is all nonsense; it is folly to try to bank upon what somebody else has done generations ago. The only truly "good blood" is that of the man or woman, who, consecrating his all to the service of his Father, remains true to the end, and who finally gains an exaltation to a crown which will never fall from his head, as all human crowns are sure, sooner or later, to do. We are <u>ancestors</u> ancestors] ourselves, and if we remain true and faithful will attain to a far higher glory than any earthly ruler who ever lived. Keep these things that I have written always in view, that you may be able to add a link to the chain from time to time; and if you do not care to labor for the dead, your children or gr-children may, in time to come.

I am able to sit up and work a little and hope soon to be well again. Aunt S's ulcer is slowly healing, and Gertie and Dora and Theo. are as usual. Give my love to all and my blessing.

Your loving father James H. Martineau
Santiago Enrique Martino[16]

Please excuse blunders.
[Blank line]

Mon. 4/ Received a telegram from Lyman, saying he would be here to day, and at 10 o'clock P.M. he arrived. He came because of my illness, and brought medicines which he

[Page B126L]

1897/ Henry Walser's death.

Oct. 4/thought would be needful. This is the first day I have been up nearly all of the day, and he was greatly pleased to see me so well. We were very very pleased to see him after four years and a half absence. Lyman has always been very good to us, and I pray God he may never want friends.

8th/ Lyman's visit is now ended, much to our regret, as he cannot be spared from his duties in Utah, especially in connexion with tithing business. He advised to build a good house at once, and offered aid to amount of $100.00 He gave me the plan of May Preston Moyle's new house as a guide. He gave Joel much good business advice, and says we have a nice place here. Says he can see great possibilities for us in Mexico, and that he will advise Jesse N. to come here from Chicago instead of to Logan. Br. Bentley showed him some of the country in his carriage and spent much time trying to get him a conveyance to the railroad at Dublan, but did not succeed until midnight.

Sat 9th/ Lyman started home at 4.30 a.m. My bowels became very loose again, but I accepted Br. Jos C. Bently's invitation to go with him to visit the mountain settlements. We started at 8 a.m. traveled 12 miles to the mouth of San Diego cañon, then 4 miles up the mountain dug way to the top, thence up hill and down to Pacheco, in all 33 miles. All the road except the first 12 miles is through timber, and road very rough and bad. Stopped at Bishop Hardy's.

---

16. The name is translated as Saint James Henry Martino. James is more commonly translated into Spanish as Diego or Jaime, but "Santiago" (a name which refers to the New Testament brother of the Apostle John) can be used for James as well. Martineau had been using the Spanish pen name "Santiago" for some time. In fact, several articles submitted to the *Contributor* had been signed with this name and it appeared on his letterhead in later years. See "Who was Santiago?" *Deseret News* (Church News Section), September 7, 1957, 3.

Sun. 10/ Held two meetings to day. I spoke in both and had much liberty of the Spirit. Br. Bently re-organized the Y.M.M.I. Association

Yesterday at 5 P.M. my son-in-law Henry S. Walser was terribly mangled by a circular saw in the Thatcher Steam Saw Mill. His right leg was almost entirely severed near the hip and the flesh fearfully mangled. He then fell forward upon the saw which cut through six ribs and into his lung, making an awful wound. Word was sent home to his father, who at 9 P.M. started to see him followed by Anna and the two children, with others. They

[Page B127R]

1897/[Blank line]

Oct. 10/arrived about 1 a.m. Henry was so weak he could hardly speak, and wished to be released from his sufferings; but after being administered to he rallied. Anna and children arrived a little later, to his great joy. He was placed upon a stretcher and willing hands carried his many miles over the rough roads—about 12 miles—and when at the bottom and on smooth roads he was placed in a carriage and taken to his own home. A messenger to Dublan telegraphed to Corralitos, 35 miles for a surgeon, and the R.R. Company sent an engine to bring him to Dublan, and in a few hours he reached this place.

He amputated the leg and dressed the wound in his side, using 26 stitches, being assisted by Dr. Mrs. Saville, our local doctor who did all she could to give aid, and was very efficient.

12th/ Tues. This morning Henry suddenly passed away at 5 a.m. in full faith and fellowship with the Saints. During his brief stay everybody did all in their power to aid, causing him to say "It is good to have plenty of friends." His funeral was very largely attended. Br. James of Dublan, paid for the run of the engine for Surgeon Stovall, and the young men paid the Surgeon's bill of $100.00, also the coffin was made gratis by
[Blank line]

Henry was universally beloved; always cheerful, loving and tender as husband and father, very industrious and helpful, prominent in the Choir and Band, and in all good works. He and Anna have had five years of very happy married life and has now gone to his reward, for his exaltation is sure. Poor Anna has been very brave all through these trying scenes, and has borne up wonderfully well.[17]

I now return to my journey.

Oct. 11/Monday. We went 8 miles to Garcia, and held meeting; also re-organized to Y.M.M.I. Association there. I here took a very severe cold and hoarseness, the altitude of Garcia being reported at 7100 feet, nearly 2000 feet higher than Colonia Juarez. My diarrea also became much worse, making me quite uneasy.

12th/ Drove 35 miles over the continental divide to Chuichupe arriving about sunset. Found Bertha and Charlie sick

[Page B128L]

1897/[Blank line]

Oct. 12/with measles, and some of Sadie's children sick with the same. Henry was at home because of their sickness. Br. Bently here re-organized the Y.M.M.I. Asson but I visited with Henry's folks. This place has altitude of about 7000 feet, and at 12 miles, on the South west foot of the range you will see palms growing. Had to leave early next morning, being only a passenger.

13/ Drove homeward as far as Garcia and held meeting, in which I spoke, with great liberty of the Spirit.

14/Thurs. Thurs] Got home at Sunset. Two hours ago we heard for the first time of the terrible accident which has left Anna a widow and her children fatherless. Found all well as usual but much depressed in spirit. For myself, I feel that the trip has done me good, as the Spirit intimated to me before I left home, or I would not have started away.[18]

---

17. Henry Walser's obituary was entered in the *Deseret News* a few weeks later. See "Obituary Notes," *Deseret Weekly* 55 (November 6, 1897): 672.

18. A few days later, Martineau sent an account of his trip to Pacheco, Garcia, and Chuichupe with Joseph Bentley to the *Deseret News*. After mentioning the tragic death of his son-in-law, Henry Walser, he wrote of the reorganization of the YMMIA and described the agricultural developments in the settlements: "In Pacheco we found apples just coming into bearing, also few peaches at Corrallis, about two miles south. We were told that small fruits, such as blackberries and strawberries, produce wonderfully both in quantity and quality, as they do in Colonia Juarez, Dublan and Diaz. I think all these mountain settlements will become great fruit producers." J. H. Martineau, "Colonists in Mexico," *Deseret Weekly* 55 (November 6, 1897): 644

Sat. 16/ Surveyed all day, the first work for many days.

Sun. 17/ Spoke in meeting to day.

22/ To day Gertrude began clerking in the "Tienda de la Colonia."—Seavy's store.

23/ I surveyed again today, but was hardly able to do so, my diarrea having returned, and having quite a fever.

24/<u>Sunday</u>. This morning, in answer to prayer, I enjoyed the manifestation of the Holy Spirit, much to my comfort. I received many good promises—renewals of those formerly promised. Among other things I was told not to fear to ask guidance even for small matters, for God delights to bless his children who seek unto him. To not fear to lay on hands to bless my family and to rebuke disease and unholy spirits, for God would seal my words in the heavens and ratify them. Also, He has called me to this land to assist in a great work, and I shall be prospered from this time forth and greatly blessed. Also many other great and glorious promises, which will all be sure unto me, unless I lose them by my own fault. I thank thee, oh Father, for thy goodness, and pray that I may so live as to have thy favor and blessing always

November

2/ To day Anna moved to her own house, as she would be more comfortable there. Theodore boards

[Page B129R]

1897/ Death of Jessie Helen Russell Anderson Grieve Maru

November/with her, and will help about the chores, +c.

5/ To day I learned for the first time of the death of my wife Jessie Helen R.A. Grieve, which occurred nearly a year ago, as I am now informed. I had never heard she was sick, as her mother would not allow any correspondence between us, and Jessie, a gentle girl, was much under her mothers influence. I do not know why her mother disliked me, and there was never an ill word between Jessie and me. It is said she died of consumption.[19] I have great pleasure in the knowledge that I have been the

---

19. Jessie Helen Russell Anderson Grieve died on October 28, 1896, and was buried in the Salt Lake City Cemetery. See entry for April 18, 1887.

means of great good to her. I caused her to receive her endowments, and her 2nd A. which last is more than we can conceive. She is past all trials, and her exaltation is sure, as a Princess and one of the Queens of heaven. She did some temple work in Logan in 1887, and may have done more since then. While a young girl in Scotland, living a few miles from Edinburg, she spent much time in making a record of her ancestry from the records in that city; and obtained over a thousand names, which I have recorded in my temple record, having been baptized for many hundreds of the males of her family. This last came about in a curious manner. Her mother wished me to do the temple work for the family, as neither her husband nor brothers would do it, and accordingly I was baptized for several hundred—nearly a thousand—of her male names. After this, a written authorization from the head of the family was required, for filing in the temple record, and Mrs. Greaves was afraid to tell her husband or brothers that I had <u>already</u> done the work, without their orders, and hardly knew what to do. She finally urged her brother John C. Anderson, to do it. He replied "I am too busy building and making money and cannot take the time. Get some one in Logan to do it. Get Br. Martineau to do it—he lives in Logan." She inwardly rejoiced at this, and told him to write the request and authority for <u>me</u> to do it, which he at once did. So I filed the proper authorization for what I had already done. I could see the hand of the Lord in all this and have since received a testimony that all I so

[Page B130L]

1897/[Blank line]

November/labored for have joyfully received the work done by me.

5/I thank the Lord for giving me this opportunity to work for the dead,—a work which to me is most delightful.

I married her at the time of the passage of the last and most stringent anti-polygamy law of congress, considering that to be the best way to show where I stood, just as I married Susan J. Sherman in 1857, when the U.S. government was about to exterminate all polygamists by aid of the army.

When Jessie and I were sealed, each of us had to go to the endowment house alone, enter by a different gate and at a different time of the night, so no one might suspect. With only two witnesses, and the person officiating concealed from our view that we might not know who it was, and by the light of a single candle, the ceremony was performed.

But I knew who sealed us, by the voice—that of Apostle F.D.R. We left the building as we came—each one going our ways alone in the darkness to our homes. When I asked consent of Prest John Taylor for her to receive her 2nd A. he at once gave it. We met at the upper room of the Historian's Office, coming there, as before, singly in the night. Apostle F.D. Richards performed the ceremony, asking me to assist by laying on my hands, which I did, and thus she received the highest ordinance possible for mortality to receive.

I did not inform any of my family in Utah of my marriage, in order that they might not be compelled to testify against me in court, should I be arrested, which they could not do, if they did not know it. I rode with her in a carriage around S.L. City a number of times, in Bishop Preston's carriage, but was not troubled by any U.S. Officers.

At one time I received an intimation from the Presidents Office that U.S. Marshals were watching me, and so I left the house of my wife, Mary E. Jones, and went to stay at Bishop Prestons, and at my Son Lyman R.'s place in Logan.

In November of 1887 Jessie Helen started for Arizona, to meet me there, but when she arrived at Vallejo, where an apostate ^aunt^ of hers lived, she was persuaded to return to Utah, which she did, and thus never came to me

[Page B131R]

1897/[Blank line]

November/in Arizona, as she first intended to do.

5/ In 1893, when Susan and I went to the dedication of the Salt Lake Temple, Susan went to see Jessie at the house of a mutual friend,—one of Brigham Young's wives—and tried to persuade her to go to us in Mexico, which she said she would do; but her mother again intervened, and prevented this. I saw her once during this time for a little while, and this was the last I saw her on earth.

Praise and blessing to Susan, for doing what she did, for it was a great—a noble act,—one that will exalt her in the heavens. She thus proved the integrity of her heart beyond all doubt.

After hearing today of Jessie's death, I received a good and comforting answer concerning her, and I know all is well with her, and she will reign with me—one of the Queens of Heaven.

6/ Saturday. Theodore came over to day, and we laid out the foundation for our new dwelling. I laid a little of the foundation wall. Although possessing little means to build such a house, I believe God will open my way to erect it, for such is the testimony to me.

10/ <u>Wed</u>. This morning, as I lay awake about 3 o'clock, I prayed, as I often do in the night, and received a glorious and comforting answer, with promise of many blessings from the heavens and from the earth. I will record some of these things, that my family may profit thereby, and learn to look to the Lord in faith, knowing that if our Father, in his goodness, will hear and answer <u>one</u> of his children, he is equally willing to bless another in the same manner.

I was told, among many other things, to look forward to the future with joy and gladness, for it is full of blessings to me and mine. That I shall be blessed and prospered from this time forth; blessed and prospered in building and furnishing my house beyond my expectations; to build it according to my present plan and Lyman's; for it shall be a house in which not only my brethren but natives of this land may sojourn, and will not be too large as I have thought it would be. That I have been brought to this land to do a great work, and shall perform it, for I shall be strengthened in body and in mind, and my age renewed

[Page B132L]

1897/[Blank line]

Nov. 10th/Wed./for that purpose. That I shall become mighty among my brethren in priesthood and in calling that I may be able to do a greater work; and that the people of this land will love, trust, honor, and defend me if necessary, with their lives; that my faith shall become like that of the brother of Jared, and I shall have power to mighty works—even to raise the dead to life if necessary and to cause the earth to shake. And that I shall never be tempted more than I can bear, nor be turned aside from the commandment I shall receive. Many other promises were given which I do not feel to write. I do not write these things in a boasting spirit. I know if I receive them it will be by the help of our Father; and if I do not, it will be because of my own shortcomings and lack of faith, which at times becomes very weak.

28/ A few days ago I received a check for $51.72 which was due me from the U.S. Government as a balance for my Surveys made in 1893–4. This amount, though justly due me, had been disallowed by the Treasury Department because, as they said, my account had been <u>closed</u>. In answer to prayer three years ago I was told I should receive my pay, notwithstanding I had been told it would <u>not</u> be paid me; and thus it seemed as if it was useless for me to hope for it. But thus has the promise of the Spirit been fulfilled; and I record it as a testimony, to assist the faith of my family and posterity.

To day I wrote to Lorenzo Snow, President of the temple in S.L. City, in regard to the principle of Sealing men and women in marriage a number of times,—as to <u>why</u> it was necessary. For instance Susan and I were first <u>Sealed</u> by Apostle Geo. A. Smith in Parowan, Utah, in May 1852, and were afterwards sealed by Prest B. Young in 1860.[20] We were endowed in March 11th 1852, and our first child born Nov. 4, 1852. The question with me is,—if the <u>first</u> Sealing is valid and of use, why must it be repeated? And if it must be repeated, as ours was, and others, is not the first sealing without value and force?

[Page B133R]

1897/[Blank line]

Nov. 28th/Also, will it not be necessary for our first born to be Sealed to us, seeing that he was begotten before our endowments.

---

20. In addition to his inquiry regarding sealings, Martineau asked about the construction of a temple in Mexico. Evidently, his letter was read in the Salt Lake Temple on the morning of December 9, in the presence of Wilford Woodruff, George Q. Cannon, Joseph F. Smith, Lorenzo Snow, Elders John Henry Smith, and Heber J. Grant: "The subject of building a Temple at Juarez, Mexico, was suggested by the reading of a letter from Bro. James H. Martineau He stated that it cost about $750 in Mexican money for a couple to come from that place to Salt Lake City, to be married or do other Temple Work. Pres. L. Snow favored the building of an Endowment House in Mexico, and perhaps another in Canada and one also in Arizona. If the people in those parts had faith and means enough to build them without calling upon the Church for funds." Journal History, December 9, 1897, p. 2.

An answer to this inquiry was made by letter dated December 24, 1897. See entry for January 12, 1898 wherein the letter is inserted.

[Blank line]

Dec./ December 1
Henry, Mellissa and 2 children came

6/ Took advantage of excursion rates to El Paso, and started for that place, having business there making it necessary to go. Stayed at the R.R. Station near Dublan

7/ In El Paso, 140m about 4 P.M. Got a bed and room for 25¢

8/ Attended to my business and bought some goods for my family, remaining also the next day, as no train went South until

10th/the tenth, Oct. (Friday) on which day I reached Dublan. Cold.

11/Sat. Arrived home and found all well as usual, except that Melissa had been very near death, from a miscarriage, but is now rapidly improving in health and strength.

I omitted to mention that on Dec. 2 the wind demolished a part of Joel's new brick and Adobe house he is building.

22/ Snowed all day but melted as it fell, also next day.

24/Snow 2 in. deep this morning. Dora had a bad fit of some kind Administered, and she soon got better, but was quite ill all day.

26/ Today Dora had a very bad fit

29/ To day Henry and family went home. The same evening we were invited to a social party at Br. John J. Walser's. A good time.

31/ Attended a Social party at Mrs. Dr. Saville's, and enjoyed it.

------------------- January 1898 -----------------

1898/[Blank line]

Jan. 1/Worked all day, and the next, lining our board room with brown sheeting, and so made it warmer and pleasanter.

8/ Got a bedstead for Gertie and Dora, for $16.00

This is our 46th anniversary of our wedding, but we did not try, as we usually do, to have a celebration, having so little means to procure eatables, and so did not expect anything. But at evening we were visited by all our children in Juarez, also by Sister Saville and daughter, and our friend John Telford, whom Theodore had caused to come from Richmond, Utah. We had a very pleasant evening, and a good supper, much of which was contributed by our visitors. I cannot realize we have been so long united, but so it it [is], the Father be praised.

[Page B134L]

1898/[Blank line]

January 12/ To day received the following in answer to the letter I Sent Prest Lorenzo Snow in November, and which he had Submitted for consideration to the First Presidency and Twelve:—

"Salt Lake City, Utah 24th Dec. 1897
Elder James H. Martineau

Dear Brother. In replying to the questions submitted by you in your letter of Nov. 28th 1897, it is not necessary to repeat them here, as you will find them covered by a decision made on Thursday, December 16th 1897, by the Council of the First Presidency and the Twelve Apostles, which was as follows:

(1st) That the Sealing of a couple outside of a temple, as husband and wife for time and eternity by one holding the requisite authority (the President of the Church, or any one deputed by him) is as valid as when performed in the House of the Lord, even when either or both of the parties have not been previously Endowed.

(2nd) That children born after such Sealing are legal heirs, even of begotten before the Sealing occurred, and it is therefore unnecessary to seal them to their parents.

(3d) No measures are at present afoot looking to the erection of a temple in Mexico.[21]

Your brother in the Gospel
Lorenzo Snow."

---

21. Lorenzo Snow to James H. Martineau, December 24, 1897. This letter was inserted at the back of Martineau's journal, book two. See Godfrey and Martineau-McCarty, eds., *Uncommon Common Pioneer*, 735–736. See note at entry for November 28, 1897. See also note at entry for September 30, 1891.

[Blank line]

This decision of the General Church Authorities sets to rest a question which has for many years been undecided in the Church. For example, Susan and I were sealed for time and eternity as husband and wife in Parowan, Utah, in May 1852, by Apostle Geo. A. Smith; and sealed again by Prest B. Young in S.L. City, Endowment House, in 1860, in order to be Sealed "over the Alter." And Susan Sherman was Sealed to me, first, in the President's Office, S.L. City, in 1857 and again in the Endowment House by Prest Young in 1860. So this question has now been settled authoritatively.[22]

[Page B135R]

1898/[Blank line]

Jan. 12/ The contention has been that a Sealing was invalid if done before one or both of the parties had been endowed; Also that it must be performed over an alter, to be legal and binding. This sets at rest all doubts relative to the Sealing of Annie B. to Henry S. Walser, neither of whom had had their endowments.

14/ Two inches of Snow this morning. Soon melted away.

15/ Col. Miguel Ahumada, Governor of Chihuahua, together with 50 or 60 leading Mexicans, Officers of the State, Military Officers and others paid us a visit. We had a good program lasting over an hour, of Speeches, Songs and music by the Band and Choir, after which tables were spread with a fine dinner, which was eaten by more than 200 Souls. Our visitors were much pleased with our town and with their reception, and praised our people highly, returning to the R.R. Station at Casas Grandes in the afternoon. I was introduced to the Governor, also to State Surveyor Senor de Bergue[23]

28/ Have been very ill with Lagrippe for almost 2 weeks But in the last 3 or 4 days copied a map for Alex. F. Macdonald, receiving $12.00 for it. Am recovering slowly.

---

22. Martineau evidently considered this letter important enough to transcribe it into his commonplace book. See Martineau, "Pearls," p. 135.

23. The visit included the governor, Col. Miguel Ahumada, and many civil and military leaders. Martineau's description of Ahumada's visit was published a few days later. "After inspecting the wire suspension bridge over the Rio Piedras Verdas the party returned to Dublan, fifteen miles distant, and thus terminated an event full of interest and possibly of importance to us as a colony." James H. Martineau to editor, January 17, 1898, "Gubernatorial Visit," *Deseret Evening News*, January 24, 1898, 2.

31/ To day Prest A.W. Ivins started to the City of Mexico, and took my map of the Colonia Juarez Survey, which is almost completed. I also sent with him a petition for appointment as official Surveyor and Engineer in the republic, hoping it may increase my power for good.

And today occurred three funerals, 2 little babies and a dear friend—Leroy Cluff, who died suddenly of pneumonia, leaving an almost helpless wife, who is a cousin of ours, formerly Maisie
[Blank line]

February/ February 1898

4/ Two funerals to day, in our little town of 600 people

5 Sat./ To day Albert unexpectedly came to us. We had not had opportunity to visit with him for many years.

11/ Henry came to day from Chiuchupe + brought Bertha to go to the Academy.

Sun. 13/ To day Gertrude was taken very sick,—great pain in

[Page B136L]

1898/[Blank line]

Feb. 13th/her spine and head, fever +c. I have been most of the time in bed for about a month, with the Grippe and also a stricture of the prostate gland, which incapacitate me almost entirely from labor, on account of intense pain. I have labored at clearing my city lot of brush and trees which have covered much of it for an hour or so at a time, then resting on a bed for most of the day, in this time and manner doing some work.

15th 17/ To night Gertrude was so much worse, with such a difficulty of breathing that Dr. Saville thought she was dying. I had her administered to many times and sat up with her all night, my hand on her head all the time, praying for and blessing her. Better next morning.

18/ Susan taken very sick with grippe, as also Theodore and Albert; so we are all sick in the house, including Dora. There are also many in the town who are also sick with the same complaint—la grippe.[24]

---

24. See Bosque, "From Colonia Juarez. Much Sickness Prevails among the Colonists—Farming Conditions," *Salt Lake Herald*, March 2, 1898, 7.

Gertrude very low.

20/ " " " Still. We deny all visitors, as she cannot endure the least noise, even of talking in a low tone in the next room. This morning she sleeps by aid of Morphine. Susan is better, but unable to sit up longer than a few minutes at a time. I do not know what we would do if Anita was not our good ministering angel. She has been with us night and day since Gertrude's first sickness. Albert is still suffering with cough and his lungs, but is able to get around, as are Dora ad myself.

22/ Gertrude begins to improve, which is because of administrations of the priesthood. Albert went up to Chuichupe to day, to see the country. Went with Henry.

23/ Gertie sat up in a chair for the first time, about an hour.

For some days Susan has been very sick also, with La grippe but she is now nearly well.

25/ By invitation of Mrs. Saville Gertrude went today to her house to remain a few days, it being more quiet and comfortable for her.

[Page B137R]

1898/[Blank line]

March/ March.

1/At the priesthood meeting today I was appointed one of a Committee of five to examine for a site for a wagon bridge over the river, and report probable cost of one.[25]

4/ Examined for site for bridge, with Committee. Apostles J.H. Smith and John W. Taylor came.

5/ Special Conference to day. Good time; also next day, Suny

7/ Susan and I visited the Apostles and had a pleasant time.

8/ I made measurements for a truss bridge over the river at a point 200 feet wide, and Commenced plan for bridge.

11/ Showed my plan for a bridge to the Apostles, who approved.

---

25. The bridge was, evidently, an important decision to the town and was critical for improved transportation across the river. See entries for March 4, 8, 11, 15, 24, and 31, 1898.

Susan and Gertie and all are well now as usual, except that Gertie is too weak to walk much. I also, am troubled with a stricture, or something, in my left groin, which prevents me from doing much work or even walking, and at times is extremely painful. But I hope I may be healed. I know that He who <u>formed</u> my body is able to renovate and Strengthen it.

Our orchard is in bloom, and is beautiful indeed. I have done much work in our garden, putting it in better shape. Theodore has done much to improve the lot I let him have, and I hope to be able to build a pleasant home.

13/ <u>Sunday</u>. This is my 70th birthday! It seems almost impossible that I have attained the full age allotted to man but so it is. As I look back upon my past, it all seems as a dream;—a dream sometimes happy,—sometimes, like a nightmare of sorrow and trouble. But I acknowledge the hand of the Lord in all, and say all is right. No doubt I have needed every sharp lesson I have had. I know it was necessary, for my Experience and perfection, as no one can profit much by another's experience.

As I review my past life, I see I have many things to be thankful for, and with all my failings, I can say I have never given any of my family evil counsel to my knowledge. I have always taught them to honor the holy priesthood, to be faithful and obedient, to be diligent in all duties of L.D. Saints

[Page B138L]

1898/[Blank line]

March 13th/ I have never upheld any in wrong doing. I myself though coming far short of what I should be, have never at any time put my own private interests before the public good or the work of the Lord. I have never raised my voice or influence against any of my leaders or authorities in Ward, Stake, or the Church. I have never brought any one before a teacher or a Bishop or High Council, but have suffered wrong rather than help to cause division among the Saints,—have paid debts twice over rather than contend. God has been wonderfully good to me. He gathered me from my kindred, who were good people according to their light, gave the gospel, with the holy Melchisedek priesthood, and the <u>fullness</u> of the priesthood; gave me my first and Second anointings and all the blessings pertaining thereto; he has given me keys of power to act as a Savior on

Mount Zion for many of the dead—about 2000 in number, with a testimony that <u>all</u> have received the temple ordinances in their behalf with joy and rejoicing, confirming this by an open vision in 1887 in Logan; He has given me a hundred wives, living and dead, Sealed and endowed, of whom six have received their Second Anointing; He has given me twenty one sons and daughters, with nearly seventy grand children, and one great grand-child, from my daughter Elvira. He has sent me noble Spirits, who, thus far, have all been true and faithful as L.D. Saints, honored and respected by all, four of whom, Lyman, Charles, Jesse and Nephi have filled foreign missions honorably, and Henry, Moroni and Elvira, called in Conference as missionaries to extend the borders of Zion. All this, and much more he has done for me, besides preserving my life by his special power, when nothing else would have saved it. Once, in 1850, when thousands died of cholera on the great plains, and I was given up to die, the angel of the Lord healed me instantaneously in the night time, telling me

[Page B139R]

1898/[Blank line]

March 13/in an audible voice three times "You will not die." to which I answered "If I do not die I will take it as a Sign the Lord has got a work for me to do." At other times miraculously preserved from death, and once actually raised from the dead—(being dead) by the power of God through the ministration of Apostle Thatcher and other brethren. At another time preserved from death by obeying the <u>audible</u> voice of a guardian angel in July or August 1888, when a heavily loaded gun discharged.

Should I not be thankful!—humble, and very obedient to all the laws of heaven! Verily—yes!

And now I pray our Father, if it is his will, to help me to live so that I may gain all that has been sealed upon me by the holy priesthood, and that all my family may be exalted with me in the celestial Glory. Amen.
[Blank line]
Yesterday I received a letter from Lyman, which I here insert:—

Logan March 7, 1898
Mr. James H. Martineau
Colonia Juarez Mexico
My dear father.

Your good letter came some time ago, but press of tithing a/cs and sickness have prevented me from writing, and am still under the pressure, and can only write you briefly so as to reach you by the time your birthday comes. I and we congratulate you on reaching 3 score and 10 years, and on a fair prospect for living several years—say 20—yet. I wish you many happy returns of the day, and that during the unfoldment of the years to come, you may take greater pleasure in life, and that your large family may be willing + able to cheer your heart, and strew flowers along your pathway, and you be able to reap the harvest from your good example, sown through many years of storms + Sunshine in the past. We honor you for

[Page B140L]

1898/[Blank line]

March 13/your integrity to the truth, for your loyalty to the cause of Christ which you espoused as a youth, and for the many virtues + good councils you have shown forth in your eventful career. I am sorry your health is bad again, and sorry, too, to hear that Aunt Susan, Gertrude, and others have been sick with the grippe. I hope you are all better by now. I was shocked to read in to day's Herald that Sister Macdonald had been strangled to death by those black fiends who Surround you on all sides.[26] It almost makes me feel like removing my objections to your staying in such a place, but I fear, as in the past, my objections would not count for much. Still, it does seem as though you were almost out of the world.

For about two months we here in Logan have had trouble, and it is

---

26. On the night of February 23, Agnes Macdonald, wife of A. F. Macdonald, was sleeping in her apartment which was adjacent to a small country store in Colonia Garcia., when an intruder took her life. According to the newspaper report, "The crime was not discovered until the following morning, when the wife of her son James went to the house and found her lifeless body upon the bed, a pillow over her face and finger marks upon her throat, showing that she had been choked to death." From "Murder of Mrs. Macdonald," *Salt Lake Herald*, March 7, 1898, 8. See also Romney, *Mormon Colonies in Mexico*, 144–145. Martineau reported that "the murderers stole a pair of horses from Joel H. Martineau, upon which to make their escape, he having camped in that vicinity the evening before the tragedy occured [sic]. Two Mexicans who had been laboring in Garcia were missing the next morning, and there is no doubt of their guilt as the murderers of our beloved sister." James H. Martineau, "A Dreadful Crime," *Deseret Weekly* 57 (March 12, 1898): 387. See also Henry Lunt, "Mrs. McDonald's Murder," *Deseret Weekly* 57 (March 19, 1898): 445. Several weeks later, writing from Colonia Juarez, Martineau tried to dispel rumors that Agnes Macdonald had been murdered by members of the "Black Jack Gang" of outlaws. See J. H. Martineau, "'Black Jack' Story Denied," *Deseret Evening News*, April 23, 8; reprinted in *Deseret Weekly* 57 (April 30, 1898): 613.

not all over yet. Lilla was confined day before yes'day, Mch. 5th but the little child, a large, beautiful boy, only lived a few moments. He was well formed and perfect in every way except there was a sort of tumor about his throat which had so Enveloped his windpipe, that he could not breathe. No medical skill could do any good, though Drs. O.C. + O.S. Ormsby's were both there. Lilla stood it pretty bravely, and to day is as well as we could expect. They gave the baby the name Dwight, and we buried him yesterday in the N.E. corner of the grave lot where mother and the other three of your dead are laid.

Charlie's baby, James Miller, is still very sick. The pneumonia left him very ~~sick~~ weak, and before he was strong, his lungs became filled with water, which if a few days treatment does not carry off, will have to be tapped. I believe he will pull through, but it is a tight place for the little fellow.

Alley's right hand is still very bad, too lame

[Page B141R]

1898/[Blank line]

Mch. 13/to write or do much with, + the doctor is giving her electric treatment, which is the only thing that has dome her any good yet. It is a sort of muscular rheumatism. I must close. All join in love to all and pray the Lord may bless + preserve you all from harm and evil. Write soon.

Your afft Son L.R. Martineau

Our children gathered in the evening, and we had a good time—a very pleasant time. I hope we may have more. Counted, living and dead, 118 in our family, one being a ^Gr.^ grandchild.

15/ Having been appointed, with others, to examine and find a place to build a wagon bridge across the river, we spent the day in so doing, and finally decided on a proper site; looking also at other proposed sites, taking levels, +c.[27]

16/ Made a plat of the Chuichupe purchase which is 5000 meters square.

18/ Henry and family, also Sadie and Sixtus returned home.

---

27. The bridge was located at the point where Snow Street intersects the Piedras Verdes River.

Perfected and finished my plan for a 2-span bridge, 66 ft each span, with approaches.

19/ Bought a saddle of J.O. Davis and two poles ($47.00) for $45.00. Cash order on Coln Company and a pair of leggins, ($5.00)

20/ Prest Ivins returned from Mexico yesterday, + preached to day. After meeting I was appointed Chairn of Committee to locate and superintend construction of an irrigation Canal for Tenaja field.

With Prest Ivins located the dividing line between Scott and Stowell. Scott gave up all claim to the land, and Prest Ivins located Stowell's N.E. line, saying that as Scott had given up all claim to the land in dispute, it should revert to the Colonization Company, for public use.

Joel laid out my garden for planting, and hauled me some lumber for a new cow shed, barn and corral.

At the land meeting a few days ago Theo. and I drew our lots contiguous, mine 14.15 Acres and his 16.+ acres. Both pieces are excellent land.

Albert started home at 3.30 P.M. We were very sorry to have him go. His visit has been very pleasant.

[Page: B142L]

1898/[Blank line]

March 23/Set out a lot of Blackberry plants.

24/at a meeting to consider the building of a wagon bridge over the river, I made my report as Engineer, which was accepted, and it was decided to build the bridge at the crossing we had selected. I and two others were appointed a Committee to receive and pass upon all plans for a bridge which might be presented by any person.

25/ Surveyed for a canal for the lower Tenaja field. Very windy.

26/ Worked on plan for bridge part of the day. High Priests meeting, and had an enjoyable time.

Have just learned from Sister Henrietta, of the recent death of my nephew, Fritz Vonwinkel, of softening of the brain. He left a wife and two little girls. He was Lois' only son, and was a good young man.

Thurs. 31/ According to previous appointment met with the two others of the Bridge Committee to examine and receive a plan for a bridge across the Piedras Verdes river in Juarez. Three plans were presented, one by me, one by R. Scott and one by F.G. Wall.[28] With us were Prest A.W. Ivins and Bishop J.C. Bentley. My plan was accepted. It provides for a bridge of two spans of 66 feet each, timber, constructed on the Whipple truss system, and will cost probably from $2000 to $3000 dollars.[29] The Committee adjourned before finally deciding what to do.

Fri. April/
1/Surveyed all day on the Tenaja field canal.

2/ Bought a saddle for $47.00 of J.O. Davis

Sun. 3. The Bridge Committee formally adopted my plan of bridge

4/ Started to El Paso with Gertrude, and went to Dublan.

5/ Very cold. Took train 8.30 A.M., third class, to save expense, $3.60 each. Car was full to overflowing of Mexicans all going to El Paso or Ciudad Juarez to spend Holy week. Very uncomfortable all day. Arrived Juarez 5 P.M.

6/+7th Attended to my business, and next day [in margin: 8th] returned home and found all well. Found a letter from Charlie, informing me of the death of his little boy James Miller, which occurred March 23 1898 at 1 o'clock P.M.

[Page B143R]

1898/ On Tues. April 5th Joel's baby boy was born. A hard time for all.

April 8th/A letter from Lilla says she has almost recovered from her attack

---

28. Probably Robert Logan Scott (1853–1940) of Fennwick, Ayrshire, Scotland, and Francis George Wall (1846–1946) of Horsely, Gloucester, England.

29. Although Martineau engineered the design of this bridge, it took nearly a decade for a bridge to be built. If Martineau's design was used it is not clear from the historical record. But Samuel Edwin McClellan is credited with building a wagon bridge that facilitated crossing the Piedras Verdes River. The bridge, which opened December 4, 1907, was built with the aid of colonists at a cost of $10,000. According to a published announcement, it was considered "a great convenience to the people who, before its erection, were frequently greatly annoyed by the sudden and often tremendous floods that commonly swept down the river after rain storms." See "The New Bridge Over the Piedras Verdes River, in Colonia Juarez, Mexico," and "The Juarez Bridge, Mexico," *Improvement Era* 12 (May 1909): 538, 540. For a brief account of the building of this bridge, see Hatch, *Colonia Juarez*, 146.

of Paralysis; can talk, but cannot sing a note. She was a fine singer before. Her left hand is also unusable from the paralysis. I hope she will soon entirely recover.

Sat. 9/ Worked on bridge plans. The Committee wish to advertise for bids on contract to build it. The following is a sketch of the proposed bridge:—

[Several blank lines—no drawing done here]

Sun. 10th/ Very warm and threatens rain.

Thurs. 7/ Last Thursday, at priesthood meeting, my plan for a bridge across the Piedras Verdes river in Juarez, was formally adopted, to be built. It will be of 2 spans, each 67 ½ feet, with approaches 65 feet, total length 200 feet.[30]

13/ Counting up my family, living and dead, including those who have married my sons and daughters. I find the numbers as follows:—self and 3 wives = 4 Children 40, Gr. children 71, Gr. Gr. Child 1, total 115. Besides these, my son Neils L. Hagberg has had 2 or three born of which I have no account at present. Truly, God has greatly blessed and added unto me, praise be to his holy name, for to him is due all the honor and glory of our salvation. In addition to the above number, I have had Sealed to me, for time and eternity 96 wives, and have had a testimony that all have received the temple ordinances with joy and rejoicing. (211 in all) Help me so to live oh my Father, that I may receive all in the end which thou hast committed into my hands. Amen.

18/ Have spent several days working up my plans for the bridge, specifications +c. Leveled to day across river

19/ Arranged about my pay for Survey of the Chuichupe purchase with Peterson the owner:—I am to receive $500. payable in Land $350.00 (100 acres) and cash $150.00

20/ Just one year since we returned home from Arizona, and in that time we have been much blessed.

[Page B144L]

1898/[Blank line]

---

30. The bridge, although it has been rebuilt and modernized, still crosses the Piedras Verdes River in Colonia Juárez.

April 21st/ Patriarch Henry Lunt, whom we have known since the spring of 1851 visited us today. When departing he said that having heard us talk and feeling our spirit he felt to prophesy upon our head. Uncovering his own head he said "I prophesy that from this day and this very hour you shall be blessed and prospered more than you have since you have been in Mexico, both spiritually and temporally, in all things. You shall see it fulfilled. Amen. I felt a testimony within me that his words will be verified, and felt very thankful for the promise.[31]

28/ Started to day to go to Chuichupe, to Survey the lands of that Settlement, with J.C. Petersen, arriving there on the

30th/30th Chilled completely through. Found Henry's family and Moroni's, all well

May 1, 1898 Sunday

May 1/ Found Prest Ivins here, and made mining maps for him, as he must start for Juarez early tomorrow. Spoke in meeting and felt well.

2/ Took Latitude, 29° 23' 30" Altitude 7505 feet. All vegetation here is only just starting, with frosty nights

3/ This morning at 4.42 a.m. made an observation on Polaris, and found variation of needle 11° 27'E. very cold. To day I began the survey, which will cover 5000 meters square,—a little over nine square miles. Much of today's work was in pine timber with tall grass among the trees. Sent to Susan for underclothing. Suffered in my groin, as climbing steep and rocky hills and deep gulches, with my heavy transit inflamed my already much inflamed and swollen prostate gland, which for weeks past has caused me at times excruciating pains, and has almost totally incapacitated me from all labor. Henry now carried my transit so I could lie down. I prayed for relief, and God heard my prayer and removed all the pain. Before I left Juarez I asked the Father if I would be able to do the work. The answer came, that I <u>would</u> be, that I should be strengthened for we work,

[Page B145R]

and that I should not suffer much pain in my groin, but it should be healed

---

31. Martineau was still reporting that, despite rumors, no act of vengeance had been perpetrated for the death of Agnes Macdonald. See J. H. Martineau to editor, April 9, 1898, "'Black Jack' Story Denied," *Deseret Evening News*, April 23, 1898, 8.

through anointing, prayer + faith, and that I should go and return in peace and safety and be greatly blessed. And I already find this blessing is being verified.

6/ To day Petersen returned home. Paid me $25.00

10/ Still surveying. In the night received glorious promises. I shall be healed of the stricture, not by surgeon's aid or Gentile physicians but by the power of God through anointing, prayer and faith. Many blessings and promises were made for my family.

This morning a prospector went hunting and has not returned. His partners fear he is lost. Great forest fires rage in the west, filling the heavens with dense smoke.

11/ Men hunted for the lost man. Unsuccessful.

12/ Two parties of Miners came in whose camps and all they contained had been burned, with heavy loss of clothing bedding, provisions, ammunition, currency + assaying outfit. Still hunting the lost man. Found where he had killed and eaten a skunk. Every man who could get a horse was hunting for him.[32]

13/ Wrote to Deseret News.[33] My party also searched for lost man, so could not work. Same on the 14th

15/ Preached and felt well. In the evening a meeting was held to devise means to build some kind of a Fort or protection against possible trouble, according to the counsel of Apostles Smith and Taylor recently given at Garcia. It was decided to build a house of adobe or brick 27 x 40 ft and surrounded it with a timber palisade large enough to hold stock and other property in case of necessity. Some of the men hunting the lost man returned, with his Burro and blankets, but did not find him. The Land Company engaged me to resurvey the town site, at $10. per day.

16/ Began the town Survey, also 17th, 18, + 19th and finished it.

---

32. On this date, Martineau wrote a letter from Chuichupa to the *Deseret Evening News* telling of the lack of progress in the search for a missing prospector near Guynopa. See J. H. Martineau, "Possibly a Tragedy," *Deseret Evening News*, May 24, 1898, 6.

33. Martineau reported on the dedication of the Juárez Stake Academy under the pen name, "Salamander." See Salamander, "Juarez Stake Academy," *Deseret Weekly* 56 (June 4, 1898): 798, and Salamander, "Juarez Stake Academy," *Deseret Evening News*, May 24, 1898, 6.

18/ Theodore arrived on the 18th Weather still very cold and windy, frost every night.

[Page B146L]

1898/[Blank line]

May 18/The lost man was found by Mexican cattle herders about 30 miles distant. Still crawling away from the Settlement. He was nearly demented and must soon have died. He felt very grateful that our people had hunted for him so long.[34]

21/ Finished the survey to day, except a little here + there. The heavy wind ceased for the first, since my arrival.

26/ Rode over the surrounding country with Henry, + families. Theodore went on a hunt with 8 others, to be gone some days. He went on the 25th Theo. Sent in 2 deer he killed

27/ Chose my land, of which I am to have 100 acres besides $150.00 Cash. I took 40 Acres (16 Hektares) of good timber the rest in open land, all of it good. I feel that I have been greatly blessed in this, and the promise made me in the beginning has been fulfilled in a manner very wonderful to me.

I have been full of life and strength and vigor, I who for so many months have been weak, feeble and filled with pain, unable to walk half a mile without having to go to bed. And I have labored hard without pain in my groin, which has for months been impossible. I know it has been only through the special blessing of the Lord in answer to my prayers. I have anointed the diseased place night and morning, in the name of Jesus, and the swelling and stricture has constantly decreased. And thus, through pain and troubles our faith is increased, therefore these so-called evils are actually blessings.

28/ As I lay awake this morning I prayed and received most glorious promises, mostly a reiteration of those given before.

29/ Theo. got back, having killed more deer than all the rest of the 8, who had chaffed him as a "tender foot." He also killed 2 Bears, with Geo. Johnson

30/ I find, by average of 63 observations of my aneroid, that the elevation

---

34. Martineau gave an account of this incident in the *Deseret News*. See J. H. Martineau, "Possibly a Tragedy," *Deseret Evening News*, May 24, 1898, 6.

of this place is 7505 feet by instrument scale and 7468 by published elevation table.[35]

31/ Recd $40.00 Cash on Survey. Started home at 1 P.M. with a deer which Theo. killed for me yesterday.

[Page B147R]

1898/I arrived (with Henry) at home on Thurs. June 2nd all [in margin: June 2] well, but quite tired. On our way home we passed for 40 miles through forest fires and smoke at times very dense. Found all at home well. Dora had had a severe fit while I was absent, and had been found senseless on the ground, by administering, she came to all right, and now is well.

3/ Paid $20.00 Cash tithing.

4/ Wrote letters and rested.

Sun. 5/ A slight thunder shower today.

15/ Went to Casas Grandes and filed application for citizenship with the Presidente. Paid 5.50

29/ Today Joel, Gertrude and Dora, also Anne Walser went with others by wagon into the Mountains to Chuichupa for an outing, to be gone 2 or 3 weeks.

July

July 3/Sunday/ I blessed Theodore Stanley, the new born child of Joel and Mary Ann Martineau, in fast meeting.

11/ Susan's birth day. We were alone, and I too poor to make her any birth day present, which I regret.

Heard that Aunt Harriet, my last living Aunt had recently died, aged 91 years. Died June 24, Fultonville.

24/ There was a celebration of Pioneer Day, but neither I nor Susan went, both being unwell, Susan real sick.

---

35. On the following day, Martineau wrote from Chuichupa and reported that the lost hunter had been found and included an elevation table of various locations in northern Mexico. He also described conditions at Chuichupa. See J. H. Martineau, "From Mexico," *Deseret Evening News*, June 20, 1898, 5, and J. H. Martineau, "Miscellaneous. From Mexico," *Deseret Weekly* 57 (June 25, 1898): 44.

Note/Aunt Harriet's first husband's name was John E. Poole. He was one of the Engineers on the Erie Canal.

August.

Aug. 17th/ Theodore went to the R.R. Station at Dublan to work for the R.R. Company. He believed he would do well and have permanent employment.

24/ Henry A. also went there to work in shops.

September

Sept. 7/A big flood in our river, the Piedras Verdas, which did considerable damage, but no lives (of people) lost.

18/ To day Theodore and I signed fresh applications for citizenship. He was at home on a visit.

For a long time I have been very unwell and scarcely able to be around, on account, mostly, of a swelling in my left groin, which the least work

[Page B148L]

1898/[Blank line]

Sept. 18/causes extreme pain. Also, my general health is very poor, and I seem to be failing fast. Susan and I have decided it best for me to go to Logan and work in the temple for awhile, if the way will open. I do not know how long my stay on earth will be, and there is much important temple work for me to do or have done and I an anxious to do it.[36]

20/ Received a letter from Jesse N. and his lately wedded wife. I record the letter of his wife, because of its genealogical value, as follows:—
[Blank line]
Chicago, Sept. 11, 1898

Dear Father

In answer to your request will give you such information as I possess in regard to my people. Have not exact date of father's birth, but will write

---

36. The following day, Martineau wrote a letter to the *Deseret Weekly* describing the Mexican Independence Day celebrations and businesses and industries in Colonia Juárez. See J. H. Martineau, "Mexican Independence," *Deseret Weekly* 57 (October 1, 1898): 493.

to my mother. I was born in Sharon, Wis. Dec. 21st 1861. My name was Eliza Belle Johnson. My father, William Warren Johnson, was a private in the 13th Wis., died of typhoid fever when I was six months old. (1862) Mother's maiden name was Mariette Leavitt, Grandfather, Peter Leavitt. Grandmother's maiden name was Sarah Spaulding.—her mother's name was Baker; all New England people of English descent.

Great Grandfather Johnson's name was William W. born Dec. 2. 1785; his wife Nancy,—have not her maiden name, born June 28 1788. My grandfather and the rest of their children in the following order:—
William E.   Jan. 24. 1812
Dewitt C.,   Feb 9. 1813
Ansil L.   Aug 14. 1814
Daniel B.   Feb. 14. 1816
Welcome W.   Oct. 26. 1817
Harty J.   May 16. 1819
David M.   Oct. 7 1821

[Page B149R]

1898/[Blank line]

Sept. 20/ John L.H.   Feb. 3. 1826
   Warren   March 5. 1830

My father had two Sisters and one brother. One Sister, Eliza, died young; the other Caroline H. Bell, is living in Hadley, Mass. The brother, Edward Eaton Johnson is ^now^ living in Los Angeles. He has the family record back to—I think—1626, when William Johnson married Nancy Eaton in London, Eng. I have one brother, Willis E. Johnson, born Dec. 8. 1859,—is now living in Myrtle, Cal.

My mother married Alexander Hyatt when I was five years old. He was killed by lightening in Syracuse, Neb. April 1883. My mother is now living in Oregon City, Oregon, with my younger brothers Willard and George Hyatt. They are both good men and very dear to me.

There has never been, so far as we know, a drunkard, a pauper, a criminal, or a disreputable person of either sex in my father's or mother's family. [blank]Enclose obituary. Please return, as it is the only one I have. Will leave news for Jess to write. We have not much of this world's goods, but are very happy together and see no reason why we shall not continue to be so. With much love to yourself, "Aunt Susan" and the rest of the family, I am yours affectionately

Belle M.
[Blank line]

22/ Answered Jesse's and Belle's letter.

24/ Sold my wagon, 2 horses and harnesses for $400.00, $100 to be cash, so I can go to Utah, hoping to renew my health. I have been quite feeble all the season, with a swelling in my left groin, which was very painful from doing any labor.

Note 16/ On Sept. 16th a daughter, Nola—was born to Albert + Emma Martineau, in Thatcher, Graham Co. Arizona.

[Page B150L]

1898/[Blank line]

Sept. 28/ To day Gertrude is 28 years of age. I gave her a carbuncle pin, which had belonged to Von Wendt. We are still putting up peaches, trying to save all we can, but many bushels go to waste. An extraordinary yield of fruit this year.

29/ Delivered 2 maps of my Chuichupa Surveys to Prest Ivins. My bill for work against the Colonization Co. is $455.00

30/ Started to go to S.L. City, Utah. In the last ten days I have two very severe attacks of pain in my left side lasting a half hour each, causing exquisite pain. I fear it is my kidneys that are affected. Stayed all night at the R.R. Station.

~~November~~/
October/1/Went by rail to El Paso, Texas, 150 miles. During the night I had another severe attack of kidney pains.

2/ Left El Paso at 10 a.m. by A.T.+S.F.R.R.

3/ Awoke this morning not far from Trinidad, Colorado.

4/ Awoke a few miles west of Green river. Arrived in S.L. City about noon. Went to Bp. Preston's to stop, not being able to find Eliza.

6/ General ^Semi^ Annual Conference. During the two previous days the great Welsh Eistedfodd was held, a great musical treat.

7/ Br. + Sister ^David^ Booth of Brigham City called to tell me about Cora, an indian girl, who died some years before in Plain City, or near there. She was the girl Wm Rice bought of the Utes in the Spring of 1851 at Parowan, Iron Co. She had been endowed and sealed to me as a wife some years previously.[37]

[The following paragraph is in left margin, sideways: <u>Sunday Oct. 8. 1898</u>. Solemn Assembly held/ Each Quorum of Priesthood voted separately in/ Confirming nominations of Presidency]

10/ Went to Logan and found all my family well and glad to see me. Found many warm friends, but many have departed this life, which makes it seem lonely to me.

[In margin to left of following paragraph says: Cora died/ March 2/67/ The boy Joseph/ was born Mch. 22/ 1866 Died May/20 1869]

14/ By letter from David Booth I learn that Cora died, March 2 1867. She had a son, named Joseph Hyrum, begotten by a gentile named Johnson, who betrayed and then deserted her. The boy died ~~Mch~~ ^May 20^ 22^22^ 1869 aged ~~one~~ ^3 years^ years ^2 months^ He was blessed in Plain City. His mother gave him to Br. Robinson, and he took his name—Robinson. On Robinson's death, his wife took him till he died. She
[Page end]

[The next page is unnumbered—two newspaper articles, "In Old Salt Lake" subtitled "The Tabernacle Thirty-Three Years Ago" has drawing of Tabernacle under construction. second article from *Deseret News* (semi-weekly) dated May 5, 1899, article "A Public Loss" about death of Ogden policeman]

[Page B151R]

1898/[Blank line]

October/gave him up to me, as the child of my wife. May God ever bless her for her kindness to the poor motherless child. At the Conference the great Solemn Assembly.

---

37. This sealing of Cora to James Martineau as a wife is not mentioned elsewhere in the Journal. However, it may have been part of a series of sealings that took place during the months of August and September 1887. See entry for August 31, 1887.

16/ Sunday. Went with Lyman and Alley to Riverdale to visit Nephi and family. Found them all well. Went over his farm of 180 acres. Attended Church, and preached. Came home in the evening. Cold weather.

17/ To day Lyman got clothing for me:—shoes, 2 shirts, 2 pr drawers, necktie, gloves, stockings, silk handkerchief + two pair Union knit garments. May our Father ever bless him.

19/ Wednesday. Went to the temple. Was endowed for Thos Corlett

20/ At the Temple. I endowed Chas H. Sherman. He and Corlett's wives having previously been endowed I had them each Sealed to their wives, I, proxy for the men, and Mary Thompson Richards for the women.

21/ Went to Richmond to visit the family of John Telford

22/ After a good visit I returned to Logan.

23/ Visited at Charley's with Lyman and Alley.

25/ Taken violently sick, with attack of excruciating pain in my left side, as before. After some hours a little rest

26/ Severe pain continues. No sleep at night. Dr. Ormsby called.

27/ Still great pain, and bloody urine, which is also very muddy. Dr. Ormsby says it is Stone in the kidney, passing and tearing its way to the bladder. Gave me morphine every 2 hours until pains abated. He made an examination of my groin and said it was a rupture, which at my age can not be healed, and I must wear a trus hereafter, to prevent an enlargement of the opening. Recd a letter from Wells Chase, in whose house Cora died, telling of her death.

28/ Still in bed, but improving. Lilla brought me fruit + oysters.

29/ Arose and dressed and went down stairs, but am very weak. In the afternoon Lyman, Charley + Frank bought me an overcoat and Lilla bought me gum overshoes.

30+31/ Attended Quarterly Conference.

November

3/I endowed ~~Antony~~ ^Jeremiah^ Sprague, and Wm Fawcet endowed

[Page B152L]

1898/[Blank line]

November/for me Anthony Sprague.

2/ I ordained John Mears, and sealed him + his wife

3/ Andena Nelson ^acted in sealing but not in endowing anyone^ ~~endowed for me Margaret Martineau ^with^ and~~ Ada Elizabeth Bott Peterson endowed for me.
[Blank line]

4/ I endowed Elijah Mears, and Sealed him and his wife. ^Margaret Martineau (Wilde)^ Ada E.B. Petersen being proxy for his wife.

    William Fawcett endowed for me William Sprague.

    Andena Nelson endowed for me Margaret Martineau.

    Ada E.B. Petersen   "   " " Mrs. Daniel G. Sprague.

I had all four couples sealed.

8/ I was baptized for 121 persons, most of them Lamanite chiefs. Of the few whites, I acted for Alex. von Wendt and his father Herman von Wendt. Also for Martinus, a Roman general who lived about the year A.D. 90 My daughter Elizabeth was baptized for his "beloved daughter Lucilla" as named upon an ancient marble tomb, between Damascus and Alleppo, in Syria, which tomb was discovered some years ago by Elder Lucander, a Greek Missionary laboring in that land. He gave me all these particulars. Elizabeth was baptized for 5 women, and Mrs. Katy Pyper Preston for four.

9/ I endowed Martinus, Eva endowed his daughter Lucilla, and the following sisters of the Relief Society endowed for me as follows:—Caroline W. Affleck, for Alicia Ann Murphy, Ada Parkinson England for Harriet Mears; Nettie T. Sloan for Pocahontas; Jean C. Thatcher for Na-do-waqua; Annie _____ for Ali-quip-pa; Catherine C. Brenchly for Mrs. Henry Schooleraft; Susan E. Terry for Sanoga, Lissetto C. Cummings for O-me-shug. I was very thankful for their aid, and they shall never lose by it. Their help was procured through the aid of Sister Affleck, Relief Socy President.

    The indian names are those of Chieftainesses of various American tribes.

10/ I endowed my uncle John Hudson Poole, and sealed him and Aunt Harriet Mears, his wife.

[Page B153R]

1898/[Blank line]

Nov. 10/Sister Mary T. Richards (wife of Apostle Richards) being her proxy.

Lyman's wife, Alley Preston, had now been very sick two days, with a severe attack of kidney disease. She has been in poor health a long time.

11/ I endowed F.T. Wilde and sealed to him <u>Margaret</u> Martineau, M.T. Richards her proxy.

Lyman sent my R.R. ticket to S.L. City to get an extension of time on it.

12/ Worked all day making out a list of names of Children to be sealed to parents,—my parents, grand-parents, uncles, aunts, +c.

13/ Alley still sick. Her father, Bp. Wm B. Preston came to see her.

14/ Went to the temple and gave in my list of names, for sealing, as children to parents.

15/ To day, myself, Lyman, Nephi, Lilla and Emma acted in the sealings, men for men, women for women.

I was sealed to my father and mother, also all my brothers and sisters.

My father was sealed to his father, also all his brothers + Sisters (my uncles and Aunts). I did not go back any farther, because I did not know the names of any other of my gr-gr. father's children, but will wait until I know them

I also Sealed to my maternal grand parents all their children—the Mears family, but went no farther back for the same reason as in the case of parental ancestors.

How thankful I am, that I now have a father and a mother, having been all these years an orphan; and they, now, have their children—before childless and alone. I thank the Father that he has permitted me to do such a glorious work! Now I can meet my father and mother without shame and confusion.

16/ I endowed <u>Alfred Higginson</u> and Eva, <u>Ellen Martineau</u>. Nephi Endowed <u>Daniel G. Sprague</u> and Emma, <u>Mrs. Danl G. Sprague</u>. I sealed both couples, Emma being proxy for both women.

[Page B154L]

1898/[Blank line]

Nov. 16/William Fawcett endd for me <u>Thomas Martineau</u>.

I had sealed to me as wives, Lucilla, Aliguippa, and Nadowaqua, Emma being proxy for them.
[Blank line]
Today I was talking with Apostle Merrill about the various gifts and offices of the church, and I remarked that I had never desired any office in the church of authority and power to sit and rule or judge the Saints, but only one. He said, you have desired power and authority to <u>bless</u>. I said yes. I had always desired the power to bless people. He said "You ought to be a Patriarch. Prest Woodruff told me to search for just such men as you, and ordain them Patriarchs.[38] But it must be done in order. Write to President Snow, tell him your desire, and tell him I consider you worthy, and that I would take great pleasure in ordaining you to that office." I said I hated to write about such a thing. He said "Write, just as I have told you. It will be all right."

In the afternoon I wrote according to his direction, and before sealing the letter spread it before me, asked the Lord to dictate the matter and inspire Prest Snow to decide as the Father wishes, to say "Yes" or "No," as the will of God will be right in either case. Then folded + Sealed and Sent the letter.

I had previously (a few days) been told by the Spirit I would be ordained a Patriarch very soon. And now I prayed, to know if I had done

---

38. As early as 1873, church leaders had determined to increase the number of patriarchs in the church. In a discourse given in the Logan City bowery, Brigham Young said:

> We have passed along now for many years with but few patriarchs in the church. At our last conference I felt very much impressed to introduce the subject of ordaining patriarchs. We talked the matter over, and we concluded we would set apart a number that were worthy—those of considerable age—and give them the blessing of a patriarch. Since that time we have ordained quite a number. We are ordaining some here, and this will be continued, probably until there is a patriarch in all the branches of the church, especially in every large branch.

From "Discourse," *Deseret News* 22 (July 23, 1873): 388.

right in the matter. I received a plain answer, in words, by the Holy Spirit, that I <u>had</u> done exactly right and had been led by the Holy Spirit. That I had been held in reserve, and gathered out from all my numerous connections for this very purpose, to take the lead in their redemption; That I had been ordained a Patriarch before I came to this Earth, and that all was according to the will of the Father. All this was a great comfort to me, and I believed all would be as I desired.

[Page B155R]

1898/[Blank line]
Nov. 17/ I endowed <u>William Henry Martineau</u>. Received my R.R. ticket, extended to Dec. 31. 1898, for which I am thankful.

18/ I endowed <u>Paul Larsen</u> for Christina Larsen, she not having any male to help her in the temple. She helped me in return by endowing for me <u>Lucy Martin</u>, and her friend endowed for me <u>Abagail Mears</u> (by Catherine L. Keller)

20/ Snow storm. Snow 14 inches deep: very cold

21/ Very cold. Zero.

24/ Thanksgiving Day. Dined at Charley's, supped at Lyman's

25/ Recd a letter from the First Presidency, saying they had written Apostle Merrill to ordain me to that priesthood, (Patriarchal) and praying that I might magnify that high and holy calling.[39]

30/ This day I was ordained a Patriarch in the Church of Jesus Christ of

---

39. This letter from the First Presidency read, in part: "Your recent letter asking the privilege of being ordained a patriarch has received our favorable consideration, and we have written to Prest. M. W. Merrill authorizing him to ordain you to that priesthood." Lorenzo Snow, George Q. Cannon, and Joseph F. Smith to Elder James H. Martineau, November 22, 1898.

In explanation, Martineau wrote the following at the bottom of the letter:

President M. W. Merrill of Logan Temple said he wished me to be ordained a Patriarch, but desiring full approbation of the First Presidency, told me to write them, asking the privilege. I said I did not like to do so. He said 'Write, and say I told you to do so.' Against my own will, as seemingly presumptuous, I did so, and the above came, and Prest Merrill ordained me. Prest Merrill said Prest. Young told him to ordain just such men as me to be patriarchs. So the office came to me, unsought.

The letter was inserted at the back of Martineau's journal, book two. See Godfrey and Martineau-McCarty, eds., *Uncommon Common Pioneer*, 747.

Latter Day Saints in the Logan Temple, by Apostle Marriner W. Merrill, Samuel Roskelly, witness. The following is my certificate of ordination:–

Office of the Logan Temple
Logan, Utah, 30th Nov. 1898

To All Concerned:

This certifies that Elder James Henry Martineau has this day been Ordained and set Apart, a Patriarch in the Church of Jesus Christ of Latter Day Saints, by Apostle M.W. Merrill in the Logan Temple.

Samuel Roskelly
Recorder Logan Temple
Witness[40]
[Blank line]
Gean's/
baby born/ Got letter from Edward Sudbury saying a daughter was born to them on 27th November, at 7.30 P.M.
[Blank line]
I endowed Thomas Preston Gentlee.

December

1/Alley very sick all night.

I endowed John May. Sealed T.P. Gentlee + Abigail Mears;– John May and Mrs. John May;– Wm H. Martineau and Lucy Martin.

[Page B156L]

1898/[Blank line]

Dec. 1/ While the Company (about 50) were passing through the vail, I and about a dozen others heard singing,—male and female voices—in the temple. It was a concert of Angels, and sounded as if in another room. I rejoice at being counted worthy of so great a blessing + honor.

2/ I endowed Mr. Webb, and sealed him to Alijay Haughout. Fanny Earl endowed for me Harriet Columbine. In all sealings Sister Mary T. Richards was my assistant, except when otherwise noted.

---

40. Another certificate of ordination (probably a replacement) was issued by Hyrum G. Smith on July 6, 1914. It was inserted at the back of Martineau's journal, book two. See Godfrey and Martineau-McCarty, eds., *Uncommon Common Pioneer*, 730.

This finishes my temple work for this time I missed very much the presence with me in the Temple of my dear wife Susan, whose absence takes away much of my pleasure.

4/ <u>Sunday</u>. Alley is still very dangerously ill. She has been unable to lie down for a long time, because of Smothering, being much bloated with dropsical water. Her heart also troubles her very much at times, and she Coughs up blood. Her father, Bp. W.B. Preston, says she can only be saved by the power of God, and this is my belief too.

5/ Nephi came for me in a sleigh, to visit his family.

6/ Very cold,—6° below zero. Blessed Nephi and Emma but had not time to bless the children.

7/ Returned to Lyman's. Very cold weather. Found Alley scarcely able to speak or move herself.

8/ Received 6$ in letter from Sudbury, for passage to visit him and Gean in Eureka, Juab Co. Utah. Could not have visited them without it, being without money.

This morning I felt very sad. A consultation of doctors decided it necessary, in order to save Alley's life, to take her unborn child instrumentally—8th month In such case, she would have only one chance in ten for life:—<u>without</u> that operation, she must die. We all felt very bad about it. This morning I asked the Father about her, and received a comforting answer,—"That she is not to pass away now, not having finished her work on Earth. Her child shall be born

[Page B157R]

1898/[Blank line]

Dec. 8/in due time, naturally, and she shall amend from this hour. I must go and seal these blessings upon her. I arose at once, and on the way to Lyman's prayed again, fearing I might have been deceived, as it seemed impossible almost, that this could be fulfilled, but received again the same answer. Once more, at the house, I prayed again, and received the same. I blessed her. She believed and wept with joy. In 12 hours, on Dec. 9th

9/ Alley's baby girl was born, 3.40 a.m. perfect on form,—weighed 5 lbs. It was a natural but unexpected birth, and was by the direct power and blessing of the Lord. The Doctor told me, in answer to my question—"It was just by good luck that it happened." It was not "luck," but the power of God in her behalf, as had been manifested to me. By request I blessed the baby, but she was not named.

In the evening I gave patriarchal blessings to Lyman and Alley. Katy Preston, Eva, and the nurse, Miss [blank]

I Sat up all night.

10/ Alley ^is^ wonderfully improved this morning. Lyman took me to photographer's, to sit for a likeness, after which took sorrowful leave of all the dear ones, including Sister Harriet Preston, and at 3.30 Started to S.L. City. There at 7.30 and stopped at Oscar Moyle's (Preston's son-in-law)

11/ <u>Sunday</u>. Meeting in tabernacle. Went to Presiding Patriarch John Smith for instruction in my duty as a patriarch, and wrote a blessing for a young man who came in.

14/ Visited the last two days, and today start 7.30 a.m. to Eureka to visit Sudbury and children, three of whom I have not yet seen. Arrived there about 10.30 a.m. Was glad to see them all—Jeannie cried when she met me.

16/ Blessed Edward, Geannie, Shurman, Lyman, Virginia and the baby, whom we named Florence. Also blessed Miss Frances G. Hovey, the hired girl.

17/ At 3.30 P.M. Started to S.L. City, arrived 7.30 P.M.

19/ Blessed Moyle's 2 children, Harriet and Elizabeth. May put up for me a nice lunch basket, by Sister Preston's direction. They all treated me very

[Page B158L]

1898/[Blank line]

Dec. 19/kindly both in Logan and S.L. City. Also every one I met. I found Eliza in very poor health, completely broken down. By her request I blessed her before I left.

20/ Started for home at 8.30 a.m. in a heavy snowstorm. Our train killed a man on the track near Provo. Noon at Helper, night on the State line. Grand Junction 6 p.m.

21/ Pueblo 5 a.m. Changed Cars. Arrived Trinidad 10.40 a.m. Changed

Cars. Arrive Raton Summit at noon in heavy snow storm. Ribera 5 P.M. Albuquerque 9.20 P.M.

22/ El Paso at 10 a.m. Sent $1.45 for Ainslee's and McClure's Magazines.

23/ Paid $5.85 duty on two dress patterns given Susan + Gertrude by Sister Preston, and by Alley and Lilla. Start 8.30 a.m. and arrived at Dublan near Sunset. Came home in mail wagon at 8.15 P.M. Very cold. Found all well. Rejoiced. The many presents sent by our loved ones caused all at home much joy + thankfulness.—Truly I have been greatly blessed in going + returning, just as I was told (Susan also) before I left home. I have greatly improved in health, and though ruptured, I am far stronger, though wearing a truss. I weigh 167 lbs, a gain of 30 lbs. Since I left home. I found Theodore, Anna and her children domiciled at home, making us crowded somewhat, but it is for the best, I think. Anna can rent her house, and can work in the store while mother tends her children.

24/ Concert and tableaus in the evening. Theo. as Santa Claus.

25/ Christmas. Spoke in meeting. Very cold weather.

26/ More pleasant this morning.

27+28/ Worked on my Temple record, inserting work recently done.

29/ Settled my tithing, amounting to about $60.00

30/ Recording blessings I gave in Utah. Almost sick with a Cold.

31/ Attended a Christmas festival—a very pleasant one.

--------------------- January 1899. ---------------------

Jan. 1/ Finished recording blessings, all but two of them

2/ Completed recording. My cold somewhat better.

3/ Very windy + threatens rain. Letter from Lyman says Alley is still very weak.

[Unpaged page. Newspaper article titled Our Neighbors/Colonia Juarez, Mexico/Chance for Homeseekers/Exceptional Opportunities for the In-/dustrious—The Poor Man's Country. Second page news- paper articles significance of which is unclear.]

[Page B159R]

1898/Jan./ While in Utah I copied a letter from Sister Henrietta to Lyman, giving all she knew relative to our ancestors, part of which I now record here:—[blank]She says:—

"My father (John Martineau) was born on Staten Island + brought up on his father's farm, until about 18 years of age, to avoid being apprenticed to a cabinet maker (I believe it was to a hatter) he ran away to England found a home in London, studied medicine (and surgery) and married a widow ten years his senior, with two children. Her name was Mrs. Hawkins, widow of Capt. Hawkins, British Royal Navy. Her two children were Samuel and Elizabeth, whom I remember as a boy. Samuel was a Warrant Officer in the U.S. Navy, and was with Commodore Wilkes in his 3 year exploring expedition in 1840 when he discovered the Antarctic Continent.[41] Mrs. Hawkins was of noble family, and had offended her family by marrying beneath her rank. (Note) She was the second daughter of Lord Charles Stanhope, 3d Earl of Chesterfield, was born 1778. When her father died he willed her 2 children (Saml + Elizh) £18000 each ($90000) but they never got it.

Father lived in England 6 years + returned to America, landed in Baltimore, where his wife soon died of yellow fever. He gave up Medicine, studied engineering, had several Govt jobs, Among them, the Muscle Shoals Canal, Tennessee, the Delaware Breakwater while he lived in Georgetown D.C. and the Croton Water Works, N.Y. City, which he surveyed, and was appointed to oversee its construction; but after six months was obliged to give up work, from Consumption, + soon died in Elbridge, Onondaga Co. N.Y. April 6, 1838. He had a Splendid physique—6'2" tall, broad in proportion, not handsome, but of sweet disposition, gentle, kindly and unassuming,—too confiding for his own good, believing every one as good + true as himself. His name was engraved on the great granite reservoir, N.Y. City, 42 st. He seemed born to command. There was nothing low, common or vulgar about him,—a nobleman by nature and by descent.[42]

Go to Staten island by ferry to Port Richmond, thence to "New Dorp" past the "old Black Horse" inn, so on to the old church

---

41. See note at entry on page 14 of the journal.
42. See notes for entries on pages 14 and 15 of the journal.

[Page B160L]

1899/Jan. 3/(Moravian) and past the Martineau and Vanderbelt farm which join each other.

Our mother, Eliza Mears, was daughter of James Mears + Lois Sprague, who were married Jan. 1. 1796. She and Gr. father Mears started on horseback (she sitting behind him) to a village to find a minister to marry them. Near the village, a small stream was swollen by rain and unfordable. They shouted until a man came to see, whom they told to bring a minister, which he did. Gr father and gr-mother got off the horse and stoon upon one bank of the stream while the minister stood on the other side, shouted the ceremony to them; they shouted back "yes" in return, were pronounced husband and wife, remounted, and went home to a little log cabin in the woods, their future home.

My gr-gr. father, John Mears, was soldier in the French + Indian War of 1756, and when Montcalm captured Fort Oswego, he and other prisoners were sent by ship to France, but on the way were taken by an English ship, taken to England penniless and naked, given license to beg, + after five years begging go enough to take him home. One lady gave him £1 "because he was so handsome." At home he found a fine tombstone erected to his memory. He afterward married + had a large family. One branch—Simeon Mears, lumber merchant, lives in Chicago. He is my mother's cousin.

[Blank line]

The Hutchinsons were the natural ancestors of my Gr. mother Mears, her mother being Lois (or Eunice) daughter of Stephen Hutchinson, younger son of Lord Hutchinson, Eng. When his elder brother assumed the title, he said he would go to America and found a family of his own. He settled in Newburyport, Mass. + had a family. One Son, Stephen, was killed at the massacre of Fort William Henry, at the head of Lake George N.Y. by the indians under Montcalm. His daughter Lois (or Eunice) Married Wm Sprague my g. g. gr. father. All the Hutchinsons were fond of music, and all could sing. Grandmother herself was a famous Singer and had a splendid voice.

[Page B161R]

1899/ The Spragues, my maternal ancestors.

Jan. 3/ They were from Dorsetshire Eng. Samuel Sprague was one of the "Boston Tea Party," and his son Charles, was a poet, 50 years ago. Major William Sprague, Son of William, married Lois (or Eunice) Hutchinson of Newburyport, Mass. my gr-grand mother. Major Sprague was a small man, active and alert and quite fearless. William Sprague was in the revolutionary Army, an Armorer. He died before the war closed, leaving a wife + nine children, six sons + 3 daughters, and a farm in Mass. His widow married Maj. Noah Allen, brother of Ethan Allen. My grandmother, Lois ^Sprague^ Mears, was the youngest of the flock, and it when she was 15 that her mother married Maj. Noah Allen. He was detailed with 30 others, to witness the execution of Maj. Andre. His sons were William (died young) Seth, James, John, Jesse, Daniel. The Spragues were all men of means. Grandmother Mears' Aunt Sprague, married Commodore Tuttle of the Navy (English or American) Rev. Wm Sprague D.D. was a famous minister 50 years ago in Albany, N.Y. was gr. ma's Cousin.[43]

[Blank line]

From British Encyclopedia I gathered items pertaining to the family connections of father's first wife, the mother of my sisters Julia and Lucretia:—

She was the second daughter of Lord Charles Stanhope, 3d Earl of Chesterfield ^and was born 1778.^ her mother being Lady Hester Pitt, the sister of William Pitt, 1st Earl of Chatham.[44] The first daughter was Lady Hester Lucy Stanhope; the third daughter was Lady Lucy Rachel Stanhope, who married Thomas Taylor, and Apothecary. The first wife was married Dec. 19. 1774. Died July 20. 1780.[45]

---

43. Rev. William Buell Sprague was born on October 16, 1795, to Benjamin and Sibyl (Buell) Sprague. He graduated from Yale in 1815 and became colleague pastor Rev. Dr. Joseph Lathrop at West Springfield, Massachusetts, August 25, 1819. After resigning from this charge in July 1829, was installed August 26, 1829, as pastor of 2nd Presbyterian Church at Albany, New York, a position he held for 41 years. He was the author of several published works, including *Letters to a Daughter* (1821), *Letters from Europe* (1828), *Lectures to Young People* (1830), *Words to a Young Man* (1848), and *Annals of the American Pulpit* (1857–1869). He died on May 7, 1876.

44. Sarah Hawkins, John Martineau's second wife, cannot be found in the peerage records of the Earl of Chatham. Nor can she be found in the records of the Manor of Chevening, Kent, England.

45. Although Lady Hester Lucy Stanhope (1776–1839) and Lady Lucy Rachel Stanhope (1780–1814) were, indeed, the first and third daughters of Charles Stanhope, 3rd Earl Stanhope, and Lady Hester Pitt, a Sarah Stanhope is not found in the peerage record; Griselda Stanhope (1778–1851) was their second daughter. Lady Griselda Stanhope was born on July 21, 1778. She married John Tickell on August 29, 1800. She survived her

Lord Stanhope's first wife died and he married as his second wife Louisa Grenville, Louisa Grenville] daughter of Hon. Henry Grenville. She was married Mch. 17, 1781. Her father was a younger brother of Earl Temple and George Grenville. She died in March, 1829. She was mother of three sons of Lord Chal- Stanhope.

Philip Dorner Stanhope, 4th Earl of Chesterfield, was a son of Philip Stanhope and Elizabeth Saville, dau. of Marquis of Halifax. He was born in London 1694. Died 24th Mch 1773.[46]

[Page B162L]

1899/[Blank line]

Jan. 3/He had an illegitimate son, Philip Stanhope, by Madame du Bouchet, born in 1732. This son died 1768.

The wife of the Earl was Melusina von Schuemberg, an illegitimate daughter of George 1st King of England. He married her 1733, but had no children by her, + adopted his illegitimate son as his heir.

William Pitt, (uncle of my wife, Lady Hester Lucy Stanhope) and Earl of Chatham, was born London Nov. 15 1708. Died May 11. 1778. He was younger son of Robt Pitt of Boconnock, and grandson of Thomas Pitt, of Madras, India.

Robt Pitt (father Earl Chatham) died 1727. His elder brother was Thomas Pitt.
[Blank line]
I am tempted to insert a letter from Lyman to Joel, not because of his praise, which I know I do not deserve, for no one on earth knows so well as I do the many imperfections I have and the many ways in which I come short; but because it shows his love, which hides or covers many failings in me, and because I think my other children feel towards me as he does; and therefore it is precious to me:—Logan, Dec. 15 1898

Letter to/Joel by/Lyman/ Dear Joel. I have not answered before because of much to do and because father was here + kept all of you fully

---

husband and died childless on October 13, 1851. See "Biographical Notice of the Late Right Honourable Earl Stanhope," 38–39; Meryon, ed., *Memoirs of the Lady Hester Stanhope*, 2:3; and Newman, *The Stanhopes of Chevening*, 136, 188–190.

46. Philip Dormer Stanhope was born at London, England on September 22, 1694. He died on March 24, 1773.

posted as to himself and us. But he has left us after two months visit, much to our regret, for his stay has been too brief entirely. We all enjoyed him so much; and the way he has improved in health is glorious; He is the best preserved man of 71 years that I know in the country. He was sick for about a week, but got medical advice that helped him much, + he soon ~~regained his~~ recovered. I have but one regret, and that is the fact that he has moved away from here. For he would live years longer if he were here in this bracing, healthful locality and so would your mother in my opinion. Besides he—they—deserve to stay here and partake of some of the fruits of the civilization they helped to plant

[Page B163R]

1899/[Blank line]

Jan./here. The Temple work is father's natural sphere, during the remainder of his life, and he ought to be able to do it. But I presume all will end well.

Of course from my stand point you boys as well as father, made a great mistake when you left Cache, for others who remained are comfortable, happy, possessers of abundance and their families near, to pluck spiritual and intellectual fruits abounding in our temples of God and temples of learning. In fact Theo. knows I told him to stay here ^+^ with me try to get you all back. But I must not dwell upon this one of my hobbies, + I only mention it because father's recent visit and departure arouses anew all the old longings for you all to be here. Father is a grand man and I must confess that a long separation of fourteen years, since he moved from Logan had made us almost strangers until this two months again brought us together, and I must say, Joel, that we boys have much to thank God for that we have such a noble father; honorable, refined, intelligent, always full of hope + charity + faith. He blends that great trinity <u>Faith</u>, <u>Hope</u>, <u>Charity</u> more perfectly than any man I know in the Church. He has gone to visit Gean at Eureka for a few days, and I believe expects to leave S.L. City for El Paso about 19th.

Alley has been very sick for 6 weeks, and for ten days we almost despaired for her life. But the Lord heard our prayers, and she has been spared to us to one inexpressible joy. Father had no doubt kept you informed so I will refrain from repeating it. She is gaining slowly, + though I do not expect her to be strong enough to do much or get out of doors till

the warm weather of April bids a friendly good bye to March winds and frosts, yet I hope that in 3 or 4 weeks she can get out of bed. Well Joel my boy, press on with hope and courage, to get out of debt, as you express a desire, + may the Lord ever be near to aid you in all things. Love to Annie and Aunt Susan, Annie W, Gertie, Dora, Theo + all Henry's and
[Page end]

[Page unnumbered. Likeness of President Brigham Young, Founder of B.Y. College.]

[Page B164L]

1899/[Blank line]

Jan. 3/Moroni's folks, and a merry Christmas to you all. write soon.
[blank]L.R. Martineau
[Blank line]

5/During this day surveyed some in lower Tenaja field

6/Blessed Joel, Mary Ann, and their children.

7/Johnney's birth day. He would be 40 years of age now. Recorded blessings in my Temple Record.

8/ Today is our 47th wedding day, and now, at noon, I think of my position just 47 years ago, when I stood solitary and alone, like a Robinson Crusoe, only I had no domain I could call my own. Now, what a change! Now, with wives, children and their companions and one great-grand child, Elbert Johnson, Elvira's gr. son, we number 115; and thus far, none have in any manner brought any shame or disgrace or sorrow upon our heads. Of the 115 total 6 of our children have passed away, 17 grandchildren and 2 wives also, making 25 who have left us, + 90 who remain, exclusive of the children my son Nels L. Hagberg has by his last wife during the last 5 or 6 years.

In addition, there have been sealed to me as wives in the temple one hundred wives for eternity and one, Mary Eliza Jones, for time only. Of the 102 wives sealed to me,—of whom I have received a testimony that all have accepted the work done for them with joy and gladness—six have received their 2nd A.,—the last and highest ordinance that can be bestowed upon Earth.[47] Among them, Nelly Benson, an indian girl raised

---

47. See notes for entries at July 4, 1884 and September 11, 1884.

by Apostle Ezra T. Benson and wife Adaline, and who died aged about 25 years, received her 2nd A. and I was told at the time, this was the first time in this dispensation that any Lamanite woman had received this ordinance, which I consider a great honor to me, as her husband. I myself having previously (July 10 1884) received the same in connection with my two wives Susan E.J. and Susan J.S. in the Logan temple. In the priesthood, I was ordained a Seventy by J. M. Grant in February 1851 in S.L. City, Utah, and a High Priest by Geo. A. Smith in May, 1854 in Parowan,

[Page B165R]

1899/[Blank line]

Jan. 8/at the time I was appointed 2nd Counsellor to Prest. of Stake John C.L. Smith. On Nov. 30th 1898 I was ordained to the high and holy priesthood of a Patriarch in the Church by Apostle Marriner W. Merrill, Saml Roskelly, Temple Recorder, as a Witness, in the Logan Temple, by direction of the First Presidency of the Church.

In temple work I and my family, have done a work more or less complete, for over 2000 of the dead, and I have had a testimony that our work has been accepted by them all. In 1887, I saw them in open vision, passing in a triumphal and joyful procession before me, a Scrolle written above their heads saying "Come unto me all ye whoa are weary and heavy laden, and I will give you rest." while the maticious [malicious?] faces of a multitude of devils glared upon them as they passed, but unable to harm them.

This temple work has been the greatest joy of my life—the thought that so many have been released from their prison house, placed beyond the power of Satan, and put on their way to an exaltation in the Celestial Glory. To me, in comparison, the wealth of a million worlds like this would be as nothing, and my soul is filled with joy and thankfulness to our Father that I have been thus permitted, in connection with my family, to be saviors on Mt. Zion. In this work, while we lived in Logan, where the temple stands, my beloved wife Susan E.J. was very Energetic, missing only one day (and that from sickness) while we remained in Logan, and considerable work at intervals, since then. Susan J. Sherman died before the temple was completed—10 years—and therefore has no record for work in the holy precincts. Truly few men have been so blessed as I,—not with temporal wealth, for we are poor in this world's goods, but have a riches that will last through all the eternities, provided I and mine do <u>our</u> part. Father help us so to do, I ask in the name of Jesus. Amen.

11/ Heard that Theodore, who is on the farm he leased in Dublan, is quite sick, pleurisy + threatened with

[Page B166L]

1899/[Blank line]

Jan. 11/pneumonia.

12/ Tried to get him home, but Dr. Keat said he must not be moved. He finally came home in a few days, recovering fast.

28/ Henry as Secretary of Chuichupa Land Comp. Settled with me as follows on my Land Survey account:—

Total Cash due me for Survey $150.00 and $40.00 = $190.00
    "   Amt to be paid in land $350.00

                                  $540.00
I have received land $280.00 $75.00 = $355.00
    "   "   Cash $164.00, now due me to settle a/c $21.00
To day I made some mining plats for A.C. Ivins $5.00

30/ This evening I blessed Henry and Gertrude, whose blessings will be found in my temple record, also those of Joel and family.

31/ Gave Sadie S. Martineau (Moroni's widow) her blessing. Henry et. al. also Theodore, went to Chuichupa. Theo. went for his health, being still feeling miserable.

February.

Feb. 23/ Dora very sick today. Had a hard fit before arising.

24/ Still very sick. Theo. Came from Chiuchupa

28/ Theo. and Gertie went to Chuichupa. Gertie has had miserable health for a long time and we hope the change may do her good. Dora is better, but not well.

    Bargained my horses to Theo, conditionally.

Mch. 1/ March

Planted peas.

2/ At Priesthood meeting it was decided to build a bridge across the Piedras Verdes river here, upon my plan. I + two others were appointed to be a building committee.

6/ Began as correspondent for El Paso Herald.[48]

13/ My 71st Birth day. In the evening I was surprised by arrival to supper of Br. J.J. Walser and his wives, Bp. J.C. Bentley's wife, Mrs. Dr. Saville and daughters and Joel and family. My folks had planned it, and we had a pleasant evening.

I cannot realize I am so aged, only I find myself tiring more quickly when I work, and my bodily strength less.

[Page B167R]

1899/ *Lyman's babe May P. died.

March 23/ Gertrude came home from Chuichupa, much improved. Henry and Charles came at Same time with Lois and Edith[49]

---

48. In what appears to be his first correspondence to the *Daily Herald*, Martineau reported of the Sierra Madre Railway extension up the Piedras Verdes River, through the town of Colonia Juárez, and into the timber region of the Sierra Madre mountains. He then described the colony's abundant yield of fruit and the progress of educating the young people in the new community:

> Our academy has an attendance of several hundred students presided over by six first class teachers, and will, in due time, furnish competent instructors for other places.
> At a recent public meeting it was resolved to build a bridge across Piedras Verdes river, a stream which unites about six miles below with the San Miguel, forming the Casas Grandes river. The bridge will be 200 feet in length, consisting of two spans 67 ½ feet each, and one of 30 feet, upon the Whipple plan, designed by Civil Engineer James H. Martineau of this place, of many years experience in civil and hydraulic engineering, as also in land and mining surveys. It is hoped, if possible, to finish the bridge this year, but it is quite an undertaking for a town of only about 700 inhabitants.

From "Colonia Juarez," *El Paso Daily Herald*, March 8, 1899, 5. Martineau also began entering an advertisement in the paper, announcing his profession as civil, hydraulic, and mining engineer. See advertisement, *El Paso Daily Herald*, March 10, 1899, 6. These advertisements appeared serially thereafter.

49. On March 24, Martineau wrote to the *Daily Herald*, describing the colonists' delight at the news that the Sierra Madre Railway would be extended through Colonia Juarez and up into the nearby mountains. See "Colonia Juarez," *El Paso Daily Herald*, March 29, 1899, 1.

25+26/ Sunday school conference. A good time. Brs. Masser and L.J. Nuttall came from S.L. City to attend it.

27/ Surveyed in the hills for McDonald and E. Taylor

28/ Made map of Survey.

April/ April

4/ Henry and family went home. Before they went I gave Patriarchal blessings to Charles, Lois and Edith, on April 3d

12/ Theodore came for me to go to Chuichupa and help him Survey some mining claims.[50]

14/ Started with him, got caught in rain and wet through. Camped on Mountain in old shanty. Elevation about 7000 ft.

15/ Rained all forenoon. Camped near Garcia

16/ Sunday. Pased over the Continental divide 7400 ft. elevation.

17/ Reached Chuichupa 9.30 a.m. Found all well as usual.

18/ Went to a party in the evening. After giving blessings to the families of Henry and Moroni, such as had not already received them.

19/ I started home with Cal. Allred, having left my instruments with Theodore to do the Surveys spoken of. Got home on

22/Saturday and found all well.

*21st/ On Friday, April 21st Lyman's little babe, May Preston, died

---

50. These surveys were reported by Martineau some months later in the *El Paso Daily Herald*:

> There has been considerable activity in mining matters during the summer and quite a number of locations have been prospected, surveyed and denounced, of which the Tres Amigos, Noventa y Nueve, Siete Hermanos, Cinco de Mayo, La Panchita, and San Agustin are highly spoken of as showing a high percentage in copper, silver and gold. These mines were surveyed by Theodora [sic] Martineau an official mine surveyor residing in Chuichupa, the nearest settlement to the mines. His surveys were mapped by J. H. Martineau of Colonia Juarez, who has had many years experience in such work in the surveyor general's offices of Utah and Arizona and for several years railway companies in the United States. He is also prepared to execute mining, land or canal surveys in northern Mexico.

From "Colonia Juarez," *El Paso Daily Herald*, October 19, 1899, 5.

suddenly, at 4.30 P.M. She weighed only 5lbs 9 oz at her death, having gained scarcely any in weight since her birth. She was born prematurely, and caused almost the Sacrifice of her mother's life.

25/ Albert, Emma and their 5 children came, having left Thatcher, Arizona, Mch 31st and traveled with 2 wagons about 400 miles. All were well, and his horses were in good condition

23/ On Sunday morning I had a very delightful dream. I was in a large building, new to me, and was told some one wished to see me in the next room. I entered and saw a man lying in a bed, aged, with white hair and long beard. I knew him as an old friend whom I had not seen for a long time, and was exceeding glad to meet him again, as he was

[Page B168L]

1899/[Blank line]

April 23/also, to see me, reaching up his arms and embracing me. I cannot describe our exquisite joy in thus meeting again; words cannot express it. As I looked I saw another man lying beside him, aged and white haired like the first, + one whom also I knew as an old, long absent friend. He and I also embraced, with the same unutterable joy, + then I saw another lying by his side, with whom I had the same joyful embrace and greeting. I knew them all, and knew they were Patriarchs, and they welcomed me as a fellow patriarch—one of that Quorum. I awoke, thrilled with exquisite joy, it all seemed so real, but could not now remember who they were, nor when I had known them. It seemed to me that they had died before I saw them.

I do not know if this means that I shall soon go to them or not, but it gives me joy to know how I shall be received when I <u>do</u> go, either soon or late. Like Abraham, I praise the Father with exceeding thankfulness and rejoicing, for the bestowal upon me of this high and holy calling and priesthood,—as Patriarch,—promised me so many years ago; and pray that I may be able to fulfill all its duties in a manner pleasing to our Father in Heaven, who has been so wonderfully good to me.

29/ Helped haul my adobes for additional house room.

May

May 2/ Began to make a map of Colonia Juarez for the Colonization Company. Worked on it all day.

[Blank line]
Note/ On April 25th Albert and his family of wife and five chil-

April 25th/-dren arrived from Arizona. He said he had dreaded to pull up and make another home, but an influence had continually drawn him to Mexico, and he had to come. I hope he will not regret coming, although he left a good home in Thatcher, Arizona.

May 5/ To day was the Cinco de Mayo celebration—the Mexican day of rejoicing over the victory achieved over the French in Puebla. Our town celebrated, also, we being now all counted Mexicans.

[Page B169R]

1899/[Blank line]

May 5/I began to lay up the adobes of my new house, but it is slow work, as I had to mix the mortar and carry it and the adobes and then lay them; but slow work is better than nothing. I have tried to get a mason to do it, but have been unable, they being engaged months ahead. I am glad I know how to do such work myself.

6/ Continued laying adobes. Theodore and Bertha Came.

7/ Blessed Albert and Emma, also their children George A. + Elzadie. Also blessed Avelina E. Mills and her daughter Carolina M. Saville

8/ Blessed Alberts children Leland A., Ernest and Nola the baby girl. In the evening ^D^ had a very severe fit + fell from her chair and hurt herself, wrenching her back. We administered at once and she soon went to sleep and rested sweetly, through the blessing of the Lord. For the first time in administering to her I blessed her that she should be entirely healed of her fits in due time, and I pray that she may be. For three years we have not felt easy to have her absent from us any length of time, as she is taken at any unexpected moment, and it is a constant worry for us. I made two maps for Theodore of a mining survey he made lately, and he took them in the evening and went to Guerrero to have them recorded. I also copied Albert's family blessings into the Blessing record, and unloaded 400 adobes. So I have had a very busy day. Got $1.00 worth of Strawberries.

9/ Finished recording Alberts blessings. Albert and family Started for Chuichupa, where he thinks of making a home if he feels satisfied there.

We have had a pleasant visit of about two weeks, and I pray that they may be blessed as they need.

10/ Blessed Dora. Laid 800 adobes today with Charlie's help, who came here on the 8th

11/ Still laying adobes. Our school term closed to day.

12/ Blessed Anna's children, Phyllis and Frederick Wenden Walser while their mother was at the school dance.

13/ Changed the foundation of front room, making it larger.

[Page B170L]

1899/[Blank line]

May 28/Gave a blessing to Sister Hannah Ballinger.
[Blank line]

June 5/While upon my scaffold to day, with Susan and Dora handing adobes from a pile of lumber the scaffold fell to the ground with a crush. I clung to the wall until everything below had settled, and then dropped upon the debris without injury, thanks to the Lord. Had I fallen with the adobes +c I would have been badly hurt, as the timbers were broken into long splinters.

16/ This morning I dreamed very vivid dream of an ancient fortification of cut stone of the Nephites. I looked at it with much interest. Its name was Atlánqui Atláya.
[Blank line]

July 1/ To day Joel and Theodore began helping me put the roof on my new house, the outside walls being done, raised 12 feet above top of foundation. I began laying the walls in April, and for three months, have labored far beyond my strength, laying foundations, hauling clay, mixing mortar, helping haul and unload adobes, then carrying them and laying the wall, carrying, too, the mortar, thus doing ten minutes work to lay adobes in the wall one minute. Sometimes Dora helped carry mortar and bring adobes, being anxious to help, as also Susan and Gertrude, but none of them were able to do much, all of them being crippled invalids. I could not get any mason or other help, having no money, scarcely, and so had to undertake the work myself, or else the rainy season would flood our poor cabin through the sieve-like roof. The Lord gave me strength, or I could not have accomplished the work. As it was, many times I was so exhausted that I could not eat. But the walls are up, all but the inside ones.

There is still a great labor:—the old walls to take down, the debris to take care of and the roof and inside wood work to make. I got my adobes little by little, and must get lumber and shingles and nails in the same way. But I hope to succeed at last.

[Page B171R]

1899/[Blank line]

July 3/Began shingling, having a few to begin with, and threatening of rains.

6/ A heavy rain, the beginning of the rainy season. The South end is covered—about one third of the roof—and so much is dry.

7/ Dora had a severe fit, or it would have been, had she not been instantly administered to, and obtained relief at once. Poor girl! She had many, fearful to behold! I pray she may be healed of them.

8/ Theodore and Joel quit work, to work for themselves, leaving me to plod on alone the best I can.

11/ Susan's 63d birth day. I pray she may have as many more, or as many as she shall desire. As I look back more than 47 years, when first we came together and wed, it all seems a dream. She was then not quite 16, plump, fair to see,—a bright, active girl; now, getting somewhat gray and quite lame with rheumatism in her knees, making it difficult for her to walk much. In all these years, in sickness and health, poverty or plenty, joy or sorrow, calm or tempest, sunshine or clouded skies, she has always been the same true, sympathetic, faithful companion, wife and mother—a helpmate indeed. And not to us alone, but to the sick or sad around her, who have many times been made to rejoice through her administrations to the sick and words of comfort to the sad. May her last days be her brightest and best. They <u>will</u>.

17/ Finished shingling the house, except a few along the comb.

20/ Have two floors laid, but have no material for the other.

To day Moses Thatcher, Lucien Farr and J.D. Haines walked in having just come from Utah.[51] I was very glad to see them again. I cannot help feeling sad at Br. Thatcher's present situation, losing his position as Apostle, even if he was rightly dwelt with, which I do not doubt. All are weak,—all liable to be overcome by evil influences, for Satan will not suffer us to gain an exaltation if he can prevent it. I do hope may come out all right—in the end. He has done much good, and shall not lose his reward.

[Page B172L]

July 20/Thurs./ Our Quarterly conference begins this morning. Apostle B. Young being present, at meeting of Relief Society Confe

Friday 21/ Meeting again today. Instructed in regard to the necessity of paying a full tithing, in accordance with instructions of Prest Lorenzo Snow at the Solemn Assembly, held July 2nd in S.L. City. Priesthood meeting in the evening.

24/ Elder B. Young and Bp. Farr dined with us after celebration of the 24th[52]

31/ Moses Thatcher, Lucien Farr and J.D. Haines dined with us, also Henry. On 25th Theo. returned to Chuichupa.

July 27th/ Dora had a bad fit to day: fell and injured collar bone.

~~September~~ August

August 1/Tues./ Moses Thatcher and friends breakfasted with us, just before their starting home to Utah.

7/ Dora had a very hard fit:—fell full length upon the floor and hurt herself badly. After administration, she soon seemed all right.

10/ Henry came last night from R.R. Station shop

11/ He began to work on my house, inside. To day I was taken very suddenly with a flux.

---

51. Moses Thatcher had served as president of the Mexican mission from 1879 to 1880 and again from 1880 to 1881. He was dropped from the Quorum of Twelve Apostles on April 6, 1896, for his refusal to comply with the political manifesto of 1896. He was allowed to retain his church membership but was stripped of his priesthood. See Lyman, "The Alienation of an Apostle," and Godfrey, "Moses Thatcher in the Dock."

52. Apostle Young's visit to the colonies was reported in the *El Paso Daily Herald*. See "Apostle Brigham Young," *El Paso Daily Herald*, July 28, 1899, 8.

12/ Very ill,—constant, copious discharges. Took much Cholera Medicine—"Sun Cholera Cure."

13/ Better to day, but much worse next day.

15/ Able to work a little.

Friday 18/ Went to Casas Grandes and paid my first tax, of $1.80 for 1899, as tax on irrigation water for one city lot.

21/ Albert bought my stock:—21 Cows, 2 3 yr. olds, 6 Yearlings and 6 horses, for $900. The Stamps on bill of sale were $5.40. The State levies tax of 2 %, = $18.00 and Republic a tax of 20 % of $18.00, = $5.40, total $23.40

29/ Dora had another fit to day.

Sept. 1st/ Hired conveyance and went with Susan and Dora to Dublan, to visit Tenney's folks, and had a pleasant time.

9/ Anna and her children went to Williams' ranch—an out.

We bought a nice dress for Bertha McClellan, who had been very good to us, in letting us have milk an in other ways.

[Page B173R]

1899/[Blank line]

Sep. 11/Gertrude also went to William's ranch in the mountains with Bentley and wife.

12/ Theo sent my transit from Chuichupa, but no key to it.

16/ Grand celebration of Mexican independence. By letter from Lyman I learn of Sister Henrietta's death some weeks ago, exact date not mentioned. He sent me Fanny's explanatory letter, which I here insert:—

Chemainus B.C.

Vancouver's Island Aug. 22. 1899

My dear Cousin Lyman

Your letter reached me yesterday and I hasten to reply now to your kind inquiries about my dear mother. I have had many letters from relatives and friends, and you can imagine how very hard it has been to write of Mama, as it brings my terrible bereavement so before me, and I have only written necessary letters.

On the steamer, coming out here between Seattle and Victoria, she fell and broke her wrist, which, with other bruises, gave a severe shock to her nervous system, from which, though she seemed to rally for a time, was hastened her death, but the failing was so gradual, and her spirits so wonderful when at all free from pain, one could not realize in the least—that is—that death was near. As she seemed so weak, the doctor advised me to take her to the hospital for more complete care than I could give her; as rheumatism had settled in her weak arm and shoulder, and she suffered most intensely,—especially during the night. So I went there with her. The next day she had a sudden sinking spell, and the following morning passed from earth to heaven,—one of the sweetest Saints that ever lived. The few people we here met were all ~~attached~~ attracted to her cheerful Spirit, bright intellect and loveable ways, and seemed to love her. All were kind to her, and to me in my desolation which I realize more every day,—over 2000 miles away from our old home and friends. Mamma
[Page end]

[Unpaged; newspaper funeral announcement of death and funeral of Emily Henrietta Lyon, dated Aug. 21, 1899]

[Page B174L]

1899/[Blank line]

Sept. 16/had been very anxious for a change to a milder climate and was so delighted to come out here, and never regretted it. It will always be a grief to me that you did not know her. She had the Martineau courage, spirit and brightness, which were with her to the last, as well as her Christian faith, ^and^ her patience during those years of misfortune have been remarked by all who knew her. I should have sent word at once to your father but did not know his address, so I shall depend upon you to let him know. According to Mama's wish I shall remain here in this family to fulfill my engagement, which closes next year. I have as pupil, the only daughter, young girl of 18, and this is her last year of study.

I hope cousin Allie and the Children are well, and that you will send me the photograph you were about to send to Mama. I have none of Mama which I can Spare at present, but the negative of the one I like best is in St Paul, and I hope long to have some more taken. With kindest regards to you all. Affectionately

Your cousin Fannie M. Lyon.

Will you not write to me once in a while? Remember, I am a stranger in a strange land."
[Blank line]
My dear Sister was born 18th Oct. 1825, and was thus in her 74th year when she died. Although not a member of the church of Christ, she loved righteousness, had a practical faith in prayer, and will, no doubt, receive the truth in the estate to which she has gone, and received the ordinances of the temple which I shall have performed for her.

Only Lois and I now remain of our mother's family, and Uncle Charles Sprague Mears alone of my grandparent (on my mother's side) Our Father only knows when my time will arrive to pass away from this mortal life and some one write of me "He was +c +c. It matters not to me—the Father doth all things well. I do not wish to live any longer than I am able to do good and help the

[Page B175R]

1899/[Blank line]

Sep. 16/work of the Lord in my weak way. When no longer able to do this I pray that I may not linger in this vale of tears.

To day we celebrated Mexican Independence.

23/ Dora had a bad fit this evening and we had hard work to get her into the house. Anna and her children came home from Williams' place in the mountains.

24/ Dora had another fit this morning—a Severe one. She fell heavily to the floor and mangled her tongue badly.

28/ To day is Gertie's 29th birth day. We had a pleasant Company and Supper in the evening.

October/ <u>October</u> 1899

10/ Joel and Gertrude went to the Mountains, Gertie for her health and Joel to Chuichupa on business.

I wrote to Asst U.S. Treasurer at New York to ~~stp~~ Stop payment of check No. 388.860 dated Mch. 17. 1899 in my favor. Mex. was pension, $24.00 I had sold same to Bentley + Harris for $50.40 Mex. currency.

For about ten days I have been glazing my windows and painting, but it is slow work for an amateur.

14/ Theodore came from Chuichupa to attend Conference.

20/ Dora had a severe fit to day. Administered, and she Soon recovered.

21+22/ Quarterly Conference in Juarez.[53]

November/ November

13/ Dora had a fit again to day.

15/ Br. David Spillsbury brought a cow which had been lost three years. I paid him $10.00 for it. I am thankful.

16/ Jos Turley began plastering my house.[54]

17/ Henry and Albert, and Sarah Came from Chuichupa for family supplies.

24/ Recd an appointment (unsolicited) as mineral Surveyor in Sabinal mineral District. Gertrude came home from Williams' mountain ranch, after absence of six weeks. She seems much improved in health.

25/ We moved into our new rooms, and thank the Lord for his blessing, enabling me, amid many difficulties, to build them.

[Page B176L]

1899/[Blank line]

---

53. In his uncredited correspondence to the *Daily Herald*, Martineau reported that representatives from the Mormon colonies and other places in Sonora were present at the conference. In addition to reporting on the good health and prosperity of the colonists, he wrote that Aaron Farr Jr., Preston Thatcher, and Lucius Farr had arrived to inaugurate Moses Thatcher's stock breeding enterprise. See "Colonia Juarez, Mex.," *El Paso Daily Herald*, November 2, 1899, 5.

54. Joseph Hartley Turley (1872–1941), the son of Isaac and Sarah (Greenwood) Turley, was one of the first settlers of Colonia Juarez. He was a mud mason and bricklayer. He and his family moved to northern Arizona in 1912 where he worked on buildings in Holbrook, Winslow, Snowflake, and Joseph City. He is buried in the Joseph City cemetery.

Nov. 26/Sunday. Apostle A.O. Woodruff and Mrs. McCune present in meeting.[55] A happy time. In the afternoon was organized a political club, of which I am one of five executive Committee. We drafted a memorial to Prest Diaz, praing [praying] him to serve another term as President of Mexico[56]

27/ Gave Mrs McClune a patriarchal blessing.

December/ December

2/Went to Dublan to attend their ward Conference. Apostle Woodruff and Mrs. McCune gave much good instruction.[57] A Change was made in the Bishopric of Dublan, Bp. Winslow Farr, retiring for age, and a new Bishop,—Saml J. Robinson ordained instead. There being some disunion in relation to Counsellors, br Woodruff called a special Council of himself, the Stake Presidency, Patriarchs and High Council. There still being a lack of unanimity, another council was called—Elder Woodruff, Stake Presidents Pratt and Eyring, and Path Stowell and myself, who finally decided the matter. Accordingly, Br. S.J. Robinson was chosen Bishop, with Jos. L. Cardon 1st and Anson V. Call 2nd Counsellors.[58] All were unanimously sustained by vote of the Conference. It was a surprise to the people, but satisfactory.

3/ Gave a blessing to Counr Call's wife,—Dora Pratt Call and came home, refreshed with my outing. Found all well at home.

7/ Made mining map for Duthie and Vance, $10.00

9/ A heavy wind today, and quite Cold.

---

55. Abraham Owen Woodruff (1872–1904), son of LDS president Wilford Woodruff, served as a church apostle from 1907 until his death. Elizabeth Ann (Claridge) McCune (1862–1924) was a member of the General Board of the Young Women's Mutual Improvement Association (YMMIA). She was the daughter of Samuel Claridge and was married to Alfred W. McCune, a mine operator and Utah politician.

56. According to an unnamed newspaper correspondent, the club was organized "to give our colonists a political status in Mexico." Anthony W. Ivins was named president, with William Derby Johnson as vice president, Henry Eyring, J. C. Bentley, H. Pratt, Dr. Keat, and J. H. Martineau as an executive committee. See "Colonia Juarez, Mexico," *Deseret Evening News*, December 9, 1899, 7.

57. A brief account of the conference was given under "Colonia Juarez, Mexico," *Deseret Evening News*, December 9, 1899, 7.

58. Samuel John Robinson (1863–1948) of Payson, Utah, succeeded Winslow Farr as bishop of the Dublán Ward. Robinson's counselors were: Joseph Samuel Cardon (1858–1908), and Anson Bowen Call (1863–1958). Anson B. Call later became bishop of the Dublán Ward, serving from 1915 to 1944.

Learn by Logan Journal that Lilla has a son.

Recd 500 lbs flour from Jarvis, the most at one time for many years.

10/ Gave a blessing to Jos A. Wooley, and he gave me $2.00

12/ Surveyed the "El Pajarito Grande" mine for Croff = $30.00

15/ Laid our new rag carpet. It gave us great pleasure, as we begin to grow more homelike and comfortable, as in days past. I thank our Father for His blessings this

[Page B177R]

[Flourish graphic under name Martineau]

1899/[Blank line]

Decr/year, in enabling to build our comfortable home without any visible means, scarcely, to build with.[59] It has been almost entirely the work of my own hands and labor from the very foundation up, my sons having done very little towards it. And one great satisfactions is that it is <u>paid for</u>. I have been engaged upon it ever since last April, and it lacks much even now, of complition, as I have another room and hall and porch to erect. I hope I shall be prospered in doing so.

16/ Made maps of the mining survey and signed them as "El perito practico, JH. Martineau," with my official Scrawl below my name, as above, which the law of Mexico requires.[60]

Also made a pair of gates and hung them.

17/ Received a letter from Theodore, who has recently been called as a Missionary, from which I insert the following paragraphs:—

"My school work keeps me very busy in connection with my work in the M.I.A. though I am still trying to find time to study the Bible, Book

---

59. In an *El Paso Daily Herald* article on settlements near Casas Grandes, a general description of the homes in Colonia Juárez read: "The houses are all cosily furnished, the little parlors are most cheerful, and here, far away from commercial centers where books can be bought, are little libraries containing the works of the best authors, and not there only to make the room more attractive as one will find in starting a conversation with the very intelligent young people of the household." See "Pretty Colonia Juarez," *El Paso Daily Herald*, June 10, 1899, 10.

60. The Spanish title "El Perito Práctico" is translated as "The Experienced Expert."

of M. Doc.+Cov. Preaching and Public Speaking, The Youth's Companion, Draper's Intellectual development of Europe, the Almanac, and a few other books, in the desperate hope of being able to catch few <u>Noble ideas;</u> Noble ideas] but alas! how meager are the results! Perhaps you can imagine the chaotic condition of my mind since I received the fateful missive!

Of course I wrote and told them I should be pleased to go at some future time, but oh dear! when will it be? With debts to pay and money for the trip, who can tell how long it will be before I shall be in condition to go? Not I, I am sure.

It almost makes me "wave and go wild" when I think how poorly I am prepared to go out into the world to carry a message which I myself So imperfectly understand. I suppose, however, that it is one of the ways the Lord has of punishing His careless children, so I shall try to make the best of my Situation and improve it as

[Page B178L]

1899/Decr 17/"much as possible in the short time at my disposal. I know the Lord will bless me with means, if I will only put my trust in Him and do my own duty, so I have no fears as to the results."

For several months Theodore has felt a desire to go on a mission, feeling he could do so better now than when he might be called and have to leave a family, deprived of his help, though always diffident as to his ability as a missionary. I pray he may go and honorably fill his mission.

31st/ I have paid $50.00 tithing this year, nearly all cash. It was a <u>full</u> tithing and something over, as all my increase this year has not been $500.00 But I would rather be over than under in my payments.
[Blank line]

1900/ January 1900.
Jany/[Blank line]

2/ To day Guy C. Taylor asked my consent to his marriage with Gertrude. Knowing his integrity and worthiness, I gave my consent. But I do not see just now, how it can be effected, as Prest L. Snow has closed the door of plural marriage.[61]

---

61. In December 1899 and January 1900, Lorenzo Snow published statements in the *Deseret News* denying that any authorized plural marriages had been performed since the

4/ Went to El Paso on business, returning on the 6th

8/ We celebrated this, the 48th anniversary of our wedding. Had a nice supper and a company of friends, and had a very enjoyable time

10/ Surveyed fence line of Lower Tenaja field, 1 day $10.

15+16/Surveyed a canal for Lower Tenaja field,—2 days 20$

18/ To day in company with Prest A.W. Ivins, I started to the new purchase of land in Sonora—the Batifilto ranch—We stayed over night at 2nd Counr H. Pratt. Very cold.

19/ Started by starlight for Diaz. Very cold weather. Got to Diaz, 55m about Sunset. I stayed at Br. Thayn's. Went to Relief Society meeting in the evening.

20+21/Attended Quarterly Conference, a very enjoyale one. On the 21st I gave blessings to Elizabeth ^Thayn^ and Nephi Tenney. I caused Elizabeth (Sen) to be ordained or

[Page B179R]

1900/Jan./blessed as a Midwife and nurse, which she had so earnestly desired might be done. I also administered to young Elizabeth Thayn, who has long been greatly afflicted.

22/ Left Diaz at 9.30 a.m. Our Company consists of Prest Ivins and Pratt, myself, as Engineer, and High Councillor Orson P. Brown and wife, Also Bishop Geo. C. Negley. Drove 25 miles and Camped. Night very cold.

23/ Started early and drove to near the Summit of Sierra Madre pass. Night Cold and windy.

24/ Drove 30 Miles to Colonia Oaxaca. The descent from the Summit, for about 3 ½ miles was steep and sometimes very rough, the descent being about 3000 feet in that distance.

25/ Reached Batipito (pronounced Bat-i-pé-to.) about 2 ½ hours after

---

manifesto in 1890. This affirmed that none of the post-manifesto marriages had been or would be sanctioned by the church. See Lorenzo Snow, "Reminiscences of the Prophet Joseph Smith," *Deseret Evening News*, December 23, 1899, part 3, p. 17; "A Sound Position," *Deseret Evening News*, January 6, 1900, 4; "Polygamy and Unlawful Cohabitation," and "Prest. Snow's Declaration," *Deseret Evening News*, January 8, 1900, 4; Cannon, "After the Manifesto," 204–205; and Hardy, *Solemn Covenant*, 186n103.

dark, a distance of 25 miles. The night was pitch dark, so I could hardly see our horses. We lost our road, and wandered until finally we heard dogs barking in the distance, and reached a Small Mexican hamlet of Mescal distillers, who directed us to the camp, about 1 mile distant, and glad indeed we were to see the bright camp fire, and to have a nice warm Supper of fresh vinison. We found 8 men, from S.L. City and Payson, Utah, who had been waiting for us about a week.

The Mescal liquor referred to is made from the century plant, or [blank] as it is known in Mexico. A piece is cut from the head of the plant, about as large as a good Sized Cabbage, which is roasted 24 hours, which makes it Sweet, as if Steeped in Molasses. Being crushed, the juice is distilled into Mescal, much like whiskey in appearance,—a strong, pure liquor, but having a smoky flavor which is disagreeable to my palate.

26/ Commenced running trial Canal lines to get water from the river, which has but little fall—about 8 or 9 feet per mile. Spent several days at this work, + finally found a suitable line for an irrigation Canal. After this I Surveyed a city plat of about 40 or 50 blocks each 100 meters square, 4 lots in a block. After this was done I laid out some hectare lots, 2 hectare and 4 hectare lots in the field, finishing our labors

[Page B180L]

1900/Jan.+Feb./on the 16th for the present, and leaving Camp near Sunset. Went 4 miles and camped.

28th/Sunday. To day was held a regular Sunday meeting on this ground,— the first, probably, since the destruction of the Nephites 1500 years ago. I opened, by prayer, and Prest Ivins and Pratt spoke, myself also. Two women, wives of Robt L. McCall, named Christina Smith + Christina Sontheimer McCall, were present, the first Colonist women in the Settlement. We met in a shanty belonging to Samuel Lewis

Feb. 4/ Meeting again to day. I spoke again

" 11/ Meeting to day. Prest Ivins organized a Branch of the Oaxaca Ward, Bishop Naegle being present. L.S. Huish was appointed Presiding Elder, E. Huish Clerk, Also Brs S.J. Jarvis, Snarr and Hunsaker an Executive committee.

F/ The bottom lands are covered with a course grass 4 to 8 feet high and so Close and thick it is hard to survey through it. This grass is called Sacation.

Sun. Feb. 18/ Meeting to day. I spoke and felt the Spirit of prophesy predicting that the rains shall increase, falling in what are now the dry Seasons, new Springs shall break forth and the Streams shall increase in volume.

I will say, that while in Colonia Batipito I blessed E. Huish + Son, JJ Huber and brother, R.L. McCall + his two wives. At Oaxaca I blessed Anna Naegle, Geo. W. and Phebe Scott by their request. I stayed with Conrad Naegle's family in Oaxaca, well treated.

Feb. 19/ Started for home in a heavy gale, which broke limbs from the trees. Drove over the mountain pass and camped after dark. Night very windy and cold

20/ Drove about 50 miles. Camp cold and windy.

21/ Started by daylight. Drove 48 miles, reaching home at 7 P.M. Very glad to be at home again. Found all well.

On this trip my labor has been very arduous, but the Father blessed and sustained me, so that I had no cause to complain.

22/ Dora had a fit at the table to day, the first in 2 mon

[Page B181R]

1900/[Blank line]

Feb. 24+25/ Apostles Grant and Clawsen, Mrs. Grant, Karl G. Maeser and J. Golden Kimball spoke by the power of the holy Spirit, and we had a glorious Conference. The Sunday Schools have an enrollment of 1591, average attendance 80%. Our Stake has paid $37000.00 tithing this year, an average of about $75.00 pr tithe payer. We were highly Complimented, but told not to become vain glorious, for we will have all the opposition we want, in Mexico.

26/ Theodore Came. He is thus far on his way to his mission in the United States.

28/ Surveyed Upper Tenaja Canal, also next day, 2 days

March 1900

Mch. 2/ Surveyed Lower (Canal.) Tenaja field, 2 days in all.

3/ To day George Orrin Jacoby, a little boy 9 years old Came to live with us. He came last fall from Ohio, with missionary E. McClellan, but they did not wish to keep him, so we take him. His family are still in the states, too poor to come to Mexico just now.

" 9/ Visited Orson Brown's family. Blessed him and his wife.

10/ Susan quite unwell, and in much pain, with cough.

11/   "   "   "   "   "   "   "

12/ Susan is recovering. It was quite severe while it lasted.

13/ My 72nd birth day. Worked hard, surveying land and at other work.

In my younger days I never expected to live to be more than 45 or 50, and now I am 72. Truly the Lord has been very kind and merciful to me. I still feel full of life and ambition, but find I tire much quickly than in years past, and my rupture incapacitates me from hard manual labor. If my faith does not fail I hope to go back to the center stake of Zion, according to the promise made me. I know that He who formed my body has power to renew and strengthen it if it is His will. And if it is <u>not</u> His will, of course I do not desire it.

16/ I have been greatly in doubt whether to go to Conference in April or not, on account of taking so

[Page B182L]

1900/[Blank line]

Mch. 16/much means that is needed at home. I prayed and received answer that it would be <u>right</u>, and that I would be blessed in so doing, and should suffer no loss. Last night Susan asked about it, and had an answer similar to mine. So now I feel to go and to trust in the Lord that it may not be injurious for my family.

17/ Attended an annual meeting of the Relief Society in honor of the organization of the Society by Joseph Smith. We had a very pleasant time.

18/ Blessed Bp. Jos C. Bentley, also Ethel and Orrin

19/ Rented my 15 acres of land to John Allen for ⅕th delivered to me at my home.

21/ Have finally determined to go to Conference. I have been undecided, because it seems selfish to use so much money for the trip, that my family ~~de~~ needs at home. I asked the Father this morning and was told in answer, to "go, you shall be blessed, your family shall be blessed in your absence, and Dora shall have no fits while you are gone, and she shall be healed entirely." I also had other glorious promises, which I hope will be fulfilled.

In the evening the girls had a party in honor of Theodore, who will soon go upon his mission.

29/ Blessed Sister Gladys Bentley and her 3 Children

April/ April 1900

1/ Blessed Manrique Gonzlez, a young Mexican man who has joined the Church. He has a great work. Also Blessed Mabel Allen.

2/ Started at 5 a.m. to go to S.L. City, with Theodore. Arrd at El Paso 4.30 P.M. Left El Paso at 8.30 P.M.

4/ Left Pueblo at noon in heavy rain, which turned to snow as we ascend the mountains along the Arkansas river.

5/ Arrived at S.L. City about noon and stopped with Bp. Preston's family.

6. 7. 8/ Attended Conference. Smoot Reed ord apostle [written above Smoot Reed is 2 and 1]

9/ Theodore was ordained a Seventy by Apostle Reed Smoot, in the mission assigned him in Southern States.

[Page B183R]

1900/April 10/ Still Snowing. Theo. and I went to Logan. Arrd 11.40 a.m. found All the family well. Went to Lyman's to stay.

12/ Began temple work. I endowed David Columbine. Theodore was endowed for himself. I had Davd Columbine and Ann Elwyn Sealed as husband and wife.

13/ I endd Mr. Webb, and sealed him and Norjay Haughout.

15/ Sunday. Spoke in the Tabernacle this afternoon. Also in the Sunday School. Blessed Charles F. Martineau ^Jun^ and Bp. B.M. Lewis.

17/ Theo. started on his mission

18/ By letter from Virginia learn She has Small pox in Eureka Her husband has got well of it, and she is quarantined. alone with her children. She feels pretty bad.

    I endd Mr. Cozine + Sealed him and Nelly Haughout.

19/ I " Mr. Stillwell. Theo. left S.L. City. Sisters Preston and May made him a nice lunch for journey. Charlie came home from sheep herd, sick with La Grippe

18/ I blessed Harriet A. and L. Royal Jr. Martineau

20/ I endd Mr. Perine, + Sealed him and wife, also Sealed Stillwell and wife.

21/ Blessed my Son Charles F. Martineau

25/ Wed. I endd Robt T. Elwyn

26/   " " John Rand

27/   " " Mr. Barlow. Sealed him + Miss Bloomfield.

    Also Sealed Mr. + Mrs. John Rand.

    Letter from Theo. His field is South Alabama Confe

29+30/ Apostles Grant, Teasdale and Lyman present. They dropped some Bishop, and ordained 3 Patriarchs. F.M. Lyman gave instructions to Patriarchs. Must set dates of events to happen:—should not give too long blessings. Must obey the Word of Wisdom and set a good and holy example to all. Saw Nephi, just from his new farm.

May/ May 1900

2/Nephi went back to Blue Creek farm.

    I endd Paul Maurice

3/ Unwell and did not go to the temple. Snowy.

4/ Charlie's boy Freeman quite sick

    I endd Mr. Dyer. Mrs. Affleck Endd Mrs. Sarah Allen

[Page B184L]

1900/ Mrs. ~~M.A. Maughan~~ ^Hibbard^ endd Maria M. Wheelock.

May 4/ Mrs. M.A. Maughan Endd Mrs. Headley

This morning I awoke very deaf, my right ear entirely

7/ Got the valise and clothes Theo. Sent home.

9/ Lyman and Alley helped me in the temple
    I Endowed Francis Columbine[62]

Lyman	" Henry H. Mears
CL Ley	" Theodora Martineau (Elwin)
Mrs. Maughan	" Catherine Barlow
Katy Preston	" Mrs. John Dexter
Mrs. Hurst	" Miss Bloomfield

I had Sealed—H.H. Mears + wife Paul Maurice and Margaret Ketettas, Mrs. Maughan prox. in Sealing.

10/ I endowed Alex. Stanhope
Lyman	"	William Martineau
Alley	"	Mrs. Joseph May
Mrs. Hurst	" "	Robt Greenhow
Mrs. Affleck	"	Ana Maria Gallega

11/ I endowed James Stanhope
Lyman	"	Mr. Hutchinson
Alley	"	Mary Clementine Stuart
Mrs. Hurst	"	Lillie Dean

I blessed Broker, Verne and Clayton Preston.
Charlie's boys Freeman and Bryant still quite sick.

12/ Blessed Alley, Preston, Martha, Allen and C.M Hurst

13/ Blessed Lyman R. Son. and wife Alley P.

14/ Lyman bought me a new suit of clothes, 2 shirts hat, pair shoes, collars, neck tie and socks. He shall never want for comfortable clothing, nor friends in time of need. My best pantaloons were broken out in the rear, displaying a flag of truce.

15/ Today Lyman Royal Jun. was baptized for 6 persons:—James Martineau, Stephen Hutchison, Charles Stanhope (Earl) ~~Giovanni Battista~~

---

62. This refers to François Colombine, the father of Paul Colombine. See entry and note at May 4, 1887.

~~Martini~~, (Earl) Philip Stanhope and ~~Simone Martini~~ Alley Martineau was baptized for my sister Emily H. Martineau, Melusina von Schulenberg. Lois Hutchinson Madame du Burchet, all rel. by blood or marriage

[Page B185R]

Harriet A. was baptized for [blank] Lady Louisa Grenville, dau. of Earl of Halifax, Lady Hester Pitt, Sister of famous William Pitt, Lady Elizabeth Saville, Countess of Stanhope, and Lady Lucy Rachel Stanhope, dau. of Earl of Stanhope, all being relatives-in-law. All the males bap. for by my grandson Royal were all relatives by blood or by marriage.

My father's first wife was daughter of ~~Philip Dormer~~ ^Charles^ Stanhope, ~~4th~~ ^3d^ Earl, and his two daughters by her, Julia and Lucretia, my half sisters, were grand daughters of the Earl. My fathers wife had first married Captain Hawkins, British Royal Navy, and was disowned by her father for the so-called misalliance. She had two Children by him, Samuel Hawkins and Elizabeth Hawkins, whom I well remember. Samuel was a warrant officer in the U.S. Navy, and was with Com. Wilkes in the Antarctic Exploring cruise, 1840, when he discovered the Antarctic continent. He used to bring us beautiful Shells, which I used to admire. Julia married a NW. Winslow, a printer, of Boston. I never knew their later lives.

When Earl Stanhope died, he willed to his daughter—my father's wife £18000 (about $90.000) and to each of the two children, Samuel and Elizabeth, £2.000 ($10.000) By some mischance these legacies were never received, and I suppose can never be recovered by any of father's family by his second wife—my own mother.
[Blank line]

16/ I endowed James Martineau (Revd Unitarian)
Mrs. Hymers   Endowed Mrs. Thomas I. Allen
"   M.A. Maughan   "   "   William Allen
"   Brenchley   "   "   James Johnson
"   Hymers   "   "   Juana Paoon

I endowed Mr. John Hutchinison

Blessed Mrs. Hibbard, and Mrs. Brenchly, who had worked for me in the temple, and Blessed Lillian Gardner, whose grandmother, Mrs. Affleck, had worked for me in the temple also.

[Page B186L]

1900/ I endowed (Earl) Philip Dormer Stanhope.
May 18/ My dau. Lilla endowed my sister Netta
Mrs. Hurst " Mad. von Schulemberg
  " Cath Preston " Mad. du Bonchet
  " Mrs. Hymers " Ana Maria Huarte

There were also Sealed nine Couples:—
Mr. Dyer + Mary Dyer, Mrs. Cath Preston Proxy
Robt T. Elwin + Theodora Martineau, Lilla proxy
Alex. Stanhope + Mrs. Alex. Stanhope   "
James Stanhope + " James " "
Mr. Hutchinson + Ann Hutchinson   "
James Martineau + Helen Higginson   "
John Hutchinson + Lucy Apsley   "
Philip Dormer Stanhope + Mrs. P.D. Stanhope "
David C. Lyon + Emily H. Martineau   "

This finishes my temple work for the present. I thank thee, my Father in Heaven, that I have been permitted to do this holy work, and pray I may be permitted to do much more, for the redemption of the dead. Could I have my wish, it would be to spend my remaining days in the temple.

May 21/ Went to Nephi's home in Riverside, King P. Office. He was still absent, but I blessed his children, as follows:—Aurelia, Mabel, Susan Elizabeth, Elva, and William Knowles Martineau.
[Blank line]

May 18/ I omitted to note above, that on May 18th I blessed my daughter Elizabeth Martineau Nebeker, her children, Frank Knowlton, Marjorie and Lyman Martineau Nebeker, and his hired girl, Mary Muffer.

23/ Howard Nephi, Nephi's oldest son, came to Logan and I blessed him. All Nephi's family are now blessed except his second son, Lee Edward, who is at the Blue creek farm with his father. Visited the Agricultural College.

At 4 P.M. I left Logan for home. Lyman gave me $10.00 for expense money. Cathe P. Preston $2.00 and Booker $1.00 Also Lilla gave me $1.00—all she had.

It was a sorrowful parting from my dear ones.

[Page B187R]

1900/[Blank line]

May 23/ Lyman and Alley invited to dinner Lilla + family, also Eva and family, also Simpson Molen, a very dear friend, and after dinner made a snap shot with his Kodak of me and my three little grand daughters—Martha, Marjorie and Clare, with little Allen between my knees.

I arrived in S.L. City about 8 P.M. and was warmly received by Br. + Sister Preston, also by May Preston Moyle.

May 24/ Visited several old friends.

25/ Went to Virginia M. Sudbury, my daughter, to stay.

26/ Visited Mrs. Emily Hill Woodmansee. Dined at Thatchers Was introduced by Frank Nebeker to Lawyer Geo. Q Rich. He said he had long known of me, was glad to meet me, and began blessing me, with much fervor, prophecying great blessings for me. Spoke of the great and good work I had performed for the Church, said it was accepted by the Lord, and that I should yet do much more, and become a mighty man in Israel. I was astonished.

27/ May Preston Moyle had a company to dinner to day, Br. + Sis. Preston, Moses Thatcher and Lettie, also their dau.-in-law Caddie and myself.

28/ Again visited Eliza

29/ Virginia's Sister-in-law—Anna Sudbury has a very sick baby, ill with Neumonia, which was thought must die. I administered, and promised life, which I pray God may grant, but the doctor and friends have no hope at all + said nothing more can be done for the child, all, save Lavina Sudbury, who is helping take care of the Child. She has faith for little Raymond. I gave her a comforting blessing. Took leave of Genie + Children, and at 8.05 P.M. left S.L. City for home! and my loved ones in Mexico. Moses Thatcher, and Sarah Farr, and her two sons also go to Mexico at same time.

Sister Preston has been as good to me as possible, and so have all in the north, may God ever bless them

At Helper, 12.25 a.m. Green River 4.45 a.m. Grand Junction, Colorado,

6 a.m. Glenwood Sps. 8.47 a.m. Tennessee Pass tunnel (Rocky mountain range) noon Pueblo, 5.30 P.M. Lay by all night.

[Page B188L]

1900/May 31/ Leave Pueblo 7.30 a.m. Change cars Trinidad 11 a.m. Raton tunnel 12.30 (noon) Raton town 12.50 p.m. Los Vegas 4.30 P.M. Albuquerique 9 P.M. and lay by 3 hours. Here 18 or 20 young indian girls entered the Car, going home from Some School. They were from 15 to 18 years of age, bright, pretty and full of talk and fun as could be—just as boys let out of school always are.

June/ June, 1900

1/ Daylight at San Marcial, New Mexico. Sunrise at Crocker. At 8 a.m. one of our Engines ran off the track which delayed us some time, but no one was hurt. At 10 a.m. at Fort Bliss, were examined by quarantine officers. Arrd at El Paso 10.25 a.m. Stay all night at Zieger Hotel.

2/ Leave Ciuidad Juarez at 8.35 a.m. Dublan 5 p.m. Home 9 P.M. Found all well as usual, and Dora has had no fit since I left home, just as I was promised before I went away. Thanks be to thee, oh Lord!

Learn particulars of Joel's injuries:—teeth broken out on one side of face, lower lip cut entirely through, large gash under chin, bruised all over and two ribs broken off spine, and spine badly hurt. Had watchers for weeks + has lately gone up to Chuichupa, being able to walk + do a little work. His escape from death was a miracle, as he fell 24 feet to solid ground, with the frame and timbers of the barn. The other man was hurt, but not seriously.

8/ Settled my Survey a/c for Sonora Survey, amounting to $275.00, of which I have had, and paid on debts, $242.50, leaving bal. due me $32.50

While absent Albert had paid me 75$ on note and $12.00 interest for 3 months on same note for $400.00
[Blank line]
On June 4th a Mr. John McComb, Agent for Smith, Davis, + Hartmann of California who have bought 500.000 acres of timber land in the mountains near our settlements, Engaged me to Survey the lands purchased, at $10. per day and board. I fear I shall not be able to do the work, unless the Lord shall strengthen me. As I hope He will.

[Page B189R]

1900/June 13/Recd 390lbs ^$25.00^ on order from Coln Company ^($25.00) I owing them $1.00 on Same. Paid Haws for hauling Same $1.50

    Have been busy, up to this date, in recording the 35 blessings and bringing up my journal to date.
[Blank line]

" 23/A Mr. John McComb, agent for Smith, Davis + Hartmann, of Cal. a timber Company, came and engaged me to survey the boundaries of a tract of timber lately bought by them joining our mountain settlements of 200.000 hectares (about 500.000 acres,—nearly 740 Sq. miles) He to pay me $10.00 pr day and also furnish me horse to ride and man to carry transit for me.

25/ Made a Small map for him, $5.00. We start on Survey today, reaching Garcia next day, and camped at old mill site.

27/ Took variations of magnetic needle by observation on Polaris + found it 10° 30' East, add Azimuth 1° 25, = total var. 11° 55' E. and Lat. 29° 59' N.

28/ Our men arrived from Chuichupa, with pack animals.

29/ Began work, by starting out to find the N.E. corner of the land to be Surveyed. We traveled all day over high ridges and deep cañons full thirty miles, without food, but with plenty of rain. Did not find the Corner.

30/ Went to an old Stone monument on a high mountain, and from it ran east, on Lat. 30°

July 1. 1900

July 1/Sunday/ Went to Garcia and spoke in the meeting on invitation of Bp. Whetton.

2/ Continued Survey east, over tremendous gorges and high ridges and in heavy timber, and on the [in margin: 5th] found the old Corner sought for, which is the N.W. Corner of Zone 6;—N.E. Cor. Zone 1, = the N.E. Cor. of our tract to be Suvd.

6/ Went to beginning point on Mountain and ran West. Camping at night near the Rio de Gavilana, (River of Hawks.)

7/ Reached the brink of the Gorge of the Rio Gavilana, but could not cross to day, as the defile is over 1000 ft deep, precipitous sides, difficult to cross either way. Thus far we have had rain every day.

8/ Rained all day, and we did not work.

9/ Triangulated across the Gorge, which took all day.

[Page B190L]

1900/July 9/The distance across, from brink to brink, diagonally, was 820 meters, = about half a mile.

10 About half a mile above where the line crossed the Cañon, and on top of a steep Conical hill in the bottom of the gorge, are the ruins of an ancient Stone fortification, with the walls about 10 or 12 feet high. It is accessible by one path only, which is only wide enough for one man to pass at a time, and so was almost impregnable to ancient force, armed only with bows, arrows, swords and spears. Oh that those gray stones could tell the scenes that have transpired in and about those walls.

Passing through the pines westward, we find many old Stone ruins of dwellings, and many places where the land has been terraced (and still is) to make level spots for cultivation. Every little hollow even, often not more than 10 or 15 feet wide between rocky ridges, have still those ancient Stone wall terraces, usually 2 to 4 feet high, to retain the earth from washing away, the terrace walls being one or two rods apart. Also all the more level spots of ground, now covered with pine and oak timber, was cultivated also in ancient Nephite times. An immense population once inhabited the land, who raised their crops by <u>rain</u>, which must have been, in ancient times, much more frequent and abundant than now.[63]

---

63. On July 15, Martineau wrote to the newspaper to describe the ruins of the former inhabitants of the area around Pacheco, south of the Corales purchase, on land owned by Smith, Davis, and Hartman:

> In running the north boundary line of the recent purchase, latitude 30 degrees, we spent a whole day triangulating and getting across the tremendous gorge of the Rio de Gavilanes (river of Hawks), about a quarter of a mile wide from brink to brink, and nearly 1,500 feet deep. Its sides are very difficult to descend or ascend. About half a mile above our line stands a hill in the bottom of the gorge, and upon its summit is an old fortification built of stone. Its walls are still ten or twelve feet in height, and access is possible at one point only, and that by a difficult way, and only for one man at a time. It is very ancient, and for those times was a place of great strength, being entirely beyond

What <u>has</u> been will be <u>again</u>, and from this time on the rains will increase in frequency and volume, new springs will break forth where water has never yet run, streams will flow in gulches now dry, and the streams now flowing will become larger. And so the thirsty desert shall become a garden, and the wilderness shall blossom as the rose.
[Blank line]

And so we continued the Survey west about 19 miles then Southward, much of the way so broken and precipitous it could not be measured with a chain, and the distance calculable only by triangulation. I remember one space, less than two miles wide, which took two of our men nearly a whole day to cross on foot. Sometimes, to go from one point to another only a mile or two distant, would require nearly a whole day of most toilsome exertion to accomplish.

[Page B191R]

1900/July 13/ this day I narrowly escaped death. I had to ascend a high + exceedingly steep mountain, and as my horse would not be led, but must be pulled along by main force, I found I must ride. I slowly zig zagged my way up over loose sliding stones, large or small, going only a few steps at a time, the mountain so steep that it made me dizzy to look down to its foot 2000 feet below. I desired to pass a small oak 8 inches diameter by going on its lower side, but my horse suddenly veered to the left, passing under a large horizontal limb which was just high enough to miss the Saddle. This brought the limb against my lower abdomen. I all the time doing my best to stop the horse and to back him, but without avail. The horse was afraid he would fall, and I could do nothing with him to stop him as he still pressed slowly forward, squeezing my abdomen harder and harder against the limb, until it seemed as if it would break my back short off. But Orson McClellan saw my situation, rushed to my rescue, seized the bridle bitts and pounded the horse over the head with a big stone until he thus forced the horse back and released me. Had the animal taken one single step

---

the reach of arrows from any besieging force. Could those gray, moss-covered stones speak what an interesting story they could tell!

A thousand evidences prove that long ago all this country was inhabited by millions of people, and that they cultivated their lands by the rains alone in most localities; and this shows that in ancient times there was much more rain than now.

From J. H. Martineau, "Millions Surely Lived There Once," *Deseret Evening News*, July 28, 1900, 4; reprinted under J. H. Martineau, "Millions Lived There," *Latter-day Saints' Millennial Star* 62 (August 30, 1900): 558–559.

farther, I would have been killed. And so the Lord has once more spared and preserved my life. It must surely be because my earthly work is not yet finished,—not because of any special worthiness in me. Many other times I rode along steep mountain sides where a misstep would have sent horse and rider tumbling down tremendous depts. It reminds me of one of the men, who, in discribing his own experience in such perilous riding, when shame prevented him from getting off his horse, and walking. Says he "I just said up all my back prayers and held my breath."

But God has been very good to me, and it must have been for a <u>purpose</u>.

The rains finally hindered us so much we abandon the Survey until the rainy season is over, and return to Colonia Juarez on Sunday July 22nd 1900, finding my family about as well as usual, though Dora had had some fits while I was absent.

When riding through the forest and grass covered earth with its flowers,—strange to me, but beautiful, I had

[Page B192L]

1900/July 22/ many seasons of delightful, heavenly communion, and glorious and comforting promises from the heavens, and at times instruction where I desired it from the voice + inspiration of the Holy Ghost. I pray that God will help me to so live as to be counted worthy to receive the blessings promised me and mine.

24/ A fine celebration to day.

25/ Recd part of my pay—$80.00 leaving still due me $170 for field work, and not including $60. due me for mapping and estimates to date of July 31st [Blank line]

August

Aug. 29/First day of our Colony Fair. I drew 1st Prize for pomegranates, mine being the first raised in the Colony. Gertrude had prize for gentleman's neck tie. Fair ended next day.

Gov. Alumada and suite, also many Mexicans were here and highly pleased.

September

Sept. 3/ Deposited check recd of timber Company for $170.00 with Bently + Harris. It is No. 1199, on Banco Minero, of Chihuahua.

Sent the names and records of birth, death + endowment of my Sisters Francis Eliza and my daughter Julia Henrietta to Joseph F. Smith, who has desired them. Julia H. to be his wife + Francis E. to be sealed to his father, Hyrum Smith.

8/ This evening we had a party in honor of Theodore's birthday about 22 guests. I wrote a few lines in an address + blessing to him, which all present signed. We thought it would please him.[64]

19/ Recd a letter from Prest J.F. Smith, thanking me, and saying he would have the sealings of my Sister and daughter performed soon, and would send me all particulars when done. I know of no one in the Church to whom I would sooner give them than to him and his father.

Both my wives—Susans—were connected to the Smith family. Their Grandmother was sealed by the prophet Joseph to his uncle John Smith, and all her children Sealed to him as a father. Br. John Smith became Patriarch to the Church after William Smith, and died in S.L. City in 1854. The blessings he gave Susan E. and Henry A. were about the last he ever gave.

[Page B193R]

1900/Oct. 19/ Blessed Susan's niece Anna S. Eager-Tenney, who has been with us about two weeks, and who returns home tomorrow. She has been a great help to us in taking care of our fruit and in nursing Gertrude, who has been very sick for about ten days, with a Spinal trouble, which has been very painful all the time.[65]

Nov—/ November 1900.

---

64. Sometime near this date, Martineau wrote to the editor of the *Deseret Evening News* to report of happenings in the colonies, including the quarterly stake conference and the annual fair. See J. H. Martineau, "The Mexican Colonies," *Deseret Evening News*, September 10, 1900, 7.

65. On October 17, Martineau wrote to the *Deseret Evening News* to expose an apparent imposter, claiming to be the self-professed healer, Schlatter. The real Schlatter died a few years earlier in Mexico, at Willow Springs, after leaving Denver. See J. H. Martineau, "Divine Healer, an Imposter," *Deseret Evening News*, October 22, 1900, 8. See entry for May 31, 1897, and J. H. Martineau, "Schlatter's Death," *Deseret Evening News*, June 11, 1897, 9.

1/Dora had two fits to day. I have prayed for her, and have been answered that she shall be fully healed.

Nov. 13/ Recd letter, (posted at end of this book) saying he had Sealed my sister Frances Eliza to his father Hyrum Smith, and my daughter Julia Henrietta to himself, in Salt Lake temple, on Wed. Oct. 31. 1900, John R. Winder officiating in both cases, Br. Smith's wife Edna L. Smith acting proxy in each case, and Geo. Romney and Wm W. Riter being witness for each Sealing. I know no man now living to whom I would sooner have given them. In January, 1885, when Prest Smith accompanied Prest Taylor + party to Guaymas, Mexico, he took breakfast with us, and looked at the photos in or Album until he came to Netta's. Here he Stopped turning the leaves, looking at her until breakfast. A week after, as about to leave us for his home I asked him if he would like to be sealed to him. He answered, "That was what I was wishing as I looked at her picture! I said "You may have her sealed to you." He said earnestly "Oh yes, if you think I would be worthy of her." He spoke very humbly, and I know he is worthy, and will remain so all his days.

It has been revealed to me that she accepts him gladly as her husband, her king and her priest through all the eternities. And now I am satisfied, as to both of them.

20th/ An important event this evening at about 9 P.M. in the union, as I understand of Gertrude to Guy Taylor
[Blank line]
This morning Br. J.F. Smith and party started home, holding meeting to night in Dublan. Before they departed they (Br. Smith and Woodruff, Bp Geo Negley and I administered to Dora, Br. Smith being mouth. Dora said she believed she would be healed if Br. Smith would bless her, and I believe she will be. Br. Smith thanked me warmly for Netta and my sister Frances Eliza. We also administered to 2

[Page B194L]

1900/Nov. 20/others before they went away, and Br. Smith gave me some important instructions in relation to the patriarchal priesthood.

Have heard that on Sunday 11th inst. two of our people killed three apaches about 10 miles from Pacheco, being attacked by 6 renegade Apaches. Prest Ivins and Apostle Woodruff helped bury the indians. The

brethren had to kill or be killed, and Br. Woodruff and Br. Smith said they were justified in defending themselves.[66]
[Blank line]

22/ I was engaged to day to survey a mining claim in the Guaynopeta District in Sonora. I believe we will not be attacked by the indians.[67]
[Blank line]

Dec. 31/I find I have paid the following tithing this year:—Cash $56.00, stock, chickens, eggs, fruit +c $22.00, = $78.00 So God has greatly blessed me in the past year in temporal things as well as spiritually. During the last 4 months I have devoted much time to visiting the sick and administering to them and comforting and strengthening them as much as I have been able, and God has blessed me in this, very greatly. It has been delightful to me, in thus helping those who need help.
[Blank line]

1901/ 1901

Jan. 6./This evening, about 8.30 P.M. Anna S. Walser, my dear daughter so early widowed in Oct. 1897, was united to Edward Turley

8/ Our 49th Wedding anniversary. Did not celebrate to day because of the absence of Henry A. and Anna S; both are absent in El Paso. They both returned on the evening of the 9th

9/ Had a family dinner this evening. Present Guy and Edward, Henry A. our own family at home and Bp. J.C. Bentley, his wives Maggie and Gladys, and Mrs. A.E. Saville Sister of Gladys. Spent a pleasant evening and had a good dinner—2 Chickens etc. Ada J East went home.

12/ Surveyed Cow pasture of about 1400 acres. I was very ill and in much pain all the afternoon.

15/ Blessed Miss Mary Richardson of Diaz. Recd letter from "Improvement Era" requesting me to write for it.[68]

---

66. For an account of this attack, see "Apaches Attack Mormon Colony," *Deseret Evening News*, November 17, 1900, 8.

67. On November 24, Martineau reported on the quarterly conference in Colonia Juarez. President Joseph F. Smith, Apostle A. O. Woodruff and Elder S. B. Young of the First Council of the Seventy attended and gave council and advice. See J. H. Martineau, "The Saints in Mexico," *Deseret Evening News*, December 1, 1900, 22.

68. The *Improvement Era* was an LDS church periodical published as the official organ

[Page B195R]

Also from "El Progresso" to act as correspondent.[69] I am already correspondent for the Deseret News, Utah, and the "El Paso Daily Herald". I was blessed and set apart in the "50"s by direction of President Geo. A. Smith, under the hands of Prest Danl H. Wells. F.D. Richards and another Apostle whose name I do not at this moment remember, to write for the "News," and I write for the El Paso Herald that I may give "our side" a public hearing when necessity demands.[70] It is for the same cause I write

---

of the Young Men's Mutual Improvement Association (YMMIA) and the Young Women's Mutual Improvement Association (YWMIA). It was published from 1898 through 1970.

69. The weekly newspaper, *El Progreso*, was published by Frederick Erastmus "F. E." Eldredge in Nuevo Casas Grandes, Chihuahua, Mexico, from about 1899–1909. According to Joel H. Martineau, the newspaper was a significant organ for transmitting news among the colonies:

> After the railroad was built into Nuava [sic] Casas Grandes, a man by the name of Eldredge brought in a Printing Press and published a news paper weekly called ~~illegible~~ ^El^Progreso.
>
> It was fairly successful and had a correspondent in each colony to keep ~~us~~ ^the people^ posted on what was going on in ~~our~~ ^the^ Stake. It carried considerable advertising for local business firms and also of El Paso.
>
> For about ten years he published it at Nueva Casas Grandes then misfortune overtook him. His wife ran away with a younger man. ~~and~~ Later his health failed and he sold the business to Elder Hyrum Harris who moved it to Colonia Dublan. A few years later Mr. Harris sold it to Prof. Guy C. Wilson and Thomas Romney who moved the plant to Colonia Juarez where it remained until the Exodus when the type and materials were scattered around and the press was dumped down by the river and all was destroyed.
>
> It was a very valuable asset to the colonies while it was being in circulation and was greatly appreciated.
>
> Mr. Eldredge was a good citizen, progressive and liberal. He later ~~investigated our religion and~~ joined ~~our~~ ^the Mormon^ Church.

From "El Progresso," Joel Hills Martineau Papers, box 1, folder 9, MS 15994, LDSCHL. For biographical information on Eldredge, see editorial note, Appendix Two.

The only extant copy of *El Progreso*, dated September 12, 1902, is found at the LDS Church History Library. The newspaper was cited by Jane-Dale Lloyd in her histories of northeastern Chihuahua, Mexico. She noted that a run of the newspaper was located in the Archivo Municipal de Casas Grandes, Chihuahua. (See Jane-Dale Lloyd, *Cinco Ensayos Sobre Cultura Material*, 318.) Noel Carmack attempted to examine this newspaper on March 13, 2008, but was not able to gain access to the storage facility where the archives are held.

70. Although they were published without attribution, Martineau's correspondence to the *Daily Herald* appeared several times over the course of about two years. In one article, Martineau described the praiseworthy work of the Ladies' Relief Society, writing: "This is a most worthy institution, and could most profitably be copied by other communities." In the same article, Martineau criticized the violence occurring on the streets of El Paso:

> A perusal of El Paso papers shows a bloody record of murders, and much crime of other character, giving your city an unenviable notoriety. It seems to an outsider that

for "El Progresso," though it is all work I would like to shun, if possible. I have not the time nor inclination for it all, but I have been able, many times, to present a public refutation of many malignant attacks upon our people, and none of my efforts have ever been refused publication by any gentile paper. Thus I have done some good with my pen, for which Our Father be praised.

My Year of Jubilee.

Jan. 19th/ To day is 50 years since I was made <u>free</u> through baptism into the church, by Elder William McBride, on the Temple block where now stands the temple, in the West Branch of City Creek, which then ran west into the Jordan.

As ancient Israel celebrated each 50th Year as one of Jubilee, wherein all slaves and bond servants became free, and where the nation could enjoy a year's rest. So I also regard this date at the era of <u>my</u> deliverance from the bonds of Satan, in that I am a partaker in the freedom the gospel gives.

As such, I desire that all my posterity after me shall forever remember and honor this aniversary, until it will no longer be best to do so.

I thank Our Father that He has preserved me thus long in the truth, and that with all my sins of Commission and omission, and many mistakes. He has been so kind and merciful to me, and has bestowed so many and so great blessings upon me. I pray that I may be true to the end. Amen.

25/ Have done several days surveying, some of it mountain work, though still feeble from continued la grippe.

[Page B196L]

1901/[Blank line]

---

the carrying of deadly weapons should be prohibited under heavy penalty, and that such a law should be strictly enforced. If any feel that it is necessary to their safety to carry arms, let such procure a license to do so in due form, such license to be made a matter of record. At present we outsiders would rather risk our lives in the heart of the Sierra Madres with jaguars and panthers for mighty companions than to walk alone at night in lonely parts of El Paso, a condition which should not and need not exist.

From "Colonia Juarez, Mex.," *El Paso Daily Herald*, November 2, 1899, 5. See also "Casas Grandes," *El Paso Daily Herald*, October 11, 1899, 5; "Colonia Juarez," *El Paso Daily Herald*, October 19, 1899, 5; "Colonia Juarez, Mex.," *El Paso Daily Herald*, December 4, 1899, 3; and "Casas Grandes, Mex," *El Paso Daily Herald*, December 30, 1899, 5.

Jan.29/ Helped a carpenter to place lumber on my barn, which is still unfinished.

Feb./ February.

5/ To day Anna moved to her new home, about a block distant. It made quite a vacancy, for she and her children had been with us so long—over two years.

   I hope she may be as happy as is consistent with weak humanity. Edward Turley, her husband for time, is a good man, and desired her years ago, also his wife Ida Eyring Turley, desired her as a sister-wife all these years. May our Father bless them all.

11/ To day Dora had three bad fits. I think they are caused by foul stomach. he will be healed of them.

12/ Recd a letter from Atty. F.W. Lake, San Francisco. He thinks he can recover $80.00 from the U.S. Govt I signed Agreement to give him half he collects,—nothing if he gains nothing. "A half loaf is better than none."

19/ A letter from Virginia, my daughter, tells me she lost her daughter Virginia, age 5 years, by pneumonia, on Sat. Feb. 9th inst. The little girl was a bright and good child. She, at least, is safe from Satan's power.

* 15/ I learn my son Albert has a new daughter, born on Friday Feb. 15th inst, in Chuichupa.

March/ March

4/ Fruit trees, viz:—Almonds, peaches, plumbs, apricots all in bloom. Apples, pears, cherries and small fruit will soon come also

7/ Dora had two slight attacks,—prevented by administration.

9/ Susan and I, went to E. Turley's and had a family dinner.

   Blessing to Nephi.

   I find a slip overlooked at the time, which I here insert:—

Feb. 5th 1901/ "Prayed for Nephi in his present distressed mind, and his financial troubles, at about 4 a.m. and was told by the voice of the Spirit to write to him as follows:—

"Write unto thy son Nephi and say unto him he shall be blessed from this time forth for more than in years past. He shall be blessed with an increase in wisdom in his business, in faith, and in all temporal

[Unpaged page signed Gertrude, from Alberta, N.W.T. Canada]
[Two written pages in Gertrude's hand]

[Page B197R]

1901/Mch./blessings, and shall be greatly prospered in all he shall put his hands to do,—he and his family. It is my will that he shall remain upon his farm for the present, and shall be prospered in his labors until it is my will for him to move to Mexico, and when that time shall come he shall sell his property and home to good advantage, and shall be blessed in Mexico in a still greater degree, he and his family, seal these blessings upon him in thy letter to him, and they shall be sealed and ratified in the heavens. Even So. Amen.

I immediately arose, lighted a lamp, and wrote as I had been instructed by the voice of the Spirit. I afterwards got a letter from ^him in^ which he expressed his great joy in what I had written to him. I pray that he may be blessed in this,—he is worthy.

He has been in debt ever since he returned from his mission in Kentucky, owing nearly $3000.00 and his crops scarcely pay interest and taxes on the land. He has about 180 acres about 9 miles from Logan, on Bear river,—a good farm, but with wheat at 35¢ pr bushel, farmers can hardly live.

16/ Albert came from chuichupa. Returned 20th To day we got a cow + calf, which will help us considerably.

19/A letter from Theo, who expects soon to be released as a Conference president, and to be called to Chattanooga office.
[Blank line]

25/This morning I start for the mountains to finish the timber Survey I began last summer, in company with Mr. John McComb, Agent of the timber Company.

During the last six months I have been constantly going among the sick and administering to them, and the Lord has greatly blessed me and the sick in all this, which has greatly increased my faith, and has given me a more perfect knowledge of the voice and inspiration of the Holy Spirit. For, before going to the house of the sick person I always asked the Father, to know if the sick would be blessed or healed under my ministration. When the reply was affirmative, of course I could administer "in faith beleaving," [sic] and so my desire was granted in behalf of the sick ones; they were blessed, and so was I.

[Page B198L]

1901/Mch. 25/ We reached Garcia next day, made our camp, and waited for our men to join us. On the 26 made an observation on Polaris to find the variation of the magnetic needle, which was 11° 15' E. On the 27th took the Lat. N. 29° 53' 30", our camp being about 4400 meters South of the North boundary of the land to be Surveyed, which is about N. 30° 0' or N. 29° 54'. On the 28th our men all arrived and on the [in margin: 29th] we moved camp, to begin the Survey of the east boundy

30/ Began our survey of east boundary running South, over high ridges and deep Cañons. I triangulated from point to point to ascertain distance, chaining being impracticable, covering, to day 10914m

April 1. 1901

Mch. 31st/Moved Camp about 12miles. In the afternoon it began to Snow with a driving. wind, piercingly cold, which by [in margin: April 1st] night became a terrible blizzard. We suffered with cold each one revoling before the fire—freezing one side and roasting the other. I went to bed with all my clothes on, but was cold all night. The snow all melted in a few days, but nights and mornings were very cold, and ice formed every nights about half an inch thick, or more. And so we continued slowly southward, over high mountains at an altitude of full 10000 feet, and crossing deep Cañons, the whole distance being through pine timber.

6/ Camped on the Las Pumas stream, which runs north with the Rio Chico.

8/ Reached the brow of South side of Rio Chico canon or gorge and built monument of Stone 6 ft. high about noon. We could not cross it. From brink to brink was over a mile + about 3000 feet in depth, with sides very precipitous.

9/ Sent two men to find a way to reach the South bank and put up a flag to be triangulated to. Edward, my grandson, was one of them. It took them all day to cross and return.

10/ Triangulated and found distance across—1976met about 1 ¼ miles. There being a deep, impossible gorge also on our right, we took all day to go around its head, crossing it where the Rio Delores joins it, and killing a deer on our way. We went south until we came to a point west of

[Unpaged letter to "My dear Grandma," dated Jan. 30. 1897 Thatcher, signed George A Martineau.]

[Page B199R]

1901/April/the flag we set the day before, and triangulated to it across the chasm,—over two miles. The country South being impracticable we ran an offset line west from our flag over a very broken + mountainous country a distance of 10394met and built a Stone monument on a ridge, then ran South 11182met to the boundary of our tract to be surveyed, then along the South line westward to the Summit of the Candelaria Mt, some 10000 or 11000 feet high. Here we were all day in another Snow storm, and we made [In margin: 17th] camp between patches of old Snow. Arrived here April 17th

21st/ Took latitude on South boundary; N. 29° 25'

22/ Moved camp about 7 miles to the Rio Guaynopa and camped in an ancient, ruinous old Spanish building, near an old Spanish mine. The Change from Snow to palms in so short a distance was very remarkable. Our way was up and down high, steep and rocky mountains, in some places dangerous to ride on horse back, but I rode all the way. As I came to the bottom of the gorge I heard one—a regular rough rider, dare devil—who had led his horse down, say to McComb "Why, Martineau rode <u>all the way to the bottom</u>." I was the only one who did so, and in some places it made my flesh creep a little on my bones. But I was not really afraid, for I asked God to bless my horse, that he might not fall stumble, or slip, and that I might ride safely, and I had a testimony that all would be well with me, I trusted it it, and all was well with me, thanks to our Father. What a blessing it is that God—the Omnipotent—will hear and answer the prayers of so weak and sinful ones as I am and others! What could we do without His goodness and mercy in our behalf![71]

---

71. The old Guaynopa trail through the Sierra de la Candelaria mountains must have seemed perilous at its roughest and highest reaches. Indeed, the region was once called "The Devil's Cauldron." The pine-covered range is situated near the northwestern border of the state of Chihuahua, south of Chuhuichupa. The summit, Cerro de Candelaria, is a

23/ Ascended a high and very steep mountain several thousand feet, then down again, and "up hill and down dale" hour after hour, Stopping from time to time to fix the packs on our eight mules. We passed a little pile of Stones with a rude cross in its top—the resting place of some poor fellow. We follow the trail that leads over into Sonora. Camped on a small rivulet, near which lay the remains of a man—his bones only. Unknown he lies—till the resurrection shall call him to life again.

24/ This morning all our animals are gone. Yesterday we Sent men to top of a high ridge back of us, to erect a monu-

[Page B200L]

1901/April 24/-ment of Stone with a tall post, to which I can triangulate today. I took my party some distance west to find a place suitable for triangulation, while others hunted the animals. They were found high up the mountain side where they could get no farther. One of my men and horse rolled a distance down the mountain, breaking his rifle to pieces, otherwise with no harm.

25/ Moved camp three miles while I surveyed onward through thick white oaks. Set a flag on West side of a deep Cañon for triangulation, after which chained onward and quit on brow of another great gorge, after placing a flag on line on its other side.

26/ Went to flag and triangulated back to last nights quitting point. Distance, nearly 2 miles. The country west being almost impossible by reason of gorges and cliffs, we concluded not to go any farther west on South boundary, and turned to the north, placing a monument of Stones and tall post with flag on South brow of a tremendous and impassible gorge, about 2 miles wide and 3000 feet deep.

We have come thus far on the South boundary 37722 meter nearly 25 miles. Most of the distance was over country impossible to Chain, and was only crossed by triangulating from one ridge to another—sometimes over 10000meter—6 or 7 miles.

---

rugged peak which reaches a height of about 8,915 feet, only rivaled by Cerro de Mohinora (or Muinora) which is the highest mountaintop in the state of Chihuahua and rises to an altitude of 10,663 feet. Rio Chico borders the Candelaria mountain range on its eastern slopes. For a description and photographs of the trail, see Slater, "The Golden Heart of the Sierra Madre," 439–442. See also Lumholtz, *Unknown Mexico*, 1:422, and Hovey, "The Western Sierra Madre," 538.

27/ As it was impossible to chain or even triangulate north, we moved camp towards the main range in order to get round the head of these deep gorges, passing through a very difficult country of rocks, difiles [defiles] and steep ascents and descents, + camped among rocks where we could hardly find place for our beds.

28/ Sent men to explore and find, if possible, a point where we could get on our western boundary line. Men came back at night unsuccesful.

29/ Ascended a high mountain ridge and went miles north along its crest, and at night camped as usual.

30/ Men hunted all day for a chance to get on line. Could not find any way to do so—so many chasms + cliffs. Camp on Ryan's Creek.

May 1/ May 1.

Ascended mountain ridge again and followed it some

[Page B201R]

1901/May 1/miles northward, to a point so steep we could follow it no longer, and we were obliged to return to Camp again.

2/ Moved camp a few miles into another cañon, but had great difficulty in getting out again to another place, climbing hills so steep our pack animals could not carry their light loads up them—men having to carry the packages up one by one. Sent men hunting for a camp ground near our west boundary line. Unsuccesfful [sic]

3/ Ascended a very high, steep ridge, and after going some miles found a place for triangulating to a monument we set last Summer. Moved camp near to this point

4/ Moved camp again. Triangulated east to point on high peak, nearly 11000 meters.

5/ Triangulated west to flag set on ridge west, 1 ½ miles. This took us all day to do.

6/ Triangulated back to last night's position on ridge east. This was a tremendously hard day's work, and sometimes dangerous. It was all I could do to get along, at much danger to life or limb. My shoes were all in rages, and the nails in the soles cut and hurt me terribly as I walked—as I had to, much of the time, as it was all I could do to get along afoot.

This finishes up our entire Survey, connecting with the point where we quit last year. The entire boundary is 196486meter about 123 miles, enclosing nearly 800 Sq. miles of mountain, timber, land—nearly 500000 acres.

This has been without exception the hardest and worst work I have ever had in all my 48 years experience as a Surveyor. Many, many times my life was in imminent danger, but God was merciful, and preserved me through it all. To Him be all the honor and glory of my Salvation.[72]

7/ Started homeward, and Camped in Bacon's Cañon.

8/ Arrived at Chuichupa about 1 P.M. hungry, tired and worn out. During the last four days we had no bread. I soon had a dish of bread and milk! A luxury indeed. Found Mary A. Joel's wife has a new baby girl, also Alberts wife the latter some 3 month's old.

9th+10/ Made a connection of Chuichupa with the eastern boundary, which finishes the field work of this Survey. And on the 11th and 12th reached home—and oh! how glad!

[Page B202L]

1901/May 10/On the 10th all our family met at Joel's and had a family dinner. About 29 or 30 being represented in this place. It was a very enjoyable time.

May 12/Sunday. At home again. I am thankful indeed

25/To date I have been working up my field notes and Map. My time, field work, 44 days, amounts to $440.00

---

72. Martineau's son Joel later wrote that, even though his party was adequately equipped, his father started out with deficient transportation:

> This tract extended from the Pacheco purchase, which was its north line to the Candelaria peaks south of Chichupa [Chuhuichupa], about fifty miles in length, and from the Sonora line it extended almost to the San Miguel River. He had an outfit for packing the necessary camp equipment and a party of eight men, and finished the job in May 1901. One of the best men was John A. Whetten, the flagman who took pity on him for the sorry horse he had to ride, and gave him a splendid little saddle mule, and rode the lazy old horse himself.

Martineau, Untitled Biographical Material on James Henry Martineau, 34.

" " 14 day office work   140.00

23d/Paid Cash, on tithing a/c $50.00 $580.00

26/Received $300.00 on account, also blankets $17.00 The same amount of time, on U.S. land Survey would have brought me 5000$,—or about $3000.00 clear.

26/ Finished a map for McComb. He wants another.

31/ Have been very busy working in garden, planting corn +c

June.

June6/ Anna returned from Chiuchupa

8/ Theodore came unexpectedly, having been honorably released by Prest Ben. E. Rich from his mission. He has been gone a little over a year. Was some month a traveling elder, then appointed President of the Alabama + Florida Conference, then called to the General Office in Chatanooga. He has been highly praised by Prest Rich.[73]

Yesterday received word from Jesse N. and Belle. They were both to be baptized on May 30th She for the first time; he, to renew his covenant. He wrote a very good letter.

15/ By letter from Elvira I learn she has a new baby boy, name is Don Charles Johnson. Born April 24, 1901.

July 1901

July 2/Anna moved to her new home, a house of two rooms, barn with abundant fruit trees, strawberries +c

Got my new chiffonier, cost $50.00 Very heavy rain in the night—the first of the coming rainy Season.

11/ Susan's birthday, her 65th. We had a good dinner. may she have many more, some, even, in New Jerusalem—Zion.

14/ Dora had another epileptic fit. I believe she will be finally healed of them.

---

73. Benjamin Erastus Rich (1855–1913) was president of the Southern States Mission from 1898 to 1908.

15/ She had another. Fell and was badly bruised.

[Page B203R]

> Eva Aileen Martineau born to Charles + Eva.
> Aug 8. [here and above in top margin]

1901/July 15/Paid $20.00 cash on tithing—$70.00 this year. I am glad I can pay it—it is no trial for me.

-----/ August

Aug 6/ Cut my ~~second~~ ^third^ crop of lucerne, and carried it all to the barn, a pitchfork full at a time, which caused rupture to pain me much. Very hot weather.

8/ Charles' wife Eva gave birth to a baby girl—Eva Alieen

13/ Finished my lucerne cutting. I used a scythe.[74]

20/ Received a letter from grandson Knowlton Nebeker, saying his mother (Lilla, or Elizabeth) has a new baby girl. She (his mother) is very ill,—paralyzed, deaf and can hardly frame sentences of more than 6 or 8 words. This is a very dreadful conditions, and I pray She may be healed.

21/ Planted beans, as an experiment as to proper time.

23/ Surveyed for B. Stowell, his pasture land.

24/ Made observation last night on Polaris, to get variation of the magnetic needle, which I find to be 11° 25' East.

25/ Gertrude was taken very sick today. It seems to be meningenetis. She suffered dreadfully. She could not sit nor lie down, but was obliged to stand on her feet to breathe at all. Finally, we had to hold ^her^ up, and she seemed as if about to die. I believe she was saved through the ordinance of administration and prayer of faith. But she still has a severe pain through her body at pit of her stomach, so bad that she can hardly breathe. Were up with her all night. I note here, that these pains continued nearly a week, gradually growing less and finally ceased, leaving her very weak. We administer frequently, and she is benifited.

---

74. Five days later, Martineau wrote to the *Deseret Evening News* to report on the quarterly conference that took place on August 17 and 18. See "Conditions in Mexico," *Deseret Evening News*, August 31, 1901, 24.

31/ In absence of A.F. Macdonald, Prest of High Priests Quo. I presided, by his direction and that of Prest A.W. Ivins.

Sep./ September

2/ Surveyed for Stovell. For about a week I have been very unwell with severe dysentery, very difficult to check, but am now much better—getting well again.

3/ Gertrud walked a little to day—a few steps only. Dora almost had a fit, twice, and would have, but for prayer and administration. She became unconscious, but did not fall, being noticed in time.

[Page B204L]

1901/ September. (contd)

Sept. 3/Oh, how thankful I would be could she be entirely healed. I believe she will be, finally
[Blank line]

5/Dora's 19th Birthday. Made her a nice dinner. I gave her a nice mirror as birthday present. She had a slight fit in the evening but we rebuked it in time. Gertie sat at the table, first time in many weeks.

13/ Gertrude had convulsions, and soon we thought her dying. Sister A.E. Saville came at 10 P.M. also Several Elders, who administered. Mrs. S. remained all night, doing what she could for her.

14–17/ Very low, almost lifeless. Too weak to speak aloud.

18/ May pass away any moment.

19/ She can speak, faintly, a little

20/ Apostle Cowley administered to her. All these days we can admit no visitors, and we speak only in low whispers, in any part of the house.

23/ She can now speak a little—very little, but cannot endure conversation around her. Some days ago we telegraphed for her husband, Guy, to hurry home He came this evening, home from Parral, Mex.

27/ This evening Gertie had a sinking spell, very bad one. We thought her dying for some hours. We could hardly perceive her breathe, or feel any pulse for full half an hour, but she finally revived

28/ Had another, also a frightening one.

-----/ Oct. 1901.

Oct. 1/Gertie sat up a few minutes, but was worse next day.

3/She talked some to day and laughed a little. Also 6th 7th + 8th

9/I went to Dublan + got some goods. Blessed Irena and Verde Pratt.

19/Gertie worse again

20/ Great hail storm. Broke Shingles and glass; killed many Small animals, birds +c, destroyed fruit and crops still unharvested. Hail piled 2 ft deep in places.

November/ November

15/Dora had a fit + fell severely to the floor.

[Page B205R]

1901/Nov. 17/Let Theo. take my transit to Survey for O.P. Brown, in the mountains.

20/ Prest Ivins engaged me to Subdivide the new purchase of land—78000 acres—at Dublan. Blessed Roxey and Myrtle Stowell. Made mining maps for Theodore's surveys.

22/ Blessed Lettie Stowell

    Anna was blessed to day with a nice baby girl at 8-15 A.M. and was much blessed in delivery.

26/Tuesday, went to Dublan and began Survey.

note/Nov. 5th/ Learn by letter that Geannie had a baby born on Nov. 5th—a son.

[Notice margin bracket]
-----/

December/ December 1901.

11/ Blessed Flossie E. Ossmen

12/ Sent a nice wire mattress cot for Dora, who is not well. Heavy gale all day. Could not work

13/ Storm continues, with snow 2 inches deep. No working.

16, 17, 18/ Surveyed part of city plat. Heard Dora is very sick. Dismissed my helpers, Started home almost sunset. Arrived home 7.45 P.M. and found Dora had died half an hour before, of lung fever. Susan had written to me to come, but I had received no letters. It was an awful shock to me, especially, that I was absent, and could not be with her to comfort her by my presence, for she loved me with intensity, as I did her

She had been sick twelve days, being taken ill on the 6th of the month, with pain in side. All that tenderest love could dictate was done for her, but without avail, for she steadily failed, day by day, until the end.

On the day she died she sat up while her hair was combed, and retained consciousness until the last. An hour before she passed away, She whispered a prayer, asking forgiveness for all her sins. She had asked Gertie to forgive if she had anything against her, and she "wished Papa would come." She suffered greatly all the time till about an hour before her death, when all pain ceased, and she passed peacefully to her rest, and to go on to her exaltation in the celestial glory.

[Page B206L]

1901/Dec. 18 cond/Oh how my heart and Susan's and Gertrude's grieved. Dora was pure in heart, if any upon earth can be, and received gladly every truth and law of the gospel. She never talked ill of any one, nor could She bear to hear it. She delighted to do all She could to help her mother, me, or Gertie, even when weak and unwell. She was very neat and tasteful in her attire, and in her hair, and delighted in all things beautiful. She was a very sweet singer, with clear, pure voice, and played the organ uncommonly well and with exceeding delicacy of touch and time, and she had a passion for music, also drew very nicely, having natural genius for music and drawing. In short, she was by nature refined, but much of the time wore an expression somewhat sad,—inherited, no doubt. What is our life here but meetings and partings! The latter almost always so sad! But to know and appreciate the sweet one must know the bitter; how else can we be qualified to sit as a King or Queen—as a judge? Thus Christ had to suffer, to enable Him to understand and to sympathise with the sorrows and troubles of a world. And it is all right and absolutely necessary to our advancement and perfection. Father! Thy will not ours be done!

" 20th/ At her funeral a large number of young ladies came to our house and walked in procession behind the coffin to the school house, and covered it with rare and beautiful flowers.

She used to say "Mama, I'm going to live with you and papa always; if I ever get married I will still live always with you." Dear girl! We will meet by-and-bye, to part no more, to mingle in love with others of our family who have gone before.
[Blank line]

24/ This is Christmas eve, but it is no Christmas for me, or my dear Susan or Gertrude. We feel too sad,—our house seems to lonely. Always before for many, many years, we have had children

[Page B207R]

1901/Dec. 24/about us, all anxious and full of expectation as to what the morrow would bring them. It is so no longer, and our souls are sad.

And yet we should rejoice, seeing God has so greatly blessed us, notwithstanding our many transgressions. Help us, Oh Father, to become pure in heart, that we may finally come and dwell with Thee!

28/ Finished papering two rooms, and put down our new tapestry bed room carpet—the first we ever had. About 25 meters cost $40.00 Our home looks much improved now.

-----/ 1902

Jan. 8th/ To day is the 50th Anniversary of our marriage, but our fond anticipations of a family reunion were not fulfilled. No one came from the North, and of our family in Mexico, outside of Juarez, only Albert + his son and Theodore were present. Anna and Gertrude were with us. Well, it makes no difference. What is the 50th Anniversary, compared with the fifty thousandth—or the 50 millionth, or a still greater number than that? for eternity is still beyond all such figures, and is truly incomprehensible to us, yet so long shall our union continue—worlds without end; and that, too, without sorrow, pain or sad partings! Oh! how happy and glorious is the the thought! And what is this short span of life here on this "dark and dreary world."

13/ Returned to Colonia Dublan to finish Survey there, the city plat to be a little over 2 miles in length and breadth. I continued this work until

Jan. 30th when I finished. I gave blessings to several while in Dublan, and received one myself from Patriarch Winslow Farr. Returned home

Jan. 31/Jan. 31st having labored in cold, disagreeable weather.

The following is my blessing from Bro. Farr:—

Brother James Martineau, by virtue of my office and calling I place my hands on thy head and give thee a patriarchal blessing, and desire that the spirit of the Lord may direct the words that may be used in this blessing. Thou wast with the Father when the foundations of this earth were laid and the morning

[Page B208L]

Jan. 19/1902/stars sang together and the sons of God shouted for joy. Thou art one of the noble sons of God selected by our Father in heaven to come forth on the earth in the dispensation of the fulness of times. Thou didst keep thy first estate with the Father, and have chosen thy parentage and the dispensation to come forth on the earth, and the eye of the Lord has been over thee from the hour of thy birth, and the Lord has seen thy integrity, and witnessed many of thy trials and tribulations and sacrifices for the gospel's sake, and great is thy reward in heaven. Thou shalt be blessed with the gift of wisdom and the Spirit of discernment to comprehend the mysteries of God, and the Lord is well pleased with thee, for thou hast filled an honorable mission on the Earth. Thou shalt have faith like unto the brother of Jared. Thou shalt have power to cast evil influences from those that are afflicted, the dumb shall speak, the deaf shall hear, the blind shall see, and the lame shall walk at thy command. Thou art of the seed of Joseph that was sold into Egypt by his brethren through the loins of Ephraim, and thou shalt receive thine inheritance with that seed. For thy name is written in the Lamb's Book of Life, and thou shalt be numbered with the 144.000, and thou shalt stand as a savior of Mt. Zion and become a mighty man in Israel, and thy name shall be handed down in honorable remembrance through future generations, and shall meet with those who have been true and faithful to the Lord. The Lord has accepted thy labors in redeeming the dead and will continue to do so until thou art satisfied. Thou shalt live as long as life is desirable, and when thou hast finished thy work on the Earth thou shalt wear the crown of eternal life. And I bless thee with the blessings of Abraham Isaac and Jacob, with power to come forth in the morning of the first ressur-

[Page B209R]

1902/Jan. 30/-rection, And I seal thee up unto eternal life, in the name of Jesus Christ. Amen.

Recorded on page 116 Book "A"
[Blank line]
 I was thankful for the promises in this blessing. They agree fully with all my previous blessings, which is, of itself, a testimony that it was given by the same spirit and power as the others,—the dictation of the Holy Spirit.

" 30th/ Returned home, having finished my work for the present.

-----/
Feb./ February 1902

3/ Began on maps of Dublan Survey.

7th/ Bertha's boy was born today about noon. This is another Gr. Gr. Child for us.

20/ Up to this time I have been mostly busy on maps. I now commence on Canal note calculations.

 Gertrude has been very sick and still is, not being able to turn in bed, unless moved by some one.

23/ She is better to day, but not able to sit up.

-----/

Mch./ March

6/ Was examined to day by Dr. Keate, as I am about to apply for an increase in pension. Found my lungs tolerably good, kidneys not first class condition, + my rupture in left groin, ample cause for increase.[75]

11/Went to El Paso to file application for increase pension. Remained in El Paso until 14th

---

75. Martineau's claim, submitted to Congress by Senator Reed Smoot in February 1904, stated that he "suffers from chronic rheumatism, enlarged prostate, hernia, and a general enfeebled condition natural in advanced age, and is totally incapacitated for labor." See US Senate, Committee on Pensions, *James H. Martineau*, 58th Cong., 2d sess., 1904. S. Rpt. 903, p. 1. The incapacitating effects of age would be quite evident during the completion of his survey contract from August 1903 to May 1906.

13/ My 74th Birthday

15/ Found Gertrude still very weak, with frequent Sinking Spells, when she seems as if dying until we can administer to her, rebuking those spells.

16/ Settled with Prest Ivins for my Dublan Surveys
Total from beginning in Nov. last, field work $380.00
                     Office work   42.50

I am to receive pay for this from $422.50
                     add—   2.50
the tithing office—no money   -------
                              $425.00

27/ Sent Small record of my narrow escape to Lyman by Bp. J.C. Bentley, going to Conference.

[Page B210L]

1902/April 18/ My grand daughter, Editha Martineau, eldest daughter of Moroni + Sarah Martineau, died to day aged about 16 years, after an illness of 16 days. She had some internal female disorder.

    She was a lovely girl in form, feature + character, foremost as a Sunday School Secretary,—in Y.L.M.I Assn and in all religious duties. I believe she has gone to assist in the work already commenced here on earth for the dead, to carry it on on the other side of the vail. She was one worthy, I think, for this work, in the highest degree

-----/

    Theo's/Marriage/Mch. 23d/ Learn that Theodore and Josephine Thurston were married (Sealed for time and eternity) by Path A.F. Macdonald, in Garcia, on the 23d day of Mch. 1902.

-----/

Apr 24th/ Gertrude had 6 bad sinking spells to day. We mush watch her every moment

25/ Blessed William and Dayer LeBaron and Adelbert Taylor.

27/ Recd letter from Fred. W. Lake, Land Atty in Washington, D.C. who says he can recover $80.00 I paid some years ago for U.S. land I did not hold, he to receive half, if he secures the claim.

[Blank line]
Mrs. M.A. Thurston + boy came; also Theo + wife Josephine, who are on the way to a place called Matachic, about 200m South.

On the day previous I was engaged by Alonzo Farnswort, acting for a Dr. Robert Nichol, of Matachic, to go there and survey a canal line for him, about 9 miles in length. My terms, as usual, $10.00 pr day + all necessary expenses.
[Blank line]

Apr. 28/ Started to Matachic, riding 16m to Dublan with Theo. Raymond A. Farnsworth, husband of my grandaughter Bertha M. Martineau, who is going to Matachic, not being ready to start, had to lay over all next day.

[Page B211R]

1902/April 30/ To day on our journey south, with Raymond + wife and my Gr. Gr. son, born Feb. 7th, also Theodore + wife. My place to ride was on a heavily laden freight wagon, and was not at all comfortable. Camped after dark, Cold.

May 1/ Passed through Galeana, on the Santa Maria river, and [in margin: 2] on next day came to El Valle, a nice place with beautiful plaza, blooming with roses and flowering shrubs.

3/ Pass to day through high, broken ground

4/ Reach the Rio Sta Maria again at noon. Had a little rain.

5/ Continue over high hills; camp in Cold, bleak place having passed through Cruces

6/ Pass Maniquipa, the last place near head of Sta Maria

Then cross the Hacienda del Toro, and camp in pass of mountains, leading West into the valley of Rio Aros

Near our camp was a huge monument or pile of Stones about 6 or feet diameter at base and same height surmounted by a rough cross made of two sticks tied together. This was to commemorate many dead Mexicans slain here some years ago by Apaches. This same pass, in 1893 or 4 was the scene of another tragedy, when Mexican troops surrounded and killed some 40 or more men whom they styled rebels. Those who surrendered were all hanged upon trees near by.

7/ At noon came to Matachic, our destination. This hamlet is several hundred years old, having been an indian village when the Spaniards first came, as its name, ending in "Chic"—a common Aztec termination.

Ten miles below is Temosochic, about 8 miles above is Tejolocachic, both of them once indian villages.

Dr. Robert Nichol, whose canal I am to survey, received us kindly, and let Raymond and Theodore each have a room, until they can build for themselves. He gave me a nice room. The house is built in Mexican Style (I like the style, too) like this:—

[Note drawing of house on left side of page, following text to the right]

a wide entrance from street, large enough for a wagon to drive through, leads into a court, into which all rooms open, they having no openings outwardly.

[Page B212L]

1902/May 7/Wealthy Mexicans make these inner courts places of fairylike beauty, with fountains, flowers, beautiful plants and shrubs and vines, the court paved and surrounded on its four sides by a broad paved court or cloister sustained by massive columns and arches.

In Chihuahua I have glanced through open entrances and beheld courts that seemed like paradise, so wonderfully beautiful were they, while the outside of the house might resemble a barn. This style has many advantages. Children need not play in the Streets with undesirable companions, but each family can be by itself, and when the one outer entrance is closed, everything about the place is safe and secure.

8/ Measured 1000 meters of a canal, to see how much fall in that distance, and took the levels.

9th/ Went to point where canal is to be taken out, and did some preparatory leveling. Was quite unwell, having been ill with a flux some days on the journey, so I was quite weak and besides had a burning fever. Very tired at night.

Sat. 10/ In bed all day. Prayed God to heal me.

Sun.11/ " " " " but my fever is gone and bowels better.

Mon. 12 + 13th/ Worked on Canal Survey. Bothered by rain. In the evening Dr. Nichol knocked my transit over, and it was so badly injured it must be sent to New York to be repaired.

13/ Tried to fix and use transit, but could not do so. Dr. Nichol agrees to pay expenses of repair in full

15/ Gave Patriarchal Blessing to Josephine, as follows:
[Blank line]
Blessing upon Josephine Thurston Martineau, daughter of Peter Franklin + Mary Ann Spendlove Thurston Martineau, born in Pima, Arizona, March 26. 1886.

Dear daughter Josephine, in the name of the Lord Jesus Christ and in the authority of the Holy priesthood I seal upon you the blessing of your father, which shall be a comfort to you in time to come, and be fulfilled according to your faith and faithfulness.

[Page B213R]

You are in the days of your youth, but the Lord hath appointed unto you power to perform a great and good work in helping to bring to pass His holy purposes. You are of noble lineage, being one of the daughters of Joseph through the lineage of Ephraim, therefore entitled by birth, being of lineal descent to all the blessings pertaining to the daughters of Joseph. The Lord has appointed a great work for you to do, and inasmuch as you will seek unto Him in faith and humility the visions of the heavens shall be opened to your view. You shall be instructed in visions and dreams, and it is your privilege to know and understand the voice and inspiration of the Holy Ghost, that when you are in doubt or uncertainty in matters appertaining to your own affairs you may ask for instruction from the Holy Spirit and receive it. I seal upon you great faith and charity, with power to heal the sick and afflicted. I seal upon you wisdom and understanding sufficient for every time and necessity. And now, my daughter, inasmuch as you have been afflicted with weakness and debility I rebuke it in the authority of the Holy priesthood and in the name of the Lord Jesus Christ and say unto you that you shall become well, healthy and strong, and filled with renewed life, spirit and vigor. You shall be a help and comfort to your husband and a wise counsellor, and dwell in his bosom as a confidant. Strive to keep all the commandments of the Lord, strive to live a holy life, and nothing that is for your good shall be denied you. I seal you up to come forth in the morning of the first ressurection, and seal you up unto eternal lives, to reign as a priestess and Queen forever in the celestial glory, upon condition of your faithfulness and endurance unto the end in the name of the Lord Jesus Christ. Amen.

Matachic, May 15, 1902
[Blank line]
May 16/Am told this morning that Mr. Nichol will send me in

[Page B214L]

1902/May 16/his carriage to Guerrero—30 miles, for which I am very glad, as I expected to have to go on a freight wagon laden with ore, taking two days, very unpleasant way of travel. Before going I sealed the following blessing upon my Gr-Gr.-son Raymond Alonzo Farnsworth,—Bertha's son.

This is notable as the first of any of my Gr.-Grand children to be blessed:—

Patriarchal Blessing upon Raymond Alonzo Farnsworth, son of Raymond Alonzo + Bertha Mondana Martineau Farnsworth, born in Dublan, Mex. Feb. 7. 1902.

Given in ~~Cola Dubl~~ Matachic, Mex. May 16. 1902

Raymond Alonzo, in the name of the Lord Jesus Christ and in the authority of the holy priesthood, I seal upon you a blessing which shall rest upon you and be a blessing indeed. You are of the blood of Joseph through the lineage of Ephraim, a lawful heir to all the blessings priesthood and powers sealed upon Abraham, Isaac and Jacob. A great work is appointed unto you in the redemption of Zion, and it is your privilege to live to assist in the redemption of Zion and in the building up of the holy city Zion,—the New Jerusalem. You shall labor there in the holy temple of the Lord and receive mighty blessings therein, even a fulness of the holy priesthood, with all the powers appertaining thereto. I seal upon you all the spiritual gifts that shall be needful for you, with blessings upon your labors. You shall never be tempted more than you are able to bear, and no power of evil shall prevail against you. The blessings that await you are great and mighty and shall be revealed to you more fully hereafter. I seal you up unto eternal lives, to reign as a King and a Priest with God through all the eternities, in the name of the Lord Jesus Christ. Amen.

[Blank line]

About 9 a.m. I started on my return home and came to Guerrero a little before sunset, 30 miles. There being no hotel, I slept in an old deserted building, awakened in the morning by the bugle calls of the troops stationed there.

[Page B215R]

1902/May 16/It is a small city though an old one, and has an elevation of nearly 7000 feet. While in Matachic I took the latitude on the 11th inst.—N. 27° 57' 30"

" 17/ Started at 7.30 a.m. in stage for Minaca, arriving there, 8miles—about 9 a.m. Miñaca is the western terminus of the Chihuahua + Pacific R.R. but it will soon be extended farther to the west. I took passage here—3d class, $3.00 to Chihuahua, about 150m and reached Chihuahua about 5 P.M.

" 18/ Started for C. Juarez 10.30 a.m. arriving there 6.40 P.M.

" 19/ Came home 9 P.M. having to face a cold wind from the R.R. Station, by which I took a severe cold. Found my family in good condition as I hoped for, Gertrude somewhat better, but still confined to her bed.

I have had a fatiguing trip of over 700 miles, over 200 of which was by wagon, camping out at night, and did not accomplish that I went for, through the breaking of my transit, but was nevertheless blessed while away + my family were also. I found Mrs. M.A. Thurston, the 2d wife of Henry, with her 10 yr old son Frank, installed at home, to assist in taking care of Gertrude and helping my dear wife, who had been quite ill while I was away.

21/ To day blessed Mary Ann Johnson, also M.A.S.T. Martineau and Frank, her son. My cold is still quite bad.
[Blank line]
Patriarchal Blessing upon Frank Thurston Martineau Son of Henry A. and Mary Ann Spendlove Thurston Martineau, born in Cola Juarez, Mexico, Sept. 19. 1891

Frank, in the name of the L. J. Christ and in the authority of the holy priesthood I seal a patriarchal blessing upon you, which shall be fulfilled upon condition of your faithfulness and endurance unto the end. You are one of those who were faithful + valiant when Lucifer fell, and for this cause you have been permitted to take part in the work of the last days. You are of Ephraim by lineal descent, a natural born heir to the fulness of the priesthood with all its blessings + powers.

The Angel of the Lord will watch over you +

[Page B216L]

May/21/1902/ preserve you in the hour of temptation and danger. No hand or voice raised against you shall prosper and no power of evil shall prevail against you, so long as you keep the commandments of the Lord. In due time you shall receive your endowments and all the holy ordinances of the temple. You shall do a great work in the redemption of the living and the dead. You shall speak with power and authority, causing the righteous to rejoice, and the wicked to tremble. You shall have great faith, like unto that of Enoch, and like him the heavens shall be unfolded to your vision, and you shall receive instruction from the heavens. The gift of healing is yours, and many of the sick and afflicted shall be made whole under your administrations. You shall understand the voice and inspiration of the Holy Ghost, and be instructed as to your duty when in doubt or uncertainty, if you will seek unto the Lord for it in faith and humility. You shall be blessed in your labors and have the comforts of life, and there is no blessing to which you may not aspire if you will ask for it in faith and humility, inasmuch as it is for your good. I seal you up unto eternal lives, to enjoy all the blessings and glories of the heavens, in the name of Jesus Christ. Amen.
[Blank line]

27/Hired team and took Susan to Dublan.

June/ June 1902

2/ Theodore and Josephine removed from us to the house they rented of B. Stovell.

I paid Cash tithing to day $15.00

3d/ The old folk Party came off today. Guy took Gertie in her invalid chair, and she remained until after dinner, though faint and fatigued, by the blessing she received. She did not feel able to go, but Guy persuaded her. She seemed to take no harm, though she previously could not sit up longer than half an hour

[Page B217R]

1902/June 6/ Elvira came to see us from St David, Arizona, bringing three children with her. We had not seen her for about seven years, and her visit was a treat, though Gertie is still very sick and cannot endure much noise

May 31/ On last Saturday, May 31st, I took charge of the High Priests meeting, in the Absence of Prest Counr Redd, having been appointed to do so in the Priesthood meeting.

June 7/ A slight sprinkling today—the first for seven months.

17/ Sold 50 lbs Apricots for $4.00, the first we ever sold.

18/ Hired team and took Susan + Elvira and children riding.

19/ Blessed Elvira, Gertrude, Guernsey and Don Charles.

20/ Elvira returned home at 10 A.M. today, her baby being quite sick with bowel complaint and sore eyes.

Gertie ill-/very-/convulsions./ At 11 A.M. Gertie had a fearful convulsion, and one at 6 P.M. both being very dreadful. She lay as one dead between them, and for several days was very low indeed, the slight appetite she previously had being gone.

[In margin by next paragraph says: Baron Alex. von Wenden was endowed/ Oct. 4. 1897. Guy Taylor/ proxy. in Salt Lake temple.]

~~22~~/ Last night Gertie dreamed of being in the next world

27/with Bp. G.W. Seary, who died a few days ago. He was very busy and happy. She told him how his family was grieving for him. He said they would cease after a while. Some one showed her two beautiful crowns, one of which was for her own reward, the other was hers because of the work she had done in the temple for the Baron Alex. von Wendt (von Wenden, true name) to whom she was at one time Engaged to be married. She tried them on, and they both fitted her beautifully. They were circlets of Gold, narrow at the back, becoming wider in front, with a magnificent stone in the front-center. She desired to have them now, but was told she must wait awhile until she had finished her work on earth.

Before this, when she heard of the death of Bishop Sevy, she cried much, saying "why cannot I die or get well and not have to suffer the agonizing pain I do."

I fear her dream indicates her speedy departure. If she cannot be healed, it would be a mercy to her, for she suffers intense pain continually. She says she cannot endure it much longer. She is too weak.

[Page B218L]

1902/June 19/ Patriarchal blessing upon Susan Elvira Martineau Johnson. Given June 19. 1902

Susan Elvira, in the name of the Lord Jesus Christ and by authority of the holy priesthood I seal upon you a patriarchal blessing. You are one of the noble spirits held in reserve from before the foundation of the Earth because you was true and faithful to our Father in Heaven when Lucifer led away many after him. You have been true and faithful these many years, sometimes in sorrow + privation, in poverty and danger, in helping to establish Zion. The Lord has accepted your labors in the past and will reward you in time to come beyond the power of any mortal mind to conceive; therefore let your mind be filled with joy + peace. The blessing of the Lord will continue upon you in a much greater degree than in times that are past. You may ask the Father for any blessing that you may desire, and if it is for your good you shall receive it. You shall never be tempted more than you can bear, and no power shall turn you aside from the truth. I reconfirm upon you all the blessings that have hitherto been sealed upon you, I seal upon you an increase of faith, an increase of wisdom and intelligence, with power to heal the sick and afflicted, to comfort the sad and brokenhearted, and to be a blessing unto all with whom you associated. You shall do a great work in the temples of the Lord and redeem from prison a Multitude of the dead, that they may attain unto to blessings pertaining to the holy priesthood. In this work, you shall have great joy, and receive a testimony that your work for the dead is accepted by them, and by your Father in heaven. You shall have power to know and understand the inspiration of the Holy Ghost, that you may ask the Father for instruction if it is needful and receive it.

[Page B219R]

And you shall walk in Light and not in darkness. And now I say unto you for your comfort, as you are about to return to your home, you shall be

blessed and prospered in your journey, and all shall be well with you and your children. You and your husband and family shall be prospered and blessed from this time henceforth with all that is needful for your comfort and happiness. Your table shall be filled with abundance; health and peace shall reign in your habitations, and you shall have plenty, to help the poor and needy. Accept every law of the Gospel and strive to live a holy life and no power shall prevent you from receiving the blessings sealed upon you. I seal you up unto eternal lives, to reign as a Priestess and Queen forever in the celestial glory, in the name of the Lord Jesus Christ. Amen.
[Blank line]
Patriarchal Blessing upon Anna Gertrude Johnson, Born May 10th 1889, in Nephi, Arizona.

Anna Gertrude, in the name of the Lord Jesus Christ and by Authority of the Holy Priesthood I seal the blessing if your father upon you. You are one of the daughters of Joseph who was sold into Egypt, of the lineage of Ephraim by lineal descent, entitled to all the blessings, powers, and priesthood that appertains to the daughters of Sarah. You have been held in reserve to do your part in the work of the last days. For this purpose your life shall be preserved through every danger, for your Guardian Angel will never desert you, but will warn you in time to escape evil. I bless you with health and strength, with vigor of body and of mind, with great faith and charity; with wisdom and understanding, that you may do good in your day and generation. I seal upon you power to heal the sick and afflicted, and to comfort those who are sad and troubled in mind. You shall be taught by visions and dreams, and shall understand the voice and inspiration of the Holy Spirit, that you may be

[Page B220L]

1902/June 19/directed in your labors and be comforted + strengthened in the hour of trial. You shall be united with a man of God, and rear a posterity that shall be mighty in Israel. No power shall turn you aside from the path of righteousness, and you shall have power to do great good, not only to the living but in the redemption of the dead. Some of them will make themselves known to you that you may do a work for their redemption. Peace and plenty shall be in your habitations and the blessings of the earth shall be yours in abundance. These are but a few of the blessings in store for you, for the Lord loves you and will make you to be a prophetess in Israel. It is your privilege to assist in building up

Zion—the New Jerusalem—and to do a great work in the temple which shall be reared there for the redemption of the dead, and to enjoy for a time the safety, peace and glory of the Holy City. All these blessings and many more are yours upon condition of faithfulness and endurance unto the end, for I seal them upon you in the name of Jesus, and seal you up unto eternal lives, even to an exaltation as a Pri[e]stess and Queen in the heavens forever, in the name of the Lord Jesus Christ. Amen.
[Blank line]
Patriarchal Blessing upon Seth Guernsey Johnson Born 24 July 1897 in Nephi Arizona.

Seth Guernsey, in the name of the Lord Jesus Christ and by authority of the Holy Priesthood I seal upon you your father's blessing, which shall be a help and comfort to you in days to come. You are of Ephraim, entitled to all the blessings that were sealed upon Abraham, Isaac and Jacob. It is your privilege to have a posterity that shall be like that of Abraham,— even like unto the sands of the sea for multitudes I seal upon you the gift of healing, that you may heal the sick and afflicted, and help and comfort those who are sad and troubled in mind. I seal upon you wisdom and intelligence sufficient

[Page B221R]

1902/June/19/for every time and duty, that you may assist mightily in the building up and redemption of Zion and in bringing to pass the purposes of the Almighty. You shall carry the words of life and salvation to those who are now in darkness, and many shall receive the truth through your instrumentality. I seal upon you health and strength, in every faculty of your mind + body. You shall be preserved in the hour of danger, and no weapon formed against you shall prosper. You shall be blessed in your labors in the building up of Zion, and it is your privilege to assist in the building up of the New Jerusalem and to labor therein for the redemption of the dead. Others shall seal blessings upon you in addition to these, even all you desire that are for your good. I now seal you up unto eternal lives, to reign + rule in the celestial glory, and to enjoy all the blessings and glories of the heavens in the name of the Lord Jesus Christ. Amen.
[Blank line]
Patriarchal Blessing upon Don Charles Johnson, born 24th April 1901 in St David, Arizona.

Don Charles, in the name of the Lord Jesus Christ and by authority of the holy priesthood I seal the blessing of your father upon you, that it shall rest upon you + enable you to fulfill every duty that shall be placed upon you. You are of the royal blood of Ephraim by natural descent, entitled to all the power, blessings + priesthood of Abraham, Isaac and Jacob. Your feet shall sand upon a sure foundation, and no power shall turn you away from the truth, for you never shall be tempted more than you are able to bear. A holy being has charge concerning you, who will preserve you in the hour of temptation and danger, that you may do your part in the work of the Lord. And now, inasmuch as you are sick and afflicted, I rebuke all disease from your body and your eyes, that you shall be perfectly healed and made whole; + I seal upon you health and strength, with vigor of

[Page B222L]

1902/June 19/body and of mind and every needful blessing. It is your privilege to do a great work for the living and the dead, whereby you may gain to yourself an exaltation in the celestial glory. You are in the days of your youth but a great and holy work is appointed unto you, and no power of evil shall prevent your fulfilling it. You are entitled to all the blessings pertaining to the priesthood, even to be a patriarch in the Church of J.C. of L.D. Saints, and to fulfill this holy office and calling I seal upon you revelation and prophesy + discernment, with every other blessing necessary to magnify this high and holy calling in the priesthood.

These are but a few of the blessings in store for you, for many others shall be sealed upon you in due time, even all that your heart shall desire, inasmuch as they are expedient for you. I seal you up unto eternal lives, to reign s a King and a Priest in the heavens for ever in the celestial glory in the name of the Lord Jesus Christ. Amen.
[Blank line]

" 26/A heavy rain today, the first for over 7 months. The drouth has caused the death of many cattle, for lack of food and water. Also, there is only a fourth of usual wheat.

Gertrudes Dream.

27/ She dreamed she had passed to the next world and was with Bp. G.W. Seavy, who died a few days previously. He was happy and very busy. Some one showed her two beautiful crowns for her, one for her self and the other given her for the temple work she had done for her friend the Baron Alex. von Wendt (true name "von Wenden) a Russian nobleman who had loved her and wished to marry her. These golden circlets were narrow behind, becoming broad and high in front, with a magnificent. (See page 217, where this is written.

July/ July 1, 1902

1/Having business in El Paso I went there today, and returned home on the 4th While in El Paso I enrolled as Correspondent for the El Paso News.

On my return found Gertrude very much worse.

[Page B223R]

1902/July 2/On Wednesday she was all day in extreme agony, and it was feared she could not survive the day, nor would she, had it not been for the administration of the Elders. She has been very weak ever since, though pain not so serious. She could only speak in a faint whisper to me, and could not bear any talking in usual tone of voice in the room. She sent a note to Bp. Bentley asking him to request all the people to pray for all the week and to pray and fast for her on the next fast day, that she might be healed and freed from her intolerable pains.

During the week the Young Ladies Assn fasted and prayed for her, also other organizations.

6/ Sunday 6th Fast day. At meeting today special prayer was offered for Gertrude, and one speaker said she was one of the noblest spirits among us. After meeting Prest Ivins, Bp. Bentley + Harris, with 6 others, came to her and administered, Prest Ivins as mouth and J.J. Waler anointing. She felt better, and not so full of pain afterwards. She is so weak she can only speak in a faint whisper, and lies as one dead, save her gentle breathing. Oh Father, if it be thy will, I pray thee heal her!

7/ Gertrude a little better, but still very weak

13/ "   Still improving, but very slowly, better one day, worse next.

28/ Went to Casas Grandes on water tax business.

Joel went to El Paso to hunt employment, with several others.

31/ Gov. Col. Miguel Ahumada and a company of 13 others, with Gen.

Angel Martinez paid us a visit. Had a fine meeting, speeches, songs, choir and instrumental music and they were all much pleased.

August/ August 1902

1/ Henry went on his way to Miñaca, for employment. He is still very weak and feeble. Hopes to get tie contract on the hew railroad. Theodore went next day, hoping to get some employment near Henry

9th/ Gertrude improving; hopes soon to be able to sit up.

(3d)/ On the 3d inst.—fast-day, the people prayed + fasted for her, and a dozen Elders administered to her at bedtime and the power of the Lord was in her behalf

[Page B224L]

1902/August 9th/ To day I was employed by Mr. Booker to survey land for him—boundaries only—a tract 360 Sq. miles = 230400 Acres salary as usual—$10.00 per day and my expenses.

" 10/ Very heavy rains ~~all~~ ^to^ day. Much needed. Gertie went out of doors a little while in her wheel chair + enjoyed it much before the rain. In the afternoon Guy became quite sick, and very much so by evening. Josephine is getting better, but cannot sit up yet. I have been quite feeble for some days past, so I could hardly go to administer to the sick around us, but feel a little better now.

11/ Still raining. Guy some better.

12/ The suspension foot bridge across the river gave way today, and three boys narrowly escaped death in the high waters. It was put up in a few days, again, in a narrower place. River unfordable still

    I appointed W.C. McClellan to preside at next meeting of high priests, as I expect to be absent.

13/ Guy still quite sick

15/ Friday. I started to Casas Grandes to go on my Survey. Found Booker not quite ready.

16/ Spent day getting ready for a start

17/ Left Casas Grandes. Crossed the river at Coralitos, Very dangerous.

Nearly 2 hours getting both wagons over. Water just at top of horse's backs, + running swiftly.

18/ Found no one in Janos who could show me any of the corner monuments of proposed survey. Camped 12 miles farther, on Palitada Springs creek.

19/ Took Latitude, and prepared Stakes. <u>Lat 30° 55' N.</u>

20/ Señor Ascanio Azcarate came and showed me one Monument on the line, and I began Survey.

21/ Sr. Zapata came, to show me corner monument. I continued the Survey, finishing on Sept. 3. The line passed in places among high and steep mountains, in other places for miles together in shallow lakes and swamps formed by the almost constant rains. Mosquitoes! No end to the clouds of them—almost unbearable. Having to move camp often, and making my bed on wet ground my bedding became wet, and for weeks I slept in wet

[Page B225R]

1902/Sept. 3/bedding, but by the blessing of the Lord I was strengthened for the toilsome work, and the wet bed did not seem to hurt me.

One day I sent my teamster to Diaz for provisions. He returned empty, and said he passed through 5 miles of water before reaching Diaz, the river having overflowed to a width—both sides of 7 or 8 miles.

On our return, we expected to Camp at the same place as before when we crossed the river at Coralitos, but found it impossible, as the water was all around us, and still pouring out from the river in a vast sheet. In the next morning our tent stood on the only dry ground for a long distance around, the water still rising. I left the men and with one team started alone for home, as I lived on same side of the river. The rest of the party all lived on the other side. A Cowboy and his horse were drowned the day before we came to the crossing. Leaving the camp I traveled miles through Water before reaching higher land.

Sept. 6/Found Gertrude still in bed, the rest of the family as usual, and our peach trees, many of them broken down by weight of fruit.

11/ Went to see Booker to get my pay for my work. He was away, so on next day I started home with Ray Pratt [in margin: 12] and carriage.

Before we reached the river, our horses got stuck in a deep mud hole, caused by overflow of the river. They went in half way up their sides, and then fell down in it. We had a hard time to get out, by help of Mexicans who came along. When we reached the river we dared not try to ford it, as the water was higher than our carriage and would have washed it away. We did not know how to get back to Dublan, through that deep mud hole, but a Mexican came along and piloted us around it through his field. May our Father ever bless him.

13/ Crossed the river in another place, not so deep but very swift and somewhat dangerous. A man's team was drowned there two days previously. A Mexican on horseback hitched a lariat to the end of our wagon tongue and to the horn of his saddle, and so with difficulty we crossed Safely, and thanked our Father sincerely. Got home

[Page B226L]

1902/Sept. 13/late at night

17/ To day Elvira's son James H. Johnson, of St David, Cochise Co. Arizona, came, to go to the Academy this term of School. He is 20 years old, and 6 ft 4in tall.

21/ To day it seems as if our long continual rains are about over. The sun Shines. Much fruit, spread out to dry has spoiled, owing to the damp atmosphere.

22/ Sold some apples, pears and peaches, to day $12.84 We have given away several wagon loads rather than have them spoil, as many bushels have, on the ground.

27/ Recd check from Booker for my pay, $259.00 Mex. equal to $105.00 in gold. This for nearly a months work, but glad indeed to get it.

28/ In looking through my papers I found the following letter from my wife Jesse Helen, explaining why she did not come home to me in Arizona, but stopped in Alameda, Cal.:—

> "1860 Central Avenue
> Alameda, Cal. Nov. 30. 1887

My dear friend

You surely have not received two letters which I sent to you. One addressed

Great Western Hotel, Sacramento, and the other to Vallejo. In my last I wanted to see you and tell you fully why I thought it safer not to go South with you. D.P.A. Sent to Vallejo a long letter telling everything. How they found it out I know not, and they sent to know if I was there and my Aunt telegraphed back to him that I was not there, that I had been and gone again, and that she knew nothing about me. They say if they find you they will make you suffer, you know in what way, I presume. That was the motive for me acting as I have done since I knew of that D.P.A's letter. My Aunt thought also it was better for me to go away, so that she would feel free, should anything serious take place. I have been expecting to see you all week, but my friend did not come. I have felt very

[Page B227R]

impatient at times, almost forget what I was about, I would be so very absent minded. Will you, my friend, Send me Bp. W. Bassett's address, so that I can write to Ma without sending it to the house. Did you see Ma, or Mrs. Russell last time you were in the city? I have Sent to Bowie for my freight, 2 boxes, both weighing 525 pounds, marked J.H. Grieve, Smithville, Arizona Via Bowie Station S.P.R.R. Via C.P.R.R. They were prepaid before I left. I sent for them on the 9th inst, but I have not received any word from the freight agent. You might make inquiry about them and confer favor upon me by so doing. When you write again sign as formerly. I was surprised that morning when I was asked about you, and they wished to know if it was so, so that she might know what was best to be done. It was immediate action, for we knew not the hour that some one might enter in to intercept me. We went to S.F.C. (San Francisco) Spent the day there, it being Thursday. On Saturday I Started for Alameda, and here I am still. I do feel so lonely at times with no one to talk to about things that are nearest and dearest to me. You know what it is, having been in the same position yourself, yet I can always find a refuge in prayer. Oh! never forget me at any time, even though we are separated by distance. I think the old adage is true "absence makes the heart grow fonder." Dont you think that California is a great Sabbath breaking State? I think it is really worse than the European Continent; hardly any one here observes the Sabbath. Last Sunday I rode on the train to Alameda Wharf. I had my book and writing tablet with me. I did feel so refreshed while sitting on the End of the pier with the sea breeze blowing upon my temples. It finally drove all my headache away. Each one seems to go to the most places of amusement on Sunday. All week it has been raining off + on. My written address is Miss Jessie Russell c/o Mrs. Wertheimer, 1860 Central Avenue, Alameda, Cal. You may guess why I take this name. I am having a little experience just now, which I think

[Page B228L]

1902/Letter of/Jessie's/may do me good in after life. I hope you will find every one well in the South, also Gertrude's leg improving. Write me a long letter as soon as you can. To night I felt I could not go to sleep without writing you a few lines. If we taste the bitter before hand we shall appreciate the sweet when it comes along. I am well, hoping you and the others are the same.

I am Your a.b.c.

P.S. Address all letters to the following address until I tell you to change. a.b.c.

Miss Jessie Russell c/o Mrs. Wertheimer
1860 Central Avenue, Alameda Cal."

    This letter from my dear wife explained to me what I could not before understand of her doings in California. She did what she considered was for the best, though it parted us forever in this life—but not in the next. Then I shall meet her again—and oh, what joy! Wicked men and women can have no power there to hurt or trouble; as she observes above "If we taste the bitter we appreciate the sweet when it comes along." And so, <u>all</u> our experiences, bitter as well as sweet, are necessary to our perfection. She was one of the pure in heart, and a dear female friend who knew her well said to me she was an almost perfect woman, if any can be found. Having received <u>all</u> the ordinances and endowments, she has made her calling and election and exaltation sure. If I meet her again in glory, I must do the same. With all my troubles and sorrows concerning her, I thank Our Father for her, and pray I may so live as to retain not only her but <u>all</u> whom God has given me.
[Blank line]

Oct. 8/ Up to this time we have been very busy taking care of our fruit, selling some and drying and preserving as much as we could. Our peaches were so plenty of the trees that many broke down, as did also Apricots. We had besides apples, pears, plums and a few almonds. We gave away one or two wagon loads of peaches, and many bushels wasted on the ground.

[Next two pages—letter to JHM from Gertrude dated Aug-5-05 C Juarez.]

[Page B229R]

1902/Oct. 17/I have been doing some mapping for various persons Lyman having recently written to me that he wished to buy my Survey and draughting instruments. I wrote accepting his offer, and telegraphed him for money to come to Utah.

I am much hampered for money in consequence of the cessation of my pension since last June. The Pension Commissioner wrote saying my pension would be discontinued because I had been actually in Mexico in the war of 1846–8, nor even on the way to "the front." I answered that I <u>had</u> been on the way there, traveling 1300 miles to Newport Barracks, where I was discharged in July 1848, and had also Served on Recruiting Service. To date I have received no reply.

Oct. 12th/ To day Gertrude had suddenly a fearful convulsion and for a long time we feared she would die any moment, by cessation of heart action; but by the power of the priesthood and our Father's blessing she was finally saved to us. She has had many suck attacks,—always striking her in an instant, beginning at the pit of her Stomach.

Nov. 27/ Bp. J.C. Bentley and his wife Gladys desiring me to bless and dedicate their home.[76] I did so to day, a numerous company being invited. We all had thanksgiving dinner. Susan walked there and back, resting several times on the way. Rheumatism in her knees, tired her much.
[Blank line]

~~Nov. 1~~/ Started with Gertrude to St Luke's hospital in El Paso Texas.

Oct. 31/Friday/Carried her on a bed to Dublan, 16 miles, over rough road. I blessed her before starting, that she might endure the journey, for it was

---

76. The dedication of a home is a blessing performed by a holder of the Melchizedek Priesthood. As a patriarch, Martineau was probably asked to perform many home dedications. For example, Maude Kenner recounted Martineau's dedicatory prayer on her home when she was a young girl: "Among the many beautiful and prophetic things he said was: 'This home will be protected from the elements, and no evil disposed persons will have power to enter; and also there will be many important events held here, and prominent people will come, and they will feel a good influence and be reluctant to leave.'" Kenner then recalled how Martineau's words were literally fulfilled when, after one of the worst storms in the history of Utah, the home was left undisturbed. See Kenner, "Dedication of Our Home." Also see entry for August 25, 1905.

feared the shaking and jolting might kill her. But the Lord blessed her so that she stood the journey much better than we hoped.

As we entered Dublan, I met Prest Helaman Pratt, who desired me to stay and survey for platting the contemplated line of canal to fill the Natural reservoirs, for Dublan fields.

Nov. 12/ Sat. I worked on Survey to day and on Monday 4th It is probably the last Surveying I will do. My dear Susan wishes me to quit surveying, as too hard and too much exposure for me; and when I ask—"how will I get means to support us all," she says "Some other way will open."

[Page B230L]

1902/Nov. 4 3d/I trust He will. I know the Lord loves her, and I believe her faith and prayers will avail much in my behalf. Returned home and found all well. On the 2nd (Saturday) Gertie went on to El Paso, on the R.R. train, arriving at the Hospital very much fatigued by the long day's travel, and Changing transit at Ciudad Juarez to cross to El Paso. Before she left Dublan, in the morning, I blessed her again, for the day's journey, and the Lord honored my ministrations in her behalf. She and her companion, Mrs. Caroline Saville Telford were given a room to themselves, and were kindly received by the Surgeon and nurses. (All this should have been noted earlier)
[Blank line]

Nov. 30/<u>Sunday</u>. Last day of Stake Conference, at which Apostle Hiram Smith, Golden Kimball, Prest Jos L. Taylor of Salt Lake, Sisters Hyde and Brixen from S.L. City were present. I blessed both those sisters at their request. After the last meeting I dedicated and blessed our house + home. Susan's brother Sixtus E. Johnson + wife and others of the family being present.
[Blank line]

Sell city lot./to E.F.T./A few days previously I sold half my residence lot, the upper city lot and Calf pasture adjourning to Edd F. Turley, Anna's husband, for a home for her, that she might be near us. The price was $1200, payable as follows:—Jan. 1, 1903, $300.00 July 1, 1903 $400.00 Jan. 1, 1904 $500.00 with interest from Jan. 1, 1903 @ 10 % pr Annum.

We intend that Gertrude shall live in our house until Guy can build home for her, he being now hardly involved, through a series of ill fortunes, in loss of stock +c Thus we may be near each other for mutual help and comfort.

[Blank line]

Dec. 1/Monday. Finished preparations for journey to Logan. Until the very last I could not make up my mind to go, tho' Lyman had sent me money for the journey, ($50.00) + I could leave Susan well provided for, in money—$50. on order on the Tithing Office, some $70. due from Harly

[Next two pages are a letter from Gertrude, at Juarez, to JHM and dated August 5, 1905. In it, she writes: "I thank Providence you won't have to go into the mountains again and the Surveyor Gen'l is a Mormon so maybe he will help you to get your work thru much sooner so you can soon come home, at least by Conference time."]

[Page B231R]

Johnson, board money from James Johnson, who boards with us and should pay $2.50 per week (equal to about 1$ Amer. money besides what Guy will help on Gertie's account. But I had a dread of leaving Susan to bear alone the care of Gertrude, and a dread of leaving my dear wife, such as I have never before felt. Is it because I am never to return? But I have asked our Father concerning my proposed journey Several times, in view of going to labor for the dead, and the answer every time has been "Go, and you shall be blessed upon your journey, and in your labors while in Utah, and shall not be hurt by change to that cold climate. And Susan and Gertrude, and your home shall be blessed in your absence, even as if you were present with them, for they are in my hands, and my blessing shall be upon them."

And such being the inspiration of the Holy Spirit to me I fear <u>not</u> to go would forfeit the promised blessings. But the parting is sad to me.

Susan and I sat up all night until 5 a.m. of Tuesday [in margin: Dec. 2] Dec. 2 to take mail wagon to the R.R. Station, except about 2 hours sleep for me.

I left Nueva Casas Grandes about 8 a.m. arriving in El Paso about 5 P.M. Went at once to see Gertrude. Found her much improved, and looking will in feature and color.

3/ Cashed Lyman's check and spent some time with dear Gertrude. Got Oranges + bananas +c for her, and left $4.00 to get some things for Susan. Blessed her in the evening and left El Paso at 9.15 P.M. on the Santa Fe

R.R. Took [in margin: 4] Sleeper. Awoke next morning near Albuquerque, + took breakfast there. Los Vegas 1.45 P.M. Trinidad 9.30 P.M. and changed Car, but not train

5/ Pueblo 6.15 a.m. and lay by until 11.55 a.m. Here I met Apostle A.O. Woodruff, just returning from New Orleans. We had a very pleasant time together all the way to S.L. City, relating mutually our experiences. He also invited me to dine on the train

6/<u>Sat</u>. Arrd in S.L. City 10.30 a.m. I went to Bp. Preston's and met a warm welcome.

[Page B232L]

1902/Dec. 7/Sunday. Visited Eliza and went to Virginia's, 9th South 942 West, close to Jordan river. She rushed out to meet me, looking in fine health. The children are fine looking and intelligent, and I feel proud—I should say—thankful for them. Edward Sudbury, her husband, in clerking in Scofield.

8/ Visited Mrs. Woodmansee, and was warmly received, as I could tell her about her daughters in our village. Sherman was taken with sore throat, and as diptheria is very prevalent and fatal, Genie was much alarmed. We were up with him till nearly 1 a.m.

9/ The doctor came and said it was only tonsilitis. I wrote to Gertie and Uncle Benjamin. Prayed for Sherman and felt he would soon recover.

12/ Snoing heavily this morning. Winter is come. Genie went and bought Christmas things for the children, also 3 neck ties for me.

13/ I tested my Aneroid at the U.S. weather bureau.

14/ Stake Conference. Preaching on priesthood by Prest Smith

16/ Went to the temple, + presented names for baptism. Lamans

19/ Saw Prest J.F. Smith about my book of "Pearls." Left it with him for examination and approval.

Yesterday, 18th met Path John Smith. He gave me permission to bless in Cache Co. Said I should ask $2.00 for blessing, stationary and recording, and giving copy. I told him I had never made any charge, and that not one in ten had ever given me anything. He said "the laborer is worthy of his hire." I have always as gladly blessed one who was unable to give anything, as though he had given gold. I esteem it a high honor and privilege to be permitted to seal a blessing upon any one in the authority of the holy patriarchal priesthood, whether I receive anything in return or not.[77] My great anxiety is that I may be <u>worthy</u> for so high and holy a privilege.

Br. Smith also gave me a key by which to know an Ephraimite when not sealing a blessing upon him[78]

21/ Sunday. Memorial service for Joseph the Prophet. Visited Eliza again + invited her to Christmas dinner

[Page B233R]

1902/Dec. 22/Sent magazine to Susan. I am sorry I have nothing else to Send for a christmas gift—except my blessing + love

" 25/ Christmas, but not much of one for me, because my dear wife is not with me. Gean had a nice dinner. I wrote to Susan and others a christmas greeting, having nothing else to send—no money in purse. I have helped Gean's table at times, when she had no money for marketing. In the evening Br. Sudbury and his daughters, Mrs. Jos E Taylor (Clara) Lavina, Gr. dau. Ruth and Lissidore + Fred. Spent a sociable evening.

27/ By invitation took dinner with Prest Jas E. Taylor's family. Also attended a funeral by his request.

---------------- [line across page]----------------------

large and bold: January 1903.
Jan./[Blank line]
1st/ The Sudbury's all came to visit us, also Mr. + Mrs. Peterson (Tip). A pleasant time.

---

77. According to historian D. Michael Quinn, local stake patriarchs charged a fee for their services. In the 1840s the fee was $1 per blessing; by the end of the nineteenth century, the fee increased to $2 per blessing. Patriarchal blessing fees ended in July of 1902, although patriarchs were allowed to accept unsolicited donations. See Quinn, *Mormon Hierarchy: Extensions of Power*, 205. See also note at entry for January 4, 1905.

78. An Ephraimite refers to a person who is of the lineage of the tribe of Ephraim by blood or who is entitled to the Abrahamic blessings of the House of Ephraim. A patriarch usually declares the lineage of the person upon whom he is giving a blessing, but in this case, Smith gave Martineau some special way to recognize an Ephraimite without having to lay hands upon them to pronounce a blessing.

Regulated my Barometer by that in U.S. Weather Office, making mine read like that in the office.

3/ Edd Sudbury came home from Scofield.

5/ Spent an hour or more in Prest J.F. Smith's office looking over my Book of "Pearls." Saw Prests Lund and Winder.

Got a ruby set placed in Susan's ring. Price of stone $10.00

6/ Received permission from the Presidency to baptize over a hundred Lamanites,—Aztecs, and other Mexican indians, Auracanians, and Incas of Peru, also North American indians. Edward + Gean gave me a suit of his clothes, also $7.00 Money to pay on ring.

8th/ My 51st Wedding anniversary, but my dear companion not with me, and this makes it not a pleasant one. To night I leave Gean's, to sleep at Bp. Preston's, so I may take the early train for Logan. I hated to leave Gean, who is lonesome and fearful of burglars and robbers. She has been good and kind to me, and I have been happy with her. Ed. will go back in 2 or 3 days to Scofield, to the store in which he is a clerk.

9/ Left S.L. City 7 a.m. At Logan 11 A.M. Found all the family but Lilla well.

[Page B234L]

1903/Jan. 9/Visited Frank and Lilla. She is almost perfectly deaf and I can hardly make her understand. She often is at a loss, in talking, for a word she needs. She can read well, but cannot write or Spell at all.

Sunday 11/ At First Ward meeting and Spoke.

12/ Wrote to Dr. Robert Nichol, at Miñaca, to pay the bill of $41.00 for repair of my transit which he broke.

Went with Nephi to his home. Cold weather. found them all well. Howard had run away again.

Their baby—James Gaston Martineau, was born April 21. 1901. One of twins. The other one died.

Nephi has nine children in all—living and dead. Lyman 8, Charles 6, Lilla 5, Gean 5 = 33 To those in Arizona and Mexico, 41, Hagberg 6 = 80

14/ Leveled a canal line for Nephi.

16/ Returned to Lyman's. Had a very pleasant visit with Nephi and family. Auretia, the eldest girl, is attending the Brigham Young Academy. Hiward is away.

17/ Sent pension papers, hoping my pension may be renewed, although the Pension Commissioner said it must cease. In Answer to my prayer I am told it shall be continued, and <u>increased</u>. I beleive it.

Recd a letter from Jas F. Smith, President, inserted in previous page.

Sunday 18/ Joined the 1st Ward in Logan, that I may continue in close touch with the Church. Found Walter Lamereaux and wife. Sister J.C. Bentley (Maggie) Specially charged me to hunt them up, as Sister Lamouraux is her sister—Edith May (Ivins) Lamoreaux. They were glad to see one who knew their sister in Mexico, and I like their spirit very much. [Blank line]

Jan. 14/ By letter I learn Theodore and Josephine Thurs--tons baby girl, named Florence—was born Jan. 14

Florence/1903 at 10.45 a.m. About 20 miles South of Miñana in born to T./State of Chihuahua, Mexico

17/ My Cousin, Anna (Mrs. Wm A. Mears) Mears, of Portland,

[Page B235R]

1903/Oregon came to visit us, to stay several days.

Jan. ~~17/~~

24/On 26 Lyman took us to see "Corianton," a Mormon play.[79]

26/[See arrow to line above]
Very cold weather and snow about 8in deep. Good play.

27/ We visited the Agricultural College

---

79. The play, written by Orestes U. Bean, was a fictional drama based on the Book of Mormon narrative described in the book of Alma. The play debuted at the Salt Lake Theater on August 11, 1902. It was produced under the direction of James H. Lewis, with music by George W. Thatcher and a libretto by Kate Thomas.

Received pension (back) $48.00 Thus is verified the word of the Spirit to me. Thus I am learning His voice.

28/With Lyman, Alley, Cousin Mears I went to a Ball of the Social Club, then to Will + Kate Preston's reception.

29/ Cousin Anna Mears went on home to Portland, well pleased with her entertainment in Logan.

31/ Finished my biographical notes for publication in Jensen's new Biographical Work, according to Jensen's request.[80]

Feb./ ------------------ February ---------------------

5/Sent my notes to Jensen.[81]

7/ Blessed Robert + wife and daughter. Very cold weather. 13° below Zero.

[Margin says: Tithing paid. $5.00]

4/ Paid $5.00 Cash tithing
[Blank line]

14/ Got my temple robes finally completed, all except cap.

20/ Endowed to day for Elias Martineau.

    Searched for family names and record in Genealogical Records in the temple. Mears Genealogy found in

Joslin's history of Poultney Vt. page 311
Keim Genealogy   "   400
Mears' Genealogy of 1873 31 pages
Savage's Genl Dictionary Vol. 3   p. 192
Secomb's History of Amherst N.H.   689
Smith's Histy of Peterborough   143
Stiles   "   " Windsor Vol. 2   p. 492

23/Blessed Wm B. Preston Jun.

---

    80. Andrew Jenson, assistant LDS Church Historian, was collecting biographical sketches and photographs for his multi-volume biographical encyclopedia.
    81. Martineau's biographical sketch appears in Jenson's *LDS Biographical Encyclopedia*, 4:156–159. The sketch is very similar to that which appeared in *Tullidge's Histories*. See note at entry for May 17, 1887.

Tues. 24/I was baptized today for 27 Aztec princes + chiefs.

25/I was Endowed for Gaston Martineau[82]

26/I "   "   " John Martineau

27/I "   "   " Peter Martineau

------------------------- March -----------------------

Mch. 2/Searched again for family names in Records.

[Page B236L]

1903/I weighed myself today = 177 lbs. the heaviest in my life.

March 3/ " was baptized for 87 Aztec Kings, princes and Chiefs.

"   4/ " Endowed Peter Martineau, Born 1727

"   6/ " "   Stephen Martineau " 1773

"   7/Blessed Martin D. Cranney

Note) " 4/Son-in-law Frank Nebeker went with others to Mexico desiring me to stay at his house while he is absent.

Mch 10th/ I endowed Peter Haughout, B. 1765.
   Nephi   "   Lord Hutchinson " 1680

12/I endowed Cornelius Martineau
Nephi "   Stephen Martineau

Mch. 13/ My 75th Birthday. My days are drawing to a close. I was invited to dinner at 6 P.M. by Br. W.S. Lamoreaux + Edith. Had a pleasant time. They gave me as birthday present a copy of the New History of the Church. This was the only remembrance received by me.

   I endowed James Guyon, Nephi Endd Dirk Haoghout I recd from Genl

---

82. Gaston Martineau was born ca. 1654 at Bergerac, France. He married Marie Pierre, daughter of Guillaume Pierre and Marie Jourdain, on September 26, 1693, at Norwich, Norfolk, England. Gaston Martineau is believed to have practiced medicine at Bergerac. A Huguenot refugee, Gaston had settled in Norwich after the revocation of the Edit of Nantes in 1685. He was buried in the French or Walloon Church, known as the Church of St. Mary-the-Less in Queen St. See Martineau, *Notes on the Pedigree of the Martineau Family*, 10–16.

Robt T. Burton an old commission of mine, as Capt in Topl Engineers, Genl D.H. Wells Staff dated in 1857.

15/ Recd notice from Comr of Pensions that my pension is disallowed by him. A great loss—my only revenue—only $8.00 per month, but my only income. He gave no reason

16/ I wrote to Senator Thos Kearns about it.

18/I endowed Peter M. Haughout, Nephi Endd Stephen Ketellas

19/Nephi Endowed Jacobus Haughout
I " Egbert "
W.S. Lamoreaux endd Peter Haughout.

In the afternoon and evening had 3 severe Chills. Some said they were Congestive Chills. I dont Know I was quite Sick all night

20/Sick in bed all day

21/Lilla gave me as birthday present a pair of Slippers and $10.00 Cash. Very acceptable in my needs. Rose this morning, but am still quite Weak. Lyman administered to me. Felt blessed.

[Page B237R]

1903/Feel much better today. Blessed Jean Spencer, [in margin: Mch. 22] who is visiting at Lyman's, from S.L. City

23/Still very weak. Sought names in Genl Record.

24/Nephi was baptized to day for 80 Aztec + Peruvian Kings, princes and Chiefs.

25/ Sent $20.00 to Susan as part of R.R. fare from Mexico to S.L. City. Only one third enough, but all I could get.

26/I endowed Nicholas Haughout, 27th Vincent Haughout

31st/Blessed John A. Gordon recd $1.00 Am not well today.

---------------------- April 1903 -----------------------

April 2/Blessed Walter S. Lamoreaux.

Fri " 3/I moved from Lilla's to Lymans, to be early to the train.

4/ Feel quite unwell

Sun. 5/ Started to S.L. City with Lyman + Alley. Arrd at noon + went to Bp. Preston's. Snow last night. Conference.

6/ Attended Conference. On the
[In margin: 7th] Attended Special (private) Priesthood meeting, where some Special instructions were given relative to temple work and garments, aprons +c Proceedings not to be public.[83]

8/ Edward Sudbury returned to Castle Gate.

10/ Spent the day trying to get employment. Tried Fred McCartney chf. Eng. Las Angeles, San P. + S.L.R.R. Nothing to be done. Also Doremus, State Engineer, same answer; Twin Falls Co. (Idaho) same; also Sur. Gen. Anderson, for U.S. Contract for Land Survey. Nothing difinite there now.

13/ Sent to Caygell for pen ($1.62) Arranged with Br. A. Jensen for extension of time for payment of my genealogical record in his book.

15/ Attended funeral of Brigham Young. Met Mrs Hubert White, daughter of Orson Hyde

17/ Recd letter from Eliza Belle Johnson (Martineau (Jesse's wife) with account of her ancestry as far as she knows:–

Her
Great Grandfather, William Johnson, Born Dec. 2. 1785 + (wife) Nancy, born June 28. 1788. Also his son, her Grandfather, William Eaton Johnson (Eldest Child) Born 24 Jan. 1812 (Their other Children were Dewitt C. Johnson. Born 9th Feb. 1813

[Page B238L]

1903/   Ansil L. Johnson. Born 14 Aug. 1814
April 16th/David B. " " 14 Feb. 1816 (Daniel B.)
    Welcome W. " " 26 Oct. 1817
    Harty J. " " 16 May 1819
    David M. " " 7 Oct. 1821
    John L.H. " " 3 Feb. 1826
    Warren " " 5 Mch. 1830

---

83. For an account of this meeting, see Rudger Clawson's diary for April 7, 1903, in Larson, ed., *A Ministry of Meetings*, 577–579.

Note/<u>Note</u>. Warren was an officer in the Confederate Army + has not been heard of since the civil war.

about two indents: Her <u>Grandfather</u> William Eaton Johnson married Mary W. Dickinson in 1832, of South Williamstown Mass.
They had four children, as follows:—Her Father
<u>William Warren</u> Johnson. Born 10 Nov. 1832. Died at Sharon, Wis. 18th July 1862, a private in 13th Wisconsin Re

Caroline H. Born 18th Sep. 1836. Now living in Hadley Mass.

Eliza Mills, " 11 July 1834 Died 18 Mch. 1843

Edward Eaton " 21st Aug. 1845. Now in Los Angeles, Cal.

note/------ Her <u>Grandfather</u>, <u>William Eaton</u> Johnson died 16 Jan. 1889. Her <u>Grandmother</u> died in 1872
[Blank line]
Her Mother was
Mary E. Leavitt, Born in Stark, N.H. 14 July 1839
and was married in Delavan, Wisconsin, 1st Jan.
1857. Her children were

Carrie B. Johnson. born 24th Dec. 1857. Died 28 Feb. 1858
Willis Eaton, Born 8 Dec. 1859. Lives now in Passadina Cal.
Eliza Belle Johnson (Martineau) Born 21st Dec. 1861 in Sharon Wisconsin.

Her Uncle Edward had family genealogy back to 1626.
when William Johnson married Nancy Eaton, in London England. All the Johnsons were early settlers in Mass.
One of them was named Barrykiah.

Her Grandmother Leavitt's maiden name was
<u>Sarah Spaulding</u>, a descendant of Hannah Dustin of early indian war (in Hadley) fame.

Five cousins have now joined the Church.

18/ Not well. In bed all day.

23/ I Endowed Garrett Cozine

[Page B239R]

1903/[Blank line]

April 23/ Lilla was nearly burned to death to day, while burning waste paper +c in the yard. A gust of wind caught a flame on her apron. She tried to extinguish the flames, but could not pull off the burning clothing. Then she ran into the house, but the hired girl was too excited to help her any. So Lilla ran out doors hoping some one would help her, and fighting the flames all the time. Fortunately a man came to her rescue + put out the flames, which had burned both arms and shoulders, right hand very deeply, also her back and side. Her corsets had partially preserved her vitals. Her eyebrows and front hair were burned, but her face escaped. Had she not been dressed in woollen skirts and underclothes she would surely have been burned to death. It happened in the forenoon, and all day she passed from one chill into another, and the doctors feared, that is her weak previous condition, the shock would kill her, but by the great blessing of the Lord + administrations of priesthood, she was saved. Prompt surgical assistance was at hand and all was done to ease her pains.

Apr. 24/ I endowed Mr. Beatly to day. Heard of Lilla's burn and tried to get to the train in time but failed to do so.

25/ Went to Logan to see Lilla

26/ She is resting easily as could be expected, and was glad to see me. Poor girl! She met me with a smile.

27/ Recd letter from Senator Kearns relative to the Stoppage of my pension. He advised a special pension bill for me in next session of Congress. I wrote him a full Statement of my case in return.

29/ I endowed Peter Cozine

Thurs 30/ I " Cora Cozine. Received letter from Susan. She is in S.L. City, having arrived last Wednesday at Midnight, with Edd Sudbury.

--------------------- May 1903 -----------------------

May 1/ Went to S.L. City, and found Susan well. I was very thankful to have her with me again after 5 months separation. We have become <u>necessary</u> to each other.

[Page B240L]

[Left margin of first paragraph sideways says: <u>May</u> 1. 1903. A girl born to G.A. + Emm Martineau/in Chuichupa, Mex. We named her Anita,/ Mexican pet name for Anna, on July 8th 1903.]

1903/May 1./Susan was four days on her journey, being detained 12 hours on the way at Pueblo. She came in company with John M. Cannon and Bp. Benion. Br. Cannon was as kind and attentive all the way as a son could have been, doing all that was possible for her comfort. May Our Father ever bless him and his. She was joined at Castle Gate, Utah, by our-Son-in-law Edward Sudbury, who took her to his house in S.L. City on arrival at midnight. They had never met previously. She said Gertrude, while desiring her mother to go, dreaded her absence, saying "Oh Ma, no one can pray for me and do for ~~you~~ me as you do." Susan had prayed for guidance as to going, and felt it right and expedient to go now, and that Gertie would suffer no ill by her going away. She was also told she should make the journey in peace, safety and comfort, and no accident should view, all which was verified. I myself, had the same testimony in answer to my inquiry. What a blessed privilege to be able to ask Our Father for guidance, and be taught! In this privilege my dear Susan is greatly blessed, as has been shown many times to my own knowledge.

Sat. May 2/ I entered temple work in my record. Susan and Virginia and myself visited Bp. W.B. Preston, but all were absent except Alley Martineau, my gr-daughter. After getting back to Gean's Susan had a sinking spell such as she has had before. Blessed by administration.

" 4/ Edward returned to Castle Gate. Sherman, his son, who has been very sick for about ten days, is about well.

5/ I found my adopted son Nels L. Hagberg to day. I had not seen him for ten years.

Thur. 12/ Visited ~~Br. +~~ Sis. H.A. White, and blessed ~~them~~ her.

Sun. 17/ Visited at Whites, and blessed him and his daughter Hazel White. Went to Gean's in a storm of rain and Snow.

Tues. 19/ Went to Sur. Genl Ed. H. Anderson to obtain a survey Contract, and to ascertain prices for work.[84] I find there must be surveyed 63 full townships, 58 fractional do. connection lines 100, besides base lines, meridians,

---

84. This is in reference to the opening of Uintah Reservation land for sale, provided by an act of Congress, May 27, 1902. The earlier discovery of gilsonite and other asphalt

[Page B241R]

Standard parallels, and meander lines, in all about 9000 miles of lines, including some resurveys + boundaries.

May 1/Note/ I learn by letter that a baby girl was born to Nephi + ^Albert +^ Emma on Friday May 1. She weighed 11 lbs.

May 19/ Conf- By letter from Charles—he says he is called on a Mission to the Middle States, to go in October next.

To day I went with Hagberg and visited his burial lot in S.L. City cemetery, and found also our own graves. May 20/Wed. Began work in S.L. temple. I endowed Robert Blake

21/ Endowed Thomas Blake. Heavy rain. Eliza endowed Lady Lucy Rachel Stanhope.

22/ Today Charles came to S.L. City and began work in Oregon Short Line R.R. Shop.

25/Monday. To day made bid for survey in Uinta indian Reservation as follows:-

For Subdivision township lines, per mile $16.00
" Connecting lines   17.00
" Township Extensions   18.00
" Meridian lines   22.00
" Standard Parallels   23.00
" Base, and Meridian lines   24.00
[Blank line]

---

minerals on the reservation attracted the interest of ranchers, water users, and farmers to the natural resources located there and in the Uintah Basin. On September 1, 1905, after a series of congressional acts, the federal government withdrew over 1,100,000 acres for the Uintah National Forest and 56,000 acres in 1909 for the Strawberry Valley Reclamation project, throwing the remaining reservation land open for public sale. See also "Opening of the Uintah Reserve," *Deseret Evening News*, March 18, 1904, 1–2. The instructions and stipulations for the disposition of unallotted lands on the Uintah Indian Reservation were outlined in Theodore Roosevelt's Proclamation, "Opening of the Uintah Indian Reservation Lands in the State of Utah." See Fuller, "Land Rush in Zion," 186–249, and Mackay, "Strawberry Valley Reclamation Project," 82–89.

Up to this time I have tried in many ways to get employment of Some kind, but unsuccessfully so far.

But in answer to my prayer that my way may be opened to obtain means for our support I have received an answer that it shall be, and speedily; but how I cannot tell. I have Small hope of obtaining a U.S. Survey contract, as there are more applicants than contracts to be let, and I am now unknown here,—a new generation has grown up, who are known in the Sur. General's Office.[85]

29th/Friday. Today Prest T. Roosevelt visited the city. A grand reception was given him, both in street parade and in the Tabernacle, where he spoke to 1200 people.[86]

June 1, 1903

Mon 1/Attended dedication of Barratt Hall. Grand.

[Page B242L]

1903/June 2/By invitation Susan and I went to visit John M. Cannon, in Granite Stake, and had a pleasant time.

Wed 3/ I endowed Wm Pitt (Earl Chatham) Susan endowed our dear Dora, and Eliza Endd Lois Hutchinson.

I had Eight couples sealed. (See temple record)

4/ I endowed Robt Pitt. Susan Endd Louisa Grenville We visited Susan West Smith, widow of Geo. A. Smith

5/ I endd Thos Pitt. Susan endd Hester Pitt.

We visited Br. Herbert A. White and remained all night. Bp. John Neff of Forest Ward was present, a good man, full of the Spirit. We blessed each other and had a glorious time. The Lord said to Sister Mary Hyde

---

85. Martineau had good reason to be doubtful of being awarded a contract. He was, by this time, aged and relatively unknown to the younger generation of surveyors. General Anderson was then compiling bids and it was made known that "Much of the work cannot be done without difficulty, especially that portion which takes in the rugged peaks of the Uintah range of mountains, some of them towering to an altitude of over 13,000 feet." From "Uintah Reservation Survey," *Deseret Evening News*, June 20, 1903, 5.

86. President Theodore Roosevelt was in Utah and made stops in Ogden and Salt Lake City as he passed through the state. See "All Hail the Nation's Chief," *Deseret Evening News*, May 28, 1903, 1.

White concerning us who were present, that we were "One with God and His son Jesus Christ."

[In margin is: June 9.1903. A girl baby born to/Nephi and Emma]

6/Sat. I blessed their daughter, Urania White, who had greatly desired a blessing from under my hands. Also blessed Sisters Lena Bell (Mrs. Davis) and C.W. Peterson Lenard. Had a time of rejoicing. Went to Gean's.

Tues. 9/ Mother, Gean and I went to Saltair bathing resort.

Wed. 10/ I endowed Charles Sprague. Too wet for Susan to go.

11/ " " Joseph May, Susan could not go.

12/ " " Richard Dexter. Susan Endd Elizabeth Mears.

I had Sealed Mr. + Mrs. Robert Pitt
  " " Wm + Mrs. Wm Pitt
  " " Thos. " " Thomas Pitt

Sat 13/Recd letter from Lyman, with $5.00. Wants to Come to Logan tomorrow, with Scandinavian excursion.

Saw President Joseph F. Smith and gave him, for his father, Hyrum Smith, my sister Lucretia, to be Hyrums wife.

[Note: margin left of above paragraph seems to say, in old, shaky hand: Changed to]

He also gave me permission to endow Lamanites for whom I have been endowed.

While in the city I had baptisms performed of 20 females of our family kindred. Sisters White and Peterson came to visit us before we should leave.

Sun. 14/ We went to Logan with excursion. Virginia also.

15/ Gean returned home.

16/ Letter from Henry, who is very sick in City of Chihuahua, Mex; he fears he may die.

[Page B243R]

1903/[Blank line]

Wed. June 7/ I endd John Dexter, Dominic Bodrero endd John Louis Pascal, a Piedmonte Martyr.

18/ I endd Robt Oguier "

19/   " John Dexter

24/ To night Lilla Nebeker's little Marjorie was lost. A large number hunted with lanterns through the city and big canal, the alarm bell rang, and there was quite an excitement until nearly 3 a.m. when she was found asleep and safe. An anxious time indeed. We feared she was drowned in the Canal.

25/ I endd Philip Henry Stanhope

26/ Susan and I went to Nephi's, at Riverside on visit.

July 1903.

July 8/We returned to Logan.

" 10/ I endd Mr. Burrows. Sister Willard Cranny End Mrs James Mears.

" 15/   " Robt Greenhow, Susan, Mrs Sarah Hutchinson.
         Mrs. Cranney, Bethia "

I had Sealed
Richd Dexter and Mrs. Richd Dexter
John Dexter   "   "   John Dexter

Susan 15/Sick/ This evening at 7 P.M. while at dinner Susan was taken Suddenly with a very serious Chill. We got her to bed with severe headach and hot fever. I sat up all night and fanned and attended her as best I could

16/ Susan very sick all day and night.

17/ Susan has congestion of the lungs with very hot fever, and is threatened with pneumonia. Lyman called Dr. Budge, who pronounced her in much danger. Does not know if she can live. I am with her every hour, night and day, doing all I can. The thought that she may leave me is agonizing.

18/ Susan Seems a little better,—fever not so hot. I am notified a contract as U.S. Dep. Surveyor is mine.[87]

---

87. Martineau was sent a letter requesting recommendations supporting his technical and financial ability to carry out the contract. The letter awarding him the contract was dated two days after this entry. The contract came with a liability of $4,453. Edward H.

19/ Wrote to Sur. Genl Anderson about Contract.[88]

20/ Susan a litter better. I laid down and slept about an hour—my first since Susan was taken sick. I have eaten scarcely anything, and Susan nothing except a little milk.

[Page B244L]

1903 July/21/Susan some better. I laid down 4 hours, a great help to me. Lyman has sat up twice, half or more the night which enabled me to lie down.

Anderson to James H. Martineau July 13, 1903 and July 20, 1903, Letters Sent, Surveyor General's Office, Vol. 39, July 6–October 20, 1903, 32 and 68. Martineau was one of eighteen surveyors, out of twenty-nine bidders, who were awarded contracts. See "Contracts Awarded," *Salt Lake Daily Herald*, July 12, 1903, 1, and "Contracts Awarded," *Vernal Express*, August 8, 1903, 2. For more on the requirements of deputy surveyors, see Agnew, "The Government Land Surveyor as a Pioneer," 370–371.

88. This letter was in response to Surveyor General Anderson's request for recommendations as to Martineau's ability to carry out his contract. Martineau wrote:

> In reply, I will say there are none able to judge, here, of my technical ability in surveying, and I must therefore refer you to previous survey contracts executed by me under direction of Sur. Genl Nathan Kimball ($6500.00) about the year 1878, and one under Sur. Genl Solomon, about 1881, which were accepted & paid after inspection in the field, without demur.
>
> I also executed several contracts in Arizona, under Sur. Genl Royal A. Johnson and Levi Manning, about 1893 and later, which were also found all right on inspection, and accepted.
>
> I have also done a geodetic survey for Smithsonian Institute, Washington D. C. in 1868, on completion of U. P. R. R. Survey, in which I acted in location and next as Construction Engineer. In this, I finished a work begun by J. B. Blickensderfer Chief of Construction, U. P. R. R. and which he left me to finish.
>
> In this I ran observations by triangulation from a point in Nevada, to Ogden, Utah. Triangulating from mountain peak to peak. The middle & highest peak in Promontory range in this range, was at this time named for me—Mt. Martineau—as the first who had triangulated to & from it. I am familiar, from 49 years practical work in all kinds of surveying except marine surveys, including hydraulic work for canals, dams & city water works-actual experience in each, from points in Idaho to Mexico, states of Chihuahua and Sonora.
>
> I will guarantee my technical work—or no pay.
>
> As to financial ability: I have previously borrowed money to begin and carry on the work at the Deseret National Bank, giving the Bank power of attorney to receive and hold pay for my contract from the Government. In Arizona, I did the same with Consolidated Bank of Tucson and a Bank in Phoenix. I expect to secure funds now in a similar manner. In my Utah Surveys Wm Jennings and Capt. Hooper were my sureties as bondsmen. I have offers, now, from two Companies to furnish bonds. My wife is quite sick at present, as soon as I can leave her I will see you in the city, and give you any other needful information.

James H. Martineau to Edward H. Anderson, July 20, 1903, Letters Received, Surveyor General's Office, Vol. 25, April 3–July 18, 1903, letter #6219, CSGUT.

22/ Susan better. An agent of a bonding company came to me, to let them be my bondsmen, to amount of $9000.00 on my Survey Contract, which is for $4453.00 I made arrangements for bonds, and must pay the Company $22.50 premium. Notified to go at once to S.L. City to file ^Execute^ Contract and bonds.

23/ Borrowed $6.00 from Frank, to go to the city

24/ Went to the city. Signed Contract, and received the "Manual" of instructions for the survey.[89] Went to Gean's but she was gone to Castle Gate. So I went to White's who received me with much joy. remaining all night. By request I blessed him and her.

25/ Filed my bond for $8906.00 My bondsmen are United States Fidelity and Guaranty Comp. Baltimore, Md.

My contract binds me to make full returns of my survey on or before Sept. 30.1904. Cannot get any money at any bank. Returned to Logan.

Eva's baby/born/At 7.45 P.M. Eva + Charles' little boy was born. All was well with Eva. Charles was in S.L. City.

Sun 26/ Quarterly Conference. Susan much better.

27/ Wrote to Coz N.B. Van Slyke to borrow money to Carry on my Survey.[90]

Blessing/on 26th/ Before starting home yesterday I visited Prest J. F. Smith and asked a blessing from him, that I may be blessed in performing my contract, and for blessings in general.

He said "Yes. I love to bless a good man." He closed the doors, and with Prest J.R. Winder gave me a grand blessing, according to my desire, ending by saying "my last days shall be among my very best days." I was greatly comforted + strengthened.

---

89. A request for Martineau to call at the Surveyor General's office and sign the contract and bond was sent two days earlier. Edward H. Anderson to James H. Martineau July 22, 1903, Letters Sent, Surveyor General's Office, Vol. 39, July 6–October 20, 1903, 85.

90. By this time, Napoleon Bonaparte Van Slyke (1822–1909) was president of the First National Bank in Madison, Wisconsin. Born to Daniel Van Slyke and Laura Mears (Martineau's aunt), he served as assistant quartermaster general of Wisconsin during the Civil War, and at various times was a member of the city council, University Board of Regents, and State Historical Society Board of Curators. See N. B. Van Slyke, Papers, Wisconsin Historical Society.

28/ Susan sat up a little while for the first time.

29/ A letter from Albey L. Sherman, Susan's cousin saying help to Survey may be had among his sons and family.

[Page B245R]

1903/Old Folks Party in Logan. A very fine entertainment.

July 31/Afternoon. I went to Nephi's, to level for a canal for him.

August

1/Leveled for him all day, and found a route by which he may bring waste water to his land! <u>Mosquitoes</u>!

Sun. 2/ Returned to Logan. Found Special instructions for my survey, which I am to sign and return.[91]

3/ Signed and mailed instructions. Made sketch of the ground to be surveyed. My work includes approx-

Base line	4 miles
Guide Meridian (special)	17 "
Township Boundaries	39 "
Section lines, subdivision	200 "
	------
	260 miles.

It consists of T.1N.–R.1E.   T.4N.–R.1E
 T.1N.–R.2E   T 2N –R.2E   T.1N –R.1W
 T.2N.–R.1E   T 2N.–R.1W   T.3N –R.1W
 T.3N.–R.1E

Much of it joins E. bdy. of Uintah Indian Reservation, and it extends North into foothills of the Uintah Mountain range, peaks of which are 13000 ft.[92]

---

91. Four copies of special instructions for his contract and bond were sent to Martineau to sign and return. A follow up letter was mailed requesting him to sign and return special instructions at once. Edward H. Anderson to James H. Martineau, July 31, and August 3, 1903, Letters Sent, Surveyor General's Office, Vol. 39, July 6–October 20, 1903, 128, 150, CSGUT.

92. Martineau's surveying contract included areas that took in some of the most rugged mountainous terrain in the Uintas. See US Department of the Interior, Map, "Part of Uinta Indian Reservation, Utah."

Aug. 4/ Susan had a relapse today. We, Lyman and I, administered, and she at once became better.

Received word from Sur. Genl Anderson my contract and bonds are accepted, all right.[93] Susan dresses herself.

10/ At this date Susan is well in lungs and body, but is very weak in her knees, and hardly able to walk. Her bosom had been blistered 15 times and she had taken much medicine to relieve congestion of the lungs. I am very thankful she is thus spared to me. We went today by invitation to Patriarch Lorenzo H. Hatch, where we blessed each other and our wives, and had a day to be remembered. We also blessed br Hatch's daughter, who was visiting there, and comforted her much.

[In margin, sideways: My/ Blessing]

My Blessing by Br. LH Hatch

Beloved Brother James, in the name of Jesus Christ of Nazareth I have placed my hands upon thy head in accordance with the desire of thy heart, and seal upon thee a patriarchal blessing.

[Page B246L]

1903/Aug. 10/ Behold I say unto thee the Lord is well pleased with thy labors and the integrity of thy heart. His guardian Angels have watched over thee, and thy life has been wonderfully preserved. Thou hast received great blessings and manifestations. The Lord has heard thy prayers and there is a crown of eternal life prepared for thee, and a mansion which has been prepared also, and in thy ministry thou hast been greatly blessed. And in thy calling as a Patriarch in the church it is the will of the Lord that you should lift up your voice as with the sound of a trumpet and bless the congregations of Israel, and lay your hands upon those who desire blessings and fear not, for whatsoever you seal

---

93. Martineau acknowledged receipt of the letter dated August 3. He signed and returned the special instructions, and asked for the map covering ground in his contract be made larger in scale so as to be more easily read. The following day, Surveyor General Anderson mailed to the commissioner duplicates of Contract No. 265, delineating all townships and ranges to be surveyed by Martineau. The letter also included Martineau's signed oath of office. James H. Martineau to Edward H. Anderson, August 4, 1903, Letters Received, Surveyor General's Office, Vol. 25, April 3–July 18, 1903, letter #6275; Edward H. Anderson to Commissioner, General Land Office, Washington, D. C., August 5, 1903, Letters Sent, Washington, Vol. 12, June 30, 1903–April 9, 1904, pp. 72–73, CSGUT.

on earth shall be acknowledged in the heavens. For this purpose thy life has been preserved, and the Lord will remember thee in thy labors and He will lengthen out thy days till thou art satisfied, for thou art entitled to every blessing that has been conferred upon thee, and thy enemies shall be confounded. The Lord is well pleased with thy labors in His holy temples. Lay the charge and responsibility for the continuation of this great work upon your sons and daughters. The Holy angels will yet minister unto them and they shall obtain the names of thy kindred, and the chain of the priesthood shall be made perfect. This day shall be a day of memorial to thee The Lord has given unto thee a numerous posterity, and of thy increase there shall be no end. They are heirs to the fulness of the priesthood, and they shall become obedient, if it needs be, with the things they suffer. Rejoice and be exceedingly glad, for this blessing is given to comfort thy heart. Thou shalt be blessed, and shall never lack for friends or means, for all things are in the hands of thy Heavenly Father. I seal all these blessings with thy former blessings, and say unto thee thou shalt obtain ^them unto^ the fulness, even unto the Godhead, for this blessing has been sealed upon thee, to reign and rule in the house of Israel forever.

[Page B247R]

There is no good gift that shall be witheld from thee. And I rebuke the power of the Enemy and say unto thee live humble and these words shall all be verified. I pronounce these blessings by the authority of the holy priesthood and in the name of Jesus Christ. Amen.
[Blank line]
Susan's blessing, same time + place.

Beloved Sister Susan in the name of Jesus Christ of Nazareth I have placed my hands upon thy head, and I seal upon thee a patriarchal blessing in connexion with all the blessings that have been promised unto thee by the Father and the Patriarchs, and say unto thee they are renewed upon thy head this day. The Lord has watched over thee and thy tribulations. He has witnessed thy tears, and thy husband has been greatly blessed by the prayers you have offered up in is behalf. Your children and your children's children shall be remembered unto the latest generation, and there shall be not one of them lost, for thou hast received all the blessings of the house of the Lord. When thou hast been in great peril the angel of the Lord has gone before thee in thy journeys. They that would have destroyed thy life have been turned aside. Lift up thy voice with thanksgiving and encourage thy children to go forth and perform their duties. Thou hast been a great comfort, + thy words have Encouraged many to walk upright before the Lord. Thy name is recorded in the Lamb's Book of Life. Thou art a descendant of Joseph that was sold into Egypt and through the loins of Ephraim. This day shall be a day of remembrance and these words shall be handed down to thy posterity. Thou shalt stand in thy lot and place with thy husband, and the holy ordinances that have been conferred upon thee shall all be verified, and then shalt be associated and reign as a Queen and priestess ~~with~~ and be exalted with thy husband + inherit the mansion that has been prepared for thee in

[Page B248L]

1903/Aug. 10./in the celestial kingdom. Continue to pray for thy husband and thy prayers shall be heard, and the Lord will watch over him in his labors, and he shall find favors with those who employ him, + everything shall be overruled for his good. I seal all these blessings with every blessing thy heart can desire in righteousness with thy former blessings by the authority of the holy priesthood and in the name of Jesus Christ. Amen.
[Blank line]

In these two blessings the spirit of revelation has been powerfully exhibited. Br. Hatch, knowing almost nothing of events in my life in the last 20 years has spoken as if well informed about them,—for instance, in my having had my life "wonderfully preserved," also Susan's and mine preserved when in "great peril,"—which was when, in the last great Apache raid Susan made me promise to kill her myself, rather than She should fall alive into their hands. Also in several other matters.

These two blessings, therefore, are an additional and very great help to my faith, and I thank God for them.
[Blank line]

16/ By invitation Susan and I visited the new home of Bishop Wm B. Preston, on his farm on Bear river + spent the night there. Also Lyman took us to his farm, beyond Bear river, leaving us at Nephi's home in Benson Ward next day, where we spent a few days pleasantly.

19/ I blessed, of Nephi's family his Sons Leigh Edward, James Easton, and baby daughter Anita.

22/ Called to S.L. City by Sur. Genl Anderson, to sign papers pertaining to my Survey contract.[94] Returned to Logan Next day.

24th/ I gave Note payable to Cache Valley Banking Co. for $600.00 payable in 8months Lyman and Frank Nebeker Endorsed it. I was hard work to get the money, and I could not, without Lyman's help.

[Page B249R]

1903 26/Aug. 26th/ Susan and L [Lyman] left Logan, I for my Survey, She to visit Gean awhile, then to visit Sariah, in Virgen city Had my chains and transit tested by Sur. Generall

29/ Finished testing instruments, and received all papers, maps, instructions +c for my Survey.[95]

I state here, that I was greatly worried as to how I would be able to get the necessary bonds for my contract, amounting to $9006.00 But to my great astonishment I received a letter from a Great U.S. Bonding Company, in Baltimore, offering to act as Such. I had never heard of them before. That Co. became my surety, I paying them $22.50 premium. Thus the Lord opened my way, when it seemed to be firmly closed against me. And there was, in part, fulfilled the blessing I had received from Presidents J.F. Smith and J.R. Winder.
[Blank line]
To day Susan Started alone on the railway to visit her sister Sariah Workman, in Virgen City, Washington Co. Utah,—a long and tedious

---

94. Enclosed were copies of the contract, bond, and instructions for surveys stipulated in his contract. Edward H. Anderson to James H. Martineau, August 21, 1903, Letters Sent, Surveyor General's Office, Vol. 39, July 6–October 20, 1903, pp. 221–222. Notice the shortened time in roundtrip travel to Salt Lake City.

On this date, the newspaper reported that nine parties of ten men each had been dispatched into the field during the week. During the following week, nine more parties would be dispatched into the field. See "Survey of the Uintah Reserve," *Deseret Evening News*, August 22, 1903, 6, and Fuller, "Land Rush in Zion," 190.

95. The testing of instruments prior to a federal survey contract was required by law. The transit would also be calibrated in the field according to the yearly and daily magnetic variations. See Martineau, "Magnetic Needle," 272–273, and Martineau's entry for September 21, 1903.

Two days earlier, General Anderson wrote to the Commissioner, informing him that Martineau had received and signed his special instructions, and that "The deputy leaves for the field tomorrow." Edward H. Anderson to Commissioner, General Land Office, August 27, 1903, Letters Sent, Washington, Vol. 12, June 30, 1903–April 9, 1904, p. 126, CSGUT.

journey for her, in her lameness and feeble condition, nearly 300 miles by rail and about 70 by wagon, over horrible roads.

I dreaded the journey for her, but she had faith she would go all right, and she did. At Lund, where she ~~found~~ left the Railway, she found her nephew Jacob Workman and wife, with a one seated buggy, waiting for her, and in that crowded little trap went to her sister's—two long days ride, over rough roads. After visiting Sariah awhile she and Sariah went to St. George, meeting her brother Nephi + wife Maggie. They took a room together, and spent some time working in St George temple, and enjoying a nice family Union, though Seth and Sixtus were absent. Then she returned to Virgen City and on Oct. 4 left for S.L. City, arriving at Lund 8.30 P.M. Oct. 6, and arrived S.L. City 9.30 a.m. Oct 7th pretty used up by so tedious a journey, Sitting up all the last night on the train. But she testified that while away her way

[Page B250L]

1903/August/was continually opened before her, and she was blessed all the time, just as had been her faith, from the first.

While Susan and I were in S.L. City, previous to her journey South, we stayed at Herbert A. White's No 462 E. 7th South S.L. City, and one night with Sister Lena B. Davis, another dear friend.

Aug. 31st/ Nephi and Howard, who will help on Survey, Started with Ether Tarbet on train for Price.[96] I was detained.

Sept. 1st/ I left S.L. City, for Price, via D.+R.G.R.R. arriving there about 6 P.M.

" 2/ I went to Huntington to hire men, not finding them at Price, as I had expected.[97] This place is 22 miles S.W. of Price. I stayed at my

---

96. Price is located between Provo and Green River, Utah, at the junction of US-6 and U-10 on the Price River. It was settled in 1877 by Mormons as the largest of several Utah mining communities. Though it was primarily supported by the mining industry and farming, its growth was spurred by the Denver and Rio Grande Railroad in 1883. See Van Cott, *Utah Place Names*, 303.

97. At least three other surveying parties had already been outfitted in Price, so it must have been difficult to find experienced, able-bodied men to assemble a full survey crew. See "Purely Personal," *Eastern Utah Advocate*, August 20, 1903, 4; "Truth and Gossip," *Eastern Utah Advocate*, August 20, 1903, 5; and "Purely Personal," *Eastern Utah Advocate*, August 27, 1903, 8.

brother-in-law Albey L. Sherman. In the evening all his family came to see me, and spent the evening pleasantly.

" 3/ Returned to Price, having engaged 6 men, sons of Albey, most of them, also Wagon + 4 horses.

" 4/ Left Price by wagon, for my field of labor, 120m dist.

5/ Camped at Brocks, in the mountain. In the night a tempest raged, of wind and rain, which wet us through Very cold and dismal

6/ Crossed another range, in cold rain, wind + snow.

7/ Camped on Duchesne river. Cold + Cheerless

8/ Arrived at Fort Duchesne about 1 P.M. and camped. Heard alarming reports of threatened Ute indian uprising,—rounding up Survey camps by them. Most of my Company were badly scared. In answer to prayer I received a testimony that no harm should come to us. All to be well with us, which so was proved in the end.

9/ Went 14m to Whiterocks Indian Agency, near which my work lies, and Camped near by.[98]

I spent Several days trying to find an old Survey Corner, at which to begin my work, hindered also by heavy rains and finally snow, which broke down my tent one night upon Nephi and me, as we lay asleep.

Soldiers had been sent out to bring in bands of refractory indians. The Utes do not want their reservation surveyed and opened to the whites.[99]

[Page B251L]

---

98. Whiterocks was established in 1868 as the first white settlement in eastern Utah. It is located near the Whiterocks River and the mouth of Whiterocks Canyon, approximately eighteen miles northeast of Roosevelt. Today it is a predominately Ute community. See Van Cott, *Utah Place Names*, 397.

It should be noted that Martineau had been listed with other deputy surveyors in a memorandum and accompanying letter from A. C. Tonner, acting commissioner of Indian Affairs, to Captain W. A. Mercer, acting Indian agent, giving authorization for survey teams to enter the Uintah Indian Reservation. William I. Hedges, Chief Clerk, to Scott P. Stewart and other U.S. Deputy Surveyors, August 14, 1903, Letters Sent, Surveyor General's Office, Vol. 39, July 6–October 20, 1903, p. 195, CSGUT.

99. A few days later, the Vernal paper was warning that "advices from the reservation are in effect that the Indians are feeling pretty sore over the presence of so many surveyors on the reserve and the prospect of opening." From "Local and Personal," *Vernal Express*, September 19, 1903, 3. See also "Truth and Gossip," *Eastern Utah Advocate*, September 24, 1903, 5.

~~August~~/1903/Sept./ They say "Pretty soon white men get all land. Injuns have no home by 'and by." They are not to blame for thinking So, judging by past experience. No white man could live or stay on the reservation (Uintah Resn) without permission, so I had presented to Capt Mercer, the Agent, my letter from the Commissioner of Interior authorizing me and my party to enter the reservation and make my survey, which was duly endorsed by Capt. Mercer, with authority to fish with hook + line, but not to kill game or prospect for minerals. Those not obeying these regulations liable to arrest by indian police, and punished.

Sat. 12/ Found an old U.S. Survey Corner, so now we may begin work of Survey, having now a starting point.[100]

I had previously sent Royal Sherman to Brown's camp to get some necessary notes of his survey, and on return of Sherman he got lost, the trail being covered with snow, but was found in the night by two Ute indians, who put him on the way to the Camp at the Agency. We had been much alarmed at his non-return two days.

Sun 13/ Today four of the men from Huntington deserted me, taking the two teams and wagon. Said our food was not good enough, though I had plenty of flour, bacon, canned tomatoes, beef, rice, sugar, coffee, tea, dried peaches +c,—far more and better than they had at home. I think it was fear of indians and of Storms that frightened them, and because of one of them—David Sherman, who was always Sulky and surley from the beginning, who led his brothers away.

So, I was left, flat,—no team or wagon, helpless. I had paid for their teams, for hay and grain $16.00 since leaving Price—only 10 days.

16th/ I started to Vernal, 40m distant, to hire new men arrived there about 5 P.M. going through a desolate land

---

100. Twenty-eight years earlier, on August 30, 1875, Charles L. Dubois, a deputy surveyor under contract with the surveyor general of Utah, had established the initial point of the Uintah Meridian and Baseline for surveys in the Uintah Indian Reservation. A series of appropriations acts had opened the way for surveys of the reservation boundaries and the creation of a baseline and meridian for use by the Utes in their own township and subdivisional surveys. Although Dubois carried out many of these Uintah surveys, other deputy surveyors, including Martineau, completed the baseline in this remote area of northeastern Utah. Seventy-five-year-old Martineau began his survey, beginning at the Dubois corner, running east on the baseline and terminating the line at the intersection of the eastern border of the reservation (the corner of Tps. 1 N. and 1 S., Rs. 1 and 2 E.). See White, *Initial Points*, 433, 438–439, and Hubbard Jr., *American Boundaries*, 340.

17th/ Hired several men, bought supplies on credit of the Vernal Co-op Store.

17th/ Returned to camp. Tested transit on Polaris at night. Find var. of magnetic needle is 15° 36' E.

[Page B252L]

1903/Sept. 19/Two of my three men whom I had hired came to day. I sent one back to bring another man.

" 20/ Moved camp about 8 miles to a point on Uinta river near which we had bound the old survey township Corner

Mon 21.] Spent the day and following night, taking observations on Polaris at its eastern elongation, to obtain true north, and to find Latitude, and ascertain variation of the needle at this point, so I can begin my Survey.[101]

Tues. 22/ Began Survey of my Contract lands, No. 265 After a few days of good weather, we had many days of rainy weather, causing at times cessation of Survey.

Quite often we were caught in cold drenching rains, miles from Camp, getting back at night cold and wet, to make our beds upon wet ground, for tho I had tents to cover us, the ground was soaked. This caused me to become almost helpless, days at a time, with severe lameness and pains in my loins, almost unbearable when the slightest motion was made by me, in trying to lie down, move in bed, rise or dress myself. But with nine men

---

101. The calibration of his transit according to declination tables was imperative for accurate readings in the field. The surveyor's transit would be adjusted according to the diurnal variations in magnetic north:

> In view of these facts the Government requires all instruments used in making surveys of the public lands or mining claims to be tested by an official standard before they can be used; and a record kept in the U.S. Land Department, Washington of the kind of instrument used, and the amount of its magnetic error. In addition to this every public land surveyor is required, frequently, to test his compass in the progress of his surveys, by observation of the polar star, to make sure that it is not getting out of adjustment. Also, in making return of any public survey, the U.S. Deputy or mineral surveyor must testify upon oath before a competent legal officer that none of his lines have been run by the magnetic needle. If they have been, all his work is liable to be rejected.

From James H. Martineau, "The Magnetic Needle," 270–273; quote from pp. 272–273. See also Carmack, "Running the Line," 300–301, and Agnew, "The Government Land Surveyor as a Pioneer," esp. pp. 370–371.

drawing pay each day, four or five horses to feed with expensive hay and grain, and the company to feed, work or no work, I could not afford to lay by and wait until better able to work. Many days.—weeks—I was on survey line working, when every step I took or motion I made was in pain. But it might have been worse; I might have been unable to do any thing, even in pain, so I had no cause to complain.

This kind of weather continued with occasional changes for the better until early in October.

Our work was very arduous. In the lower part of my work we had miles at a time of dense cedars through which constant use of the axes was required and one or two miles advance in a day was all we could accomplish and when near to top of the Uintah range of mountains, where about half my work must be done we had to continue with the most dense undergrowth of pines and aspens I

[Page B253R]

1903/ever saw in all my life,—so dense that a man could hardly get through it on foot. So we had to cut every foot of the way a path through the thicket. And all this was made still more impassible for men, and totally so for horses in many places by fallen trunks of timber lying every way, over which it was often difficult to pass. Sometimes heavy labor all day gave us only a mile advance. In other places, where was no timber, we had to go over huge boulders with no earth among them, making it difficult to pass on foot;—totally impossible for horses or mules.

I had a horse to ride, but much of the time had to tie him and go all day climbing over fallen trees or boulders, or forcing my way through dense thickets, and all this, much of the time over ground so Steep that to up or down it was very toilsome and sometimes dangerous. I had a sure footed, strong man to carry my transit, (which I could not safely do myself,) and even then had many falls, sometimes quite painful ones among the rocks. One especially, I was carefully making my way down a steep slope of the mountain, elevation 12000 feet above the sea, when in clambering over a high breastwork of dead timber I fell headfirst down the mountain. As I fell I caught at a small bush, which partially broke my fall, so that instead of striking my head upon the rock below and probably killing me, I only nearly broke my leg. As they helped me to get up, I found myself scarcely able to stand or walk, my left knee being apparently badly injured. But I had to walk a long distance to camp, pain or no pain. This injury was painful to me for about five weeks. I think the bones were cracked or otherwise injured. For weeks I was unable to rise without help, nor could I mount a horse without efficient help from a strong man. Thus this injury caused me to pain in every movement I made each day. Had I been at home I would not have thought of doing anything, or even of walking about.

[Page B254L]

1903/October/But when we work in rough mountains we must expect hard knocks and make the best of them. It was a great blessing to me that heavy fall did not kill me, leaving my work not half completed, and a strong probability my dear wife would receive no material benefit from what I had already accomplished

It was mostly for her sake I undertook such work at an age of almost 76 years. I wished she might not be left dependent should I pass away before her, and feel herself a burden upon our children. For, to one who for many years had presided in her own home, to become an inmate of that of some one else, with nothing to do or say about matters, must be anything but pleasant or agreeable.

Some of our work was in places actually dangerous. And sometimes our lines lay across gorges and defiles actually impossible—so precipitous + sheer. This is notably the case in the Whiterocks river cañon, a tremendous gorge about 2000 feet, or more deep; its sides bordered for miles with precipices from 100 to 600 or 700 feet in height. In the bottom of this Cañon, in one place, are a number of beaver dams and artificial ponds, with acres of aspens cut down by them, lying in all directions. Some of our party caught a beaver, which we ate The beaver tail is Counted a great delicacy. We saw tracks of deer, but did not hunt any, as contrary to regulations, but our boys caught many fine brook trout, a pleasant addition to our larder.

The foregoing general description applies to work not only in October, but to all our work in general, till in November, when forced to discontinue Surveying by snow.
[Blank line]

Oct. 12/ Was unable to rise from my bed on account of severe pain and lameness in my loins and back, which caused excruciating pain at the least and slightest movement. This continued several days; in this interval Nephi ran the transit on open grounds and was a considerable help to me.

[Page B255R]

1903/Oct. 15/To day I attempted to go out on line, and did so, but became worse again, and unable to leave my bed.

18/ Able to sit up, Nephi says he must go home to save his crop of potatoes and other vegetables. How can I spare him? is the question with me. Two other men left me.

19/ To day Nephi started home. I was able to go with him to the Indian Agency, to see him off, riding in a spring seat.

And now, with the absence of Nephi and the two other men, I am unable to go on with my survey, the five remaining being too few. I was promised two men—said they were sure to come—but after waiting some [in margin: Oct. 31st] days in vain, I went again to Vernal, to hire more, with a Mr. Washington Caldwell, staying at his house in Vernal. They were all very desirous to receive patriarchal blessings from me, and I accordingly gave them to Br. Caldwell, his wife Almira, daughter Pearl, and sons Earl and Alonzo. Also to the woman who wrote for us, Sister Holgate, her son, and daughter. I was able by the blessing of the Lord, to help them and do them much good, as they all testified to me time and again. And so I felt much blessed myself. Brother Caldwell left of liquor, teas, coffee and tobacco, on his own volition, altho for many years a user of them all. I pray that he may be able to continue to the end.

Nov. 1/ I obtained three men, and resumed survey on return to Camp Nov. 5th

11/ Went to work this morning, snowing gently. It soon became a regular blizzard, with piercing wind. We had often to stop, light a fire and thaw ourselves out from our benumbing condition. We did not reach Camp till dark—glad indeed when we saw our camp fire the blinding snow, and terribly tired. We were at an elevation of over 12000 feet all day—an elevation cool in the heat of Summer,—how, then winter, which had set in some time ago!

12/ Still snowing, with prospects of a long continuance. My men, familiar with the mountains and climate at this time of the year, decided we could hope for nothing

[Page B256L]

1903/Nov. 12/more favorable, and that we were in great danger of a being snowed in, unless we immediately broke camp and sought the low lands. This was afterwards proved correct, as one survey party had to be dug out by settlers, from Snow five feet deep; and another party was snowed in eleven days, on very light rations all that time.

We accordingly broke Camp, loading all upon our pack horses, and began our toilsome way. It required a labor of over half a day to go a little over 3 miles to lower altitude, reaching there utterly tired and worn,—but out of the deep snow and safe. I looked back up to the higher mountains we had left, and was glad indeed to be out of them for the time, but very Sorry the snow had come to stop the survey, for the snow fallen will remain until next summer, besides that which will yet fall.

" 13/ Moved Camp today down into the open valley, hoping to continue the survey in lower altitude, and did a few days work, But the days are now so short we can at best put in but a half day's work, at cost of a full day—expense daily of party for food for men and five horses. And as we cannot under any circumstances finish the Survey this season, but must come again next year, I concluded it best to stop survey now, + did so.

18th ~~17th~~/ I took final oaths of my men, and disbanded.
[Blank line]

Sat. 21/We started for Price, by Caldwell's wagon and team.

Tues. 24/arriving at Price on Wednesday Nov. 24th We had very cold weather all the way, in an open wagon, camping long after dark. At The Well, where we camped one night A Mrs. Odekirk, hearing I was a Patriarch, was anxious to

23d/obtain a Blessing under my hands, which I Sealed upon her on Monday 23d.

Before leaving the Agency, I gave my note to the Store of W.P. Coltharp + Co. for $245.90 payable on or before July 1. 1904, with 10 % interest from maturity. My indebtedness at Vernal store is

[Page B257R]

1903/Nov./$216.16, while I owe my men about $500.00 payable when my work is finished and paid me. I have paid them in all about 250 or $300.00 dollars. And I paid the Price Store for Supplies about $80.00.

There was no grass for our horses on the whole time of Survey, so I had to buy several thousand pounds of oats and hay to feed them all the time much of which cost me $40.00 to $60.00 per ton. And thus, in connexion with our 20 days lost by desertion of men, my expenses have been abnormal—far too much. But I was unable to help myself, and my men took advantage of it.
[Blank line]

Nov. 25/ I reached S.L. City, with Howard, Nephi's son, and was overjoyed meet again my beloved wife and my daughter Virginia, and be again in a pleasant home for the time, to sit at a table, on a chair, not exposed to chilling wind nor stifling smoke, nor the many other discomforts of Camp life in winter time,—for it *was* winter in the Uinta elevated plateau and mountains—the highest in Utah.

Susan said she never for years, had seen me look so worn, thin and haggard as when I entered the house, and when I felt that a time of rest had come I nearly collapsed, but in a few days was all right again, my long continued worry and anxiety being over for the time.

7th/ Susan and I remained at Virginia's until Dec. 7th and on that day went to Lyman's, in Logan, and met a warm reception there

" 10/ We went to Nephi, in Benson Ward, and had a very pleasant visit there until Thurs. Dec. 17

18th/ Returned to Lyman's

24/ Susan sick in bed with severe cold and cough.

25/ Christmas at Lyman's. A pleasant day + good dinner.

28/ Letter from Co-op Store in Mexico, showing I have a stock interest in the Store of about $1100.00.

30/ This morning Susan was able to come down to breakfast for the first time since she was sick, but came down yesterday to dinner. I am very thankful.

[Page B258L]

Joseph's prophecy. May 6. 1843.

1903/December/31/ I find among my papers a copy of a prophecy of the Prophet Joseph, copied from the original in possession of Samuel W. Richards by Mary Eliza Brown Jones (Martineau) I have been for many years acquainted with the brother Edwin Rushton, and believe his words are true:—
[Blank line]
"A prophecy by Joseph Smith Jr. related to Edwin Rushton and Theodore Turley, on or about May 6. 1843.

A grand review of the Nauvoo Legion was held in Nauvoo. The Prophet, Joseph Smith, complimented them for the good discipline and evolutions performed. The weather being hot he called for a glass of water. With the glass of water in his hand he said "I will drink you a toast to the overthrow of the mobocrats." which he did in language as follows:—"Here's wishing they were in the middle of the sea, in a Stone coffin with iron paddles (padlocks) and a shark swallow the coffin, and the Devil swallow the Shark, and him locked up in the northeast corner of hell, the key lost, and a blind man hunting for it."

The next morning a man who heard the prophet give the toast visited the mansion of the Prophet, and so abused him with bad language that he was ordered out by the prophet. It was while the two were out that my attention was attracted to them, and hearing the man speaking in a loud voice I went toward them + the man finally leaving. There were then the prophet Joseph Smith, Theodore Turley, and myself. The Prophet began talking to us of the mobbings and drivings, the persecutions we as a people had endured. "But," said he, "we will have worse things to see. Our persecutors will have all the mobbings they want. Don't wish them any harm, for when you see their sufferings you will shed bitter tears for them." While the conversation was going on we stood near his south wicker gate in a triangle. Turning to me he said, "I want to tell you something. "In the future I will speak in parables, like John the Revelator." (Little did I think then the Prophet of the

[Page B259R]

Lord would so soon be slain in cold blood.) Continuing, he said

"You will go to the Rocky mountains, and you will see a great and mighty people established, which I will call the <u>White Horse of Peace and Safety</u>." When the Prophet said "You will see" I asked him where he would be at that time. He answered "I shall never go there. Your enemies will continue to follow you with persecution, and they will make obnoxious laws against you in Congress, to destroy the White Horse, but you will have a friend or two to defend you, and throw out the worst part of the laws, so they will not hurt much. You must continue to petition Congress all the time, but they will treat you as strangers and aliens, and they will not give you your rights, but will govern you with strangers and Commissioners. You will see the Constitution of the United States almost destroyed; it will hang by a thread, and that thread as fine as the finest silk fibre."

At this point the Prophet's countenance became sad, as he said "I love the Constitution. It was made by the inspiration of God, and it will be preserved and saved by the efforts of the White Horse and the Red Horse, who will combine in its defense. The White Horse will raise an ensign on the mountains of peace and safety, where all the nations may flee for safety. The White Horse will find the mountains full of minerals, and they will become very rich. You will see silver piled ^up^ in the streets."

(At this time it must be remembered that it was not known that the precious metals existed either in the Rocky mountains or in California.) "You will see gold shoveled up like sand. Gold will be of but little value, even in mercantile capacity, for the people of the world will have something else to do in seeking for Salvation. The time will come when the banks in every nation will fail, and only two places will be safe, where the people can deposit their gold and treasures. The places will be with the White Horse and England's vaults. A terrible revolution will take place in the land of America, such as has never been seen before; for the land will be left without a supreme government, and every species of

[Page B260L]

<u>Joseph's prophecy. May 6. 1843.</u> (Contd-

wickedness will run rampant; it will be so terrible that father will be against son and son against father; mother against daughter, and daughter against mother. The most terrible scenes of murder, and bloodshed and rapine that has ever been looked upon will take place. Peace will be taken from the earth, and there will be no peace, only in the rocky mountains. This will cause hundreds and thousands of the honest in heart of the world to gather there, not because they would be saints, but for safety, + because they would not take up the sword against their neighbors. They will be so numerous that you will be in danger of famine, but not for the want of seed time + harvest, but that so many will have to be fed. Many will come with bundles under their arms to escape the calamities, and there will be no escape, only by fleeing to Zion. Those that come to you will try to keep the laws + be one with you, for they will see your unity and the greatness of your organizations. The Turkish Empire, or the Crescent, will be one of the first powers that will be disrupted as a power, for freedom must be given for the gospel to be preached in the holy land. The Lord took of the best blood of the nations and planted them on the small island now Called ^England, or^ Great Britain, and gave them great power in the nations for a thousand years, and their power will Continue with them that they may keep the balance of power; that they may keep Russia from usurping power all the world. England and France are now bitter enemies, but they will be allied together in order to keep Russia from Conquering the world. The two popes, Greek and Catholic, will come together + be united. The protestant religions do not know how much they are indebted to Henry 8th for throwing off the pope's rule and establishing the protestant faith. He was the only monarch that could so at that time, and he did it because the nation was at his back to sustain him. One of the peculiar features in England is the established red coat, a uniform making so remarkable a mark to shoot at, and yet, they have conquered wherever they have gone. The reason for this will be known by them some day. The

[Page B261R]

Lion and the Unicorn of England is the ensign of Israel. The wisdom and statesmanship of England comes from there being so much of the blood of Israel in the nation. While the terrible revolution of which mention has been made is going on, England will be neutral until it becomes so inhuman that she will interfere to stop the shedding of blood. England and France will then unite together and come with the intention to make peace, not to subdue the nation. They will find the nation so broken up, and so many claiming government. Still, there will be no responsible government. Then it will appear to other nations or powers as though England had taken possession of the country. The Black Horse will flee to the invaders and join ^with^ them, for they will have fear of becoming slaves again, knowing England did not believe in slavery; fleeing to them, they believed, would make them safe. Armed with British bayonets the doings of the Black Horse will be terrible, so the Prophet said he could not bear to look longer upon the scene as shown him in his vision, that he asked the Lord to close the Scene. Continuing, he Said

"During this time the great White Horse will have gathered strength, sending out elders to get the honest in heart among the Pale Horse, or people of the United States, to stand by the Constitution of the United States, as it was given by inspiration of the Lord. In these days, God will set up a kingdom never to be thrown down, for other kingdoms to come unto, and those kingdoms that will not let the gospel be preached will be humbled until they will. England, Germany, Norway, Denmark, Sweden, Switzerland, Holland and Belgium have a considerable amount of the blood is Israel among their people which must be gathered. These nations will submit to the kingdom of God. England will be the last of these kingdoms to surrender, but when she does, she will do it as a whole, in comparison as she threw off the Catholic power. The nobility know the gospel is true, but it has not enough pomp and grandeur and influence for them to embrace it. They are proud, and will not acknowledge the kingdom of God or come into it, until they see the power which

[Page B262L]

Joseph's prophecy. May 1843

it will have. Peace and safety in the Rocky mountains will be protected by a Cordon band of the White Horse and the Red Horse. The Coming of the Ten Tribes
(illegible for a space)

[Several blank lines]

The coming of the Messiah will be so natural that only those who see Him will know he has come; but he <u>will</u> come, and give the law unto Zion, and minister unto His people. This will not be His coming in the clouds of heaven to take vengeance on the wicked of the world. The temple in Jackson Co. will be built in this generation. The Saints will think there will not be time enough to build it, but with all the great help you will receive you can put up a great temple quickly. You will have all the gold, silver and precious stones, for these things only, will be used for beautifying the temple. All the skilled mechanics you want, and the Ten Tribes of Israel to help you build it. When you see this land bonded with iron you may look towards Jackson County."

At this point he made a pause, and looking up as though the vision was still in view, he said—

"There is a country beyond the rocky mountains that will be invaded by the heathen chinese. Great care + protection is given [blank]" Speaking of heathen nations he Said "Where there is no law there is no condemnation: this will apply to them. Power will be given the White Horse to rebuke nations afar off, and they will obey, not that they will be one with the White Horse, but when goes forth they will obey, for the law will go forth from Zion. The last great struggle Zion will have to contend with will be when the whole of America will be made the Zion of our God. Those opposing will be called 'Gog and Magog. The Nations of the world will be led by the Russian Czar, and this power ~~will be just~~ but all opposition will be overcome, and this land will be the Zion of our God."

[Page B263R]

These words of the Prophet made a strong impression upon me, which I have never forgotten. In about two weeks later I was at a meeting where he preached a sermon which he said would be the greatest of his life. On that occasion he reiterated the matter which I have now written, so that the subject became firmly rooted in my memory and I know them to be true. Now therefore I testify these are the inspired words of the Prophet Joseph Smith as he stood looking up into heaven. His countenance became white and transparent He looked as if he had as much of the heavenly influence as he could bear, and stay with the Saints. His voice was powerful, and his words cut like a two edged sword. (Signed) Edwin Rushton

Witness Signature
 A.G. Giauque
[Blank line]
 I have skipped several pages in my journal to write the foregoing prophecy, and now continue my journal.
[Blank line]

Dec. 31/ Susan mending rapidly, and will, I hope, soon be well.

1903/ 1904

=====/

1904/Jan. 1st/ January 1st Had and enjoyable day, but would much rather have been, with Susan, at our own Mexican home.

" 19th/ Am still without my pension, which was dropped last March, without any reasonable Cause. Today I wrote to Senator T. Kearns, asking his help to have it reviewed.

" 27th/ In the Logan temple, to day endowed Herbert Martineau

Lyman Endd Henry Martineau, and Alley, his wife, endowed Berthia Martineau

" 28th/ I endd A.Y. Thompson; Lyman, Peter Martineau; Alley, Hannah Hutchinson; Ann Hymers, Mrs. Sarah Martineau

~~Feb~~ " 30/ Gean's baby girl born to day, weight 8 ½ lbs. All doing well.

I secured affidaivts from Drs. Calderwood + Budge, as to my need of pension, through infirmity.

Yesterday (29th) We came back to Lyman's to stay awhile.[102]

Feb. 2/ Sent Affidaivts to Kearns.

Jan. 29th/ I Endowed David Martineau Blackburn; Lyman, John Martineau Blackburn; Alley, Abagail Hutchinson; Ann Hymers

[Page B264L]

Jan. 29/04/Mrs. Susannah Archer.

Feb. 6th 1904/ Blessed Emeline B. Rich

Feb. 8th 1904/ This morning I dreamed of holding a cup while one poured into it, long after it was full, but not running over the while. I had the interpretation, which was for good to me.

Mch. 12th/04/ We moved to Eva's, by her invitation

---

102. Sometime during his visit to Logan, Martineau wrote of Benjamin Johnson's experiences during the Missouri persecutions of the Mormons. See James H. Martineau, "Is There Power in Prayer?" *Improvement Era* 8 (November 1904): 337–340.

" 13/ My 76th Birth day, Lyman + Alley made a nice family dinner, <u>all</u> our family in Cache being present. Good time.

" 16/ I endowed John Scott

" 17/ " " Francis Martineau

18/ " " Edd Marsh "

=====/ <u>April 1904</u>

~~April 29th/~~
March 29th/[Blank line]
1904/Gave Lyman a deed for an alley, on my old place. I had previously, by his help, obtained $50.00 for right to use it, by Logan Journal Co. which was great help to me

-----/ <u>April</u>.

April 1st/ Blessed Br. and Sister Harrison

2/ " Br. Guy Thatcher and Florence, his wife

3/ " Sister Needham, (widow

4/ Susan and I went to Gean's, in S.L. City

5/ Attended Special Meeting in the New Barratt Hall

6/ Genl Conference. Manifesto again sustained by U. vote

7/ Visited H.A. and M.A.H. White and blessed them

10/ Met Jesse N. Smith and his wife, friends of my youth. Had not seen them for about 40 years. Happy meeting.

   Blessed Albey and Mary Sherman, Susan Julias, brother

11/wwi]Wrote to Senator Smoot, about my renewal of pension.

12/ Lyman enabled me to borrow $600.00 of the Utah Natl Bank. He and Prest Anthony Ivins Signing my note as Sureties, on my first assigning my property to them, security.

13/ Albey and Mary Sherman returned home to Huntington.

   Note. I assigned as security on Note for $600.00 the following:–

1115

Stock in Union Mercantil Store, Dublan Mex.	$11.00
" " Tannery, Juarez "	150.00
My home (house & ½ lot) " val. In Mex. Money	1200.00
	$2450.00
Value, Mexican Money	$1225.00

Note. 10 % interest from date.

[Page B265R]

1904/April 20/ Recd word Congress, by special act, renewed me pension at rate of $12.00 per month.[103] Previously it was at $8.00 and on the [in margin: " 22] I sent my old pension papers to Pension Agt. John R. King, ^D.C.^

26/ Opened an account with Utah Natl Bank.

28/ Gave Check for $300.00 to apply on my $600 note due in the Cache Valley Bank.

-----/
May/ May. 1904

5/Susan and I met, at Whites, with Bp. John Neff, and Christina Pyper. Had a glorious time. Blessed each other. The voice of the Holy Ghost said we were "One with the Lord and his Son Jesus Christ." It was a glorious time, never to be forgotten.

---

103. The bill to grant Martineau a place on the pension roll and increase his pension to $12 was passed on March 12, 1904. See US Congress, Senate, *Congressional Record*, 58th Cong., 2d sess., 1904, 38, pt. 3: 2668, and *idem*, pt. 4:3205. The fuller Senate report stated:

> James Henry Martineau, of Logan, Utah, served during the Mexican war from January 4, 1848, to June 23, 1848, as a private recruit in the general service of the United States Army. He was granted bounty-land warrant for 160 acres on account of this service, and was also allowed the pension of $8 per month provided by the service act of January 29, 1887, which pension he continued to receive until December 4, 1902, when his name was dropped from the roll on the ground that he did not serve in Mexico, on the coasts or frontier thereof, or en route thereto for sixty days during the war with that nation.

Since for six months Martineau had traveled to Newport Barracks, Kentucky, and was armed and drilled in preparation for duty at the front, it was argued that this was indeed "service en route to the war with Mexico" and that he was entitled to the benefits of all survivors of the Mexican War. See US Senate, Congress, Committee on Pensions, *James H. Martineau*, 58th Cong., 2d sess., 1904. S. Rpt. 903, 1–2.

6/ Blessed Esther, Vitate, Albert + Lorenzo Elggren, also E. Iverson, Alice Schied, a little girl 7 years old, who desired it.

7/ Blessed A. Lewis Elggen. Yesterday blessed Br. + Sis. Elggren. Susan anointed and blessed Sis. ~~Peterson,~~ ^Brown^ for confinement.

8/ Blessed Mary E Bassett, and Sister Brown, whom Susan had anointed and blessed the day previous. She had been, for 5 months under care of doctors with a complication of several serious disorders, and her case declared entirely hopeless, without taking into account her near confinement, through which it would be impossible for her to pass. She lay very low and lifeless, but Susan, in blessing her, said she should be blessed in her confinement and have the easiest time that she had ever had with any of her children; and that should soon be fully healed. Sister Brown desired me to give her a patriarchal blessing, which I did, and without knowing what Susan had promised her, gave her substantially the same.

Note./ I will say here, that all this was fulfilled to the very letter, to the great joy of herself + husband, and wonder of all the doctors, who had said she must die. It was a great testimony to Susan and me.

9/ Blessed David Brown, her husband. Also Mrs. Sainsbury and sealed Susan's anointing and blessing upon Mrs. Peterson Also blessed Br. Sainsbury.

16/ Got my final papers from Sur. Genl Anderson. Got a Bro. Snarr, of Sonora Mex. to help Susan on her way home, as she wishes to go home to Mexico.

[Page B266L]

1904/May 17/To day I started for my Survey, to finish it up, leaving Susan, who will start for Mexico in a few days. It was a trial for us to part, she to journey near 2000 miles without my help and company, but it had to be. How glad will I be when we can part no more. God grant that time may soon come.

I went by the Denver and Rio Grande R.R. to Price 130m From Price I went by Stage 130 miles to Vernal, Uinta Co. to get my company and supplies. Fare $12.50

23/ Started out with 2 wagons and teams and 10 men. Drove to Deep Creek, about 26 miles

24/ Started Survey of the Uintah Special Base Line, finished next day, 3 miles, over very rough ground + in rain.

26/ Susan started home 8.05 P.M. Had to walk alone 2 ½ blocks which was very hard for her to do. No one helped her.
[Blank line]
    From the 24th inst. I continued my survey, the ground being exceedingly bad. The lower and more level parts were covered with a dense growth of Cedars, making progress very slow. The mountains, on which most of my work lay, was exceedingly rough + precipitous, covered, almost totally—with pine or quaking aspens, and in many places almost impossible for dense growth of young pines, one to two inches diameter, 10 to 20 ft high, and so thick as to be almost impenetrable, so that we had to cut a passage every foot of the way. Also large areas were covered with fallen timber, impossible to get a horse through without much chopping. In other places, great tracts of huge boulders were almost impossible to cross on foot. The altitude 12000 to 13000 feet. Made warm, heavy winter clothing necessary, even in July while the Clouds of mosquitoes were almost unbearable to men or our horses. We also had much heavy rain and cold sleet. Although my men were robust, strong frontiersmen, inured all their lives to hardship three of them broke down and quit for sickness. Many wondered how I, at 77, stood these hardships so well, without breaking down also.

[Page B267R]

My Survey

1904/ It was a simple thing:—In the morning I asked the Father to bless and strengthen me for the days work. And He did. The others neglected this—never thought of it, I suppose, but trusted in their own strength. Sometimes, for miles at a time it was very difficult to get over the ground because of the dense mass of fallen timber, crossing in every way. Even in July we crossed old snow. Sometimes our way was along slopes so hard, Smooth and steep that it was only with great difficulty I could pass, even afoot, with a possible slide or tumble of a thousand feet. Added to all this, two cañons crossed one Township, each of them over 2000 feet deep, with slopes inaccessible in many places;—huge precipices 500 to 800 feet—barring the way. At one point, the only one to get from the bottom of the Whiterocks river Cañon to the top of it, the trail we made was very steep, so much so, that in ascending it with my pack train, one of the horses fell backwards down the mountain. Although the oaken, strong pack saddle was between the body of the horse and the pack, it was broken into small pieces. I <u>rode</u> up this trail the previous fall, being unable to ascend it afoot, but it was a very dangerous thing to do: Many times my life was in extreme danger in the mountains, but through faith I was preserved,—by the mercy of the Lord alone.

Having finished my field work, as I supposed, I came back to S.L. City, and was there informed I had left out a small separate tract I had not known of, and must return and survey that also, as I will not farther on.[104]

While in the city I gave patriarchal blessings to quite a number, visited and blessed the sick, and worked very hard and late on my Survey notes for Sur. General's office.

Aug 14/04/ To day I was received as a member of 2d Ward, Liberty Stake, as I wish always to be in track with the Church, in every place, when I can.

Sept. 16/ To day I started back to Uintah, to finish my field work going by wagon, with Br. Harden Benion.[105] Our road was all in ^was all in^ the mountain, and occupied 5 days hard and late driving, cold nights, and much bad road. Arrived at Vernal at 9 P.M. just ahead of a great tempest

[Page B268L]

1904/which caused me four or five days detention in Vernal, while I was engaged in getting up a new survey party.[106]

---

104. Martineau was requested to call at the surveyor general's office about standard lines in Tps. 4 and 5 N. W. J. Hedges to James H. Martineau, August 5, 1904, Letters Sent, Surveyor General's Office, Vol. 42, July 12–December 10, 1904, 88, CSGUT.

105. Evidently, Martineau had not adequately documented the courses, distances, and topography on the west boundary of Tp. 2N, R. 1W. He was asked to furnish notes and drawings of this western boundary but probably had to go back into the field to obtain the information first-hand. Edward H. Anderson to James H. Martineau, August 24, 1904, W. J. Hedges to James H. Martineau, August 26, 1904, and W. J. Hedges to James H. Martineau, August 31, 1904, Letters Sent, Surveyor General's Office, Vol. 42, July 12–December 10, 1904, 162, 167, and 192, CSGUT.

Harden Bennion (1862–1936) was born to John and Esther Ann (Birch) Bennion in Taylorsville, Salt Lake County, Utah. He married Vilate Kimball Nebeker on May 31, 1893.

106. In early September, Utah Surveyor General Anderson reported that he had an appropriation of $16,000 for the survey of public lands in Utah, provided he could get applications from at least three actual settlers on each township. See "Money on Hand for Surveying Townships," *Eastern Utah Advocate*, September 8, 1904, 1. Two weeks later,

On the journey to Vernal, I noted elevations at points on the way, established by the U.S. Geological Survey party, on metal plates set on iron posts:—as follows:—

Ridge, (on wagon road, South of City ^Park City^ 7310 feet
" at S.E. entrance of Strawberry valley 8100 ft.
1st Crossing of Duchesne river: 5517
2d " " " 5378
" Uintah river bridge, Fort Duchesne 4994
" Sand ridge 5 m. from " " 5305
" Vernal 5500

Sept. 27/1904/ Started out from Vernal with only 5 men and 1 team + wagon, as my alterations of corners and additional work will not need much time or labor. Reached the Forks in Whiterocks Cañon on next day, 28th and began work same day.

I arranged with Dep. U.S. Surveyor Wm Dallas to Survey the Small tract North of my Survey (now finished) to save time, and finished the few corrections required on Oct. 8th

Oct. 8/Arriving in Vernal, and started on return home Oct. 9th [in margin: " 9] by Stage to Price, 130 miles. In this short period of work I had a hard time, being at time drenched with cold, sleety storms, but had no accidents. I visited Kirkpatrick, the U.S. land Examiner, and had a pleasant time[107]

My journey from Vernal to Price, 130 miles in 2 days by a miserable stage, in very cold weather, in rains, Snow storms and mud, driving long

---

Anderson reported that work was progressing, with thirty-nine out of one hundred and twenty-five completed. Survey reports for thirty-one had been submitted to his office for review. "Reports for the remaining fifty-five townships have not yet been filed by the surveyors, although the work of all engineering parties on the reservation is finished, except in the case of one party and the engineers are now working up their reports for filing here." From "Pushing Work Along," *Eastern Utah Advocate*, September 22, 1904, 1.

107. A few days earlier, Martineau had written to General Anderson to acknowledge receipt of an empty pasteboard map case for his drawings. He also noted that he had not submitted notes of solar observations because he was unable to get a reading for three days due to the constant obstruction of clouds. Both solar and Polaris observations were "impossible." James H. Martineau to Edward H. Anderson, October 4, 1904, Letters Received, Surveyor General's Office, Vol. 28, July 25, 1904–January 11, 1905, letter #7082, CSGUT.

General Anderson reported only two-and-a-half weeks earlier that four parties of government inspectors were going over the work of the surveyors. The only work that remained was establishment of this boundary line, pending Brown's corrections. See "Pushing Work Along," *Eastern Utah Advocate*, September 22, 1904, 1.

after dark and starting in the morning long before sunrise in the cold, was very hard and tedious, but might have been worse. Arrived [in margin: Oct. 11th] at Virginia's in S.L. City pretty tired, but well.

" 13/ Quite sick all night, with severe pain. Lyman came to see me, Said Bp. Preston has asked for me many times, as he has long been sick, almost unto death, wishing me to administer to him, and to give him a patriarchal blessing Said the Bishop remarked "I dont know of any man in the Church whom I would rather bless me. He is one of the few honest men in the world, and I'm trying to be another." I feel much gratified for his confidence in me. Truly, I

[Page B269R]

1904/Oct. 13/striving with my might to live as a true L.D. Saint, but I know I fall short of what I should be. I pray continually that I may become one with the Lord, even as was Enoch of old.

" 20/ I blessed Bp. Preston and comforted him much. He shed tears of joy and said "That has the right ring, that sounds right." His blessing will be dependant upon his own faith and the blessing of the Lord.

Nov. 9/ I went to the temple today, to A.W. Morrison's wedding, and endowed David Martineau (no. 177) Morrison Endd another David Martineau for me. In the evening attended wedding reception at Elgreen's.

" 17/ I endowed Edwd Wamsey

" 18/ Finished my writing of field notes, giving the rest of it to a Mr. John Benson to be type written.

Up to this time I have labored every day, writing, at my table, continuing at night until 11 P.M. to 2 a.m. Much of this time is occupied in Complicated calculations, making my labors, so long continued, very exhausting, bodily and mentally. The days noted above, and Sundays, were the only days Exempt.

19/ Blessed Bishop John Neff and his daughters Frances and Eugenia, the latter about to go on a mission. Sister Mary A. Hyde White also blessed the two girls in tongues. We had a delightful time.

" 22/ Up to this time I have visited and blessed the sick daily, and to day I blessed Sister Sears with P. Blessg

" 24/ Thanksgiving Day. Lyman's family being invited to Preston's and Gean's to Andersons. I was left alone, so took my dinner at Br. + Sis. H.A. White's friendly table, and in evening visited Preston's, who apologised for not inviting me with Lyman.

Dec. 5/ Today put all my survey notes in Sur. Genl office + Sent my pension papers to Washington.[108]

" 8/ My son-in-law E. Guy Taylor, from Canada, Called to see me.

" 10/ Sold my transit to Joel for $300.00 Mexican money equal to $150.00 American, and less than half it cost me, being in perfect order. Sell him my drawing instruments at same rate, he to pay as he can, from time to time.

" 20/ Sent transit to Joel by express.

[Page B270L]

1904/Dec. 20/Paid John Benson in full for type writing field notes +c $33.75, making total paid him, $78.75. His total bill was $83.75, but he deducted $5.00 It was all I could do to raise the money for him

Today I removed from Virginia's (who is going soon to Castle Gate foe awhile) to Lyman's.

I learn by "El Progreso" newspaper that my grandson James Edward, Moroni's eldest son, was married on 12th

Dec. 12th/to Myrtle Clark, daughter of Joseph Clark, of Colonia Chuichupa, Chihuahua State, Mexico.

---

108. Two days later, Martineau was asked to call at the office regarding his contract, presumably to sign the paperwork. Edward H. Anderson to James H. Martineau, December 7, 1904 and W. J. Hedges to James H. Martineau, December 8, 1904, Letters Sent, Surveyor General's Office, Vol. 42, July 12–December 10, 1904, 492 and 496. Near the end of the month, Utah Surveyor General Anderson sent Martineau's completed contract (No. 265) to Washington for approval. The papers, in two separate packages, contained eighteen transcripts of field notes and eight township plats. Anderson reported that Martineau executed work in the amount of $182.07 "over and above" the estimated $4,453 liability of his contract. He recommended that Martineau be allowed this additional amount, as he appeared to be "justly entitled to it." Edward H. Anderson to Commissioner, General Land Office, Washington, DC, December 28, 1904, Letters Sent, Washington, Vol. 13, April 9, 1904–January 19, 1905, 460–461, and Edward H. Anderson to James H. Martineau, December 28, 1904, Letters Sent, Surveyor General's Office, Vol. 43, December 10, 1904–May 31, 1905, 38, CSGUT.

Dec. 25/ Albert was released from his mission in Kansas where he presided over that state Conference.

I spent Christmas at Lyman's

" 29/ Lyman + Alley and children, and I, spent afternoon by invitation of Bp. Preston and wife, at their house, in celebrating Lyman + Alley's wedding day—the 23d one.

-----/
1905/ 1905

Jan. 1/ At Lyman's, Bp. Preston, Moyle and families present.

" 2/Bp. Preston took me through the New L.D.S. Hospital, the finest West of Chicago, and best appointed.

" 4/ With Sister Mary Hyde White visited her Sister Zina Virginia Hyde Bull, widowed recently, who has Cataract growing over her eyes and is losing her sight. She wished me to rebuke blindness and to bless her, which I did, Her Sister Mary also blessed her in tongues, with the interpretation. I know Zina may be healed, through faith. She felt very happy. I enjoyed my visit very much, as I always do in visiting and blessing the Sick.

Ever since I was free from my press of Survey notes and mapping, I have rarely missed a day when I was not visiting + administering to the sick, or giving blessings, and I know I have given great comfort + help to many. Especially do I delight to visit and bless the poor. The rich can (they think) take care of themselves. and need no special blessings from a Patriarch. I never accept any remuneration from the poor for blessing, and the rich very seldom give me anything, so I spend much time in recording blessings and making copies for people.

[Page B271R]

1905/January/4/I do not make, nor wish to—my holy office of Patriarch a matter of dollars.[109] It is too sacred and holy a labor for that, and a precious privelige from our Father, to have a right to seal blessings upon

---

109. In November 1877, LDS church president, John Taylor, criticized the motivation of some stake patriarchs for accepting money for blessings, but it wasn't until 1943 that such fees and gratuities were discontinued. See John Taylor to George Q. Cannon, November 7, 1877, in Bates and Smith, *Lost Legacy*, 136, and Quinn, *Mormon Hierarchy: Extensions of Power*, 205.

others,—an office which reaches into the eternities,—the only office I have desired. I have never desired an office which would require to sit as a Judge ^over^ others. I desire rather, to be as a Father,—eventually, to become as a Father in heaven, as those who have gone before.

6/ Paid $2.00 tithing, which covers all my increase for 1904, as I have not yet received anything for my last Year's work.

7/ Sent 111 names to Anna Woods, at Manti, to baptize and endow

8/ Gean's baby Marjorie quite sick, I went to her

11/ Marjorie getting well, and I return to Lyman's

16/ I went to Bp. Neff's at East Mill Creek by his request, and blc remained until the 18th Bp Neff told me he heard Apostle John W. Taylor prophecy, on his return from Mexico that

"The time will come when ships of was commanded by officers wearing the Mexican uniform will be seen in New York harbor."

Blessed Sisters Neff, Spencer, Elaine, and Br. and Sister Hixon. Recd $1.00

22/ Attended (our) Liberty Stake Conference

25/ I endowed (no. 197) Richard Martineau

26/   "   "   (199) Meadows Martineau

27/   "   "   (205) James Martineau Lee

[Left margin has written sideways, between next line and Jan 6: On Jan. 31st 1905 I had 146 Males Baptized in S.L. Temple]

February

Feb. 1st/ I endowed Philip Martineau. Ellie came home from New York

2/   "   "   Meadows Martineau No. 237

3/   "   "   John Martineau

4/ Lyman and I went to Logan with Legislature to Ag. College

8/ I endowed Edward Mears no 253

9/   "   "   Robert Mears no 254 I blessed Sister Majors and her daughter Clara JM Larson; also Beatrice Sears.

10/ I endd Oliver Mears no 255. Blessed Estella Sears.

11/ Was at Sister Harriet A Preston's 66th birthday dinner. Was notified of error in one corner Stone, of my Survey in the Uintah Reservation.[110]

[Page B272L]

1905/Attended meeting in Emerson Ward. Very Cold,—below Zero Feb. 12/[Blank line]

13/Presented papers to draw $11.74 Sent by Mail from Mexico. Could not get it. Some trickery, I fear.

[Left margin has written, sideways: Feb. 14. ^1905^ My son Nels L. Hagberg died in the L.D.S. Hospital S.L. City, of an operation. I had not known he was sick. He was true as steel to the truth.]

15/ I endd John Mears No. 256

16/ " " Nathaniel Mears, No 257

17/ " " Oliver M. Hyde

18/ Recd a blessing from Apostle John H. Smith. Visited

19/ I worked all day on my temple records.

20/ I gave 56 names of males and females for temple baptism. 33 men

---

110. Martineau was requested to call at the surveyor general's office in Salt Lake City and bring his notes of the western boundary of Tp. 2 N., R. 1 W. in the Uintah Reservation. He was then given thirty days to show cause as to why he should not return to the field to correct the error. W. J. Hedges to James H. Martineau, February 8, 1905 and Edward H. Anderson to James H. Martineau, February 23, 1905, Letters Sent, Surveyor General's Office, Vol. 43, December 10, 1904–May 31, 1905, pp. 150 and 197, CSGUT. On February 10, Martineau acknowledged the receipt of the letter calling attention to his error in stating the length of the southern boundary of sec. 36 in Tp. 4 N., R. 1 W:

> On the day on which said line was run I forgot my note book, and had to use a small pocket tablet for note taking. The paper was poor and pencil marks easily blurred by handling. In transcribing my notes from it into my usual field book, in my tent, and with a poor light, I inadvertently made a mistake in copying, writing 54.40 chains instead of 63.40 chains, the distance originally noted, as reported to me by the chainmen as the true distance, and so noted at the time.
>
> I trust the 35 lks. difference between my measurement and that of the Examiner as reported by him,—by different sets of chainmen, over very broken and difficult ground, will not be regarded as excessive, and I trust this explanation will be satisfactory.

James H. Martineau to Edward H. Anderson, February 10, 1905, Letters Received, Surveyor General's Office, Vol. 29, January 14–May 5, 1905, letter # 7236, CSGUT.

23 women. This makes 202 in all, baptized this Year. By request I visited and blessed Sister Isabel P. Kenner. At the temple I was told of Hagberg's death. Poor fellow, he had much grief in his life time. His first wife Josephine Rodhine left him when her baby was only [blank] days old, deserting it, and it soon died. His next wife, Sarah Westwood died in childbirth + her baby also, about 14 months after marriage. His next wife Emilia Sophia [blank] died next. He thus lost by death 2 wives and four children, leaving one boy only, about 12 years old, of all his family. He was a true L.D. Saint, had done much Missionary work in Sweden, and was a good, industrious man. His Mother was sealed as my wife, and he sealed to me as Son. A letter of his gives particulars of himself and family. [Blank line]

21/ Went to Mrs. Zina V. Hyde Bull's to meet her sister, Mrs Lulla Hyde Hess, of Farmington, who has come to the city for me to administer to her in Blessing, she being in very bad health, her kidneys almost without action, and threatened with dropsy and some other severe complications, making her a great sufferer. She had fasted 3 days for this occasion, and one day also her Sisters Mary A. Hyde White and Zina Virginia. Her husband also came. After prayer we all laid hands upon her, I being mouth, and a good blessing was sealed upon her causing her to shed tears of joy. Then we blessed each other, and had a time of heavenly rejoicing. I hope she will recover

[Next two pages are a letter to JHM from N.L. Hagberg, mentioned above]

[Page B273R]

1905 22d/I endowed Richard Webb, next day <u>Peter Haughoubon</u> 23d inst.

Feb. 22/ Mrs. Clara JM Larsen Endd <u>Alice Hutchinson</u>
    " Mary Ann Owen   " <u>Mehitable Hutchinson</u>
    " Mary E.L. Neff   " <u>Alice Barnett</u> and
    " Amelia L.M. Turner " <u>Sarah Baker</u>

24/ I endowed Nicholas Haughout. Today Cora's son, Joseph Hyrum Robinson, was sealed to her and to me by Asst President Mattison. Sister Wilcox, as proxy for Cora and JB Adlard [blank] as proxy for the child. Now Cora, knowing she has her child secure, may rejoice exceedingly. and I am thankful also.

26/ Sunday. Attended the funeral of my dear friend—one of the friends of my youth, L. John Nuttall. His sudden death was a shock to all, to me especially. It seems as if all my old friends are leaving me.

March. 1905.

Mch. 1/I endowed David C. Lyon, husband of my sister Henrietta. He was a Presbyterian minister in high standing in his church, an honorable man, who treated me very kindly when I visited him in 1879. He believed in many of the principles of or faith—all except plural marriage an the divine mission of Joseph Smith, the Seer. He has now received the word of God in Paradise—the Spirit World. Of this I have testimony.

 I also sealed him and Henrietta, Christina M.F. Ericson proxy for my sister, I for him.

Also Sealed Lord William Russell + Rachel Russell.
 " " Louis Paschal + Camilla Guarina (martyrs)

Mch. 2/I endd my uncle Charles Sprague Mears. Also D. Murphy. Sealed Uncle Charles S. Mears ~~and~~ to his father James + mother Lois Sprague Mears, my mother's parents. Maria W.R. Wilcox, proxy for Lois S. Mears. I for grandfather.

" 3/ I endd John Russell (Lord) Sealed Danl Murphy and Alicia Murphy, old friends of mine. Also " Lord John Russell and Lady Frances Anna Maria Russell, also had sealed to me Lilla Dean, distant relative, unmarried, as all have been whom I have thus taken to wife by the holy ordinance of Sealing.

[Page B274L]

1905/March 8/ I endowed John Grant, father of Mrs. Jane S. Hill, a friend; and she endowed for me Mrs. Hawkins.

" 9/ I endowed Capt. Hawkins, father of Samuel + Elizabeth Hawkins, and husband of my father's first Wife, Sarah Stanhope, daughter of the Earl of Stanhope He was Captain in the British Navy. The Earl of Stanhope disinherited his daughter Sarah, for marrying out of the nobility.

 By my father she had Julia and Lucretia, my ½ sisters and died in Baltimore soon after father returned from England. Samuel became an officer in the American navy and was in Commodore Wilkes Exploring

Expedition in 1839-40-41 during which the Antartic Continent was discovered. Elizabeth married, but all trace of her is lost

As I have Sealed the wife and two children of Capt Hawkins to my father, I seal a Miss Bloomfield to him as wife, she being dead also, and believe they will accept the ordinance.

Sisters Jane S. Hill, Mary E.L. Neff, Nancy NL Neff and Mary Ann Brown also endowed for names for me, as shown in Sealing and endowment record.

" 10/ I endd Capt James Johnson.

In the Sealing of John Grant and wife for Jane S. Hill. I was proxy for him and she for the wife.

March 1st (overlooked)

[Margin shows a drawing like a hand with finger pointing to following paragraph]

Mch. 1/ I sealed Julia and Lucretia Martineau, my half sisters to father, John Martineau and Sarah Stanhope, widow of Capt. Hawkins, noted on previous page. M.W.R. Wilcox proxy for her, I for father, Evelina L. Babbitt for Julia and Eliza D. Fletcher for Lucretia.

Mch. 10 (Continued) Sisters Owens, Neff, Williams, and Larsen also worked for me.

Mon. Mch. 10/ Gave 8 more names for baptism, making 210 in all.

" 15/I endd Mr. Winslow, husband of my Sister Julia. I have lost all trace of them since their marriage in the 30s (Years) I believe he was a printer, and lived in Boston.

Sealed Capt Hawkins + Miss Bloomfield
   "   Samuel Hawkins + Lucy Mears
   "   David M. Blackburn + Elizabeth Martineau

[Page B275R]

1905/Mch. 15/Sealed Samuel and Elizabeth Hawkins to Capt and Mrs. Bloomfield Hawkins.

Also Sealed to William Sprague and Lois Hutchinson Sprague their children, as follows:-

Seth Sprague	proxy	J.B. Adlard
John "	"	J.C. Petersen
William "	"	George Burt
James "	"	William Hodge
Daniel "	"	Peter A. Burt
Jesse "	"	John James
Esther Sprague (Babcock)	Proxy,	Evelina L. Babbitt
Eunice Sprague (Crittenden)	"	Eliza D. Fletcher
Lois Sprague (Mears)(My gr. mother)	"	Elixabeth M. Cooper

" 16/ I end. Andrew Y. Thompson, my Aunt Laura Mears Van Slyke's f Second husband. Also I

Sealed Elie and Marguerite Barbesson, our Norman ancestors, of Dieppe, France. I proxy for Eliza + M.R. Wilcox for Marguerite. Also sealed to them their children

1 Marie Martineau (Columbine, Proxy. Evelina L. Babbitt
2 Gaston Martineau   "   J.B. Adlard

Also Sealed to Peter + Maria Martineau Columbine
~~son~~ Columbine (Hilyard) proxy E.L. Babbitt

Francis "	"	Jabez B. Adlard
Mary " (Rand)	"	Eliza D. Fletcher
Paul "	"	Jens C. Petersen
David "	"	Geo. Burt
Peter Columbine	"	William Hodge

" 17/ Sealed Andrew Y. Thompson + Mrs. A.Y. Thompson
Sealed Oliver M. Hyde + Julia Sprague and <u>Endowed</u> Mr. Marturin, a martyr (Waldensees)

Sealed Gaston Martineau and Miss Hoyle + children

Gaston Martineau	proxy	J.B. Adlard
John "	"	J.C. Petersen
Fanny " (Holland)	"	E.L. Babbitt

Susan   "   (Cunningham)   "   E.D. Fletcher

Sealed to David + Elizabeth Finch Martineau their children, as follows:–

[Page B276L]

1905/   Peter Martineau   Proxy J.B. Adlard

March 17/Mary Martineau (Martineu)   "   Eliza D> Fletcher
    Elizabeth " (Blackburn)   "   Evelina L. Babbitt
    Daniel   "   "   J.C. Petersen
    Peter   "   " - Burt
    Hannah   " (Blackburn)   "   Elizabeth M. Cooper

" 18/ Paid my tithing up to date, in full, in Liberty Stake.

Blessed Zina Hyde Bull and Jane S. Hill, widows I recd recommend from Bp. Iverson to change my membership to Emerson Stake, it being close to my present home, Lyman's house, so I can attend Ward meetings

Sun. 19/ Joined Emerson Ward

Harriet's baby girl born, my Gr.Gr. child

Mon. 20/At 11.40 P.M. the baby was born. 9 lbs. Hard time.

Thurs./
~~Wed~~. 23/I endowed Peter Haughout. Sealed
Robert   Mears and Abagail Hutchinson
Nathaniel   "   " another Abagail Hutchinson
John Mears "   " Hannah Hutchinson

Fri. " 24/I end. Egbert Haughout also Seal
John Martineau + Nelly Haughout
Egbert   "   " Elenor Garebrantz

         ------------ Also Sealed

To John Martineau (my father) and Eliza Mears Martineau (mother)

Caroline Martineau Babcock |
              |-Children born to my mother by her
Chas Sprague Babcock | second husband William Babcock.

Caroline died about 3 years old. Charles S. died a soldier in the Union Army, near Stone river battlefield, of dysentery. He has been endowed, and a wife sealed to him.

Sealed to William Sprague + Mrs. Wm Sprague their Children

William Sprague Jun.   proxy J.B. Adlard. M.WR. Wilcox acting for Mrs. William and I for him.
[Blank line]
Sent answer to Sur. General's Office about my Survey, which is to be altered somewhat, Uinta Resn[111]

[Page B277R]

1905/Mch. 27/Copied plats in Sur. Genl Office. Administered to Bp. Wm B. Preston who is again quite ill.

28/Went to Theatre, free ticket to Old folks. Enjoyed it.

29/ I endd Nicholas Haughout

---

111. This refers to a letter, dated March 20, in which he replied to Surveyor General Anderson's request for him to show cause why he should not be required to make his corrections. "I beg leave to say it is evident to me that said corrections are necessary," Martineau wrote, "and I will return to the Uintah Indian Reservation and make them in conformity with the regulations prescribed in the 'manual', at the earliest moment practicable." After clarifying the conditions of disputed locations of missing corners, Martineau reported that many corners had been destroyed by the Indians:

> … the indians, being very hostile to the subdivision of the Reservation, destroyed many of the corners, which I rebuilt, some of them several times, especially those near their homes … I reported this to the Examiner, as Mr. Kirkpatrick will doubtless remember. How many others have been thus destroyed I cannot say, but doubtless there were others I did not see. The words of a leading indian to me expressed the feelings of the tribe. He said "Washington (U.S. Govt.) gave this land to indians, now you make piles of stones all around. By'me bye white man come-take land, and me have no home."

James H. Martineau to Edward H. Anderson, March 20, 1905, Letters Received, Surveyor General's Office, Vol. 29, January 14–May 5, 1905, letter #7309, CSGUT.

30/   " "   Wynant   "   Sealed Spragues to fathers

31/To. Edward + Mrs. Edward Sprague
William Sprague   proxy JB Adlard
[Blank line]

"/To William and Mrs. William Sprague
  Anthony   proxy J.B. Adlard
[Blank line]
"/To Anthony and Mrs. Anthony Sprague
   Jeremiah Sprague   proxy JB Adlard
[Blank line]

"/To Jeremiah and Mrs. Jeremiah Sprague
William Sprague   proxy JB Adlard

who was husband of Lois Hutchinson, my gr.gr. grmother

[See line pointing from William Sprague to above sentence]

This carries an unbroken line of ten generations, including my great-grand-children, to the year 1600 A.D.

My Gr.Gr.mother Lois Hutchinson, was Gr. dau. of Lord Hutchinson; also a relative of Gov. Hutchinson, of Mass.
[Blank line]

April 1905.

April 1/Attended Priesthood meeting in Granite Stake house.

" 4/Joel arrived, Sister Thurston and two children from Mexico.

Received the following from my son Nephi, which I insert, as testimony of his spiritual standing and love:–

"King April 1. 1905.

Dear Father. I received your welcome letter and felt sorry that you have to make another trip to Uintah, as it will be very hard on you to ride that long distance ~~on~~ ^over^ such a rough road and through such a bleak country, to say nothing of the expense. I can see that you are worried, but go ahead and you will do good on your trip. Your work will be received and you will get your pay, and your trip will be of a benefit to you. I feel impelled to write you these words, + they will be fulfilled to the very letter. You feel down, but the Lord has'nt forgot you and mother. You cannot

[Page B278L]

1905/April 1st/measure the good you do. You have great knowledge in the things of the Lord, few men equal you in sound judge- -ment, and by coming in contact with men your influence is felt, and the Lord is glorified through your precept and example. I feel to bless you with life, health, an an increase both temporally and spiritually. Your last days shall be your best days, with power to be saved in our Father's kingdom. Amen. Peace be to you dear Father, may our love for one another grow stronger through time and all eternity[blank]From Nephi.

P.S. Tell Joel and family to come along. I cannot come down." Blank line]

    This letter gave me great comfort. His words of promise are exactly in line with blessings I have received from the holy priesthood, and I believe they will be fulfilled.

Apr. 5/I endd Richard Williment. Also Sealed David C. Lyon, my brother in law to Eliza Shiland, his first wife

    At the Conference to day it was said there are 55 Stakes and 629 Bishop's Wards

"9th/Joel and Company went North to visit Thurston's relatives.

" 12th/Worked all day on my temple record

13/I endd William Williment family—children to parents. Also Endowed Simeon Mears, and sealed him + Mrs Simeon Mears.

    Gave blessings to Maria W.R. Wilcox, Eveline L. Babbitt and Eliza D. Fletcher, dear friends who have helped me in my temple work. They are women whom God loves.

Sat 15/ Quite unwell to day—kidneys—and lay in bed all day.

Sun. 16/ Still in bed all day. Obstruction in urinating

Mon. 17/ "   "   "   "   " Have eaten almost nothing for 3 days. No appetite.

Tues. 18/ Felt stronger, but kidneys no better. Went up town, but was tired, and accomplished nothing.[112]

Wed. 19/ Still weak, and kidneys apparently dead. I must again go up town. Lyman wants me to see a doctor.

Yester I got from Susan Joel's recommend to temple, and to day I sent it to him in Charlie's care. Logan.

[Page B279R]

1905/Apr. 20/Recd a demand from Cache Valley Bank to pay $358.49 with interest at 10 %. Cant pay it—no money.

21st/ Lyman's 46th birth day. Preston and wife came. Named and sick/ blessed Harriet's baby, Lyman spokesman. Named her Harriet Louise. I was just able to get around, by holding to things My kidneys seem absolutely dead. No power to pass urine. Unless this can be changed, it means death by dropsy, or the filling up of my body with fluid.

I got my blessings and read them. Much in them still remains to be fulfilled. I prayed the Father to make known to me if I have forfeited any of them, or if they are still for me. I received answer, that altho I have come short in many way, I have *not* forfeited any of my blessings,—they are still all mine by promise. Therefore, to fulfill them I must live and be healed. And so I received faith, an actual, living faith, to ask in faith that my kidneys renew their action and pass the fluids from my system. I went to sleep, and on awakening found it possible to urinate, + not with the severe pain, as before, but in a natural manner.

Sun. 23/ then I thought of my sister-friend Zina V.H. Bull, who has power in healing. I went to her, and asked her to bless me. She did so, and spoke in power. I felt better at once and the next day felt like a new man.

25/ Went to Gean's.

---

112. On this date, Martineau wrote to General Anderson to acknowledge receipt of instructions from the Department of Interior regarding the opening of the Uintah Indian Reservation. He also acknowledged receiving Anderson's letter of April 11, requesting corrections to his survey Contract No. 265. Since corrections to his survey depended on corrections to be made by Deputy Brown, Martineau wrote: "I cannot rectify *my* closing upon his erroneous (as alleged) lines until *they* are rectified. I will do my part of the work as soon as snow in the mountains shall sufficiently melt to permit work." James H. Martineau to Edward H. Anderson, April 18, 1905, Letters Received, Surveyor General's Office, Vol. 29, January 14–May 5, 1905, letter #7347, CSGUT.

[In margin, sideways: 26th Lilla's baby born]

Wed. 26./ Went to temple and endd Jan Haughout, and Jos Hutchinson next day. I sealed Jan + Elizabeth Haughout, also sealed children to Hewett Rand, on Thurs. 27th

Fri. 28/ Endowed John Hutchinson, and Sealed Fanity D. Columbine and Paul Columbine. Also two couples in marriage.

Sat. 29/ Visited Gean's with Mary A Freeze and her daughter.

Sun. 30/ Wrote to Susan, and looked over my temple work.

-----/

May 2/Attended by Special invitation of Bp. Iverson the reunion held in honor of Path J. Leach, Age 90. Banquet, speeches and flowers.

" 4*/ Blessed Phebe Woodruff Snow, wife of Prest Snow. She said had greatly desired it of me. Also blessed her daughter Florence Snow Critchlow and Mary Forster. I endowed Jos Sprague Sealed 3 coples.* Yesterday Sealed 3 families

[Page B280L]

1905/May 5/I endd Thos Hutchinson. Had 2 women helping, Ford + Hansen also and they endowed 2 women

" 6/ Lyman, Member of Commercial Club, went with them to Los Angeles, on Excursion, by invitation of Senator Clark. I am still quite feeble from my late attack of kidney disorder. Was in home all day.

" 8/ Gave 40 names for Baptism in the temple, males, paid 40¢

9/ Rain and Snow

" 11/ Endd Wm Mears. Ford Endd Ann Hutchinson, Eva H. for Susan H.

" 10/ Not well yet. Visited Gean, who will go to Castle Gate to live tomorrow, taking cow, and some furniture. May stay there a year.

" 11/Endd Wm Mears. Eva Hanson Endd Rishworth. Ed + Gean went in a cold rain storm. I blessed Zina Hyde Bull.

12/ End Jos Sprague. 8 Sisters worked for me in temple.

13/ Lyman returned home.

" 15/ Gave 21 female names for baptism for Sister S.J. Russell also 4 males + paid for same.

Blessed Miss Afton Young, who is very lame, rheumatism of 5 years standing, and much money spent. A cripple.

Gave a comforting blessing to Eva K. Hanson

17/ Endd Abraham Taylor and Mr. Abrams on 18th Sisters Bessie H Brown, Maddox assisting in Endowments for women.

19/ I end. F.J Blake. Assisted by Sisters Brinton, Pierce, Murphy, Bassett, Henderson, Carter, Maddox, and Reed. ^and Jenkinson^ Sealed Stanhope + family, 3 daughters. Blessed Lucille Critchlow, daughter of Florence, and Gr. Dau. of Prest Snow, a little girl, who had greatly desired a blessing from me.

20/ Got garments and hose for Susan

22/ Gave names of 2 men, + 5 women for Baptism in temple. Joel, Mary Ann, his wife, 2 children, Sister Thurston + her father came.

23/ Gave 20 female names for baptism in temple.

24/ Endd David Martineau, Joel for T.A. Corlett, Sisters Bassett, Henderson and Maddox assisted for female dead.

25/ Endd John Hilyard, Joel's wife Endd, also Bassett, Hanson, Madox, Perreninal,[?] Henderson + Naylor.

Sister Wooley, very low, sick over a year, wished me to come and administer to her at her house. Sent me word.

[Page B281R]

1905/May 25/I sealed Blake family, David Martineau family and P.M. Martin family to day. Sisters Pierce and Fletcher assisted. End 2 women.

26/ I End. Henry Columbine

29/ Sister Badger came with carriage to take me to her Sister Mrs Wooley who had wished me to come, and who is low and feeble—ner.[nervous] prostrations for more than a year. I went, blessed her, also Sister Badger.

Also went to Mary A.H. White, who last night stuck a garden rake tooth into her foot two inches; then administered at homes of E.K Hanson, who has diabetes, Sister Ford, ruptured. Sister Jane Hill + V. Zina Hyde Bull, who has cataract growing over her eyes. Then went over 6 miles and gave P. blessing to Helen Babbitt. Got home 9.30 P.M.

30/ Went up town and saw grand decoration parad[e]. Then to Saltair.

31/ Endd Henry Columbine. Mary Bassett for Susan Hutchinson. Also Sealed 3 couples. Patl Blessing to Evadne Henderson Hart

June/[Blank line]

1/ Endd Phillip Stanhope. Sisters Stevens, ~~Larsen~~, Iverson, Gave P.Bls to Sister Cooper and Langton. Gave Langton $1.00 for some Huguenot Martineau names she found in her Huguenot record

2/ I endowed Marinus, Duke of Rome, year 720. Marinus is same as Martinus, (Latin for Martineau). Sister Bassett for Farnun. I Sealed 3 families.

In the evening attended closing, graduation exercises of the High School, Class of 1905, of which Loyal is head. Over 70 graduates. In S.L. Theatre, which was full. All Lyman's family but Harriet + Gowan were there.

3/ Graduation exercises in Theatre again tonight. Royal is head of Class for 1905, graduating with highest honors and a record of 98 out of possible 100 points in all his branches of study. He has studied indefatigably to accomplish it + has succeeded.

20/ Went to Lagoon, on Nauvoo Legion excursion, 16m 25¢. Met my old friend—Wm K. Rice—with whom I lived in 1850 and with whom I went South and helped Settle Iron Co. in Spring of 1851. Saw also his eldest daughter. Mrs. Lucy A. Clark, also of Farmington, now a matron of 55, then, a little baby. Br. Rice is now over 80, and very feeble.

21/ By invitation of David Hess and wife of Farmington, visited them in company with Sisters Zina Hyde Bull and Mary Hyde White, sisters of Mrs. Hess. The widow of Orson Hyde was present.

[Page B282L]

1905/June 21st/whom I blessed, and gave a Patriarchal Blessing to Sister David Hess, her daughter. Had a very pleasant time.

" 22/ Again went to Farmington and Brigham City on Old Folks Excursion, 22 passenger cars—all filled—1148 people.

" 24/ Visited and blessed my patients, as tomorrow I go away.

" 25/ Started for Uintah reservation to do a little work.[113] Price

26+27/ On the road from Price to Vernal 130 miles—very bad ones.[114]

29/ Start out with Survey party and camp at Dry Fork. 15m

30/ Drove to forks of Whiterocks river and camped.

July 1/ Lay by, waiting for one of my men.

" 2/ Moved down to Farm Creek and Camped. Began work.

" 3/ Surveyed, also next day, 4th

" 4/ Today I was preserved from death by the direct aid of my Guardian Angel. I had to ascend a high mountain, very steep—too steep foe me to Climb on foot, so I started to ride up. I came to a wide belt of flat rocks, sloping downwards, and as I could see no way round it, attempted to ride up over it, but after a little my horse began slipping, got Scared and lost his wits and fell with me repeatedly. I sticking to him as he fell and rose again, doing my best to control him. Each time he fell, we tumbled farther down the rocks, the horse plunging frantically. After his last fall I found myself lying full length upon the rocks, at the horse's back, and above him. How I was laid there so carefully, without his falling upon my leg, or my brains not being dashed out, or any bones broken, and how my feet were loosed from the stirrups I cannot even guess, only that my Guardian Angel did it all, during all the plunging, falling, getting up, and falling again down the rocks. Had my feet hung in the stirrups nothing could have

---

113. Approval of Martineau's contract, No. 265, was withdrawn, presumably until corrections were made to comply with his instructions. Edward H. Anderson to James H. Martineau, May 13, 1905, Letters Sent, Surveyor General's Office, Vol. 43, December 10, 1904–May 31, 1905, 460; Edward H. Anderson to James H. Martineau, June 30, 1905 (two separate memoranda), Letters Sent, Surveyor General's Office, Vol. 44, June 1–November 21, 1905, 98 and 101, CSGUT.

114. From Whiterocks, Martineau wrote to General Anderson to request a manual and blank forms for swearing in his men. In his hurry to leave town, he had neglected to obtain the forms from the Land Office. James H. Martineau to Edward H. Anderson, June 27, 1905, Letters Received, Surveyor General's Office, Vol. 30, May 6–July 31, 1905, letter #7510, CSGUT.

saved me, and had I fallen under my horse, as was seemingly unavoidable, I might have lain there, crushed, till death.

I was somewhat to blame. For years, when about to ride over or along a dangerous place, as many times I have had to do, I always blessed my horse, that he might not stumble, fall, or cause me any hurt, but this day, I never once thought of doing it, and paid penalty.

In my tumbles I got some bruises, and a severe wrench over my middle caused not by falling but by struggles of the horse.

[Page B283R]

1905/July 4th/ It shows how careful we should always be, even about what we may esteem small things. My miraculous escape shows to me that I have still some work to do here on Earth. That is why my life was spared, by the mercy of Our Father.

" 6/ Must go to Vernal and take one of my men who fell down the rocks on foot yesterday and got badly hurt, reaching Vernal

" 8th/on the 7th Broke up party and engage a new one, as several quit. Some of my party were taken as Jurors, causing me loss of 4 days more, so that my man's fall cost me about $30.00[115]

" 13/ Start out again, finishing my work and returning to Vernal

" 17/on the 17th We had to camp on Water (Deep Creek) full of Alkali and tasting like a cow yard. Nearly all my me were made sick by it, excepting me,—another blessing from the Lord.

" 19/ Started home to City, reaching Castle Gate on the 20th and there I stayed two days with my daughter Virginia, husband + family, +

[In margin: 23] reaching City on the 23d Found Lyman's family away,

---

115. The following day, Martineau wrote to General Anderson to acknowledge receipt of a letter dated June 30 containing a telegraph from the GLO and blank forms. He also indicated that corrections to Contract No. 265 in Tp. 3 N., R. 1 W., and Tp. 2 N., Rs. 1 W. and 1 E., were finished. He had predicted only a few days more to complete corrections in Tp. 1 N., R. 2 E., which would finish all of his work. "I would have finished earlier," he wrote, "had I not been obliged to bring one of my party to Vernal, who was seriously hurt by falling in the rocks on July 6th." James H. Martineau to Edward H. Anderson, July 9, 1905, Letters Received, Surveyor General's Office, Vol. 30, May 6–July 31, 1905, letter #7542, CSGUT.

camping, Harriet, baby and husband Chas A. Gowan, at Lyman's house—baby with whooping Cough.

30/ To date have been writing up my field notes etc.[116] Has been very hot,—one death from heat in the city. Had a good celebration on the 24th but very hot, and I felt, too, a stranger among the 20.000 people that day in the Park. Visited Lagoon.

August 1905

Aug. 1st/Went to White's. Sisters A.M. Musser and Carter desired me to bless them, which I did. Sister White had just blessed them, too.

2/ Lyman took me to Barnum's circus. I then went to Bp. Preston's to see his sister Annis Chantrel, who had come from Cache Co. for me to bless and administer to her for a great swelling on her neck, which Surgeons Say Cannot be operated upon for fear of certain death. I blessed her, with Bp + Sister P. assisting.

10/ Up to date I have been working on my field notes. Today got word from Washington that part of my survey = $540.70 is ready for payment. I shall be glad to pay even part of my debt.

14/ Sister Julia Wooley, widow, Sent carriage for me to come to her, some miles, and bless her, sick, very, for 15 months. I promised her recovery, through faith.

Recd check for $540.70 from Govt. Sent. I paid Cache Valley Bank for $300.00 and with $72.29 interest. Glad it is paid.

[Page B284L]

1905/Aug. 15/ A few days ago I received Several letters from Susan dated in June and July, one contained a dream that to her seemed very impressive:—as follows:—"I thought I was living in a house in a canyon with very large trees whose branches were interlaced overhead. They seemed to be oaks, only they seemed to be so tall. I heard a strange sound and looked out of the window and saw one of those trees rise from the ground, and I went to the door and heard the sound of cracking limbs overhead, and

---

116. Martineau had been requested to file his corrective notes of surveys as soon as they were made. See Edward H. Anderson to James H. Martineau, July 21, 1905, Letters Sent, Surveyor General's Office, Vol. 44, June 1–November 21, 1905, 171, CSGUT.

saw 3 other trees rise up from the ground, their limbs still entwined together, and they sailed away in a southrty [southerly] direction and were Soon lost to sight. x x x The impression I had was that some of our leaders would leave us suddenly. Strong, sturdy oaks represent men and their leaving no roots shows that their families were left behind." Study and see if you can get the same feeling I have about it."

I believe it was a true dream, and that her interpretation is correct. I believe Changes will take place among our leading men, but whether by death or by some other way I cannot tell. But this is the work of our Father, and He knows just how to carry it on to a successful finish. So I house [sic] no fear or doubt,—only that I may be true to the end, according to promises made to me.
[Blank line]
Went to Calder's Park with temple workers to reunion of the B. Young family. Prest Smith spoke, with others. I became acquainted with many there and enjoyed myself much.

19/ Bought shoes, 3.50$ and pants 4.00$ first I have bo't for years.

20/ To Farmington, and saw my old friend Wm K. Rice, with whom I lived in 1850, when he had only 2 Children, William and Lucy A. the latter being only a few (6) months ago. He and I went and helped settle Iron Co. in the Spring of 1851, and had times of great danger with indians. Also with him when he bought Cora aged 9 yrs, and got Moshien, age 4 or 5 yrs.[117] We talked of old times. He is 2 or 3 yrs. older than I, and very feeble.

[Page B285R]

1905/Aug. 23/Went by invitation to Saltair on Butcher's + Grocers outing. About 20.000 there during the day. Had a fine bath in the lake, first for over 20 years. Had an enjoyable time with friends.

24/ Blessed Eva Hanson, who is ill with diabetes—quite low.

25/ Lyman and Allie went to Portland. I felt impelled to go to Br. H.A. Whites and there found Sisters A.M. Musser and Carter. They said they were hoping I would come, desiring blessings from me, which I gave them. Also blessed Sister White, who is quite ill. At 3 P.M. Met with

---

117. See entry at September 4, 1852.

temple workers and Stake and Ward officers at S.A. Kenner's house, to its dedication. About 40 present. Br Tollman, Patriarch dedicated the house. I opened by prayer, and later being placed in charge of the meeting by Bp. Warburton, who had to go. We had a grand time. Sisters Babbitt, W.W. Phelps, A.M. Musser, In. A. White and others spoke in power, also the few brothers there. Br. Foster and I blessed by request Several of the Sisters. One was deaf and desired hearing restored, another desired children, others were ill. Three other sisters have come to me for blessing that they may become mothers,—Frances Neff Smith, Florence Thatcher, of Logan, Florence Snow Chithlow, daughters of Prest Lorenzo Snow and Gr.dau. of Prest Woodruff. I pray their desires may be granted.

28/ Blessed Several sisters today

29/ Sent $5.00 for Wilson Ear Drum. My hearing is so poor Blessed Sisters Cummings and Knight. Also some others

31/ Quite unwell all day.

September 1905.

2/Paid $5.00 Cash tithing. Lyman and Alley got home.

5/Royal Martineau went to Harvard College. Bp + Sis. Preston were here. He blessed Royal and I gave him patriarchal blessing having his father lay on hands with me.

6/ Got word I must return to Uintah Reservation and make Some Changes in the Survey.[118]

7/ Blessed Mrs. Zina Hyde Bull, for her threatened blindness by Cataract growing over both eyes. Doctors say She must get blind. My faith is—she shall not become blind, for she may be healed through faith

8/ Visited temple. Administered to Julia Wooley, very sick for almost two years.

[Page B286L]

---

118. In reply to a letter of instructions for corrections to be made on his contract, Martineau wrote that he would make the corrections at the earliest possible time, "being at present physically indisposed." James H. Martineau to Edward H. Anderson, September 19, 1905, Letters Received, Surveyor General's Office, Vol. 31, July 7–November 27, 1905, letter #7658, CSGUT. See note at entry for September 20, 1905.

[Page has a small graphic, 26 Sept]

Sept. 9/1905/ Sister Wooley sent for me again. She is very low. Can speak only in a whisper. I blessed her again.

Sun. 10/ Blessed J. Wooley again. Bp Sheets sent urgent request to bless his little boy, whose legs are paralyzed. I went and blessed him and believe he will be perfectly healed.

Tues. 12/ Went to Farmington to funeral of Mary T. Richards, widow of Willard Richards. She was a dear friend of mine, who assisted me very many times in my Logan temple Sealings.

Wed. 13/ Worked in temple for Joseph Hutchinson. Next day for John Hutchinson. Miss Afton Young worked for Lois Martineau, Henry's daughter. Also she assisted me in Sealing 3 Couples.—1506+921–1547 +1009 and 313+918. (numbers on Names in my temple record.)

Fri. 15/ Endd Bartholomew Hutchinson. Blessed Fanny Palmer.

16/ Had my teeth (11 of them) Extracted. Only 5 left. Visited Evelina Babbitt, who is sick. While there blessed Margaret Caine and Jessie T.Y. Driggs.

17/ Recorded blessings. Visited Sisters Wooley and Fanny Blair Stringham and blessed them.

20/ In answer to my prayer this morning, before day, I received a glorious blessing. I desired, among other things, that I might good weather while upon my next trip to Uintah valley, Surveying,[119] and not be caught in equinoctial storm while camping out. Was told my prayer should be granted.

21/ Visited and blessed sister Babbitt, who is very sick.

Learn that Charles' baby was born Aug. 10. 1905

Tues. Sept. 26/ I start for Uintah 10P.M. Ride all night and arrived at Mack in Colorado 7 a.m. There I took Uintah R.y. 54 ½ M. to Dragon So

---

119. On this trip, Martineau was to make corrections on his contract and resurvey all boundaries of section 1, Tp. 3 N., R. 1 W., "including a retracement of the Reservation boundary," so as to show the actual conditions as they existed on the ground. Edward H. Anderson to James H. Martineau, September 18, 1905, Letters Sent, Surveyor General's Office, Vol. 44, June 1–November 21, 1905, 319–320, CSGUT. See note at entry for September 6, 1905.

named from the Dragon Asphaltum Mine. This R.R. Crosses the Book Cliff Mts. at Baxter Pass, Elev. 8500 ft. This road has an ascent of 450 ft per mile, with 60° curves and one of 70°, the line ascending the steep mountain side in a series of letter S lines, like this, [see graphic], as many as four lines at once being one above another.

28/ Leave Dragon by Stage 7 a.m. and reach Vernal 7 P.M. after 65 miles drive over a rough mountainous country. Just as I entered the house in Vernal, the rain fell in a deluge, continuing all night and for two days and nights, during which time I made up another survey party, and started anew on Oct. 2d to

Oct. 2/finish alterations required.

[Page B287R]

1905/Oct. 3/Began work in the Deep Creek country; finishing there on the 12th I moved up into Whiterocks Cañon, and finished my work up in the mountain locality, over 10000 ft altitude, and finished

" 20th/Oct. 20th and returned to Vernal. Here I remained Several days working up my notes.

During all my survey the promise made me before I started—that I should have good weather and no storm of Snow or rain while on my work was literally fulfilled, thought at times storms seemed inevitable Storming all around us, but not upon us, and we returned to Vernal on ground <u>dry</u>, not wet, as had been promised me. For all this, all praise be to Our Father, who condescended to hear the prayer of one so small as I am.

For some days the weather was intensely cold,—22° below Zero, and I had to dress in a double Suit of under clothing and over clothing too. But I took <u>no hurt</u>, even as I had been promised. To Our Father be all the praise.

During this work I had extraordinary experiences of deep anxiety and dread, followed by corresponding joy and peace, fear, lest I had been mistaken,—misled by false spirits causing me to think their whisperings were the voice of the Holy Spirit, or that what I supposed to be the voice of the Holy Spirit was <u>not</u>, and there, how should I ever learn to know His voice. This was to teach me how to <u>know</u> and judge the Spirits which operate upon me.

The Holy Spirit, in His influence, brings peace, joy, trust, faith and courage and trust in God; desire to do His will and to works of righteousness. The evil spirit incites exactly to the Opposite. I was told that when filled with fear, doubt and dread to rebuke that evil influence in the name of Jesus, + it should depart. And I found this true.

When I inquired why I should be thus troubled + afflicted I was plainly shown by a smile or parable by the Spirit, who said to me "Which is the better seaman, he who has all his life been only upon a small, unruffled lake, where he had no storm or danger to comfort him,—or a sailor, upon a tempestuous ocean, exposed often to hurricanes, shipwreck, and constant danger, accustomed to meet and overcome danger and death." The comparison and the

[Page B288L]

1905/Oct. 20th/answer—both plain as the noon-day sun, Satisfied me completely. I see it is absolutely needful to meet and learn to overcome difficulties if we would reach perfection and victory. Thus was I strengthened in faith, and in courage to strive for victory, and to learn to know the voice of the Holy Sprit, to be my strength, guide and comfort, as has long been my constant prayer.

During this time, when praying, I received many great and priceless promises, often while laying awake at night in Camp while all others slept; promises so great that I dare not write them now, but which were promised or foreshadowed in my patriarchal blessings, especially the last one given by Patriarch Chas W Hyde, who foresaw what was in Store for me, but feared to tell me, and whe he desired me to bless him, which I did, very unwillingly, fearing I was doing something I had no right to do, as I was not then a Patriarch except to my own family, causing me great dread until he said to me "Br. Martineau, that is word for word the blessing sealed upon me by Hyrum Smith in Nauvoo." I had told him things it seemed to me to be impossible of fulfillment, and thought I had been misled by an evil spirit for acting in an office not appointed me.

And so, although a hard and expensive trip, there has blessing been because of it. Truly "God moves in a mysterious way."

27th/ Left Vernal 7 a.m. Dragon 7 P.M. Next day to Mack

28/ Took D+R.G train 4 P.M. and arrived in City next morning

29th/at 4 A.M., long and tedious night ride + no sleep. Elev. of Mack, Col. = 3540 ft. Distance to S.L. City = 271m to Denver 469m

30/ Was sent for to administer to Julia Wooley, sick for 2 years nervous prostrations. Also visited and blessed Sisters Ford and Hansen.

31st/ Registered to vote at Election.

Nov. 7th/ Up to date I have gone to administer to the sick every day Sometimes to Several. One, a little boy 3 yrs old, paralyzed in both legs—limp as rags when I blessed him just before I left for Uintah the last time, can now stand on his legs.

[Page B289R]

1905/Nov. 7/And when I blessed him yesterday said "Now I can walk" + got sown on floor and <u>did</u> walk several steps. To God all the praise and Oh! how thankful I am that God deigns to show His mercy and power through one so weak and sinful as I. The boy will be fully healed, I fully believe, for he has great faith, tho so small. And Miss Afton Young, who was so almost helpless when first I blessed her is now very much improved and will soon be healed of the rheumatism, which for 5 years has resisted all the power of the doctors. Thus is the one great desire of my soul being granted—the power to bless, comfort and help the Sick and the afficted, the Sad and weary of Our Father's children.

I would do good, if possible, to the wickedest of men,—those who would even desire my death, Yet, to every son + daughter of Our Father. If they in, let Our Father judge them, not I ^me.^
[Blank line]
Today was election, and Lyman has gained great prestige as the Chairman and leader—manager of the Democratic party in S.L. City. He is credited with having made a magnificent fight against great odds, and great generalship, the Gentile (American) party were victorious. To Lyman, personally, it is a great victory politically, and his party give him unstinted praise.

The "American" party, gotten up by the Apostate, adulterer, and whoremonger Frank Cannon, is now in power, enemies to the Church. But God has permitted it, and He will not suffer His Church to be overthrown. He will continue and finish His work, no matter what may be the desire of our enemies.

[Blank line]

Note/ I think I should record here a comforting vision or dream given me about day break, Nov. 6, I had been praying, about 3 am for health and power to do great good, and that I might be fully healed and Strengthened in my kidneys, which have long been Seriously affected. The dream or vision was Short, but marvelously effective, showing perfect health and power in those organs, with promise never to have kidney disease.

At times the Father has given me other instruction and comfort in the same manner, a scene but momentary, but full of Significance, and so I have been helped when in deep distress of mind.

[Page B290L]

1905/Nov. 11/ This morning I received words of comfort and blessing that filled my soul with gladness,—that the Father approves my ministry as Patriarch—a Father among the Saints, and will open my way that I may greatly increase in power to do good in healing, comforting, blessing and helping the Saints, and in my work for the dead and the living, with approval of my Survey by the Government, and means in abundance, so I may devote the rest of my days to the work of the Lord, + to the living and the dead, with other promises, in Connection with the Lamanites and the Three Nephites so great that I hesitate to write them.[120] Oh that I may have power to do good to the fulness of my desires. I believe that I shall, for so said the voice of the Spirit to me, and I know He deceiveth not.

By letter from Susan, received today I find we have 10 great-great grand Children:—5 from Elvira's Son Joseph, 3 from Bertha, Henry's eldest daughter, and 1 from Harriet Lyman's daughter, and one from James Edward, Moroni's eldest Son. Truly God blesses me greatly. I pray all the time that I may increase all the time in heavenly gifts + in power to do good.

---

120. The Lamanites refers to one of four groups of ancient peoples in the Book of Mormon who, according to the narrative, repeatedly fell into iniquity—causing them to be marked with dark skin—but ultimately won favor with God. They were promised to inherit the Promised Land and initiate the gathering of Zion in the last days. The Three Nephites refers to three righteous individuals from the favored group of peoples—bearing white skin—who would be gathered from the four corners of the earth to help build Zion. These men were blessed by Jesus to "never taste of death" saying "ye shall live to behold all the doings of the Father unto the children of men, even until all things shall be fulfilled according to the will of the Father, when I shall come in my glory with the powers of heaven" (3 Nephi 28: 7). Church members believe that they roam the earth, giving aid to those in need. See Lee, *The Three Nephites*.

16/ Edd Sudbury came, with Florence. He gave me 2 prs. Each of undershirts, drawers and garments, which came very seasonably, as I had only one old, ragged undershirt and 1 old pair of drawers. I was very glad, and blessed him, that he shall never be without good clothing, which may God grant.

Lyman R. my son, was ordained High Priest by Apostle Moses Thatcher in Nov. 1881, on his appointment as President of the M.I.M.I. Association of Cache Co. of 32 Wards.

21/ Blessed Lillian V. Jones and Miss McKnight.

24/ Attended Priesthood Meeting of Granite Stake and was invited to Speak, which I did

25/ At Quar. Conference of the Stake. A grand time and a good dinner with visiting officials of the Church.

Nov. 21/ To day, by invitation of little Mary White, 2 years old 15 day, I attended her "Birf day party," organized by herself. She invited br. Motino, Aunty Kenner, Sister Sears and Fido (the dog) Several others Came also. A pleasant time.

[Page B291R]

1905/Nov. 21/ Tho only 2 years old little Mary has prayed daily for me. I think it is because I brought bananas for her at times, when she Could not eat anything else, hardly, and she could not get them. She prayed at various times to God for "Bannas," and it was so that always shortly after, I was impressed to bring her some, + this, to her, was an answer to her prayers. I believe it <u>was</u>. She has wonderful faith, naturally born in her.

" 25/ Recd a letter from my Cousin Napolion B. Van Slyke, one of my few remaining relatives of the olden time. He is 83, shortly (born Dec. 21. 1822) still an active business man.[121] He sent me information relative to his progenitors and family, and of my Sister Lois M. Voswinkel's family, which I insert here.

Children of

Lois Elena Martineau ^Born Aug. 10, 1838^ and John Peter Voswinkel, married 1860

---

121. Napoleon B. Van Slyke (1822–1909) was the son of Daniel Van Slyke, who married Laura Mears, the sister of Eliza Mears, James Martineau's mother. See note at entry for July 27, 1905.

Frederick William Voswinkel, B. Jan. 27 1862. Died Feb. 25 1895
Bertha Martineau   "   B. Jan. 9. 1864 – [no death date]
Adlienne   "   " May 26 1866 Died July 22 1866
Louis   "   " May 15 1868   " Sept. 11 1868
Caroline Whittlesey "   " Sep. 13. 1869 – – – – [no death date]
Alexander   "   " Dec. 25. 1870 D. July 1 1871
William   "   " June 2   1872 "   Aug. 5. 1872
Jenny Louise   "   " – 22 1873 – – [no death date]
 (married Donald Roderick Osborn July 28. 1878. has
 two children)
Lois Elenor   "   B. June 26 1876 – – – [no death date]

Note. She (Lois) says our half brother Charles Augustus, died in the last year of the civil war, before Richmond, of disease.

Cousin Napoleon Bonaparte Van Slyke's family.

He was son of Daniel Van Slyke and Laura Mears. ^Daniel was^ Born about [blank] Died 1831. Daniel Van Slyke's record.[122]

---

122. In November 1828, Daniel Van Slyke, a civil engineer, was appointed to the first division of resident engineers who worked on the Chesapeake and Ohio Canal. See Sanderlin, *The Great National Project*, 62.

By 1830, John Martineau and Daniel Van Slyke (both married to daughters of James Mears) had finished their service on the canal. John wrote to Daniel regarding another engineering project:

> We closed our business a month ago, very much to our loss, a loss entirely brought about by the want of good faith on the part of the government, who gave us the entire contract for this season; + then forsooth, before the ~~season~~ ^proper time^ of beginning in the spring lett [sic] three other contracts on the Delaware, + one at this place in direct violation of good faith with us. The opperation [sic] of ^this^ state of things was to our prejudice in many ways.
>
> I have thought of a plan for a dry dock and naval arsenal to be located at this city [New York] which unites all the desired requisits + facilities to make it a "*ne plus ultra*" I have shewn a sketch of it to Com: Chauncey [probably Captain Isaac Chauncey, 1772–1840], who highly approves it. In order to bring it into notice it must be submitted to the government, now I would be glad to have your views as to the proper mode of introducing it in order to its most favorable reception.
>
> I have thought that if Martin Van Buren Could be convinced of its ability he might be in some way interested in it so as to give it all his influence, by having which, if the government are not dead set against incurring further cost for valuable public works, till the debt is paid off, it would be [illegible] to take, particularly as the navy is one of a most decidedly popular character.
>
> Give my best respects to Laura Mary and James, not forgetting my love to Napoleon. It would afford me much pleasure to see all of you.

John Martineau to Daniel Van Slyke, November 9, 1830, Daniel Van Slyke Papers, New York Public Library.

His father Daniel's parents were Garrett and Catherine: their children were <u>John,</u> <u>Peter,</u> <u>Catherine</u> + <u>Daniel,</u> in the order ^above^

Napoleon's first wife was Laura Sheldon. His next wife is Annie Corbett, Still living. Their children—by Laura were Laura, Mare ^died^, Sheldon ^died^, and James. by Annie

(names of other 2 not given in letter)

Napolean's Grandchildren,—James' Children:—

[Page B292L]

1905/Children of James Van Slyke:–

Nov. 25/Ruth, age 18, John, 16. Maie 13. Elizabeth 5yrs.^1900^ of Age.
   B 1887   1889   1892   1900

" 27/ Winter Commences today—Rain, followed by Snow storm.

December/[Blank line]

3th/ We all went to Bp. Preston's for family dinner. Pleasant.

4/By invitation I visited Sister Maria W. Richards Wilcox, sister of Saml W. Richards, and while there blessed her two daughters, Matilda W. Wilcox—Cummings and Ellen A.W. Wilcox Hyde, also Br. Horace H. Cummings. Also administered to Sister Wilcox, suffering from indigestion. Had a pleasant time.

" 16/ Visited Sister Zina Hyde Bull, who has cataract, and can hardly see. She said, "Oh! I'm so glad you've come." She wanted me to bless her; also to bless her sister Delia Ellis, who has joined the Christian Science nonsense and is now visiting her, from Seattle, Oregon. She said her sister, still feeble from a recent hospital operation, wished me to bless her, for her health. I did so, having asked Our Father about it, and being told to do so, and that she should be blessed. I then visited a widow, Jenny Hill who also was very glad I came. She was very sad,—husband, daughter and son taken by death. I was full of pity, and sealed a comforting blessing upon her, and she <u>was</u> blessed indeed. I then walked about 2 miles or more (to save car fare, which is scarce with me now) to See Sister White. Found her children sick, and blessed them. Then walked about a mile to see a little boy of 3 years, whose legs are paralyzed, and blessed him. Then walked about 2 miles home, several hours after dark.

I give this day's work as a sample of what I have done for two years in this city, few days passing without visiting and blessing the sick. Often so tired, but always glad to help and comfort others. It is what I live for. I wish to live no longer than I can do good to others, and God has greatly blessed me and my labors in this, all praise be to His holy name, for all good is from Him.

19/ Visited Sister Hill, who feels much happier since I blessed her a few days ago. Mrs. Delia Ellis and

[Page B293R]

1905/Dec. 19/Zina Hyde Bull were also there. Mrs. Ellis wished me to bless her, that her knees might be healed—weak and painful from her operation in hospital. She said she was very much better since I blessed her some days before, + believed she could be blessed now. So I blessed her again, and believe God will bless and heal her, and hope she may come back again to the Church.

Today I finished the following verses, and sent to Susan in place of other Christmas gifts, which I am unable to Send:—

[Poem follows:]
[Blank line]
Lines to my wife for our Wedding day, Jan. 8. 1852
[Blank line]
Susana guerida! Thou wife of my youth
How blessed was the day in its dawning.
When, youthful, we plighted our love our truth
In the brightness of Life's early morning.
[Blank line]
How changeful the scenes since the hour we met—
Grim darkness the light oft succeeding!—
Gay laughter so joyous—then our pillow soon wet
With tears that would come without seeking.
[Blank line]
The friends of our youth—from Earth they are gone—
From this sphere now so darksome and dreary;
While we we who remain feebly totter along
To our haven of rest, worn and weary.
[Blank line]

But there is a clime—oh! blissful and bright!
Where dwelleth out Father and Mother,
Where be ameth [becometh?] forever that radiant light
That shineth in heaven forever
[Blank line]
Then let us take courage—in Father we'll trust
Whose acts are all pure, just and holy
When our work here is finished gain heavenly rest
With our Savior—once homeless and lowly

[Page B294L]

1905/Nov. Dec. 23/Visited and blessed Julia Wooley, who said "Oh! I'm glad you have come! You have done me so much good—more than one has ever done. She gave me a handkerchief to send to Susaying [Susan saying] "Tell her I love her, tho I never have seen her." She said "She is a good woman,—pure in spirit as this handkerchief, and I love her."

24/ Visited Gean's after Tabernacle meeting.

25/ Christmas again. I wonder if I will see any or many more on this life. I had a few presents. Bp. Preston fell down stairs early this morning, and was unconscious when picked up. I hope nothing serious may result. Wrote letters to nearly all my children.

--------------- line across page ----------------

1906/ January 1906.

Jan. 8th/ To day in the anniversary—54th—of our marriage, Susan E. Johnson's and mine. But no beloved wife was near nor any one to care for it. Seemingly, but I felt lonely all day. Well, when we both go to the "other Side" sad lonely lives and partings will be no more for us. What a comforting thought! 54 years is a good while for people to live together as husband and wife, and in all these years she never, even once, gave me any wrong or evil counsel, but <u>always</u> her counsel was for good, not evil.

11/ I started to day to go to administer to Bp. Preston, but felt to stop by the way and see Sister Maud Patterson, a widow. I did not know where she lived, but felt I must go there.

When I found her house I found why I went there. A woman, Lydia E. Carter White was in an agony—four days and nights—peritonitis in dangerous form, and some internal complication—female—also dangerous in nature.

When I came in the woman exclaimed "Oh! I'm so glad you have come! The Lord has surely sent you to help." I found the doctor had just gone, his last words were—"If the pain continues, dont wait for me—get to the hospital just as quick as you can, if you would live, and have an operation at once." I asked out Father about her case. The answer was,—"She is <u>not</u> appointed unto death, but may be healed by my power and not by that of man, nor need

[Begins with 4 unpaged pages of a letter from Joel dated Jan 8, 1906, from Guerrero to JHM 819 Logan Ave, SLC, on the occasion of JHM's 54th wedding anniversary, has some business information]

[Page B295R]

1906/[Blank line]

go through any surgical operation." I told Sister White this and asked if she believed it. She said. I then administered to her, and she was healed almost instantly of all pain, which till then, had caused her to writhe in agony. Peritonitis was perfectly healed, and the trouble in her abdomen. But she still felt she must go to the hospital for an operation. But I Said she could be healed without it, by faith. And she was, + is now, a month later, well, praise be to our Father above for to Him all the praise and glory.

Jan. 18th/ Attended a Social meeting of temple workers, at Knight's Peasant time. I spoke and felt blessed

Jan. 14/ Was invited by Br. and Sister Morris B. Young to bless their children, and was urgently desired to go and administer to a young woman, Miss Stella Wickel, very Sick and in agony.[123] I went there from Young's and found Stella in great pain in her loins, and doctor said—appendecitis, another—inflammation of the ovaries. Both said she must have surgical operation if she wished to live. I obtained a testimony regarding her like that of Lydia E.W. Carter, (see previous page), told Stella, she said she believed, was prayed for, and mended from that time, + is now well—and no surgeon required.

---

123. This probably refers to Morris Brigham Young (b. 1874) who married Olive Edith Forbes (b. 1878). Estella Fannie Wickel (1884–1981) was born to Richard Wickel and Charlotte Ann Stevens and later married Charles Elmer Mongomery on May 22, 1907.

While with Stella, another woman sent urgently for me. I found her in a very dangerous condition, she fearing lest she lose her unborn babe. I blessed her also, and she felt better at once, and is now doing well.

I record these cases—all desperate ones—that my children may see how our Father blesses those who put their trust in Him, and that they make great faith also
[Blank line]
During the past month I have given patriarchal blessings to many—40 or 50—and scarcely a single day has passed that I did not visit and administer to the sick, often 3 to 5 a day, traveling miles at night on foot, in mud or snow, while it was counted very dangerous to do so because of thugs + murders committed almost Every night. But I had a promise, by the voice of the Holy Spirit saying no one would harm or molest me, and thus far, it has been So.

[Page B296L]

1906/Feb. 2nd/Today a woman ^Mrs. Langton^ came from home several miles distant + brought her married daughter ^Mrs. Elizabeth Driggs^ for me to bless and help if I could, she being in a very bad condition, enciente, broken down, bloodless, and so nervous she shook all over like one in a heavy chill, and afraid she was going crazy.[124]

She had been told she must have an operation to get rid of her babe—unborn—was told she would be justified, as it was as lawful to kill a babe to save its mother's life. I could not consent to this, but she quoted examples in town, and felt it must be done. After, or while administering to her she felt much better and her nervous spasms and jerks ceased. I gave her then a Patl Blessing, and she went away like an entirely different person, and could smile + Even laugh. The change was wonderful indeed, all praise to our Father in heaven.

" 4/ I blessed Sister Maud Patterson, her two children and Lydia Carter's little girl, who asked for a blessing.[125]

" 6/ I was called to visit Sis. Stillman, who was in great need of help, soon

---

124. Elizabeth E. Langton (1871–1922) was born to Fredrick and Elizabeth Emily (Downes) Langton; she married Benjamin Woodbury Jr. Driggs on June 25, 1894.

125. This could refer to Maud Patterson (b. 1876), Lydia Estelle (Carter) White (1874–1957) and her seven-year-old daughter, Dorothy.

to be confined, and at times unable to talk, or use words she wished—could not remember her own name, and feared she would lose her mind. I blessed her, and she was at once much better, her mind clear, and filled with hope and faith, and I feel sure all will be well with her in her confinement.

And thus I am called for continually, and I thank Our Father I am enabled, by His blessing, to do some good.

9/ Attended a meeting of temple workers at the house of the Mourie [Maori] prince lately deceased.[126] About 40 present and a lovely time. His widow and family very much pleased. Several were administered to. Mrs Ida White wished me to bless her, that she might have children. I did so.

10/ I visited Sister Elizth Driggs, whom I blessed on the 2d and the change in her, for good, was astonishing to me although I had fully expected her to be healed. She was another woman—no one would think she had been sick. Words could not express her joy and thankfulness. It was a great testimony to <u>me</u> also.

[Page B297R]

1906/Feb./ By recent letter from Susan, I learn that Moroni's Son, James Edward's wife's maiden name is Myrtle Clark

His baby boy is named Edward Bernard Martineau and was born Oct. 6. 1905 in Chuichupa, Chihuahua Mex.

11th/ Sunday visited and blessed sister Julia Wooley, also her daughter Jessie, whose eyes are very weak. Then to our Ward meeting, then to Elizth Driggs, who is doing finely. Got home quite late at night, as Driggs lives about 6 or 7 miles off.

14/ A Mrs. Murdock, unknown by me, phoned for me to come and bless her. I found her, weak and feeble, and troubled because of a tumor in her body, which she was told must be removed at the hospital—a place she dreaded to visit. Her husband, James B. Murdock, is not a Mormon, but seems a good man.

---

126. This refers to the death of Hirini Whaanga, a former Maori chief, who had converted to Mormonism in 1882. He traveled from New Zealand to Salt Lake City in 1894 to do temple work and chose to reside there until his death on October 17, 1905. See "Maori Chief Passes Away," *Salt Lake Herald*, October 18, 1905, 5, and "Ex Chief of Maoris Dies in Salt Lake," *Salt Lake Tribune*, October 18, 1905, 3.

I blessed her and her mother. She is promised her tumor shall pass away naturally, and she become healthy and strong as she was in girlhood, through faith. he said she believed. If she does and continues she shall be fully healed, without and Surgery or knife.

On my way home I visited and blessed Fanny Blair Stringham, an old friend who had phoned, also, for me to come and visit and bless her. She is feeble, with a boy a few weeks old. She has a swelled neck, and har [hard] of hearing, for which she wished to blessed and healed. I did so, and believe she <u>will</u> be fully healed. Some 2 months ago, she wished me to bless her for her approaching confinement, feeling them greatly in fear of that trial. I blessed her that she should have the quickest, easiest and best confinement she ever had had. She now told <u>every word</u> of my blessing at that time had been fulfilled. Oh! how thankful I am to Father for blessing the Sick, fearful and suffering and showing forth His power + goodness through so weak a one as I, and that He enables me to help and comfort those who need it!

15/ By letter from Susan and Gertrude I learn G. is getting well. How thankful I shall be, when she <u>is</u> well and my dear wife be relieved from the wearing care and anxiety she has born so long.

[Page B298L]

1906/Feb. 17th/and 18th/Attended Quarterly Conference of Granite Stake. Spoke Sunday 18. Conference continued. A grand time. Prest J.F. Smith Spoke in mighty power. He wept, I, and others also. He spoke of Ruth's Covenant with Naomi, in power. At close of meeting I took his hand and blessed him. He pressed my hand. I then said to him, "Brother Smith, the covenant Ruth made with Naomi I make with you." He pressed my hand so warmly! and gave me such a look! I cannot describe it, but it was full of love, glad surprise and joy. Afterwards I felt as John when he baptized Jesus—it was for him to bless me, not for me him—the less to bless the greater. But it was done on the inspiration of the moment.

I afterwards asked the Father about it, and the answer was "It was right, and was pleasing to thy brother."

Fri. 23/ Blessed Victor and Norma Cummings. Heavy Snow.

Sun. 25/Ward meeting. Assisted in blessing and setting apart Several Sisters, as officers in Relief Society, also for washing and anointing the sick, and other duties. Then about 6 miles to visit a very sick woman who had Sent for me to visit her, a Mrs. Jenny Brooks. She was very sick, weak and frail, hardly able to walk or even talk—Cancer on both breasts. I tried to cheer her, and blessed her, to be healed, live + labor in the temple to be built in Zion—Jackson Co. Mo.

I had obtained this testimony before I went. She was very much better when I left her. I thank thee, oh God for the privilige thou hast given me to comfort + heal the afflicted. After meeting, to day, I was requested to go and bless two Sisters, who are in precarious health, South and Kimball.

March/ March 1906

1/Heavy snow storm, worst of the winter. Snow nearly 1 ft deep. I am quite ill with rheumatism, and can hardly walk.

2/ Alley's birth day.

6/ Am better, but walking hurts me a little. Visited Sister Brooks. A desperate condition. In Constant, heavy pain in breast and stomach (she thinks indigestion) hardly able to breathe, and each breath with much pain, can only talk a little and in whisper very faintly. Blessed her again, to be healed. I believe she will be.

[Page B299R]

1906/March 8/ E Guy Taylor came, on his way home from Canada. With him came a young woman, introduced to me as Miss Watts. They Spent the Evening with us and went on to Mexico at 11 P.M.

Sun. 11/ A hard day for me. Started out after breakfast, and spent most of the day visiting the sick. Walked Several miles to get to the afternoon meeting, and then to the sick again. Got home at about 10 P.M. But I was greatly blessed, in giving comfort to those Sisters who needed it so badly, so very ill and low with disease.

12/Was told in the Sur Genl office they could not approve my Survey. It was owing to erroneous work of a Mr. Brown, who Surveyed the Bdy. [boundary] line of the Uintah Ind. Reservation upon which my work joined.[127] I felt much distressed, for to go over part of it again could not

---

127. Martineau had received letters from Surveyor General Hull reminding him that he had yet to file returns on corrections he was directed to make on Contract No. 265. See

be done before next June because of Snow at so great an elevation (over 10000 feet), and the trip would cost over $200.00 which I knew not how to obtain; and I would be unable to pay the $3000.00 I already owe, to those who need it, and gave me help in my Survey.[128] But worst of all, I feared I had been misled by some delusive spirit, for in answer to prayer I had been told I should not have to go again to make any corrections, and that my Survey should speedily be accepted and paid in full. And now it seemed as if I had been deceived by some evil power, and how can I learn to know the true from the false! How can I know, as I bless one, that I am led by a good and not by an evil spirit! It seems all very dark to me as I pray during the night.

13th/ But as I wake I seem to see a letter from the Land Commissioner in Washington, saying my work is accepted there, and will be paid. If so, then I know I have been led by the true spirit and not the false one, and that when I bless, that my words are dictated by the Holy Spirit.

Cold, stormy and Snowing. Well any weather is better than none, but it seems dismal to me.

My 78th Birthday! And I used to think I would never be older than 45 or 50! It is truly the blessing from the Lord.

(12th)/ Yesterday, I was called to see a sister who fears miscarriage, and had faith I could help her. I blessed her that all will be well with her, and her frequent miscarriages shall cease from this time forth. Her mother, Sister Maria W. Richards Wilcox told me that she herself was perfectly healed of indigestion since

[Page B300L]

1906/Mch. 13/I blessed her and rebuked it. She had for years suffered from it. Could eat scarcely anything, and even that put her in excruciating pain. I blessed her about Jan. 10th and she is now perfectly healed, even from

---

Thomas Hull to James H. Martineau, January 5, 1906 and January 24, 1906, Letters Sent, Surveyor General's Office, Vol. 45, November 28, 1905–May 11, 1906, 123 and 196.

128. Martineau's worry about paying for his expenses caused him to ask Hull for a "personal favor" to help him obtain partial payment on his contract. The expense to complete the corrections on his contract, he wrote, "will be as much, or more than $450.00 judging by my previous experience." Anything that Hull could do in his behalf would be much appreciated. "I wish to get to work soon as possible and make a final end," he wrote. James H. Martineau to Thomas Hull, May 29, 1906, Letters Received, Surveyor General's Office, Vol. 34, June 2, 1906–September 22, 1906, letter #8087, CSGUT.

that very day. She is full of life + like a young woman, tho now about my age. Thanks to to Thee! Oh, my Father in Heaven, that Thou hast permitted me to be an instrument through whom to show Thy power, mercy and goodness to her and so many others! And I thank Thee for the power to do good, for <u>that</u> is all I desire to live for! Help me to continue and to increase in doing good, my Father, and all the glory be to Thee forever. Amen.

14/ My survey notes were sent to Washington today.

17/ For several days I have been almost sick, with very bad cold and cough. To day I was phoned to go to Walnut Ave to see some unknown person, presumably sick, altho I was quite unwell I went, and found a sister with a heart trouble—leakage of the heart. I blessed her that she should be healed. Also present another Sister in Some trouble whom I comforted all I could.

18th/ After visiting Virginia I went to the Tabernacle meeting and met a Sister Sharp, who wished me to go with her and bless some one. I went to Mr. Murdock's and met two young ladies and a Brother Paradise who desired P. Blessings. I blessed them all, and felt well.

20/ Went to Logan, and went to Lilla's to stay. Have a very bad cough and cold. Cold and Stormy—snow.

21/ Visited Charles and family, also Lamoreaux's and Will Preston's. Very cold and Stormy. Snow all over valley.

22/ Quite unwell. In house all day. Lilla had her tooth drawn yesterday, and is now better. She had feared a stroke of paralysis, last Sunday.

23/ Nephi came from Benson Ward. Roads almost bottomless. I visited Aurelia, his eldest daughter, training as nurse in the hospital.

24/ Spent day at Charles's

25/ At meeting, Spoke, and felt well. After meeting, letter from Susan, saying Gertrude is very low—fading away, and I must come soon if I would see her again. Still raining.

[Page B301R]

1906/Mch. 26/Returned to S.L. City at noon. Find that Virginia is very sick danger of miscarriage. Went to her after dinner. Next, I bid good bye to some dear friends in Emerson Ward, + others.

27/ Still quite unwell. In bed all day till 5 P.M. then walked to LeGrand Young's to See Afton, whom I had before blessed for her rheumatism. Found her greatly improved. I blessed her again. She, her father and mother were very glad I came. Still raining, cold and Muddy. Walked over two miles.

28/ Visited Gean. Also Eliza Jones, and blessed the last, for heart disease, from which she has Suffered 8 years.[129] Was also Sent for to Forest Dale, to administer to Sis. Gardner, for heart trouble. Also blessed a sister Brum for cancer in the breast. Thus I have visited and blessed parties many miles apart.—have walked some miles, but feel better.

29/ Sent for again, to Forest Dale. Blessed Alice Grover, who has had 3 bones taken from her spine, and suffers much. Thence I went about 6 or more miles to See Sis. Bliss (Cum) threatened with miscarriage. Found her mother, En. W.R. Wilcox very Sick. Blessed her. Thence 5 miles home to Lyman's. <u>tired</u>.

30/ Went to See Gean, who is rather worse today. Thence to Preston's From there to While's. Found her and Hazel very sick. Blessed them. Then to Eva Hanson, very sick—diabetes. Then to Matilda Ford, very weak from Severe operation in hospital. Blessed her, then to Lyman's at night—9 P.M.

There are so many sick who desire my help, though I am quite ill myself, but the Lord blesses my labors.

April/ <u>Sunday April 1st 1906.</u>

1/Snowing heavily all day, and last night. I am still quite unwell, and did not get up fro breakfast, lying abed till noon. Was called by telephone to go to Sis. Julia Wooley. I went up to town, got two sisters to accompany me + we then went about 4 miles to Sis. Wooley's. Blessed her, then went to Fanny Blair Stringham, blessed her for swelling on her neck and deafness. Thence (Snow nearly a foot deep) about 5 miles up City Creek Cañon to Br. F.E. Barker's, whose wife fears a miscarriage, blessed her, and her son, who has a hot fever. Then to Sis. Anderson, whose left arm is totally paralyzed and her side and leg partially, blessed

---

129. This is the last mention of Mary Eliza (Brown) Jones (1836–1916) who had married Martineau as a plural wife on December 27, 1877. She died on November 18, 1916. See entries at March 5, 1877 and December 22, 1877. She had been married to Nathaniel Vary Jones (1822–1863), whom Martineau met while staying at the home of Almon W. Babbitt during the winter of 1856–1857. See entry for July 23, 1877.

[Page B302L]

1906/April 1st/Cond/Started home but stopped to White's and found her very ill, also her baby. Blessed both; then went to Eva Hanson who is very low, and blessed her; also Sis. Ford, who is very weak from a Severe operation in the hospital, and blessed her. Thence home, quite late—10 or 11 P.M. Thus I have often gone, traveling miles at night, sometimes in mud,—Snow—or rain, when men were sand bagged and robbed almost every night. Lyman's family were worried lest I come to grief, but I trust in the blessing of the Lord, in doing His work among the sick, and so I have no fear. Still quite ill with cold on my lungs.

3d/ Lay all day in bed till 5 P.M. Thought of Afton Young, who is still rheumatic. Arose and visited and blessed her, returning home about 9 P.M. Walked two miles. She and her parents were very glad I came, as all are whom I visit.

4/ Attended funeral of my dear Sister, Eva Hanson. Spoke and was blessed in so doing, and believe others felt well.

5/ Went about 6 miles to Lydia Brooks, who fears miscarriage + blessed her. Then visited Sis. Driggs, whom I had blessed previously, and found her wonderfully improved. Home.

6/ Attended Conference. Then to Bp. Sheets, and blessed his son partially paralyzed, but greatly improved since my last visit. Blessed him. He can now walk, and play out of doors. Was entirely paralyzed when I first blessed him. To God be all the praise, for His mercy to the boy. I walked all the way home, 4 miles. In the evening I went to Kimball's and gave patl Blessing to his wife, Miss M.M. Merrill and a Sister Harper. Home 10.30 P.M.

Albey, ^+^ Mary Sherman, and daughter Elvira Came.

7th+8th/ Conference. 3 New Apostles chosen, two dropped from Apostleship.—M.F. Cowley and J.W. Taylor.[130] About 15000 present at Conference.

10/ In temple, to do a work for Susan Julia's (my wife) father Lyman R. Sherman and his wife (Susan's Aunt) Delcena D. Johnson, who have long

---

130. Mathias F. Cowley and John W. Taylor openly opposed the Second Manifesto of 1904 and were dropped from the Quorum of the Twelve. Taylor continued to oppose the Manifesto and was excommunicated in 1911. See Cannon, "After the Manifesto," 201, 209–210.

been waiting for their blessings. He died in 1839, Jany, a martyr, as Prest H.C. Kimball told me, also Prest G.A. Smith, his death

[Page B303R]

1906/April/11/came by the exposure and hardship consequent upon his constant labors in guarding and protecting Joseph Smith and the Saints in the persecution of 1838. He and she had never been sealed as husband and wife, though married by the law of the land, in the church. He had not been endowed. She, his widow, was endowed in Nauvoo. In addition, I have greatly desired their 2n A. feeling they are worthy if any are, and I made application to Prest Jos. F. Smith in their behalf. He desired something written, in support of my application, and I wrote what I knew in favor, and said I would hold myself responsible. Last evening I was told over the phone my wish is granted.

I endowed Nathaniel Hutchinson, Albey Sherman endd Seth, his brother, Mary Sherman endd Amy Johnson and Elvira Cox endd Elizth Blackburn. Also Sister Wessman endd Elizth H. Freak for me.

Mary Elvira, Albey, Seth and Susan Julia, LR Sherman's Children, were Sealed to him and Delcena, his wife

I acted for the father, + Mary E. Cox for the mother.

13/ To day two infant children were also Sealed to L.R. and D.D. Sherman, viz. Alson, a boy, and Sarah, each about 1 yr. of age.

I also had the unspeakably great pleasure to act as proxy for Lyman R. Sherman, and Mary E. Cox as proxy for Delcena Diadama Johnson Sherman, in the holy 2d A.

Words cannot tell my joy. Now, they are united never to Sevor; their children are now theirs, Susan, my wife, now has father and mother legally in the line of the priesthood; they have gained their exaltation and glory. How wonderfully good Our Father has been to me, in permitting me to bring all this to pass, Albey giving his assent, he being legal heir to labor for his father, but not eligible to act in the last + highest ordinance given on Earth.

Lyman Sherman joined the church in 1831, was the first who ever spoke in tongues in this dispensation. Prest Kimball told me that LRS. was the Sweetest Singer in tongues in the Church, and was Joseph's "right hand man," in Missouri.[131]

Prest Smith said L.R.S. was appointed an apostle, but

[Page B304L]

1906/April 13/his untimely death occurred before there was opportunity for his ordination.

While Widow Sherman lived in Nauvoo, Joseph Smith came to see her, while Susan, her little daughter (my wife) was sick and bribed the child to take some medicine by promise of a plate with letters around the edge, as she sat upon his lap. Joseph had a sister—Almera—sealed to him as wife, Sister of Delcena Sherman,—my wife's Aunt. She died in Parowan about 1878 if I remember the date rightly. She had married a Mr. Barton.[132]

---

131. See Compton, *In Sacred Loneliness*, 291–294, and Cook, "Lyman Sherman," 123–124.

132. According to Todd Compton, both Delcena Diadamia Johnson Sherman and Almera Woodward Johnson were married to Joseph Smith. Although Delcena's union to Smith is poorly documented, Benjamin Johnson wrote that Delcena was sealed to Smith "by proxy" sometime in early July 1842. Compton speculates that this would have been "something of a Levirate marriage, marrying the widow of a brother in the gospel." He also suggests that the marriage was "an early proxy marriage in which Delcena married Lyman for eternity, with Smith standing proxy for the dead man, after which Delcena and the Mormon leader would have been sealed for time." Delcena lived with Louisa Beaman, during which time he provided for their care and comfort.

In answer to a query regarding the rumored marriage of Delcena to Joseph Smith, Martineau wrote:

> The oldest sister of Uncle Ben was Nancy Maria Johnson born Aug. 1, 1803, died 30 Oct. 1836, before plural marriage was revealed, so, if she was sealed to Joseph it was after her death, not while living. While my wife Susan E. and I were in [his] house in Mesa, she asked him if his sister Delcena was ever sealed to Joseph. He said if that was so he '[Page chipped and word missing] never heard of it.' He was better informed upon such [word missing] than most men, Joseph loved L. R. Sherman very dearly and I do not believe he would take his wife from him. If he took her at all it would be for time only, not as his very own. She was 'wife for time' to Almon Babbitt, but I know he had sister Almera Johnson (I mean Joseph) I knew her myself while she lived + died in Parowan, Utah. Joseph also wished sister Esther to marry him, but she declined him. As you say Delcena, was spoken of by Uncle Ben as his oldest sister, probably because she was his eldest, Nancy having died long before, and I this [sic] is where the error may possibly be. In all my intercourse with Uncle Ben He never referred to any marriage of Delcena to Joseph Smith, and in writing his journal we had many talks 'on the side'— other than his own special items.

James H. Martineau to Charles S. Sellers, November 1, 1911, Johnson Family Correspondence, MS 14631, LDSCHL.

13/ And so this is a grand "red-letter" day in my life, this 13th day of April 1906. Father, I thank Thee for thy goodness.

Today Albey endowed his father, and Mary S. endd—Hutchinson [appear that JHM left blank line at first, later added Hutchinson]

This finishes—for the present, my temple work here + I took leave of some of my fellow laborers.

12th/ Blessed Frances A Langton[133]

14/ Busy in Sur. Genl Office. Sent my last Sur. Notes.

15/ Sunday Admd to Lydia Smith, Julia Wooley, Pat. Bl. to her Son Claude.[134] Admd to Fanny B. Stringham, also to Walter Sheets (paralyzed partially) Thence Home. I had walked 4 miles and was tired.

16/ Mon. Sent additional items of life of Lyman R Sherman to Prest Jos. F. Smith, taken from life of H.C. Kimball, who says Sherman was appointed an Apostle in place of Tho. B. Marsh by the Prophet Joseph while he was in Liberty Jail, date, Jan. 16. 1839. Sherman was sick at the time and died in a few days, (about) Feb. 15. 1839. before he could be ordained.[135]

In the evening, at 6.30 P.M. went several miles in Br. Best's Carriage to bless his wife, bedfast 9 yrs. in Heavy rain storm, in Winder Ward. Attended Dr Kerte's funeral, and spoke.

17/ Visited Gean and family for good-bye. Then to Br. Best's Gave her Patl Blessing, also to Br. R.S. Horne.[136] Admd Sis. L. whos feet are partially paralyzed. Thence 7 miles to Sis. H.A. Ensign, very sick, + admd to her, then to Mary White Bld, her and Hazel. Home 10.30 P.M.

Almera's marriage to Smith, on the other hand, was better documented. Compton dates Almera's marriage sometime in April 1843. She married James Reuben Barton for time on November 16, 1845, in Nauvoo. She died on March 4, 1896, of "paralytic stroke" in Parowan at age eighty-three. See Compton, *In Sacred Loneliness*, Chapter 12, "Loving Sisters," 288–305; photographs of Delcena and Almera appear in the photo section.

133. Probably Frances Ellen Langton (1886–1906), who was born to Isaac and Phoebe (Lindsey) Langton and married James O'Connor on October 31, 1906.

134. Lydia Smith, Julia Wooley, son Elande, and Fanny B. Stringham are not found in extant sources. Walter Taylor Sheets (1902–1943) was born to Edwin Spencer and Alice (Taylor) Sheets.

135. See Orson F. Whitney, *Life of Heber C. Kimball*, 250–251.

136. Probably Richard Stephen Horne (1844–1925) who was born to Joseph and Mary Isabella (Hales) Horne.

[Page B305R]

1906/Apr. 17/ Felt a slight Earthquake shock about 5 P.M. but did no damage.

18/ Visited LeGrand Young and family + Bld. Aften. Her chronic rheumatism is almost healed. Sick 5 years.

19/ Paid San Pedro RR. $21.55 for half rate ticket to Colton 781 miles. Also $5.50 for Pullman berth; $1.25 to get baggage to depot. Also $2.60 for 50 lbs excess weight.

In the afternoon Bp. W.B. Preston and wife, Gean, and Sister Moses Thatcher visited me. Sis. Preston gave me $15.00 and Lyman lent me $25.00, making a little more than R.R. fare with what I had before. I blessed Lyman and his family, and dedicated his house, also Dr. Chas Gowen's (Harriet's husband) At 10 P.M. Went to Depot and

20th/left Friday Morning, Midnight 12 1' a.m. Lyman helped me till train started. He and Alley also Gean gave me a good lunch, also some hdks, ties, hose +c for Susan, Anna and Gertrude. We all felt bad at Parting.

21/ Awoke near Lynn. Arrd at Colton 10.30 a.m. 5 hours behind time. Road washed badly. Took S. Pacific train At 3 P.M. for El Paso, 755 miles. Arrd Yuma 9 P.M.

Sun. 22/and El Paso 1 P.M. I crossed into Mexico, at Juarez, and stopped at Pierce's. Just in time to attend a meeting of the few L.D.S. in that vicinity. Spoke. In evening I gave Patl Blessing to Br. I.W. Pierce and his wife.[137]

23/ Left Juarez 9.30 A.M. Arrd Casas Grandes 6 P.M. and home in Cola Juarez 10.30 P.M.

Found family better than I expected. Gertrude some better, but unable to sit up. My dear Susan seemed much broken down by Constant care, anxiety and watching with Gertrude for almost 2 years.

26/ Visited Sis. Ivins and admd to her. Quite Sick. Also visited my children Anna, Emma. Theo + wife came.

29/ At meeting and Spoke.

---

137. Isaac Washington Pierce (1839–1906) was married to Elna Carlson, Caroline Done, and Hannah Carlson.

<u>May 1906</u>.

May 6/ To day I became a member again, of the Juarez Ward by vote, as usual.[138]

8/ Susan and I visited Apostle Teasdale + wife. This is the first time Susan has walked so far, for years.

[Page B306L]

1906/Had a pleasant visit with them.

May 9/Gertrude had a nervous chill, quite serious, by prayer and what else we could do she passed a good night.

Blessings received by Gertrude, not yet recorded herein. Patriarchal Blessing by Patriarch James N. Skowson[139] given in Cloa Juarez, Mex. upon Gertrude Martineau Taylor:—

Dear Sister, in the name of Jesus Christ I place my hands upon your head and give you a patriarchal blessing. Thou art a daughter of the House of Israel thru the loins of Ephraim, and legal heir to all the blessings of the holy priesthood according to your sex. Rejoice, dear Sister, that you are placed on mother Earth in the fulness of times, when God has again spoken from the heavens thru Jos Smith the Prophet. You are a legal heir to all the blessings that have ever been pronounced upon the daughters of Zion, according to your Sex. Thy Guardian Angel shall follow thee by day and by night and thou shalt live so that in a short time God will permit thee to walk upon Mother Earth like the rest of the daughters of Zion, even thou shalt walk on the streets of the New Jerusalem, and be troubled no more of the infirmity of your body, and God is well pleased with you because of the integrity of your heart. Thou art barren for the present, but the time will come when your offspring shall be great and numerous, like the stars of the heavens. You shall have no sorrow on mother Earth, only the Sins of your fellow beings. The Gospel shall be sweeter unto You day by day. Thou shalt have visions and dreams, and the Eternal World shall be opened to thy vision, + you shall behold the great glories of the

---

138. It would have been difficult for Martineau to establish residency or feel a sense of permanence in a ward, since he was regularly traveling to Utah to finish his surveying contract.

139. This was James Niels Skousen (1828–1912), born to Niels Hansen Kappel and Johanna Jens (Jenson) Skousen. He served as a patriarch from the time of his ordination on January 12, 1894, until his death on October 21, 1912.

Heavenly Host. If you be taken before the Son of Man come I seal up to eternal life, to receive all the glories and exaltation of a priestess and queen, and receive them under the crown of your husband. If it is the will of the Father that you shall wait till the Son of Man Come you shall be changed from Mortality to immortality + shout hosannah in His glorious presence, all these

[Page B307R]

blessings, and all your former blessings I seal upon you by authority of the holy priesthood in the name of Jesus Christ. Amen.
[Blank line]
Blessing by Path Wm. R.R. Stowell given in Cola Juarez Mex. June 6, 1897.

Sister Gertrude, I place my hands upon Your head in the name of the Lord Jesus Christ, and by authority of the holy priesthood vested in me, in in my office as a Patriarch in Israel I pronounce upon you a blessing, and pray God my heavenly Father that the words which I may speak may be dictated by the holy Spirit, and be a comfort and a pleasure to you, both now and hereafter. You are of the blood of Israel and have been reserved in the world of Spirits to come forth in this, the dispensation of the fulness of times. You have been born of goodly parents, and are an heir to all the blessings of the gospel, even the new and everlasting covenant, pertaining to your sex. Your Guardian Angel has watched over you from your infantile moments, and preserved you from dangers, both seen + unseen. You have had many afflictions, but do not despair, nor think that the arm of the Lord is shortened. Think over the many afflictions that the Saints of God have passed through in the past, and the many kind blessings from the hand of the Lord which you have enjoyed. Turn to the bright side of the picture + reflect upon the future, and ask God in humble prayer that your physical nature my be strengthened, that you may be able to endure and prove faithful to your covenants which you have made with God, to the end of your days. You have been permitted, dear sister, to come to this Earth for a wise purpose. You are one of those noble spirits now tabernacled in the flesh, + when you have finished your earthly career, you, through your faithfulness, will be entitled to many great, noble and grand blessings and positions. You shall be numbered with the Queens of Israel,

[Page B308L]

Gertrude's Blessing Cond

also with the princesses, and enjoy those grand blessings that you have so long desired. Let your aspirations be high. Your natural inclinations and disposition is to acquire knowledge and intelligence that you may enjoy the highest position of womanhood. Do not despair of these noble ideas. God is able to bring about all the noble purposes, and to your great astonishment the future shall bring to you blessings that you have almost despaired of. Ask God for wisdom, take the advice and Counsel of your parents, whose object is to counsel you in righteousness. Your life shall be spared on the Earth and you will live as long as you desire life; and you shall overcome the weakness of nature and the pain and afflictions that you are and have been subject to in the past. And you shall rejoice and be comforted, and feel to acknowledge the hand of God in all things. Many blessings are for you, + you shall rise up in the strength and power of God, + shall see many happy days, and when you have finished your earthly career you shall go as a shock of corn fully ripe to the garner, with a hope and a bright prospect of the future. I seal these blessings upon your head, + reseal every blessing that has hitherto been conferred upon you, and seal you up to come forth in the morning of the first ressurrection, clothed with glory, immortality and eternal life in the kingdom if God, with many friends and kindred, through your faithfulness, in the name of Jesus Christ. Amen.

<u>Recorded in his book A, page 149</u>.

Blessing by Path Alex. Jameson upon Gertrude M. Taylor, given Aug. 20. 1904.

 Sister Gertrude, by virtue and authority of the holy priesthood and in the name of Jesus Christ I lay my hands upon thy head and shall proceed to bless thee, agreeable to the mind and will of the Lord, and I seal upon thee thy former blessings that have been given thee thru the channel of the holy priesthood, + say unto thee, thou art of Ephraim, and no blessing

[Page B309R]

that belongs to his posterity shalt thou be deprived of, unless it be that the Lord thy God should order otherwise, but I say unto thee thy sins are forgiven thee, for thy has come up before the Lord, and thou art accepted

of Him, and if thou wilt continue to hold fast to the faith + be willing in thy heart to multiply blessings unto thy husband, and falter not in faith in the Lord I say unto thee thou shalt stand with him in Holy places. These blessings are given to thee as an aim + object upon which thou mayest look forth in hours of affliction in order that thy faith may not falter for thy comfort and thy blessing; and by virtue of my calling s a Patriarch, and in the name of Jesus Christ our Lord do I rebuke the powers and influences that have preyed upon your system, and command them to depart from thee, and bless thee from the crown of they head to the soles of thy feet, that thy heart, the Stomach, thy head + blood in thy arteries and veins may be filled with the vigors of life, and with the blessing of health, peace and contentment in thy mind, to the end that thou mayest be comforted, yea, and be made whole. These are thy blessings at this time, and I seal them upon thee and seal thee up unto eternal life, even to a part in the glorious ressurrection of our Lord, there to Enjoy all that thou hast merited, forever, even so. Amen.
[Blank line]
Blessing by Winslow Farr, given Aug. 28. 1904

    Sister Gertrude M. Taylor, in the authority of the holy Melchisedek priesthood and in the name of Jesus Christ of Nazareth I place my hands upon thy head and seal a Patriarchal blessing, and desire that God our Eternal Father dictates by His Spirit the words that may be used in this blessing. Thou art a chosen vessel of the Lord, selected from the Courts of heaven, and given the privilege to choose thy parantage and dispensation to come forth on the earth, and thy Guardian Angel that was given thee at thy birth has watched over thee, ^and^ for a wise purpose thy life

[Page B310L]

has been preserved. Thy lineage is of Joseph, through the loins of Ephraim, born a legal heir to the keys of the priesthood and the blessings of the Gospel according to thy sex, and I say unto thee, dear Sister, if thou wilt exercise faith, the blessing thou so much desire shall come to pass, even to be healed in body and mind, and become a Mother in Israel, that you might be able to answer the measure of thy creation, and bring joy to thy household. The Lord is well pleased with thy mission on the Earth, and will sanctify thy afflictions to thy good. Thy faith s^h^all increase and thy heart made to rejoice. Thou shall have power over this disease and live to fill a good mission on the Earth. Thou shalt be blessed with exceeding faith and wisdom and understanding to comprehend the things of God. Thou shalt have power over evil influences + unclean Spirits. Thou shalt have the privilege of going into the temple of God and assist in redeeming the dead who died without the gospel. Thou shalt have visions and dreams to comfort thee. The time shall come that you shall comprehend the things you desire of the Lord, and as thy days so shall thy strength be, for thou shalt stand as Queen to thy husband in the kingdom of God. Thou shalt be comforted, and shall receive all blessings promised. If thy faith fail not it is thy privilege to live to see Zion redeemed, in power and influence here on the Earth. I say unto thee, dear Sister, cling to the promises made unto thee, for thou shalt live as long as life shall be desirable. Thy name is written in the Lamb's Book of Life. Thou shalt stand as a Savior on Mt. Zion and wear the crown of eternal life. I bless thee with health and strength, with power to overcome this disease and affliction, and I bless thee with the blessings of Abraham, Isaac and Jacob, with power to come forth in the morning of the first ressurrection, and say unto thee let thy faith fail not and all of these blessings shall be fulfulled on thy head. I confirm all of thy former blessings and this blessing, for I seal them upon thee in the name of Jesus Christ.

[Next two pages are unpaged letter to JHM from Gertrude, at Colonia Juarez, dated Feb. 4. She says: "I am better in many ways in fact in every way than I have been since I have been sick almost five years now. I cling to the promises I have received and know they will be realized in time, but I get impatient." Near the end of the letter, she continues: "Guy will be home in about a week to stay—he has sold everything in Canada it is so far away. Dublan is going to build an ice plant this year and we have a dynamo for electric light mabe we will soon have street cars just imagine."]

[Page B311R]

Note/ When Br. Farr gave this blessing he said Prest Snow said "in 50 years the savior will be here and he will visit from house to house, just like we are now." Br. Farr says this was said by Prest Snow 3 or 4 years ago. (1902- or 1901)

also/ That 54 years will complete the 6000 years according to the chart of the Pyramid.[140]

---

140. This could refer to estimated epochal timetables by Charles Piazzi Smyth, Joseph Seiss, and others, but it may directly reference Orson Pratt's estimates, published under "The Great Pyramid and the Last Dispensation," *Deseret News* 28 (May 28, 1879): 264-265.

May 16/ Up to date Gertrude seemed to be much better + talked, laughed, curled her hair, and seemed quite well, except her weakness, which made her unable to sit up any.

But today she seems much worse, and talks in a faint voice, and but very little during the day, with much pain in her head.

21/ Gertrude very low. Can not bear to hear the clock tick so we stop it. She seems near to death[141]

23/ Somewhat better to day Ate a few mulberries.
[Blank line]
   As an invitation from the Young Ladies Journal for <u>Personal Recollections of the Prophet Joseph</u>, Susan contributed her "recollections" in the following:—
[Blank line]
My Recollections of the Prophet Joseph Smith

   I was born in Kirtland in 1836, and as a child of ten saw the prophet in the Sunday meetings in the temple and also at the house of my father Joel H. Johnson, but my more distinct recollections begin about 1841, when we lived in Ramus, afterwards named Macedonia, about 20 miles from Nauvoo where father was Presiding Elder. The Prophet frequently came to our house and sometimes stayed over night, but usually with his uncle John Smith, who was Patriarch in S.L. City up to 1854. On one occasion Joseph, with H.C. Kimball, Jedediah M. Grant and some others from Nauvoo whose names I do not now remember, partook of a Christmas dinner at my father's, and standing at the head of the table he carved the turkey. Fearing his clothing might accidentally be soiled, my step mother, Susan Bryant Johnson,

[Page B312L]

1906/May 23/tied a long apron upon him. He laughed and said it was well, for he did not know what might happen to him. My brother Seth

---

141. Three days later, Martineau wrote to the surveyor general, acknowledging receipt of a letter dated May 11 with instructions for him to go back into the field to correct apparent errors in Tp. 3 N., Rs. 1 E. and 1 W. He responded: "I cannot do so at once, as my daughter lies very ill—dangerously so,—and I cannot leave her at present, but will inform as to the time I can return." James H. Martineau to Thomas Hull, May 24, 1906, Letters Received, Surveyor General's Office, Vol. 33, February 28–May 28, 1906, letter #8080, CSGUT.

and I were in the room, admiring, in our childish way, him whom we thought the greatest man on Earth.

My father was present when Joseph received the "Word of Wisdom," and testified to the day of his death, 1883, that instead of "hot drinks," the words as received were "tea and coffee," which at that time were the only "hot drinks" in common use. Also, that the change in language was on suggestion by Oliver Cowdery who said "Why not write it "Hot drinks? that will cover it." He also said Joseph afterwards regretted having allowed the change, as it let to controversy even in his day

The revelation given in Sec. 131 Doc. + Cov. was given in my father's house in Ramus, when Joseph came, to preach next day.

It was in Ramus that Joseph taught my father and grandmother Julia Hills Johnson the principle of plural marriage, both of whom accepted it, and Joseph sealed my grandmother to his uncle John Smith, afterwards Patriarch. She was sealed as his second wife for eternity. The Prophet married my Aunt Almira Johnson as a plural wife with my father's consent, to my certain knowledge, living as such until his martyrdom. She died a few years ago in Parowan, Iron Co. Utah, and was proud of her union with him.[142]

[Blank line]

" 24/Visited and blessed three sick children.

---

142. The foregoing article was published, with slight variation, under "Joseph Smith, the Prophet," *Young Woman's Journal* 17 (December 1906): 541–542. The published article included three additional paragraphs on Joseph Smith's desire to be married to another daughter of Ezekiel Johnson and Julia Hills:

> Joseph Smith desired my Uncle [Benjamin F. Johnson] to explain the law to another aunt of mine, and have her consent to be sealed to him, but she refused, preferring to marry a young man then paying her attention. She did marry the young man, and according to her conversation with me, regretted it all her life.
>
> When I was but a child, I had a positive testimony that Joseph was a Prophet of God, and as I looked at him he seemed to me like a heavenly being. And at the age of eighteen I had a positive testimony that the principle of plural marriage as revealed through Joseph was a pure and holy one.
>
> In conclusion I declare myself a living witness to the fact that Joseph Smith the Prophet not only taught but also practiced plural marriage, any one to the contrary notwithstanding.

The other aunt would have been Esther M. Johnson who was fifteen at the time she refused to marry Smith. She married David LeBaron on March 28, 1844 at age sixteen. See Benjamin F. Johnson, *My Life's Review*, 85, and Compton, *In Sacred Loneliness*, 298 and 711n.

" 25/Anna's baby/born/At 12.30 a.m. Anna's boy baby was born, in severe labor he weighed 9 ½ lbs. and is a fine well-developed child. She is getting along all right. Susan was with her. I was left thus with Gertrude, who suddenly collapsed [in margin: " 26] and at 2 a.m. had a collapse, and thought she was dying I thought so too, and sent for Guy's wife Minna. She and his wife Lilly remained all night, doing all we knew how, and she gradually improved little. Guy also ^came.^

[Page B313R]

1906/May 26/Picked the last of our early Cherries. Others are just beginning to ripen. We also have ripe mulberries.

I blessed my grandson, George, Albert's son, as he is about to go to Temosachic, to obtain employment.

" 29/ Gertrude is much better, and does up her hair, and has sung a little. She has wonderful faith still.

June 1906.

June 4th/Gertrude had a fit at 10.30 P.M., another next day at 6.20 P.M. with two other light ones.

6/ Emma came to see how much Albert owes me. We found the amount due, on June 10th next to be $262.97 bearing 10 % interest pr annum.

7/ Today and at night Gertrude had 8 fits, most of them light ones. In the morning she said she heard singing not of Earth, and said to her mother "Cant you hear it, I hear it plainly."

8/ She had a bad fit, and 4 others at various hours.

9/ "   " a light attack at 11 a.m.

10/ She was very bright and cheerful this morning and all day until 6 P.M. when she suddenly felt like death, and wanted Guy, Minna and Lilly sent for, thinking she was dying. They all came. We were with her all night. She said, "I want to kiss you all while I can." Her pulse almost ceased, and she wanted us to dedicate her so she might be released. We did so. Then she rested, and seemed to sleep till morning.

11/ Very weak this morning, but seemingly better.
[Blank line]

13/ Began picking Apricots, and sell them at 8 cts per kilo, (kilo = 2 ½ lbs)

Lyman writes me he has engaged a Mr. Stewart to go to the Uintah Survey, and remedy an incorrect closing corner, which will save me considerable expense, by not having to go myself from Mexico, to do the work.[143]

14/ Went to home of John W. Taylor, and blessed his wife Rhoda. She sent her carriage to bring Susan + me, also sent us in the same way she had also present Sister Saville and daughter, and

[Page B314L]

1906/ Prest J.E. Robinson and wife. He is President of the California Mission. We had a pleasant time.

June 15/ Gertrude said that last Sunday when she sank away, a feeling like death came upon her, unlike anything she ever felt before, and some one told her she must die. It seemed horrible to her, but after she had prayed a long time all dread ceased, and she felt at peace. She could see her body lying on the bed, dead, and had a glimpse of heaven, and Saw Dora and others of our dead.

It was on that morning she heard the singing. She says a change for her is coming, and is willing for any

15 + 16/ Quarterly Conference. Apostles Teasdale + Clawson were present. Susan went on the second day by the kindness of the Sisters JW Taylor, who gave us use of their carriage, and took us to their home for dinner.

19/ Gertrude had a bad fit at 9.40 P.M. Guy and Minna Went to El Paso yesterday.

20/ She seems passing away.

25/ " had a fit 1 a.m. Very weak all day.

I went to Heber F. Johnson's and gave Blessings to him and four of his family. At 10 P.M. G. had another fit, also several light ones.

---

143. In response to Martineau's letter, dated May 29, requesting a "personal favor," Thomas Hull wrote to the Commissioner of the GLO for Martineau to receive partial payment on his contract, but it was probably too late, as his returns had to be filed before the end of June. Thomas Hull to James H. Martineau, June 4, 1906, Letters Sent, Surveyor General's Office, Vol. 46, May 11, 1906–October 12, 1906, 84, CSGUT. See note at entry for March 12, 1906.

26/ She had two, 6.20 P.M. and 10.30 P.M.

27/ " 8 fits from 1 a.m. until 10.40 P.M.

28/ " one at 5 a.m., 9 a.m. and 11 p.m.

29/ " " 12.30. She gave me names for temple work for Alex. von Wenden, our friend, whose sweetheart Margaret Leavitt, a Scotch girl whom he loved when he was in Scotland at age of 20, died of a broken heart, because his parents forbade their marriage. Gertrude wants Margaret to be Sealed to von Wenden.

We obtained these data by a remarkable way. A Young woman, Isabel Fowler, came from Ireland with Frank Stowell, whose Mother was Margaret's aunt Barbara Leavitt by name. She told Gertrude how her cousin Margaret Leavitt had loved a young Russian nobleman, but whose father prevented their marriage, and she died of grief.

[Page B315R]

1906/June/And we found she was the same girl von Wenden had told us of. It seems brought about by the Lord.

29/ Gertrude still very weak.

30/ " sinking spell at about noon. She said "Do plead with the Lord for my release. I can't endure it." Guy and I did so, praying God to release her. She then lay for hours as if asleep, but was not really so.
[Blank line]

July/ July 1906.

To day Apostle Teasdale blessed Anna's baby with the name Aubrey Franklin Turley, and said he was much impressed to give him a great blessing as he did.

Gertrude rallied some in the night, but is very weak.

2/ I was taken suddenly with cholera morbus. I continued so, in bed on 3d and 4th Rainy Season began with heavy rain all night.

We have found, from a Miss Isabel Fowler, the name of the girl the Baron Alex. Von Wenden loved and wished to marry, but was prevented by his parents. She was the cousin of Miss Fowler, her name Margaret

Leavitt, age about 17 or 18, lived in Kirkaldy, near Edinburg, Scotland.[144] She died of a broken heart. I wish to have her united with the Baron, her lover, in the holy order of marriage. It seems as if our meeting with Miss Fowler, lately from G. Britain, was ordained by the Lord that the union may be brought about.

Wed 11/ Susan's 70th Birth day. Had a nice dinner, with Anna, Edward Turley and Ida, Emma, Albert's wife. I thank thee Oh Father, she is preserved to me thus long, a blessing and comfort to all who know her, filled with faith and beloved of the Lord.

Gertrude had a fit at 3.15 P.M. the first in 13 days. Up to this time she had seemed very bright and cheerful. For several days after, she was very low and weak.

[Page B316L]

1906/July 15th/ Emma paid me $265.00 which Albert has been owing so long, for my cattle sold him.

20/ Albert came home from Sonora, where he has been grading on a railroad several months.

Gertie had a light fit, on 16th Also 1 at 10 P.M. to day

21/ " " " " 5 a.m., 9.30 P.M. and 3.20 P.M.

22 + 23/Slight fits 10 p.m. 23d fits 2.45 a.m. 10.45 a.m. 11.20 a.m. 1.15 P.M. 3.30 P.M. 5.30 P.M. 6.35 P.M. 11.0 P.M.

24/fit 5.0 a.m. Recd dun [sum?] from Coltharp + Co $378.46 per F.G. Luke Collector for Merchants Protective Assn I wrote him I am unable to pay till Govt pays me.

Susan and I visited Alberts. Gertrude f. at 6.30 P.M.

31st/ Blessed Helen M. Clark

August 1906

Aug. 1st/ I was suddenly attacked with inflamy rheumatism.

---

144. Margaret Leavitt was born at Leith, Midlothian, Scotland, in 1851. She is believed to have died in 1869.

6th/ I Able to sit up a little to day

Recd Statement from Co-op. Mercantile Ist, thus:–

"May 1st 1903   By E. Turley $110.00
    Oct. 1st   ($1048.00)   938.00
Dec. 15 1904   Dividend $47.16
April 1   "   "   120.49   167.65
Total Capital Stock $1215.65

8/ Gertie fit 9 P.M. Sent letter to F.S. Luke. Wrote Lyman. Sur. Genl tells me all my survey accepted but 2 PPS.[145] Wrote to Afton Young, to be Endowed for Margaret Leavitt.

9/ Gertie f. 5 a.m. 10.00 P.M. Sent Express receipt to Lyman for my chain and pins

10th, 11th, 12th/ Gertrude a fit each day.

13th/   "   3 to day 14th 2 fits

22/   " fit 6 P.M. 23d 24th + 25th a fit each day

25/ I sent draft $1.25 for Ladies Home Journal. Bt Bedstead + M.

30/ Received the following letter from a Sister who had been confined in bed two years and given up to die three times, with nervous prostration. I had visited and blessed her many times, having testimony she could be healed. She said I was the first and only one who had Ever promised she should be healed.

[Page B317R]

1906/ It is a sample of others from my "patients" in the City (Salt Lake) whom I had administered to, and whom the Lord had healed; some of deadly tumors others of deadly disease when the doctors said they must surely die, or have an operation in the hospital,—many marvelous healings of paralysis and kidney diseases, goitre Etc.

    I insert this to show how my labors there, in visiting the Sick were appreciated:—

---

145. Two-and-a-half months later, Martineau acknowledged the receipt of the Commissioner's approval (dated October 19) of part of Contract No. 265. James H. Martineau to Thomas Hull, October 29, 1906, Letters Received, Surveyor General's Office, Vol. 35, September 20, 1906–February 24, 1907, Letter #8348, CSGUT.

Salt Lake City Aug. 18. 1906

Dear Brother Martineau

 Not another day shall pass till I write you a note. I have been thinking of you all day and for several days. Your teachings and counsels come to me every day, and the promises Our Father made me through you. I am so very thankful to you for the faith + hope + patience you instilled into me. I am getting better just as you said I would, and can again walk around the house and look after my children a little. They are glad that I can eat at the table with them, and ride, and I can also go to Sunday School, and have been to meeting several times. I am so thankful for these blessings, dear Father Martineau, for I look upon you as a Father. What could I have done without you some days! I cannot tell how just and merciful is our Heavenly Father. He alone knows what his children need, at least this is so in my case. I have not stopped wavering yet, but I sleep pretty well and can often sleep in the day time. I wish you lived near. I would enjoy having you come and talk to me on those sacred principles. It seems people have so little time for such things here. We would so love to her from you. I will take this letter to your son's wife and get your address. You have my faith and prayers, as also your dear wife. I shall never forget how you expressed your love for her. Br. Martineau accept my thanks and the gratitude of my heart

[Page B318L]

1906/Aug. 30/for your kindness and care over me. x x I was very much disappointed at not seeing you before you left, and not seeing you again.

With kind love Julia S. Wooley
1169 S., 3d East S.L. City. Utah
[Blank line]
 I take no credit for my ministrations, as I only had power as God in his mercy to the sick made manifest through me,— privilege, which to me is of inestimable worth For very many years my greatest desire has been for power to do great good to all who will receive it. And the only office in the Priesthood I have desired was that of Patriarch, which would give me power to Seal blessings upon others.
[Blank line]

Sept./ September 1906

3/ Paid Tannery Compy $21.78 for Capital Stock, which makes our interest in the business $200.00

6/ Today Guy Taylor moved Gertrude to his house She stood the change very well, in her wheel reclining Chair. To her mother and me the change was a Sad one, for she has lived at home with us all her life.

Alone/Again/we two/ Now, after about (or over) 54 years of married life, Susan and I are alone again,—just us two.

For years our family increased until in Logan we ate at a long table—18 of us. Then as children married and left the family hive we decreased until now we are but <u>two</u> again. I hope the time may never come when there shall be but One. Far better for both to pass away together. We have become necessary to each other that for either to be left alone would be dreadful.

Anna's little boy Freddy is still very sick with a hot fever,—now about two weeks.

By letter from Lyman I learn my last corrective work is finished. Glad.

[Page B319R]

1906/Sept. 10/ My left leg is still lame with rheumatism, and feels cold, numb and lifeless, which seems to me to threaten paralysis, but I hope not, as I am promised renewed health and strength, and that I shall labor in the temple to be built in Zion.

Phyllis, Anna's eldest daughter, comes to stay at night, and to help Susan.

26/ To this date we have been very busy drying fruit, + selling some, at 3¢ per pound. Agreed to let Gruel have my apples at 6¢ per pound.

29/ Sat. Left home for S.L. City, and to finish up my Survey business. Started 2.30 A.M. by mail wagon. Reach the Sierra Madre R.R. at Nueva Casas Grandes at Sunrise and reach Ciudad Juarez and El Paso at 3 P.M. Got my ticket to the City, via California, (return ticket) $43.05. Sleeper to Colton $5.00 Too tired to go on to night and stayed in El Paso.

30/ <u>Sunday</u>. Start 8.45 a.m. Colton, Cal. next day.

Oct. 1/ <u>Monday</u> 11.15 a.m. 2 hrs. late 884 miles. Found 2 women of our party stranded at Colton,—lost their train and did not know what to do, never having traveled, and but little money. I let <u>my</u> train go on and remained to help them through. We had hot weather here, 108° in shade. Left Colton at midnight.

" 2/ <u>Tues</u>. Summit of mountains 2 a.m. at 8.30, Haydn, Cal. Caliente 6.20 P.M.

" 3/ Arrd in S.L. City 7.10 a.m. Very cold—40°—Found Lyman's family ad Virginia's, well. Met Charles also.

" 5/ At 5.30 A.M. My Great-gr. dau. Ruth Crismon, dau. of Ollie, Lyman's eldest dau. was born, but lived only 4 hours. Was delayed 2 weeks in birth, and lacked vitality. Allie was dangerously ill in confinement.

I visited two of my "patients," Julia S. Wooley and Fanny Blair Stringham, and blessed both. They are getting well.

Little Ruth's funeral was at 12.30 P.M.

" 6/ Visited Several "patients," as I call them, persons sick, and blessed them. I thought this was better than going to church. One, Sister Driggs, who has been in so desperate and helpless condition when I blessed her last April, when the doctor said she must die in her approaching confinement, or her Child

[Page B320L]

1906/October/must be taken instrumentally, and that if she <u>lived</u>, after She would be a helpless invalid all her life, but whom I had blessed, Saying she should go her full time, be blessed in her confinement, and her son should be a child of promise and she become healthy and well, even as in your young day I found her well and strong, her babe a <u>Son</u>, as promised, whom they had named Arthur Martineau Drigs, a large 12 lb. boy. Thus was fulfilled, exactly, a promise given by inspiration of the Comforter, but which seemed at the time almost presumptuous. To Our Father be all the honor.

By all who knew the circumstances, it was Called an absolute miracle. I had been shown to her in dream before she had ever seen me, as one who would heal her, and this gave her faith when I blessed her, and me, also

Oct. 10/ In Temple to day. Afterwards visited and blessed Sis. Garringe, nearly a lunatic, who became quiet. Then to Eve Winberg, who is about to undergo an operation in the hospital which she dreads. Blessed and Comforted her and her mother. Gave P. blessing to Br. Dixon and wife, who live about 7 miles from "home," as I style Lyman's while I am with him and Alley.

" 11/ Blessed Sis Driggs for a special purpose. Met F.A. Mitchell and agree to go to Cache Valley and make a Survey for him.

" 12/ Visited and ^blessed^ J.S. Wooley, who is still improving. Lives in the country, near Waterloo. Weather very cold + cloudy. Spent 13th and 14th in visiting and blessing the sick.

15/ Went to Logan and began Survey for Mitchell. Cold

16/ Surveyed line over high, rugged hills. Very cold + windy.

17/ Too stormy to work. Paid some debts and wrote letters. Next day Nephi came to see me. Still very cold to 19th

20/ Snow 4 ins. deep in morning, and snowing all day. I am Staying in Logan with Lilla (Nebeker) who is very good to me. She is still badly afflicted in speech and hearing.

29/ Return to S.L. City. Found letter from Land office. Part of my Survey allowed to amount of $2316.43 and am't disallowed $186.89 from account Sent by Sur. Genl of Utah. It should have <u>not</u> been disallowed by the Clerks in Washington.

[Page B321R]

1906/Paid ~~Budge~~ Gowans $10.00 Also S.L. Herald $1.05 in full.

Oct. 31/ Blessed Zina Bull and Jenny Hill, also went, as sent for to bless Nelly Nicholson, said to be dying of quick consumption. She is 24 yrs. of age, has cough and bad bleeding of the lungs, also great pain her lungs. All say she cannot live much longer. I asked a testimony, and was told she could be healed by administration. I told her she could be, and she said she <u>believed</u>. I blessed her with that promise, and she at once felt better, both in lungs and mind—was actually happy. So was <u>I</u>.

Nov. 1/ In temple. Endd Edd Wells. Sister Watson, a temple <u>worker</u>, took me in afternoon, to see and bless a Sad case,—Lillie Anderson, who has for weeks wished for me. She seems melancholy—mad, almost. Deserted by her husband, poor and ill. I did all I could for her, but with little effect. Also went to and bld Nelly Nicholson, who is better, pain less, bleeding less.

2/ I endd Sylvander Hutchinson, Dyar LeBaron endd Joseph Hutchinson; Richd S. Horne endd Benjamin Hutchinson.

 I visited and blessed Nelly and Lilly. Gave Patriarchal blessing to Nelly Nicholson and to Grant M. Weiler

3/ Visited and blessed Nelly N. who is improving daily. Then to Eve Winberg, who has returned from hospital. Said my blessing had been literally fulfilled. She is rapidly recovering. She and Nelly live about 6 miles from Lyman's, and I have to walk several miles, in visiting my "patients," who sometimes do not live on the Car line. I get tired, my lame leg causing me to limp. It feels lifeless below the knee, and sometimes I fall suddenly as my knee gives out without warning.

4/ Sun. Visited and bl. Nelly N. Went to Gean's. Visited and blessed Lilly Anderson, but she will not cease to yield to evil spirits, though she says she knows she ought to do so. They tell her to do wrong, and not to do right, and she yields. I cannot do her any good while she yields to such powers.

5/ Went to Fanny Wessman and blessed her. She is recovering from typhoid fever. She and her mother have endowed 20 females for me. May Our Father ever bless them. Visited and blessed Nelly, who is better day by day and is getting well. Bleding [sic] only once or twice a day and pain

[Page B322L]

1906/in lungs almost ceased. Thanks to Our Father

Nov. 5/ Was caught in a heavy cold sleety rain at Wessman's over Jordan, and nearly fell, several times, in the mud.

" 6/ Election day. Republicans win. Visited and blessed Nelly. Lilly. Eve, Hazel White and Sister Coulam, miles separated. Walking Snowy, muddy, and slippery.

7/ Took my last Survey notes to the office. Bl. Nelly and Coulam. Visited Sister ash by request. It was a Surprise party in my honor. My leg Still weak. Fell down on my way home.

8/ Signed my last Survey notes in Office. Admd to Nelly W. also to ~~Ann~~ Mary Wickel, who fears miscarriage.

9 Was invited to visit Sisters Bull, white and hill—close friends—at Sister Bull's home. I found it was a Surprise party for me, the house full of ladies, mostly temple workers and friends of mine, with several of high standing whom I had not known before. It was given as a party testimony of regard for me, in view of my soon return to Mexico. A nice lunch, pleasant time. A Small parcel was given me, instructed not to open till I get home. It contained $10.00 given by various ones. I felt unworthy so much honor. Four of Prest B. Young's daughters were there. Also Sis McCune, Julia Smith and Dougall. Patriarch Lawson also there. I had to go before over, to visit and bless Nelly N. and to be at a Relief Society entertainment to which I was invited in Emerson Ward 5 miles away, which I reached at 8.30 P.M. Home about 11 P.M. Somewhat tired, having walked Several miles, with nearly 10 miles street Car.[146]

10/ In temple a little while to bid good bye to many there. Visited and blessed Sister Kimball, Barker, Sharp, Hazel White, and Lydia White, 3 to 5 miles separate necessitating much walking, but warmly greeted, as I always am, and blessed myself always in blessing others.

11/ Went to Elgren's in 2d Ward, and gave Patl Blessing to A.W. Morrison, Martha Elggron and D.F. Wissman.

Next to Br. Saniger, 3 miles distant, and gave P. blessings to his Children L.M. Saniger and Violet Saniger. then to see Nellie Nicholson, who says she is now well. I gave

[Page B323R]

1906/Nov./11/her a parting blessing. Then to 2d Ward and admd to Hazel White, Urania White, and Lewis Elggren. So I have had a busy day. But I am sent for, for miles around, + have to spend dollars for Car fare, besides much walking.[147]

Mon. 12/ Admd to Nelly once more, because of sudden change in weather for heavy Snow Storm, also admd to Urania White and Mary Wickins, 5 miles apart.

Tues 13/ Bld Fanny B. Stringham, who had me go with her 6 miles to adm. to her daughter, Mrs. Mainwaning, who is in danger of miscarriage.

---

146. Evidently Martineau did not have any other mode of transportation besides walking or riding the street car to reach his "patients."

147. See entry for November 9, 1906.

Gave patriarchal blessing to Fanny. Thence to Geans 4 miles away, and stayed all night. Cold storm

14/ <u>Wed</u>. Bld. Nelly Nicholson once more. Gave ^P.^ blessing to C. Eden Richards her nurse

15/ Endd Nathaniel Hutchinson. Mrs. Wessman End Mary Hutchinson. Sealed Margaret Leavitt and Alex. Von Wenden to each other. I proxy for him. Afton Young proxy for her. I am very glad

This was brought about, I believe, by the power of God, and in a wonderful manner. In 1895 the Russian Baron Alex. von Wenden, who boarded for a time with us told of his visiting Scotland when he was twenty years old, + there fell in love with a Scotch girl—Maggie, he called her, but never gave her full name—and would have married her; but his father hearing of it came from Riza, Russia, and took him home, unwilling for him to marry one not of noble blood. He often spoke of her with sorrow for his blighted love. He died in 1897.

In 1901 a girl came from Ireland, a new convert—named Isabel Fowler—came direct to Colonia Juarez, our home, and related that a cousin of hers, Margaret Leavitt, of Leith, near Edinburg, met there a young Russian nobleman who fell in love with Maggie, + would have married her, but his father came and took him from her, and She pined away and died of a broken heart. We found she was that girl von Wenden had spoken of. Miss Fowler remained with us only a short time, went to Utah, and we never heard of her again. The Lord sent her to us, who of all, were the only ones who knew Von Wenden's story—and she gave all data

[Page B324L]

1906/needful to complete the story—then departed.

Nov. 15/ By E. Guy Taylor, my son-in-law, von Wenden was endowed Oct. 4. 1897 in S. Lake temple. On Sept. 11. 1906 Margaret Leavit was endowed by Miss Afton Young, on Nov. 15th they were sealed in marriage. Thus was finally finished a love story, giving us all very great joy.

Since then I have had testimony that both he and she accepted with joy what we had done for them.

I endowed Nathaniel Hutchinson ^1518^, Mrs Wessman Endd Mrs. Jane Taylor

Visited and blessed Maria Y. Dougal + dau. Clarissa who were both much pleased. Heavy rain Storm began at eve.

Nov. 16/ I endd Bartholomew Hutchinson. Snowing today. Visited Nelly Nicholson to see if storm made her worse. It did not.

Sat. 17/ Snowed all night and till 10 a.m. 7in deep

Sun. 18/ Blessed Violet and Lona Saniger (Patriarchal) Went to see Nelly Nicholson. She says she is fully healed, but weak yet.

19/ Visited and blessed Virginia Zina Bull. She blessed me.

20/ "   "   " Jenny Hill also went to Sis. Julia Wooley and blessed her, farewell.

Wed. 22/ Went to Temple and got my temple clothes. Bid good-bye to many. Sis. Dougall bl. me and I her. Bl. Nelly. Got some things for Susan. Also Pullman car ticket $5.50 Spent some time with Gean. Got temple record from Afton Young, for 21 names she endowed for me.

24/ Got my return ticket via San Pedro R.R. 43.05 to E. Paso Blessed Mary A.H. White. In afternoon Bp. W.B. Preston and Wife, Edd Sudbury + Gean, Gowans + Harriet, Crisman and Ollie met at Lyman's, who is absent in Star Valley, Wyo. as a farewell to me. Dined at 7 P.M. + then went to train.

Sun. 25/ Left city at 3 a.m., 5 hrs behind time. Awoke near Milford. Snow all the way, 130 miles

Mon. 26/ Arrived at Colton, 58 m. east of Los Angeles + took SPRR train at 3 P.M.

27 Tuesday/ Arrived El Paso 3.15 P.M.

28 Wed.   "   home 9 P.M. Found all well as usual. "There's no place like home, be it ever so humble."

Nephi's baby/boy/ I learn Nephi's baby boy was born Nov. 20

[Page B325R]

1906/Nov. 28/ I learn that Theodore + Josephine's girl baby was born + died Oct. 13. 1906. Her name given was Mary Ellen Martineau. It was a difficult birth, but the mother lived,—a blessing.

29/ Thanksgiving day. We had a family dinner, with Anna and her children, and Emma and hers. A pleasant time, It was sad our dear Gertrude, still confined to her bed, cannot be with us. But we sent her some of our dinner. She seems stronger than when I went to the City.

Dec 31st/ Sat as a High Councillor in a case to day. Settled tithing amounting to $75.48 I have not yet received my Survey money from the Govt hence my tithing account is Small. But it was in full, as I always pay, year by year.
[Blank line]
Since my home coming nothing beyond usual home matters has occupied my attention. I have administered to the sick around me, and given some Patriarchal blessings, and spent some time examining my survey maps, of my Mexican work. For one thing especially I feel thankful—that Our Father has so greatly blessed me during the past year in my ministrations among the Sick, and for the dead, a work for which I would exchange uncounted gold. Gold is fleeting—the work I have done is for an eternity, and eternal.

1907/ January 1907.

Jan. 1/ Had a nice family dinner to day. Lyman's daughter Harriet's child was born, I believe, Jan. 2d

" 8/ Our 55th wedding day. When a young man I believed that I would never reach the age of fifty,—felt sure of it—and I have instead reached my 55th wedding anniversary, through the special blessing of the Lord, whose angel saved my life in the Uintah Mountains while on my Survey, when my horse fell with me on his back down the steep rocky side of the mountain. Nothing but the Special power of God saved my life, and in a miraculous manner. We had a nice dinner again, and Anna and Emma gave us presents.

In December last I sold my land in Chuichupa to Henry for $875.00 payable in two years. Interest 10 % from date. There was 92 ½ acres farm land and a vacant city lot. I sold cheaper to him than I would to others not in the family.

[Page B326L]

1907/The sale was made Dec. 18. 1906. The land was worth full $1000.00 but I am to infirm to handle it.

January/8th/ 55 years ago I stood alone. Now head of a family of about 150, including 100 grandchildren and 14. Gr-Gr. Chiln Truly has God blessed us, tho both of us are quite infirm. I have not yet recovered the full use of my left leg, from the rheumatism of last Summer. But we might be much worse—Sick, perhaps.

15/ Leveled for a canal in the Canyon for Prest Ivins, very tired, walking so much among rocks and sand.

16/ Leveled another canal for him in our town.

17/ Made estimates of cubic yds. in proposed canal.

18/ Finished estimates, + received $21.00 Mex.
[Blank line]

Feb. 1907/ February 1907.

Sun. 3d/ To date have spent much time revising my maps.

" 12/ Received word from Sur. Genl Hull my survey contract is approved in full. Approved Jan. 8. 1907.[148]

16/ Letter from Lyman, says he has recd a draft from Govt on my Survey, for $2334.50, and has paid my bank a/c of $1119.00 which has long been drawing interest.

23/ Had telephone put in today. Cost $1.50 per month Susan and I both sick with Lagrippe.

March 4/ Just able to be about, but must go to El Paso to file papers. Stayed all night with Jos Cardon, in Dublan. Blessed his wife, who fears cancer near the Eye and nose.

5/ Reached El Paso late in afternoon. Very Tired.

---

148. On February 2, General Thomas Hull wrote that the commissioner of the General Land Office by his letter "E", dated January 28, 1907, "has duly approved the surveys executed by you under your contract No. 265, in Tps. 3N., Rs. 1E. and 1W." Hull wrote, "This approval closes up your contract." Four days later, Hull wrote that he was in receipt of the Commissioner's letter "M", dated January 31, 1907, which read: "The final account of James H. Martineau, D. S., for surveys within the Uintah Indian Reservation, executed under contract No. 265, dated July 20, 1903, has been examined by this office and approved without difference for $1571.91, making the total account approved under this contract $4448.13. The account will be transmitted to the Commissioner of Indian Affairs for his action." Thomas Hull to James H. Martineau, February 2, and 6, 1907, Letters Sent, Surveyor General's Office, Vol. 47, October 12, 1906–April 26, 1907, 288 and 300.

6/ Finished my business. Met Mr. Boyd, who wishes me to do Some Surveying for him at Carretas Hacienda.

8/ Start home. Stopped off at Dublan to attend Quar. Conference.

9 + 10/ Conference in Dublan. Apostle H.J. Grant present. Very good Visited and blessed Sister Josephine Mc M. Hilton who is very low.

11/ Got home late to day. Found letter from Lyman, which causes me to return at once to El Paso. Must start 2.30 a.m. So I did not take any sleep, but started out, in cold night for Station.

12/ Reached Nueva Casas Grandes before sun rise. Soon took train and reached El Paso about 5.0 P.M. nearly worn out with 2 days and night, without sleep and almost constant travel.

[Next two pages comprise a letter from Lyman dated 3/13/1907, 918 Logan Ave., SLC, to Col. J.H. Martineau, Colonia Juarez. Birthday greetings on 79th]

[Page B327R]

1907/March/Fixed up my business same evening, very tired. Met Albert in Ciudad Juarez, on his way home from Sonora, where he is working on the new railway along the Pacific Coast.[149] Emma, his wife, went there to meet him with me.

15/ Reached home again. No place like home.

19/ Got letters from Lyman and Allie, Gean, ~~Niece~~ Gr. daughter Susan Martineau (Nephi's dau.) and son Theodore, congratulating me on my 79th birthday, which occurred while I was in El Paso. All were full of love and good wishes.

Up to this time I have visited among the Sick + administered to them, and have spent much time in working on my maps of Surveys I have made

---

149. This refers to the Southern Pacific Railroad of Mexico (Ferrocarril Sud-Pacifico de México), which was then under construction along the west coast of Mexico. In 1903 the Southern Pacific acquired control over the Cananea, Yaqui River, and Pacific. On October 27, 1905, the Southern Pacific interests obtained a concession for a line from Guaymas to Guadalajara, Mexico. The extension from Guaymas was begun in 1905 and was completed to Mazatlan in 1909. See Powell, *Railroads of Mexico*, 9, 161–162; Trennert, Jr. "Southern Pacific Railroad of Mexico," esp. pp. 268–270; and Zonn, "Railroads of Sonora and Sinaloa," 5–8.

here, to correct any possible errors, So that who may come after me as a Surveyor here may find nothing to my discredit as an Engineer.

27th/ On the 5th inst. I went to El Paso to file pension paper and again, about a week after, on Surveying business, and there met Albert, just on his way home on a visit from Sonora.

Today I bought Some fruit trees, to replace those killed this winter by the cold snap. Up to this time I have ministered to the sick and have worked on the new maps of my Surveys here I am making for the Colonization Company.[150] Gertrude is much better, and I believe she will yet recover. If so, it will indeed be a veritable miracle to all who have known her. She is now able to go out Short distances in her invalid Chair

April/ April 1907.

1st/ Have been awake all night. Insomnia. I lately got a letter from Sister J.S. Wooley, S.L. City, telling how wonderfully God had fulfilled to her the promises I made in blessing her, and her unbounded Joy for it. It gives me great joy also, showing I have been led by the Holy Spirit in my ministrations as a Patriarch. God has been wonderfully good to me

23/ Obliged to go to El Paso again on my Pension business, and on Sunday 28 attended meeting in private house in Ciudad Juarez. Spoke and felt well. Blessed Lulu Johnson, dau. of Coz. W.D. Johnson, of Diaz.

[Page B328L]

1903/May 5/[note error in year. Should be 1907] Got home again, and found all about as usual. Soon after getting home I became very lame, all through back and legs, continuing so about two weeks.

27/ Made mining survey for J.C. Peterson.

June 6/ Start to Cola Diaz, to Conference, to camp out on way

7/ Arrived 4.30 P.M. Spent two following days in Confern Blessed (Patriarchically) eight persons, who gave me $3.00 in all. Arrived home, camping on Casas Grandes river Cold night. I stood the whole trip very well, although on leaving home I could hardly climb into the wagon.

---

150. These maps were made by the Mexican Colonization & Agricultural Company, which was then under the management of Anthony W. Ivins. As vice president and general manager of the company, Ivins issued deeds to unsettled land near Colonia Juarez.

18/ Received a letter from Young Women's Journal asking me to become a contributor, per Ann M. Cannon Editor[151]

July 1907

July 11th/ To day a number of relatives and friends came as a Surprise party in honor of my dear Susan's 71st birth day. She is certainly worthy. Born in Kirtland, tried in all the Church tribulations to this date. She has always been true to Mormonism, a great blessing + help to me. May she see many more birth days.[152]

August 1907.

Aug. 1/ Quite ill with a flux, which is prevalent now.

15/ Sent articles to Y.W. Journal. Poem "Boyhood's Days" and "A Sunday dance."[153]

28/ Received word that Joel's baby girl, born Aug. 28th/07 died in birth. She was named Ruth. Joel and his family are in Madera, a new mountain town. He is superintending 30 Carpenters working for the Green-Silver Co. at that place. Annie, his wife, nearly died.

Up to this date I have done considerable mapping for the Colonization Comp. A.W. Ivins, Manager.[154] And have done much administering to sick and injured, some whose condition seemed hopeless. But by the mercy and goodness of the Lord they recovered. One was Sister Charles Whipple, thrown to the ground in a Run away, her spine so injured her least move caused exquisite pain. Through faith and prayer she was healed. I have visited the Sick when myself hardly able to walk, but always was blest in doing so.

[Page B329R]

---

151. See note at entry for September 24, 1907.

152. Two weeks later, Martineau wrote to F. E. Eldredge, editor of *El Progreso* newspaper in Nuevo Casas Grandes, Mexico, about the Mountain Meadows Massacre. See James H. Martineau to F. E. Eldredge, "The Mountain Meadows Catastrophy" [sic], July 23, 1907, MS 163, LDSCHL. A Photocopy is held at BYUSC, MSS 467. This letter is reproduced in Appendix II.

153. See J. H. Martineau, "Truth," *Young Woman's Journal* 19 (February 1908): 69, and James H. Martineau, "Our Girls. A Dance on Sunday," *Young Woman's Journal* 19 (February 1908): 72–74.

154. These maps were for documenting the subdivision of land and issuing deeds for the company. See Martineau's entry for April 27, 1907.

1907/[Blank line]

Sept. 21/Heard the sad news of my son's wife, Allie Preston Martineau, who expired on 13th almost instantly, from something affecting her head.¹⁵⁵ I here insert a letter received since from Lyman. (Insert below extracts from his letter.)

She was loved by all who knew her, and those who knew her best loved her most. She blessed the poor and did more good, unostationly, [?] than many who attain 80 or 90 Years.
[Blank line]

24/ Went to El Paso, on pension business. Regulated my barometer by the U.S. weather office. Returned 27th

Found letter from Y.W. Journal, enclosing $3.00 and a letter expressing pleasure from my articles sent for publication relating to Early scenes in Settlement of Utah, privations, troubles with indians, etc¹⁵⁶

Extracts from Lyman's letter of Sept. 21st 1907

x x "Just returned from Logan where we laid her (Allie) away in my family plat by the side of our two little girls.¹⁵⁷ Oh! how I mourn! Oh what anguish of soul her loss has brought to us all. Words of course utterly fail me. I am crushed. I am */undone utterly. x x x She died Sunday* morning at [In margin: (Note* 15th)] half past 7 o'clock, of the breaking of a blood vessel in her brain. You must know that for a number of days we had been arranging for Allie and Kenneth to go to Philadelphia on the 15th at noon, where Kenneth was to enter Jefferson Medl College. Also, that Royal was to go East for his 3d year in Harvard on the 19th inst. x x x On Friday the 13th we dined with May and Oscar Moyle. On Saturday evening some of the family were up to see us + stayed till 9 o'clock. Alley was feeling more cheerful than usual, altho all day Saturday I was much distressed in mind without knowing why. I went home early but felt awfully bad. x x x Alley woke at 6.30 on Sunday and spoke to me. I arose and went down stairs to make a fire telling her to hurry, but she soon got up and came down Stairs and began to prepare breakfast. I staid 15 or

---

155. See "Mrs. Martineau Claimed by Death," *Deseret Evening News*, September 16, 1907, 5, and "Mrs. Martineau Dies Suddenly," *Salt Lake Herald*, September 16, 1907, 2.

156. These articles didn't appear until 1908. See note at entry for August 15, 1907. See bibliography for other articles.

157. See "Internment at Logan," *Deseret Evening News*, September 17, 1907, 2.

20 minutes with her, and Royal and Martha came in the room as I was excusing myself to go up stairs to take my morning cold bath. I turned the cold water on but before I

[Page B330L]

1907/undressed I was startled by Martha calling me to hurry to her mother who "was fainting." I was at her side in less than two minutes, but too late to hear her last words to Royal as she sank in his arms "Oh Royal." We thrust her feet in hot water, gave her some whiskey, prayed for her and phoned for the doctor all at once, almost, for Alley came to our rescue also. But all was to no avail. She expired without regaining consciousness She did not expect it I am sure, nor did she suffer more than one or two seconds. The doctors Richard, Stephen + Gill soon came but said nothing could have saved her. Oh, dear Father, how I thought of you and wished you were here! I seemed to be utterly alone, lost! To lose my darling, my companion of 25 years! She and I had spent a happy life together. We were mated and loved each other devotedly, as you and Aunt Susan and all know. What to do seems a harrowing uncertainty. I shall have to have time and the Lord's help to heal the wounds, and the Scar can never be effaced. I think Will's sudden death on Aug. 13th caused her so much grief that it finally took her away. Now if I can only live to be worthy of her hereafter I shall be so thankful. x x x Praying God to bless you all. Your loving son L.R. Martineau.
[Blank line]

Oct. 1/ Took observations on Polaris and find Var. of needle is 11° 54'E.

Wrote to Prest J.R. Winder to see if he approved of sending names to the Temple, to be worked for there by temple workers.

3/ Received answer approving, also blanks for names.

2/ Wrote to Cyril Martineau to see if we are kindred.

3d/ Recd complimentary letter from Young Woman's Journal and a check for $3.00, which last was unexpected by me.[158]

Aug. 25/ Susan was suddenly taken with bleeding at the nose

---

158. Mary E. Connelly to James H. Martineau, September 28, 1907. This letter was inserted in Martineau's journal after p. 330, book two. See Godfrey and Martineau-McCarty, eds., *Uncommon Common Pioneer*, 716.

1907/in a stream and it took two hours to Entirely stop it. She lost fully 2 pints of blood, and was very faint and weak

I learn by letter that Harriet's baby girl Allie Martineau Gowens was born May 12. 1907.

Oct. 8/ Sent a genealogical article to Deseret News[159]

21/ Albert came home from his R.R. work in Sonora for a visit and to pay for his house + lot here.

[Unpaged typed letter from Mary E. Connelly, editor, dated Sept. 28, 1907, to JHM, Col. Juarez, Chihuahua, Mex. thanking him for articles and looking forward to articles about Pioneers and experiences with Indians]

[Page B331R]

1907/Oct. 9/Old Folks reunion. A pleasant time and nice dinner. Susan was the only one who had ever been in Kirtland, and but a few who had ever seen Joseph the Seer or Nauvoo. The Pioneers and veterans are rapidly passing away.

Nov. 12/ Received answer to my letter to Cyril E. Martineau and a beautifully gotten up Genealogical record, dating back in unbroken line to the year 1450, when Romain Martineau Seigneur or Sieur de Romas, in Middle age was one of the Court of king Charles 7th of France and of Louis 11th, and in the time of Jeanne DArc. He was of the ancient

---

159. Martineau's article appeared under the following: James H. Martineau, "Genealogy," *Deseret Evening News*, October 19, 1907, 13. In it, he wrote of his family history research on Martineau, Hutchinson, and Mears lines. He also wrote of his hatred for Native Americans—a hatred he grew to overcome:

> Many years ago the writer was blessed by patriarchal authority at three several times to lead forth and do a great work for the Lamanites, a prophecy at that time very distasteful, as I was filled with hatred against them; but our Father in His mercy took from me that hatred by a dream, or vision, I know not which, and gave me instead love and desire for their redemption through the ordinances of His holy house. Authorized by the presidency, I have acted in behalf of several hundred of the blood of Lehi, including all the noted Lamanites of the United States, Mexico, the Incas of Peru, and a noble line of Auracanian chieftains of South America who for centuries defied the efforts of Spain to conquer them. The Mexican names include the Montezuma emperors, their wives and children, with many subject kings, princes and chieftains; also Hidalgo, Allende, Morelos, Guerrero and others who died for their country, and President Benito Juárez, their second liberator.

nobility. This record gives unbroken line of descent for me from 1450 to the present date, giving me knowledge of Seven generations antedating my former records, and supplying the one name that was needful to make the correction complete.

This name was Francis Martineau, living in 1700, who with his Father Denis Martineau came to America from Holland, Amsterday^m^, to which place he fled in the persecution of the huguenots in 1685–1690. No words can express my joy for this record, compiled by David Martineau, who is one year older than I, and was assisted by a noted French Genealogist in his researches in France.[160]

I regard the coming of this record as a miracle, for I had no knowledge either of Cyril or David. I simply saw the name—Mrs. Cyril E. Martineau, as the name of a lady guest in a Woman's Club in New York City, and wrote on a mere chance that she would get my letter, as I knew not her address, but directed to her in New York City or New Jersey. She sent my letter to London and instantly the volume was sent me, with Nearly or fully a thousand names. Thus Our Father opens the way for the redemption of the dead, and to Him be all the honor and glory. The address of him in London in <blank to end of line> "David Martineau Esq. No. 122 King's Avenue, Clapham Park. London S.W. England.

22/About midnight Susan awoke Struggling for breath and for over an hour I was struggling for; she in her agony was fighting for breath, I praying for her. I was alone, could not go for help nor call any one. It was either congestion of

[Page B332L]

1907/Nov. 22/the Lungs or pneumonia. He life was saved only by the mercy of the Lord. She could lie down, and sat up all night, I with her. Albert and Emma came early, staid all day and all night, all next day and night, before they could leave her.

I also, for two weeks have been hardly able to move about or rise from

---

160. Martineau is referring to David Martineau's *Notes on the Pedigree of the Martineau Family Descended from Gaston Martineau Who Emigrated to England in 1686*, which was published in London in 1907 and revised by Anthony C. Crofton in 1972. Crofton's edition, however, is extremely scarce, with no known extant copies in North America. See Crofton and Martineau, *Pedigrees of the Martineau Family*. See note at entry for March 5, 1910.

a chair without help—a pain and weakness in my back. We are a couple of almost helpless cripples.

26/ So helpless, suffering acute pain on the least motion Albert had to undress me for bed like a little child.

29/ To night Gertrude went to a Social party—the first time in years. She is greatly improved in health, greatly to the wonder of all who know her, for no one thought she could live. It is all by the blessing of the Lord, administration and her wonderful faith.

Dec./ December.

2/ Albert and Emma gave a Social dinner to which Susan, Gertrude and I went, Albert bringing us in a carriage.

I learn from the newspaper of the birth of another Gr-Grand Child, a daughter of Henry's oldest daughter Bertha [in margin: Nov. 2] Farnsworth, who was born Nov. 2nd, last month.

3/ Recd a letter from a Miss Mary Bruyire Wikoff, Cream ridge, N.J. who had read my genealogical article in the Des. News of Nov. 26, and desired information relative to temple work.[161] Thus is interest increasing in this holy work. I recd same mail, a letter on the same subject from Utah who also had read my article.

5/ Letters from Persis L.Y. Richards and others asking particulars of my temple work, for indians and those of their families. Thus my article published in the "News" is bringing forth increased interest in the work for the dead. Thanks to God.

8+9/ Quarterly Conference. Present from S.L. City Apostles G.A. Smith and Geo. F. Richards, also H.H. Cummings Gen Supt. Church Schools and Sister E.C. McCune. A good time. Pleasant visits with Br. Cummings. Blessed him, that his wife Barbara shall know the Law of Plural Marriage is true and from God. Br. C. was greatly rejoiced + happy.[162]

---

161. No article appears under this date. The article to which Martineau refers appeared on October 19, 1907. See note at entry for October 8, 1907. Another article appeared later in December. See James H. Martineau, "Genealogy," *Deseret Evening News*, December 21, 1907, 31.

162. For Martineau's full report of the conference, see J. H. Martineau, "Juarez Conference," *Deseret Evening News*, December 28, 1907, 27.

[Unpaged letter from Mary E. Connelly dated Feb. 2, 1908 on Young Woman's Journal letterhead. payment for article "A Dance On Sunday" which appeared in the Feb Journal.]

[Page B333R]

1907/Dec. 9/Had a good interview with Sister McCune about temple work. She was glad to see and talk with me.

10/ Blessed Sister I.W. Pierce who was distressed in mind, and She was made happy. It makes me happy to make others so.

23/ Recd of Prest A.W. Ivins Store orders for mapping, amounting to $118.00 Paid tithing $6400 and all debts and had $17.00 left. Thankful to be able to do so.

25/ Susan and I took dinner at Guy Taylor's. Gertrude able to sit at the table. Albert also brought us some nice eatables.

30/ Sent a temple sheet, male names, to Nephi, also a list to him of women, hoping he may get some to endow them. I hope So.

During the past month I have spent most of my time arranging my names for baptism and endowment, and hope I may interest my children warmly in the holy work.
[Blank line]

January/ January 1908

1st/ Spent the day quietly and wrote letters.

3/ Sent 60 female names and 20 male, to temple (S.L. City) for baptism. Rain, and warm weather.

6/ Surveyed for Allred

11/ Sent 20 male names to B.S. Johnson for bap. + Endd

15/ Electric lighting beam

16/ Albert returned to his R.R. work in Sinaloa, Mex.

22/ Electric lights finally in working order.

25/ Sat in High council, hearing 3 cases.

27/ Susan suddenly very sick. Billious attack. Went to Bp. J.C. Bentley's and blessed his wife for her confinement. Promised a boy baby, being thus impressed to do.

Went 10 miles to measure cub. meters in a reservoir dam of Gov. Terrazas. A dispute as to true Contents.

27/ Again at the dam. Susan still sick, but better

31/ Susan able to sit up most of the day.

February/ February

8/ Sent 20 female names to Jennie S. Hill, S.L. City for baptism and Endowment. Recd from temple the list of 80 males and females baptized there

[Page B334L]

1908/Feb. 15/ Wrote to Prest JF. Smith about removing to S.L. City, so I may be near the temple and genealogical records, for I wish to spend my last days in the work for the dead.

March/ March

20/ Sent temple sheet to Sister Amanda Wessman, for her to endow for me, 20 female names.

20/ F.R. Society entertainment. Very pleasant. Gertie went in her wheel chair, and was very happy. Letter from 1st Presidency, who say come to the City if you want, in reply to my letter.[163]

April/ April

8th/ Went to EL Paso to file my pension papers. returned [in margin: 10] home, 11 P.M.

18/ Recd my pension check for last 6 months $72.00

20/   "   5 % dividend from Store ($1240.00 Stock) $62.00

23/ Surveyed pasture line of G.C. Wilson 1 day

---

163. In reply, the First Presidency wrote: "Inasmuch as you desire to change your residence from Colonia Juarez to this city, we know no reason whatever why you should not do so, and as far as we are concerned therefore you may consider yourself at perfect liberty to come and live here." Joseph F. Smith, John R. Winder, and Anthon H. Lund, to James H. Martineau, March 13, 1908. This letter was inserted at the back of Martineau's journal, book two. See Godfrey and Martineau-McCarty, eds., *Uncommon Common Pioneer*, 731.

24/ "   plat of land for B.Y. Whipple 1 "

May/ May

1/ Recd my temple sheet from Mrs. Wessman, work all done, most of it by Mrs. M.W.R. Wilcox. God bless them.

5/ Received temple sheet (20 names) from Jane S. Hill, work all done. May Our Father ever bless her.

March 13. 1908

Mch. 13/ My 80th Birth day. Most of our children came from the [note horizontal lines in margin] mountains. We had a very nice dinner and an enjoyable time. We sat in a group for a photograph,—about 50 in number, including my two sons in law, E. Guy Taylor and E.F. Turley and their families.[164]

May/ May

24/ I will here note two cases in my ministrations to the sick, wherein two young women given up to die by the doctor and relatives were healed in a marvelous manner by the power of the Lord. The first was a daughter of P.C. Hancy ill with typhoid pneumonia, age about 17 years. Sent for. I asked the Father if it was His will for her to live and if He would bless my ministration to her. (This as I always do) An Affirmative answer by the Holy Spirit gave faith to bless her with full assurance of healing for her. I blessed her that she should be healed, and amend from that hour, all of which was fulfilled to the letter, and to the astonishment of

[Page B335R]

1908/May/the doctor, a man of great experience. He said "I can't understand how she could live. Nothing to build hope upon."

The other case was that of Mary Pierce, age 22, sick unto death with dropsy at the heart combined with rheumatism.

I obtained a favorable answer for her, that she should live and be perfectly healed. I blessed her accordingly + she revived so she could speak and said she believed. Next day she relapsed, and was apparently dying,

---

164. This photograph was comprised of James Henry and Susan Ellen, with more than fifty children and grandchildren. See photograph section.

suffocating with the water around her heart and lungs. Sent for again and told she was dying. I said to myself "Have I been misled by my sympathy for her in pronouncing upon her, life, health and speedy recovery? Has some other Spirit—not of God—deceived me? How then shall I know the true voice of the Holy Ghost—the Comforter? I prayed to know how it was, and received a plain answer from the spirit.—"You have not been deceived. The voice which spake yesterday to you was truly the voice of the Comforter. She <u>Shall be fully</u> healed. Fear not to bless her with recovery for thy words of blessing shall be ratified in the heavens."

I found the family in deep distress, with the father, mother and other relatives sent for from Diaz. I told them not to fear—she should be healed. Mary said she believed me. I then blessed her that she should amend from that hour and be perfectly healed. Next day I found a wonderful change. She seemed an entirely new woman, the dropsy nearly gone and all pain. Next day dropsy entirely gone, and she sitting up, and the next morning went home by wagon to Diaz 70 miles distant, camping out one night on the way.

How merciful is Our Father! To Him be all the praise.

May 24/ Visited and blessed Br. and Sis. Longhurst and Elizth Johnson. Not feeling well myself, in bed all forenoon.

" 19/ This morning about 3 a.m. my father and his mother visited me, either in dream or vision I know not which, and approved my temple work in their behalf.

29/ Susan and by invitation went to Dublan Old Folks party. Visited Iris Call, suffering from an operation for apendicitis and in dangerous condition from inflamation of kidneys and rheumatism. I had testimony she should be healed

[Page B336L]

May 29/1908/but the hospital surgeon wrote Br. Call to bring her back to the hospital, as an abscess was forming and must be removed before too late. She (Iris 17 yrs old) had faith to be healed,—and was healed, for the pain ceased before we removed our hands from her head. This was at noon, and that evening Came to the reunion (Ward) seeming pretty well, and danced once. Next evening she danced every time,—as well as the other girls. How good and merciful is Our Father.

I also visited Julia Jones, the blind woman of 20 yrs continuance, and she said "When you was here last time (6 weeks) I could only distinguish a chimney or window of a house; now I cam see writing." I thank Thee of God

I also blessed a boy who had fits and a woman who was suffering from apparent appendicitis.

June 1/ Visited Sister Longhurst—very sick and much pain—and she felt better immediately and soon was well

20/ Up to this time I have been quite unwell + very feeble, lying in bed much of the time, but visiting the Sick when asked for. One case of special note—Eva, the daughter of Joseph Cardon, who has been very ill for 14 months, most of the time in bed, eating nothing but a little Mellen's infant food. She was in bed, too weak to sit up longer than a few minutes at a time. But after administration she felt stronger, and when I visited her next day she was walking about in the garden, much stronger and better every way. She said she was no longer taking any of the doctor's medicine. All praise to Out Father

Albert came and told us to get ready to go to the mountains tomorrow, and have a change for our good.

21st/ Started 8 a.m. Over a very rough road, which shook up Susan very badly. Twenty miles of our route was in the mountains—ridges to cross and deep gorges. Reached Sister Lunts and had a warm welcome. Susan could hardly get out of the wagon.

22/ Arrived at Theodore's, in Garcia, 8 miles over mountain. Remained in Garcia until 30th and enjoyed ourselves very much, with Change of Climate and associations.

[Page B337R]

June 1908/Gave 16 patriarchal blessings, and were invited out to dinner 5 or 6 times. Garcia is a beautiful Gem of the mountains—a Scene of rare sylvan beauty, with an altitude of over 6000 feet above the sea. A village only.

30/ Went 40 miles to Chuichupa over high mountains ranges of the Sierra Madre Mts. some passes of over 8500 feet altitude. Pine timber all the way, with occasional beautiful grassy glades. Reach Henry's home about 9 P.M.—gladly received by all + glad to get to a resting place. It is just the beginning of the "rainy season." Chichupa's altitude is over 8000 ft.—on the top, so to speak, of the Sierra, though peaks rise above us 2000 feet higher, notably, the Candelaria's.

This altitude gives pleasant days and cool nights, and one can eat and sleep well, with pine scented air and clear mountain water.

While here, enjoying the Society of our Children and grand and great grand children we felt at rest and spent 25 days very pleasantly. It rained a while almost every day—an hour or so at a time. I blessed many + went out a few times to dinner. I spent much time in getting indian names for baptism, from an ethnological work of the U.S. Government—Several hundred.[165]

July 25/ Started homeward, and reached Garcia at sunset.

Mon. 27/This evening, at 10 P.M. Josephine, Theodore's wife, presented us with another grand child—a girl—8 lbs.—all being well with mother and Child.

August 4/ I Blessed and named the baby <u>Lucilla</u>, after my most ancient Martineau, who died in Syria in the year A.D. 70, her marble tomb Still intact in the desert between Damascus and Allippo, as noted previously in my journal. She was "the beloved daughter of Martinus, Roman General." So says the inscription on her tomb.[166]

" 5/ Start home and camped at Kartchener's camp.

6/ Reached home. "No place like home." Theodore brought us home, and started back. Soon returning + going to the Summer School until 22d Aug. [Page end]

---

165. This could have been one of a number of publications issued by the Bureau of American Ethnology. See, for example, Powell, *Indian Linguistic Families*.

166. No known inscriptions can be found bearing the name Lucilla Martinus. Martineau apparently confused a sketchy description of a gravestone in Cyrrhus, Syria, with Lucilla, the daughter of Marcus Aurelius. Lucilla's name and image is found on Roman coinage of the second century.

Annia Galeria Lucilla (148–182), the second daughter of Marcus Aurelius and Faustina the Younger, married Lucius Verus in 164 at the age of seventeen. Verus and princess Lucilla lived in Syria from 163–166. Verus was an *imperator* or general in Syria and was involved in the Parthian wars. After Verus's death in 169, Claudius Pompeianus, a Syrian, married Lucilla and became a Roman general under Lucilla's father.

8
"To the Father Be All Glory"
Sunset Years, 1908–1918

[Page B338L]

1908/Sept. 7/Start to El Paso to file pension papers. Stayed over night in Dublan and administered to Eva Cardon who is very sick.

8/ In El Paso. Remained until the 10th and came home.

12+13th/ Quarterly conference in Cola Juarez.

Joel's wife and children—Annie—came on Tues 8th from Madera, Joel remaining there to close up affairs. She will stay in our house, and relieve Susan of the housework, which is hard for her, she being so lame

18/ Henry returned home. I loaned him $15.00

29/ Started to S.L. City with Conference Company,

Oct. 2 (2)/arriving 2d Oct. in a cold, rainy time. Went to Gean's who made me Welcome. Visited a few of the family + on

4/ attended Conference, also on 5th and 6th

10/ Up to this time I have been very busy, visiting the sick and giving several blessings. Especially, visited Sister Alice Bowman, near the L.D.S. Hospital, in a very precarious state of health for several years. She desires children, but the doctors tell her that to conceive is to invite almost certain miscarriage and if not miscarriage, death at time of confinement. Consequently very despondent. Blessed her with promise she shall conceive, go safely her full time, be blessed in confinement, and all shall be well. Sister Margaret Sharp, whom I brought with me, blessed her also, confirming the same which I had sealed on her.

16/ Attended a reunion of Temple workers, at which the Wid. of W.W. Phelps was present and Spoke in tongues.

28/ Today, in the Temple, Prest Madsen took my hand and blessed me, Saying:—"You shall never want for a dollar when you need it." This promise rejoices me very much, for I believe it will be fulfilled.

30/ I learned today that the name of Romain Martineau, father of Francis Martineau, and the name of my Romain Martineau was Madaleine Bucher, her father's name being Denis Bucher, with wife Mrs. Geneveive Bucher.

Nov. 2/ Had 80 male names in temple for baptism, and paid $15.00 for endowment of 20 males. Also $20.00 endment of 40 women, by Sis. Wessman.

[Page B339R]

1908/Nov. 13/ Admd to Sister Wetzel, who lies very dangerously ill. She shall be healed, and this I sealed upon her. Also Sister Quist, that she need not be operated upon in hospital for removal of tumor in abdomen. (note. Fulfilled, both cases.)[1]

Dec. 21/ Up to this time have spent my time in the Temple or in the Genealogical Rooms, obtaining names of our dead. Also, nearly every day visiting and administering to the afflicted, and in giving many Patl blessings. Have had many endowed, and many baptisms for the dead.

31/ Attended social party at Prest Winder's—I being the only man present. A lovely time and holy Spirit. After close of meeting Prest J.F. Smith's wife Edna asked me to bless a Sister McDonald—in great distress—which I did. I learned Sister Marie Young Dougall—a dear friend, was in Los Angeles in a very dangerous condition, and her sisters Susa and Zina wished me to bless and write to her, which I did next day, promising she should be healed + greatly blest.

January 1909.

Jan. 1st/ Went to Lilla's, in Logan. Spent much time visiting and blessing the sick, and had temple work done for about 100 persons. I had previously joined the genealogical Society as a life member. I sent money, $8.00 + 2.00 = $10.00 also for a life membership for Susan.

---

1. Six days later, Martineau noted in his pocket diary: "Had first ride in automobile." Entry for November 19, 1908, Martineau Pocket Diary, January 25, 1908–January 11, 1911, Joel H. Martineau Papers, MS 15994, box 3, fd. 17, LDSCHL.

25/ Learn from Susan that Anna's boy was born Nov. 8 1908,—named Lawrence Edward Turley.

31/ At Conference in Logan I blessed Prest J.F. Smith. He was pleased, and told me to go on with my work for Lamanites—baptisms and sealings of husbands and wives + children.

Feb. 11/ Recd word from Union Mercantil Co. Mexico, that my Stock of 1240.00 had dividend of 10 %, making my stock $1364.00

I learn from my eldest daughter—that her dau. Gertrude Johnson Roberts has a son—Tillman Snowden Roberts—born

19 feb. 1808, at Buckeye Arizona. Blessed 31 March 1908 by Elvira's [Note year error. 1808 should be 1908] husband—B. Samuel Johnson.

Her son Joseph + wife Cora Allred, have 7 Children

March 13/ My 81st birth day. A beautiful time, as Charlie's baby Dorothy is very Sick. I spent the day visiting the sick. Up to this date I have obtained over 2000 new names of the dead.

[Page B340L]

1909/Sun. Mch. 14/Today was held funeral of Charlie and Eva's baby Dorothy who died on 11th aged about 18 months.

23/ Worked on my temple records, but still ill with lagrippe.

24/ In bed all day.

25/ Better. Visited and blest the sick

27/ Gave Patl Blessings to Aileen, Eldon and George, children of Charles and Eva.

April 1/ Went to S.L. City and went to Jean's.

3/ Was present at receptions of Admiral Robley Evarts and the reunion of High School Cadets, of which Gean's Son Sherman is a member.

6/ At banquet at Social Hall—"Founders Banquet"—Interesting time, and on 8th at temple party at Bp. Brinton's

12/ Temple workers reunion at Bp. Brinton's. Good time

21/ Lyman's 50th Birth day. Visited and blessed him.

28/ Heavy snow storm

May 8/ Went to Logan, who is struck with paralysis, but better

15/ Lilla is healed of her paralysis, but still weak. I went to Nephi, at Benson. Cold.

16/ Snowing and dismal, but good for crops soon. Nephi had all his family at home, including Susa'a husban [sic] Wm Chantrill. Went and looked at his late purchase [in margin: ~~15/~~] of 380 A. of land, with good brick house + flowing wells.

18/ Returned to Charles' in Logan.

20/ Got three Martineau names—a <u>side line</u>—as follows, Edward Martinewe, + wife Thankfulle Martinewe who died in London Eng. May 5. 1545. He was son of Edwarde + Cecilia, son of John + Genevieve, son of Francois Martineau + Madaleina—

I knew long ago that Martineau's had come to England before the Sons of Elie + Margurite came in 1685, but did not know how to connect them with the main Romain line.

From records in Genealogical Library I find that I am by marriage connected with Oliver Cromwell through the line the French family Bucher, wife of Romain 1st + Margurite Bucher B. 1420, as follows:—

"Sir James Bucher, of Filsted. Eng. had daughter, Elizabeth Boucher, who married Oliver Cromwell, who was then 21 ys of age"

[Page B341R]

1909/May/I find also that a Martin (Martineau) came over to England with William the Conquror, and became a Lord of a large domain in Wales, where he built a large castle.

Note/ The Family name in the old Roman empire, held by a Roman General in Syria A.D. 70 was Martinus, (male) and Martina (female) at which date he erected a marble tomb in honor to the "Manes" (Spirit) of his daughter Lucilla who died there. The tomb is still in that land

The British Encyclopedia gives the following as the names translated in various languages:—Latin <u>Martinus</u> Italian and Spanish, <u>Martino</u>; Portuguese, <u>Martinho</u>, German, English and French—<u>Martin</u>. How did the name become Martin<u>eau</u> in France? For centuries much intercourse occurred between Italy and France, + Italian Martineaus who removed to France adopted the French—eau (o) in their new spelling, using "<u>Eau</u>" (the French Sound of "O" But others, not moving from Italy spelled the name <u>Martin</u>, as St Martin, tutary Saint of France. So all named <u>Martin</u> in England, Germany and France, are of the same Martinus stock of old Rome.

From other records I learn that a Grandson of Columbus married a Martineau, and by my father's marriage with the daughter of the Earl of Stanhope he became connected by marriage with the Earls Minto Chesterfield, Bedford, Halifax and Lord Chatham, the most noble of the aristocracy of England, + by an intrigue of Geo. the Second, with him and his Mistress,—a thing not to boast of, however.

Sat. 22/ My daughter Lilla Nebeker again a mother—a girl born 12.30 a.m. She had been several weeks very ill, was greatly blessed at delivery.

I returned to S.L. City. I have been quite ill for several days, but not Enough to be in bed. Lyman came to me at Gean's, and invited me to come and stay at his home. Moved there next day to 918 Logan Ave. Still quite feeble.

30/ By invitation attended meeting of Genl Board Y.M.I.A. at

[Page B342R]

1909/May/31/the home of Marie Y. Dougall Pleasant time. Blessed Sister Bennett, also her daughter, who desires children Also blessed several others.

June 1/ Sent 800 names if indians to Manti temple for baptism

Went with Sister M.Y. Dougall + Mary White to see Julia D. Wooley, long ill and feeble. Administered to her, each of us. Had great outpouring of the Holy Spirit.

2/ By request of Sisr Dougall I was today endowed for one of her father's family—Prest Brigham Youngs—a Mr. John Young.

3/ Jos. F. Smith's wife Julina sent for me to visit her daughter Donetta who is very sick. Administered.

4/ Went again, found daughter much better. It was a painful tumor on an ovarian tube or veins to the uterus. Julina asked me to come every day and dine with her family + Prest Smith.

My gr. dau. Ale M. Crissman's baby, named Jefferson. He was born Feb. 4 1908 in Philadelphia P.A.

About this time Sistr Dougall who had been very sick + I went to see her. She was only able to sit up, but had not been out of doors,—very feeble. She said how much she wished she could go to a committee meeting tomorrow but she dared not go out of doors yet. I asked the Father if she <u>could</u> go safely to the meeting, + got answer she could, (privately) So I said to "yes, you can go to the meeting and anywhere you desire from this time henceforth, and not take any hurt." She said "I believe you. I'll go." She went next day without detriment + from that time was well and strong God was merciful because of her faith, and <u>He</u> healed her.

A few days later she wished me to go with her to the hospital to see a friend there, who had had a severe operation performed. We went, administered to the woman and to three others who heard I was there and believed I could help them, and they truly <u>were</u> very greatly blessed and left the hospital much sooner than the surgeons thought possible. God healed them very speedily.

Shortly after this Sistr Dougall took me to see her

[Page B343R]

1909/June/friend—Mrs. Wright, of Ogden, in a very desperate condition, who had come to have two severe operations in the hospital. She had been ill five years and for last five months had her stomach pumped out every day. The opening from Stomach to bowels was closed + must be cut open. Also, she had a tumor <u>in</u> her uterus, large and painful. The doctor came daily to see if she was strong enough to go through these two severe operations, she being in bed, unable to dress herself. I asked and got a testimony she could be healed of <u>all</u> her troubles by the power of God and without having any surgical operations at all. Sister Dougall also had the same testimony. So we blessed Sisr Wright, telling her she could + should be healed by administrations. It was hard for her to have faith, for the surgeons said she could not live without surgical aid. She prayed all that afternoon and night, and when we came next day to bless her again she was greatly changed for the better and said she had faith to be healed. She had dressed herself, came down stairs without help, could walk about lively—entirely like another woman. We blessed her again, and in three days dismissed the doctor and went home feeling fine.

From Sister Wright we went about a mile to a woman very sick with appendicitis—going next day to be operated upon for that disease. Having testimony I sealed health + recovery upon her—<u>without</u> operation in hospital. She said "I believe—I know Ill be healed." And she was. A few days after this she came to see me—said she felt no pain from that moment (blessing)—was perfectly well + going on a pleasure trip to California tomorrow.

From her we went to another very sick woman ^woman^ and blessed her. She was healed immediately.

All these miracles were simply manifestations of the power and goodness of God, and to him be all the glory and honor. I, of myself could do nothing

[Page B344L]

June 1909/I have given so detailed an account of these cases as a sample of almost daily experiences for month as I am sent for constantly, when hope from doctors fail people. The blind have been made to see, the paralyzed to instantly walk, ossification of joints in a case (Miss Afton Young) which for years had defied the efforts of the most skillful surgeons in the United States; seven persons with tumors the surgeons said must be removed surgically, all healed by administration and the power of God, without going to a hospital; one worn an given up by doctors and relatives to die of consumption speedily healed,—oh, so many cases, too many for enumeration. People from towns north and south of S.L. City coming + being healed. To Father be all glory.

I cannot express how thankful I am to be the poor humble, unworthy instrument in the hands of Father in healing + comforting the afficted and sad. It is all I live for, this, and helping the dead, of course, first of all, I must labor for my <u>own</u> salvation

Time not thus occupied I spend in hunting the names of my dead kindred in the genealogical library, and have thus obtained thousands. I have expended considerable time and money in getting Temple work done for me, and have scrimped in food, going many days without dinner to save money to be used for the dead, but fasting thus has not hurt me any. I am feeble, and walk with difficulty, my legs below the knee being partially paralyzed + without feeling, except that my feet are always very cold. I have fallen several times on the side walks, as the least thing causes it. But—I might be sick in bed! So I can't complain, but only be thankful to be as well as I am. There but a very few men so greatly blessed as I, though poor financially. I am laying up my treasures in heaven, where no one can cheat or rob me, as many have done here. But I have not contended. I trust my Father to bless me if He thinks best to do so

[Letter inserted here from GAR dated August 2, 1909 saying JHM has a seat (possibly two) on Grand Stand at the parade and will send a carriage to your residence at 918 Logan Ave., City]

[Page B345R]

1909/Fron cousin Napoleon B. VanSlyke's last letter I learn that my cousin Laura Perel Starin in 1898, and her husband John Starin in 1909. I learn from others that Coz. Van Slike died in 1908. I am now the last living member of our extensive cirle [circle] of relatives.

June 23/ Invited to a reunion of the Genealogical Society at the old "Lion House" Prest Youngs old residence

29/ Attended "Old folks Day." About 3000 dined on the Tabernacle grounds.

July 13/ Visited and blessed a Sister Hinkley who was very ill with appendicitis, + going soon to hospital for operation. Was in much pain which instantly ceased, + she was perfectly healed, as she told me a few days later as she was about to go on a pleasure trip to California. Also blessed another that she might conceive.

22/ I learn that my gr. daughter Bertha's (Henry's daughter) last child was born June 2 1909; also that my Gr. Son James Edward's Son was born June 17, 1909. 22 Gr. Grands.

Aug. 2/ Visited G.A.R. head quarters to see if there is to be any place in the Grand Parade on Aug. 11 for Mexican War veterans. Was told by Col. Stetson, manager, that he would give me a carriage in the procession and tickets for the grand stand.

5/ Visited Sistr Adkins sick baby, which three doctors say cannot live. Had testimony the child should be healed by a Administration. Met there

Sister^s^ Dougall and Sharp and Levi Richards I was speaker, in blessing, and sealed life upon the Child, who immediately opened his every eyes with new life + was healed soon. To Father be all the honor and glory for it.

11/ At 8 a.m. a carriage came for me to go to the place where the procession was to form, hour miles distant. Our procession was full two hours in passing a given point. Thousands of the veterans of the civil war, U.S. troops from Camp Douglas and the Utah military organization, more than 30 Brass Bands A grand display. Two other Mexican War veterans were also in the procession. A grand event.[2]

16/ Sent for at day light to bless Sistr Knight, very sick with typhoid fever—104°. She was instantly healed.
[Page end]

[Page B346L]

Aug. 1909/Visited and blessed Sisr Grover. Weak, dangerous flooding.

17/Went to see her next day and found her healed of her trouble.

20/ Sent for to bless Sisr Stevens, of Ogden, who came for this purpose. She has cancer in the womb. Sealed full healing upon her, and she believed. I had previously blessed a friend of hers, Sisr Wright, of Ogden, who had cancer in the womb and serious stomach trouble, said to require surgical operation, who had been healed, the Cancer quickly healing + disappearing

25/ Went to Logan, to Moses Thatcher's funeral. Returning, I got off at Ogden to see my patient, Mrs. A.T. Wright. Found her in fine spirits and looked well.

30/ Visited Sisr Dougall. Found two of her family sick, one nearly blind. Blessed them. Sis. Dougall, very glad, said "Surely the Lord must have sent you in this, our time of need." To Him be all honor.

31/ Met Miss Marian E. Martins, of Eng.—one of our Martineau kindred

Sept. 29/ Attended a reunion in 19th Ward in honor of the widow of W.W. Phelps, a veteran of Missouri persecution times. She spoke in tongues, interpreted by a daughter of Orson Hyde, Sis M White.

---

2. For descriptions of the day's parade and celebrations, see "Silver Grays March Erect," *Deseret Evening News*, August 11, 1909, 1, and "Caught on the Street," *Deseret Evening News*, August 11, 1909, 2.

Was then taken to see a Sister very ill. Blessed her + she was well next day. Found there a young girl of 17 years, from Mexico. She Came to have her leg amputated above the knee. I had testimony she could be healed of the tuberculosis of the knee by the power of God, and without amputation, and blessed her to that End. It seemed pitiful for a young girl to go through life with only one leg.

Received telegram from my beloved wife, saying she will meet me here Oct. 1 at 6.30 a.m. Oh how thankful I am for it.

Oct. 1/ Susan came at 6.30 to the R.R. Station. I was not able to meet her, being in bed, quite weak, but Lyman met her + brought her to me. Now I believe I shall become stronger For weeks I have been scarcely able to walk without some one to hold to, I am partially paralyzed below the knees. But before this, for over 6 months, my legs have been very bad in condition—swollen and almost without sensation to the touch. An Osteopath, by examination, says my spinal cord is affected. It has been all I could do ever since April last to walk a block or two and climb

[Page B347R]

1909/the stairs to the Genl Library rooms, which I have never missed doing a single day, except when called to visit the sick. This I am constantly called to do, usually when the person has been given up by the doctors. I have thus prevented seven persons, whose tumors must be removed, the doctors said, by surgical operation. All of them were healed—the tumor gradually disappeared. Many other wonderful manifestations of the power and goodness of God have occurred in my experience here, which I have not noted in my memorandum, and so cannot tell of them here, even if I wished to, which I do not care to do, only as a testimony of the Gospel Ordinances, + that God is to day, as of old, able and willing to bless His people.

Dec. 31/ Sister Nelson telephoned me saying Lura was worse, and suffering much pain in her knee. She had also fallen and hurt her hip very badly. I asked Susan to ask for a testimony concerning her. I did not wish to have her leg amputated. I had visited her several times, with Sisters Dougall, Sharp, Susan and Clayton, and we had blessed her that she should be fully healed by the power of God, for such was the testimony to us all. Could it fail?

I asked God to give to me and to Susan testimony concerning Lura.

After a time I asked if She had an answer. She said Yes. What was it I asked. She said "She shall be healed by my power, for there is no other way. Therefore fear not. All shall be well."

The answer to me was:—"<u>Fear not concerning thy Sister. She shall be perfectly healed by my power, and not by any surgical operation.</u>"

I wrote this to Sister Dougall, hoping she could convey it to Sister Weson, [Weston?] to strengthen her faith which she did. I am unable, for the last 2 months to go out, as I cannot stand alone nor walk without holding to some one, so I could not go to see the poor girl. When I had visited her before I had to cling to my companion to enable me to walk,—could not alone. My

[Page B348L]

1909/ trouble is in my legs and feet below my knees, which are paralyzed, the doctor says and he calls it <u>Locomoter Ataxia</u>, and says nothing can be done, as it is an affection of the spinal cord.[3] When he said this, a voice said to me, "You shall be healed by my power saith the Lord," and from that moment began to grow in my heart. I have had the gift to heal the sick, but not for myself, hence I could not pray for myself in <u>real</u> faith as I could for others. I believe I shall be healed, and if I am not, it will be because of failure in me and not in the Lord. My great desire is to live + bring souls to God, who has been so wonderfully good and merciful to me, and that I may help and bless the living. All else earthly is as nothing to me, save my beloved wife. I have gone scores of times to visit the sick when I was scarcely able to stand, but glad to do so because I could thus make others happy, as was always the case. Letters have come to me from Ogden, Logan and Los Angeles from those whom I have administered to, full of joy that my words were fulfilled in their cases, all of them desperate—internal cancers and one of Severe internal complication of long standing. To Our Father be all the honor and glory.

Dec. 25/ Christmas, and many tokens of remembrance from almost all

---

3. This refers to locomotor ataxy, a disease of the spinal cord and central nervous system caused by tabes dorsalis in the dorsal columns (posterior columns) of the spinal cord, which causes (among other symptoms) the atrophy of cerebral, auditory, and olfactory systems. The primary symptoms, however, are temporary paralysis in the limbs, numbness, and involuntary movements of the arms and legs. See Kuh, "The Pathology of Locomotor Ataxy," *Medical News* 64 (March 3, 1894): 227–230.

my dear ones. Thankful I am I was admitted, with Susan, as members of Emerson Ward. S.L. City about the middle of December, and paid $7.50 tithing, acrued since I came from Mexico, having previously sent money to Bp. Bently, of Juarez, Mexico to pay my tithing in full there. I can say, thankfully I have paid full tithing all my church life,—almost 60 years, and in the early 50's I consecrated all I had to the Church, by deed, as required at that time.[4]

[Page B349R]

Jan. 1/ 1910 Tribune Conspiracy

1910/Before commencing my daily record for this year I will narrate how the Lord, through my humble labors, [blank to end of line]

In the 70's the "Tribune" clique of our enemies laid a plan to either destroy the Church or drive us from Utah, by bringing upon us another army. To accomplish this they published daily reports that we were organizing for rebellion and were secretly drilling every night for an uprising.

Every day were published letters purporting to come from every town and hamlet, almost, in Utah crying for help, saying every night might be their last, for in each place Mormons were preparing to massacre them all. These letters were all written in the Tribune office. Every Mormon town or village was in perfect peace, and there was no thought of evil to any non-mormon, anywhere. There was no no friction—no cause for trouble. The Tribune continually called upon Government for help by an Army to be sent quickly, or all non-mormons in Utah would be killed.[5]

---

4. Here Martineau refers to a time when he gave nearly all that he had to the church. See entries for June 3 and 18, 1852.

5. These rumors of secret drills appear to have reached a crescendo during the months of May and June 1877. They reportedly stemmed from Brigham Young's alleged response to the John D. Lee trials and investigation of the Mountain Meadows Massacre. See "Defying the Law," *Salt Lake Daily Tribune*, April 24, 1877, 4; "The Nauvoo Legion," *Salt Lake Daily Tribune*, May 1, 1877, 6; "Treason in Logan," *Salt Lake Daily Tribune*, May 3, 1877, 4; "Drilling," *Salt Lake Daily Tribune*, May 3, 1877, 4; "Mormon Militia," *Salt Lake Daily Tribune*, May 3, 1877, 4; "Will Resist," *Salt Lake Daily Tribune*, May 3, 1877, 4; "Drilling at Home," *Salt Lake Daily Tribune*, May 4, 1877, 4; "Obeying the Priesthood," *Salt Lake Daily Tribune*, May 4, 1877, 4; "Time to Act," *Salt Lake Daily Tribune*, May 5, 1877, 1; "Miscellaneous," *Salt Lake Daily Tribune*, May 6, 1877, 1; "The Nauvoo Legion," *Salt Lake Daily Tribune*, May 13, 1877, 2; "The Public Peace in Danger," *Salt Lake Daily Tribune*, May 13, 1877, 2; "More Troops Asked For," *Salt Lake Daily Tribune*, May 15, 1877, 1; "Ogden," *Salt Lake Daily Tribune*, May 17, 1877, 2; "Beaverites Alarmed," *Salt Lake Tribune*, May 25, 1877, 2; "Mormon Uprising," *Salt Lake Daily Tribune*, May 26, 1877, 4; "An Inquiry Ordered," *Salt Lake Daily*

Before sending an Army the President sent Gen. Crook to investigate, before expending millions in a military crusade which might be needless.

I was a resident of Logan and one day received a telegram from Genl Kimball, U.S. Surveyor General, requesting me to visit him at once, but giving no reason. I went to him on the next day in his private office. He said:—Martineau, there is a great deal of talk about a Mormon uprising. I know you are one of the leading military men in Cache Co. and will know as much or more than anybody about the matter, and I want you to tell me what you know about it.[6] You and I were comrades in the Mexican War, and I know I can depend

[Page B350L]

Conspiracy Contd

1910/upon what you tell me. Now, is there any truth in these reports about a Mormon uprising?"

I smiled and replied "Do you think Brigham Young is a fool?" He said "No he is no fool, leaving religion out of the question he is by far the Smartest and most able man in the U. States" "Do you think said I "that he would be so foolish as to attempt to accomplish what 12 great states attempted, with millions of money, men, munitions of war and they sympathy of all Europe, and attempted in vain? What could Brigham do with 8000 or 10000 militia, undisciplined, no arms of any value, ammunition for not to exceed half an hour's firing, no supplies of ammunition, food, transportation supplies of food or clothing—not enough for a week's campaign! What could such a force do in opposition to the united States, with its millions of men and means? Do you think Brigham Young such an idiot as that"?[7] "No," said he "I dont believe it for a moment, but I thought that where there was so much smoke there might be some fire."

Tribune, May 26, 1877, 2; "Governor Emery and General Crook," *Salt Lake Daily Tribune*, June 16, 1877, 2; and "Troops for Utah," *Salt Lake Daily Tribune*, June 27, 1877, 2.

    6. General Kimball, having known Martineau for a number of years, may have asked him directly, after reading reports that the Cache Militia had been drilling for an impending confrontation. See "Treason in Logan," *Salt Lake Daily Tribune*, May 3, 1877, 4, and "Ogden," *Salt Lake Daily Tribune*, May 17, 1877, 2.

    7. For editorials in opposition to the spurious reports of drilling, see "The Great 'Uprising,'" *Deseret News* 26 (May 23, 1877): 242; "There is No Trouble but Let the Troops Come," *Deseret News* 26 (May 23, 1877): 249; and "The Bosh from Salt Lake," *Deseret News* 26 (May 23, 1877): 249.

Gen Kimball, said I, "you may depent [?] upon what I tell you. I am next in authority to Gen Hyde who is the Brig. Genl Commanding in the Cache Militia District, a brigade of two full regiments of infantry and one of mounted men, termed by us "Minute Men" expected to go any hour, day or night, against the indians, and as Chief of Staff receive reports from every company and regiment. Every military order pertaining to the Brigade or District is written by me. Therefore I know all that is going on in the whole District, more perfectly than any one else. If you doubt come to Logan and inspect our military records and you will have no room for doubt."[8]

"I believe you" said he, "I'll put a stop to

[Page B351R]

Conspiracy Contd

1910/all this infernal business. It's all that infernal Tribune Clique,—they ought to sent to Hell—they want an army here so they can take the property and homes of the Mormons, and get rich out of army contracts for supplies of all kinds. But I'll block their game. Genl Crook is on the way here to investigate. He and I were bosom friends in the civil war. I'll go and meet him, and post him about the whole thing." He thanked me warmly for my coming a 100 miles to see him, and, true to his word, soon started to meet Gen. Crook, which he did at Cheyenne, and fully explained to him the situation. At Ogden a special train was awaiting Gen. Crook with some 35 or 40 of the Tribune Conspirators ready to pump him full. He declined for the present to talk of the uprising, was tired by the journey, and would talk later. Which he did. In two or three days the Tribune ^Clique^ called him a "Jack Mormon"—"Bought with mormon gold" etc. etc.

So vanished the roscate [?] hopes of a few bold bad men, anxious for wealth, even if it be obtained by injustice to a whole community, always loyal and true to the Government.

While at Corinne on Some Engineering business one day, a non-mormon whom I met at the railroad station who supposed me to be a Gentile, took me one side and said "Somehow I've taken a liking to you, and I want to put you on to something perhaps you don't know, for it isnt made public yet. "Any money in it" said I, "if there is, I'd like to know

---

8. Martineau's journals of the Cache Military District are on microfilm at the Utah State Archives and Records Service; a copy is held at USU Special Collections.

about it. I want money myself, just now." "I will tell you, but don't talk about to any one you dont fully know. We're going to have a big army here before long and the Mormons have got to get out. They cant sell out for we wont need to buy. We'll just take such places as we like and they

[Page B352L]

Gen. Axtell

1910/cant help themselves. Some of my friends [In margin: Jan 7] and I have picked out some good places. The best ones are rapidly being chosen already, and if you dont hurry up you'll lose some good chances."

"Well," said I, "I hope no one has picked out my home." "Your home?" said he "Where is your home?" "I Logan City" I said "and if any body tried to take my home, I'll kill him if I can." "Why," Said he, "You are not a Mormon"! "Yes, I'm a full blooded Mormon," and I tell you right now, if you or your chums try the game you are telling me about, you'll never live to enjoy it nor the plunder you hope to get."

His countenance underwent a sudden change and he muttered "It's all a joke" and got away speedily as possible.

To my personal knowledge there was at one time in Logan assertions by a Presbyterian minister resident there and by some apostate Mormons, that they would take the Tabernacle and the Temple, and devote the Temple to various secular uses.

The foregoing sketch should have been inserted years ago. Also my experience with Gov. Axtell in 1875 which I now write:—

About the middle of June 1875 the County Court, and Logan City Council, of which I was a member, determined to invite Gov. Axtell to visit with his friends, Cache Valley. I being appointed to write the invitation, as I did, soon receiving from the Governor a note ~~oth~~ of thanks and acceptance. Apostles Brigham Young, Moses Thatcher and I were appointed a Committee to wait upon him and go with him through Cache County. But before his arrival to Logan both Elders ^Thatcher^ and Young were unavoidably compelled to be absent, therefore Prest W.B. Preston and Judge M.D. Hammond were appointed in their

[Page B353R]

places. Gov. Axtell arrived in Logan June 22/75 and took apartments prepared for him at the Blanchard Hotel. During the Governor's visit we visited many towns in the county in his company, at all of which he addressed large audiences, and was especially desirous to see the children, which wish of his was gratified, the school or Sunday school children being marshaled before him for his inspection. In addressing them, he spoke always as would a L.D. Saint elder,—told them to avoid profanity, liquor, obscene language, tea, coffee or tobacco as being injurious to health; to observe and keep holy the Sabbath day, to honor the aged and to be good, true citizens obedient to the laws. Any one not know who was speaking would have thought him a Mormon elder. And he was sincere, as I found in my personal interviews and conversations during his visit. He was not a member of any church, but was one of the "Honorable men of the Earth," full of broadminded integrity.

But our last and most pleasant interview occurred the day previous to his departure. He said to me "Mr. Martineau, I am satisfied the highest and most perfect ~~examples~~ ^type^ of the Anglo-Saxon race will be found in three or four generations among you mormons." I thought—that's taffy, because he's among us today—so I said "Why do you think so"? He replied in a manner which surprised me beyond measure

"Well," said he, "I see it this way. I don't know anything practically about polygamy, but I can understand that if a man has several wives he can only be present with one at a time, which would place the others in the position of spinsters or widows for the time being, placing upon them the responsibility of governing and teaching their children, planning their welfare, and in short,

[Page B354L]

Gen. Axtell

bring into exercise facilities otherwise lying dormant because of disuse. Now back East where I came from such women are just as good "business men", so to speak, as men—often more so, And simply because they exercise their facilities A tailor, who wields only a needle or a pressing iron has not so muscular an arm as a blacksmith, who swings all day a heavy sledge or other heavy tool.

In like manner mental facilities become weak and dwarfed for lack of exercise. Women who thus exercise their mental facilities endow their children at birth with mental facilities above the average through natural laws; and their children produce a generation still superior, and so, upon natural principles, a few generations should show a surprising excellence, far above the average of the human race—at the very head of all."

I saw he was a man of profound thought. He had unwittingly given a powerful, philosophic testimony in favor of the Law of plural marriage.

He told me of his early life, and how he first became ambitious to obtain education. His father, a well-to-do but uneducated farmer, thought that a little country school education was all a man needed, and he gave his son little opportunity for instruction—no candle or lamp light for study at night, so pitch pine knots burning in the fire place had to furnish the light for study. The final impetus for education came one day in the corn field. Tired and perspiring from hoeing corn he was resting in the shade of the road fence when two gentlemen came slowly along the road, one of whom—a Jude of the Supreme Court, related how he had obtained his high position, his father giving him no encouragement. He had spent Every spare dollar he could earn for books which he studied by fire light; had gained a place as Errand boy and general help in a lawyer's office who finally

[Page B355R]

Gen. Axtell

1910/became interested in him,—made him clerk and finally admitted him to partnership and to general prosperity.

Gov. Axtell said that the Judge told his story the thought came to him—"if one boy can do that so can I," and from that time never ceased the struggle till he too, had gained the goal of his ambition,—first, a lawyer—next, Governor of Utah.

Before leaving Logan he gave me another and most agreeable bit of information. Said he "I will tell you why I wanted to see the children in every place I visited. I had been told in the East that the Mormon children, especially polygamous children, were very inferior, mentally and physically, to the children of Non-Mormons and I wanted to see for myself." I said "Govr—what do you think of the children you saw?" "I never saw finer," said he, healthy, intelligent, and bright; and a high school teacher of seven years experience and eleven years in public schools of Chicago told me he could bring the Mormon children up to a point in two thirds the time required by the gentile children. I asked him his theory, and he said he had no theory, but knew it was true." I said, "Well, Governor, what is your theory"? He answered "I'm like the other fellow. I have no theory, but I know I'm correct."

Gov. Axtell was all unknown to himself, a natural born Mormon, a man of true integrity.

I have thought it right to insert the foregoing two retrospects even at this late date, in honor of Gen. Kimball and Gov. S.B. Atell.

Jan. 8/ To day is the blessed anniversary of Susan E.s and my marriage—58 years ago. Nothing done in remembrance—none is needed. She is with me.

" 18/ This is the anniversary of my marriage with Susan Julia Sherman, who died 35 years ago in her comparative youth of 39 years. But she has

[Page B356L]

Jan. 18/1910/escaped many years of Sorrow and care, and for many years rejoiced with the just + in the companionship of her loved ones. She obeyed cheerfully every law of God made known to her, and will go on to her exaltation as one of the Queens of Heaven, and in due time become Eve to an Earth, peopled by her spiritually born children, over whom she will preside forever as a Priestess and Queen, having received every ordinance that of the 2nd A, by Susan E. in Logan temple.

She is to be greatly congratulated—not mourned
for she has passed all danger,—her exaltation is sure. Our faithfulness is yet to be proved.

Fri. 13/ This morning, while awake about 3 A.M. as I often do, I was wondering whether my place, as capable for doing the most good, is here in S.L. City or in Mexico, seeing that I am not able now to go about as before among the Sick, or to do any work in the temple, and as having no real home here for myself and Susan. I asked for a testimony, and received this answer plainly given by the Holy Spirit.

"James, My Son, thy prayer is heard + accepted and thou also art accepted, for I know the secret desires of thy heart, for they are all for good + none for evil, and that thy great desire is to do good to the living and the dead, even to all who will receive it at thy hand; and there are not too many who have so great a desire to do so. Be of good cheer, for all shall be well for thee, for thou shalt remain here, near to the temple and the records of the dead, that thou mayest do a great work for them in the future as thou hast in the past, for thou wast appointed and set apart for this work before thou didst take thy temporal body because thou wast valiant for thy Father when Lucifer drew away so many after him. Thou shalt live and labor many years in this holy

[Page B357R]

Jan. 18/1910/work, though Satan desires to hinder thee, and has brought thine affliction upon thee for this purpose, but the power of thy Father is still greater, and thou shalt do the work appointed thee yet many years to come. Thou shalt labor not only here but in my holy house in Jackson county, even until the coming of my beloved Son. Thy way shall open up before way to thine own wonder. Thou shalt not lack for a comfortable home nor for means to obtain abundant help in thy temple work, even to the fulness of thy desires, for thou shalt be fully healed of all thy present infirmities and become strong as in thy prime. Amen.

This gave me much joy. I know it was from the Lord by the Holy Spirit, and if it is not fulfilled it will be because I prove myself unworthy of these blessings promised.

Jan. 19/ Sister Needham from Logan visited me and said her daughter, Mrs Mae Earl, Sick so long, was much better. My words of blessing had been fulfilled, also, in the case of Miss Marian Martines, whom I had blessed, to the least particulars.

These things give me great joy and strengthen my faith, as showing my ministrations were approved of the Lord.
[Blank line]

26th/ This morning at 1.10 a.m. my dau. Virginia Sudbury's girl baby was born, all being well.

Feb. 8/ Received my temple sheets from St George, 599 Baptisms for me.

" 7/ To day Sisters Buel, White and Hill visited me. I had at times greatly blessed them in times of trouble and sorrow, and we are dear to each other. I blessed Virginia, the little daughter of Sister Buel for diseased throat.

Sis. Hill pleased me greatly in telling me her dau-in-law is pregnant, after many years of longing for a child. This was in fulfillment of a

[Page B358L]

1910/Feb. 7/promise I had sealed upon her last summer. I had met the young wife at the home of Sis. Buel, and she had unburdened her trouble to me of "hope deferred" and apparently vain, for motherhood. A few days later I felt so strongly impelled to visit and seal upon her her conception and motherhood, that went several miles to her and told her and husband what I had come to do, if they desired it, and had faith in the holy ordinance of blessing. They were both greatly pleased and said they believed.

I sealed upon her the promise she should become a mother to a noble spirit, and should be greatly blessed in child bearing. Sister Buel told me all is being literally true, and great is my joy that Our Father enables me thus to help and comfort others, and deigns to make known His will to one so little and unworthy as I am.

How could I dare to make such a promise? I had so promised, by blessing, several times before, and my words had literally been fulfilled. I asked the Father to thus bless them if was His will so to do, and if so, to manifest it to me by the Holy Spirit. I received testimony it <u>was</u> His will, and not to fear, but bless the woman to that End and to fear not, for my words should be fulfilled. And so they were. I never go to administer to the sick without asking first for a testimony concerning the Sick one, + when I obtain it, I speak as one having authority, and if the sick have faith, they are healed, even at the gates of death. All praise to Our Father, from whom all good comes.

8/ Sister Pola brought Sister Newton and her baby 3 months old apparently blind, born so. She

[Page B359R]

1910/Feb. 8/wished me to bless her baby to restore or give sight. I did so. The result is with the Lord.

In the afternoon Sis. Alice Bowman came with her baby—a fine one—which she claimed as a child of promise in answer to a blessing sealed upon her by me, after physicians had declared she could never become a mother, or if she should become pregnant, she surely would die in confinement, her system so disorganized. She is now the picture of health, more so, she says, than in many years.

She brought her niece, who desired + obtained a Patriarchal blessing.

10/ Sis. Maria Dougall telephones to me that our friend, Sister Wright, is perfectly recovered from her cancer in Uterus and her closed stomach, which doctors all said must each be operated upon to save her life Her recovery is a miracle.

13/ Lyman received from my cousin, Mrs. W.A. Mears, of Seattle, Washington, data which will Enable me to join the "Sons of the Revolution, as follows:—my great gr. father, John Mears, was born in Connecticut in 1734 or 1735 and served in the American Army in Capt. Joseph Boynton's Comp. Col. Nathaniel Wade's regiment from June 26. 1778 to Jan. 6. 1779 (including 100 miles travel home) 6mo 11d. His name is on the muster rolls of the Company on Nov. 6. 1778 at North Kensington R.I.; also in East Greenwich, R.I. Sept. 17 + 28; Nov. 6th to 12th, and Dec. 1778 and Jan. 1. 1779. He died in Poultney Vt. He was a Sergeant. Our Mears tradition, told me by his son—my Gr. father James Mears, said he was at the execution of Maj. Andre, on a detail from each Regt
[Blank line]

Feb. 11/Filed application with Mexican War Commission for pension, for Ind. War service in 1860.

19/Sent 940 names to be baptized for n St George temple. This number baptized for me there about 2000

[Page B360L]

1910/Feb. 23/ My gr. daughter Alle M. Crismon and son Jefferson, who is nearly 3 years old Started to go to rejoin her husband Kenneth, who is studying medicine there. A sad parting. Will she see me again in this life? Who can tell

23/ Sent to Local Branch of "Sons of American Revolution," to ascertain how to obtain membership.
[Blank line]
In searching the genealogical records of our Society I find the name of Romain Martineau (1st) was Francois Martineau, born about 1376, his wife's name Madeleine.

Also, that one of the family came to England with William the Conqueror in 11th Century, and conquered for himself a part of Wales and erected two castles, the ruins of which still exist.

From "Gibbon's Dec. + fall of Roman Empire" I learn of an ancestor—General Martinus, who served under the great Roman general Belisarius, AD. 538. Also of a Byzantine (Eastern Roman empire, Constantinople) Empress Martina daughter of Heraelino, Exarch (Viceroy) of Africa at Alexandria, and wife of his son Heractius Emperor, living A.D. Another Martin was an officer serving under the Roman Emperor Maximim.

Feb. 14/ Sent 940 names for baptism at St George. Had previously had 599 baptized there, recently besides several hundreds previously.

In making out these lists, with all data, I was so weak I could hardly hold a pen or write legibly. Could not stand alone or walk alone.

When Dr. Richards pronounced my trouble a disease in spinal column, Locomotor Ataxia, and said the nerves branching from it and giving life and sense of feeling to my legs + feet below the feet were dead, and nothing could be done. The same cause made me unable to balance and stand alone.

[Page B361R]

Pedigree

1910/Feb. 23/ When he said I was incurable a voice said to me "You may be healed by the power of God." Then faith sprang up in my heart. This was in January last/10. Since then I have gained considerably so that to day, Feb. 23d I can walk across the floor without touching any thing with my hands, and I believe I shall be healed. All honor to <u>Father</u>.

March 2/ I walked about 40 rods to day alone, first time without help since Oct 1. 1908

4/ Florence Sudbury, (gr. dau.) was accidentally shot by her brother Lyman, with 22 caliber gun. Hit at base of nostril, thru roof of mouth. "Didn't know gun was loaded," as usual. Lyman went to her and stayed all night.

5/ <u>Tracing back my pedigree</u>.

I have now completed my Pedigree back for many generations, both Paternal and Maternal, + God has blessed me wonderfully in doing so

On my father's side I have been aided by the work of Basil and David Martineau, of London, who have spent thousands of pounds in their researches, David, especially, who employed the best experts in France, discovering that my French ancestry of 14th and 15th Centuries were of most eminent nobility, in the French Court, and one was a Knight of St John (or Malta. Also that a grand son of Columbus married a Martino.[9]

The following is Paternal lineage from myself to year 1376, an unbroken line.
[Note brackets following:]

John Martineau (my father Born 22 Mch. 1793 D. 1838
Eliza Mears. B. 13 Apr. 1806, in Fabius, N.Y. D. 1848

son of
Stephen Martineau B. 22 Mar. 1761 N.Y.   1st Gr father
Elenor Haughwout B.[blank] D. 1832

Son of
Stephen, B. 22 Mar. 1727   1st Great Grand Father
Mrs. Stephen Martineau

Son of

[Page B362L]

Pedigree contd
1910/
[In margin: 2GGF]
Cornelius Martineau   B. 1704. Staten isl N.Y.
Mrs. Cornelius "   B. 1704
Son of
[In margin: 3GGF]
Cornelius Martineau   B. 1676 Holland
Mrs. "   "   1677
Son of
[In margin: 4thGGF]
Denis Martineau   B. 1651 France
Mrs. "   "   1656

---

9. It is evident from this entry that Martineau had his own copy of David Martineau's *Notes on the Pedigree of the Martineau Family.* See note at entry for November 12, 1907.

Son of
[In margin: 5thGGF]
Sieur Pierre Martineau   1642 France of
Lady " "   1630 Peronne
Son of
[In margin: 6thGGF]
Sieur (Lord) Francis Martineau B. 1597 "
Lady (Demoiselle) " " 1605
Son of
[In margin: 7thGGF]
Sieur Louis Martineau   1570 "
Lady Catherine Alleaume 1574
Son of
[In margin: 8thGGF]
Sieur Francois Martineau 1532
Lady Claude du Boulay   1533
Son of
[In margin: 9thGGF]
^Sieur^ Denis Martineau   1493
Lady Marie Chartelier   1500
Son of
[In margin: 10thGGF]
Sieur Romain Martineau   1470
Lady Marie Chartelier   1468
Son of
[In margin: 11thGGF]
Sieur Jean Martineau   1440
Lady Genevieve —   1445
Son of
[In margin: 12thGFF]
Sieur Romain Martineau   1415
Lady Marguerite   1420
Son of
[In margin: 13thGFF]
Sieur Francois Martineau 1376
Lady Madeleine "   1380

[Blank line]

Note/In ancient France, Sieur corresponded to German "Baron" or English—"Lord." Demoiselle, feminine title, of not

[Page: B363R]

1910/Mch 5/less than nine generations of nobility, direct descent. The term "Damsel" applied to unmarried ladies of less noble standing or to the commonalty.

The men noted "Sieur" were high officials of the court, and one was a "Chevelier" in the celebrated order of the "Knights of St John" (or "Knights of Malta."

Hutchinson Line.
and Sprague.

James Mears (my Gr. father)   B. Sharon Conn. ^Apr. B. 1804^ 1774
Lois Sprague Mears (Gr. mother) " Lebanon "   ^26 feb.^ 1779
dau of
William Sprague	B. 1740	U.S.
Lois Hutchinson	1745	"
dau of		
Jeremiah Sprague	1700	"
Mrs. " "	abt 1705	"
dau of		
Anthony Sprague	1660	"
Mrs. " "	1665	"
dau of		
William Sprague	1620	Eng.
Mrs. " "	1625	
dau of		
Edward Sprague	1604	"
Mrs. " "	1605	"
dau of		
Edward Sprague	1579	Upway Dorset Eng
Christina "	1574	" " "

[Blank line]

Hutchinson Pedigree of Lois Mears Sprague
She was dau. of

	{ Lois Hutchinson B. 1745 My 2d Gr. Mother
	William Sprague (noted above) and B. 1740
no. 2251	{ Stephen Hutchinson B. 14. Aug. 1714
no. 2252	Abigal Haskins " 1720 My 3 Gr. mother
	dau of

[Page B364L]

1910/
March/
5/

[In margin: 920–2056]

    { Richard Hutchinson B. 10 May 1681
      Rachel Bance (My 4th Gr. mother) 1691
dau. of
No. 1408   { Joseph Hutchinson B. 1658
            Mrs. Joseph   "   5th Gr. Mother 1662
               dau of
No. 1300   { Richard Hutchinson B. 1633 D. 22 Oct ^1680^
            Alice Bosworth   6th Gr. Mother 1635

[In margin: Note]
Stephen Hutchinson (no. 1251) had childn
Lois B. 1739 (my ancestor) Stephen 1740 Daniel
B. 1742—Richard 1744—Lydia 1746.
Abigail 1748—Joseph 1750—Joseph 1752.
[Blank line]

6/ Before I arose I received a holy testimony regarding my Gr. dau. Florence Sudbury, age 11, who was accidentally shot on afternoon of 4th inst., the ball entering at base of nostril and passing through roof of mouth, and for which it is feared blood poisoning will ensue. I asked to know the will of the Father concerning her, and also others, partly or wholly blind, barren, tumors and cancers, for whom I had administered + blessed to be healed and the barren to be fruitful.

The answer came to me, that <u>all</u> who I had blessed thus should be healed; that Florence should not have blood poisoning but be fully healed; that my sisters, now barren shall bear noble spirits, that the tumor of Sister Pola shall disappear and not, as she has feared, injure her unborn babe; also that Gertrude shall be perfectly healed, strong and healthy and be mother to a Son of Promise; that Freddy and Elzadie, and all others whom I had blessed through faith and the power of God. Also that Susan, my beloved wife, shall be healed, by the power of God and not by medicine, and that I, too, shall be healed and live to do a great work for the living and the dead, to the fulness of my

[Page B365R]

1910/Mch. 6/desires, especially the work for the living and the dead, as far back as shall be needful, for names now unknown to me shall be made known.

This was by the still small voice of the Spirit, the Holy Ghost, who deceiveth not. I know that all this may be fulfilled through faith, hindered only by transgressions not repented of. Other precious promises also were given. Help us, Oh Father, in our weakness, that we may become strong and receive what is our privilege to receive.

My mother had the following Uncles and Aunts:—
1 Seth Sprague B. 1764 lived in N.Y. State

2 John	"	"	1766	Pa.
3 William	"	"	1768 died in Elbridge N.Y.	
4 James	"	"	1770	
5 Daniel	"	"	1772 died 1857. Vt had wife	
	Hanna Maxon			
6 Jesse B.	"		B. 1774	
7 Esther	"	"	1776 had hus. I Ichabod Babcock. F. of Wm Babk	
8 Eunice	"	"	1777 (hus. Crittenden	
9 Lois	(my Gr. Mother	"	1779 (hus. James Mears, my gr. father	

Daniel + Hannah Maxon had childn:–
1 Harriet Sprague, B. 1796 (hus. Henry Stanley

2 George	"	"	1798
3 Isaac Newton	"	"	1800 (my mother's coz. sent pedigree
4 Mary Ann	"	"	1803 (hus Benj. Withwell of Mch.
5 Julia	"	"	1805 (hus Oliver M. Hyde. He died 1867 Mich.

She had chiln Henry and Lewis, living 1879, Springfield Mass.

29/ Filed application for membership in "Sons of Amer. Revolution" paid $5.00 fee. The annual fee is $1.50[10]

31/ Recd $5.00 (U.S. cur.) from Joel, on a/c of things sold him. Susan and I went to funeral of Pres J.R. Winder. Henry came to day.

Apr. 7/ At conference with Susan
   Sent 1340 names for baptism to St George

" 19/ Attended Banquet of "Sons of Amer. Revolution."

[Page B366L]

Mch. 1910 13d/(omitted by accident) My 83 birth day.[11] Lyman gave dinner. In the evening Patriarch Jos E. Taylor and Miss Afton Young (dau. of LeGrand Young) called to see me

Mch. 9th/ Met Sister Robinson to day, in perfect health. I administered to her for cancer of the uterus when doctor said she must die. She was healed by the power of God immediately. Also received a letter from a Sister Stevens, of Ogden, who came to me for administration. She says she is perfectly healed. She also had Cancer in the womb, and doctor stai said she could not live over three months. I blessed her only twice. To God be all honor and glory.

Baptisms not noted in proper place, St George temple Nov. 1909, 820:– Apr. 1910 1340:– March 680:

April 30/ Recd letter from Genl Register of Society of "Sons of Amer. Rev." in Washington DC. saying my application is accepted and I am now a member, my number is 19322. I take pride in this membership of an Association acknowledged by Special act of Congress. My number the Utah State Branch of the Society is 122.

I visited and blessed LeGrand Young. Severely injured by a horse stepping on his breast and foot. He healed immediately, to surprise of himself + all.

---

10. Martineau's application for membership in the Utah Society of the Sons of American Revolution is included with his July 23, 1907 letter to F. E. Eldredge, MS 163, LDSCHL.

11. This was actually his eighty-second birthday. For an announcement and brief sketch of his life, see "Pioneer J. H. Martineau Celebrates His 82nd Birthday," *Deseret Evening News*, March 12, 1910, 31.

May 5/ Received notification from Washington D.C. that I may obtain gold badge of the Society of "S. of A. Rev. with the number inscribed "19322."

    Ichabod Babcock, B. Dec. 12 1731 was father of Ichabod, who married my Great Aunt Ester Sprague He was born Jan. 15 1758 in Westerly R.I. He had Son William Babcock, my Step father, who died 1864

May/ Recd $5.00 (gold) from Joel on a/c.

" 24/ Susan and I went to Old Folks theatre—free

" 15/ Henry returned home to Mexico

Apr. 30/ Sent 1200 names to St George for baptism

" 28th/ Recd note from Joel for 375.00 (Mex. = half that of U.S. gold) $87.50 (gold) ~~Also, May 26 $10.00 Mex—$5.00 U.S.~~

May 20/ Total number names of my dead in my records 21233 Of these about 16.000 have been added since I came from Mexico last time. Of these added over 4000

[Page B367R]

May/1910/have been baptized, most of them in the St George temple, some in Manti, Logan and Salt Lake temples, also many sealed.

    During the long winter, when unable to walk about unassisted, and hardly able to hold a pen, I made all or most of these baptismal records. For all these names dates of birth, + death, where born, when baptized and relationship were required to be sent to a temple, + again to be noted in my temple record. From first to last each name must be recorded 5 or 6 times:—1st record, baptism, endowment, sealing; also, in some cases, 2nd Anointing. So that to date my list shows a great deal of time and labor—a labor of love indeed, to accomplish which I have expended considerable money—treasure laid up in Heaven, where no thief can steal. I have positive testimony that all, thus far, have received my temple work in their behalf—recompense to me in full, yes, far more than full.

May 22/ Two light Earthquakes rattled dishes, some plaster fell in houses. No one hurt. Time 7.25 A.M.

    In trying to trace Susan's ancestry, back from her father—Joel Hills Johnson, Son of Ezekiel, born 12th Jan. 1776, in Uxbridge, Mass. Died

1848 in Nauvoo Ill. He was Son of [blank] Johnson, who was killed in battle of Bunker Hill, 1775. His widow [blank] remarried [blank] and they removed to Canada, since then all trace of her family is lost.

"/ I learn from my daughter Elvira Martineau Johnson that her Son Joseph Johnson became father to twins on April 13. 1910, a boy names (2d) Barnard Lavern, the first born, a girl named Verde Viscelia. The wife of Joseph is Cora Johnson. They have eight children, Grandchildren to Elvira, Great Gr. Children to making, to me in all 22 Gr. Grd Children.

Early arrivals in America of Mears + Johnson's noted in the Genl Library,—[blank to end of line]
[In margin: hus. and wife]

/Suzan Johnson, B. 1612, Eng. in Ship "Abigail" in 1634
/John Johnson " 1612 " " "
/Edmond Johnson " 1612 " " "James" in 1635

[Page B368L]

/Edmund Johnson (see previous page, bottom
May 1910
/Suzan Johnson, Born 1612 Eng. in ship "James." 1635
/Eliza " their child (These were husband, Wife + child)

William Johnson, of London Eng. came 1635 in Ship "Robert Bonaventura"

Neile Johnson. 1635, ship "John + Sarah."
Edward Johnson, 1635, " " (from Sandwich, Eng.)
Susan, his wife, 7 children and 3 servants 1635 " "

Abram Johnson, of London, came 1634
John Johnson, came 1634 in ship "Hopewell"
John Johnson " " age 23 yrs. "
Robert Johnson " " " 26 " "
James Johnson " " " 28 " "

Mears family.

{ Robert ^B. 1592^ Mere came 1635 age 43 yrs. ^ship "Abigail to Boston^
{ Mrs. Elizabeth " (wife) ^B. 1605^   "   30   "
                    Ohio.
{ Samuel Mere ^B. 1630^ " 3 "
{ John Mere ^B. 1635^   " 3 months

<u>Note</u>. Mears is spelled in old records in more than 15 ways as noted by genealogists.

In reply to my letter to Orrin P. Allen, Genealogist, of Palmer, Mass. relative to the Johnson ancestry, he says no doubt Joel H. Johnson, my wife's father, are descendants of William Johnson, who in 1634 or 1635, settled in Charlestown, Uxbridge or Boston. Probably descended from William Johnson, of Charlestown, Mass. Came 1635 from London, ship "Robt Bonaventura." His posterity all settled in eastern Mass, in vicinity of Uxbridge Mass.

Those who defended Bunker Hill we militia, farmers, who lives near at hand,—not regular soldiers—organized, And undoubtedly Gr. Grd F. Johnson, who fell in that battle, lived near by, in or near Uxbridge.

Mr. Allen gives names of other early Johnson settlers:—

John William Jun. came 1634, of Charlestown; Edward of Woburn Mass.—John, of Roxbury;—John, of Ipswich Mass. and Sea. Solomon Johnson, Sudbury, Mass. He died 1687.

June/ Lyman wishes to go to his farm near Benson to stay until school recommences in Sept, so Susan and 3 are to go to Logan on Sat. June 10th

" 9th/ Sister R.J. Grant Sent for me to come and bless and name her baby, 8 days old. I did so.

[Page B369R]

1910/June 9/This was a child of promise. Doctors had told her she could never conceive again, but I had blessed her last year that she <u>should</u> again become a mother, and she soon became pregnat [sic] in response to her faith. To Our Father be all praise.

This is the Sixth case in which my blessing has been verified in like manner, in all of which doctors said it could not be. And at this time (July 15. 1910) I have caused 18 persons to have no hospital operation performed by blessing them to be healed without any Surgical operation. In every case doctors declared the operation was imperative, or death would surely result. No doubt such would have been the case, leaving the power of God out of consideration. I am more thankful than I can express that God has made one so weak as I ~~am~~ am the instrument of God's goodness and mercy. To Him be all honor and praise.

June 10/Saturday. Went to Logan, to my Son Charles + wife Eva.

" 20/who made us welcome. On 20th June went to stay a few days with Nephi and Emma, Benson Ward.

" 23/ Received $61.38, dividend for past year on my $1364.00 stock in the "Union Mercantile" store in Dublan, Mexico.

My sons Nephi and Charles have rented for Susan + me a small house in Logan, for $8.00 pr. month. I fit it with furniture, so this money comes in good time.

" 25/ Sent article for "Era" on the "Death valley" tragedy of 1849.[12]

July 1910

July 5/Recd check from Joel and Guy Taylor $17.50 and $25.00 (U.S. gold

9/Began getting furniture. To date July 15th $91.05 pd by me, besides several dollars for provisions, etc. since moving into our house July 11th 1910. We left Nephi's place July 8th

" 11/ Susan's 74th Birth day. Eva made a dinner but I was not able to attend, having to be with men at the house.

I pray my dear wife may have many more + happier birth days, for she is worthy, if any woman is

A few days ago I wrote to Prest J.F. Smith, asking that my Bro-in-law Sixtus E. Johnson may be ordained Patriarch, reciting his eminent worthiness, also told the visit of Nephi, the Nephite apostle who, the indians said visited them in Nevada, at the time of the "Ghost Dances"

[Page B370]

1910/July/some years ago, and suggested that Sixtus be asked to write a statement of what the indians told him.

---

12. This article didn't appear for another eighteen years. See James H. Martineau, "A Tragedy of the Desert," *Improvement Era* 31 (July 1928): 771–772.

In reply Prest Smith said he would have the first apostle who shall visit Mexico ordain him, and interview Sixtus about Nephi's visit to the indians.

He also said he had mailed my book, "Pearls" which he had been examining.

" 15th/Yesterday and last night, rain, first for several months.

24/ To day Susan and I were admitted members of the 1st Ward in Logan,—Cache Stake

August/ Sent several hundred names to St George for Baptism in the Temple.

26/ Lyman and family returned from his Preston farm to S.L. City.

27/ Letter from Prest Jos F. Smith. Says he has left my book of "Pearls" with his Son Jos S. Jens [?] for examination by a Church Committee as I wished

Oct. 2/ My Gr. Son James Henry Johnson, son of B.S. Johnson + my eldest daughter Susan Elvira, and his wife Stella Clark, have their first child born + blessed in Mesa Ariz.

" 7/ Lyman's dau. Harriet Gowan's baby girl born 12.30 am

" 24/ Up to this date there have been born to us, besides Harriet's daughter just above noted eight Gr. Grand children during 1910 to date, as follows: some of whom are noted above:—also in 1909

To Chas H. Martineau, dau. born 27 Sep. 1910, Chuchupa,
"   Saml J. Johnson, twins, Bernard Lavern and Verde Visalia Johnson, B. 13th April, Buckeye, Ariz.
"   Edward Martineau, <u>Ivans</u>, B. 12 June 1909, Panguich
"   James H. Johnson, a dau. (?) " 10 Sep. 1910 Mesa, Arz.
"   Edward F. Turley, <u>Lawrance</u> B. 1909 Juarez, Mex.
"   T.S. Roberts, son Tillman S. Roberts B 1909 Buckeye Ariz.
"   "   dau   B 1910   "   "
"   James H. Johnson, Louise Elvira (?) B Oct. 3 1910 Mesa "
"   Ray Farnsworth, dau   B 1909 Chichupa ^Mex^
"   William Chantril, dau, Annis B. 27 Sep. 1910 Benson ^Utah^
Besides these births Several other Grand children have married in 1910:—Howard Martineau + Mary [blank] Clark

[Page B371R]

1910/Oct./married in Logan temple, Utah, 29 Sep. 1910, and Emma Vilate Johnson + Chas Morton Lewis, were married in Salt Lake temple 24th Sept 1910.

Thus is being fulfilled the blessing promised of a mighty posterity. I Pray all may be true and faithful.

24/ Up to date I have been confined much in the house, but am gradually gaining in health, tho Dr. Richards declared that as my infirmity is Locomater Atxia, nothing could be dome for its healing. This may be true, usually, but I know the Lord is able to heal me entirely, if it be His will. If not His will, be it done, for it is always best.

I have been able to administer to some and they have been healed by the power of the Lord.

One woman came to me from Salt Lake City for me to administer to her, 6 doctors saying she must be operated up. But she does not need any doctor, being on the way to speedy recovery.

Also a little girl, very low with typhoid fever, is now almost entirely well. To God be all honor.

24/ Blessed my Great Grand child Annis, dau. of Susan, Nephi's dau. and wife of William Chantril. She is the first Gr. Grand Child of our 29, that I have blessed. By marriage Annis is Gr. dau. of Bp. WB Preston's Sister Annis Chantril.

Mabel/(Oct 9)/ I should have noted that on Oct. 9. 1910 Nephi's daughter Mabel married James Chantril in Logan temple. He, also William, were sons of Annis Preston Chantril.

Recd my certificate of membership of Society of "Sons of the American Revolution from Washington D.C.[13]

Oct. 30/ Prest F.M. Lyman advised me to have my name and sons in the Book of Utah Pioneers.

---

13. Martineau's membership (#19322) was through John Mears, Sergeant, Capt. Boynton's Company, Col. Nathaniel Wade's Mass. Regiment. See *National Year Book, 1910* (National Society of the Sons of the American Revolution, 1910), 236.

Nov. 10/ Recd from Gr. Son Chas Henry $25.00 on land account. His baby girl is named Lois,—my sister's and Gr. Mother Mears first names.

" 15/ Recd letter from Señor Gahan a Porfirio Diaz of Mexico relative to his land for sale, which Susan's cousin Wm D. Johnson is endeavoring to colonize.

[Page B372L]

1910/ Ate our Thanksgiving dinner at Charlie's + Eva's.

Nov. 24/ Sent my petition for an increase of my Invalid [In margin: Dec. 12] pension as a Mexican War Soldier to Congressman Joseph Howell.[14]

19/ Susan suddenly very sick, Charles and Eva came I was up nearly all night with her, until she began to amend.

" 22/ This evening a miracle was wrought in my behalf through faith and blessing by Susan. For about ten years I have had an incipient rupture in left groin, a break being in the envelope of the bowels, which were prevented from emerging through the opening by a truss. By a strain by lifting and displacement of the truss my bowel gushed out forming a large swelling upon the abdomen with agonizing pain. I was unable to force it back through the small opening of about two inches or move the bowel in the least, and a light pressure upon it caused excruciating pain. All effort failing, I asked Susan to pray that the bowel might be replaced, knowing she had great faith and that she was beloved of the Lord.

She had prayed not longer than a minute, when some power—supernatural—forced the bowel back through the aperture manifestly two small for its passage, as if forced through by considerable force and yet without the least pain. I know this was done by some personage of the spirit world, probably my Guardian Angel, who has saved me from death so many times before. And to God be all praise.

---

14. Joseph Howell or Morgan (1857–1918) was born at Brigham City, Utah, on February 17, 1857, to William and Martha (Williams) Morgan. He was elected as a Republican to the Fifty-eighth and to the six succeeding Congresses. Howell taught school, engaged in the mercantile business, and was mayor of Wellsville, Utah, from 1882 to 1884. He served in the Territorial House of Representatives from 1886 to1892. He served as a regent of the University of Utah from 1896 to 1900 and was a member of the State senate from 1896 to 1900. He died in Logan, Utah on July 18, 1918. For the result of Martineau's pension claim, see notes at entry for June 14, 1915.

Now, I thank the Lord for this experience, though so painful a one, for it gave me a faith to pray for healing of this affliction I did not have before, for I had never had faith before to hope for its healing by faith and prayer.

And thus, also, have I learned by many trials to trust in the Lord and to know the voice of the Holy Spirit far better than before.

[The following is in the margin at bottom of page:]

Dec. 23 1910/Sent $5.00 to help pay/for name in Pioneer Book

[Unnumbered page, letter dated January 9th, 1911, from office of First Presidency, noting the Historian's Office has verified the date of the murder of Dr. Whitmore and Robert McIntire.]

[Page B373R]

1910/Dec. 24/ The Relief Society sent us a chicken and other things for our Christmas dinner. Quite unexpected.

" 25/ Susan and I ate our dinner alone, save Vere, a son of Charles, who happened in, Charles family were sick and Nephi to far away—at Benson.

[The following is in margin left of next paragraph: Dec. 23d Sent $5.00/ to Frank Eshom, SL. City/to apply for space/in "Pioneer Book,"/to be published soon.]¹⁵

26/ Sent my pedigree to St George temple, going back, on father's side to 1376, and on mother's side, Spragues, to 1255, in the reign of King Edward 1st This I did that others in the Church might be able make connection of their lineage with mine, for scores thus are connected by intermarriage with my ancestry.

January/ ------------- 1911 --------------

Sent my genealogical record for publication in the "Pioneer Book" to Lyman to give to the publisher.

10/ Received letter of thanks from Prest Lund for sending him an account of the discovery of the bodies of Dr. Whitmore and Robt McIntire, killed by Navajoe indians.¹⁶

---

15. See note at entry for August 2, 1911.
16. This refers to an Indian raid that took place in January 1866 near Pipe Spring, Arizona. Dr. James M. Whitmore and Robert McIntyre were allegedly attacked and killed

Deep snow last night.

Jan 8/ On our 60th Wedding day Nephi and Charles and wives dined with us.

" 21/ Wedding dinner of Charles + Eva—their 25th anvy

" 19/ By letter from Henry learn his daughter Ida married [blank] on Jan. 19 1910

31/Susan began using obesity belt, on trial[17]

Bertha's (Farnsworth) baby born Jan. 19th 1911

February 1911

Feb. 27/[Blank line]

1911/By letter from Mexico I find my stock in Tannery Co. is $248.00

28/ By invitation went to S.L. City to banquet of the "Sons of Amern Revolution," in which I numbered ^17322^

Still very feeble. Can hardly walk. During much of the winter I have been confined to my bed the most of the time. Charles has been very good to us, sweeping snow paths, bringing in coal + water, for all which may our Father bless him and his forever. I do not know what we would have done without him + Eva, his good wife.

[Page B374L]

1911/[Blank line]

Mch. 1/Snow 4in deep. Still very feebl, scarcely walk.

3/Walked round the city block. Fell, but was helped by a woman who saw me fall.[18] Administered to several who were ill.

by Navajo Indians, after they went out to recover stolen sheep. A company of militiamen under the command of James Andrus recovered the bodies. See "Story of Indian War in the Arizona Strip," *Salt Lake Herald*, February 26, 1905, Section Two, p. 7, and Gottfredson, *Indian Depredations in Utah*, 179–180, and *Nuwuvi: A Southern Paiute History*, 89.

17. See entries for January 3, 1896, and May 4, 1911.

18. For the past few months, Martineau was becoming more feeble and indigent. Earlier in the fall, on September 9, 1910, he wrote to his son, Joel, of the difficult financial straits he and Susan Ellen were experiencing:

Yesterday I had only 254 in the world and in debt over $30.00 for food, etc. I felt alone, I can tell you, but your mother said, 'don't worry the Lord will provide for us.' I prayed and

4/ A brother (Church) came to see me. He blessed me, saying I <u>shall</u> be healed of Locomotor Ataxia,—the only man with faith to say so. His name is A. Clark, of Idaho. I believe him.

8/ Up to this date I have blessed several sick every day, as they come to me for help, + God has thus healed them all. To Him be all praise.

Preston/Married/ This evening Lyman's Son Preston married Miss Elenora Heringer, a Catholic girl, much the surprise of his father and all of us. He is the first of my family to marry out of the Church. His father was much displeased.

9/ Before I was up a messenger came for me to go to see a woman very sick—Typhoid fever. Her temperature 105 ½°. Her fever instantly abated + was absolutely normal in 20 minutes, and in less than an hour she was perfectly healed. God is merciful.

10/ Sister Julia S. Woolley + dau. Lucille came. Lucille has goitre of long standing. Blessed her. She will be healed, for she has faith. Her mother took me to Dr. Gambl, she gave me osteopath treatment, which helped my lameness.[19]

11/ Visited and blessed Maria Y. Dougal, dau. of Prt Young also bld her daughter Catherine, whose heart beat was 160 a minute, and she very ill. Bless + promised her perfect recovery. Her heart beat was soon reduced to 80.[20]

---

had testimony that I speedily would receive money. And sure enough—today Bp. Neff of East Mill Creek sent me a letter with $5.00. He did not owe me anything, but said he had just been reading a blessing I sealed upon him 5 or 6 years ago and it caused him tears of joy and comfort & felt so to send me a little remembrance. We were made to rejoice. … I can hardly stand alone or walk, and [it is] very difficult to pick anything up from the floor, and this last is hard for your mother too. We two live alone, doing the best we can.

James H. Martineau to Joel H. Martineau, September 9, 1910, Martineau Collection, MS 4786, box 1, fd. 6, LDSCHL.

19. This probably refers to Dr. Mary Elizabeth (Good) Gamble (b. 1865), an osteopath and ex-wife of Dr. Gustavus Alonzo Gamble (1860–1923), also an osteopath practicing in Salt Lake. In the spring of 1908, the two doctor-spouses were involved in a highly publicized divorce. See "Mrs. G. A. Gamble Talked Too Much," *Deseret Evening News*, May 22, 1908, 2; "Mrs. Gamble Now Makes Charges," *Deseret Evening News*, June 10, 1908, 1; "Doctors Disagree," *Salt Lake Herald*, May 23, 1908, 12. Evidently, Dr. Mary Gamble regularly treated the aging Martineaus. See entry for April 10, 1911.

20. Clarissa Maria (Young) Dougall (1849–1939) was the daughter of Brigham Young and Clarissa Ross. She married William B. Dougall (1843–1909) a telegraph superintendent on June 1, 1868. Their daughter, Catherine Macswain Dougall, was born on August 11, 1878.

16/ Blessed Sisr Witzell, also her son having "St Vitus Dance" very badly.[21] Note. He was healed perfectly Also blessed Mrs. that she may conceive. Also a woman, for her insanity, and another for approaching confinement, as I have several others lately; in every case words fulfilled.

[Page B375R]

1911/[Blank line]

Mch. 17/ At Relief Society A sister who had long been childless and whom I had blessed to become a mother, came up to me with a baby, Saying "Here's the baby you promised me. Every word you uttered came true." I was so thankful God had been merciful to her, and heard my prayer.

" 19/ Visited Sisr Pola. She showed me her promised baby boy-a large fine one. Learned Susan is very ill. Applied for pass to go home.

" 24/ Home 8 P.M. Susan had lost much blood, bleeding a stream from the nose for two days. But it had left her very feeble and bedfast. Better.

" 23/ Blsd Mrs. King, very sick, Typhoid. Soon to be be confined. Also Emma S. Hughes, sick 7 months very low, soon a mother, if she lives. Doctors say she cannot survive the ordeal in her weak state. I had promise for good for both, and blessed both with safe deliverance. They both had faith.

28/ I feared for the little unborn ones, their mothers having been sick so long—so little nourishment for the little ones, and by consent of the mothers of each baby and <u>their</u> mothers. I blessed each child in the womb, with promise they should be born safely, speedily and perfect in body and mind, (afterwards exactly fulfilled, for mothers and babies. In the case of Emma, the doctor declared it a miracle. It was the power and goodness of God alone.

30/ At this date I have blessed the sick, several every day, and they have been healed.

31/ Susan and I went to Lyman's, in City.

April/Attended one meeting of Conference, Susan + I too feeble to go.

---

21. St. Vitus' Dance is another name for Sydenham Chorea, a neurological disorder causing involuntary movements and spasms. Chorea is often a disorder of childhood resulting from the complications of rheumatic fever.

17/ Susan taken very sick. Since we came I have administered to many, some every day.

Her sickness is Erysipelas, great swelling in face and neck and violent pain. (See p. 378)

[Page B376L]

1911/ During our stay in Logan numbers have come to me for Patriarchal blessings, and very many administrations for healing the sick, in which the power and goodness of God has been shown in mighty power. In one case a Sister having heart disease for a long time were healed at once.

4th Mch/ To day a Bro. A. Uwik [?] felt impelled to come and bless me, though a stranger, promising I shall be fully healed. I felt better immediately.

8/ Got medal as "Indian War Veteran" from Gov. Spry. Should have had it earlier. Blessed 3 persons suffering from sickness.

My grand son Preston, (Lyman's 2d Son) was married to Eleanora Henager,—a good girl, but not a member of the church—a Catholic. I am sorry, but she may finally receive the Gospel. The wedding was at her father's house, and most of the guests stranger to me.

10/ Sis. Julia A Wooley took me to Dr. Mary Gamble an Osteopath, for a trial treatment. She feels sure it will benefit me. I think it will, and she gave it freely. May God bless her.

11/ Visited Catherine Dougall Platt, dau. of Sister Maria Young Dougall. She has goitre with a pulse 160 per minute. I blessed her that she shall be healed by the power of God. She has great faith and has before been greatly blessed, in becoming a mother, where was no hope of it.

13/ Three women came for blessing for motherhood and conception.

14/ Blessed Sis. Jewkes for confinement. Almost weekly, women came for blessing, that they may conceive and bear children, many have done so previously, and had their blessings fulfilled in every case. So the Lord has been wonderfully good to me, in giving me power to bless and comfort my Sisters, barren, but desirous of motherhood.

[Page B377R]

1911/Mch. 15+16/ Blessed Irene Adkins and Mrs. Smot who expect to be soon confined that all may be well. I will note here, that all <u>was</u> well, as promised. Also blessed Son of Sis. Wetzell, who has St Vitus dance, St Anthony's dance, so called. Also blessed Mrs. Peterson, barren, that she may conceive, and a Mrs. Horton for insanity which she fears.

20/ Up to this time I have blessed from 2 to 6 or 7 daily, and Our Father has greatly blessed me in blessing others.

Albert's/boy baby/ By letter I learn that Albert + Emma his wife are the happy parents of another Son, born Mch. 15 1911. All well, at 5.30 A.M. Born in Colonia Juarez, Chih. Mexico

21/ Susan phoned she was dangerously bleeding from the nose for two days. Got to Logan same day, 8 P.M. I found the Doctor had stopped the bleeding, but she was very weak, having lost a great deal of blood. She is now out of danger but very weak

28/ Administered + blessed Emma Smith Anges, about to be confined. Very sick for Seven months, and legs much swollen. Dr. says if she ~~can~~ can be confined + live it will be a miracle in very deed,—no strength or visiting. I obtain good testimony for her, that she shall live and be safely confined and all be well with her. Next day I thought of her poor unborn child all this time of its mother's illness, and in the next day [blank to end of line]

29th/Went and blessed the baby in the womb, that it may be blessed, perfect in body and mind. Also blessed three women from Box Elder County.

30/ Bl. Mrs. McCrary from Box Elder County. For the last week Aurilia, Nephi's eldest daughter, who has helped us all last week, went home. She has greatly blest us.

31/ Susan + I went to Salt Lake City for Conference. She is still very weak, but I hope will be able to go. Very cold and heavy blizzard. Arrived safely in the city, met by Lyman and went to his house.

April/ April 1911.

1/ Blessed son of Sister Witzell for St Vitus. He has greatly improved, and I hope will soon be healed.

[Page B378L]

~~1911/2d April/ Blessed Cath. D Platt for heart + Goitre. Also to Sis. Burton (Sis. Dougall's niece) for general debility. Also to M.Y. Dougall.~~

[Note above paragraph appears to be crossed out.]

April/27/ Drs S.L. Richards and [blank] opened the gathering on Susan's face. She had suffered greatly up to this time, and I, in my feeble state nearly worn out with anxiety + little sleep.

May/ May 1911

4/ Lyman's hired girl left to day, and we had to go to Virginia's to stay. We moved in Sist Burton's Auto, as Susan could not get in carriage[22]

10/ Mrs. Dr. Gamble gave Susan Osteopath treatment for severe pains in her legs.[23] Susan growing worse all the time in her whole body, also on the 11th 12th + 13d by which all pain in legs was gone.

15/ Dr. Richards said she must get to the hospital quick as possible, she is in great danger.

In the night she saw her mother in vision who died when Susan was four years old.

Susan saw herself small and dressed as a little girl of that age, just as her mother saw her last. She stood looking upward among the exceedingly white and beautiful clouds like flowers and trees, and standing between two trees that arched over her stood her mother robed in robes of exquisite whiteness, looking down at Susan a little while, then all vanished. All was far whiter and more clear than snow.

It troubled me, fearing her mother had come for her, though I said nothing. All who saw her thought she was beyond all hope.

Lyman came with auto and took her to the hospital at 6 P.M. None but I thought she would ever return alive. She <u>was</u> very near death.

18/ Susan very low, almost unconscious and able to articulate with difficulty and a

---

22. Susan's obesity appears to have affected her mobility. See entries for January 3, 1896, and January 31, 1910.

23. Dr. Mary Gamble's office was located in the Templeton building in Salt Lake City.

[Page B379R]

1911/[Blank line]

May 18/strange, weird look in her eyes. She told me afterwards she could die, but felt one little spark of life in her breast. Then thought of me—alone—no one to care for me as she could, and she decided to stay—for my sake. From that time she began slowly to mend. May the choice blessings of heaven be her's forever!

21/ She seems a little better, but can hardly speak yet. Learned our house in Logan is sold, + our things carried to Charlie's and piled under a shed. Must go to Logan. I blessed and dedicated her, that all may be well with her while I am away

22/ Went to Logan. Visited + blessed 2 women and babies also another on 23d and to Emma S. Hughes whose milk had totally ceased, through cold, and doctors said nothing could be done to restore. Hath ceased 7 weeks. She was blessed that her breasts shall ^be^ renewed and supply abundant and healthy milk for this and all her future children. She believed.

24/ To S.L. City. Found Susan still very low, I fear. Her eyes have so strange a look. Can scarcely speak. I got my Cluthe [?] Truss

28/ Susan better. But very weak. I visit her every day at 20 m. from the very first, but can stay but 2 hours.

June 2/ June

    Susan now able to sit up a little, if lifted from bed. Henry and Melissa, Charles his son and wife Florence Whelton came to Hospital. It gave Susan new life They had just come from Mexico.

7/ Charles baptized, also Melissa 20 men + 15 females (dead) and 8th were endowed for John Mears and Martha Mears. Charles + Florence baby Lois, born previous to their sealing in S.L. temple (they having married in Mexico) was sealed to her parents.

10/ Moved Susan to her niece Margaret Smith Jensen in Auto, by Nebeker's auto. We hire rooms there. Margaret nurses her tenderly, our meals free.

[Page B380L]

1911/[Blank line]

June 12/ Susan now able to walk to next room and sit at table. I am obliged to go to Logan to day.

13/ Visited Emma Hughes again. Her milk had gain filled her breasts as promised, and she and baby doing finely. The doctor had tested her milk, and found it perfect. Was astonished and "Cant understand it! its a miracle." His mistak[e]—the power and goodness of the Lord. To Him be praise

   I also Blessed three others the same day

" 14/ At Old Folks Party in Agricultural Bldg. but did remain to end. Felt impressed to leave and found and blessed 5 persons, who had been seeking me anxiously.

" 15/ Returned to City and found another swelling on Susan's face becoming very serious. The doctor said it must be lanced at once or serious consequences would follow. Susan and objected feeling it was not necessary. She sits up a little.

" 18/ The doctor again insisted on an operation, but we declined. Seth Johnson and family visited. Dr. Rich sent his bill $ [blank] Hospital bill $78.40—Graft, too much for so poor attenance [sic] at the hospital (L.D.S. Groves) As our room was let to another person before we took it, we went
[In margin: " 26] to board with Widow Robinson, to whom I had administered (and healed) for cancer of the room. While living with her we applied antophlo ^gistin^ to Susan swelling, and it healed it. We had one room in the 18th Ward, S.L. City. Lyman sent total bills for Susan's sickness,—Richards $62.00 Hospital $79.40

July/ July

1/ Note/Nephi's daughter Aurelia married F.W. Stock Slvira's dau. married—Emma Vilate Johnson to

Charles Lewis 13 Sep. 1910 Arizona

11/ Susan's 75th birthday. Henry dined with us may she have as many more as she shall wish in increased health, strength and prosperity.

[Next unpaged photograph of three men and a boy, back says Myself, Charles, Vern, Mary + dolly/4 generations/Taken on porch of Vern's residence in Salt Lake, 1920]

[Page B381R]

1911/[Blank line]

July 13/ We removed to Charlie's, Logan, to stay until Nephi can be ready for us on his farm a few miles north of Logan. Found all well.

" 24/ Susan and I went to 24 Celebration in the Logan Tabernacle in an auto.[24] This is the first time she has been out anywhere, being still quite feeble, and the first day she has left the bandages in her face necessitated, by the last abcess on it.

Aug./ August 1911

" 2/Had my photo taken for insersion in "Pioneer Book of Utah."[25]

" 7/ Moved to Nephi's farm between Logan and Hyde Park, in Greenville Ward.

29/ Up to this time since the 24th all Nephi's horses (3) have died, leaving only a small pony.

    I learn Albert has exchanged all my stock in the "Union Mercantile" Store in Dublan, Mexico for land in Sonora, Mexico, value $1314.00 and its dividend at 8 % $55.12 total value $1419.12 and this without my knowledge or consent. It places me in straightened circumstances.

Sept./ September 1911

9/ By letter from Gr. Son James Johnson I learn that his Sister Gertrude Johnson Roberts has a son—3d child born 3d Sept. 1911 at Buckeye Ariz.

" 12/ Sixtus ordained Patriarch, at San Jose, Sonora, by Apostle Richards.

" 18/ Albey Sherman, my bro-in-law, died 7.30 P.M. in Huntington, Utah, aged 78.

" 21/ Lyman Royal Jr. my Gr. Son, married Zayde E. Bothwell, and next day they went to Harvard [in margin: Note 12th] College, Mass. He has a year yet in San [law] course Geo. Albert, my son to day ordained Bishop of San Jose, Sonora, Mex. by Apostle Richards

---

    24. This is one of the first times Martineau had ridden in an automobile. See note at entry for November 13, 1908.

    25. This refers to Frank Esshom's *Pioneers and Prominent Men of Utah*. Martineau's photo appeared on page 255. See also marginal note at December 23, 1910.

Signor di Martins, Italian Charge de Affairs at Constantinople may be of our family.

[Page B382L]

1911/[Blank line]

Oct. 7/ Went to Salt Lake City, and went ^to^ my son-in-law Frank K. Nebeker and Lilla by Frank's invitation

8th/ At Church conference. Next day met Henry and Seth Johnson, Susan's brother from Southern Utah

2d/ Administered to and blessed Clara, dau. of Maria Young Dougall, for blessing approaching maturity who fears miscarriage.

13/ Blessed Sis. Bull, Anna Knight + boy and Mrs Wickell and her child. Also Irene Adkins.

14/ Blessed Sis. Billings

16/ " Sister M.Y. Dougall, also Sis. Burton, and Son Julian, who is in great danger from blood poison.

17/ Attended funeral of Prest J. Henry Smith

20/ To date have been continually blessing the sick

21/ Gave Prest Lund an account of the visit of Nephi, of ancient days, to the indians of Southern Nevada. The account was given by them to my bro-in-law Sixtus E. Johnson, who for over 60 years, has been a trusted friend to them. They said this visitor said his name was Nephi; he told the Mormons were their friends—not to steal from them; told them of ancient Nephites and Lamanites, and taught them many days. Messengers were sent to gather indians from hundreds of miles around, in several states

Prest Lund was greatly pleased.

30/ Up to date I have been daily administering to the sick, many of them seriously, but all are healed, + it is by the goodness and power of God, not by me.

I start home, staying all night with Charles. I blessed Sis. Ellen Nibley, Str Moses Thatcher and daughter

31/ At home and found all well.

Nov./ November

16/ After a stay with Nephi of about 3 months we remove to Salt Lake City, to make it our final home, as Lyman has rented a house for us, and we go to the city, staying in Logan a few days, part of the time with Sister Ellen Nibley,

[See note in margin—difficult to read—may say: "home/Salt Lake/Nov. 17/1911"]

[Page B383R]

1911/Nov./but most of the time with our son Charles, who was quite ill with a swollen leg.

25th/ Saturday. Arrived in the city, and Lyman took us to our new home 545 ½ 6th S, whiche + Alle, his daughter had made habitable with our furniture and some furnished by them; 3 rooms, bath and pantry. A nice, pleasant place, 3 rooms + toilet +c.

Note/ I note that during our 5 days in Logan I gave several blessing, admd to several cases of kidney and womb disease, and blessed Jessie Knowles, sick for 5 weeks and recently with inflammatory rheumatism all over her body. All these were healed at once, by the power of the Lord. Blessed also Mrs. Afton Knowles, in critical condition, who was wonderfully benefited. She was pregnant + fearing.

Dec./ December. (Error, too soon)

2/ To day Lyman presented me a new suit of clothes.

17/ Sunday attended High Priests meeting of Liberty Stake. We are members of 9th Ward, Bp. Woolley.

Dec. 31/too soon/ Up to this time have lived quietly, knowing very few of our neighbors, occasionally giving a blessing or visiting the sick

[Notice margin bracket]

Nov. 20/ November

Note/My gr. dau. Ida Martineau Jesperson's baby girl, her first child, was born in Chiuchupa, Mexico. She is Henry's daughter

1912/[Blank line]

Jan. 6/ January 1912

Became almost totally deaf, could scarcely hear my own voice. Susan blessed me, and I soon regained my hearing. She has great faith.

8/ Our 60th Wedding day. Made dinner for Lyman Lilla and Gean (Elizth and Virginia)

11/ Visited Widow of Prest W. Woodruff and blessed her. My cousin Wm A. Mears and wife met me in Hotel Utah—first time I ever saw either. They were returning home to Seattle Wash. from a business trip (Panama Canal) in Washington D.C.

[Page B384L]

1912

Jan./12/ Received a letter from Mrs. Anna Louisa Mears Thompson, of Washington D.C. She is Natl Sect of "Daughters of American Revolution" in Washington D.C. Her address is 715 Pine St. She wrote me that a Mears (John Mears) fought under Paul Jones in "Bon Homme Richard" against the Serapre in Rev. War. Also that a Mears came to England with William the Conqueror in 1066.

I have since seen the record of the battle of Hastings, when three French Lords (Mears) fought with their knights and retainers.

13/Joel wrote. Wishes to buy our home in Juarez.

Note/ I learn that Susan's mother (Anna Pixly Johnson) was born Aug. 7 1800 in Canaan N.H. She married George G. Johnson, and [blank to end of line] Sarah Sophie Johnson Apr. 22 1820, Keen, Essex Co. ^N.Y.^

22/ As requested by Cousin Annie W. Mears I began search for family names of her line of Whippl [Whipple?] and others, intermarried She is not a Mormon, but has spent much time and money in genealogical research, also in the Mears line of her husband, my cousin, Wm A. Mears. She found the name of John Mears, who served in the army in the Burgoyne Campaign, 1777, under Gen. Gates By this I obtained membership in the Society of "Sons of the American Revolution," of which I am proud. I will state here, that I have since found other names, Samuel

and Thomas Mears, both in the battle of Lexington. My mother's Grand Uncle, also one who was with Washington, at Valley Forge, a boy of only 16 years. I have also a record of 3 others, French Lords with William Conqr at battle of Hastings, 1066, one of whom gained an estate in Wales and built three castles now in ruins. Another, a Martineo, was a Knight of St John of Jerusalem, a Crusader. His crest
[Page end]

[Page B385R]

[This page is blank]

[Page: B386L

[Page has a graphic}

1912

Jan./1912/or armorial bearing was a shield, argent ^(silver)^ with three towers, stable (black).

Three Roman generals, one under Emperor Maximin, one under Belisarius, and another in Syria—Catullus Martinus, A.D. 70, where his daughter Lucilla died A.D. 70, age 18 years. Her marble tomb still stands with ancient ruins as seen by a Mormon elder some years ago, who described it to me as like this:—[graphic here] It is more fully described, with its inscription in a former entry of this record.[26]

Feb. 24/ Susan had nose-bleed—started Suddenly, first [?] up with her all night.

Mch. 3/ Administered to Jessie Sterling, a young woman who 15 years has been badly twisted bodily by paralysis. Also blessed two others.

12/ Blessed Mrs. Kirkpatrick for falling of uterus to the open air. Believe she will be healed.

Apr. 9/ Blessed Clara Bergstrum, lately confined that her milk should be restored. It was, almost at once Also blessed her sister, Catherine Platt, (both were gr. daughters of Prest Brigham Young) that she might conceive, which soon occurred. She had long been barren and hopeless[s], I

---

26. The name Lucilla Martinus cannot be found in surveys of Roman inscriptions. See entry for August 4, 1908, and its accompanying note.

had thus previously blessed her Sister Clara, as noted above, who had been told by physicians she could never again conceive since the birth of a son years before. For all this all praise be to God, for He brought all to pass.

Note 28/ I find my maternal Gr. Mother Mears was daughter of Stephen Hutchinson, 2d Son of Lord Hutchinson, who was an officer killed at the massacre of the British garrison of Fort George by Montcalm's indians, 1757

Genealogical. On a tomb of Catacomb of Rome is the body of Aurelia Martina, Christian martyr inscribed "To the well deserving the chamber of Aurelia Martina wife most chaste + modest who lived in wedlock 23 years 12 ~~months~~ days.

[Page B387R]

1912

To the well deserving one who lived 40 yrs. 11 ^months 13 days^

April/Her burial was on the third Nones of October, Nepotianiss and Farnudus being consuls. In peace. A.D. 360." (From the Cemetery of Calixtus, Pope and martyr

Note/ The name of the mother of Lucilla Martinus wife of Gen. Catullus Martinus, was <u>Sempronia</u>

May/ May 1912

1/ Up to this date I have administered to the sick or troubled in mind almost all the time since Coming to the city to live. Many have been desperate cases, given up to die by the doctors, but almost all have been healed by faith + the power of God, to whom be all the praise. Several cases of Cancer of the womb, falling of the same, quick consumption, blindness, paralysis, appendicitis, barrinnes, typhoid fever and other troubles.

Elizabeth (Lilla Nebeker) has Sent food to us weekly for the last two months, a great help to us. May God bless + heal her.

3/ Fredk J Holton called to see me today, as the U.S. Surveyor who in 1877 noted land as "Mineral" where he is now tunneling for gold. He said it was shown to him in a dream several times, and he found the ground just as he dreamed.

I finished my family list of names for the "Pioneer Book" of early Utah Settlers.

4/ Kenneth Crismon came home from Medical College in Philadelphia, where graduated at the head. He is Lyman's Son-in-law

June/ June 1912

11/ Learn that a son was born to Nephi and Emm on [blank] weighed 8 ½ lbs.

19/ Went to Lagoon with Susan. Beautiful place.

25/ " " Hooper on excursion Ind. War veterans

26/ " to War dance, "Old folks excursion.

27/ At 2.30 A.M. Susan taken very sick, and continue so till July 6th. Then I took my turn

[Page B390L]

[Note: top line says "(Pages 388 and 389 are blank)"]

July/ July 1912

8/ My cousin Wm A Mears sent me $10.00 for Genealogical names of Mears ancestry I sent him.

10/ Susan's sister Janet Johnson Smith, the widow of my dear Bro. Jesse N. Smith, + several daughters came from St Johns, Ariz.

11/ Susan's 76 birth day. Aged in years but to me always young. May she have many more, with the choice blessings of heaven.

13/ Miss Marian Martino gave me treatment with electric Vibrator, and lent it me

24/ I am still very feeble

August/ <u>August 1913</u>

My electric stove, cost $8.00 burns Elc power 80 watts per hour— From 80 Watts—We use the electric heater to save coal.

15/ Our first letter from Annie since she, with 60 of my family, was driven from homes in Mexico.[27] All had good homes some worth $25.000.00 to $300.000.00 She had a nice brick residence, well furnished, orchard of 3 acres choice fruit, cows fowls, and plenty. Left her home as it stood, herself and 7 children, taking 1 trunk, 1 pillow and 7 quilts + the clothes they stood up in. Escaped to El Paso, Texas lived weeks under open shed, no privacy and at last given money by U.S. government to come, finally to Logan Utah[28]

My other children and married Grand Children are scattered I know not where, in Arizona, Texas + New Mexico[29]

21/ finished paying for 2d hand Sewing machine $15.00 price. Administered to Mrs Dorothy Kenner, suffering greatly in her whole arm for several weeks. She instantly was healed. Her mother gave me $5.00

[Page B391R]

1912/ August

29/ Letter from Joel. Sent my damage list (Rebel plunder) but not in full. I wrote him not to return to Mexico till peace is fully restored.[30]

---

27. Martineau's wife Susan had to flee Colonia Juárez in 1910 and their son Henry was forced to abandon his property Chuichupa. In July, their son Lyman sent a telegram to President William Taft asking for protection for the colonists: "Besides property interests that are suffering, I have fifty blood relatives in the state of Chihuahua and Sonora, and I appeal to you for such immediate protection as the United States owes and can give to her subjects without waiting for longer delays of diplomacy." See "Local Man Protests Against Inactivity in Mexican Matter," *The Evening Telegram*, July 18, 1912, 3.

28. This refers to Annie Sariah (Martineau) Walser Turley (1875–1963), who was born to James Henry and Susan Ellen (Johnson) Martineau on May 4, 1875, and married Edward Franklin Turley (1869–1940) as a plural wife on January 6, 1901. Edward had married Ida Isabel Elizabeth Eyring on October 11, 1893. Edward took both of his families to El Paso and intended on returning to Colonia Juárez after the crisis was over. Annie did not want to return to the colony and asked his permission to leave. Although he was unhappy at the thought of separation, he reluctantly gave her a signed "letter of divorcement" giving her permission to leave. She returned to North Logan and later married Alvin James Hawkes. See Turley, "A Brief History of Edward Franklin Turley," 15–16.

29. For accounts of Mormon colonists who sought refuge in border states, see Karl E. Young's, *The Long Hot Summer of 1912*, and *Ordeal in Mexico*.

30. It wasn't until August 12, 1912, that the American consul informed colonists that federals occupied Ciudad Juárez and that railroad transportation had been resumed, signaling secure conditions for their return. But many colonists still felt it unsafe to return to the colonies to reclaim their homes. Moreover, the settlement of claims for damages sustained by Mormon colonists during the Revolution was prolonged until 1938, when a Special Mexican Claims Commission concluded its review of cases filed. Land which had been abandoned could be reclaimed by the American colonists, as long as they paid back

Sept./ September

4/ Am very unwell and nearly helpless.

16/ The Kindergarten children + teachers came as a surprise to us. Sang Songs + gave us their little presents—an apple, a few grapes, a flower, etc. It was sunshine to us.

27/ George and Ernest, my grand sons, with each a girl they would marry, came + saw us a few hours. They married in Salt Lake temple, to Miss Langferd + [blank]

30/ Went to the fair. Very tired + feeble.

Oct./ October

2/Georg and Lilly May Langford, and Ernest and Stella May Jones and blessed both [In margin: 4] girls Oct. 4

16/ Learn Henry's dau. Bertha Farnsworth has boy baby born Sep. ~~27~~ 27 1912

30/ Snow this morning.

Nov./ November

3/ Got letter from Albert, from Douglas Ariz. Sent $10.00 on account due me.

4/ Mrs Martins has endowed 20 of my dead. Gave her 20 more names to endow for me.

5/ Susan and I voted

16/ Elzada, Albert's daughter, came to Stay with us. During the past week I got about 500 names for baptism. Elzalda was baptized for 40. I also sent 620 to St George temple, for baptism.

    I am very feeble—hardly able to in the house.

    Phyllis, Anna's daughter, was married to William Preston.

---

taxes and expenses, but many were not in a solvent position to do so. Martineau's son Joel, who had become a Mexican citizen in 1897, remained in the colonies during the revolution, except for a period of two weeks. Others became discouraged and searched for homes elsewhere in the states. See Mills, "Mormon Colonies in Chihuahua after the 1912 Exodus," esp. pp. 172–175 and 301–310, and Smith, "Impacts of the Mexican Revolution," 91–101.

19/ Anna came with 6 children ^from^ refugee camp in El Paso, and in afternoon went to Logan, 4 P.M.

[Page B392L]

1912/November/It was a time of rejoicing, tho she had left a good home, with 3 acres of choice fruit trees, cows, chickens and good furniture, dishes +c.

She and her 7 children left home in haste with 7 quilts, 1 pillow and one trunk, left fruit cooking on the stove—fruit jars to be filled, word had come to get away as quickly as to not risk death by Mex. bandits. She and 4000 others had shelter for a time in an old and open lumber shed, with no privacy, lying on a quilt spread on bare ground—one quilt as cover

El Paso people gave clothing, bedding, [and?] milk for children, and were very kind, + the U.S. government gave R.R. transportation free to any part of United States.

The Church gave $5.00 to each person.

Anna felt well—not murmering. I blessed her, her Son Louis Osborn. I learn that my Grandson Joseph Johnson + Cora have another daughter born Aug 17 1912.

Nov 24/David Johnson my wifes brother came. He gave $10 for a life membership in the Genealogical Society and some money to me to do Temple ~~wor~~ work for his Mothers family the Bryants of Vermont. I paid for his membership in the Genealogical Society. Later sent it to him

30/ First snows. Bro CH Dunn has been baptized in the temple for 20 dead

Dec 14/ Sick in bed with very bad cough

19/ Still in bed. Susan suddenly taken very sick with Lagrippe. Our neighbors were very kind to give us food + doing good in many [In margin: 25] ways. A sorry Christmas both feeble but able to be up + about the house. Lyman invited us to dinner but we were unable to go.

30/ I went out to day for first time for about 3 weeks walked 2 blocks administer to a sick woman, though still feeble.

[Page: B393R]

[Note handwriting change on this page—to end]

1913

Jan 1/Lillie invited us to dinner but we were too feeble to accept the invitation

" 8/ Our 61st wedding day. Several friends not our relatives remembered us and brought picnic and we had a very pleasant time.[31]

" 25/ Mrs Fowkes, who has had no children for several years, and desiring to become a mother, and whom I have blessed that she should be, came and brought to show me a fine boy s in fulfillment of the promise.

30/20/ Received a letter from Mrs. Sterling in Alberta Canada Saying She Saw our picture in the Desert News and remembered that 33 years ago She arrived late one night in Logan on a R.R. train and found no one to meet her as she expected and did not know where to go. She Said we took her home and cared for her till her friends came and She had never forgotten it. Susan and I had forgotten it long ago.

29/ Attended banquet of Sons of American Revolution.

Febuary

Feb. 5/ Blessed a child for curvature of the Spine.

25/ Received lists of 620 names baptised for in St George Temple. The Sisters in the temple had voluntary endowed 154 female names without charge. May God bless them forever.

[Page B394L]

Oct 3/ October 1913

3/ My granddaughter Elzada my Son Albert's daughter, who has been with us about a year went home to her parents in Arizona.

6/ Phyllis Preston, Annies daughter has a girl born Sept 26 1913 in Pima Arizona.

9/ My brother in law Nephi Henson has examined the records in Charleston, Marlboro, Haverhill Leving Leominster, Southboro Worcester Longhill in Mass. Also in Truro N.S.

---

31. The anniversary party was described under "Sixty-One Eventful Years Spent Happily as Man and Wife," *Deseret Evening News*, January 11, 1913, 3.

up to this date there has been little daily change. The Sick and troubled have come almost daily to be administered to, meny cases being very dangerous but almost every one departed feeling greatly blessed. And I have visited great meny habitations of the afflicted and troubled and God has greatly blessed my labors. To Him be all the honor praise and glory.

Nov/ November

4/ Elzada was baptised for a 133 names

Dec/ December

12/ David W. Johnson my brother in law desires me to assist him in doing temple work for his mothers family. Her fathers name was Charles Bryant and his wifes name Susan Fuller. There childrens names were Daniel Alfreda Charles Martha Ada and Willard [Note extra space between names]

[Page B395R]

December ~~1914~~ 1913

Dec/16/ Cousin William A Mears writes me that his wife Annie O [?] Mears died Dec 4 1914 in Seattle Wash. She had done much in obtaining the genealogy of her fathers family and had given me help in my genealogy. It was through her investigation that I was able to find out the connection of my ancestors with the Revolutionary War. I found that my Great Grand-father John Mears Served in the Burgoyne Campaign in 1777 and that another grand uncle John Mears was with Paul Jones in his battle with the Serapis on the coast of England. In obtaining her information She had spent much time and money

----

Jan 1914/ January 1914

20/ Bought a Sewing Machine price $65 payable monthly installments. Due 44.00

Feb/ February 1914

6/ My Grand Son Royal Martineau's Son was born weighed ten pounds[32]

---

32. Lyman Royal Martineau Jr.'s son, Glenn Bothwell Martineau, was born on March 14, 1914, not in February as JHM indicates here.

27/ Dressed my self to day all but coat vest and Shoes having for months been unable to do so either to dress or undress my self for nearly a year. Some of the time I could not even wind my watch or feed my self. Kidney trouble

[Page B396L]

Nov. 23./ November 23, 1914.

"/Today removed to No. 1 Gudgells Ct. We were compelled to move as the owner of the present residence was going to demolish it + build a new house. Our new residence was more pleasant than the other. Rent $15.00 month. Close to street car line + near the 2nd Ward Chapel.

June 14./Recd information that my pension has been increased to $30.00 a month instead of $12, for which we were very thankful, as our former pension of $12 was insufficient.[33] The increase was obtained by Senator Reed Smoot.[34] I pray that he may never need a friend, without having one + that he may be greatly prospered. Susan has had a very severe fit of sickness + Mrs. Steele a lodger in the same house has been very good + attentive every day. She is not a Mormon but is a good woman + I pray that the choice blessings of Heaven may rest upon her. I also had a very severe attack + very dangerous one of bladder trouble, but was relieved by surgical aid. In other respects our daily life has been about the same as usual. My time being mostly spent in visiting the sick + blessing + comforting those who came to me, for help in their afflictions, bodily + mentally; many in a very serious condition, but all who came in sorrow + distress left me in smiles + peace of mind. Ah Father in Heaven, I thank thee for this power to bless those sad or afflicted in mind; and numbers of these afflictions were very serious indeed. I will state one case: A young woman came to me about 10:30—her mother very sick + in great pain; desiring me to go to her mother's assistance. The side walk were icy + I did not dare to go in the dark for fear of falling. I said to her, "Do you ever pray?"

[Page B397R]

She said, "You bet I do." I said "Put your hands upon her head + ask God in the name of Jesus Christ to heal her + I believe it will do her good."

---

33. Martineau's change in pension was read before Congress on June 16, 1914. See U.S. Congress, *Statues at Large*, Vol. 38, pt. 2, 1915, p. 1286.

34. The bill (S. 2502) had been introduced by Reed Smoot as early as June 13, 1913. See U.S. *Senate Journal*, 63rd Cong., 1st sess., June 13, 1913, 90.

She came early next morning. I said, "What did you do?" She said, "I just put my hands on mother's head + said 'Be healed in the name of Jesus Christ, Amen. She was." All pain instantly ceased + she was instantly healed. Thus God hears + answers the prayers of faith. Many other cases equally serious have been healed by faith in my experience One young woman paralyzed from head to foot unable to move, healed perfectly by one administration. A woman stone blind twenty years her sight perfectly restored. Two women, each with an internal cancer (one sentenced to die in three months + the other in five months, by counsels of doctors) were both perfectly healed, one in two days + the other in three. Many other cases of healing were miraculous. In all this, all the praise + honor + glory be ascribed to our Father in Heaven, for He it was not me who showed forth His power + mercy. I have been repaid in my labors in the joy that I have experienced in helping to make others happy. One of my greatest delights is this.[35]

1918./ [Blank line]

Nov. 21./ I come now to the saddest occurance in my life. A week before Thanksgiving Day (1918) having a chicken some one sent us + Susan said "We'll have our Thanksgiving dinner today."

" 22./ Daughter Annie + husband Alvin J. Hawkes + son Louis Osborn Turley, together with my granddaughters Clara Turley + Elzada Martineau Jackson + her husband Hyrum Jackson were here to a big dinner, which Annie brought down in honor of Clara's 17th birthday, but Susan couldn't partake of it. Her stomach was upset. Her trouble was a clogging of the bowels which caused an entire stoppage of the

[Page B398L]

contents of the bowels so that they couldn't be moved. And the two doctors had no hope for her from the start. She suffered agonizing pains almost without cessation. Her daugh—Annie + granddaughter Elzada, myself + others were increasing in attempts to help her. During the last

---

35. Martineau had become more feeble and his daily entries had ceased, but sometime during this period he submitted an article to the *Deseret Evening News*, giving an account of the discovery of a stone box in the southern Utah desert. On another occasion, he gave what would be his last interview about his long life on the Mormon frontier. See J. H. Martineau, "Pioneer Incidents—A Mystery of the Desert," *Deseret Evening News*, September 30, 1916, Section Three, 11, and "Veteran Engineer and Surveyor Tells of Stirring Days in Long and Active Life," *Salt Lake Herald-Republican*, April 2, 1916, Magazine Section, p. 8.

four days she was partially unconscious, with occasional short spells when she was conscious + in one of those conscious moments; as I sat by her constantly fanning her; she looked up with an expression of joy beyond measure saying "Oh how lovely, how beautiful everything is up there, so beautiful, so lovely, no words can tell." A glimpse of a better world had been opened + the day before she said as I said by her she was conscious for a short time + she lay pointing with her finger up to the Heavens with an expression upon her countenance of infinite joy. I said "Susan, what do you see?" She said, "I see the face of my Savior," + then she became again unconscious + slept for several hours as peacefully as a little baby, breathing naturally but a little quicker than usual, taking apparently full breath when suddenly she stopped breathing the next day at 4:10 P.M. + was gone.[36] (the awful death gurgle was in her throat from 5 a.m. till 4:10. Dec. 5, 1918. While in her semi-conscious state I sang several of our old familiar songs to her, hoping it might tend to quiet her excited nerves + it did, for although she was unconscious the sound of my voice seemed familiar to her + several times she weakly joined in with me + repeated one or two lines that I had sung. Now she can sing with the angels

[Page B399R]

of Heaven. Thus was fulfilled the blessing she received in 1865 from Patriarch Chas. W. Hyde, who told her she should live to be eighty and three years old, + should see the face or the coming of the Savior.[37] She did die in her 83rd year + did see the face of her Savior.

I had often wondered in reading her blessing how it could be fulfilled + did not expect the coming of the Savior so soon as that; but to fulfill the promises of the patriarch did show her His face by vision.

No one can realize except by experience such a loss to me, but gain to her. For sixty-seven years lacking a few days had we been united. She only 15 ½ yrs. old + I twenty three when we married. In all that time she never once gave me evil counsel, nor held me back from my duty, when at times it is difficult to obey them. Numbers of times we faced death together from the Indians; once when she reentered the house she saw her little

---

36. Susan Ellen Johnson Martineau died on December 5, 1918. See "Mrs. Susan E. Martineau Pioneer Woman, Passes," *Deseret Evening News*, December 6, 1918, 8; "Funerals: Susan Martineau," *Salt Lake Herald*, December 6, 1918, 6; and "Pioneer Utahn is Called by Death," *Salt Lake Tribune*, December 6, 1918, 16.

37. A transcription of this blessing is included in the entry for August 6, 1865.

daughter Elvira, about 6 years old, crouching down on the floor crying bitterly, an Indian holding above in one hand, threatening to kill her with a big butcher knife. Unarmed she flew at him like a tigress, seizing him by the shoulders, dragged him from her child + with a piece of stove wood beat him over the head + face, until he was glad to escape on the run. And for a year Indians came from a distance to see + admire the white squaw who beat an Indian. Upon another occasion she rescued a little child two years old, which a squaw had concealed under her blanket + was carrying away. She passed our house + was about to enter the willows, from which

[Page B400L]

if once safe there, she couldn't be found. The child was a Curtis boy + is a grown man today. She desired + was granted a badge as an Indian war veteran.

She received every ordinance of the Church. The highest that was given,[38] and will sit upon a throne of glory as one of the queens of Heaven; to become mother to innumerable spirits born, who will eventually people a new earth + pass through an experience similiar [sic] to ours as we have done, + as Our Father in Heaven has done, who in His earthly experience feared + trembled lest He should fail.

[See marginal note: _?_was it 1913 at 4 a.m.]

In 1915, ~~one evening~~ I suddenly awoke at 3. a.m. and as I lay ~~reading in bed~~ I felt a strange sensation + plainly saw about an inch of thumb + fore finger which turned out the light + I said "What is all this?" A voice answered "I am your son John Wm Don't you remember your little Johnny who died so long ago?" [He died in 1863 at the age of 5 years.] He said "I came to visit you first, because I died first. Della was come next, because she died next to me." He told me much that would happen, much of which I have forgotten, which I should of written. But he said as I well remember that mother should live to be eighty-three + should die in peace without any pin, which she did, + that I should live twenty years longer + should die in ~~smoke~~, but without pain. I said, "Will I burn?" He said "No, you'll die just as if asleep." Then he said, "I must go now" + I again saw his thumb + finger ^seize +^ turn on the switch of the lamp re-

[Page B401R]

---

38. This refers to the second anointing, which is considered the highest priesthood ordinance conferred upon a married man and woman in the LDS temple. See note at entry for July 4, 1884.

[Top margin says "which I was unable to do"]

lighting it.

I feel very sad to be left alone, once I had fourteen at the table, now I sit alone. I have many children who are good + loving, but they cannot fill the place of wife. I pray thee O Father in Heaven to help and comfort me the rest of my days + that I may be able in due time to rejoin my loved ones, never more to separate.

During her sickness and after her death, my son Lyman was of very great assistance to me, but in care for her while living + in arranging details of her funeral. My daughter Annie was also present + also my granddaughter Elzada; also my sons, Nephi from St. Anthony Ida. + Joel from Mexico. She was buried Dec. 7, 1918 in the City Cemetery; Nephi + Joel paying the funeral expense of more than two hundred dollars.[39] Inasmuch as all this occured during the influenza scourge, during which schools + churches were closed, her funeral was not public but private attended by especial loved friends. Lyman took me to his own house + gave me a room for my own comfort, with Annie's daughter Clara to assist; for which I am to pay him $35.00 a month. For a long time I have been almost helpless myself. For a long time unable to ^un^dress myself alone, but now so able to do so, but with difficulty of putting on my coat + vest. I can't stand or walk alone, but expect to be finally healed, that I may do the work which is appointed me in the future,[40]
Add
[Page end and end of written mss]

---

39. Graveside services were held on Saturday, December 7, 1918. See "Pioneer of Utah in 1849 Will Be Buried Today," *Salt Lake Tribune*, December 7, 1918, 11. Susan Ellen (Johnson) Martineau's death certificate is preserved at the Utah State Archives and Records Service, Department of Health, Office of Vital Records and Statistics, Death Certificates, Series 81448, box 24, fd. 18, certificate file #2417.

40. James Henry Martineau died on June 24, 1921, at 1:30 p.m. at the home of his daughter Virginia. His body was taken from her home and moved to Lyman's, where a funeral was held on June 26. He was buried in the Logan City Cemetery next to Susan Julia. See "Aged Pioneer of 1850 Called by Death," *Deseret News*, June 24, 1921, 2; "Pioneer Civil Engineer Dies," *Salt Lake Tribune*, June 25, 1921, 2; "Funeral to be Held at Residence of Son," *Deseret News*, June 25, 1921, 10; "James Henry Martineau," *Deseret News*, June 27, 1921, 4; and "Colonel James Henry Martineau," *Improvement Era* 24 (August 1921): 956. Martineau's death certificate is preserved at the Utah State Archives and Records Service, Department of Health, Office of Vital Records and Statistics, Death Certificates, Series 81448, box 30, fd. 29, certificate file #990.

Appendix 1
Conversations with John C. Frémont

Editorial Note

On his fifth and final expedition to find a route for a railroad to the Pacific, Colonel John Charles Frémont, the Great Pathfinder, and his party met a tragic fate. The survey began on the Missouri frontier, at the mouth of the Kansas River, and almost came to a disastrous conclusion at the head of the Little Salt Lake Valley (present-day Parowan Valley), fifteen miles north of Paragonah, Utah. Frémont and his men moved west across the Continental Divide, following a route roughly between the 38th and 39th parallels. The group approached the Wasatch Mountains on reduced rations during the height of winter. They spent almost two weeks (from January 24 to February 7, 1854) working their way across the snow-covered Wasatch Mountains eating porcupine and salvaged mule and horse meat from the party's pack train. The men crossed the frozen Awapa Plateau connecting with the Fish Lake branch of the Old Spanish Trail where it turns south through Grass Valley and runs along Otter Creek. Reaching Circle Valley, Frémont and his party continued south, following the Sevier River through Circleville Canyon, then departed from the river somewhere north of Bear Valley Junction. They probably moved west through Hell Hole Canyon, across Dog Valley, traversing the adjacent peak, and through a dry wash defile (now called Frémont Canyon) before they came into view of the tiny Mormon fort settlements of Paragonah and Parowan.

Starving and suffering from severe exposure, the men moved south toward the walled Mormon forts on the valley horizon. As they passed the foothills west of Anderson Mountain, one man, Oliver Fuller, fell dead off his horse. Fuller had to be left where he fell as the men continued on through the snow past Muley Point to the valley plain, at Buckhorn Flat, where they found a dry stream bed. During the night, a number of

Parowan residents heard Frémont's cries for help, and by late morning, searchers had gone out and brought the twenty-one survivors of the party in to be placed in the homes of helpful settlers. Frémont and his men then spent the next two weeks being nursed back to health by the people of Parowan before resuming their course into California.[1]

The following article is James H. Martineau's firsthand account of John C. Frémont's ill-fated fifth expedition of 1853–54. It was published in the *Deseret Evening News*, February 17, 1917, Section Two, page 14.

A Meeting With Fremont
Pioneer Experiences
For The Saturday News by Col. J. H. Martineau.

About the fifteenth of February [1854] the people of Parowan were astonished by the sudden arrival of Col. Fremont with a party of [illegible] whites and 11 Delaware Indians.[2] The party was in an almost starving condition, having been nearly three months in the snows of the Rocky and Wasatch mountains, and on the day previous to their arrival one of the men fell from his horse from starvation and hardship and died. Having no means to dig a grave his comrades spread a blanket over his body and left it to the mercy of the elements and wild beasts. When this sad event became known, a party of colonists went out and discovered his body and buried it.[3]

---

1. For various accounts of Frémont's stay in Parowan, see Driggs, "When Captain Fremont Slept in Grandma McGregor's Bed"; Hinton, "Parowan Mormons Rescue the Great Pathfinder"; Stegmaier, ed., *James F. Milligan*, 92–94; and Spence, ed., *Expeditions of John Charles Frémont, Volume 3*, 458–464.

2. Frémont and his men evidently came into view of Parowan watchmen on February 8, 1854. See "Col. Fremont's Railroad Exploration," *Daily Alta California*, April 21, 1854, 2. John Calvin Lazelle Smith's account, however, placed Frémont coming into the valley two days earlier: "On the 6th of February, the man on the lookout at Parowan reported a company, supposed to be Indians, coming into the north end of the valley, twenty miles distant from Parowan, and about 11 o'clock on the morning of the 7th, Col. John C. Fremont, with nine white men and twelve Delaware Indians, arrived in Parowan in a state of starvation." J.C.L. Smith to editor, "Editor of the News," *Deseret News*, March 16, 1854, 3; reprinted as J.C.L. Smith, "News from Utah—Sufferings of Col. Fremont's Party," *New York Daily Times*, May 15, 1854, 5.

Martineau described the company's route and their point of entry into the valley near the present-day juncture of I-15 and Fremont Road (Exit 100): "He has travelled in a straight line across the plains and entered this valley about seventeen miles north of where Major Beale came into it last spring on the Spanish trail." From "The Central Route to the Pacific," *Daily National Intelligencer* (Washington, DC), April 13, 1854, 3.

3. Party member Oliver Fuller suffered from frostbite and exposure and fell dead from his horse. Parowan stake president John Calvin Lazelle Smith provided more details regarding his death: "[O]ne of his men had fallen dead from his horse the day previous, and several

The night previous to his arrival the party encamped near a band of Ute Indians from whom, by a payment at an exorbitant price in ammunition and blankets they obtained about 50 pounds of flour and a small dog. The flour was divided equally among the 25 persons, and the dog being killed made about a mouthful to each of the party. They were all taken in by the colonists and received the most tender care which their limited means would permit for about three weeks until sufficiently restored to continue their journey to California.[4] The colonists furnished Col. Fremont horses and other needed supplies to the amount of $3,000, receiving nothing in payment, but a promise from the colonel of full payment as soon as he should reach the coast, when he would send payment in full. But he never paid one dollar.

Tell Story of Journey.

I had many interesting conversations, not only with Fremont himself, but with most of his party, both whites and Indians, the latter of whom spoke English passably well, and their reports of the journey were in complete unison.

---

more must inevitably have shared his fate had they not had succor that day." J.C.L. Smith to editor of the News, *Deseret News*, March 16, 1854, 3. Joseph Fish remembered, "some distance up in Fremont's Canyon the party met some Ute Indians and obtained a very little dried meat. Fuller ate some of it which immediately physicked him and he was so weak that he fell from his horse and died. After Fremont got into Parowan Simeon F. Howd and Mr. Davis went out and buried Fuller at a point about 22 miles from Parowan, about a mile and half above what is known as mule point." Krenkel, ed., *Life and Times of Joseph Fish*, 46–47.

On February 9, Frémont wrote to his father-in-law from Parowan, describing what happened:

> Until within about a hundred miles from this place we had daguerreotyped the country over which we passed, but were forced to abandon all our heavy baggage to save the men, and I shall not stop to send back for it. The Delawares all came in sound, but the whites of my party were all exhausted and broken up, and more or less frost-bitten. I lost one, Mr. Fuller, of St. Louis, Missouri, who died on entering this valley. He died like a man, on horseback, in his saddle, and will be buried like a soldier on the spot where he fell.

John C. Frémont to Thomas Hart Benton, February 9, 1854, "Colonel Fremont," *Daily National Intelligencer*, April 12, 1854, 3; reprinted in Spence, ed., *The Expeditions of John Charles Frémont, Volume 3*, 470.

4. Frémont was taken in by the family of J.C.L. Smith. He was given a bed and nursed back to health by Smith's wife, Sarah (Fish) Smith. See Driggs, "When Captain Fremont Slept in Grandma McGregor's Bed," and Hinton, "Parowan Mormons Rescue the Great Pathfinder." According to one published account, Frémont's party left Parowan on February 21. See "Col. Fremont's Railroad Exploration," *Daily Alta California*, April 21, 1854, 2; reprinted in the *Deseret News*, June 8, 1854, 2. This date is corroborated by Solomon Carvalho who left Parowan on February 21 for Salt Lake City with a wagon company heading for conference. He noted that Frémont left Parowan on the same day. See Carvalho, *Incidents of Travel*, 139.

They had joined the party during the autumn and had expected to cross the mountains before any snow should fall; but they did not enter the mountains until Dec. 1, being delayed by several trips of Fremont to the eastern states made by the colonel. In conversation with the colonel he admitted this was the fact for he knew his men would refuse to go if they would have to encounter the snows and snows of winter. But as his point of departure was at the foot of the mountains and his men had no means of travel independently they were compelled to go on. He told me it was his special and sole desire to test the possibility of locating a railroad line across the mountains that would be practicable for traffic in the winter, or whether the snows would be too deep.[5]

He employed the Indians as hunters in the expectation that plenty of game killed would obviate the necessity of taking a large supply of meat along. In this he was greatly disappointed, scarcely any game was seen and none at all was killed, as the elk and deer had sought lower levels to escape the snows.[6]

Their progress was toilsome in the extreme, struggling through the snows with excessive labor their pack animals soon began to give out and when at length a mule or horse did succumb it was killed and eaten, everything except hair, bones, and the contents of the entrails. All his men declared that he did not favor himself in the least, either in choice bits of

---

5. Frémont's plan is confirmed by Martineau's contemporaneous letter to the *National Intelligencer*: "His [Frémont's] report is *highly favorable*, the more so as he waited until winter set in too cross the mountains in order to test the depth of the snow in the passes, and in the worst and most elevated pass (which he crossed some time in December) he found the snow only four inches deep in the shade on the summit." From "The Central Route to the Pacific," *Daily National Intelligencer* (Washington, DC), April 13, 1854, 3. It was repeated again a week later in the San Francisco newspapers: "The purpose of undertaking the journey at such a time was to ascertain what amount of snow lay on the proposed route in the depth of winter, and to demonstrate completely that the road could be traversed at all seasons of the year." From "Col. Fremont's Railroad Exploration," *Daily Alta California*, April 21, 1854, 2.

6. Martineau later wrote:

The only winter we have in the months of December and January, the snow rarely lying on the ground more than a week at a time. Last winter the snow fell in all to the amount of twenty-seven inches, and in the previous winter to the depth of thirty-three inches. This winter has been the most severe ever experienced in Utah since its settlement, as much snow having fallen as in the two previous winters put together, and it has not exceeded eleven inches at any one time, and then only a few days.

From "The Central Route to the Pacific," *Daily National Intelligencer* (Washington, DC), April 13, 1854, 3.

food or quantity, but on their arrival in Parowan he appeared to me as the best, physically, of any of the party—"tough as a knot."

Used a Camera.

In order to make his explorations of the mountains of greater value, he daily took photographs to the front and rear,[7] thus giving a perfect view of his entire line of march until, compelled by lack of transport animals, he abandoned his photographic outfit and much other valuable property,[8] and finally when within a few days' march of deliverance from their toils

---

7. The daguerreotype photographs were taken by Solomon Nunes Carvalho (1815–1897), a portrait painter, expedition artist, and daguerreotypist who was active in both the eastern and western United States. He was born in Charleston, South Carolina, and moved with his family to Baltimore in 1828, and in 1835, to Philadelphia, where he was a portraiture student of Thomas Sully. From 1838 to 1850, he worked as an artist in Philadelphia and was also active in Charleston, Washington DC, and Baltimore where he had a daguerreotype studio. Carvalho was selected to accompany John Charles Frémont on his fifth expedition and photographically document the party's route. See Greenspan, *Westward with Fremont*; Sturhahn, *Carvalho*, 70–93; Macnamara, "First Official Photographer," 73–74; Rolle, "Two Explorers on the Trail to California"; and Shlaer, *Sights Once Seen*, 39–58.

The views were re-photographed by Robert Shlaer between 1995 and 1999, based on the illustrations in Frémont's Memoirs, and a retracing of the party's course across the Rocky Mountains into Utah. See Shlaer, *Sights Once Seen*, 76–153.

8. Although some or all of the daguerreotype photographs were preserved and taken to California, it is not clear that the cached photographic equipment was ever recovered. A comment in Carvalho's published account indicates that Wakara had sent a Mexican named José back with a party of several Indians to retrieve the equipment and plates but they had been gone thirty days and had not been heard from. Carvalho later reported that he took daguerreotype photographs during his stay in Salt Lake City, but he did not indicate if the equipment was his or if it was provided by Lieutenant Edwin G. Beckwith who supplied him with painting materials before returning south to finish Captain Gunnison's survey. See Carvalho, *Incidents of Travel*, 140, 195–196, and Sturhahn, *Carvalho*, 100. See also Rolle, "Two Explorers on the Trail to California: Carvalho and Frémont."

After Frémont returned to California, one early report stated that the daguerreotypes would be printed and published with the notes of the journey. "These views will carry in themselves conclusive evidence of the correctness of the report in regard to the topography, timber, &c., of the more important localities." From "Further Facts in Regard to the Exploring Expedition of Col. Fremont," *Daily Alta California*, April 24, 1854, 2. The daguerreotypes of Solomon Nunes Carvalho were the basis of the illustrations in Frémont's *Memoirs*. In her introductory essay to her husband's *Memoirs*, Jessie Benton Frémont wrote that these daguerreotype plates were "beautifully clear" and had made it to California through near-calamitous circumstances: "These plates were afterward made into photographs by Brady in New York. Their long journeying by mule through storms and snows across the Sierras, then the searching tropical damp of the sea voyage back across the Isthmus, left them unharmed and surprisingly clear, and, so far as is known, give the first connected series of views by daguerre of an unknown country, in pictures as truthful as they are beautiful." Jessie Benton Frémont, "Some Account of the Plates," in *Memoirs of My Life*, xv–xvi. Unfortunately, the whereabouts of these photographs is unknown. See Sturhahn, *Carvalho*, 111–113.

and arrival to the lowlands, he cached all of his property not absolutely necessary, amounting in value to more than a thousand dollars, consisting of blankets and articles intended for trade with the Indians to procure horses or other things necessary.

He appeared very grateful to the colonists for their kindly assistance and I believe that much of his former hostility to the "Mormons" had ceased.

The valuable cache of goods referred to was the cause of a tragedy. One of his men, a Spaniard, Carvalho by name, refused to accompany him as he continued his journey from Parowan and remained for some time, for the purpose, as I believe, of obtaining possession of the goods cached.[9] As none of the colonists would go with him to obtain the property, saying that they would not steal it, he made an agreement with some Ute Indians, who agreed to go with him and get the prize upon the condition of having one-half of the plunder. They went with him and found the goods, but evidently concluded it better to keep the whole without the bother of dividing it. This they did and killed him.[10] This was the report the Indians made some months afterwards. They said they were many and needed the goods, and that he being neither a "Mormon" nor an Indian, had no need of any of it. Thus the greed of Carvalho was his undoing.

Sees Military Drill.

It happened that while the colonel was in Parowan, one of our usual company and battalion drills occurred, in which I acted as military instructor. As one of the veterans, the war with Mexico in 1846–48 had given me experience. I felt much annoyed, as to their presence on the occasion, for he was an officer used to seeing men standing in stiff military order—"eyes front," while our boys on such occasions were apt to talk, stand unsteadily and lean forward to look up and down the line. We went through our evolutions all

---

9. Carvalho undoubtedly suffered from dehydration and starvation during the expedition. He traveled to Salt Lake City to convalesce and to observe the Mormons under the shadow of church leadership. See Carvalho, *Incidents of Travel*, 139–145, passim, Sturhahn, *Carvalho*, 99–109, and Macnamara, "First Official Photographer," 73–74.

10. Martineau's version of the events is incorrect. Carvalho was not killed and, according to Joseph Fish, "During his [Frémont's] stay in Parowan a party was sent back to recover the instruments and goods that he had cached some distance back in the mountains, but the articles were not found. It was thought that Utes that Fremont met when he came in had found the cache and had, of course, appropriated them to their own use." From Krenkel, ed., *Life and Times of Joseph Fish*, 47. This statement, with the fact that the daguerreotypes were recovered, suggests that the equipment was pilfered by Indians and the photographs were left where they were cached with the other goods.

right, and upon dismissal of the men, I invited him to accompany me home and have something to eat, which he very willingly did.

I excused our unmilitary appearance on drill, but he cut me short saying, "Mr. Martineau, if I had five thousand men like those I saw on drill today, I could march through Mexico, and with ten thousand, I could conquer Mexico." "Why," said he, "they move just like that," moving his finger to and fro. It appeared to me as if he did not notice our unmilitary style of drill but that in some way he felt the spirit of unity. He expressed a very ardent desire to see a railroad connecting the east and the west, and I am glad he lived long enough to see his wish fulfilled.[11]

While at my house he said to me, "I never eat the whole of any meal. I save a piece in my pocket in case I accidentally miss my next meal, which has happened a number of times on expeditions like my present one. A number of times the piece saved at breakfast was all I had for supper. I have made this my invariable rule on my long trip, the bit saved from one meal was all I had for the next."

Since then I have found it best in my own experience to always keep at least "one shot in the locker."

---

11. Although he admitted to experiencing an abnormally severe winter that year, Martineau wrote of typically mild snowfall in other years: "You will see by this that the snow is no impediment to the construction or operation of a railroad through this country, and when you take into consideration the mountains of iron ore and coal beds eight feet high, both being of the first quality, and the vast forests of pine at this point also, the conclusion must be evident to a candid and public-spirited mind that this is the best, most central, and most national route for the Pacific Railway; at least such is the unanimous opinion of the people of Utah, and you must remember that the 'Mormons' are one in thought, feeling, and action." From "The Central Route to the Pacific," *Daily National Intelligencer* (Washington, DC), April 13, 1854, 3.

Appendix 2
Letter to F. E. Eldredge, 1907

Editorial Note

The following letter was sent to F. E. Eldredge, editor and publisher of *El Progreso*, a weekly newspaper published in Nuevo Casas Grandes, Mexico, from about 1899–1909. The newspaper reported news and events in the Mormon colonies of northern Mexico. The letter was presumably published in the paper, but no issues of this date are known to exist; one extant issue, dated September 12, 1902, is held at the LDS Church History Library. A photocopy of the handwritten letter is held at the Harold B. Lee Library Special Collections (MSS 467). Previous to publishing the *El Progreso*, Eldredge published the Panguitch *Progress*, a weekly paper he established in 1897.

Frederick Erastmus Eldredge (1853–1923) was born at Salisbury, New Hampshire, on May 1, 1853, to Rev. Erastmus Darwin and Isabella Tappin (Hill) Eldredge. After living for a time in the south, Eldredge moved to New York and later to Montana. Eldredge was a settler of Orting, Washington, and served as its first mayor. He also served as secretary of the Territorial Board of Education in Washington. Eldredge married Ellen "Nellie" Mavette McCausland on April 4, 1888, in Tacoma, Washington. In 1897, he moved to Panguitch, Utah, where he established the Panguitch *Progress*. He was baptized a member of the LDS Church on June 17, 1913. In 1917, he was elected mayor of Panguitch and served one term. He later moved to Marysvale to be near his daughter. There, he founded the Marysvale *Progress*. He died at Marysvale on December 1, 1923.[1]

Martineau's account of the Mountain Meadows Massacre contains a number of inaccuracies. The letter was written fifty years after the

---

1. For more on Eldredge, see "Pioneer Editor Laid to Rest," *Garfield County News*, December 21, 1923, 1, and note for Martineau's journal entry of January 15, 1901.

massacre, with all the deficiencies that come with a poor memory. Based on the abundant strikeouts and emendations, Martineau carefully crafted this report to agree with many widely circulated accounts of the massacre. A portion of this letter was previously published in Bigler and Bagley's massacre narratives, but is included here in its entirety.[2] The letter has been lightly edited to remove hyphens at the end of lines, extra spaces, and indentations; all other spelling, grammar, and punctuation is retained.

The Mountain Meadow Catastrophy [sic].

Mr. F.E. Eldredge
Nueva Casas Grandes, Chih. Mex. July 23d 1907

In response to your request for information relative to the so-called Mountain Meadow Massacre I give you a brief statement of the causes of that most lamentable occurrence, which you may depend upon as Substantially correct, ~~though~~ ^I was^ not present at the scene myself, being absent at the time with [words illegible and crossed out] a scouting party, watching for the advent of a portion of the Army sent by the President to harass or expel the Mormons from Utah. My position as Adjutant of the Iron Military District, which embraced all of Utah south of Fillmore, and the fact that all military orders therein were issued by me as Adjutant ~~to the Colonel commanding,— Col.~~ Wm. H. ~~Dame,~~ ^commanding^ ~~and~~ to whom also all subordinate reports were sent, gave me exceptional opportunities for authentic information.

At this time (1858) [1857] a State of war virtually existed ^in Utah^. The Govt of the United States had dispatched an army under Col. [Edmund] Alexander to "subdue the Mormon rebellion" as they termed it. (a rebellion which never existed, even in thought.) and Utah was placed under Martial law. The Government had stopped all mail service to or in Utah, and no travel was permitted in the Territory ~~to any one~~ without a Pass signed by Col. Dame, myself, or Battalion commanders.— The uncertain attitude of the indians, who seemed halting between the General government and the Mormons,—liable at any moment to side against the weaker party—rendered it unsafe for any one to travel alone. I state these facts, not specially connected with the subject of this paper, to show the general condition existing in Utah.

---

2. A portion of this letter was previously published in Bigler and Bagley, eds., *Innocent Blood*, 388–390.

The Company which perished at the Mountain Meadows was a part of a still larger company which entered Salt Lake City ~~int he autumn~~, and which there ^divided.^ [three words erased and illegible] Those who came to the Meadows were such a disreputable lot that the more respectable part of the original party refused longer to travel with them, and remained at S.L. City while the others came South through Utah, making themselves very offensive to the Settlers as they journeyed.

At their camp at or near Corn Creek in Millard County an ox died, and the indians asked for the carcass for food. A man said "No, leave it till morning and I'll fix it for them." He <u>did</u> fix it for them, inserting poison all through the carcass.[3] Next morning it was given to the indians, a large number partaking of it. Six or Seven warriors died, with several Squaws and children, and many were made very ill, and the indians, knowing they had been poisoned without provocation became furious for revenge. To an indian, to revenge the death of a friend is a duty, imperative and sacred, a curse to rest upon him who

[Page 2]

neglects or refuses to redress the wrong; not necessarily upon the party actually guilty, but upon any one—man or woman—of the same race.

Accordingly the indians attacked the emigrants as they went onward, day after day as opportunity offered, at the same time sending out rumors to all surrounding bands, detailing the outrage and calling on them to come and help avenge it, only discontinuing when the travelers reached the Mormon colonies in Iron Co.

Arriving at Cedar City the company remained a week or more, their conduct becoming very offensive;—saying they would remain … until the U.S. troops arrived and then help kill every man and take the wives and daughters to do with as they pleased. Consequently altercations with the citizens were frequent, and the presiding authorities had all they Could do to prevent actual fights, until the situation became so unbearable a message was sent to Col. Dame showing the situation, and asking what could be done.[4]

---

3. This claim was never fully substantiated during the initial investigation by Judge John Cradelbaugh, nor by subsequent inquiries by Brevet Major James Henry Carleton and others. See Carleton, *Mountain Meadows Massacre*, 12–13, 17. It appears to have been a rumor spread by suspicious immigrants, such as Elisha Hoopes, who alleged that a man had inserted poison into an ox carcass at Corn Creek. See Walker, Turley, and Leonard, *Massacre at Mountain Meadows*, 119–124; Bagley, *Blood of the Prophets*, 295.

4. This was Colonel William Horne Dame (1819–1884) who was first mayor of Parowan, second president of the Parowan Stake, and head of the Iron County Militia. He is believed to be one of the masterminds of the attack on the Fancher party. In 1874, Dame

By Col. Dame's ~~order~~ ^direction^ I wrote an order directing that all possible means should be used to keep the peace until the emigrants should leave and proceed upon their journey, and remember perfectly part of that order, which was in these words,—"Do not notice their threats, <u>Words</u> are but wind—they injure no one; but if they (the emigrants) commit acts of violence against citizens inform me by express, and such measures will be adopted as will insure tranquility."

This order was directed to the authorities at Cedar City, from Col. Dame's head quarters in Parowan, 18 miles distant.[5]

About this time the Emigrant party proceeded onward to the Mountain Meadows, camping there [erased word] a considerable time to recruit their teams for the desert country South. This delay was fatal. Had they not made these long halts, the indians would not have gathered in Sufficient strength to have done them much harm, but during the ^two^ weeks of ^their^ Stay ^indians^ gathered from a hundred miles around, until, emboldened by ^their^ numbers ^over 1000^ they attacked the party.[6] These things we did not understand or know of until afterwards, but learned ^that^ the emigrants parked their wagons in a circle, one behind another closely joined ^and^ dug a trench inside the wagon line throwing up the earth as a wall beneath the wagons, thus making a strong

---

was indicted by a grand jury for his alleged involvement in the massacre and, in 1876, was brought to Beaver to stand trial, but was never tried. See biographical note at entry for March 4, 1853.

5. No such order from Martineau could have been issued between September 3 and September 9, 1857, since he was in a scouting party on the upper Sevier River. See Martineau's journal entries for September 4–8, 1857.

6. Despite many firsthand testimonies to the contrary, Martineau had chosen to hold to the story that he had told in the days following the massacre: that Indians had attacked the party. In September 1857, as part of the official Parowan Stake History, Martineau wrote:

> This morning [September 7, 1857] at daylight the indians attacked a company of emigrants on their way to California four miles beyond Mountain Meadows, numbering about 118 men, women and children, and killed them all but 15 small children from 2 to 6 years old, which the brethren ransomed. The company had poisoned the Indians at Corn Creek, killing 6 Pahvantes, without cause, which was the cause of the massacre. As the Company were traveling through the various settlements, they were very abusive in their language, swearing they would help kill the Mormons if the troops were in, saying "old Jo Smith ought to have been killed long before he was etc; and profaning the name of God. At Cedar they were fined for swearing but swore they would not pay it, and the rest of them swore they would protect them. On Friday the 11th Col. Dame and others went to the place of action to try and save them, but met the news that all was over.

From Martineau, "James H. Martineau Record & Negotiations, 1855–1860," Part B, September 7, 1857, p. 34, SUUSC.

fortification. Its fatal weakness was its distance from water, which could only be obtained by men going out in plain view of the enemy [00 yds. in left margin and number not complete] without the slightest shelter from their fire. But water they <u>must</u> have, and day after day men were killed or wounded in getting it. This desultory warfare continued three or four days, with loss on both sides.

[Page 3]

But indians cannot long continue a siege. Without a food supply they cannot long continue an attack upon a fortification, and although hundreds in number did not dare attempt to assault their enemy. Enraged and determined not to allow their ~~enemy~~ ^coveted prize^ to escape, they sent a demand to Maj. John D. Lee, of Harmony to bring to their aid some of the settlers, with the threat that if help was not furnished, they would destroy the few Mormon Settlements in ^the South of Utah^ ~~Iron County~~. It ~~suppose~~ ^is probable^ they ~~come~~ ^sent^ to him because he spoke their language and ^were ~~was~~ well known to him^[7] ~~frequently got them to work for him~~ I do not know if, in going to help the indians, he knowingly [word in left margin] disobeyed Col. Dame's order to preserve peace ^as he lived some distance South from Cedar City.^ ~~But~~ I do know ^however^ he did not [word in left margin] communicate with Col. Dame, but acted solely upon his own volition. And the few whites ~~men~~ he took with him to the Meadows have all testified they had no idea of what ^was expected of them^ ~~they were expected to do,~~ ^or^ ~~and think had they known~~, they would not have gone with him, ~~or turn any part in the tragedy~~. But ~~that~~, when ~~once arrived~~ ^on arrival, surrounded by the^ upon ~~the Scene, they had no alternative from death by~~ ^hords of infuriated savages were compelled to charge between certain death at the hands of^ the indians or ^to^ help~~ing~~ them in the fight.

Col. Dame was all this time in Parowan entirely ignorant ~~of what was going on,~~ ^the situation at the meadows^ but when finally an express ~~came to~~ ^brought^ him ~~with the~~ intelligence, he instantly set out for the Meadows to put a stop to all hostilities. But he arrived too late. The tragedy was completed. The responsibility, so far as the settlers was concerned rests upon ~~Mr.~~ Lee and a man of ^great^ ~~some~~ influence ^named^ ~~named Smith~~, commonly ~~known as~~ ^called^ Klinkensmith

---

7. John Doyle Lee (1812–1877) was charged and tried as the instigator and perpetrator of the September 7–11, 1857, attack upon the Fancher wagon train. See biographical note at entry for 1852, Book One, stamped page 32L.

[Klingensmith], who soon left the country and the church and died a miserable outcast in California.[8]

Col. Dame arrived in time to save from the indians about 40 little children, but it was with great difficulty. The indians having tasted blood and lost numbers in the fight, were insatiable for more, like so many beasts of prey. The children thus saved were taken by various charitable disposed families and tenderly cared for until friends and relatives came and claimed them.

Strenuous attempts were made by the Anti-Mormon officials of the Territory to implicate Brigham Young and Col. Dame as instigators of the tragedy, both of whom, to my certain knowledge were absolutely ignorant of it until ^informed^ too late to prevent it.

As soon as Col. Dame received intelligence of the attack, he Sent a Messenger, a Mr. Haslam, well known to me, to inform Gov. Young. Haslam had orders to lose not a moment, ^but ride for life^ no matter how many horses he might kill; and he ^and he^ did so, making a record rarely of ever equaled by any white man. He reached Salt Lake City, a distance of 300 miles in 3 days Acquainting instantly Gov. Young on his arrival. The Governor in horror and tears streaming down his cheeks ordered Haslam's instant return, with

[Page 4]

orders to all men in authority on his way back to furnish him [word in left margin: swift] horses and all necessary aid to expedite his journey. Haslam made the return trip in three days, but three days too late. I believe no man ever before rode 600 miles in six consecutive days and lived. But Mr. Haslam did so. I saw him as he went through Parowan as he went and ^as he^ returned.[9] He brought an order to Col. Dame to stop the attack upon the emigrants if it should require the entire military force of the Iron Military District to accomplish it. While Lee was imprisoned for ^his offense^ several months before trial and during that time persistent effort was made to ^cause him to^ sign a statement that Brigham Young had authorized the tragedy. He was offered a full pardon, $50.000 in gold, and ^safe^ conveyance to any place he might designate for his safety. The alternative for

---

8. Philip Klingensmith (1815–1881) was the first bishop of Cedar City. He is believed to have been a witness and participant in the massacre at Mountain Meadows. He reportedly died in Sonora, Mexico, in 1881. See biographical note at entry for September 1852.

9. For more of his comments on Haslam's remarkable ride, see Martineau's journal entry and accompanying notes for September 12, 1857. See also Martineau [Santiago], "A Wonderful Ride."

Refusal ^was^ to be certain death. His wife Rachel was with him in prison the last 6 months, and she told me, herself, that she implored Lee to sign the paper and save his life for the sake of his family—implored him on her knees and in tears. But he said "No! I cannot implicate an innocent man, not even to save my life. This she told me her self.

And when Lee was about to be shot, he was again offered pardon and reward if he would sign the statement required, but he still said "No," and was shot. This I heard the U.S. marshal say after he returned from Lee's execution.

At Lee's trial, at Beaver, Beaver Co. Utah, at which I was present fo as a witness for Col. Dame, no proof whatever was produced to implicate Gov. Young, and Col. Dame was released, after ^waiting^ 8 months awaiting trial in prison, without being brought to trial. I was his witness, but was never required to testify in his case, as his opponents feared my testimony. [Blank line]

In connection with the foregoing I will state that the other part of the original Company which had remained for a time in S.L. City finally proceeded on their way to California by the same route as those slain at the Mountain Meadows. When they arrived at Parowan, fearful lest they also might be attacked they applied to Col. Dame for an escort through the dangerous part of the way. Col. Dame knowing the indians had all dispersed said he believed there would be no danger, but to satisfy the party he sent five young men with them who understood the language of the Pah Utes and were acquainted with many of them, as guides+ interpreters. Thus assisted the company consisted of about 140 families proceeded on its ^way in safety.^ Indians frequently visited their camps, ostensibly
[Page 5]
to sell buckskins for ammunition and other things, but in reality as Spies, to know their force, and resources, and fighting strength. On these occasions the Mormon guides counseled Peace, magnifying the power of the emigrants for defense, and showing the hopelessness of successful attack.

Thus they escaped attack, but on several occasions indians in great number surrounded the camp in the night, the first intimation of their presence being demoniac yells on every Side as if the devils of hell had been let loose, presaging death to all. It was only by the heroism of the young guides who ventured among them, exposing themselves to ^all^ human appearance to frightful death, that they could turn aside the threatened cyclone of destruction. But in this they always succeeded, thanks to an overruling Providence, and the Company safely reached the Muddy and another tribe of natives not imbued with the lust for plunder and murder, +finally attained their journey's end in California. At the Muddy the Mormon guides left the party and returned to their homes, without recompense from any one. Had it not been for the assistance thus rendered by the Mormons another bloody page would have been added to frontier history, for although the party was too strong to be massacred, many lives must have been lost by ambuscade and midnight attack as well as great loss of Cattle and horses.[10]

Although not myself present with this party, I was well acquainted with all five guides, who gave me full particulars of their mission of peacemakers, all of whom were of undoubted veracity and good character. [Page end]

---

10. The wagon company referred to here was probably the William Dukes train, which followed the ill-fated Fancher train by only about three days. Sometimes called the Collins–Turner company, the Dukes and Turner train, and the Honea Davis train, the composite company had divided into three units before arriving at Beaver. Upon hearing of the approach of Nicholas Turner's wagons six miles north at Indian Creek, Philo Farnsworth, bishop of Beaver, sent five men to assist the train and accompany them down to Beaver. Before the guard could reach the train, the company was attacked by Indians. While under attack, the Turner wagons moved to join Dukes's camp just below Beaver. During a break in the skirmish, captains Turner, Dukes, and Collins went into town and were attacked. Turner was shot in the hip and Dukes was grazed by two or three bullets. Wilson Collins was shot and seriously wounded. The joined Dukes–Turner train was later accompanied by interpreters David Carter, Nephi Johnson, and Carl Shirts, who agreed to guide the party to the divide between the Santa Clara and Virgin Rivers. See Brooks, *Mountain Meadows Massacre*, 114–123, Bagley, *Blood of the Prophets*, 164–168, and Walker, Turley, and Leonard, *Massacre at Mountain Meadows*, 175–176.

James Henry Martineau's Family Pedigree

Grandparents (spouses listed in italics)

- Stephen Martineau (1761-1785)
  Eleanor Haughwout (1765-1832)
- James Mears (1774-1779)
  Lois Sprague (1779-1861)

Parents, Aunts and Uncles (spouses listed in italics)

- Stephen Martineau (1787-1822)
  Charity Christopher (1787-1857)
- Elizabeth Martineau (1788-1846)
  Abraham Merrill (1788-1862)
- Ann Martineau (1791-1864)
  Abraham Decker (1789-1834)
- Egbert Martineau (1795-1826)
  Eleanor (1795-1826)
- Abraham Martineau (1798-1853)
  Ann Simonson (1798-1875)
- Maria Martineau (1800-1832)
  Joseph Christopher (1800-1832)
- **John Martineau (1793-1838)**
  Jane Varley (1796-1815)
  Sarah Stanhope (1783-1819)
  Eliza Mears (1806-1848)
- Peter G. Martineau (1803-1874)
  Mary Ann Mears (1812-1882)
- Cornelius John Martineau (1805-1860)
  Elizabeth Amelia Betts (1811-1871)
- Catherine Hanna Martineau (1808-1811)

James Henry Martineau and His Brothers and Sisters (spouses listed in italics)

- Emily Henrietta Martineau (1825-1899)
  David Calderwood Lyon (1809-1888)
- **James Henry Martineau (1828-1921)**
  *Susan Ellen Johnson (1836-1918) - Children ***
  *Susan Julia Sherman (1838-1874) - Children ****
  Jessie Helen Russell Anderson Grieve (1765-1832)
  Mary Eliza Brown Jones (1836-1916) — Two adopted native
  Cora Rice (1841-1867) — daughters, Post-
  Dora Martineau (1883-1901) — mortem marriages (sealings) by proxy
- Charles Augustus Martineau (1831-1831)
- Frances Eliza Martineau (1831-1847)
- Lois Eleanor Martineau (1838-1919)
  John Peter Voswinkel-Dorselen (1832-1924)
- Harriett Martineau (1835-1837)

Children of James H. Martineau (spouses listed in italics)

- Henry Augustus Martineau * (1852-1941)
  Melissa Editha Johnson (1859-1920)
  Mary Ann Spendlove (1855-1923)
- Cora Colorado Martineau * (1854-1867)
  Adopted: 1854
- Moroni Helaman Martineau * (1854-1896)
  Sarah Sophia Johnson (1863-1944)
- Susan Elvira Martineau * (1856-1942)
  Benjamin Samuel Johnson (1853-1939)
- John William Martineau * (1859-1863)
- Lyman Martineau * (1859-1926)
  Alley Thatcher Preston (1863-1907)
  Emeline Cannon (1893-1972)
- Nephi Martineau * (1862-1951)
  Emmaline Pamela Knowles (1869-1954)
  Eveline Eliza Holman (1869-1954)
- Charles Freeman Martineau ** (1861-1935)
- George Albert Martineau * (1864-1957)
  Emma Pauline Allred (1868-1922)
  Verna Maud Boyce (1886-1965)
  Mary Ella Hickman (1865-1941)
  Emeline E. Ellsaesser (1872-1948)
  Ida Billingsley (1876-1952)
- Joel Hills Martineau, Sr. * (1867-1955)
  Mary Ann Thurston (1875-1963)
- Gertrude "Tillie" Martineau * (1870-1927)
  Ernest Guy Taylor (1872-1963)
- Theodore Martineau (1872-1954)
  Josephine Thurston (1886-1925)
  Nellie Ann Gurr (1884-1954)
  Leonora Horne Spencer (1871-1898)
- Virginia Murphy Martineau ** (1870-1947)
  Edward Sudbury (1869-1953)
  John S. Murphy (1873-1938)
- Annie Sariah Martineau * (1875-1963)
  Henry Samuel Walser (1873-1897)
  Edward Franklin Turley (1869-1940)
  Alvin James Hawkes (1872-1947)
- James Edward Martineau * (1877-1880)
- Delcena Diadamia Martineau ** (1857-1865)
- Elizabeth Lillian Martineau ** (1867-1953)
  Frank Knowlton Nebeker (1870-1962)
- Jesse Nathaniel Martineau ** (1863-1928)
  Eliza Belle Johnson (1862-1927)
- Dora Martineau (1883-1901)
  Adopted: 1884
- Julia Henrietta Martineau ** (1865-1885)
- Joseph Herbert Martineau ** (1873-1873)

Source: Contributors to FamilySearch

Photographs and Illustrations

Portrait of James H. Martineau. Probably taken by Thomas B. Cardon, in his Logan studio on July 18, 1875. See JHM's journal entry for that date, stamped page 367R.

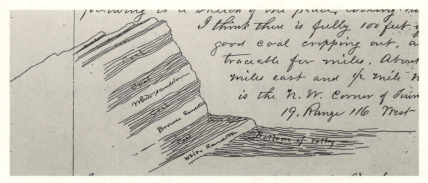

A line drawing of the strata at "Coal Mountain" (Crocker's Point, Wyoming), the location of JHM's mining claim. See description and drawings at entry on June 12, 1875, stamped page 358L.

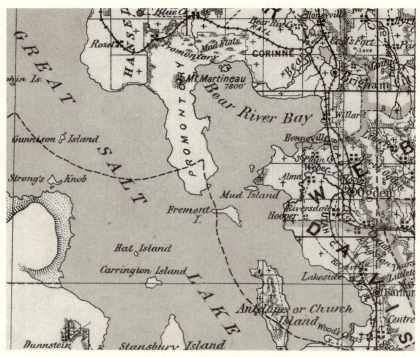

Detail Showing "Mt. Martineau" as a peak in the Promontory Range at an Elevation of 7,800 feet, north of the Great Salt Lake, from the 1879 General Land Office Map of the Territory of Utah.

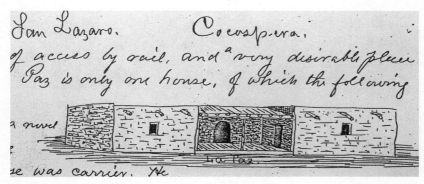

A line drawing of an adobe structure at an abandoned ranch locale, La Plaz, near San Lázaro, Sonora, when JHM visited that area south of Nogales, on January 8, 1883. The drawing is on stamped page 517R.

A drawing of the Cocóspera Mission Church, described by JHM on January 9, 1883, when he was in Sonora with an exploring party headed by Moses Thatcher. See the entry for that date on stamped pages 517R–519R.

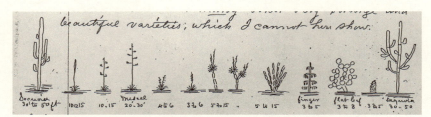

A series of line drawings showing the different varieties of cacti at Cocóspera. The drawing is found under an ink sketch of the Mission Church, stamped page 519R.

Martineau family portrait, taken on September 15, 1884, at the studio of David Lewis in Logan, Utah. Back row: Joel Hills, Nephi, Charles Freeman, Lyman Royal; middle row: Gertrude, Susan Ellen, James Henry, Julia Henrietta, Elizabeth; front row: Theodore, Annie Sariah. Photo courtesy of Daughters of Utah Pioneers.

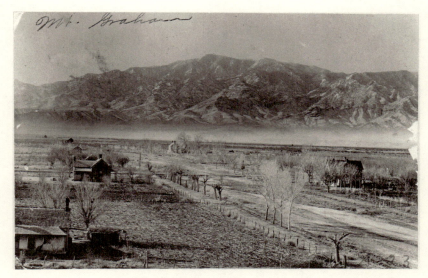

View of Pima, Arizona, looking down Main Street, toward Mt. Graham, ca. 1895. Courtesy of Eastern Arizona Museum & Historical Society.

Royal A. Johnson, Arizona surveyor general (Tucson), and his office staff, 1892. Left to right: Morris Wilson, chief clerk; General Johnson; Daniel Drummond, deputy surveyor; Philip Contzen, draughtsman; States Morrison, clerk; Ignacio Valencia, janitor. Martineau worked in this office as a clerk and mineral draughtsman on several occasions in 1893, under Johnson's direction, and from 1893 to 1896, under the direction of Levi Manning. AHSL.

George J. Roskruge, Arizona surveyor general (1896–1897), eating his grub while on a surveying trip, ca. 1896. AHSL.

An aging James Henry Martineau sitting with his rifle in Sabino Canyon, Arizona. Photo taken by George J. Roskruge, ca. April 1891. AHSL.

Portrait of Lieutenant Colonel Emilio Kosterlitzky taken in 1896 in Nogales, Sonora, and given as a gift to Mr. John Slaughter and family. Kosterlitzky and Slaughter worked together in the unsuccessful pursuit of the "Apache Kid." AHSL.

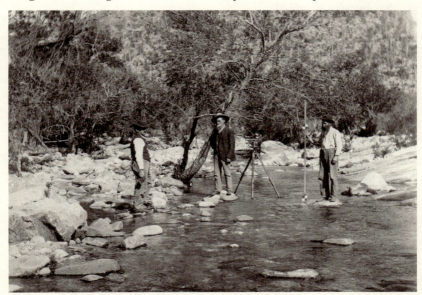

James Henry Martineau (center) with unidentified members of the survey crew, Sabino Canyon, Arizona. Photo taken by George J. Roskruge, ca. April 1891. AHSL.

Emilio Kosterlitzky, the Russian-born soldier of fortune known to American troops as the "Mexican Cossak," is shown here (on white horse) with his mounted gendarmes. Under Kosterlitzky's approbation, Martineau surveyed lands near Bavispe for Mormon colonization. AHSL.

Photograph of Susan Ellen (Johnson) Martineau, probably taken on January 8, 1893. Photo courtesy of Marcella Martineau Roe.

Photograph of James H. Martineau, probably taken on January 8, 1893. Photo courtesy of Marcella Martineau Roe.

Photograph of Benjamin Franklin Johnson (sitting front, center) and family in front of his home in Mesa, Arizona, ca. 1890. His wife, Harriet Naomi Johnson, is on his right. Daughter-in-law Rebecca Sybil Johnson, wife of Benjamin Farland Johnson, is on his left. BYUSCA.

Vol. 2, - Fig. 19. Photograph of the James Henry Martineau family in Colonia Juárez, March 13, 1908. Photo courtesy of Marcella Martineau Roe.

Photograph of James H. Martineau, taken later in life (ca. 1910). Photocourtesy of Marcella Martineau Roe.

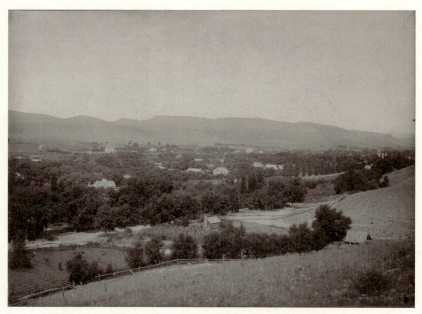

A View of Colonia Juárez, taken ca. 1917. USHS.

BIBLIOGRAPHY

Adkins, Marlowe C., Jr. "A History of John W. Young's Utah Railroads, 1884–1894." Master's Thesis, Utah State University, 1978.

Agnew, Dwight L. "The Government Land Surveyor as a Pioneer." *Mississippi Valley Historical Review* 28 (1941–42): 369–382.

Aird, G. Merkley, ed. *Monuments to Courage: A History of Beaver County*. Beaver, UT: Daughters of the Utah Pioneers, 1948.

Albright, George. "Plans and Official Exploration for Pacific Railroads." Master's Thesis, University of California, Berkeley, 1916.

Alexander, Thomas G. *A Clash of Interests: Interior Department and Mountain West, 1863–96*. Provo, UT: Brigham Young University, 1977.

———. "Conflict and Fraud: Utah Public Land Surveys, the Subsequent Investigation, and Problems with the Land Disposal System." *Utah Historical Quarterly* 80 (Spring 2012): 108–131.

———. "Stewardship and Enterprise: The LDS Church and the Wasatch Oasis Environment, 1847–1930." *Western Historical Quarterly* 25 (Autumn 1994): 340–364.

Allen, Barbara. "The Heroic Ride in Western Popular Historical Tradition." *Western Historical Quarterly* 19 (November 1988): 397–412.

Alter, J. Cecil, ed. "Journal of Priddy Meeks." *Utah Historical Quarterly* 10 (1942): 145–223.

Ambrose, Stephen E. *Nothing Like It in the World: The Men Who Built Transcontinental Railroad, 1863–1869*. New York: Simon & Schuster, 2000.

American Biographical History of Eminent and Self-Made Men with Portrait Illustrations on Steel. Michigan Volume. Cincinnati, OH: Western Biographical Publishing Co., 1878.

Ames, Charles Edgar. *Pioneering the Union Pacific: A Reappraisal of the Builders of the Railroad*. New York: Appleton-Century-Crofts, 1969.

Anderson, Nels. *Desert Saints: The Mormon Frontier in Utah*. Chicago: University of Chicago Press, 1942.

———. "The Mormon Family." *American Sociological Review* 2 (October 1937): 601–608.

"Andrew Jackson Stewart." *Tullidge's Quarterly Magazine* 3 (April 1885): 451–452.

Arizona Bulletin Supplement, Solomonville, Ariz. Jan. 12th, 1900: Special Illustrated Edition. Solomonville, AZ: Bulletin Publishing Company 1900.

Arizona Construction Company. *Irrigated Lands: The Best in the World for Fruit and Vine Culture are Found Under the Gila Bend Canal on the Lower Gila River.* Peoria, IL: J. W. Franks & Sons, 1892.

Armstrong, Belle Joseph and Estella Jones Grimshaw. "A History of Johnson's Fort or Enoch as it is Known." N.p., 1958; copy held in Special Collections, Sherratt Library, SUU.

Arndt, John Stover. *The Story of the Arndts: The Life, Antecedents and Descendants of Bernhard Arndt who Emigrated to Pennsylvania in the Year 1731.* Philadelphia: Christopher Sower Company, 1922.

Arrington, Leonard J. *Brigham Young: American Moses.* New York: Knopf, 1985.

———. *Great Basin Kingdom: An Economic History of the Latter-day Saints, 1830–1900.* Cambridge: Harvard University Press, 1958.

———. "Iron Manufacturing in Southern Utah in the Early 1880s: The Iron Manufacturing Company of Utah." *Bulletin of the Business Historical Society* 25 (September 1951): 149–168.

———. "The Mormon Tithing House: A Frontier Business Institution." *Business History Review* 28 (March 1954): 24–58.

———. "Utah's Coal Road in the Age of Unregulated Competition." *Utah Historical Quarterly* 23 (January 1958): 35–63.

———. "Planning an Iron Industry for Utah, 1851–1858." *The Huntington Library Quarterly* 21 (May 1958): 237–260.

———. "The Transcontinental Railroad and the Development of the West." *Utah Historical Quarterly* 37 (Winter 1969): 3–15.

———, and Larkin, Melvin A. "The Logan Tabernacle and Temple." *Utah Historical Quarterly* 41 (Summer 1973): 305–310.

Arsenault, David Joseph. "Unlawful Cohabitation Arrests in Cache Valley, 1885–1890." Master's Thesis, Utah State University, 1995.

Athearn, Robert G. "Contracting for the Union Pacific." *Utah Historical Quarterly* 37 (Winter 1969): 16–40.

———. "Opening the Gates of Zion: Utah and the Coming of the Union Pacific Railroad." *Utah Historical Quarterly* 36 (Fall 1968): 291–315.

———. "Railroad to a Far Off Country: The Utah and Northern." *Montana: A Magazine of Western History* 18 (Autumn1968): 2–23.

Augst, Thomas. *The Clerk's Tale: Young Men and Moral Life in Nineteenth-Century America.* Chicago: University of Chicago Press, 2003.

Bagley, Will. *Blood of the Prophets: Brigham Young and the Massacre at Mountain Meadows.* Norman: University of Oklahoma Press, 2002.

Bailey, L. R. *Indian Slave Trade in the Southwest: A Study of Slave-Taking and the Traffic in Indian Captives*. Los Angeles: Westernlore Press, 1966.

Bain, David Haward. *Empire Express: Building the First Transcontinental Railroad*. New York: Viking, 1999.

Bair, Jo Ann W., and Richard L. Jensen. "Prosecution of the Mormons in Arizona Territory in the 1880s." *Arizona and the West* 19 (Spring 1977): 25–46.

Baker, Doran J., Charles S. Peterson, and Gene A. Ware, eds. *Isaac Sorenson's History of Mendon: A Pioneer Chronicle of a Mormon Settlement*. Logan, UT: Cache County Historical Preservation Commission and Utah State Historical Society, 1988.

Ball, Larry D. *Ambush at Bloody Run: The Wham Paymaster Robbery of 1889; A Story of Politics, Religion, Race, and Banditry in Arizona Territory*. Tucson: Arizona Historical Society, 2000.

Ballard, Henry. Journal, 1852–1888. Typescript, Special Collections and Archives, Merrill–Cazier Library, Utah State University.

Ballweg, John A. "Extensions of Meaning and Use for Kinship Terms." *American Anthropologist*. New Series, 71 (February 1969): 84–87.

Bancroft, Hubert Howe. *History of the North Mexican States and Texas*. Volume XV of the Works of Hubert Howe Bancroft. San Francisco: The History Company Publishers, 1884.

———. *History of Arizona and New Mexico, 1530–1888*. Volume XVII of the Works of Hubert Howe Bancroft. San Francisco: The History Company Publishers, 1889.

———. *History of Utah, 1540–1887*. Volume XXVI of the Works of Hubert Howe Bancroft. San Francisco: The History Company Publishers, 1890.

Barber, George. Journal, 1861–1885. Typescript, Special Collections and Archives, Merrill–Cazier Library, Utah State University.

Barnes, Will C. *Arizona Place Names*. Tucson: University of Arizona Press, 1988.

Barnett, Alan B. "'We Must Do Right and Be Guided by the Priesthood': A Study of the Parowan Meeting House and Its Role in the Mormon Community." Master's Thesis, University of Utah, 1994.

Bartlett, Richard A. *Great Surveys of the American West*. Norman: University of Oklahoma Press, 1962.

Bate, Kerry William. "John Steele: Medicine Man, Magician, Mormon Patriarch." *Utah Historical Quarterly* 62 (Winter 1994): 71–90.

Bates, Irene M. "Patriarchal Blessings and the Routinization of Charisma." *Dialogue: A Journal of Mormon Thought* 26 (Fall 1993): 1–29.

———. "Uncle John Smith, 1781–1854: Patriarchal Bridge." *Dialogue: A Journal of Mormon Thought* 20 (Fall 1987): 79–89.

———, and E. Gary Smith. *Lost Legacy: The Mormon Office of Presiding Patriarch*. Urbana: University of Illinois Press, 2003.

Baxter, Robert Wright. "Life History of Robert Write Baxter, Son of John and Margaret Baxter." Typescript in my possession.

Beal, Merrill D. "Cache Valley Pioneers: The Founding of Franklin in 1860." *Idaho Yesterdays* 4 (Spring 1960): 1–7.

———. *A History of Southeastern Idaho: An Intimate Narrative of Peaceful Conquest by Empire Builders*. Caldwell, ID: Caxton Printers Ltd., 1942.

———. *Intermountain Railroads: Standard and Narrow Gauge*. Caldwell, ID: Caxton Printers, 1962.

———. "The Story of the Utah Northern Railroad." *Idaho Yesterdays* 1 (Spring 1957): 3–10; and idem, *Idaho Yesterdays* 1 (Summer 1957): 16–23.

———, and Merle W. Wells. *History of Idaho*. 3 vols. New York: Lewis Historical Publishing Co., 1959.

Bean, Lee L., Geraldine P. Mineau, and Douglas L. Anderson. *Fertility Change on the American Frontier: Adaptation and Innovation*. Studies in Demography, No. 5. Berkeley: University of California Press, 1990.

Bean, Orestus U. *Corianton, An Aztec Romance; a Romantic Spectacular Drama*. S.I.: s.n., 1902?

Bean, George W. *Autobiography of George Washington Bean a Utah Pioneer of 1847, and His Family Records*. Compiled by Flora Diana Bean Horne. Salt Lake City: Utah Printing Company, 1945.

Bedini, Silvio A. *With Compass and Chain: Early American Surveyors and Their Instruments*. Frederick, MD: Professional Surveyors Publishing Company, 2001.

Beecher, Maureen Ursenbach, ed. *The Personal Writings of Eliza Roxcy Snow*. Logan: Utah State University Press, 2000.

Beeton, Beverly. "Teach Them to Till the Soil: An Experiment with Indian Farms, 1850–1862." *American Indian Quarterly* 3 (Winter 1977–78): 299–320.

Belk, Russell W. "Moving Possessions: An Analysis Based on Personal Documents from the 1847–1869 Mormon Migration." *Journal of Consumer Research* 19 (December 1992): 339–361.

Bemis, Samuel Flagg. "Captain John Mullan and the Engineer's Frontier." *Washington Historical Quarterly* 14 (July 1923): 201–205.

Bennett, Richard. "Line upon Line, Precept upon Precept." *BYU Studies* 44, no. 3 (2005): 38–77.

Bentley, Joseph Charles. Journal, 1875–1911. MS d 1499, LDS Church History Library, Salt Lake City.

Bernstein, Peter L. *Wedding of the Waters: The Erie Canal and the Making of a Great Nation*. New York: W. W. Norton & Co., 2005.

Bernstein, Samuel. "American Labor in the Long Depression, 1873–1878." *Science and Society* 20 (Winter 1956): 59–83.

Bidlack, Russell E., and Everett L. Cooley, eds. "The Kinter Letters: An Astronomer's View of the Wheeler Survey in Utah and Idaho." *Utah Historical Quarterly* 34 (Winter 1966): 62–80; and idem, *Utah Historical Quarterly* 34 (Spring 1966): 169–182.

Bigler, David L. *Forgotten Kingdom: The Mormon Theocracy in the American West, 1847–1896.* Spokane, WA: Arthur H. Clark, 1998.

———, and Will Bagley, eds. *Innocent Blood: Essential Narratives of the Mountain Meadows Massacre.* Norman, OK: Arthur H. Clark Company, 2008.

A Biographical Dictionary of American Civil Engineers, ASCE Historical Publication No. 2. New York: Committee on History and Heritage of American Civil Engineering; American Society of Civil Engineers, 1972.

Biographical Review of Dane County, Wisconsin; Containing Biographical Sketches of Pioneers and Leading Citizens. Chicago: Biographical Review Publishing Co., 1893.

"Biographical Notice of Late Right Honourable Earl Stanhope." *The Scots Magazine, and Edinburgh Literary Miscellany* 79 (January 1817): 36–39.

"Biographical Sketch of John Lyman Smith." *Latter-day Saints' Millennial Star* 56 (August 13, 1894): 524–527, idem, *Latter-day Saints' Millennial Star* 56 (August 20, 1894): 539–542, idem, *Latter-day Saints' Millennial Star* 56 (August 27, 1894): 556–559, idem, *Latter-day Saints' Millennial Star* 56 (September 3, 1894): 573–575, idem, *Latter-day Saints' Millennial Star* 56 (September 10, 1894): 588–590.

Bishop, M. Guy. "Building Railroads for the Kingdom: The Career of John W. Young, 1867–91." *Utah Historical Quarterly* 48 (Winter 1980): 66–80.

———. "More than One Coal Road to Zion: The Utah Territory's Efforts to Ease Dependency on Wyoming Coal." *Annals of Wyoming* 60 (Spring 1988): 8–16.

Bissell, Hezekiah. Reminiscences. Film 0056–33–0205, Wyoming State Archives, Cheyenne.

Blair, Roger P. "'The Doctor Gets Some Practice': Cholera and Medicine on the Overland Trails." *Journal of the West* 36 (January 1997): 54–66.

Blair, Seth Millington. Diary and Autobiography, 1853–1868. Typescript, MSS 1316, L. Tom Perry Special Collections and Manuscripts, Harold B. Lee Library, Brigham Young University.

———. Reminiscences and Journals, 1851–1868. MS 1710 1–3, LDS Church History Library.

Blickensderfer, Jacob. *History of the Blickensderfer Family in America.* S.l.: s.n., 1896?

Boyer, Dorothy Fillerup, ed. *William Derby Johnson, Jr.: Journal Excerpts, 1850–1894.* Mesa, AZ: The editor, 2005.

Bowen, Patrick K., Helen J. Ranck, Timothy J. Scarlett, and Jaroslaw W. Drelich. "Rehydration/Rehydroxylation Kinetics of Reheated XIX-Century

Davenport (Utah) Ceramic." *Journal of the American Ceramic Society* 94 (August 2011): 2585–2591.

Bozzuto, Robert T. "Geology of the Skull Point Mine Area, Lincoln County, Wyoming." In *Rocky Mountain Thrust Belt Geology and Resources; Wyoming Geological Association Twenty-Ninth Annual Field Conference Guidebook*, ed. by E. L. Heisey, Don E. Lawson, et al., 673–678. Casper: Wyoming Geological Association, 1977.

Brand, Donald. "The Natural Landscape of Northwestern Chihuahua." *University of New Mexico Bulletin, Geological Series*, 5:2 [no. 316], University of New Mexico Press, 1937.

Briggs, Robert H. "The Fog of War: Invasion Hysteria in Southern Utah at the Outbreak of the Utah War." Unpublished manuscript delivered at the Annual Conference of the Utah State Historical Society, Salt Lake City, Utah, September 14–16, 2006; copy in the editors' possession.

———. "The Mountain Meadows Massacre: An Analytical Narrative Based on Participant Confessions." *Utah Historical Quarterly* 74 (Fall 2006): 313–333.

Britton, J. Blodget. "Water in Coals." *Transactions of the American Institute of Mining Engineers* 5 (May 1876–February 1877): 97–99.

Brooks, Juanita. "Indian Relations on the Mormon Frontier." *Utah Historical Quarterly* 12 (January–April 1944): 1–48.

———, ed. *Journal of the Southern Indian Mission: Diary of Thomas D. Brown*. Western Text Society, Number 4. Logan: Utah State University Press, 1972.

———. *The Mountain Meadows Massacre*. Stanford, 1950; new edition, Norman, OK: University of Oklahoma Press, 1970.

———, ed. *On the Mormon Frontier: The Diary of Hosea Stout, 1844–1861*. 2 vols. Salt Lake City: University of Utah; Utah State Historical Society, 1964; reprint edition, 1982.

———. "A Place of Refuge." *Nevada Historical Society Quarterly* 14 (Spring 1971): 13–24.

Brooks, Juanita Leone Leavitt Pulsipher Brooks. Papers, 1928–1981. MSS B-103, Utah State Historical Society.

Brown, Lisle G. "'Temple Pro Tempore': The Salt Lake City Endowment House." *Journal of Mormon History* 34 (Fall 2008): 1–68.

Brown, Noral Lee. *Jacob's Legacy: An Intimate Portrait of the Blickensderfer Family*. Colorado Springs, CO: The Grumpy Dragon, 2006.

Brown, Randy. *Historic Inscriptions on Western Emigrant Trails*. Independence, MO: Oregon-California Trails Association, 2004.

Bruce, William George. "Memoirs of William George Bruce." *Wisconsin Magazine of History* 17 (June 1934): 402–432.

Budge, Seth. "Perception of the Boundaries of the Mormon Cultural Region." *Great Plains-Rocky Mountain Geographical Journal* 3 (1974): 1–9.

Buerger, David John. "'The Fulness of the Priesthood': The Second Anointing in Latter-day Saint Theology and Practice." *Dialogue: A Journal of Mormon Thought* 16 (Spring 1983): 10–44.

———. *Mysteries of Godliness: A History of Mormon Temple Worship*. San Francisco: Smith Research Associates, 1994.

Burgess, Glenn, ed. *Mt. Graham Profiles: Ryder Ridgway Collection, Volume 2*. Safford, AZ: Graham County Historical Society, 1988.

Burgess-Olsen, Vicky. "Family Structure and Dynamics in Early Utah Mormon Families, 1847–1885." PhD diss. Northwestern University, 1975.

Burn, John Southerden. *The History of the French, Walloon, Dutch, and other Foreign Refugees Settled in England*. London: Longman, Brown, Green and Logmans, 1846.

Burns, Barney T. and Thomas H. Naylor, "Colonia Morelos: A Short History of a Mormon Colony in Sonora Mexico." *The Smoke Signal* [Published by the Tucson Corral of the Westerners], No. 27 (Spring 1973): 142–179.

Cache County Surveys. Recorder's vault, County Recorder's Office, Logan, Utah.

Cache County, Utah. County Books "A" and "B," 1857–1891. Typescript. 2 vols. Special Collections and Archives, Merrill–Cazier Library, Utah State University; originals in the Cache County Recorder's vault.

Cache County, Utah. Land Surveys, 1860–1879. Special Collections and Archives, Merrill–Cazier Library, Utah State University; originals in the Cache County Recorder's vault.

Calabasas Land and Mining Co. *Prospectus and Reports of the Property of the Calabasas Land and Mining Co. Located in Pima County, Arizona Territory*. San Francisco: Francis & Valentine, 1878.

Campbell, Eugene E. *Establishing Zion: The Mormon Church in the American West, 1847–69*. Salt Lake City: Signature Books, 1988.

Cannon, Brian Q. "Adopted or Indentured, 1850–1870: Native Children in Mormon Households." In *Nearly Everything Imaginable: The Every Day Life of Utah's Mormon Pioneers*, edited by Ronald W. Walker and Doris R. Dant, 347–357. Provo, UT: Brigham Young University Press, 1999.

Cannon, Donald Q. "Zelph Revisited." In *Regional Studies in Latter-day Saint Church History: Illinois*, edited by H. Dean Garrett, 97–111. Provo: Department of Church History and Doctrine, Brigham Young University, 1995.

Cannon, Kenneth L. II. "Beyond the Manifesto: Polygamous Cohabitation among LDS General Authorities after 1890." *Utah Historical Quarterly* 46 (Winter 1978): 24–36.

———. "After the Manifesto: Mormon Polygamy, 1890–1906." *Sunstone* 8 (January/April 1983): 27–35.

Carleton, James Henry. *The Mountain Meadows Massacre: A Special Report by J. H. Carleton, Bvt. Major U. S. A. Captain 1st Dragoons, 1859*, with an Introduction by Robert A. Clark. Spokane, WA: Arthur H. Clark, 1995.

Carmack, Noel A. "James Henry Martineau and the Cache Expeditions of 1862." Unpublished manuscript delivered at the Cache County Historical Society, Logan, Utah, August 6, 2008.

———. "Labor and the Construction of the Logan Temple, 1877–1884." *Journal of Mormon History* 22 (Spring 1996): 52–79.

———. "A Long Course of the Most Inhuman Cruelty: The Abuse and Murder of Isaac Whitehouse." *Utah Historical Quarterly* 82 (Fall 2014): 272–87.

———. "Running the Line: James Henry Martineau's Surveys in Northern Utah, 1860–1882." *Utah Historical Quarterly* 68 (Fall 2000): 292–312.

Carpenter, J[ames]. Estlin. *James Martineau, Theologian and Teacher: A Study of His Life and Thought.* London: Philip Green, 1905.

Carrington, Albert. Papers, 1847–1887. MS 0549, Special Collections and Manuscripts, Marriott Library, University of Utah.

Carter, Kate B., comp. "Diary of Albert Carrington." *Heart Throbs of the West* 8 (January 1947): 77–132.

———. "Early Pioneer Photographers." *Our Pioneer Heritage* 18 (February 1975): 249–305.

———. "Journal of Mary Ann Weston Maughan." *Our Pioneer Heritage* 2 (February 1959): 345–420.

Carter, Robert W. "'Sometimes When I Hear the Winds Sigh': Mortality on the Overland Trail." *California History* 74 (Summer 1995): 146–161.

Carter, William A. "Diary of Judge William A. Carter." *Annals of Wyoming* 11 (April 1939): 75–110.

———. "Fort Bridger in the Seventies." *Annals of Wyoming* 11 (April 1939): 111–113.

Carvalho, Solomon Nunes. *Incidents of Travel and Adventure in the Far West: with Colonel Fremont's Last Expedition across the Rocky Mountains, Including Three Month's Residence in Utah, and a Perilous Trip across the Great American Desert to the Pacific.* New York: Derby & Jackson, 1858; reprint, Lincoln: University of Nebraska Press, 2004.

Cazier, Lola. *Surveys and Surveyors of the Public Domain, 1785–1975.* Washington, DC: Dept. of the Interior, Bureau of Land Management, 1976.

Chaffin, Tom. *Pathfinder: John Charles Frémont and the Course of American Empire.* New York: Hill and Wang, 2002.

Chesapeake and Ohio Canal Company. *Reports and Letters from the Engineers Employed in the Revised Location of the Western Section of the Chesapeake and Ohio Canal.* Washington, 1829.

Chittenden, Samuel H. "The Chittenden Correspondence." *La Posta: A Journal of American Postal History* 14 (August 1983): 44–48; idem, 14 (October 1983): 42–44; idem, 14 (December 1983): 69–72; idem 15 (February 1984): 71–73; idem, 15 (April 1984): 57–59; idem, 15 (June 1984): 53–57; idem, 15

(August 1984): 81–84; idem 15 (October 1984): 21–26; idem, 15 (December 1984): 85–89; and idem, 16 (April 1985): 66–69.

———. Correspondence, February 25, 1868–December 8, 1868. Office Vault, Postal History Foundation, Tucson, Arizona.

Christensen, Keith. "Courageous Moments." *Friend* 6 (November 1976): 28–29.

Christensen, Scott R. *Sagwitch: Shoshone Chieftain, Mormon Elder, 1822–1887*. Logan: Utah State University Press, 1999.

Christopherson, Victor A. "An Investigation of Patriarchal Authority in the Mormon Family." *Marriage and Family Living* 18 (November 1956): 328–333.

Christy, Howard A. "Open Hand and Mailed Fist: Mormon-Indian Relations in Utah." *Utah Historical Quarterly* 46 (1978): 216–235.

City of New York, Board of Aldermen. *Documents of the Board of Aldermen, of the City of New York*. Volume IV. New York: The Common Council, 1838.

Claridge, Samuel. Papers, 1828–1919. MSS 228c, Special Collections and Archives, Utah State University.

Clayton, Roberta Flake. *Pioneer Men of Arizona*. S.l.: Roberta Flake Clayton, 1974.

Cleary, John B. *United States Land Surveys*. Pts 1 and 2. Scranton, PA: International Textbook Company, 1943.

Cleland, Robert Glass, and Juanita Brooks, eds. *A Mormon Chronicle: The Diaries of John D. Lee, 1848–1876*. 2 vols. San Marino, CA: Huntington Library Press, 1958; reprint, 2003.

Clinton, Dewitt. Letters to Daniel Van Slyke, 1824–1826. Chicago History Museum, Chicago, Illinois.

Coates, Lawrence G. "Brigham Young and the Mormon Indian Policies: The Formative Period, 1836–1851." *BYU Studies* 18 (Spring 1978): 428–452.

———. "The Mormons and the Ghost Dance." *Dialogue: A Journal of Mormon Thought* 18 (Winter 1985): 89–111.

Coatsworth, John H. "Indispensable Railroads in a Backward Economy: The Case of Mexico." *Journal of Economic History* 39 (December 1979): 939–960.

Codman, John. *The Mormon Country. A Summer with the "Latter day Saints."* New York: United States Publishing Company, 1874.

Cohen, Paul E. *Mapping the West: America's Westward Movement, 1524–1890*. New York: Rizzoli International, 2002.

Cole, Helen R., ed. *100 Years in Thatcher, 1883–1983*. Thatcher, AZ: The Town of Thatcher, 1983.

Collins, Dabney Otis. *Great Western Rides*. Denver, CO: Sage Books, 1961.

"Colonel James Henry Martineau." *Improvement Era* 24 (August 1921): 956.

Colvin, Verna Rae. "First Came the Water and then the People: History of Water in Graham County." Unpublished manuscript, copy in the Graham County Historical Society Museum, Thatcher.

Compton, Todd. *In Sacred Loneliness: The Plural Wives of Joseph Smith*. Salt Lake City: Signature Books, 1997.

Conant, Helene M. "The Locational Influence of Place of Work on Place of Residence." PhD diss., University of Chicago, 1952.

Cook, Lyndon W. "Lyman Sherman: Man of God, Would-be Apostle." *BYU Studies* 19 (Fall 1978): 121–124.

Correspondence of the Surveyors General of Utah, 1854–1916, Records of the Bureau of Land Management, Record Group 49. National Archives and Records Administration, Rocky Mountain Region, Denver.

Correspondence of the Surveyors General of Arizona, 1860–1950, Records of the Bureau of Land Management, Record Group 49. National Archives at Riverside, Perris, California.

Cotter, Michael David. "George A. Smith and the Founding of Parowan, Utah." Honors Thesis, History Department, University of Utah, 2003.

Cox, Clarence William, Jr. "The Mormon Colonies in Chihuahua, Mexico." Master's Thesis, University of Southern California, 1969.

Crofutt, George A. *Crofutt's Transcontinental Guide, Containing a Full and Authentic Description of Over Five Hundred Cities, Towns, Villages, Stations ....* New York: The American News Co., 1871.

Crofton, C. Anthony, and David Martineau. *Pedigrees of the Martineau Family: A Revision and Continuation of Pedigrees Set Forth in 1907 by David Martineau in "Notes on the Pedigree of the Martineau Who Emigrated to England in 1686."* Northampton, UK: Archer and Goodman Ltd., 1972.

Cross, Gary. "Worktime and Industrialization: An Introduction." In *Worktime and Industrialization: An International History*, edited by Gary Cross, 3–19. Philadelphia: Temple University Press, 1988.

Cuch, Forrest S., ed. *A History of Utah's American Indians*. Salt Lake City: Utah State Division of Indian Affairs; Utah State Division of History, 2000.

Daines, Richard. "Heroes and Horse Doctors: Medicine in Cache Valley, 1857–1900." In *Cache Valley: Essays on Her Past and People*, edited by Douglas D. Alder, 64–76. Logan: Utah State University Press, 1976.

Dalton, Luella Adams, comp. *History of the Iron County Mission and Parowan, the Mother Town*. 5th Edition. Parowan, UT: Daughters of the Utah Pioneers; Parowan Old Rock Church Museum, 2001.

Dame, William H. "Cedar City Plat B. Surveyed May 30, 1855 by Wm. H. Dame." Recorder's vault, County Recorder's Office, Iron County Courthouse, Parowan, Utah.

———. "Coal Creek Survey Iron Co. U. S. 1851–53 by Wm. H. Dame." Recorder's vault, County Recorder's Office, Iron County Courthouse, Parowan, Utah.

———. County Surveyor. "Parowan City Survey Iron Co. U. S. Jan 1853 by Wm. H. Dame, County Surveyor." Recorder's vault, County Recorder's Office, Iron County Courthouse, Parowan, Utah.

———. Diaries, 1850–1857, 1860–1861. Microfilm, 920 no. 57, Harold B. Lee Library, Brigham Young University.

———. Diaries, 1854–1858. MSS 820, L. Tom Perry Special Collections and Manuscripts, Harold B. Lee Library, Brigham Young University.

———. "Journal of the Southern Exploring Company for the Desert," April–June 1858. Manuscript in Martineau's hand, but probably dictated by Dame. MS 4953, fd. 1, LDS Church History Library.

———. Papers, 1846–1884. Vault MSS 55, L. Tom Perry Special Collections and Manuscripts, Harold B. Lee Library, Brigham Young University.

———. Papers, 1838–1884. MS 2041, LDS Church History Library.

Dame-McBride Family Papers, 1828–1978. MS 0515, L. Special Collections, Marriott Library, University of Utah.

Davidson, Karen Lynn, and Jill Mulvay Derr. *Eliza: The Life and Faith of Eliza R. Snow*. Salt Lake City: Deseret Book, 2013.

Davies, Charles, and J. Howard Van Amringe. *Elements of Surveying and Leveling*. New York and Chicago: A. S. Barnes & Co., 1883.

Davis, Arthur Powell. *Irrigation Near Phoenix, Arizona*. Water-Supply and Irrigation Papers of the United States Geological Survey, No. 2. Washington, DC: Department of the Interior; U. S. Govt. Printing Office, 1897.

Davis. W. R., Jr. "The Sutler at Fort Bridger." *Western Historical Quarterly* 2 (January 1971): 37–54.

Dawdy, Doris Ostrander. *George Montague Wheeler: The Man and the Myth*. Athens, OH: Swallow Press; Ohio University, 1993.

Dean, Lindley Richard. "A Study of the Cognomina of Soldiers in the Roman Legions." PhD diss., Princeton University, 1916.

Deckert, Emil. *Nordamerika*, Allgemeine Länderkunde, vol. 1. Leipzig: Bibliographisches Institut, 1904.

Dewey, Louis Marinus, comp. "Inscriptions from Old Cemeteries in Connecticut." *New England Historical and Genealogical Register* 60 (October 1906): 370–372.

Dodge, Grenville Mellen. *How We Built the Union Pacific Railway and Other Railway Papers and Addresses*. Council Bluffs, IA: n.d., ca. 1910; reprint, De`nver: Sage Books, 1965.

———. Papers, 1851–1916. Dodge, Special Collections, Council Bluffs Public Library, Council Bluffs, Iowa; originals at the State Historical Society of Iowa.

Donnelly, Joseph L. and Karl J. Lietzenmayer. *Newport Barracks: Kentucky's Forgotten Military Installation*. Covington, KY: Kenton County Historical Society, 1999.

Dowdle, John Clark. Journal, 1844–1908. Special Collections and Archives, Merrill–Cazier Library, Utah State University.

Driggs, Nevada W. "When Captain Fremont Slept in Grandma McGregor's Bed." *Utah Historical Quarterly* 41 (Spring 1973): 178–181.

Eckhart, George B. "A Guide to the History of the Missions of Sonora, 1614–1826." *Arizona and the West* 2 (Summer 1960): 165–183.

Eckhart, George Boland and James S. Griffith. *Temples in the Wilderness: The Spanish Churches of Northern Sonora, Their Architecture, Their Past and Present Appearance, and How to Reach Them.* Historical Monograph, No. 3. Tucson: Arizona Historical Society, 1975.

Edmonds, Michael. "The U.S. General Land Office and Commercial Map Making: A Case Study." *Government Publications Review* 13 (September–October 1986): 571–580.

Eggenhofer, Nick. *Wagons, Mules, and Men: How the Frontier Moved West.* New York: Hastings House, 1961.

Ehrenberg, Ralph. "Taking Measure of the Land." *Prologue* 9 (Fall 1977): 129–150.

Ellison, Robert Spurrier. *Independence Rock: The Great Record of the Desert.* Casper, WY: Natrona County Historical Society, 1930.

Ellsworth, S. George. *Samuel Claridge: Pioneering the Outposts of Zion.* Logan, UT: By the author, 1987.

———, ed. *The Journals of Addison Pratt: Being a Narrative of Yankee Whaling . . . .* Publications in Mormon Studies, Volume 6. Salt Lake City: University of Utah Press, 1990.

Esshom, Frank. *Pioneers and Prominent Men of Utah, Comprising Photographs—Genealogies—Biographies.* Salt Lake City: Utah Pioneers Book Publishing Company, 1913.

Essin, Emmett M. *Shavetails and Bell Sharps: The History of the U.S. Army Mule.* Lincoln: University of Nebraska Press, 1997.

Ewing, Floyd F., Jr. "The Mule as a Factor in the Development of the Southwest." *Arizona and the West* 5 (Winter 1963): 315–326.

Eyring, Henry. Journal. MS 8, Special Collections and Manuscripts, Marriott Library, University of Utah.

Farmer, Jared. *On Zion's Mount: Mormons, Indians, and the American Landscape.* Cambridge: Harvard University Press, 2008.

Farnham, Wallace D. "Grenville Dodge and the Union Pacific: A Study of Historical Legends." *Journal of American History* 51 (March 1965): 632–650.

Fels, Rendigs. "American Business Cycles, 1865–79." *American Economic Review* 41 (June 1951): 325–349.

Ferguson, Arthur. Journals, 1865–1869. MSS A-1168, Utah State Historical Society; original at the Union Pacific Railroad Museum, Council Bluffs, Iowa.

Fielding, R. Kent. *The Unsolicited Chronicler: An Account of the Gunnison Massacre, Its Causes and Consequences, Utah Territory, 1847–1859: A Narrative History.* Brookline, MA: Paradigm Publications; Distributed by Redwing Book Co., 1993.

Fife, A[ustin]. E., "The Legend of the Three Nephites among the Mormons." *The Journal of American Folklore* 53 (January–March 1940): 1–49.

First Presidency. John Taylor Presidential Papers, 1877–1887. CR 1/180, LDS Church History Library.

First Presidency. Letterpress Copybooks, 1881–1890. CR 1/20, LDS Church History Library.

"The First Settlements in the Sevier Valley." *Utah Genealogical and Historical Magazine* 6 (April 1915): 83–87, and idem, *Utah Genealogical and Historical Magazine* 6 (July 1915): 141–145.

Fish, Joseph. "History of Arizona Territory." MSS-86, Arizona Collection, Arizona State University; microfilm copy, Utah Reel 533, Special Collections and Archives, Utah State University.

———. Journal, 1840–1926; 1857–1926. MS 34\10: 4, Utah State Historical Society.

———. Journals, 1840–1936. MIC A-337, Utah State Historical Society.

Fleisher, Kass. *The Bear River Massacre and the Making of History*. Albany: State University of New York Press, 2004.

Fleming, L. A., and A. R. Standing. "The Road to 'Fortune': The Salt Lake Cutoff." *Utah Historical Quarterly* 33 (Summer 1965): 248–271.

Flicker, Sandra Kuntz. "Economic Backwardness and Firm Strategy: An American Railroad Corporation in Nineteenth-Century Mexico." *Hispanic American Historical Review* 80 (2000): 267–298.

Flores, Dan L. "Agriculture, Mountain Ecology, and the Land Ethic: Phases of the Environmental History of Utah." In *Working the Range: Essays on the History of Western Land Management and the Environment*, edited by John R. Wunder. Westport, CT: Greenwood Press, 1985.

Foster, Craig L. "'That Canny Scotsman': John Sharp and the Union Pacific and the Union Pacific Negotiations, 1869–72." *Journal of Mormon History* 27 (Fall 2001): 197–214.

Fox, Feramorz Young. "The Life of Jessie W. Fox, Sr." Copy held at the Utah State Historical Society.

Fox, William L. *The Void, the Grid, and the Sign: Traversing the Great Basin*. Salt Lake City: University of Utah Press, 2000.

Francaviglia, Richard V. *The Mapmakers of New Zion: A Cartographic History of Mormonism*. Salt Lake City: University of Utah Press, 2015.

———. *Mapping and Imagination in the Great Basin: A Cartographic History*. Reno: University of Nevada Press, 2005.

———. *The Mormon Landscape: Existence, Creation, and Perception of a Unique Image in the American West*. New York: AMS Press, 1978.

———. *Over the Range: A History of the Promontory Summit Route of the Pacific Railroad*. Logan: Utah State University Press, 2008.

———. "'Surely There is a Vein for Silver and a Place for Gold': Mining and Religion in the Nineteenth Century Intermountain West." *John Whitmer Historical Association Journal* 26 (2006): 194–213.

Franklin, Selim Maurice. Papers, 1873–1931. AZ 336, Special Collections, University of Arizona Libraries, Tucson.

Frémont, John Charles, and Jessie Benton Frémont. *Memoirs of My Life by John Charles Frémont.* ... Vol. 1. Chicago, New York: Belford, Clarke & Company, 1887.

"From Mules to Motorcars: Utah's Changing Transportation Scene." *Utah Historical Quarterly* 42 (Summer 1974): 273–277.

Fuller, Craig Woods. "Land Rush in Zion: Opening of the Uncompahgre and Uintah Indian Reservations." PhD diss., Brigham Young University, 1990.

Gannett, Henry. *Results of Primary Triangulations*, Bulletin of the United States Geological Survey, No. 122. Washington, DC: U.S. Govt. Printing Office, 1894.

Gardner, A. Dudley, and Verla R. Flores. *Forgotten Frontier: A History of Wyoming Coal Mining.* New York, Routledge, 1989.

Gilbert, G. K. "Art. XXXVI.—The Ancient Outlet of the Great Salt Lake." *American Journal of Science and Arts*, Third Series, Vol. 15, no. 88 (April 1878): 256–259.

———. "Art. XLII.—The Outlet of Lake Bonneville." *American Journal of Science*, Third Series, Vol. 19, no. 113 (May 1880): 341–349.

Gillespie, W[illiam] M[itchell]. *A Treatise on Land-Surveying: Comprising the Theory Developed* .... New York: D. Appleton and Co., 1855.

Gleave, Ray Haun. "The Effect of the Speaking of George A. Smith on the People of the Iron Mission of Southern Utah." Master's Thesis Brigham Young University, 1957.

Godfrey, Donald G., and Kenneth W. Godfrey, eds. *The Diaries of Charles Ora Card: The Utah Years, 1871–1886.* Provo, UT: Religious Studies Center, Brigham Young University, 2006.

Godfrey, Donald G., and Rebecca Martineau-McCarty. *Uncommon Common Pioneer: The Journals of James Henry Martineau, 1828–1918.* Provo, UT: Religious Studies Center, 2008.

Godfrey, Kenneth W. "The Coming of the Manifesto." *Dialogue: A Journal of Mormon Thought* 5 (Autumn 1970): 11–25.

———. "Moses Thatcher and Mormon Beginnings in Mexico." *BYU Studies* 38, no. 4 (1999): 139–155.

———. "Moses Thatcher in the Dock: His Trials, the Aftermath, and His Last Days." *Journal of Mormon History* 24 (Spring 1998): 54–88.

———. "William Bowker Preston: Pioneer, Colonizer, Civic Leader, Church Official, Husband and Father." *Mormon Historical Studies* 5 (Spring 2004): 87–126.

———. "The Zelph Story." *BYU Studies* 29 (Spring 1989): 31–56.

Goetzmann, William H. *Army Exploration in the American West, 1803–1863*, Fred H. and Ella Mae Moore Texas History Reprint Series, Number 9. Revised edition. Austin: Texas State Historical Association, 1991.

———. *Exploration and Empire: The Explorer and the Scientist in the Winning of the American West*. New York: Knopf, 1966.

———. *The Topographical Engineers and the Western Movement*. New York: The Westerners New York Posse, 1958.

Gottfredson, Peter. *History of Indian Depredations in Utah*. Salt Lake City: Skelton Publishing Co. 1919.

Graham County Surveys. Recorder's vault, County Recorder's Office, Graham County Offices, Safford, Arizona.

Greenwell, Scott L. "A History of the United States Army Corps of Topographical Engineers, 1843–1859." Master's Thesis, Utah State University, 1972.

Greer, Leland H. "The Explorations of Gunnison and Beckwith in Colorado and Utah, 1853." *The Colorado Magazine* 6 (September 1929): 184–92.

———. *The Founding of an Empire: The Exploration and Colonization of Utah, 1776–1856*. Salt Lake City: Bookcraft, 1947.

Grey, Alan H. "Roads, Railways, and Mountains: Getting Around in the West." *Journal of the West* 33 (July 1994): 35–44.

———. "The Union Pacific Railroad and South Pass." *Kansas Quarterly* 2 (Summer 1970): 46–57.

Grover, Susan Hendricks, and A. Garr Cranney. "Reading on the Utah Frontier, 1850–1877: The History of the Deseret Alphabet." Unpublished study, Brigham Young University, 1982.

Gudde, Erwin G. *California Place Names: The Origin and Etymology of Current Geographical Names*. Revised and expanded by William Bright. Berkeley: University of California Press, 2005.

Hafen, Althea. *History of Bellevue*. St. George, UT: Works Projects Administration, 1950.

Hafen, LeRoy R., and Ann W. Hafen. *The Old Spanish Trail: Santa Fé to Los Angeles....* Glendale, CA: Arthur H. Clark, 1954.

Hardy, B. Carmon. Cultural 'Encystment' as a Cause of the Mormon Exodus from Mexico in 1912." *Pacific Historical Review* 34 (November 1965): 439–454.

———, ed. *Doing the Works of Abraham: Mormon Polygamy: Its Origin, Practice, and Demise*. Norman, OK: Arthur H. Clark Company, 2007.

———. "The Mormon Colonies of Northern Mexico: A History, 1885–1912." PhD diss., Wayne State University, 1963.

———. *Solemn Covenant: The Mormon Polygamous Passage*. Urbana: University of Illinois Press, 1991.

———. "The Sonora, Sinaloa and Chihuahua Railroad." *Jahrbuch für Geschichte von Staat, Wirtschaft und Gesellschaft Lateinamerikas* [West Germany] 12 (1975): 253–283.

———. "The Trek South: How the Mormons Went to Mexico." *Southwestern Historical Quarterly* 73 (July 1969): 1–16.

———, and Melody Seymour. "The Importation of Arms and the 1912 Mormon 'Exodus' from Mexico." *New Mexico Historical Review* 72 (October 1997): 297–318.

Harstad, Peter T., ed. *Reminiscences of Oscar Sonnenkalb, Idaho Surveyor and Pioneer.* Pocatello: Idaho State University Press, 1972.

Hart, Neell. "Rescue of a Frontier Boy." *Utah Historical Quarterly* 33 (Winter 1965): 51–54.

Hartley, William G., and Lorna Call Alder. *Anson Bowen Call: Bishop of Colonia Dublán.* Provo, UT: Lorna Call Alder, 2007.

Hatch, Charles M. "Creating Ethnicity in the Hydraulic Village of the Mormon West." Master's Thesis, Utah State University, 1991.

Hatch, Lorenzo Hill. Journal, 1855–1906. 921 H 28, Utah State Historical Society.

———. "Utah Northern Railroad." *Idaho Yesterdays* 22 (1978): 26–28.

Hatch, Nelle Spilsbury. *Colonia Juarez: An Intimate Account of a Mormon Village.* Salt Lake City: Deseret Book Company, 1954.

———, comp. *Stalwarts South of the Border.* El Paso, TX: Distributed by M. Knudsen, 1985.

Haver, Sherri. "Exploring Southern Utah, 1872: The Diary of William Derby Johnson, Jr." *Rangelands* 15 (June 1993): 111–119.

Haycox, Ernest, Jr. "'A Very Exclusive Party': A Firsthand Account of Building the Union Pacific Railroad." *Montana: The Magazine of Western History* 51 (Spring 2001): 20–35.

Heap, Gwinn Harris. *Central Route to the Pacific; by Gwinn Harris Heap, with Related Material....* Glendale, CA: Arthur H. Clark, 1957.

Heaton, John W. "'No Place to Pitch Their Teepees': Shoshone Adaptation to Mormon Settlers in Cache Valley, 1855–70." *Utah Historical Quarterly* 63 (Spring 1995): 158–171.

Henck, John B. *Field-Book for Railroad Engineers.* New York: D. Appleton and Company, 1854.

Hendricks, J. E. "Land Surveying." *The Analyst* 3 (July 1876): 109–111.

Hinton, Richard J. *Progress Report on Irrigation in the United States. Part I.* Washington: Government Printing Office, 1891.

Hinton, Wayne K. "Parowan Mormons Rescue the Great Pathfinder." *Southwest Utah Magazine* 2 (Winter 1994): 8–10.

Hirschfelder, Arlene B. *Photo Odyssey: Solomon Carvalho's Remarkable Western Adventure, 1853–54.* New York: Clarion Books, 2000.

Hirshson, Stanley P. *Grenville M. Dodge: Soldier, Politician, Railroad Pioneer.* Bloomington: Indiana University Press, 1967.

A Historical and Biographical Record of the Territory of Arizona. Chicago: McFarland & Poole, 1896.

Hodges, Almon D., Jr., ed. *Almon Danforth Hodges and His Neighbors: An Autobiographical Sketch of a Typical Old New Englander.* Boston, MA: Privately Printed, 1909.

Hodges, Frederick. Journals, 1867–1869. Levi O. Leonard Papers. Coll. MSC0159, box 20, fd. 2, Special Collections & Archives, University of Iowa Libraries.

Hoffman, Charles. "The Depression of the Nineties." *Journal of Economic History* 16 (June 1956): 137–164.

Holt, Ronald L. *Beneath These Red Cliffs: An Ethnohistory of the Utah Paiutes.* Logan: Utah State University Press, 2006.

Hooker, Bill. "The Journal of Mrs. Peter Martineau." *Wisconsin Magazine of History* 17 (September 1933): 72–76.

Horton, Zachary Ryan. "'Wherein Shall We Return?': A Historical and Analytical Examination of Lorenzo Snow's 1899 Reemphasis of Tithing." Master's Thesis, Brigham Young University, 2015.

Hotchkin, James H. *A History of the Purchase and Settlement of Western New York, and of the Rise, Progress, and Present State of the Presbyterian Church in that Section.* New York: M. W. Dodd, 1848.

Hovey, Edmund Otis. "A Geological Reconnaissance in the Western Sierra Madre of the State of Chihuahua, Mexico." *Bulletin of the American Museum of Natural History* 23 (June 1907): 401–442.

———. "The Western Sierra Madre of the State of Chihuahua, Mexico." *Bulletin of the American Geographical Society* 37, no. 9 (1905): 531–543.

Hovey, Merlin R. "Early History of Cache County." Typescript of serialized articles published in the *Herald Journal*, from January 1, 1923, to January 1, 1925. Bound copies held in Special Collections and Archives, Merrill–Cazier Library, Utah State University.

Hoyt, Franklin. "San Diego's First Railroad: The California Southern." *Pacific Historical Review* 23 (May 1954): 133–146.

Hubbard, Bill, Jr. *American Boundaries: The Nation, the States, the Rectangular Survey.* Chicago: University of Chicago Press, 2009.

Hudnutt, Joseph O. Letters to Grenville M. Dodge, 1868–1869. Microfilm copy, State Historical Society of Iowa.

Hunsaker, Q. Maurice, and Gwen Hunsaker Haws, eds. *History of Abraham Hunsaker and His Family.* Salt Lake City: Hunsaker Family Organization, 1957; Reprint, 2008.

Hurd, D. Hamilton, *History of Rockingham and Strafford Counties, New Hampshire with Biographical Sketches of Many of Its Pioneers and Prominent Men.* Philadelphia: J.W. Lewis & Co., 1882.

Hyde, Louis Howard, comp. "A Compilation of the Letters of Samuel B. Reed and Notes Concerning His Life." Unpublished compilation, 1895. Photocopy held in Special Collections & Archives, Merrill–Cazier Library, Utah State University.

Hyde, William. Journal, 1818–1873. MS d 1549, LDS Church History Library.

Ibsen, Charles A., and Patricia Klobus. "Fictive Kin Term Use and Social Relationships: Alternative Interpretations." *Journal of Marriage and the Family* 34 (November 1972): 615–620.

Iron County. Probate Court Minutes, 1853–1868, Series 17477, Utah State Archives and Records Center, Salt Lake City, Utah; originals in County Clerk's Office, Parowan, Utah.

Iron County. Surveys. Recorder's vault, County Recorder's Office, Iron County Offices, Parowan, Utah.

Irving, Gordon. "The Law of Adoption: One Phase of the Development of the Mormon Concept of Salvation, 1830–1900." *BYU Studies* 14 (Spring 1974): 291–314.

Ivins, Anthony W. Papers, 1875–1934. MSS B2, Utah State Historical Society.

Ivins, H. Grant. "Polygamy in Mexico as Practiced by the Mormon Church, 1895–1905." *Doctrine of the Priesthood* 1 (March 1981): 1–40.

Jackson, A[braham]. W[illard]. *James Martineau: A Biography and Study*. Boston: Little, Brown, and Co., 1901.

Jackson, Richard H. "Mormon Perception and Settlement." *Annals of the Association of American Geographers* 68 (1978): 317–334.

———. "The Mormon Village: Genesis and Antecedents of the City of Zion Plan." *BYU Studies* 17 (Winter 1977): 223–240.

———. "Myth and Reality: Environmental Perception of the Mormon Pioneers." *Rocky Mountain Social Science Journal* 9 (1972): 33–38.

———. "Religion and Landscape in the Mormon Culture Region." In *Dimensions in Human Geography*, edited by Karl W. Butzer, 100–127. Chicago: University of Chicago Department of Geography, Research Paper No. 186, 1978.

Jackson, W. Turrentine. *Wagon Roads West: A Study of Federal Road Surveys and Construction in the Trans-Mississippi West, 1846–1869*. Yale Western Americana Series, 9. New Haven and London: Yale University Press, 1964.

Jenson, Andrew, comp. *Church Chronology: Or, A Record of Important Events pertaining to the History of the Church of Jesus Christ of Latter-day Saints*. Salt Lake City: Andrew Jenson, 1886.

———. *Encyclopedic History of the Church of Jesus Christ of Latter-day Saints*. Salt Lake City: Deseret News Publishing Company, 1941.

———. *Latter-day Saint Biographical Encyclopedia: A Compilation of Biographical Sketches of Prominent Men and Women in the Church of Jesus Christ of Latter-day Saints*. 4 vols. Salt Lake City: A. Jenson History Co., 1901–36; reprint: Western Epics, 1971.

———. "Origin of Western Geographic Names." *Utah Genealogical and Historical Magazine* 10 (January 1919): 6–16; idem 10 (April 1919): 81–85; idem 10 (July 1919): 120–128; idem 10 (October 1919): 181–190; idem 11 (January 1920): 34–40; idem 11 (April 1920): 82–91; idem (July 1920): 141–144; idem 11 (October 1920): 170–177; idem 12 (January 1921): 41–48; idem 12 (July 1921): 125–130; idem 12 (October 1921): 188–192; and idem 13 (January 1922): 38–43.

Johnson, Annie Richardson. *Heartbeats of Colonia Diaz*. Mesa, AZ: By the author, 1972.

Johnson, Benjamin F. *My Life's Review: Autobiography of Benjamin Franklin Johnson*. Provo, UT: Grandin Book Co., 1997.

Johnson Family. Correspondence, 1896–1938. MS 14631, LDS Church History Library.

Johnson, J[ohn]. B[utler]. *The Theory and Practice of Surveying: Designed for the Use of Surveyors and Engineers Generally. But Especially for the Use of Students in Engineering*. New York: J. Wiley & Sons, 1886.

Johnson, Joel Hills. *Excerpts from a Journal or Sketch of the Life of Joel Hills Johnson (Brother to Benjamin F. Johnson)*. Dugway, UT: Pioneer Press, 1970?.

———. *Voice from the Mountains: Being a Testimony of the Truth of the Gospel of Jesus Christ, as Revealed by the Lord to Joseph Smith, Jr*. Salt Lake City: Juvenile Instructor Office, 1881.

Johnson, Royal A. *Adverse Report of the Surveyor General of Arizona, Royal A. Johnson, upon the Alleged Peralta Grant: A Complete Expose of Its Fraudulent Character*. Phoenix: Arizona Gazette Book and Job Office, 1890.

Johnson, Susan Elvira Martineau. Autobiography, 1874–1930s. MS f 164, item 1, LDS Church History Library.

Johnson, William Derby, Jr. Correspondence Typescripts, 1883–1915. MSS 1506, L. Tom Perry Special Collections and Manuscripts, Harold B. Lee Library, Brigham Young University.

———. Diaries, 1871–1894. Photocopy of holographs. MSS 1506, L. Tom Perry Special Collections and Manuscripts, Harold B. Lee Library, Brigham Young University.

Jones, Gerald E. *Animals and the Church*. Salt Lake City: Eborn Books, 2003.

Jones, Larry. "Site of Utter Party Massacre." *Idaho State Historical Society Reference Series*, No. 233, June 1993.

Jones, Sondra. *The Trial of Don Pedro León Luján: The Attack Against Indian Slavery and Mexican Traders in Utah*. Salt Lake City: University of Utah Press, 2000.

———. "'Redeeming' the Indian: The Enslavement of Indian Children in New Mexico and Utah." *Utah Historical Quarterly* 67 (Summer 1999): 220–241.

———. "Saints or Sinners? The Evolving Perceptions of Mormon–Indian Relations in Utah Historiography." *Utah Historical Quarterly* 72 (Winter 2004): 19–46.

Judd, Zodak Knapp. Autobiography, 1827–1884. MSS 18, Box 4, fd. 17, Special Collections and Archives, Merrill–Cazier Library, Utah State University.

Kearl, J. R., Clayne L. Pope, and Larry T. Wimmer. "Household Wealth in a Settlement Economy: Utah, 1850–1870." *Journal of Economic History* 40 (September 1980): 477–96.

Keen, Effie R. "Arizona's Governors." *Arizona Historical Review* 3 (October 1930): 7–20.

Kelly, Charles, ed. *Journals of John D. Lee, 1846–47 and 1859.* Salt Lake City: Western Printing Company, 1938; reprinted by University of Utah Press, 1984.

Kelly, Isabel T. "Southern Paiute Bands." *American Anthropologist* 36 (October–December 1934): 548–560.

Kelson, Aaron R. "'A Plea for the Horse': George Q. Cannon's Concern for Animal Welfare in Nineteenth-Century America." *BYU Studies* 38, no. 3 (1999): 47–61.

Kenner, Maude. "The Dedication of Our Home." *Chronicles of Courage* 5 (1994): 253–354.

Kenney, Scott G., ed. *Wilford Woodruff's Journal.* 9 vols. Midvale, UT: Signature Books, 1983.

Klein, Mary-Jo. *A Guide to Documentary Editing.* Second Edition. Baltimore, MD: Johns Hopkins University Press, 1998.

Klein, Maury. *Union Pacific: Birth of a Railroad, 1862–1893.* 2 vols. Garden City, NY: Doubleday, 1987.

Knack, Martha C. *Boundaries Between: The Southern Paiutes, 1775–1995.* Lincoln: University of Nebraska Press, 2001.

Knapp, Martin A. "The Social Effects of Transportation." *Annals of the American Academy of Political and Social Science* 20 (July 1902): 1–15.

Knecht, William L. and Peter L. Crawley, eds. *History of Brigham Young, 1847–1867.* Berkeley, CA: MassCal Associates, 1964.

Koepp, Donna P., ed. *Exploration and Mapping of the American West: Selected Essays.* Occasional Paper No. 1, Map and Geography Round Table of the American Library Association. Chicago: Speculum Orbis Press, 1986.

Koeppel, Gerard T. *Water for Gotham: A History.* Princeton, NJ: Princeton University Press, 2000.

Kolb, Franz. "The Northern Ute Indian Reservation: Establishing Portrayal and Change." Master's Thesis, Brigham Young University, 1983.

Korns, J. Roderic, and Dale L. Morgan, eds., *West from Fort Bridger: the Pioneering of the Immigrant Trails across Utah, 1846–1850.* Revised and updated by Will Bagley and Harold Schindler. Logan: Utah State University Press, 1995.

Kosterlitzky, Emilio. Collection, 1883–1959, AZ 333, Special Collections, University of Arizona Libraries, Tucson, AZ.

Krenkel, John H., ed. *The Life and Times of Joseph Fish, Mormon Pioneer.* Danville, IL: Interstate Printers and Publishers, 1970.

Kuh, Sydney. "The Pathology of Locomotor Ataxy." *Medical News* 64 (March 3, 1894): 227–230.

Kytle, Elizabeth. *Home on the Canal.* Baltimore: Johns Hopkins University Press, 1983.

Lane, Dixie Dillon. "Protecting the Family in the West: James Henry Martineau's Response to Interfaith Marriage." *Journal of Mormon History* 36 (Fall 2010): 1–17.

Larsen, Stan, ed. *A Ministry of Meetings: The Apostolic Diaries of Rudger Clawson.* Salt Lake City: Signature Books, 1993.

Larson, Gustive O. "Building of the Utah Central: A Unique Cooperative Enterprise." *Improvement Era* 28 (January 1925): 217–227.

———. ed. "Journal of the Iron County Mission, John D. Lee, Clerk." *Utah Historical Quarterly* 20 (April 1952): 109–134; idem, *Utah Historical Quarterly* 20 (July 1952): 253–282; and idem, *Utah Historical Quarterly* 20 (October 1952): 353–383.

———. "Land Contest in Early Utah." *Utah Historical Quarterly* 29 (October 1961): 309–325.

Lavender, David. *The History of Arizona's Pipe Spring National Monument.* Springdale, UT: Zion Natural History Association, 1997.

Lavis, F[red]. "The Construction of the Chihuahua & Pacific Railroad." *Engineering Record* 55 (March 2, 1907): 241–243.

LeBaron, E. Dale. *Benjamin Franklin Johnson: Friend to the Prophets.* Provo, UT: Grandin Book Co., 1997.

Lee, Hector. *The Three Nephites: The Substance and Significance of the Legend in Folklore.* Publication in Language and Literature, No. 2. Albuquerque: University of New Mexico Press, 1949.

Leighton, Albert C. "The Mule as a Cultural Invention." *Technology and Culture* 8 (January 1967): 45–52.

Leonard, Levi O. Collection, 1850–1942. MsC 159, Special Collections and Archives, University of Iowa Libraries.

Lewis, David. Journal, 1854–1857. MS 4598, LDS Church History Library.

Liepmann, Kate. *The Journey to Work: Its Significance for Industrial and Community Life.* New York: Oxford University Press, 1944.

Linford, Lawrence L. "Establishing and Maintaining Land Ownership in Utah Prior to 1869." *Utah Historical Quarterly* 42 (Spring 1974): 126–143.

Lippincott, Joseph Barlow. Papers, 1882–1942. Coll. LIPP, Water Resources Center Archives, University of California, Berkeley, CA.

Livermore, Lin. *Running Line: Recollections of Surveyors.* Washington, DC: U.S. Department of the Interior, Bureau of Land Management, 1991.

Lloyd, Jane-Dale. *El Proceso de Modernización Capitalista en el Nortoeste de Chihuahua, 1880–1910.* Mexico: Universidad Iberoamericana, Departamento de Historia, 1987.

———. *Cinco Ensayos Sobre Cultura Material de Ranceros y Medieros del Noroeste de Chihuahua, 1886–1910*. Mexico: Universidad Iberoamericana, Departamento de Historia, 2001.

Logan, Deborah Anna. *The Hour and the Woman: Harriet Martineau's "Somewhat Remarkable" Life*. Dekalb: Northern Illinois Press, 2002.

Logue, Larry M. "Modernization Arrested: Child Naming and the Family in a Utah Town." *Journal of American History* 74 (June 1987): 131–138.

Long, William Rodney. *Railways of Mexico*. Washington, DC: Government Printing Office, 1925.

Ludlow, Daniel H., ed. *Encyclopedia of Mormonism*. 5 vols. New York: Macmillan, 1992.

Lumholtz, Carl. *Unknown Mexico: A Record of Five Years' Exploration Among the Tribes of the Western Sierra Madre*. 2 vols. London: Macmillan and Co., 1902.

Lunt, Henry. Journal, 1850–1851. MSS HM 66417, Henry E. Huntington Library and Gallery, San Marino, California.

———. "Journal of the Journey of the Pioneers from Great Salt Lake City to Little Salt Lake." MSS SC 3046, L. Tom Perry Special Collections, Harold B. Lee Library, Brigham Young University.

———. Diaries, February 1, 1852–October 20, 1859. Uncatalogued, Special Collections and Archives, Gerald. R. Sherratt Library, Southern Utah University.

Lyman, Amasa Mason. Collection, 1832–1877. MS 829, LDS Church History Library.

Lyman, Edward Leo. "Alienation of an Apostle from His Quorum: The Moses Thatcher Case." *Dialogue: A Journal of Mormon Thought* 18 (Summer 1985): 67–91.

———. *Amasa Mason Lyman, Mormon Apostle and Apostate: A Study in Dedication*. Salt Lake City: University of Utah Press, 2009.

———. "Chief Kanosh: Champion of Peace and Forbearance." *Journal of Mormon History* 35 (Winter 2009): 157–207.

———. "The Demise of the San Bernardino Mormon Community, 1851–1857." *Southern California Quarterly* 65 (Winter 1983): 321–339.

———. "George Q. Cannon's Economic Strategy in the 1890s Depression." *Journal of Mormon History* 29 (April 2003): 4–41.

———. "Outmaneuvering the Octopus: Atchison, Topeka and Santa Fe." *California History* 67 (June 1988): 94–107.

———. *The Overland Journey from Utah to California: Wagon Travel from the City of Saints to the City of Angels*. Reno: University of Nevada Press, 2005.

———. *San Bernardino: The Rise and Fall of a California Community*. Salt Lake City: Signature Books, 1996.

———, and Larry L. Reese. *The Arduous Road: Salt Lake to Los Angeles, the Most Difficult Wagon Road in American History*. Victorville, CA: Lyman Historical Research and Publishing Co., 2001.

MacDonald, Alexander Findley. Collection. MS 9548, LDS Church History Library.

———. Journal, 1877–1885. MS 1450, fd. 2, LDS Church History Library.

Mackay, Kathryn. "The Strawberry Valley Reclamation Project and the Opening of the Uintah Indian Reservation." *Utah Historical Quarterly* 50 (Winter 1980): 68–89.

MacKinnon, William P. "'Lonely Bones': Leadership and Utah War Violence." *Journal of Mormon History* 33 (Spring 2007): 121–78.

———. "Sex, Subalterns, and Steptoe: Army Behavior, Mormon Rage, and Utah War Anxieties." *Utah Historical Quarterly* 76 (Summer 2008): 227–46.

———. *At Sword's Point, Part 1: A Documentary History of the Utah War to 1858.* Norman, OK: Arthur H. Clark Company, 2008.

———. *At Sword's Point, Part 2: A Documentary History of the Utah War, 1858–1859.* Norman, OK: Arthur H. Clark Company, 2016.

Macleod, William. *Catalogue of the Paintings, Statuary, Casts, Bronzes, &c. of the Corcoran Gallery of Art.* Washington, DC: Gibson Brothers, 1878.

Macnamara, Charles. "The First Official Photographer." *Scientific Monthly* 12 (January 1936): 68–74.

Madeira, Crawford Clark. *The Delaware and Raritan Canal: A History.* East Orange, NJ: Eastwood Press, 1941.

Madsen, Brigham D. *Gold Rush Sojourners in Great Salt Lake City, 1849 and 1850.* Salt Lake City: University of Utah Press, 1983.

———. "The Northwestern Shoshoni in Cache Valley." In *Cache Valley: Essays on Her Past and People*, edited by Douglas D. Alder, 28–44. Logan: Utah State University Press, 1976.

———. *The Shoshoni Frontier and the Bear River Massacre.* Salt Lake City: University of Utah Press, 1985.

———. "Shoshoni-Bannock Marauders on the Oregon Trail, 1859–1863." *Utah Historical Quarterly* 35 (Winter 1967): 3–30.

Maricopa County. Canal Books, Recorder's vault, Maricopa County Offices, Phoenix, Arizona.

Marquardt, H. Michael. *Early Patriarchal Blessings of the Church of Jesus Christ of Latter-day Saints.* Salt Lake City: Smith–Pettit Foundation, 2007.

Martineau, David. *Notes on the Pedigree of the Martineau Family Descended from Gaston Martineau Who Emigrated to England in 1686.* London: Elsom & Co., 1907.

Martineau Family Papers, 1884–1941. MS 18303, LDS Church History Library.

Martineau, George A. Autobiography, 1864–1906. Msd 2050, 7, 13, #15, LDS Church History Library.

Martineau, James Henry. "A Night of Anxiety." *Young Woman's Journal* 18 (October 1912): 445–47.

———. "A Stolen Child." *Contributor* 12 (December 1890): 75–78.

———. "A Tragedy of the Desert." *Improvement Era* 31 (July 1928): 771–72.

———. "A Wonderful Ride." *Contributor* 11 (August 1890): 397–98.

———. "Additional material written about Susan Johnson Martineau by her husband James H. Martineau." Special Collections and Manuscripts, Harold B. Lee Library, Brigham Young University.

———. "An Engineer's Tribulations." *Contributor* 12 (June 1891): 317–20.

———. Articles. MS 3784, LDS Church History Library.

———. "A Thirst in the Desert." *Contributor* 12 (February 1891): 155–58.

———. "Boyhood's Days." *Contributor* 12 (January 1891): 113.

———. "Chart Showing the Explorations of the Desert Camp," June 2, 1858. MS 4953, fd. 3, LDS Church History Library.

———. "Chasing Indians." *Young Woman's Journal* 20 (June 1909): 290–91.

———. Certificates, 1851–1876. MSS 235, L. Tom Perry Special Collections and Manuscripts, Harold B. Lee Library, Brigham Young University.

———. "Ciudad Chihuahua." *Contributor* 13 (September 1892): 501–503.

———. "Col. James H. Martineau." *Tullidge's Histories, (Vol. II)* (Salt Lake City: Juvenile Instructor, 1889), Biographical Appendix, pp. 68–79.

———. Collection, 1822–1932. MS 4786, LDS Church History Library.

———. Correspondence, 1848–1883. MS 9532, LDS Church History Library.

———. Diary, "My Life. James H. Martineau," 1850–1918. MS FAC 1499, Henry E. Huntington Library and Gallery, San Marino, California; location of original is currently unknown.

———. "Discourse by President Brigham Young, Delivered on Tuesday December 30, 1856, at the Legislative Assembly in the Social Hall. (Corrected) reported by James Henry Martineau." MS 5104, pp. 387–393, LDS Church History Library; transcription kindly provided by Michael Lyman.

———. "Frontier Life in Utah." *Contributor* 10 (July 1889): 349–352, idem, 10 (August 1889): 364–67, and idem, 10 (September 1889): 404–406.

———. "Genealogical Data of J. H. Martineau." Original manuscript in the possession of Elma Martineau Jones of Pima, Arizona; a photocopy kindly provided by Kevin C. Jones.

———. "History of the Mission Exploring the Southwest Deserts of Utah Territory &c in 1858." MS 4953, fd. 2, LDS Church History Library.

———. "History of the Parowan Stake, 1859–1860." Vault MS 56, L. Tom Perry Special Collections and Manuscripts, Harold B. Lee Library, Brigham Young University.

———. "How Wonderful Are Thy Works, Oh Lord!" *Improvement Era* 27 (August 1924): 955–956.

———. "Important Chronology." *Contributor* 14 (November 1892): 44–45.

———. "Is There Power in Prayer?" *Improvement Era* 8 (November 1904): 337–340.

———. "James H. Martineau Record & Negotiations, 1855–1860." Typescript; includes part A: "Book of Spoken Words"; and part B: Minutes of Meetings in Parowan. William Rees Palmer Collection, MS 1, Box 90, fds. 3 and 4, Special Collections and Archives, Gerald R. Sherratt Library, Southern Utah University.

———. Journal, 1859–1860. MS 320, LDS Church History Library.

———. "Journal of the Cache Military District, Reorganized August 5, 1869." Brigade muster rolls, returns, journal 1865–76; microfilm copy, Utah Reel 3, Special Collections and Archives, Merrill–Cazier Library, Utah State University.

———. Letter to Mr. F. E. Eldredge, July 23, 1907, "The Mountain Meadow Catastrophy [sic]." MS 467, Special Collections and Manuscripts, Harold B. Lee Library, Brigham Young University; transcription kindly provided by Will Bagley.

———. Letters, 1855. MS 5164, LDS Church History Library.

———. Map, 1858. MS 979, L. Tom Perry Special Collections and Manuscripts, Harold B. Lee Library, Brigham Young University.

———. "Modern and Ancient Arizona." *Contributor* 10 (February 1889): 130–33.

———. "Organization of the Iron Military District, June 1857." Iron County Militia Roster. Vault MSS 801, L. Tom Perry Special Collections and Manuscripts, Harold B. Lee Library, Brigham Young University.

———. "Our Girls. A Dance on Sunday." *Young Woman's Journal* 19 (February 1908): 72–74.

———. "Our Girls. An Indian Dinner Party." *Young Woman's Journal* 20 (February 1909): 88–89.

———. Oxford, Idaho, Survey of the City, 1864, Utah Reel 18, item 3, Special Collections and Archives, Merrill–Cazier Library, Utah State University.

———. "Pearls Collected from Church Works," 1887–1917. MSS 238, no. 108, Special Collections and Archives, Utah State University.

———. "Pioneer Sketches. A Ball in Early Days." *Young Woman's Journal* 1 (December 1889): 78–81.

———. "Pioneer Sketches. II. A Journey in 1854." *Contributor* 11 (March 1890): 180–84.

———. "Pioneer Sketches. III. A Time of Fear and Death." *Contributor* 11 (April 1890): 224–227.

———. "Pioneer Sketches. IV. Seeking a Refuge in the Desert—I." *Contributor* 11 (May 1890): 249–251.

———. "Pioneer Sketches. Utah in 1850." *Contributor* 12 (January 1891): 93–96.

———. "Pioneer Sketches. V. Seeking a Refuge in the Desert—II." *Contributor* 11 (June 1890): 296–300.

———. "Pioneer Sketches. VI. A Mystery of the Desert." *Contributor* 11 (July 1890): 342–344.

———. "Pioneer Sketches. VII. A Scouting Party." *Contributor* 11 (August 1890): 395–397.

———. "Pioneer Sketches. VIII. A Leap for Life or Death." *Contributor* 11 (September 1890): 419–423.

———. "Plat of College Lands." Survey made August 28–30, 1873. Cache County Archives Collection, Box 315.

———. "Pre–historic Races of Arizona." *Contributor* 10 (April 1889): 204–206.

———. "Prophecy Fulfilled." *Improvement Era* 5 (November 1901): 115–118.

———. "Report on the Logan Temple." CR 308/21, LDS Church History Library; copy in S. George Ellsworth Collection, Special Collections and Archives, Utah State University.

———. "Settlements in Arizona." MS P-F 63, Bancroft Manuscripts, Bancroft Library, University of California, Berkeley; transcription kindly provided by S. George Ellsworth.

———. "Song of the Torrent." *Contributor* 13 (March 1892): 215.

———. "The 'Big Olla' in Cave Valley." *Improvement Era* 24 (April 1921): 640–641.

———. "The Cross." *Contributor* 13 (September 1892): 487–488.

———. "The Magnetic Needle." *Contributor* 5 (April 1884): 270–273.

———. "The Military History of Cache Valley." *Tullidge's Histories, (Vol. II)* (Salt Lake City: Juvenile Instructor, 1889): 361–376.

———. "The Old Pueblo." *Contributor* 12 (September 1891): 423–426.

———. "The Resurrection Day." *Latter-day Saints' Millennial Star* 30 (September 26, 1868): 640.

———. "The Title of Liberty." *Contributor* 11 (June 1890): 312–313.

———. "To My Wife on Her Fiftieth Birthday." *Young Woman's Journal* 1 (May 1890): 246.

———. "To My Wife." *Young Woman's Journal* 1 (August 1890): 405.

———. "Traditions of the Deluge. I. The Chaldean Story." *Contributor* 12 (March 1891): 167–171.

———. "Traditions of the Deluge. II. Greek and Other Traditions." *Contributor* 12 (April 1891): 213–217.

———. "Truth." *Young Woman's Journal* 19 (February 1908): 69.

———. "Truth." *Young Woman's Journal* 2 (October 1890): 10.

———. "Twilight Memories." *Western Galaxy* 1 (April 1888): 193–194.

———. "Wisdom Tersely Expressed." *Young Woman's Journal* 1 (March 1890): 174–175.

———. "Woman's Power." *Young Woman's Journal* 1 (August 1890): 405–407.

Martineau, Joel H. "Colonia Oaxaca Settled." *Improvement Era* 53 (November 1950): 889–890, 892, and 894.

———. "History of the Mormon Colonies and Missionary Work in México." Microfilm, FHL INTL Film 35110, LDS Family History Library, Salt Lake City.

———. "Mormon Colonies in Mexico, 1876–1929." MIC A-410, Utah State Historical Society.

———. Untitled Biographical Material on James Henry Martineau. M270.1 M385m, held in the LDS Church History Library.

Martineau, LaVan. *Southern Paiutes: Legends, Lore, Language, and Lineage.* Las Vegas: KC Publications, 1992.

Martineau, Susan E. Johnson. "Joseph Smith the Prophet." *Young Woman's Journal* 17 (December 1906): 541–542.

———. "Almost an Indian Bride." *Young Woman's Journal* 18 (June 1907): 264–265.

———. "Autobiography." MSS 587, L. Tom Perry Special Collections and Manuscripts, Harold B. Lee Library, Brigham Young University.

———. Papers, ca. 1908–1972. MS 15994, LDS Church History Library.

———. "Record of Susan Ellen Johnson Martineau." L. Tom Perry Special Collections and Manuscripts, Harold B. Lee Library, Brigham Young University.

———. "Record of Susan E. Martineau." Original manuscript in the possession of Elma Martineau Jones of Pima, Arizona; a photocopy was kindly provided by Kevin C. Jones. Varies slightly to one of nearly the same title above.

Matheson, Annie I. "A History of Johnson Fort." Cedar City: Iron Camp of the Daughters of the Utah Pioneers, 1960.

Maxwell, James Riddle. Papers, 1867–1900. MS 170, Special Collections, University of Delaware Library.

McClintock, James H. *Arizona, Prehistoric—Aboriginal, Pioneer—Modern.* 3 vols. Chicago: S. J. Clarke Publishing Company, 1916.

———. *Mormon Settlement in Arizona.* Tucson: University of Arizona Press, 1985.

McDannell, Colleen. *Material Christianity: Religion and Popular Culture in America.* New Haven & London: Yale University Press, 1995.

McIntyre, Myron W., and Noel R. Barton, eds. *Christopher Layton.* Kaysville, UT.: Christopher Layton Family Organization, 1966.

McNeeley, John Hamilton. "The Railways of Mexico: A Study in Nationalization." *Southwestern Studies* 2 (Spring 1964): 1–53.

"Measures of Economic Changes in Utah, 1847–1947." *Utah Economic and Business Review* 7 (December 1947).

Meinig, D. W. "The Mormon Culture Region: Strategies and Patterns in the Geography of the American West, 1847–1964." *Annals of the Association of American Geographers* 55 (June 1965): 191–220.

Merrill, Mariner Wood. Diary, 1886–1890. Coll V Book 378, Special Collections and Archives, Merrill–Cazier Library, Utah State University.

Merrill, Melvin Clarence, ed. *Utah Pioneer and Apostle Marriner Wood Merrill and His Family*. Salt Lake City: N.p.: n.p, ca. 1937.

Meryon, Charles Lewis, ed. *Memoirs of the Lady Hester Stanhope, as Related by Herself in Conversations with Her Physician*. 3 vols. London: Henry Colburn, 1845.

"Mexico and the Mormons." *Western Galaxy* 1 (April 1888): 145–153.

Middleton, C. H. "Railroad Surveys—Camp and Field Life on the Union Pacific." *Scientific American Supplement*, No. 653, Vol. 26 (July 7, 1888): 10427–10428.

Miller, David Henry. "The Impact of the Gunnison Massacre on Mormon-Federal Relations: Colonel Edward Jenner Steptoe's Command in Utah Territory, 1854–1855." Master's Thesis, University of Utah, 1968.

Miller, Elbert E. "Agricultural Geography of Cache Valley, Utah-Idaho." PhD diss., University of Washington, 1952.

Mills, Elizabeth H. "The Mormon Colonies in Chihuahua after the 1912 Exodus." *New Mexico Historical Review* 29 (July 1954): 165–82; idem, 29 (October 1954): 290–310.

Milikien, Herbert C. "'Dead of the Bloody Flux': Cholera Stalks the Emigrant Trail." *Overland Journal* 14 (Autumn 1996): 4–11.

Mitchell, Albert O. "Pioneers and Players of Parowan." *Utah Humanities Review: A Regional Quarterly* 1 (January 1947): 38–52.

Moehring, Eugene P. *Urbanism and Empire in the Far West, 1840–1890*. Reno: University of Nevada Press, 2004.

Monkkonen, Eric M. *America Becomes Urban: The Development of U.S. Cities and Towns, 1780–1980*. Berkeley: University of California Press, 1988.

Moody, Francis W. Autobiography and Journal. MS 9137, LDS Church History Library.

Morgan, Dale L. *The Humboldt, Highroad of the West*. New York: Farrar & Rinehart, 1943.

Morris, Roland S. Papers, 1856–1988. MC214, Rare Books and Special Collections, Princeton University Library.

Morris, Thomas Burnside. Family Letters, 1862–1923. (Phi)1950, Historical Society of Pennsylvania.

———. Papers, 1861–2000. Coll. C1416, Special Collections & Manuscripts, Princeton University Library, Princeton.

Muhlestein, Robert M. "Utah Indians and the Indian Slave Trade: The Mormon Adoption Program and Its Effect on the Indian Slaves." Master's Thesis, Brigham Young University, 1991.

Naylor, Thomas H. "The Mormons Colonize Sonora: Early Trials at Colonia Oaxaca." *Arizona and the West* 20 (Winter 1978): 325–342.

Nelson, Peter Udall. *Arizona Pioneer Mormon: David King Udall, His Story and His Family.* Tucson: Arizona Silhouettes, 1959.

Nelson, William G. Dictation, 1903–1906. Microfilm of holograph, Utah Reel 106, pt. 10, Special Collections and Archives, Merrill–Cazier Library, Utah State University.

Newman, Aubrey. *The Stanhopes of Chevening: A Family Biography.* London: St. Martin's Press, 1969.

Nibley, Preston. *Stalwarts of Mormonism.* Salt Lake City: Deseret Book Company, 1954.

Nielson, Emma Cynthia. "The Development of Pioneer Pottery in Utah." Master's Thesis, Brigham Young University, 1963.

Norman, V. Garth. *The Parowan Gap: Nature's Perfect Observatory.* Salt Lake City: Cedar Fort, 2007.

Nuwuvi: A Southern Paiute History. Reno: Inter-Tribal Council of Nevada, 1976.

O'Donnovan, Connell. "The 1855 Murder of Isaac Whitehouse in Parowan, Utah." *Journal of Mormon History* 40 (Fall 2014): 130–157.

Olsen, Robert W., Jr. "Winsor Castle: Mormon Frontier Fort at Pipe Spring." *Utah Historical Quarterly* 34 (Summer 1966): 218–226.

O'Neal, Floyd A., and Stanford J. Layton, "Of Pride and Politics: Brigham Young as Indian Superintendent." *Utah Historical Quarterly* 46 (Summer 1978): 236–251.

Pace, D. Gene. "Changing Patterns of Mormon Financial Administration: Traveling Bishops, Regional Bishops, and Bishop's Agents, 1851–1888." *BYU Studies* 23 (1983): 1–12.

Packer, Murland R. *Life History of Elisha Hurd Groves (November 5, 1797–December 29, 1867) & Lucy Simmons (February 1, 1807–July 20, 1883): Special Bicentennial Edition Issued on the 200th Birthday of Elisha Hurd Groves.* Tehachapi, CA: By the author, 1990.

Palmer, William R. "Indian Names in Utah Geography." *Utah Historical Quarterly* 1 (January 1928): 5–26.

Palmquist, Peter, and Thomas R. Kailbourn. *Pioneer Photographers of the Far West: A Biographical Dictionary, 1840–1865.* Stanford, CA: Stanford University Press, 2000.

Parkin, Louise, and Beulah Gibson, eds. *A Voice from the Mountains: Life and Works of Joel Hills Johnson.* Mesa, AZ: Joel Hills Johnson Arizona Committee, 1982.

Parkinson, Samuel Rose. Journal, April 1873–October 1876. MS 17364, LDS Church History Library.

Parshall, Ardis E. "'Pursue, Retake & Punish': The 1857 Santa Clara Ambush." *Utah Historical Quarterly* 73 (Winter 2005): 64–86.

Partridge, Scott H., ed. *Thirteenth Apostle: The Diaries of Amasa Lyman, 1832–1877*. Salt Lake City: Signature Books, 2016.

Pattison, William D. *Beginnings of the American Rectangular Land Survey System, 1784–1800*. Department of Geography Research Paper No. 50. Chicago: University of Chicago Press, 1957.

———. "Use of the U.S. Public Land Survey Plats and Notes as Descriptive Sources." *Professional Geographer* 8 (January 1956): 10–14.

Pease, Harold W. "The Life and Works of William Horne Dame." Master's Thesis, Brigham Young University, 1971.

Peden, Linda Sue. "Land Laws, Water Monopoly, and Lewis Wolfley in Gila Bend, Arizona." Master's Thesis, Arizona State University, 1997.

Pelzer, Louis. "Pioneer Stage-coach Travel." *Mississippi Valley Historical Review* 23 (June 1936): 3–26.

Pendleton, Mark A. "Dr. Calvin Crane Pendleton." *Utah Historical Quarterly* 10 (January–October 1942): 34–36.

Peterson, Charles S. "A Mormon Town: One Man's West." *Journal of Mormon History* 3 (1976): 3–12.

———. "The Valley of the Bear River and the Movement of Culture Between Utah and Idaho." *Utah Historical Quarterly* 47 (Spring 1979): 194–214.

———. *Take Up Your Mission: Mormon Colonizing Along the Little Colorado River, 1870–1900*. Tucson: University of Arizona Press, 1973.

Peterson, F. Ross. *A History of Cache County*. Salt Lake City: Utah State Historical Society and Cache County Council, 1997.

Peterson, Janet, comp. "Clarence King's 40th Parallel Survey Across the Great Basin and the Rediscovery of Lake Marian." *Northeastern Nevada Historical Society Quarterly* (2001): 2–21.

Peterson, John Alton. *Utah's Black Hawk War*. Salt Lake City: University of Utah Press, 1998.

———. "Warren Stone Snow, a Man in Between: The Biography of a Mormon Defender." Master's Thesis, Brigham Young University, 1985.

Peterson, Paul H. "Brigham Young and the Mormon Reformation." In *Lion of the Lord: Essays on the Life and Service of Brigham Young*, edited by Susan Easton Black and Larry C. Porter, 244–261. Salt Lake City: Deseret Book, 1995.

Pfefferkorn, Ignaz. *Sonora: A Description of the Province*. Translated and annotated by Theodore E. Treutlein. Albuquerque: University of New Mexico Press, 1949.

Pletcher, David. M. "The Development of Railroads in Sonora." *Inter-American Economic Affairs* 1 (March 1948): 3–45.

———. *Rails, Mines, and Progress: Seven American Promoters in Mexico, 1867–1911*. Ithaca, NY: Cornell University Press; American Historical Association, 1958.

Portrait and Biographical Record of Arizona. Chicago: Chapman Publishing Co., 1901.

Powell, Fred Wilbur. *The Railroads of Mexico*. Boston: Stratford Co., 1921.

Powell, John Wesley. *Indian Linguistic Families of America, North of Mexico*. Seventh Annual Report of the Bureau of Ethnology. Washington, DC: Government Printing Office, 1891.

———— et al. *Report on the Lands of the Arid Region of the United States*. 2nd ed. Washington, DC: Government Printing Office, 1879.

Powers, Ramon, and Gene Younger. "Cholera on the Overland Trails, 1832–1869." *Kansas Quarterly* 5 (Spring 1973): 32–49.

Preston, William B. Papers, 1857–1919. MSS 268, Special Collections and Archives, Merrill–Cazier Library, Utah State University.

Pulsipher, Lynn. "Post-1890 Plural Marriage in Mexico between 1890 and 1904." Senior seminar paper, Brigham Young University, 1977.

Pusey, Merlo J. *Builders of the Kingdom: George A. Smith, John Henry Smith, George Albert Smith*. Provo, UT: Brigham Young University Press, 1981.

Quinn, D. Michael. *Early Mormonism and the Magic World View*, Revised and enlarged. Salt Lake City: Signature Books, 1998.

————. "LDS Church Authority and New Plural Marriages, 1890–1904." *Dialogue: A Journal of Mormon Thought* 18 (Spring 1985): 9–105.

————. *The Mormon Hierarchy: Extensions of Power*. Salt Lake City: Signature Books; Smith Research Associates, 1997.

Ramenofsky, Elizabeth L. *From Charcoal to Banking: The I. E. Solomons of Arizona*. Tucson, AZ: Westernlore Press, 1984.

"Recent Works on Topographical Surveying." *Science* 8 (November 19, 1886): 463–66.

Reed, Samuel B. "Biographical Material." Levi Leonard Collection, MsC 159, box 58, University of Iowa Libraries.

Reid, Robert K. "Letter No. 3. Official List of Killed and Wounded at the Battle of Bear River." *Tullidge's Quarterly Magazine* 1 (January 1881): 194–196.

Reinhartz, Dennis, and Charles Colley. *The Mapping of the American Southwest*. College Station: Texas A&M University Press, 1987.

Reeder, Clarence A., Jr. "The History of Utah's Railroads, 1869–1883." PhD diss., University of Utah, 1970.

Reeder, Ray M. "The Mormon Trail: A History of the Salt Lake to Los Angeles Route to 1869." Master's Thesis, Brigham Young University, 1966.

Reese, Robert E., and Osborne, George E. "Early Utah Materia Medica: Priddy Meeks." *American Journal of Pharmaceutical Education* 18 (July 1954): 401–409.

Reeves, Brian D., ed. "Two Massachusetts Forty-Niner Perspectives on the Mormon Landscape, July–August 1849." *BYU Studies* 38, no. 3 (1999): 123–144.

"Reminiscences of Morris R. Locke." *Prairie Schooner*, Jersey County Historical Society, Spring 1986.

Reps, John W. *The Forgotten Frontier: Urban Planning in the American West Before 1890.* Columbia: University of Missouri Press, 1981.

Resneck, Samuel. "Distress, Relief, and Discontent in the United States During the Depression of 1873–1878." *Journal of Political Economy* 58 (December 1950); 494–512.

———. "Unemployment, Unrest, and Relief in the United States during the Depression of 1893–1897." *Journal of Political Economy* 61 (August 1953): 324–345.

Richards Family. Collection, 1837–1961. MS 1215, LDS Church History Library.

Richards, Heber G. "George M. Ottinger: Pioneer Artist of Utah." *Western Humanities Review* 3 (July 1949): 209–218.

Richards, Franklin D., and James A. Little, comps. *A Compendium of the Doctrines of the Gospel.* Salt Lake City: George Q. Cannon & Sons, 1892.

Richmond, Katharine Fall. *John Hayes of Dover, New Hampshire: A Book of His Family.* 2 vols. Tyingsboro, MA: Higginson Book Company, 1936.

Ricks, Joel Edward. *The Beginnings of Settlement in Cache Valley*, Twelfth Annual Faculty Research Lecture. Logan, UT: Utah State Agricultural College, 1953.

———. *Forms and Methods of Early Mormon Settlement in Utah and the Surrounding Region, 1847 to 1877.* Monograph Series, Volume XI, no. 2. Logan, UT: Utah State University Press, 1964.

———. Papers, 1850–1972. MSS 114, Special Collections and Archives, Merrill–Cazier Library, Utah State University.

———, and Everett L. Cooley. *The History of a Valley: Cache Valley, Utah-Idaho.* Logan, UT: Cache Valley Centennial Commission, 1956.

Riedesel, Paul L. "Who Was Harriet Martineau?" *Journal of the History of Sociology* 3 (Spring–Summer 1981): 63–80.

Riggs, Effel Harmon Burrow. *History of Hatch, Utah and Associated Towns Asay and Hillsdale.* Beaver, UT: Beaver Printing Co., 1978.

Ristow, Walter William. *American Maps and Mapmakers: Commercial Cartography in the Nineteenth Century.* Detroit: Wayne State University Press, 1985.

Roberts, Peter J. "Colonia Juárez: A Mormon Enclave in México." Master's Thesis, University of Kansas, 1970.

Robinson, Phil. *Sinners and Saints. A Tour Across the States, and Round Them; with Three Months among the Mormons.* Boston: Roberts Brothers, 1883.

Roediger, David R., and Philip. S. Foner. *Our Own Time: A History of American Labor and the Working Day.* New York: Greenwood Press, 1989.

Rogers, W. Lane. "From Colonia Dublán to Binghampton: The Mormon Odyssey of Frederick, Nancy, and Amanda Williams." *Journal of Arizona History* 35 (Spring 1994): 19–46.

Rolle, Andrew F. "Two Explorers on the Trail to California: Carvalho and Frémont." *California History* 73 (Fall 1994): 182–187.

Rollins, George W. "Land Policies of the United States as Applied to Utah to 1910." *Utah Historical Quarterly* 20 (July 1952): 239–251.

Romer, Christina. "Spurious Volatility in Historical Unemployment Data." *Journal of Political Economy* 94 (February 1986): 1–37.

Romney, Thomas Cottam. *The Mormon Colonies in Mexico*. Salt Lake City: University of Utah Press, 2005.

Rosenberg, Charles E. *The Cholera Years: The Unites States in 1832, 1849, and 1866*. Chicago and London: University of Chicago Press, 1962.

Rosenvall, Lynn A. "Mormon Settlement Plats: Their Design and Origin." Typewritten manuscript, University of Calgary, n.d.

———. "Mormon Settlement Plats: Their Design and Origin." *Great Plains-Rocky Mountain Geographical Journal* 1 (1972): 88–93.

Roskelly, Samuel. Family Papers, 1859–1908. MSS 65, Special Collections and Archives, Merrill–Cazier Library, Utah State University.

Roskruge, George James. Papers, 1881–1897. AZ 535, Special Collections, University of Arizona Library, Tucson.

———. Papers and Surveying Documents, 1872–1900. MS 0697, Arizona Historical Society, Southern Arizona Division, Tucson, Arizona.

———. Photo Collection, 1875–1900. PC 114, Arizona Historical Society, Southern Arizona Division, Tucson.

Roth, Mitchel. "Cholera Summer: Independence, St. Joseph, and the Path of Contagion." *Gateway Heritage* 15 (Summer 1994): 20–29.

———. "Cholera Treatment in the Nineteenth Century." *Gateway Heritage* 15 (Summer 1994): 27.

Rushton, Patricia. "Cholera and Its Impact on Nineteenth-Century Mormon Migration." *BYU Studies* 44 (2005): 123–144.

St. Joseph Stake. Letterpress Copybooks, 1885–1888, 1898. LR 7781/21, LDS Church History Library.

Salas, Miguel Tinker. *In the Shadow of the Eagles: Sonora and the Transformation of the Border during the Porfiriato*. Berkeley: University of California Press, 1997.

Sanderlin, Walter. *The Great National Project: A History of the Chesapeake and Ohio Canal*. Baltimore: Johns Hopkins Press, 1946.

Scales, John, ed. "Some Descendants of Deacon John Dam of Dover, N. H., 1633." *New England Historical and Genealogical Register* 65 (July 1911): 212–219, idem, 65 (October 1911): 311–314.

Scarlett, Timothy James, Robert J. Speakman, and Michael D. Glascock. "Pottery in the Mormon Economy: An Historical and Archaeometric Study." *Historical Archaeology* 41, no. 4 (2007): 70–95.

Schindler, Harold. "The Bear River Massacre: New Historical Evidence." *Utah Historical Quarterly* 67 (Fall 1999): 300–308.

Schivelbusch, Wolfgang. *The Railway Journey: The Industrialization of Time and Space in the 19th Century.* Berkeley: University of California Press, 1986.

Schneider, David M., and George C. Homans. "Kinship Terminology and the American Kinship System." *American Anthropologist* 57 (December 1955): 1194–1208.

Schnore, Leo F. "The Separation of Home and Work: A Problem for Human Ecology." *Social Forces* 32 (May 1954): 336–343.

Schubert, Frank N. *Vanguard of Expansion: Army Engineers in the Trans-Mississippi West, 1819–1979.* Washington, DC: Historical Division, Office of Administrative Services; Office of the Chief of Engineers, 1980.

Schulman, Frank. *James Martineau: "This Conscience-Intoxicated Unitarian."* Chicago: Meadville Lombard Press, 2002.

Schwendiman, Anita Martineau. *Family History of Nephi Martineau and Emmeline Knowles Martineau.* Newdale, ID: By the author, 1987.

Scott, Robert F. "What Happened to the Benders?" *Western Folklore* 9 (October 1950): 327–337.

Seegmiller, Janet Burton. *A History of Iron County: Community above Self.* Salt Lake City: Utah State Historical Society; Iron County Commission, 1998.

Seegmiller, William Henry. "Fish Lake and Surroundings." *Juvenile Instructor* 13 (July 15, 1878): 165.

———. "Peace Made with the Indians at Fish Lake, Sevier County." *Juvenile Instructor* 37 (August 1, 1902): 472–473

Shannon, Donald H. *The Utter Disaster on the Oregon Trail: The Utter and Van Ornum Massacres of 1860.* Snake Country Series, Vol. 2. Caldwell, ID: Snake Country Publishing, 1993.

Shirts, Morris A. and Parry, William T. "The Demise of the Deseret Iron Company: Failure of the Brick Furnace Lining Technology." *Utah Historical Quarterly* 56 (Winter 1988): 23–35.

Shlaer, Robert. *Sights Once Seen: Daguerreotyping Frémont's Last Expedition through the Rockies.* Santa Fe: Museum of New Mexico Press, 2000.

Shoumatoff, Alex. *The Mountain of Names: A History of the Human Family.* New York: Simon and Schuster, 1985.

Simkins, Larry Dean. "The Rise of Southeastern Salt River Valley: Tempe, Mesa, Chandler, Gilbert, 1871–1920." PhD diss. Arizona State University, 1989.

Simmonds, A. J. *The Gentile Comes to Cache Valley: A Study of the Logan Apostasies of 1874 and the Establishment of Non-Mormon Churches in Cache Valley, 1873–1913.* Logan: Utah State University Press, 1976.

———, ed. *History of Weston, Idaho, by Lars Fredrickson.* Western Text Society, Number 5. Logan: Utah State University Press, 1972.

———. "Idaho's Last Colony: Northern Cache Valley under the Test Oath, 1872–1896." *Idaho Yesterdays* 32 (Summer 1988): 2–14.

———. "Southeast Idaho as a Pioneer Mormon Safety Valve." *Idaho Yesterdays* 23 (Winter 1980): 20–30.

Slater, H. D. "The Golden Heart of the Sierra Madre." *The American Monthly Review of Reviews* 17, no. 99 (April 1898): 439–442.

Smaby, Beverly P. "The Mormons and the Indians: Conflicting Ecological Systems in the Great Basin." *American Studies* 16 (Spring 1975): 35–48.

Smart, Charles E. *The Makers of Surveying Instruments in America Since 1700*. 2 vols. Troy, NY: Regal Art Press, 1962–67.

Smart, Willam B., and Donna Toland Smart, eds. *Over the Rim: The Parley P. Pratt Exploring Expedition to Southern Utah, 1849–1850*. Logan: Utah State University Press, 1999.

Smiles, Samuel. *The Huguenots: Their Settlements, Churches, and Industries in England and Ireland*. New York: Harper & Brothers, 1867.

Smith, Cornelius C., Jr. *Emilio Kosterlitzky: Eagle of Sonora and the Southwest Border*, Frontier Military History Series, 7. Glendale, CA: Arthur H. Clark, 1970.

Smith, George A. Diary, 1850–1851. MSS A-654, Utah State Historical Society.

———. Family Papers, 1731–1968. MS 0036, Special Collections and Manuscripts, Marriott Library, University of Utah.

———. Papers, 1834–1875. MS 1322, LDS Church History Library.

Smith, Hyrum G. "Patriarchs and Patriarchal Blessings." *Improvement Era* 33 (May 1930): 465–466.

Smith, Jeffrey S., and Benjamin N. White. "Detached from Their Homeland: The Latter-day Saints of Chihuahua, Mexico." *Journal of Cultural Geography* 21 (Spring/Summer 2004): 57–76.

Smith, Jessie Nathaniel. Papers, 1845–1970. MSS 503, L. Tom Perry Special Collections and Manuscripts, Harold B. Lee Library, Brigham Young University.

———. "An Adventure Among the Pah Utes." *Juvenile Instructor* 13 (February 15, 1878): 40–41.

Smith, John Lyman. Letter to James H. Martineau, August 24, 1857. MS 16651, LDS Church History Library.

Smith, Karen L. "The Campaign for Water in Central Arizona, 1890–1903." *Arizona & the West* 23 (Summer 1981): 127–148.

Smith, Lucy Toulmin. "The Walloon Church at Norwich in 1589." In *The Norfolk Antiquarian Miscellany*, edited by Walter Rye, Ser. 1, Vol. 2, pt. 1, 91–148. Norwich: A. H. Goose and Co., 1880.

Smith, Oliver R., ed. *Six Decades in the Early West: The Journal of Jesse Nathaniel Smith, Diaries and Papers of a Mormon Pioneer, 1834–1906*. 3rd edition. Provo, UT: Jesse N. Smith Family Association, 1970; second printing, revised, 1997.

Smith, Oliver R. and Dorothy H. Williams, ed. *The Family of Jesse Nathaniel Smith, 1834–1906*. Snowflake, AZ: Jesse N. Smith Family Association, 1978.

Smith, Ralph. Diary, 1859–1897. Vault Coll MS 43, Special Collections and Archives Merrill–Cazier Library, Utah State University.

Smith, William Lelanel. "Impacts of the Mexican Revolution: The Mormon Experience, 1910–1946." PhD diss., Washington State University, 2000.

Snow, William J. "Some Source Documents on Utah Indian Slavery." *Utah Historical Quarterly* 2 (July 1929): 76–90.

———. "Utah Indians and the Spanish Slave Trade." *Utah Historical Quarterly* 2 (July 1929): 67–75.

Soltow, Lee, and Dean L. May. "The Distribution of Mormon Wealth and Income in 1857." *Explorations in Economic History* 16 (1979): 151–162.

Sorensen, A. N., ed. "The History of Isaac Sorensen: Selections from a Personal Journal." *Utah Historical Quarterly* 24 (January 1956): 49–70.

Sorensen, Isaac. "History of Isaac Sorensen and Mary Jacobsen Sorensen." 920 So68, bk. 1, Special Collections and Archives, Merrill–Cazier Library, Utah State University.

———. History of Mendon, 1857–1919. Vault Coll MS 43, Special Collections and Archives, Merrill–Cazier Library, Utah State University.

Specht, George J., Arthur Sherburne Hardy, John Bach McMaster, and Henry Francis Walling. *Topographical Surveying*. New York: D. Van Nostrand, 1884.

Spence, Mary Lee, ed. *The Expeditions of John Charles Frémont, Volume 3: Travels from 1843 to 1854*. Urbana and Chicago: University of Illinois Press, 1984.

Spencer, Joseph E. "The Development of Agricultural Villages in Southern Utah." *Agricultural History* 14 (October 1940): 181–89.

Sprague, Warren Vincent. *Sprague Families in America*. Rutland, VT: The Tuttle Company, 1913.

Spude, Robert L. "A Land of Sunshine and Silver: Silver Mining in Central Arizona, 1871–1885." *Journal of Arizona History* 16 (Spring 1975): 29–76.

———. *Promontory Summit, May 10, 1869: A History of the Site Where the Central Pacific and Union Pacific Railroads Joined to Form the First Transcontinental Railroad*.... Santa Fe, NM: Cultural Resources Management, Intermountain Region, National Park Service, 2005.

Standing, A. R. "Through the Uintas: History of the Carter Road." *Utah Historical Quarterly* 35 (Summer 1967): 256–267.

Staack, J. G. *Triangulation in Utah, 1871–1934*. United States Geological Survey, Bulletin 913. Washington, DC: Government Printing Office, 1940.

Stanhope, Ghita, and George Peabody Gooch. *The Life of Charles, Third Earl Stanhope*. New York: Longmans, Green and Co., 1914.

Stapley, Jonathan A. "Adoptive Sealing Ritual in Mormonism." *Journal of Mormon History* 37 (Summer 2011): 53–117.

———, and Kristine Wright. "The Forms and the Power: The Development of Mormon Ritual Healing to 1847." *Journal of Mormon History* 35 (Summer 2009): 42–87.

Steele, Ian K. *Betrayals: Fort William Henry and the "Massacre."* New York: Oxford University Press, 1990.

Steele, John. Papers, 1847–1936. Vault MSS 528, L. Tom Perry Special Collections and Manuscripts, Harold B. Lee Library, Brigham Young University.

———. "Extracts from the Journal of John Steele." *Utah Historical Quarterly* 6 (January 1933): 3–28.

Steeples, Douglas. "Origins of the Depression of the 1890s: An Economy in Transition." *Essays in Economic and Business History* 14 (1996): 167–183.

Steeples, Douglas, and David O. Whitten. *Democracy in Desperation: The Depression of 1893*. Westport, CT: Greenwood Press, 1998.

Stegmaier, Mark Joseph, ed. *James Milligan: His Journal of Fremont's Fifth Expedition, 1853–1854; His Adventurous Life on Land and Sea*. Glendale, CA: Arthur H. Clark, 1988.

Stevens, Michael E., and Steven B. Burg. *Editing Historical Documents: A Handbook of Practice*. Lanham, MD: AltaMira Press, 1997.

Stewart, Andrew Jackson. Dictation, 1886. MS P-F 56, Bancroft Manuscripts, Bancroft Library, University of California, Berkeley.

Stewart, Lowell O. *Public Land Surveys: History Instructions, Methods*. Ames, IA: Collegiate Press, 1935.

Stoffle, Richard W., Kristine L. Jones, and Henry F. Dobyns. "Direct European Transmission of Old World Pathogens to Numic Indians During the Nineteenth Century." *American Indian Quarterly* 19 (Spring 1995): 181–203.

Stolebrand, V[asa]. E. "Irrigation in Arizona." Arizona Agricultural Experiment Station, Bulletin No. 3. Tucson: University of Arizona, October, 1891.

Stott, Clifford L. *Search for Sanctuary: Brigham Young and the White Mountain Expedition*. Salt Lake City: University of Utah Press, 1984.

Stout, Wayne Dunham. *A History of Colonia Dublán and Guadalupe, Mexico*. Salt Lake City: By the author, 1975.

Strack, Don. *Ogden Rails: A History of Railroads in Ogden, Utah from 1869 to Today*. Ogden, UT: Railway & Locomotive Historical Society, Golden Spike Chapter, 1997.

Sturhahn, Joan. *Carvalho, Artist—Photographer—Adventurer—Patriot: Portrait of a Forgotten American*. Merrick, NY: Richwood Publishing Company, 1976.

Sudweeks, Leslie L. "The Miracle of the Piedras Verdes: The Story of the Founding of Colonia Juarez." *Improvement Era* 49 (November 1946): 28–29, 40–41.

Surveyor's Notebooks and Maps of Cache Valley, 1856–1915, Utah and Idaho. Microfiche copy, Special Collections and Archives, Merrill–Cazier Library,

Utah State University; originals at The Bureau of Land Management, Salt Lake City.

Talbot, E. H., and H. R. Hobart. *The Biographical Directory of the Railway Officials of America*. Chicago and New York: The Railway Age Publishing Company, 1885.

Taylor, Fenton W., ed. *The 25th Stake of Zion, 1883–1983*. Thatcher: Thatcher Arizona Stake, 1983.

Taylor, John. Letter to Christopher Layton, February 20, 1883. MS 13744, LDS Church History Library.

Teasdale, George. Papers, 1770–1984. MS 678, Special Collections and Manuscripts, Marriott Library, University of Utah.

Teeples, C. A. "The First Pioneers of the Gila Valley." *Arizona Historical Review* 1 (January 1929): 74–78.

Tenny, Ammon M. Papers, 1884–1923. MS 785, Arizona Historical Society, Tucson, Arizona.

Thatcher, Moses, Sr. Diary and Notebook, 1884–1885. MS 17375, LDS Church History Library.

———. Family Papers, 1866–1923. MSS 22, Special Collections and Archives, Merrill–Cazier Library, Utah State University.

———. Letters, 1882–1884. MSS A-2268, Utah State Historical Society.

Thompkins, Christopher R. *The Croton Dams and Aqueduct*, Images of America. Charleston, SC: Arcadia Publishing, 2000.

Thrapp, Dan L. *Encyclopedia of Frontier Biography*. 3 vols. Glendale, CA: Arthur H. Clark, 1988.

Tingey, Willis A. "Early Land Surveys and Land Allotments in Cache Valley." Typewritten manuscript from the Papers of the Cache Valley Historical Society, vols. I–II, 1951–1953, 29–36. MSS 43, Special Collections and Archives, Merrill–Cazier Library, Utah State University.

Trennert, Robert A., Jr. "The Southern Pacific Railroad of Mexico." *Pacific Historical Review* 35 (August 1966): 265–284.

Truett, Samuel. "Transnational Warrior: Emilio Kosterlitzky and the Transformation of the U.S.-Mexico Borderlands." In *Continental Crossroads: Remapping U.S.-Mexico Borderlands History*, edited by Samuel Truett and Elliott Young, 241–270. Durham: Duke University Press, 2004.

Tullidge, Edward William. *Tullidge's Histories, (Vol. II), Containing the History of all the Northern, Eastern, and Western Counties of Northern Utah; also the Counties of Southern Idaho*. Salt Lake City: Juvenile Instructor, 1889.

Tullis, F. LaMond. "Early Mormon Exploration and Missionary Activities in Mexico." *Brigham Young University Studies* 22 (Summer 1982): 289–310.

———. *Mormons in Mexico: The Dynamics of Faith and Culture*. Logan: Utah State University Press, 1987.

Turley, Clarence F., and Anna Tenney Turley. *History of the Mormon Colonies in Mexico (The Juarez Stake), 1885–1980*. Salt Lake City: Publishers Press, 1996.

Turley, Richard E., Sr. "A Brief History of Edward Franklin Turley (1869–1940) & Ida Elizabeth Eyring Turley (1874–1952)." Unpublished compilation, Salt Lake City, Utah, 2006.

Turley, Richard E., Jr., and Ronald W. Walker, eds., *Mountain Meadows Massacre: The Andrew Jenson and David H. Morris Collections*. Provo: BYU Studies; Brigham Young University Press, 2009.

Turner, D. L. "Forgotten City of the Saints: Mormons, Native Americans, and the Founding of Lehi." *Journal of Arizona History* 47 (Spring 2006): 57–82.

U.S. Bureau of the Mint. *Report of the Director of the Mint Upon the Statistics of the Production of the Precious Metals in the United States*. Washington, DC: Government Printing Office, 1882.

U.S. Coast and Geodetic Survey. *The Plane-Table and Its Use in Topographical Surveying. From the Papers of the United States Coast Survey*. New York: D. Van Nostrand, 1869.

U.S. Congress. Senate. Committee on Pensions. *James Henry Martineau*. S. Rpt. 903, 58th Cong., 2d sess., 1904.

U.S. Congress. Senate. *Congressional Record*. 58th Cong., 2d sess., 1904, 38, pt. 3: 2668, and idem, pt. 4:3205.

U.S. Congress. House. *Report Chief Engineer of the Union Pacific Railroad*. H. Ex. Doc. 132, 41st Cong., 2nd Session, 1870.

U.S. Congress, *Statues at Large*, Vol. 38, pt. 2, 1915, p. 1286.

U.S. Senate. *Senate Journal*, 63rd Cong.,1st sess.,13 June 1913, 90.

U.S. Department of the Interior. Map, "Part of Uinta Indian Reservation, Utah, to be disposed of under Act of March 3, 1905 and President's Proclamation, dated July 14, 1905." [drawn by I. P. Berthrong]. Scale ca. 1: 130,000.

U.S. Department of the Interior. General Land Office, J.A. Williamson, Commissioner. Territory of Utah. 1879. Compiled from the Official Records of the General Land Office and Other Sources by C. Roeser, Principal Draughtsman G.L.O. Photo lith & print by Julius Bien 16 & 18 Park Place N.Y. Scale 1: 950,400.

Udall, David King. Papers, 1875–1930. MS 294, Special Collections, University of Arizona Library, Tucson.

Union Pacific Coal Company. *History of the Union Pacific Coal Mines, 1868–1940*. Omaha: The Colonial Press, 1940.

Union Pacific Railroad Company. Utah and Wyoming Surveys, 1865–1868. MSS 4181, Box 1, L. Tom Perry Special Collections and Manuscripts, Harold B. Lee Library, Brigham Young University.

United States, Surveyor General, Arizona. Register of Survey Requests, 1880–1914. Microfilm copy, FHL US/CAN Film 1639163, LDS Family History Library, Salt Lake City.

Upton, Larry T., and Larry D. Ball. "Who Robbed Major Wham? Facts and Folklore Behind Arizona's Great Paymaster Robbery." *Journal of Arizona History* 38 (Summer 1997): 99–134.

Urbanek, Mae. *Wyoming Place Names*. Missoula, MT: Mountain Press Publishing Company, 1988.

Utah Territorial Militia. Records, 1849–1877, 1905–ca. 1917, Series 2210, Utah State Archives and Records Service, Salt Lake City.

Van Cott, John W. *Utah Place Names: A Comprehensive Guide to the Origins of Geographic Names: A Compilation*. Salt Lake City: University of Utah Press, 1990.

VanHoak, Stephen P. "And Who Shall Have the Children? The Indian Slave Trade in the Southern Great Basin, 1800–1865." *Nevada Historical Society Quarterly* 41 (Spring 1998): 3–25.

Van Slyke, Daniel. Papers, 1795–1880. Uncatalogued, Humanities-Manuscripts & Archives Division, New York Public Library.

Van Slyke, Napoleon B. Papers, 1822–1909. M75-329, 376; M76-139; M79-362; M82-363, Wisconsin Historical Society.

Van Wagoner, Richard S. *Mormon Polygamy: A History*. Salt Lake City: Signature Books, 1989.

Vaughn, Jerome H., comp., *Resources of Graham County*. Solomonville, AZ: Board of Supervisors, 1888.

Veatch, A[rthur]. C[lifford]. *Geography and Geology of a Portion of Southwestern Wyoming with Special Reference to Coal and Oil*. United States Geological Survey, Professional Paper No. 56. Washington, DC: Government Printing Office, 1907.

Verite, "The Battle of Bear River." *Tullidge's Quarterly Magazine* 1 (January 1881); 190–193.

Vetter, Jeremy. "Science Along the Railroad: Expanding Field Work in the U. S. Central West." *Annals of Science* 61, issue 2 (2004): 187–211.

Wagoner, Jay J. *Arizona Territory, 1863–1912: A Political History*. Tucson: University of Arizona Press, 1970.

Wahlquist, Wayne Leroy. "Settlement Processes in the Mormon Core Area, 1847–1890." PhD diss., University of Nebraska, 1974.

Waldron, Adelaide Cilley. "Farmington." *The Granite Monthly* 19 (October 1895): 259–290.

Walker, Henry P. "Pre-Railroad Transportation in the Trans-Mississippi West: An Annotated Bibliography." *Arizona and the West* 18 (Spring 1976): 53–80.

Walker, Ronald W. "Brigham Young Writes Jefferson Davis about the Gunnison Massacre Affair." *Brigham Young University Studies* 35 (1995): 146–170.

———. "Crisis in Zion: Heber J. Grant and the Panic of 1893." *Arizona and the West* 21 (Autumn 1979): 257–278.

———. "Toward a Reconstruction of Mormon and Indian Relations, 1847–1877." *Brigham Young University Studies* 29 (Fall 1989): 23–42.

———. "Wakara Meets the Mormons, 1848–52: A Case Study in Native American Accommodation." *Utah Historical Quarterly* 70 (Summer 2002): 215–237.

Walters, Daniel Leigh. History of Daniel Leigh Walters and Family, 1843–1917. MSS 238, no. 15, Special Collections and Archives, Merrill–Cazier Library, Utah State University.

Ward, George Washington. *The Early Development of the Chesapeake and Ohio Canal Project*. Baltimore: Johns Hopkins Press, 1899.

Wasserman, Mark. "The Social Origins of the 1910 Revolution in Chihuahua." *Latin American Research Review* 15, no. 1 (1980): 15–38.

Weech, Guy et al., eds. *Pioneer Town: Pima Centennial History*. Pima: Eastern Arizona Museum and Historical Society, 1979.

Wegmann, Edward. *The Water-Supply of the City of New York, 1658–1895*. New York: John Wiley & Sons, 1896.

West, Robert C. *Sonora: Its Geographical Personality*. Austin: University of Texas Press, 1993.

Westwood, Brad. "The Early Life and Career of Joseph Don Carlos Young (1855–1938): A Study of Utah's First Institutionally Trained Architect to 1884." Master's Thesis, University of Pennsylvania, 1994.

Wheat, Carl I. *Mapping the Trans-Mississippi West, 1540–1861*. 5 vols. San Francisco: The Institute of Historical Geography, 1957–63.

Wheeler, George Montague. *Report upon United States Geographical Surveys West of the One Hundredth Meridian: in Charge of First Lieut. Geo. M. Wheeler . . . under the Direction of the Chief of Engineers, U.S. Army*. 7 vols. Washington, DC: Government Printing Office, 1875–1889.

Whipple, Squire. *An Elementary and Practical Treatise on Bridge Building*. 2nd edition, revised and enlarged. New York: D. Van Nostrand, 1873.

White, C. Albert. *A History of the Rectangular Survey System*. Washington: U.S. Department of the Interior, Bureau of Land Management, 1983.

———. *Initial Points of the Rectangular Survey System*. Westminster, CO: The Publishing House for Professional Land Surveyors of Colorado, 1996.

White, Gerald T. *The United States and the Problem of Recovery after 1893*. Tuscaloosa: University of Alabama Press, 1982.

White, Jean Bickmore, ed. *Church, State, and Politics: The Diaries of John Henry Smith*. Salt Lake City: Signature Books, 1990.

Whitney, Orson F. *Life of Heber C. Kimball, an Apostle*. Salt Lake City: Kimball Family; Juvenile Instructor Office, 1888.

———. *History of Utah*. 4 vols. Salt Lake City: George Q. Cannon & Sons, 1892–1904.

Whittaker, David J. "The Bone in the Throat: Orson Pratt and the Public Announcement of Plural Marriage." *Western Historical Quarterly* 18 (July 1987): 293–314.

Wilford, John Noble. *The Mapmakers*. Revised edition. New York: Vintage Books, 2001.

Wilkes, Charles. *Narrative of the United States' Exploring Expedition, during the Years 1838, 1839, 1840, 1841, 1842*. London: Whittaker and Co., n.d.

Wilkins, Thurman, *Clarence King: A Biography*. Revised and enlarged. Albuquerque: University of New Mexico Press, 1988.

Wilkinson, Melvin, and William C. Tanner III. "The Influence of Family Size, Interaction, and Religiosity on Family Affection in a Mormon Sample." *Journal of Marriage and Family* 42 (May 1980): 297–303.

"Will of the Late Earl Stanhope." *The Scots Magazine, and Edinburgh Literary Miscellany* 79 (March 1817): 187–88.

Willcox, William B. *Portrait of a General: Sir Henry Clinton in the War of Independence*. New York: Alfred A. Knopf, 1964.

Williams, Mentor L. "'A Shout of Derision': A Sidelight on the Presidential Campaign of 1848." *Michigan History* 32 (March 1848): 66–77.

Williams, Oren A. "Settlement and Growth of the Gila Valley in Graham County as a Mormon Colony, 1879–1900." Master's Thesis, University of Arizona, 1957.

Winslow, Arthur. "The Art and Development of Topographic Mapping." *Engineering Magazine* 6 (October 1893–March 1894): 24–31.

Winter, William. *In Memory of John McCullough*. New York: The De Vinne Press, 1889.

Winther, Oscar O. *The Transportation Frontier: Trans-Mississippi West, 1865–1890*. New York: Holt, Rinehart and Winston, 1964.

———. *Via Western Express & Stagecoach*. Stanford, CA: Stanford University Press, 1945.

Woodford, Robert J. "The Historical Development of the Doctrine and Covenants." 3 vols. PhD diss. Brigham Young University, 1974.

Woodward, William. Papers. Microfilm of original holographs, Utah Reel 104, pt. 2, and 105, pt. 1, Merrill–Cazier Library, Utah State University.

Wright, John B. "Mormon 'Colonias' of Chihuahua." *Geographical Review* 91 (July 2001): 586–596.

Wrighton, Scot, and Earl Zarbin. "Lewis Wolfley, Territorial Politics, and the Founding of The Arizona Republican." *Journal of Arizona History* 31 (Autumn 1990): 307–328.

Wrigley, Robert L., Jr. "Utah and Northern Railway Co.: A Brief History." *Oregon Historical Quarterly* 48 (September 1947): 245–253.

Young, Brigham. Letterpress Copybooks, 1844–1879. CR 1234/1, LDS Church History Library.

———. Office Files, 1832–1878. CR 1234/1, LDS Church History Library.

Young, John W. Papers, 1874–1889. Caine MSS Coll 26, Special Collections and Archives, Merrill–Cazier Library, Utah State University.

Young, Karl E. "Brief Sanctuary: The Mormon Colonies of Northern Mexico." *American West* 4 (May 1967): 4–11, 66–67.

———. "Early Mormon Troubles in Mexico." *Brigham Young University Studies* 5 (Spring/Summer 1964): 155–167.

———. *The Long Hot Summer of 1912: Episodes in the Flight of the Mormon Colonists from Mexico.* Charles E. Merrill Monograph Series in the Humanities and Social Sciences, No. 1. Provo, UT: Brigham Young University Press, 1967.

———. *Ordeal in Mexico: Tales of Danger and Hardship Collected from Mormon Colonists.* Salt Lake City: Deseret Book, 1968.

Zonn, Leo E. "The Railroads of Sonora and Sinaloa, Mexico: A Historical Survey." *Social Science Journal* 15 (April 1978): 1–16.

Newspapers and Periodicals

Daily Alta California (San Francisco)

Alexandria Gazette (Alexandria, VA)

Arizona Bulletin (Solomonville, AZ)

Arizona Daily Star (Tucson, AZ)

Arizona Daily Gazette (Tucson, AZ)

Arizona Weekly Citizen (Tucson, AZ)

Deming Headlight (Deming, NM)

Deseret News (Salt Lake City)

Deseret Evening News (Salt Lake City)

Deseret Weekly (Salt Lake City)

El Progreso (Nuevo Casas Grandes, Mexico)

Frontier Index (Kearney, NE)

Graham County Bulletin (Solomonville, AZ)

Graham Guardian (Safford, AZ)

Daily Independent (Helena, MT)

Irrigation Age (Chicago)

Journal of the Franklin Institute of the State of Pennsylvania and Mechanics' Register (Philadelphia)

Logan Leader (Logan, UT)

Liberty Weekly Tribune (Liberty, MO)

The Mechanic (Boston)

Mechanics' Magazine, and Journal of the Mechanics' Institute (New York)
Mechanics' Magazine, and Register of Inventions and Improvements (New York)
Mechanics' Magazine, Museum, Register, Journal, and Gazette (London)
Mexican Financier (México)
The Mormon (New York)
Daily National Intelligencer (Washington, DC)
New York Farmer (New York)
Ogden Daily Herald (Ogden, UT)
Ogden Junction (Ogden, UT)
Oregon Argus (Oregon City, OR)
Phoenix Gazette (Phoenix)
Preston Citizen (Preston, ID)
Salt Lake Daily Telegraph (Salt Lake City)
Salt Lake Daily Herald (Salt Lake City)
Salt Lake Herald (Salt Lake City)
Salt Lake Herald-Republican (Salt Lake City)
Salt Lake Tribune (Salt Lake City)
Semi-Weekly Telegraph (Salt Lake City)
Transactions of the American Institute of Mining Engineers (New York)
Utah Church and Farm (Salt Lake City)
Utah Journal (Logan, UT)
Utah Mining Journal (Salt Lake City)
Valley Bulletin (Solomonville, AZ)
Vernal Express (Vernal, UT)

INDEX

A

adultery, 86, 120–21
Agricultural College (Logan, Utah), 850, 864, 957, 1030, 1081
Ahumada, Miguel, 973, 1036, 1069
alcohol, 29, 234, 239, 569, 574, 914, 1023; *see also* Word of Wisdom
Allen, Ethan, 5n3
ambrotypes. *See* photography
American Party, 1146; *see also* elections
American Revolution, 5; *see also* Sons of the American Revolution
Anderson, Edward H., 1085, 1088, 1093, 1096, 1099, 1117, 1120n107, 1131n111
Angell, Truman O., 437, 439
Apache, 652, 670, 811, 818, 819, 1038, 1058, 1098
apostasy, 36, 55
apostles. *See* Quorum of Twelve Apostles
army. *See* US Army
astrology, 34, 62, 78, 228
astronomy, 100
automobiles, 1204, 1244, 1245, 1247
Axtell, Samuel B., 397–98, 403, 406–9, 1217–20

B

Babbitt, Almon W., xxii, 40, 77, 79, 80; death, 135
Baker, Samuel G., 95, 96, 97, 98n117, 99
Bates, Thomas H., 296
Bean, George W., xxvii, 183
Bear River, xxxv, 24, 252, 254, 272

Bear River Massacre, 261–65, 591
bears, xxxiv, 150, 182, 235, 250, 259, 505, 799–800, 985
Benson, Ezra T., 132, 231, 239, 244, 245, 247, 263; colonel in Cache Militia branch of Nauvoo Legion, 282, 345; death, 346
Bentley, J. C., 981, 1008, 1015, 1018, 1019n56, 1025, 1075, 1196, 1214
Black Hawk War, xxiv, 140n157
Blair, Seth M., xxviii, 229, 231, 240, 244, 247, 266, 399
Blickensderfer Jr., Jacob, xxix, 297, 302, 304, 308n96, 313, 318, 324n132, 397, 523, 592
blood atonement, 121, 123
Book of Mormon, 25, 557, 693, 745, 755, 777, 809, 831, 843, 903, 1012, 1023, 1034, 1080, 1091, 1147, 1234, 1248
brass bands. *See* music
Brigham Young College (Logan), 542, 550
Buchanan, James, 193; *see also* Utah War

C

Cache Valley, Utah, xxviii, xxxiv, 597
Camp Douglas. *See* US Army: Camp Douglas
canals, 5, 36, 186, 268, 272, 273, 377, 431, 465, 504, 516, 603, 606, 608, 610, 637, 655, 656, 658, 714, 734, 765, 775, 776, 788, 833, 980; *see also* irrigation
cancer, 850, 1157, 1160, 1187, 1211, 1213, 1223, 1228, 1230, 1246, 1252, 1260
Cannon, Angus M., 540

Cannon, Frank J., 1146
Cannon, George Q., 379, 403, 504, 521, 616; shows JHM around Washington, DC, 471, 473, 474
Cannon, John M., 1088, 1090
Cannon, John Q., 642, 644, 665, 671
canoes, 87–88, 544
Cass, Lewis, 15n22
Catholicism, 745, 751, 921–22, 1112, 1240, 1242
cattle, 22, 49, 50, 54, 91, 111, 192, 197, 433, 469, 652, 701, 702, 806, 957, 1015
Cedar City, Utah, xxvii, 39, 51
Celestial Marriage. *See* plural marriage
Chicago, Illinois, 17, 470, 482–85, 498
choirs. *See* music
cholera, 19, 22, 873–74, 1015, 1175
Christmas, 71, 72n75, 360, 419, 451, 563, 638, 678, 806, 822, 851, 869, 914, 999, 1054, 1079, 1108, 1123, 1152, 1213–14, 1238, 1256
Church Farm (Logan, Utah), 243, 376, 457
church (LDS) finances, 79
circus, 1140
Civil War, 318, 485, 497, 548
Clawson, Rudger, 1024, 1174
Clinton, Sir Henry, 4n1
Cluff, Benjamin, 71, 251
coal. *See* mining
Colonia Dublán, Mexico, 821n110
Colonia Juarez, Mexico, xix, xxxi, xli, 945, 955, 1292; JHM describes, 798n89
Colorado, Cora, xxxvii, 211, 212, 224, 234, 919–20
Colorado River, 162, 556, 602
Confederacy. *See* Civil War
conferences, 53, 55, 85, 91, 100, 101, 236, 238, 508, 536, 608, 638, 671, 821, 822, 947, 1018, 1024, 1050n74, 1076, 1148, 1156, 1188, 1189, 1195; *see also* general conference
Connor, Patrick E. *See* Bear River Massacre

constitutional conventions. *See* Utah statehood
Cora (Indigenous girl), 37–38, 990
Corianton, 1081
cotton. *See* crops: cotton
Cowley, Matthias, 1051, 1161
crime, 157, 244, 257, 562, 575, 606, 751, 978; *see also* violence; Wham Robbery Trial; Whitehouse, Isaac, murder of
crops, 35, 54, 100–1, 116, 135, 154, 192, 210, 229, 260, 464, 604, 652, 959, 1036, 1050, 1074–75, 1173, 1179; cotton, 35, 147, 196, 211; destroyed by insects and weather, 70, 88, 93, 94, 198, 213, 228, 300, 651; *see also* farming
Croton Aqueduct, xx, 8–9, 585
Curtis, Arizona, 607, 633, 634

D

daguerreotypes. *See* photography
Dame, William H., xxvii, 45, 50, 67, 106, 116, 140, 158, 194, 524, 532, 925, 938; accusations of misconduct and trial, 195–96; desert mission with JHM, 168, 177, 180, 183, 186, 188; and Mountain Meadows Massacre, 149n170, 395, 403, 411, 423, 1274, 1275–79; photographs, 588; Parowan stake president, 106, 109, 134, 165, 208; surveyor, 111; teaches JHM surveying and topography, 74, 76; *see also* Mountain Meadows Massacre
dancing, 18, 29, 32n, 210, 419, 610
Deseret alphabet, 61n65, 70, 88, 89, 211
Deseret News, 44, 634, 657, 790, 864, 888, 889, 891, 900, 906, 913, 920, 934, 939, 947, 951, 984, 1040, 1193, 1195, 1257, 1266
Deseret University, 550
desert mission, 168–94; *see also* JHM: desert mission; Utah War
Diaz, Porfirio, 818, 820, 1019, 1237
disease, 602, 778, 873–74, 1015, 1213n3, 1252; *see also* cancer; cholera; medicine; typhoid
Dodge, Grenville M., xxix, 297n77, 304,

309, 312n106, 313, 315, 316; *see also* Topographical Corps
Doremus, Abraham F., 332, 335, 395, 440, 527
Dougall, Clarissa Maria Young, 1183, 1185, 1204, 1207, 1208, 1211, 1212, 1213, 1223, 1240, 1248

E

earthquakes, 223, 723, 812, 954, 1165, 1231
Edmunds Act. *See* plural marriage: Edmunds Act
Eldredge, Frederick E., 1273
elections (territorial, state, and federal), 32, 56, 90, 117, 135, 195, 206, 211, 231, 245, 247, 254, 345, 346, 379, 421, 460, 484, 521, 730, 731n102, 793, 849, 910, 1146, 1182, 1255
electricity, 871, 979, 1170, 1196, 1253
El Paso Daily Herald, 1008, 1040
El Progreso, 1273
Endowment House, 59, 60, 127, 381, 451n114, 540n153, 548
Ensign, Marius, 92, 111, 193, 199
Erie Canal, 5, 487
executions, 69
Eyring, Henry, 725, 820, 953, 956, 1019

F

Fancher/Baker Party. *See* Mountain Meadows Massacre
farming, xl, 70, 114, 136, 164, 188, 192, 208, 604, 606, 607, 609, 649, 650, 652, 654, 656, 676, 811, 813, 814, 816, 946, 953, 976, 1008; *see also* crops
Farr, Lorin, 295n71, 312, 330, 383, 388, 389, 396, 518
Farr, Lucien, 1014
Farr, Winslow, 1019, 1055, 1069, 1070
Farrell, George L., 236, 240, 241, 251, 341, 402, 403, 503, 513
ferries, 249, 261, 327, 474, 475, 482
Fillmore, Utah, 98, 104, 134, 200; territorial capital, 116
firearms, 47, 53, 93, 194, 203, 220, 230, 408–9, 420, 421, 444, 459, 503, 504, 638, 801
First Presidency, 612
Fish, Hannah, 85
Fish, Joseph, xxiii, 148, 149n172, 150nn173–74, 151n175, 221
Fox, Jesse W., xxix, 229, 238, 373, 377
Fremont, John C., xxvi, 149n172, 1265–71
Froiseth, Bernard A. M., xxix, 400–1

G

Gamble, Mary Elizabeth, 1240, 1242, 1244
gambling, 659, 745, 771n32, 924
Garfield, James A., 538
garments. *See* temple work: garments
Genealogical Society, 1204, 1206, 1209, 1210, 1212, 1223, 1256
general conference, 79–80, 134–35, 164n191, 240, 246, 284, 344, 356, 373, 376, 455, 506, 512, 535, 611, 614, 705, 828, 990, 1025, 1115, 1133, 1161, 1203, 1241, 1243, 1248
Gibbs, George F., 547
Gila Valley, Arizona, xxx, 606–7
Gillespie, Robert, 37, 52; slaughters Indigenous People, 53
gold, xl, 46, 175, 179, 1110, 1252; *see also* JHM: gold seeker; mining
Grant, Heber J., 611, 698, 1024, 1027, 1188; visits Arizona, 634, 635, 636, 641–44
grasshoppers, destroy crops, 70, 88, 93, 94, 300
Great Salt Lake, 311
Grieve, Jessie Helen Russell Anderson. *See* Martineau, Jessie Helen Russell Anderson Grieve
Groves, Elisha H., 30–31
Guiteau, Charles J., 538
Gunnison, John W., 54; *see also* Walker War

H

Habgerg, Niels L., 627, 1088, 1089; death, 1125, 1126

Haight, Isaac C., 73, 116, 146; elected mayor of Cedar City, 56
Hamblin, Jacob, 147, 154, 162n189, 661
Harrison, Benjamin, 791
Harvard, 1142, 1191, 1247
Haslam, James, 153
Hatch, Lorenzo Hill, 354, 372, 408, 1096
Hawkes, Alvin J., 1260
Hawkes, Annie "Anna" Sariah Martineau Walser Turley (daughter), 518, 524, 801, 809, 820, 860, 943, 1253–54, 1256, 1260; birth, 401; blessings, 718–19; character, 811, 1205; children, 839, 947, 1012, 1052, 1173, 1179; divorce from Edward Turley, 1254n28; health and illnesses, 460, 525, 528, 532, 549, 771; marriage to Edward Turley, 1039; marriage to Henry Walser, 821; photographs, 1286
Hayes, Rutherford B., 473
Holladay, J. D., 632, 652, 654, 664
horses, xxxv, 80, 82, 198, 201, 209, 220, 250, 257, 260, 604, 606, 670, 723, 814, 1247
Hotel Utah, 1250
Hughes, Louis Cameron, 879–80
Hull, Thomas, 1157, 1158n128, 1174n143, 1187
hunting, 21, 52, 250, 253, 510, 511, 801, 985, 1268
Hyde, Orson, 59, 123, 127, 225, 241, 1137
Hyde, William, 295n71, 319, 320, 323n131, 326, 380; Cache Militia branch of Nauvoo Legion, 345, 346; death, 347

I

Improvement Era, 801n91, 1039, 1234
Indians. *See* Indigenous Peoples
Indigenous Peoples, xxiv, xxviii, 24, 33, 40, 45, 73, 77, 79, 81, 86, 87, 91, 151, 174, 176, 185, 192, 224, 242, 243, 244, 383, 416, 562, 566, 574, 652, 874, 1032, 1059; blamed for Mountain Meadows Massacre, 152–53, 1274–79; children bought, sold, or traded, xxxvii, 37–38, 211, 212, 224, 234, 383, 938, 990, 1005–6; conflicts with settlers, 30, 37–38, 42–43, 47–48, 49, 54, 68–69, 93–94, 140, 195, 230, 234, 257–60, 266, 271, 591, 604, 653n50, 660, 661, 670, 673, 743, 811, 814, 818, 823, 889, 1038–39, 1101–2, 1131, 1238; conflicts with US Army, 261–62; guides, 172, 176, 1266, 1267; intertribal conflict, 44, 73, 880n149; JHM records earlier encounters with, 923–28, 936–38, 942n191; JHM reports rumors of violence by, 668, 669; kidnap white children, 283; missionary work to, 55, 56, 605, 903, 1080; sold or traded as slaves, 37n26, 106; temple work for, 1195, 1201, 1205, 1207; trade with settlers, 88, 245; traditions, 182–83; *see also* Apache; Black Hawk War; Kanosh; Paiutes; Pahvants; Shoshone; Utes; violence; Walker War
Iron County Militia. *See* Nauvoo Legion
iron works, 39, 40, 42, 45, 49, 73, 82, 146
irrigation, 605, 609, 746, 788, 789, 811, 813, 833n120, 935, 980; *see also* canals
Ivins, Anthony W., 956, 974, 1022, 1115, 1190; stake president, 953, 980, 983, 1051, 1196

J

Jackson, Margaret, 336, 337
Jenson, Andrew, 1082
Johnson, Benjamin F., xxii, 40, 76, 80, 83, 142, 201, 242, 378, 382, 383, 394, 417, 558, 742, 756, 940; JHM records history of, 846, 847, 849, 850; patriarchal blessing, 764–65; photograph, 1291
Johnson, Benjamin Samuel (son-in-law), xxxvii, 379, 381, 394, 419, 735, 737, 815, 840, 842; called on mission to Arizona, 420–21
Johnson, Joel Hills, xxi–xxii, 55, 71, 426, 528, 876, 962; death, 551; photographs, 588
Johnson, Joseph E., 248, 254, 525, 556,

558; called on mission to Mexico, 548; death, 566
Johnson, Nephi, 46, 55, 83, 111, 113, 194, 219, 220, 242, 1100, 1280n10; health and illnesses, 321; interpreter on desert mission, 168, 169, 172, 174, 178, 180, 183, 186, 188
Johnson, Royal A., 746, 767, 780, 788, 823, 825, 1287
Johnson, Sixtus E., 201, 242, 260, 526n145, 723, 808, 821, 885, 886, 953, 979, 1076, 1234, 1235, 1247, 1248; mission to Sandwich Islands, 188
Johnson, Susan Elvira Martineau (daughter), xxxvi, 284, 299, 353, 356, 363, 377, 394, 401, 419, 548, 712, 735, 737, 739, 740, 753, 793, 840, 863, 1064, 1261; baptism, 275; birth, 112; blessings, 115–16, 215–16, 759–60, 762–64, 1065–66; children, 435, 677, 742, 810, 849, 894, 940–41, 1049, 1072; health and illnesses, 159; marriage to Benjamin Samuel Johnson, 379, 381; mission to Arizona, 420–21; poetry, 750
Johnson, William D., 790, 793, 794, 815, 883; stake counselor with JHM, 636, 638, 640, 641, 644, 645, 646, 652, 655
Johnston, Albert Sidney. *See* Utah War
Johnston's Army. *See* Utah War
Jones, Mary Eliza Brown. *See* Martineau, Mary Eliza Brown Jones
Jones, Seth C. (stepson), 601, 602, 603, 605, 607, 609, 610, 628, 631, 647, 650

K

Kanarra, 924, 925, 938
Kane, Thomas L., 160, 161n186; *see also* Utah War
Kanosh (Pahvant leader), 140, 224
Kearns, Thomas, 1084, 1087, 1114
Kimball, David P., 558–59, 566; bishop, 565, 603, 609; death, 613
Kimball, Heber C., 29, 36, 60, 120, 121, 127, 128, 935; seals JHM to Susan Julia Sherman, 131–32, 135
Kimball, J. Golden, 1024, 1076

Kirtland, Ohio, xxii, 55n58, 872, 938, 1193
Klingensmith, Philip, 39n29, 1277–78
Kosterlitzky, Emilio, 807, 808, 809n100, 810, 811, 812, 818, 1289, 1290

L

Lagoon (amusement park), 1137, 1140, 1253
Lamanites. *See* Book of Mormon
Law of Adoption, 102, 618, 701
Layton, Christopher, 559, 561, 565, 607, 610, 736, 939; accuses JHM of mismanaging tithing funds, 682, 695, 699; hides on the underground, 635, 658, 660; St. Joseph stake president, 576, 577, 579, 603, 632, 634, 644, 657, 661, 712, 715
LDS Hospital, 1123, 1203
LeBaron, David T., 629, 631, 648, 658, 760, 793,
Lee, John D., 31n13, 35, 114, 146, 162n189, 209, 1214n5; 1277, 1278–79; *see also* Mountain Meadows Massacre; *Salt Lake Tribune* "conspiracy"
Lewis, James, 39, 40, 56, 57, 64, 67; accuses JHM of theft, 225–26
Lewis, Samuel, 48, 68, 86, 91, 112n134, 148, 150, 169
Lewis, Tarlton, 42; bishop, 40, 92, 116, 163
Little, James A., 31, 48
Little Salt Lake, 90, 91
Logan, Utah, xli, 232, 236, 542, 598, 615, 827; city council, 397, 406, 420, 423, 453, 516, 542, 543, 1217
Los Angeles, California, 555–56, 575, 602, 797
Louisa, Utah. *See* Parowan, Utah
Lund, Anthon H., 1080, 1238, 1248
Lunt, Henry, 44, 45, 46n43, 211, 267n48, 425, 428–29, 524, 616, 805, 947, 983
Lyman, Amasa, 29, 43, 48, 98, 159–60, 161, 195, 209; commander of Southern Utah, 163; home in Parowan, 205;

sermons, 210; trial of Dame, William H., 195–96
Lyman, Francis M., 661, 662, 776, 1027, 1236
Lyon, Emily "Nettie" Henrietta Martineau (sister), 11, 13, 14, 25, 487, 495, 497; correspondence with JHM, 16n23, 18n25, 75, 89, 114, 384, 390, 416, 543, 547, 575, 770, 855, 980, 1000; death, 1015–17

M

MacDonald, Alexander F., 557, 639, 644n45, 648, 798, 855, 956, 978n26, 1051
Madison, Wisconsin, 6, 26n4, 48, 337, 384, 485–86, 495–96, 545
Maeser, Karl G, 1024
Manning, Levi H., 832, 850, 852, 862, 870n144, 880n150; *see also* US Surveyor General's Office
Maricopa, Arizona, 556–57, 558, 581
martial law. *See* Utah War
Martineau, Alley Preston (daughter-in-law), 539, 540, 543, 549, 582, 623, 629, 687, 708, 979, 991, 1123; death, 1191–92; health and illnesses, 993, 996, 997–98, 1004; photographs, 589
Martineau, Annie "Anna" Sariah (daughter). *See* Hawkes, Annie Sariah Martineau Walser Turley (daughter)
Martineau, Charles Freeman (son), 388, 399, 431, 435, 517, 1159, 1234, 1237, 1239, 1245; baptism, 415; birth, 245; blessings, 278; children, 678, 772, 981, 1050, 1094, 1143, 1205; health and illnesses, 612, 754, 1027, 1249; marriage to Eva Rice, 663; missionary work, 542, 545; photographs, 1286; surveys with JHM, 534
Martineau, Delcina "Dellie" (daughter), 198, 220, 267, 284; birth, 159; blessings, 166, 216; death, xxxvi, 285–87, 289, 422
Martineau, Dora (adopted daughter), xxxvii, xxxviii, 551, 726, 747, 753, 781, 818, 839, 848, 863, 1032; baptism, 809, 810; blessings, 721–22, 1038; death, 1053–54; epilepsy, 971, 986, 1007, 1011, 1013, 1014, 1015, 1017, 1018, 1024, 1036, 1042, 1049, 1050, 1051, 1052; health and illnesses, 582, 612, 614, 715, 771, 974; schooling, 866, 903; sealed to JHM and Susan Martineau, 618
Martineau, Eliza Belle Johnson (daughter-in-law), 1085–86
Martineau, Elizabeth "Lillie" Lillian (daughter). *See* Nebeker, Elizabeth "Lillie" Lillian Martineau
Martineau, Eliza Mears (mother), xix, xx, 11, 12, 13, 14, 492–93, 993, 1001, 1225; death, 16
Martineau, George Albert (son), 551, 608, 609, 645, 652, 663, 731, 957, 974, 1010, 1011, 1043, 1188, 1193, 1200, 1247, 1255; baptism, 412; birth, 271; blessings, 277, 718; children, 727, 782, 789, 797, 837, 891, 989, 1088, 1173, 1243; ecclesiastical callings, 663, 664; marries Emma Allred, 703; missionary work, 712, 1123; moves to Arizona with JHM, 604
Martineau, Gertrude "Tillie" (daughter). *See* Taylor, Gertrude "Tillie" Martineau
Martineau, Henry Augustus (son), xxxvi, 55, 57, 97, 228, 231, 275, 353, 652, 794, 799, 942, 983, 987, 1200, 1203, 1231, 1245, 1246; birth, 41, 42; baptism, 275; blessings, 60, 213–14, 279–80; children, 436, 670, 777, 798, 805, 818, 862, 1210, 1255; ecclesiastical offices, 658; health and illnesses, 61, 159, 161, 1091; marriage to Melissa Edith Johnson, 419; missionary work, 379, 381, 394, 664; work grading railroads, 327, 330, 341, 355, 392
Martineau, James "Eddie" Edward (son): death, 517–18; health and illnesses, 515; photograph, 1286
Martineau, Jane Varley, 7n6, 545
Martineau, Jessie Helen Russell Anderson Grieve (fourth wife), xxxvii, 385,

683, 684, 685, 705, 766, 1072–74; blessings, 691; death, 966–67, 969; JHM recalls sealing to, 967–68; mother refuses to let her see or correspond with JHM, 767, 825, 829, 830, 831, 967, 968; sealed to JHM, 686, 687, 709

Martineau, Jesse Nathaniel (son), 446, 448, 449, 506, 604, 657, 660, 668, 683, 849, 915, 920, 987–88; attends college, 820; baptisms, 415, 1049; birth, 267; blessings, 278, 529–30; health and illnesses, 270, 459; missionary work, 614, 730, 732, 780, 793; moves to Arizona with JHM, 602; surveys with JHM, 445, 447, 460, 465, 509, 510, 511, 513, 514, 515, 534, 610, 652, 656

Martineau, James Henry: accused of theft, 225–26; accused of tithing mismanagement, 682, 695, 699, 727; actor, 109–10, 246–47; ancestry, extended family, and genealogy, 3–11, 128, 384–88, 390–91, 463, 465–66, 477–79, 485, 490–92, 496–97, 522, 543–44, 547, 616–18, 619, 726, 782–83, 793, 860, 959–62, 987–88, 1000–3, 1029, 1082, 1127–28, 1148–50, 1193–94, 1204, 1206–7, 1223–28, 1231, 1238, 1250–51, 1252, 1258; arrested, 753; autobiography, 3–26; baptism, xx, 25–26, 933, 1041; biography, xix–xliv; xxn1, 226–27; birth, xix, 3; blessings, 27–28, 57–58, 60, 105, 128, 165, 217–18, 241–42, 255–57, 275–76, 280–81, 426–28, 429–30, 506–8, 512, 580, 623–24, 633, 691, 729–30, 733, 756–57, 1055–56, 1096–97; bridge engineer, 975, 980–81, 982, 1008; canal surveyor and engineer, xli, 185, 186, 238, 268, 272, 273, 377, 431, 457, 464, 505, 508, 509–10, 516, 603, 656, 658, 679, 712, 713, 730, 735, 740–41, 742, 744–45, 754, 766, 769–70, 771, 778, 780, 788, 790, 810, 820, 832–33, 834, 844, 956, 981, 1022–24, 1058–60, 1081, 1095, 1187; cartographer, xix,

xxix, 109, 186, 188, 192, 195, 198, 254, 314, 317, 378, 389, 392, 397, 586, 590, 597, 787, 835, 851, 974, 1010, 1190; character and personality, xliii, 1004; clerk and recorder, xxi, 32, 34, 40, 53, 65, 86, 92, 97, 145, 146, 148, 163, 168, 205, 206, 210, 226, 231, 236, 238n18, 239, 240, 241, 242–43, 247, 254; county assessor, 114, 226, 255, 261, 263; daily activities, xlii; death, xli, 1263n40; desert mission, 168–194, 195; diarist, xx, xxiv–xxvi, xl, 22, 838; dramatist, 65, 110; dreams and visions, 35, 102, 119, 130, 164, 207, 269, 703, 768–69, 831, 833–34, 839, 843, 860, 879, 890, 922–23, 1010, 1114, 1147, 1199; ecclesiastical offices, xxi, xxiii, xxxix, 80, 82, 85, 134, 994, 1006; education, 13; endowments, 61; faith and prayers, xxi, xxxiii, xxxix, 20, 26, 103, 181, 246, 257, 268, 339, 420, 426, 464, 484, 508, 511, 527, 535, 546, 693, 743, 747, 752, 772, 773–74, 776–77, 780–81, 782, 783, 792, 798, 813–14, 824, 834, 840–41, 852, 853, 854, 865, 880–82, 884, 892, 895–96, 900, 901–4, 905, 906–9, 911–12, 914–15, 917, 933–34, 958, 966, 969–70, 976–77, 983–84, 1025, 1043–44, 1045, 1090, 1118, 1143, 1144–45, 1147, 1156, 1186, 1212–13, 1220–21, 1224, 1228–29, 1237; family and home life, xxvi, xxxvi–xxxviii, 33, 57, 161, 167, 197, 209, 356n14, 370–71nn23–24, 411–12, 439, 454, 466–67, 500, 540, 576, 662, 705, 713, 732, 761, 842, 979, 982, 1005, 1030–31, 1064, 1080, 1165, 1176, 1179, 1186–87, 1188, 1198, 1263, 1235–36, 1254; fears deception by evil influences, 783, 835, 881, 902–3, 905, 916–17, 1014, 1145, 1158, 1182; finances and poverty, xxi, xl–xli, 35, 41, 46, 63, 71, 105, 111, 197, 201, 205, 206, 223, 233, 234, 282, 344, 355, 401, 428, 449, 452, 456–57, 501, 523, 541, 550, 577, 580, 601, 627,

646, 673, 737, 760–61, 765, 769, 770, 773, 776–77, 784, 787, 796n84, 797, 811, 813, 824, 825–26, 855–56, 859, 861–62, 870, 891, 900, 901, 905–6, 909, 910–11, 917, 986, 1072, 1107–8, 1115–16, 1134, 1140, 1158, 1176, 1177, 1181, 1186, 1239n18, 1246, 1247; gold seeker, xix, xx, 17, 19; grandparent, 435–36, 576, 611, 623, 669, 675, 677, 727, 730, 732, 771, 772, 777, 778, 797, 805, 815, 837, 839, 853, 862, 864, 866, 884, 894, 1057, 1147, 1179, 1201, 1228, 1257; health and illnesses, xix, xxxi, 19–20, 22, 29, 114, 160, 195, 198, 401, 426, 468, 510, 576, 611, 677, 680, 693, 714, 715, 729, 743–44, 782, 784, 806, 821, 840–41, 865, 900, 957–59, 963, 965, 966, 973, 983, 987, 991, 999, 1004, 1014–15, 1041, 1056, 1059, 1084, 1085, 1103, 1104–6, 1121, 1133–34, 1135, 1143, 1159, 1160, 1175, 1176, 1179, 1187, 1189, 1194–95, 1200, 1205, 1207, 1210, 1212–13, 1224, 1237, 1239, 1250, 1255, 1256, 1259; home in Arizona, 608, 609, 610, 631, 650; homes in Logan, 236, 238n18, 242, 270, 380, 388, 416, 451, 455, 464, 466, 523, 583, 601, 1234; homes in Mexico, 725, 767, 784, 806, 812, 819n105, 854, 912, 945, 969, 974, 985, 1010, 1011, 1012–13, 1018, 1020, 1042, 1054, 1250; home in Parowan, 33, 39, 45, 62, 94, 112, 161; home in Salt Lake City, 225, 229, 233, 1249, 1259; horse named "Jack," 259–60, 266; journals, xlii; learns French, 239; legislative clerk, 116; mayor of Pima, Arizona, 679; meets President Rutherford B. Hayes, 473; mineral and mining surveyor, 462, 463, 468, 513, 533, 549, 606, 791n69, 792, 793, 845, 849, 1009, 1011, 1018, 1020, 1284; military service, xix, 14, 15, 31, 34, 82, 110, 112, 142, 145, 154, 157, 226, 240; move to Arizona, 548, 552, 576–77, 581–82, 583, 601–3, 629–30; move to Mexico, 713n94, 715, 722, 728, 737, 739; musician, 67; notary public, 61, 205, 206, 226, 239, 423, 514, 663; overland travel to Utah, 19–23; Patriarch and blessings given, 994–96, 1009, 1012, 1019, 1022, 1024, 1025, 1026, 1027, 1030, 1033, 1038, 1060–61, 1062–63, 1066–68, 1075, 1078, 1094, 1106, 1107, 1114, 1117, 1119, 1121, 1123–24, 1126, 1130, 1135, 1136–37, 1141, 1142, 1146, 1148, 1150–51, 1153–55, 1156, 1157, 1158–59, 1160, 1161, 1164, 1165, 1177–78, 1180–82, 1183–84, 1187, 1188, 1190, 1198–99, 1200, 1203, 1204, 1205, 1207–9, 1210, 1211, 1221–23, 1230, 1233–34, 1236, 1240, 1245, 1248, 1249, 1251, 1256, 1257, 1258, 1260; "Pearls" collection of quotes, 694, 695, 697, 702, 709, 732, 769, 771, 1078, 1235; photographer, xxiii, 268–69, 293, 338, 342; photographs, 130, 548, 592, 593, 594, 629, 755, 824, 871, 998, 1198, 1247, 1283, 1286, 1288, 1289, 1290, 1291, 1292; physical appearance, xxiii; poetry, xxxviii–xxxix, 66–67, 74, 83–85, 107–9, 135, 138–39, 141–42, 155–57, 167–68, 169–71, 172–74, 177–78, 187–88, 189–91, 202–3, 287–88, 289–93, 293–94, 302–3, 305–7, 310–11, 316–17, 333–34, 334–35, 352–53, 402, 480–81, 515–16, 521, 531, 549, 558, 578, 619, 672, 674–75, 685–86, 724–25, 741, 750, 792, 800–1, 802–4, 806–7, 892–94, 918–19, 1151–52; political offices of, xxi, 82, 91, 195, 226, 231, 397, 406, 420, 421, 460, 542; printer's devil, xix, 14; probate judge, xxxi; railroad leveler, surveyor, and engineer, 295–96, 298, 301–23, 324–28, 329–35, 340, 341–43, 353–55, 375, 376, 392–93, 439–41, 450, 468, 500, 513, 514, 785, 789–90, 791, 794–96; rebaptisms, 59, 116, 127, 412, 727; recalls near-death experiences while surveying in southern Utah, 928–33; receives prophecy from seeress, 199–200; reminisces his early years in Utah, 923–38; scout, 148–51, 166, 249–54, 261; settler, xxiv; smoking habit, xxxi; speaker, 88, 89, 966, 984, 1148, 1156, 1161, 1165; stake counselor, 576, 581, 607, 644, 645, 646, 650, 657, 715; surveyor and topographer, xix, xxvii, xxviii–xxix, xxx, xliii, 74, 76, 111, 142, 196, 197, 202, 208, 211, 212, 221, 227, 229–30, 231, 243, 246, 250, 254, 263, 268, 269, 271, 272, 275, 282, 283, 284, 293, 294–95, 325–27, 328–29, 339, 355, 376, 377, 388, 395, 396, 401, 402, 410, 411, 417, 418, 419, 432, 433, 442–44, 445–49, 451, 453, 455, 457, 458, 460–62, 463, 465, 468, 501, 505, 506, 508, 511, 518, 522, 523, 526–27, 533, 534–35, 549, 586, 596, 597, 603, 607, 610, 632, 633, 634, 635, 650–51, 653, 654, 659, 711–12, 713, 714, 715, 767, 772, 777, 783, 788, 792, 799, 800–5, 832, 839, 840, 842–44, 852, 853, 855, 861, 946, 953–55, 956–57, 966, 983–84, 985, 1005, 1009, 1022, 1032, 1033–36, 1044–48, 1050, 1052, 1054–55, 1057, 1070–71, 1076, 1088–89, 1092, 1094, 1099, 1100–8, 1117–20, 1121, 1138–39, 1142–46, 1157–58, 1179, 1181, 1182, 1188–89, 1197; teacher, 17–18, 44, 45, 72, 90, 239, 246; temple record, 615, 705, 708, 748, 752, 796, 967, 999, 1005, 1007, 1088, 1090, 1125, 1133, 1143, 1205, 1231; travel habits, xxxiv–xxxv; travels East and visits family, 468–99; travels through Arizona and Mexico, 556–75; travels through California, 553–55; travels to Iron County (1851), 26, 29–30; US Deputy Surveyor, xli, 832, 833n119, 836, 891; Utah Territorial Militia, xix; visits Utah for health and rejuvenation, 682–709, 989–99; war pension, 730, 762, 814, 818, 854, 1075, 1081, 1082, 1084, 1114, 1116, 1189, 1197, 1223, 1237, 1259; writer and columnist, 202, 219, 541, 657, 689, 690, 733, 748, 755, 762, 766, 767, 775, 777, 779, 781, 820, 864, 865, 888, 894, 900, 906, 920, 939, 947, 951, 984, 1008, 1040, 1190, 1191, 1193, 1260n35; *see also* canals; desert mission; Iron County Militia; Nauvoo Legion; railroads: surveying; Sons of the American Revolution; surveys and surveying; tithing: JHM responsible for in Arizona; temple work; Topographical Corps; US Surveyor General's Office

Martineau, Joel Hills (son), 550, 613, 614, 639, 711, 734, 739, 945, 971, 1122, 1134, 1203, 1231, 1250; baptism, 412; birth, 289; blessings, 719–20; bookkeeper, 614; children, 816, 841, 866, 981, 986, 1190; ecclesiastical callings, 663, 664; health and illnesses, 389, 729, 1032; marriage to Mary Ann Thurston, 805; missionary work, 712; photographs, 1286

Martineau, John W. (father), xix–xx, 3–4, 7, 8–9, 12, 13, 494–96, 993, 1000, 1225

Martineau, John William (son): birth, 205; blessings, 215; death, 267–68; health and illnesses, 212, 267; reinternment, 518

Martineau, Joseph (son), 343, 344

Martineau, Josephine Thurston (daughter-in-law), 1060

Martineau, Julia "Nettie" Henrietta (daughter), 375, 535, 550, 582; birth, 274; baptism, 412; blessings, 278; death, 637–41; health and illnesses, 284, 368, 612–13; photograph, 1286

Martineau, Lyman Royal (son), xxxvi, xli, 379, 432, 443, 444, 455, 546, 566, 582, 614, 623, 629, 708, 827, 963, 978–79, 991, 1093, 1108, 1115, 1123, 1134, 1165, 1174, 1206, 1207, 1234, 1241, 1249, 1263; birth, 207; blessings, 217; children, 732, 771, 808, 821, 823, 921, 1009–10, 1186, 1224, 1240, 1242, 1247; health and illnesses, 236; marries Alley Preston, 540; missionary work, 500, 501, 502, 503, 536; photographs, 1286; political career, 1146; travels East with JHM, 468, 470, 475

Martineau, Mary (aunt), 11, 72, 392, 496, 497, 498, 537, 538, 547

Martineau, Mary Eliza Brown Jones (third wife), xxxvii, 433, 437, 438, 462, 532, 533, 579, 708, 826, 1031, 1078, 1079, 1089, 1109; death, 1160n129; health and illnesses, 499, 1160; sealing to JHM, 451

Martineau, Moroni Helaman (son), xxxvi, 272, 284, 363, 388, 400, 420, 433, 506, 548, 611, 731, 798, 818, 820, 983; baptism, 275; biography and character, 885–88; birth, 68; blessings, 70–71, 86, 214–15, 502; children, 730, 910, 1122, 1155; death, 884–85, 888, 889; health and illnesses, 92, 113, 209, 369; marriage to Sarah S. Johnson, 522; missionary work, 420

Martineau, Nephi (son), xxxvi, 431, 433, 465, 518, 549, 582, 615, 629, 779, 827, 828, 867–69, 991, 1027, 1084, 1095, 1098, 1132–33, 1159, 1181, 1196, 1206, 1234, 1239, 1246, 1247, 1249; birth, 247; blessings, 276–77, 1042–43; children, 837, 838, 865, 1080, 1091, 1185, 1253; missionary work, 810, 867, 896–900; photographs, 1286; surveys with JHM, 460, 465, 1106

Martineau, Peter (uncle), 11, 14, 17, 75, 384, 498

Martineau, Sarah S. Johnson (daughter-in-law), 522

Martineau, Susan Elvira (daughter). *See* Johnson, Susan Elvira Martineau

Martineau, Susan Ellen Johnson (first wife), xxi, xxxviii, 45, 89, 91, 143, 205, 221, 223, 228, 238n18, 240, 247, 269, 289, 338, 344, 356, 375, 411, 434, 455, 503, 512, 518, 524, 550, 601, 655, 664, 674, 747, 753, 778, 816, 824, 828, 830, 839, 845, 846, 848, 851, 892, 1013, 1075, 1077, 1087, 1088, 1099–1100, 1165, 1176, 1190, 1212, 1253; biography and family history, 872–78, 883, 1231–33, 1250; blessings, 58–59, 60, 276, 528–29, 624–25, 717–18, 757–59, 1097–98; church service, 548; death, xli, 1260–63; dreams, prophecies, and visions, 244, 519, 622, 669, 768, 771, 775, 860, 1140–41, 1244; health and illnesses, 96, 113, 157, 159, 160–61, 195, 430, 526, 528, 543, 614, 619, 657, 658, 660, 714, 754, 771, 850, 863, 869, 900, 901, 921, 939, 974, 975, 1025, 1062, 1092, 1093, 1096, 1108, 1114, 1192–93, 1194, 1196, 1241, 1242, 1244–46, 1251, 1256, 1259; marriage to JHM, 33, 57, 103, 213, 541, 569, 851, 970, 1152, 1186, 1220, 1257; photographs, 589, 755, 871, 1286, 1290, 1291; rebaptisms, 59, 116, 412, 628; recollections of Joseph Smith, 1171–72

Martineau, Susan Julia Sherman (second wife), xxii, xxxiii–xxxiv, xxxvi, 73, 130, 133, 143, 159, 188n203, 198, 207, 209, 218, 229, 234, 238, 247, 254, 261, 267, 338, 343, 878–79, 1220; blessings, 134, 136–38, 143–44, 277, 281, 285; death and burial, 357–69; family history, 1162–63, 1164; health and illnesses, 134, 144–45, 155, 157, 158, 160, 195, 197, 229, 232, 233, 239, 240, 245, 268, 269–70, 274, 344, 356–57; JHM proposes marriage, 119–20, 131; marriage to JHM, 131–32, 973; meets JHM and is courted, 77–78, 79, 80, 81; photographs, 589; rebaptism, 275; receives temple endowments, 232

Martineau, Theodore (son), 399, 436, 612, 639, 661, 732, 798, 811, 818, 820, 838, 841, 985, 987, 1063, 1200; attends college, 850, 862, 864, 957; birth, 344; blessings, 720–21, 848; children, 1081, 1185, 1201; health and illnesses, 974, 1007; marriage to Josephine Thurston, 1057; missionary work, 1020–21, 1024, 1026, 1043,

INDEX

1049; photographs, 1286; poetry, 816–17; rebaptism, 840; surveys with JHM, 799, 801, 805, 842, 1009
Martineau, Virginia "Gean" (daughter). *See* Murphy, Virginia "Gean" Martineau Sudbury
Maughan, John, 294
Maughan, Peter, 132, 231, 237, 239, 244, 247, 263, 271, 320, 345; death, 346
Maughan, William H., 251, 282, 380, 457, 592
Maxwell, James R., 308, 309, 312nn105–6, 313, 315n112, 316n115, 318, 594
McBride, William, 632–33, 649, 681, 729
McCune, Elizabeth, 1019, 1183, 1195, 1196
McKinley, William, 910
medicine, 46n44, 113n136, 157, 198, 236, 637, 651, 778, 847, 863, 1015; *see also* disease
Meeks, Priddy, 46, 48, 106, 113, 158n184
Merrill, Marriner W., 621, 994, 996
Mexican War, xli, 14, 16; *see also* Mexico
Mexico, 1285; Cinco de Mayo, 946; independence, 1015, 1017; LDS church in, 560, 566–75, 807–8, 1023, 1165; revolution, xli, 1253–54; ruins, 562, 568, 571–72, 808, 1034, 1045; *see also* conferences
militias. *See* JHM: military service; Nauvoo Legion; US Army; Utah War
Millennial Star, 140
mining, xl, 39, 462, 506, 513, 533, 534, 845, 855, 863, 871, 901–3, 920, 948; coal, 403, 404, 405, 406, 413–15
Minneapolis/St. Paul, Minnesota, 487–89, 495
missionaries and missionary work, 39–40, 64, 65, 80, 83, 97, 98, 379, 420, 458, 603, 799
Morley, Isaac, 140, 213, 241
Mormon Battalion, 75–76
Mormon Reformation, 117n139, 118n141, 121–22; *see also* blood atonement
Mormon Robbery Trial. *See* Wham Robbery Trial
Mormon, The, 72, 87
Morris, Thomas B., xxix, xxxi, 297, 300, 313, 314, 324, 592, 593
mountain lions, 150
Mountain Meadows Massacre, xxvi, 151, 152–54, 395, 403, 411, 1273–80
Murphy, Virginia "Gean" Martineau Sudbury (daughter), 355, 655, 766, 827, 828, 829, 998, 1031, 1078, 1108, 1135, 1159, 1203, 1244; birth, 338; children, 815, 866, 1042, 1052, 1114, 1221; health and illnesses, 369, 1027, 1160; marriage to Edward Sudbury, 781, 782, 787; poetry, 749
music and concerts, 67, 68, 70, 88, 89, 161, 236, 237–38, 321, 370–71, 408, 483, 503, 508, 655, 682, 780, 999

N

Native Americans. *See* Indigenous Peoples
Nauvoo Legion, 31, 282, 284n62, 344–51, 380–81, 417, 418, 592, 1137, 1270–71
Nebeker, Elizabeth "Lillie or Lilla" Lillian Martineau (daughter), 438, 452, 602, 660, 668, 991, 1181, 1204, 1248, 1252, 1257; baptism, 457; birth, 289; children, 892, 979, 1020, 1092, 1135, 1207; health and illnesses, 293, 323, 356, 369, 604, 605, 979, 981–82, 1050, 1080, 1087, 1159, 1206; marriage to Frank Nebeker, 768, 775, 794; moves to Arizona with JHM, 583, 601; photographs, 1286
Nephites. *See* Book of Mormon
Nephi, Utah, 61, 62
New Mexico, 653n50, 709, 785n56, 822, 1032, 1254
New York City, 474–75, 476
Niagara Falls, 481
Nibley, Charles W., 396
Nuttall, L. John, 542, 1009, 1127

O

opera. *See* music; theater
Order of Enoch. *See* United Order
Oregon Short Line. *See* railroads: Oregon Short Line
oxen, 235, 272, 937

P

pack mules, xxxv, 37, 251, 258, 317
Pahvants, 66, 79, 86, 91, 140, 152, 183, 224
Paiutes, 32n17, 44, 63n68
Panic of 1893, xl, 835–36
Parowan, Utah, xx, xxi, xxvii, 109, 163, 194, 226, 424, 425, 524, 876, 923; fort, 64; founding, 30–32; hardships in, 36, 67n72; people of rescue John C. Fremont party, 1265–66, 1267n4, 1271; stake, 53
Patriarchs, 623, 632, 633, 649, 681, 691, 717, 821, 876, 931, 994–96, 1123n109; *see also* JHM: Patriarch and blessings given
Pendleton, Calvin C., 56n59, 67, 90, 92, 93, 146, 161, 196, 226; desert mission, 175; physician, 95n112, 113; stake counselor, 109
Penrose, Charles W., 508
Perris, Frederick T., 196
phonograph. *See* music
photography, 241, 242, 268–69, 629, 1269
Pioneer Day (July 24), 67, 88, 89, 816, 955, 986, 1014, 1140, 1247
Platte River, 20, 51n50, 469
plural marriage, xxiii, xxxvii, 43, 83, 102, 118, 134, 467, 614–15, 635, 707, 967–68, 1195, 1218; Edmunds Act, 542, 543; Edmunds–Tucker Act, 682; post-manifesto, 1021; Second Manifesto, 1115, 1161n130; underground to avoid prosecution, 635, 636, 645–46, 653n50, 705, 712n93, 778–79
Political Manifesto, 880, 1014
polygamy. *See* plural marriage
pottery, 96
Powers, Ridgley C., 810, 840, 848, 849
Pratt, Helaman, 805, 945, 953, 1019, 1022, 1023, 1076
Pratt, Parley P., 25n1, 29, 30
Pratt, Orson, xxiii, 508
prayer circles, 63, 179
pregnancy and miscarriage, 971, 997, 1154, 1158, 1159, 1160, 1161, 1182, 1183, 1203, 1228, 1241, 1242, 1243, 1248, 1249, 1251–52
Preston, William B., xxiii, xxxiv, 235, 261, 320n124, 340, 372, 380, 398, 412, 421, 454, 501, 540, 589, 652, 668, 705, 829, 989, 1026, 1088, 1098, 1122, 1123, 1140, 1142, 1165, 1185; health and illnesses, 1121, 1131, 1152; presiding bishop, 615, 656, 670, 701
prophecy, 200

Q

Quorum of Twelve Apostles, xxii, 104, 579, 612

R

railroads, xl, 15, 308, 310n102, 353, 373–74, 388–89, 390, 442, 469, 514–15, 553, 595, 710, 753, 1180, 1265; Central Pacific, 314, 315, 319, 320, 323, 581; daily life building, 313n108, 318n120, 319n121; Denver and Rio Grande, 530; North Mexican Pacific Railway, 786, 789, 791, 794; Oregon Short Line, xxx, 297n79, 1089; Sonora, 567, 569, 573, 603; surveying, xxix; Transcontinental, xxxix; Union Pacific, xxix, xxxv, 295, 297nn77–79, 299n82, 309, 317, 370, 383, 396, 581, 593, 594; Utah and Nevada, 527; Utah Central, xxix, 370, 374, 595; Utah Northern, xxx, 339–40, 351, 353–54, 370, 372, 378, 383, 396, 408, 431, 439, 450, 458, 459, 468; Utah Southern, 423, 430, 500; Utah Western Railway, 395, 434; *see also* surveys and surveying: Union Pacific Railroad

Relief Society, 323, 548, 650, 653n50, 664, 671, 676, 712, 793n88, 992, 1014, 1022, 1025, 1040n70, 1156–57, 1183, 1238, 1241; *see also* women's callings; women's meetings

remedies. *See* medicine

Reynolds v. United States. See plural marriage

Rice, William K., xxi, 24, 38, 260, 928, 932, 935, 1137; purchases Indigenous slave girl, 37–38, 990, 1141; travels with JHM to Iron County, Utah, 26, 27, 29, 30

Rich, Charles C., xxiii, 29, 43, 48, 196, 269, 512

Richards, Franklin D., xxv, 42, 52, 54, 55, 123, 211, 500, 512, 547, 579, 652, 871, 905n173, 1040; seals JHM to Jessie Grieve, 686, 968

Richards, George F., 1195

Richards, Willard, 29, 61, 1143

Ricks, Thomas E., 243, 249, 250, 251, 261, 282, 345, 380, 417

riots, 72

road development and improvement, 76n87, 91

Robinson, Joseph E., 1174

Robinson, Samuel J., 1019

Roosevelt, Theodore, 1090

Roskruge, George J., 787, 888, 890, 894, 901n167, 956n1s, 1288

S

Sagwitch. *See* Bear River Massacre

Salomon, Frederick C., 455, 458, 459, 469, 542n154

salt, 90, 91

Saltair, 1091, 1137, 1141

Salt Lake City, Utah, xli, 117, 301, 334; JHM relocates to, 219, 223

Salt Lake Herald, 865, 1181

Salt Lake Tabernacle, 538, 612, 694, 998, 1090, 1210; old tabernacle, 25, 79

Salt Lake Tribune "conspiracy," 1214–17

San Bernardino, California, 29, 43, 98, 159, 160, 162

San Francisco, California, 553–54, 575–76, 630–31, 710, 1073

Santa Clara, Utah, 147

Scupham, James R., 390, 396n44

second anointing. *See* temple work: second anointing

sheep, 54

Sherman, Delcena Diadamia Johnson, xxii

Sherman, Lyman Royal, xxii

Sierra de la Candelaria, xxxii

silver, xl; *see also* mining

Silver-Money Panic, 904; *see also* Panic of 1893

slavery, 337, 548; *see also* Civil War; Indigenous Peoples: sold or traded as slaves

sleighs, xxxvii, 133, 239, 265, 270, 470, 478

small pox. *See* disease

Smith, Bathseba W., 546

Smith, George A., xxiii, xxvi, 26, 30, 31, 42, 69, 82, 86, 104, 109, 195, 209, 330; Church Historian, 77, 201; commander of southern Utah, 50, 52, 145–46; death, 417; seals JHM to Susan Ellen Johnson, 33; sermons, 210; tours Southern Utah with JHM, 146–47; trial of Dame, William H., 195–96

Smith, George Albert, 1195

Smith, Hyrum, 1038

Smith, Hyrum M., 1076

Smith, Jesse N., 33, 104, 146, 161, 193, 211, 425, 642, 643, 645, 647, 685, 921, 1115; JHM names a son after, 267

Smith, John, 60, 998, 1078

Smith, John C. L., xxi, 43, 44, 45, 49, 1267n4; death, 102; Parowan stake president, 69n74, 82, 83, 86, 99; photograph, 587

Smith, John Henry, 705, 727, 975, 984, 1125, 1248

Smith, Joseph, xxii, 25, 962, 1037, 1079, 1109, 1113, 1163, 1171–72

Smith, Joseph F., 422, 536, 540, 546, 579, 616, 1037, 1080, 1091, 1141, 1156, 1208; visits Arizona and Mexico, 641, 1038, 1039
Smith, Julina, 1183, 1207–8
Smith, Mary, 85
Smith, Samuel, xxxiv, 248
Smith, Silas S., 204
Smoot, Reed, 1026, 1115, 1259
Snake River Massacre, 262nn40–41
Snow, Eliza R., xxxvi, 287, 364, 546, 962
Snow, Erastus, xxiii, 42, 54, 55, 102, 196, 274, 403, 565; apostle, 661, 670; mission to Mexico, 552, 557, 561, 565; visits Arizona, 641
Snow, Lorenzo, 118, 121, 123, 240, 416, 970, 972, 994, 1014, 1170; blesses JHM, 127–28
Sons of the American Revolution, 1223, 1230, 1236, 1239, 1257
Spencer, Orson, 24n35
spiritualism, 144–45
Spry, William, 1242
Stanford, Leland, 323
steamboat, 17
Steele, John, 37, 43, 45, 52, 68, 83, 226, 332, 525; temporary commander, 53
St. David, Arizona, 563–65, 579, 602, 631, 657, 735; JHM describes, 605
St. Joseph Stake, Arizona, 576–77, 652
St. Paul, Minnesota. See Minneapolis/St. Paul, Minnesota
Stout, Hosea, 56
Sudbury, Edward, 782, 787, 827, 998, 1078, 1079, 1088
surveys and surveying: Gila Valley, Arizona, 603, 607, 610, 632, 633, 634, 635, 650–51, 653, 654, 659, 711–12, 713, 714, 715; federal resurveys, 1088–89, 1094, 1099, 1100–8, 1117–20, 1121, 1138–39, 1142–46, 1157–58, 1179, 1181, 1182; northern Mexico, 946, 953–55, 956–57, 966, 983–84, 985, 1005, 1009, 1022, 1032, 1033–36, 1044–48, 1050, 1052, 1054–55, 1057; northern Utah, 231, 243, 246, 250, 254, 263, 268, 269, 271, 272, 275, 282, 283, 284, 293, 294–95, 325–27, 328–29, 339, 355, 376, 377, 388, 395, 396, 401, 402, 410, 411, 417, 418, 419, 432, 433, 442–44, 445–49, 451, 453, 455, 457, 458, 460–62, 463, 465, 468, 501, 505, 506, 508, 511, 518, 522, 523, 526–27, 533, 534–35, 550; railroads, 295–96, 298, 301–23, 324–28, 329–35, 340, 341–43, 353–55, 375, 376, 392–93, 439–41, 450, 468, 500, 513, 514, 785, 789–90, 791, 794–96; southern Arizona, 767, 772, 777, 783, 788, 792, 799, 800–5, 832, 839, 840, 842–44, 852, 853, 855, 861; southern Utah, 111, 142, 196, 197, 202, 208, 211, 212, 221, 227; see also JHM (bridge engineer; canal surveyor and engineer; cartographer; mineral and mining surveyor; railroad leveler, surveyor, and engineer; surveyor and topographer; US Deputy Surveyor); Topographical Corps; Uintah Indian Reservation; US Surveyor General's Office
Surveyor General's Office. See US Surveyor General's Office
Syracuse, New York, 5n5

T

tabernacles, 261, 275, 397, 431, 459, 615n14, 681, 687, 1247; see also Salt Lake Tabernacle
Tabernacle Choir, 825
Taylor, Gertrude "Tillie" Martineau (daughter), xxxviii, 338, 736, 742, 801, 818, 821, 828, 844, 857, 989, 1017, 1063, 1068–69, 1076, 1077, 1088, 1189, 1196; blessings, 649–50, 652, 812–13, 823, 1069, 1166–70, 1195; courted by non-Mormon Alexander von Wendt, 854, 855, 856–58; heath and illnesses, 389, 549, 648, 650, 652, 656, 677, 715, 743, 754, 771, 813, 822, 846, 847–48, 850, 863, 864, 921, 946, 974, 975, 1007, 1050, 1051–52, 1056, 1057, 1064, 1075, 1156, 1165, 1166, 1171, 1173–77; lives with her brother

Lyman, 549; marriage to Guy Taylor, 1021, 1038; works with JHM, 661
Taylor, Guy, 957, 959, 1021, 1038, 1063, 1070, 1122, 1157, 1173, 1175, 1179, 1184, 1196
Taylor, John, 459, 499, 504, 533, 534, 552, 564, 578–79, 611, 616, 683, 968, 1123n109; visits Arizona, 641–44
Taylor, John W., 700, 975, 984, 1124, 1174; removal from Quorum of the Twelve, 1161
Taylor, Joseph E., 1230
Teasdale, George, 664, 680n64, 798, 805, 813, 814, 821, 830, 1027, 1166, 1174, 1175
temples, 246, 373, 437, 500, 525, 547, 614, 615, 665, 1231, 1255; Logan Temple dedication, 616; Salt Lake Temple dedication, 826–27, 968
temple work, xxxviii, xliii, 232, 382, 451, 504, 540, 546, 548, 616–23, 626–28, 629, 665–68, 684, 688, 689–91, 692–93, 695–703, 704, 705, 706–8, 709, 752, 771, 827–28, 836, 970, 972–73, 991–94, 995, 996–97, 1005, 1006, 1026, 1027–30, 1083–84, 1086, 1087, 1089, 1090, 1091, 1092, 1114–15, 1121, 1124–26, 1127–32, 1133, 1135–36, 1137, 1143, 1153, 1161–62, 1164, 1184–85, 1195, 1196, 1197, 1204, 1209–10, 1223, 1230, 1231, 1235, 1245, 1255, 1256, 1257, 1258; clothing, 1082; garments, 54n56, 59–60, 63, 75; second anointing, 620, 621, 628, 629, 665, 687, 693, 700, 709, 915, 968, 976, 1162; *see also* JHM: ancestry, extended family, and genealogy
Thatcher, Moses, 258, 378, 380, 395, 406, 419, 437, 454, 518, 582–83, 612, 659, 679, 723; apostle, 500, 536, 1217; death, 1211; health and illnesses, 827; mission to Mexico, 503, 552, 557, 565, 566, 575, 577; removed from Quorum of the Twelve, 258n38, 1014; travels East with JHM, 469, 471, 474, 475; and Utah Northern Railroad, 374, 396, 439; visits Arizona, 641–44; *see also* Political Manifesto
theater, 65, 75, 92, 93, 109–10, 246, 247, 248, 302, 357, 470, 473, 475, 476, 483, 486, 546, 554; 687, 826, 1231
theft. *See* crime
timber mining, 462, 474
tithing, 239, 240, 611, 1014, 1021, 1039, 1049, 1082, 1124, 1130, 1186, 1196, 1214; JHM responsible for in Arizona, 614, 646, 650, 655, 656, 663, 673, 675, 676, 679, 680, 713n94, 714, 715, 716, 717; *see also* Layton, Christopher: accuses JHM of mismanaging tithing funds
tobacco, 239; *see also* Word of Wisdom
Tombstone, Arizona, 604, 606, 611, 658, 668
tongues, speaking in, 83, 114
Topographical Corps, 76, 78, 142, 202, 227, 304, 441; *see also* JHM: surveyor and topographer
transportation, 15, 17, 61, 62, 80, 133, 228, 234–35, 422, 581, 608, 609, 711n92, 753, 1179, 1256; *see also* canoes; ferries; horses; pack mules; railroads; sleighs; steamboats; wagons
typhoid, 952, 988, 1182, 1198, 1211, 1236, 1240, 1241, 1252

U

Uinta Indian Reservation, 1088n84, 1089, 1095, 1102, 1125, 1142, 1157, 1174
Uinta Mountains, xxxii, 1095
Union Pacific. *See* railroads: Union Pacific
United Order, 375, 379, 412, 416
US Army, 14–15, 69n73, 72, 75, 79, 204, 207, 208, 228, 234, 261, 262–63, 482, 565; Camp Douglas (Salt Lake City), 262, 266, 416, 829; conflict with Mormons, 80, 145, 159, 266; deserters, 203; Newport Barracks, 15n21; *see also* Utah War
US Capitol. *See* Washington, DC
US Constitution. *See* White Horse Prophecy

US Department of the Interior, 506
US Magnetic Observatory (Madison, Wisconsin), 486
US Surveyor General's Office, 433, 434, 435, 436, 443, 452, 455, 459, 467, 518, 533, 535, 541, 661, 668, 746, 769, 775, 777, 788, 823, 824, 829, 830, 832, 849, 860–61, 864, 870, 880, 906, 921, 1088, 1093, 1099, 1122, 1287, 1157, 1164, 1177, 1182
Utah; demographics, xxviii
Utah Central. *See* railroads: Utah Central
Utah Northern. *See* railroads: Utah Northern
Utah statehood, 247, 546; *see also* Utah Territorial Legislature: constitutional conventions
Utah Territorial Legislature, xxiv, 117, 121, 127; congressional memorials, 129; constitutional conventions, 106, 247
Utah territorial militia. *See* Nauvoo Legion
Utah War, xxiv, xxvii, 144, 145, 148, 154, 158, 159, 161, 163, 164n191, 194, 1274
Utah Western Railway. *See* railroads: Utah Western Railway
Utes, 30, 42, 47–48, 54n55, 64, 73, 79, 1101, 1267, 1270n10, 1279

V

Van Slyke, Napoleon, 26, 336–37, 384
Varley, Jane. *See* Martineau, Jane Varley
violence, 54, 73, 94–95, 200, 300, 374n27, 459, 519–20, 743, 811, 814, 819, 864, 978
von Wendt, Alexander, xxxviii, 790, 791n69, 793, 824, 836, 845, 846, 849, 851, 855, 858–59, 861, 863, 864, 866, 869, 889–90, 900, 902n168, 904, 914, 917, 920; temple work for, 957, 1064, 1069, 1175, 1176, 1184; courtship of Gertrude Martineau, 854, 855, 856–58, 890; death, 939, 948–52, 953
Voswinkel, Lois "Lotie" Martineau (sister), 11, 26, 416, 470, 482–84, 496, 498, 499, 980, 1017, 1148

W

wagons, 17, 22, 27, 80, 146, 160, 163, 168, 220, 228, 229, 234, 245, 999, 1010
Wakara. *See* Walker (Chief)
Walker (Chief), 32, 42, 47–48, 64, 65, 913, 920, 927–28; death, 73, 906
Walker War, 49–50, 52, 53, 54, 64
Walser, Henry, 821, 964–65
Washington, DC, 471–72, 473–74
Washington, George, 4, 472
Weber River, xxix, 297, 299
Wells, Daniel H., 64, 76, 78, 129, 148n169, 202, 219, 282, 416, 419, 579, 1040
West, Margaret, 85
Wham Robbery Trial, 751
White, Herbert A., 1085, 1088, 1090–91, 1094, 1100, 1115, 1116, 1122, 1140, 1141
Whitehouse, Isaac, murder of, 95–96, 97, 98, 99; *see also* Baker, Samuel G.
White Horse Prophecy, 1109–13
Whiterocks, 1101, 1105, 1118, 1120, 1144
Whitney, Orson F., 723
Williams, Frederick G. II, 821–22
Winder, John R., 1080, 1094, 1192, 1204, 1230
Wolfley, Lewis, 786, 787, 790, 808, 832
women's blessings, 652, 1117, 1156, 1250, 1259–60
women's meetings, 86, 654, 662, 664, 1183; *see also* Relief Society
Woodruff, Abraham Owen, 1019, 1038, 1039, 1078
Woodruff, Wilford, 123, 416, 579, 705, 748, 836, 994
Wooley, Julia, 1136, 1140, 1142, 1143, 1146, 1152, 1155, 1160, 1164, 1178, 1180, 1181, 1185, 1189, 1207, 1242
Word of Wisdom, xxxi, 359, 428, 1172

Y

Young, Brigham, xxiii, xxvii, 29, 34, 39, 61, 63, 82, 104, 129, 130, 175, 260, 261, 274, 302, 328, 330, 397, 432,

1210, 1215; and astrology, 62, 78; and Indigenous Peoples, 47, 54, 64, 65; and Mountain Meadows Massacre, 153, 1278; proclaims martial law, 154; sermons, xxiv, 104, 123–26, 142, 246, 379, 403, 416; territorial governor, 72n75; *see also* Utah War

Young, Brigham Jr., 380, 397, 403, 419, 433, 437, 634, 635, 636, 656, 661, 662, 671, 711, 1085, 1217

Young, John W., xxxi, 339, 353, 354, 401, 404, 413, 523, 547, 714, 733, 786, 789, 797n86; *see also* railroads

Young, Joseph A., 342

Young Ladies' Mutual Improvement Association (YLMIA), 664, 1057

Young Men's Mutual Improvement Association (YMMIA), 536, 641, 650, 664, 712, 732, 964, 965

Z

ZCMI, 344, 533, 629, 663
Zelph, 684
Zion, 28, 508, 1111